African American Literature

AN ENCYCLOPEDIA FOR STUDENTS

Hans A. Ostrom and J. David Macey, Editors

GREENWOOD

An Imprint of ABC-CLIO, LLC

Santa Barbara, California • Denver, Colorado

Library of Congress Cataloging-in-Publication Data

Names: Ostrom, Hans A., editor. | Macey, J. David, editor.
Title: African American literature : an encyclopedia for students / Hans A.
   Ostrom and J. David Macey, editors.
Description: Santa Barbara, California : Greenwood, an imprint of ABC-CLIO,
   LLC, [2020] | Includes bibliographical references and index.
Identifiers: LCCN 2019029439 (print) | LCCN 2019029440 (ebook) | ISBN
   9781440871504 (paperback) | ISBN 9781440871511 (ebook)
Subjects: LCSH: American literature—African American
   authors—Encyclopedias.
Classification: LCC PS153.N5 A33644 2020 (print) | LCC PS153.N5 (ebook) |
   DDC 810.9/896073003—dc23
LC record available at https://lccn.loc.gov/2019029439
LC ebook record available at https://lccn.loc.gov/2019029440

ISBN: 978-1-4408-7150-4 (print)
      978-1-4408-7151-1 (ebook)

24 23 22 21 20   1 2 3 4 5

This book is also available as an eBook.

Greenwood
An Imprint of ABC-CLIO, LLC

ABC-CLIO, LLC
147 Castilian Drive
Santa Barbara, California 93117
www.abc-clio.com

This book is printed on acid-free paper ∞

Manufactured in the United States of America

Contents

Introduction

It would be impossible to tell the story of African American literature in a single volume or indeed in multiple volumes. Like the great rivers in Langston Hughes's famous poem "The Negro Speaks of Rivers" (1921), "ancient as the world and older than the flow of human blood in human veins," the rich network of texts, authors, and traditions that comprise African American literature flow from numerous headwaters through multiple intersecting channels. This rich and varied literature reflects the lived experiences of African Americans from the beginning of the colonial period through the present day, and it has enriched and transformed the social, cultural, political, intellectual, and aesthetic landscape of America.

What, then, is "African American literature"? It is writing produced by persons whose identities and heritage are linked to the African diaspora—the spreading out of people from Africa, the influence of cultural practices they brought to the places they went, and the social and political circumstances that have shaped their lives. It is writing produced by persons of the diaspora whose background is chiefly American, as opposed to British or French. That said, many African American writers have been immigrants, and many of these have come from Caribbean islands, so that the "American" part of African American literature has always been interpreted expansively. By "literature," we mean published writing in a wide variety of forms, including essays, poems, autobiographies, short stories, novels, plays, monologues, folktales, and works for children and young adults. "Literature," understood in this inclusive sense, encompasses writing of every sort, including comic, tragic, satiric, humorous, realistic, surrealistic, absurd, religious, speculative, introspective, and political texts.

African American Literature: An Encyclopedia for Students offers an overview of some of the major writers, genres, issues, and historical events that have defined the course of African American literature over the past three centuries. No single volume can do justice to the richness, variety, and complexity of African American literature; the five-volume *Greenwood Encyclopedia of African American Literature* (2005), upon which the present encyclopedia is to a large degree based, was itself only an introduction to and overview of the field. Both encyclopedias might best be understood as points of embarkation—"jumping off" points, if you will—for a lifelong exploration of the expansive network of texts and contexts that define African American literature's vast and varied geography.

This volume is intended as a resource for students, particularly high school students and college and university undergraduates, who are beginning to conduct research on topics in African American literature. In preparing this volume, we have selected crucial entries from the *Greenwood Encyclopedia of African American Literature* that address major writers, genres, and critical and historical contexts, and we have added a handful of new entries on contemporary writers in order to help readers form a solid foundation in African American literary studies.

Any principle of selection will be, to some degree, both partial and inadequate. We have had to exclude writers whose achievements have been extraordinary, but we have deferred to broad scholarly consensus regarding the importance of figures and movements in selecting entries for this volume. No encyclopedia of African American literature could reasonably exclude such writers as James Baldwin, Frederick Douglass, Langston Hughes, Zora Neale Hurston, Harriet Jacobs, Toni Morrison, or Phillis Wheatley. The same is true of the Harlem Renaissance and the Black Arts Movement. So, too, the lasting and still controversial impact of public intellectuals, including W.E.B. Du Bois and Cornel West, made their inclusion in this volume critical. Many other writers, movements, and events might have been included in this volume, and it is our hope that the resources provided in this encyclopedia will encourage readers to conduct further research and to learn more about other topics in African American literature.

African American Literature: An Encyclopedia for Students offers several different points of embarkation for students of African American literature. While the largest number of entries focus on individual writers, other entries provide introductions to groups of authors who formed a particular movement in literature and culture such as the Chicago Renaissance or the Black Atlantic Movement. Some entries provide a window into a genre such as the slave narrative, the novel, or drama. Still other entries explore links between literature and historical events such as the Civil War or the Civil Rights Movement, literary tropes or movements such as feminism and Black feminism or the trickster, or important centers of literary and social activity such as Chicago, Illinois, or New Orleans, Louisiana.

By providing up-to-date bibliographies for each entry, a general bibliography, and a detailed timeline of African American literary history, we hope to offer readers the resources they will need to identify and refine research topics; recognize connections among authors, genres, periods, and social, cultural, and political movements; and formulate and support critical arguments about African American literature. These bibliographies, together with the chronology, will help readers find additional sources to enlarge their understanding of a particular writer, work, genre, group, critical vantage point, or era. When an entry only briefly mentions related writers, contexts, or critical approaches, the bibliography will provide a roadmap for further investigation.

We hope that *African American Literature: An Encyclopedia for Students* will open up for readers a range of new resources, approaches, and contexts for studying African American literature and for pursuing an exciting voyage of discovery—or rediscovery—of the richness, variety, and profound power of the African American literary tradition.

Hans A. Ostrom, Tacoma, Washington
J. David Macey, Edmond, Oklahoma

Chronology

ca. 35,000 BCE

The Lemombo bone, one of the earliest known mathematical instruments, is in use in what is now known as Swaziland in Africa. In this same period, the Egyptians and Sumerians invent writing, using clay tablets.

8th Century BCE

Nubians become pharaohs in Egypt's 25th dynasty. They were instrumental in the trading that went on between sub-Saharan Africa and Egypt and the Mediterranean. By this time, the Yoruba civilization was well established in West Africa, where the nations of Benin and Nigeria are now situated. The Yoruba developed an advanced agricultural society and also practiced sophisticated blacksmithing, leather-working, glass-making, and bronze casting.

8th Century BCE–6th Century CE

The Ancient Greek culture flourishes.

ca. 600–500 BCE

Genesis and *Exodus*, the first books of the Hebrew Bible (Old Testament), are thought to have been written in this period.

ca. 558–ca. 491 BCE, or ca. 400 BCE

Gautama Buddha, on whose teaching Buddhism is founded, is believed to have lived in what is now called India.

550 BCE

Cyrus the Great establishes the first Persian dynasty.

ca. 380 BCE

Plato writes his work, the *Republic*.

ca. 335 BCE

Aristotle writes his work of literary criticism, the *Poetics*. His material on rhetoric dates from this period as well.

100 BCE

Julius Caesar is born in Rome. He is assassinated there in 44 BCE.

ca. 4 BCE–30 CE

Jesus of Nazareth lives at this time.

ca. 66–70 CE

The Gospel of Mark, the earliest gospel of the New Testament, is written.

80

Construction of the Roman Colosseum is completed.

325

The Nicene Creed, a foundational Christian text, is published in Nicea, which is now known as Iznik, Turkey.

450
Attila the Hun invades Western Europe.

609–632
The Quran, the central text of Islam, is revealed to Prophet Muhammad.

711
The Moors, a Muslim people of western North Africa, conquer southern Spain and rule there into the late 1400s.

ca. 1162
Genghis Khan, founder of the Mongol Empire, is born.

ca. 1450
In Mainz, Germany, Johannes Gutenberg develops and uses the first printing press.

1517
Slave trade to the New World (Western Hemisphere) begins.

1526
Spanish ships bring slaves to North America.

1543
On the Revolutions of the Heavenly Spheres, by Copernicus, is published, establishing that Earth orbits the sun.

1564
William Shakespeare is born. Galileo Galilei is born.

ca. 1602
William Shakespeare writes *Hamlet*.

1605
Don Quixote, by Miguel de Cervantes, is published.

1616
William Shakespeare dies.

1619
A Dutch ship brings the first Africans to Jamestown, Virginia.

1620
The *Mayflower* docks at Cape Cod, Massachusetts.

1641
The Colony of Massachusetts legally recognizes slavery. *Discourse on Method*, by René Descartes, is published.

1652
Rhode Island adopts a law prohibiting slavery.

1667
Paradise Lost, by John Milton, is published.

1689
The Japanese poet Basho writes *The Narrow Road to the Deep North*.

1712
Pennsylvania adopts a law against slavery. A slave revolt occurs in New York City.

1726
Gulliver's Travels, by Jonathan Swift, is published.

ca. 1730
Lucy Terry [Prince] is born in Africa.

1732
George Washington is born.

1734
Daniel Boone is born.

1743
Thomas Jefferson is born.

1744
Lucy Terry writes the poem "Bars Fight," considered to be the first written African American poem.

ca. 1753
Phillis Wheatley is born.

1755
Samuel Johnson's *Dictionary of the English Language* is published in England.

1769
Napoleon Bonaparte is born.

1770
Crispus Attucks, an African American, is killed in the Boston Massacre.

1773
Poems on Various Subjects, Religious and Moral, by Phillis Wheatley, is published. Sally Hemings is born.

1775–1783
The Revolutionary War.

1776
The Declaration of Independence is written.

1779
Articles of Confederation are ratified.

1789
George Washington is elected president. The French Revolution begins. *The Interesting Narrative of the Life of Olaudah Equiano; or, Gustavus Vassa, the African*, by Olaudah Equiano, is published.

1791
The Private Life of the Late Benjamin Franklin (later known as the *Autobiography of Benjamin Franklin*) is published. *The Rights of Man*, by Thomas Paine, is published.

1793
The first Fugitive Slave Act is passed into law. It makes harboring an escaped slave a crime in the United States.

1797
Sojourner Truth is born.

1798
Lyrical Ballads, by William Wordsworth and Samuel Taylor Coleridge, is published.

1799
In France, Napoleon's coup d'état succeeds.

1803
Louisiana Territory is purchased from France by the United States; the land mass of the United States thereby doubles.

1812
Charles Dickens is born. Napoleon invades Russia. The War of 1812, in which both slaves and free Blacks fight, begins.

1815
Napoleon's army is defeated at the Battle of Waterloo.

1818
Frederick Douglass is born.

1819
Queen Victoria and Walt Whitman are born.

1820
George III, king of England, dies.

1822

Denmark Vesey organizes a slave revolt in Charleston, South Carolina, but he is betrayed, and the revolt fails.

1826

Thomas Jefferson dies.

1827

Tamerlane and Other Poems, by Edgar Allan Poe, is published.

1829

Published this year: *The Hope of Liberty*, a collection of poems by George Moses Horton; and *An Appeal to the Colored Peoples of the World* by David Walker. Native American tribes are driven from their homelands to "Indian Territories," including what is now Oklahoma.

1831

Nat Turner leads a slave rebellion in Virginia. He is subsequently captured and executed.

1835

Sally Hemings, Thomas Jefferson's mistress, dies.

1845

Narrative of the Life of Frederick Douglass, an American Slave, Written by Himself, is published.

1849

David Copperfield, by Charles Dickens, is published.

1851

"Ain't I a Woman?," a speech by Sojourner Truth, is delivered in Akron, Ohio.

1853

Clotel; Or, the President's Daughter: A Narrative of Slave Life in the United States, a novel by William Wells Brown, is published.

1854

Poems on Miscellaneous Subjects, by Frances Ellen Watkins Harper, is published.

1855

Leaves of Grass, by Walt Whitman, is published.

1857

The U.S. Supreme Court reaches its decision in the infamous *Dred Scott* case. *Madame Bovary*, by Gustave Flaubert, is published.

1859

On the Origin of Species, by Charles Darwin, is published. John Brown's raid on Harpers Ferry occurs.

1860

The total population of African American slaves is roughly four million. South Carolina secedes from the United States; it is the first state to do so.

1861

Incidents in the Life of a Slave Girl, by Harriet Ann Jacobs, is published.

1861–1865

The American Civil War takes place.

1863

The Emancipation Proclamation is issued by President Abraham Lincoln; it declares slaves to be free, except for those in the Border States: Delaware, Maryland, Kentucky,

West Virginia, Missouri, Tennessee, the "Indian Territory," and Kansas.

1864

The Fugitive Slave Laws are repealed.

1865

April 9: General Robert E. Lee surrenders to General Ulysses S. Grant. The Civil War ends.
April 15: Abraham Lincoln dies from gunshot wounds suffered the night before at Ford's Theatre in Washington, DC.

1867

The period of Reconstruction begins in the South.

1868

The U.S. Congress passes the Fourteenth Amendment to the U.S. Constitution, granting African Americans equal citizenship and civil rights. The Meiji Restoration begins in Japan. W.E.B. Du Bois is born.

1869

The National Woman Suffrage Association is established. *War and Peace*, by Leo Tolstoy, is published.

1872

Paul Laurence Dunbar is born.

1874

Robert Frost is born.

1876

Alexander Graham Bell invents the telephone.

1877

The U.S. military withdraws from the South, and Reconstruction ends.

1881

The Tuskegee Institute is founded, under the leadership of Booker T. Washington.

1884

The Adventures of Huckleberry Finn, by Mark Twain, is published.

1892

The *Baltimore Afro-American* is established. Walt Whitman dies. *A Voice from the South*, by Anna Julia Cooper, is published.

1893

Oak and Ivy, by Paul Laurence Dunbar, is published.

1894

Jean Toomer is born.

1895

Frederick Douglass dies in Washington, DC. Booker T. Washington speaks at the Atlanta Exposition. *Violets and Other Tales*, by Alice Moore Dunbar-Nelson, is published.

1896

The U.S. Supreme Court issues its infamous decision in *Plessy v. Ferguson*, reaffirming the concept of "separate but equal" public accommodations for African Americans.

1897

William Faulkner is born.

1898

The Spanish–American War takes place. Melvin B. Tolson is born.

1899

The Conjure Woman, by Charles Waddell Chesnutt, is published. Ernest Hemingway is born. Edward Kennedy "Duke" Ellington is born.

1901

Queen Victoria dies. *Up from Slavery*, by Booker T. Washington, is published. Langston Hughes is born.

1902

Arna Bontemps is born.

1903

The Souls of Black Folk, by W.E.B. Du Bois, is published.

1904

Lyrics of Life and Love, by William Stanley Braithwaite, is published.

1905

The *Chicago Defender* is founded.

1906

Paul Laurence Dunbar dies.

1908

Richard Wright is born.

1909

The National Association for the Advancement of Colored People (NAACP) is founded, led by W.E.B. Du Bois.

1910

Mark Twain dies. *The Crisis* is established.

1912

James Weldon Johnson's novel, *Autobiography of an Ex-Colored Man* is published.

1913

The First International Exhibit of Modern Art, also known as the Armory Show, takes place in New York City. *Complete Poems*, by Paul Laurence Dunbar, is published.

1914

World War I begins. Ralph Ellison is born.

1915

Booker T. Washington dies.

1916

Rachel, a play by Angelina Weld Grimké, is performed. Frank Yerby is born. *The General Theory of Relativity*, by Albert Einstein, is published.

1917

The United States enters the Great War, later known as World War I. Over 365,000 African Americans are drafted into the military during this war, serving in segregated divisions. The Russian Revolution begins.

1918

World War I ends. *The Heart of a Woman*, by Georgia Douglas Johnson, is published.

1919

The Volstead Act is passed, beginning the era of Prohibition. John Reed's *Ten Days That Shook the World*, concerning the Bolshevik Revolution, is published.

1920

The beginning of the Harlem Renaissance is often dated to this year.

1922

Published this year: *The Book of American Negro Poetry*, edited by James Weldon Johnson; *Harlem Shadows* by Claude McKay; and *The Waste Land*, by T. S. Eliot.

1923

Cane, by Jean Toomer, is published.

1924

James Baldwin is born. *The Fire in the Flint*, by Walter White, is published. The *Opportunity* magazine awards banquet is held in Manhattan, celebrating Black writers, so that this year is also often counted as the beginning of the Harlem Renaissance.

1925

Published this year: *The Great Gatsby* by F. Scott Fitzgerald; and *The New Negro*, an anthology edited by Alain Locke.

1926

Published this year: *The Sun Also Rises* by Ernest Hemingway; *The Weary Blues* by Langston Hughes; and the single issue of the magazine *Fire!!*, edited by Wallace Thurman.

1927

Published this year: *Caroling at Dusk*, edited by Countee Cullen, and *Ebony and Topaz*, edited by Charles Spurgeon Johnson.

1928

Maya Angelou is born.

1929

Published this year: *The Sound and the Fury*, by William Faulkner; Walter White's *Rope & Faggot*, a landmark study of lynching; and *Plum Bun*, by Jessie Redmon Fauset. The U.S. stock market crashes. The Great Depression begins. Martin Luther King Jr. is born.

1930

Not Without Laughter, a novel by Langston Hughes, is published. The Nation of Islam is established.

1931

The case of the Scottsboro Boys begins in Alabama. *Black No More*, by George Samuel Schuyler, is published. Toni Morrison is born.

1932

Published this year: *The Southern Road*, by Sterling A. Brown, and *The Conjure-Man Dies*, by Rudolph Fisher.

1933

Adolf Hitler becomes chancellor in Germany. National Prohibition ends in the United States. President Franklin Roosevelt institutes New Deal policies.

1934

The Ways of White Folks, by Langston Hughes, is published. Rudolph Fisher dies.

1935

Mulatto, a play by Langston Hughes, is produced in New York.

1936

Black Thunder by Arna Bontemps, an historical novel based on an actual slave uprising, is published.

1937

The College Language Association is established. *Their Eyes Were Watching God*, by Zora Neale Hurston, is published. In Spain, Langston Hughes writes articles about the Spanish Civil War for *The Baltimore Afro-American*.

1939

World War II begins. *The Grapes of Wrath*, by John Steinbeck, is published.

1940

The Big Sea, by Langston Hughes, and *Native Son*, by Richard Wright, are published.

1941

The Japanese air force attacks Pearl Harbor, Hawaii, in December. The United States enters World War II. The first commercial television broadcast occurs. Approximately one million African American soldiers serve, as draftees or volunteers, in the war. As in World War I, the troops are segregated based on race.

1942

Published this year: *Dust Tracks on a Road*, by Zora Neale Hurston, and *For My People*, by Margaret Walker.

1943

Langston Hughes begins writing columns for the *Chicago Defender* newspaper. Many of these columns feature brief comic short stories featuring Jesse B. Simple.

1944

Published this year: *Rendezvous with America*, by Melvin B. Tolson, and the short story "King of the Bingo Game," by Ralph Ellison.

1945

Published this year: *Black Boy*, by Richard Wright; *If He Hollers Let Him Go*, by Chester Himes; and *A Street in Bronzeville*, by Gwendolyn Brooks. The United States drops two atomic bombs on Japan. World War II ends. The United Nations is established.

1946

The Street, by Ann Petry, is published. Countee Cullen dies. *The Foxes of Harrow*, by Frank Yerby, is published.

1947

Jackie Robinson breaks the color line in professional baseball, playing for the Brooklyn Dodgers.

1948

Claude McKay dies. *The Living Is Easy*, by Dorothy West, is published. *Death of a Salesman*, by Arthur Miller, is produced.

1949

The Chinese Revolution occurs.

1950

Gwendolyn Brooks wins the Pulitzer Prize for her book of poetry, *Annie Allen*, published in 1949.

1950–1953

The Korean War takes place.

1951

Montage of a Dream Deferred, by Langston Hughes, is published.

1952

Published this year: *The Old Man and the Sea*, by Ernest Hemingway, and *Invisible Man*, by Ralph Ellison. Dwight Eisenhower is elected president.

1953

Go Tell It on the Mountain, by James Baldwin, is published. Langston Hughes is called to testify before Senator Joseph McCarthy's Permanent Subcommittee on Investigations.

1954

The U.S. Supreme Court issues its landmark decision in *Brown v. Board of Education, Topeka, Kansas*.

1955

Notes of a Native Son, by James Baldwin, is published. Walter White dies.

1957

On the Road, by Jack Kerouac, and *Black Bourgeoisie*, by E. Franklin Frazier, are published.

1957–1958

The desegregation of public schools in Little Rock, Arkansas, occurs.

1958

The Book of Negro Folklore, edited by Langston Hughes and Arna Bontemps, is published.

1959

A Raisin in the Sun, by Lorraine Hansberry, is produced on Broadway. *Brown Girl, Brownstones*, by Paule Marshall, is published.

1960

Zora Neale Hurston and Richard Wright die. Students in North Carolina stage sit ins at lunch counters to protest Jim Crow Laws ("separate but equal" accommodations).

1961

Preface to a Twenty Volume Suicide Note and *Dutchman*, both by LeRoi Jones (Amiri Baraka), are published. Ernest Hemingway dies.

1962

Ballad of Remembrance, by Robert Hayden, is published. James Meredith becomes the first African American to enroll at the University of Mississippi. William Faulkner dies.

1963

Martin Luther King Jr. writes "Letter from Birmingham Jail." *The Fire Next Time*, by James Baldwin, and Amiri Baraka's *Blues People: Negro Music in White America* are published. John F. Kennedy is assassinated. W.E.B. Du Bois dies. Medgar Evers is assassinated. Robert Frost dies.

1964

Martin Luther King Jr. wins the Nobel Peace Prize. The Free Speech Movement begins at the University of California, Berkeley. *The Dead Lecturer*, by Amiri Baraka, is published.

1965

Harlem Gallery, by Melvin B. Tolson, is published. *The Autobiography of Malcolm X*, which Alex Haley helps write, is published. The Vietnam War begins. Malcolm X is assassinated. Winston Churchill dies. Lorraine Hansberry dies. The Selma to Montgomery, Alabama, protest marches take place. Dudley Randall establishes the Broadside Press in Detroit.

1966

The Black Panther Party is established. *Jubilee*, by Margaret Walker, and *The Book of Negro Humor*, edited by Langston Hughes, are published. Melvin B. Tolson dies.

1967

Thurgood Marshall becomes a Justice of the U.S. Supreme Court. *The Best Short Stories by Negro Writers*, edited by Langston Hughes, is published. Langston Hughes dies. *Think Black*, by Haki R. Madhubuti, is published. Jean Toomer dies. *Soul on Ice*, by Eldridge Cleaver, is published.

1968

Poems from Prison, by Etheridge Knight, and *The First Cities*, by Audre Lorde, are published. Richard M. Nixon is elected president. Martin Luther King Jr. gives his renowned "I Have Been to the Mountaintop" speech. He is assassinated the next day in Memphis. Robert F. Kennedy is assassinated in June. Shirley Chisholm is elected to Congress.

1969

The first Black Studies program at a four-year university is established at San Francisco State College. *home coming*, by Sonia Sanchez, and *Black Pow-Wow: Jazz Poems*, by Ted Joans, are published. The U.S. agency NASA lands a man on the moon. A riot breaks out after the Stonewall Inn is raided by police in Manhattan; the event is associated with the beginning of the Gay Pride movement. *Black Boogaloo: Notes on Black Liberation*, by Larry Neal, is published.

1970

Published this year: *I Know Why the Caged Bird Sings*, by Maya Angelou; *Dear John, Dear Coltrane*, by Michael S. Harper; *I Am a Black Woman*, by Mari Evans; and *The Bluest Eye*, by Toni Morrison.

1971

Published this year: *The Black Aesthetic*, by Addison Gayle; *The Black Poets*, edited by Dudley Randall; and *The Autobiography of Miss Jane Pittman*, by Ernest James Gaines.

1972

Published this year: *Mumbo Jumbo*, by Ishmael Reed, and *Gorilla, My Love*, by Toni Cade Bambara.

1973

A treaty between the United States and North Vietnam is signed in Paris, France, ending the Vietnam War. *The Lynchers*, by John Edgar Wideman, and *In Love and Trouble: Stories of Black Women*, by Alice Walker, are published. Arna Bontemps dies.

1974

President Nixon resigns because of the Watergate scandal. Duke Ellington dies. *Ark of Bones and Other Stories*, by Henry Dumas, is published.

1975

for colored girls who have considered suicide/when the rainbow is enuf, by Ntozake Shange, is produced in New York City. *Corregidora*, by Gayl Jones, is published.

1976

Roots, by Alex Haley, is published. It is turned into a television miniseries in 1977. Black History Month (February) is established in the United States, based on Black History Week, founded by Carter Woodson in 1926. Gil Scott Heron writes and records the poem "Bicentennial Blues."

1977

Published this year: *Elbow Room*, by James Alan McPherson; *Dhalgren*, by Samuel R. Delany; and *Song of Solomon*, by Toni Morrison.

1978

James Alan McPherson wins the Pulitzer Prize for *Elbow Room*.

1979

Kindred, by Octavia E. Butler, is published.

1980

The Salt Eaters, by Toni Cade Bambara, is published. Ronald Reagan is elected president.

1981

Published this year: *The Chaneysville Incident*, by David Bradley; *A Soldier's Play*, by Charles Fuller; *Ain't I a Woman: Black Women and Feminism*, by bell hooks; and *Women, Race, and Class*, by Angela Davis.

1982

Published this year: *The Color Purple*, by Alice Walker, and *The Women of Brewster*

Place, by Gloria Naylor. Charles Fuller wins the Pulitzer Prize for *A Soldier's Play*. *Ma Rainey's Black Bottom*, by August Wilson, is produced.

1983

Alice Walker wins the Pulitzer Prize for *The Color Purple*.

1984

Sister Outsider: Essays and Speeches, by Audre Lorde, is published. The human immunodeficiency virus (HIV) is identified as the cause of AIDS.

1985

Published this year: *Linden Hills*, by Gloria Naylor; *Afro-American Folktales: Stories from Black Traditions*, edited by Roger D. Abrahams; and *Annie John*, by Jamaica Kincaid.

1986

Published this year: *Thomas and Beulah*, by Rita Dove; *Our Dead Behind Us*, by Audre Lorde; and *In the Life: A Black Gay Anthology*, edited by Joseph Beam. *The Oprah Winfrey Show* debuts on television.

1987

Rita Dove wins the Pulitzer Prize. James Baldwin dies. *Heavy Daughter Blues*, by Wanda Coleman, and *Beloved*, by Toni Morrison, are published.

1988

The Signifying Monkey, by Henry Louis Gates Jr. is published.

1989

The Berlin Wall is torn down, signaling the dissolution of Communist regimes in the Soviet Union and Eastern Europe.

1990

August Wilson wins the Pulitzer Prize for the play *The Piano Lesson*. Charles R. Johnson wins the National Book Award for the novel *Middle Passage*. *Devil in a Blue Dress*, by Walter Mosley, is published.

1991

Frank Yerby dies.

1992

William Jefferson Clinton is elected president. Published this year: *Technical Difficulties*, by June Jordan; *Waiting to Exhale*, by Terry McMillan; *Jazz*, by Toni Morrison; and *Through the Ivory Gate*, by Rita Dove.

1993

Toni Morrison wins the Nobel Prize for Literature. Rita Dove is named Poet Laureate of the United States.

1994

Race Matters, by Cornel West; *The Portable Harlem Renaissance Reader*, edited by David Levering Lewis; and *Juba to Jive: A Dictionary of African American Slang*, by Clarence Major, are published. Ralph Ellison dies. Yusef Komunyakaa wins the Pulitzer Prize for his book of poems, *Neon Vernacular*.

1997

The first edition of *The Norton Anthology of African American Literature*, edited by Henry Louis Gates Jr. and Nellie Y. McKay, is published.

1998

Margaret Walker and Dorothy West die.

1999

The Intuitionist, by Colson Whitehead, is published.

2000

Step into a World: A Global Anthology of the New Black Literature, edited by Kevin Powell, is published. Gwendolyn Brooks dies. *In the Blood*, by Suzan-Lori Parks, is published.

2001

Giant Steps: The New Generation of African American Writers, edited by Kevin Young, is published. The University of Missouri Press begins to publish *The Complete Works of Langston Hughes* in 16 volumes. September 11: Terrorists from the group al-Qaeda hijack airplanes, two of which destroy the Twin Towers of the World Trade Center in New York City. October 7: In response to the attacks, the United States begins its invasion of Afghanistan.

2002

Quincy Troupe's *Transcircularities: New and Selected Poems* is published this year, as is *Black Like Us: A Century of Lesbian, Gay, and Bisexual African American Fiction*, edited by Devon W. Carbado, Dwight A. McBride, and Donald Weise. Hannah Crafts's *The Bondwoman's Narrative* (ca. 1853–1861) is published for the first time. Carl Phillips receives the 2002 Kingsley Tufts Poetry Award for *The Tether*.

2003

Love, by Toni Morrison, and *The Other Woman*, by Eric Jerome Dickey, are published. On March 20, the United States begins its invasion of Iraq. Edward Jones receives the 2003 National Book Critics Circle Award for Fiction for *The Known World*, which also receives the 2004 Pulitzer Prize in Fiction. Lynn Nottage's play *Intimate Apparel* premieres at Baltimore's Center Stage.

2004

American Smooth, by Rita Dove; *Don't Let Me Be Lonely: An American Lyric*, by Claudia Rankine; and Carl Phillips's *The Rest of Love* are published. Henry Louis Gates Jr. receives the 2004 Carl Sandburg Literary Award. Yusef Komunyakaa receives the Poetry Society of America's 2004 Shelley Memorial Award, and Anthony Butts receives the Poetry Society of America's 2004 William Carlos Williams Award.

2005

African Voices of the Atlantic Slave Trade: Beyond the Silence and the Shame, by Anne C. Bailey; the short-story collection *God's Gym*, by John Edgar Wideman; Tananarive Due's *Joplin's Ghost*; and Samuel R. Delany's *About Writing: Seven Essays, Four Letters, & Five Interviews* are published. August Wilson dies.

2006

Nathaniel Mackey receives the 2006 National Book Award in Poetry for *Splay Anthem* (2006). Barack Obama publishes *The Audacity of Hope*. Ishmael Reed's *New and Collected Poems, 1964–2006* is published. Octavia E. Butler and Nellie Y. McKay die.

2007

Brother, I'm Dying, by Edwidge Danticat, is published and receives the 2007 National Book Critics Circle Award for Autobiography; Harriet Washington's *Medical Apartheid* receives the National Book Critics Circle Award for nonfiction. Natasha Trethewey receives the Pulitzer Prize in Poetry for *Native Guard*, and Nikki Giovanni receives the 2007 Carl Sandburg Literary Award.

2008

Maya Angelou's *Letter to My Daughter*, Toni Morrison's *A Mercy*, and Patricia

Smith's *Blood Dazzler* are published. U.S. Senator Barack Obama becomes the first African American to be elected president of the United States. Michael S. Harper receives the Poetry Society of America's Frost Medal, and Annette Gordon-Reed receives the National Book Award for Nonfiction for *The Hemingses of Monticello: An American Family*, which also receives the 2009 Pulitzer Prize in History.

2009

Rita Dove's *Sonata Mulattica* is published. Anna Deavere Smith's solo show *Let Me Down Easy* premieres. President Barack Hussein Obama receives the Nobel Peace Prize. Lynn Nottage receives the 2009 Pulitzer Prize for Drama for *Ruined*, which also receives the Lucille Lortel and Drama Desk Awards for Outstanding Play and the 2009 Obie Award for the Best New American Play; E. Lynn Harris dies.

2010

Michelle Alexander's *The New Jim Crow: The Warmth of Other Suns*, a new history of African Americans' Great Migration to the North by Isabel Wilkerson, and *Wench*, by Dolen Perkins-Valdez, are published. Terrance Hayes's *Lighthead* receives the National Book Award in Poetry, and Lucille Clifton, who dies in 2010, receives the Poetry Society of America's Frost Medal.

2011

Jesmyn Ward receives the National Book Award for Fiction for *Salvage the Bones*. Nikky Finney receives the National Book Award for Poetry for *Head Off & Split*.

2012

Barack Obama is elected to a second term as president of the United States. Toni Morrison's *Home* and *The Collected Poems of*

Lucille Clifton 1965–2010 are published. Tracy K. Smith receives the Pulitzer Prize in Poetry for *Life on Mars*, and Toi Derricotte receives the PEN/Voelcker Award for Poetry. Natasha Trethewey is named Poet Laureate of the United States.

2013

The House Girl, by Tara Conklin; *Chasing Utopia: A Hybrid*, by Nikki Giovanni; and *Who Asked You?*, by Terry McMillan, are published. The activist group Black Lives Matter is established.

2014

Black Girl Dreaming, by Jacqueline Woodson, and *Citizen: An American Lyric*, by Claudia Rankine, are published. Rankine receives the Jackson Poetry Prize, and *Citizen: An American Lyric* receives National Book Critics Circle Award in Poetry, the NAACP Image Award, the *Los Angeles Times* Book Prize, and the PEN Open Book Award. Maya Angelou and Amiri Baraka die.

2015

Between the World and Me, by Ta-Nehisi Coates; *God Help the Child*, by Toni Morrison; *The Sellout,* by Paul Beatty; and *How to Be Drawn*, by Terrance Hayes, are published.

2016

Colson Whitehead's *The Underground Railroad*, Jacqueline Woodson's *Another Brooklyn*, and Rita Dove's *Collected Poems 1974–2004* are published. Margo Jefferson receives the National Book Critics Circle Award for Autobiography for *Negroland*.

2017

Loving Day, a satirical novel by Mat Johnson; *Difficult Women*, a collection of stories by Roxane Gay; and *The Fire This Time*, by Jesmyn Ward, are published. Colson Whitehead receives the Pulitzer Prize in Fiction for *The Underground Railroad*, and Jesmyn Ward receives the National Book Award for Fiction for *Sing, Unburied, Sing*. Tracy K. Smith named Poet Laureate of the United States.

2018

An American Marriage, by Tayari Jones, is published, as is *Barracoon: The Story of the Last "Black Cargo,"* a previously unpublished book by Zora Neale Hurston. Former first lady of the United States, Michelle Obama, publishes *Becoming*.

2019

Monument: Poems New and Selected, by Natasha Trethewey; *John Woman*, by Walter Mosley; *Bivouac*, by Kwame Dawes; and *Stony the Road: Reconstruction, White Supremacy, and the Rise of Jim Crow*, by Henry Louis Gates Jr., are published.

A

Angelou, Maya (1928–2014)

Autobiographer, poet, actress, producer, director, scriptwriter, political activist, and editor. Angelou, having overcome exceptional adversity, has emerged as one of the most remarkable self-affirming literary and cultural voices in contemporary American literature.

Angelou was born Marguerite Johnson on April 4, 1928, in St. Louis, Missouri. At the age of three, she was sent to Stamps, Arkansas, with her brother, Bailey, to live with their grandmother, Momma, after her parents' divorce. Momma was the owner of a small convenience store and managed to scrape by during the Great Depression.

Five years later, her father took Maya back to her mother in St. Louis. In 1936, she was raped by her mother's boyfriend, Mr. Freeman. This event was confusing to Maya, because Freeman had made prior sexual advances toward her that were unrecognized or misinterpreted as love. Angelou writes, "He held me so softly that I wished he would never let go. I felt at home. From the way he was holding me I knew he'd never let me go or let anything bad happen to me. This was probably my real father and we had found each other at last" (*I Know Why the Caged Bird Sings*, 71). After his ensuing trial, Freeman was murdered. Angelou felt responsible for his death and became mute for a period of about five years and was sent back to Stamps to live with her grandmother.

Angelou's muteness was finally broken by Bertha Flowers, a woman who not only brought speech back into her life but also initiated a new romance with literature and a profound sense of self. Angelou writes, "I was liked, and what a difference it made. I was respected not as Mrs. Henderson's grandchild or Bailey's sister, but just for being Marguerite Johnson" (*I Know Why the Caged Bird Sings*, 98). This sense of self-awareness and pride, in turn, brought Angelou literary fame.

Angelou was reunited with her mother in San Francisco, California, in 1940. She became the first female streetcar conductor in San Francisco and gave birth, at sixteen, to her son, Guy. To support her family, she held a variety of jobs, such as working as a cook, a waitress, and even a madam. She finally settled into performing as a professional dancer.

Angelou spent most of the early 1950s performing at the Purple Onion and touring with the musical *Porgy and Bess*. During this time, she adopted the name Maya Angelou. Maya is derived from her childhood nickname, "My," given to her by her brother, Bailey. Angelou was the last name of her first husband, Tosh Angelou, a White former sailor to whom she was married for two and a half years.

After touring for several years, Angelou moved with her son to New York, where she became actively involved with the Harlem Writer's Guild. Her association with such respected authors as James Baldwin, John Henrik Clarke, and Paule Marshall led to the beginnings of her writing career. Baldwin introduced Angelou to Judy Feiffer. Feiffer and one of her friends at Random

House encouraged Maya to write not only poetry but also her autobiography.

During this time, Angelou became a social activist. She was asked by Martin Luther King Jr. to serve as the northern coordinator for the Southern Christian Leadership Conference after Cabaret for Freedom with Godfrey Cambridge, a comedian. In 1961, she wrote (with Ethel Ayer) and acted in an off-Broadway production, *The Blacks*, with Louis Gossett Jr., Cicely Tyson, and James Earl Jones. The production was highly successful, but Angelou stayed for only a short time due to the director's refusal to pay for music she had written for the show with Ayer.

As her writing accelerated, Angelou met and moved to Africa with Vusumzi Make, a South African freedom fighter, in 1961. The relationship did not last, and Angelou moved with her son to Ghana, where she wrote articles for *The Ghana Times* and was features editor of *The African Review*. She also taught courses at the University of Ghana before returning to the United States in 1966.

In 1969, Angelou's first autobiography, *I Know Why the Caged Bird Sings*, was published. The book was a best seller and was nominated for the National Book Award. In 1971, Angelou became the first Black woman to have a feature-length screenplay produced. *Georgia, Georgia* was well received by critics. *I Know Why the Caged Bird Sings* was followed by other autobiographies that continued to narrate the extraordinary circumstances of her life: *Gather Together in My Name* (1975), *Singin' and Swingin' and Gettin' Merry Like Christmas* (1976), *The Heart of a Woman* (1981), *All God's Children Need Traveling Shoes* (1986), and *A Song Flung Up to Heaven* (2002). These autobiographies

catalog her extraordinary life experiences and have been lauded by critics as a significant contribution to African American literature because of Angelou's profound sense of self and her environment. Her work has been compared to that of Frederick Douglass and Richard Wright in its emphasis on the effect of the external environment, including the culture and the people, on the narrator. In 1979, she wrote the script and composed the music for the television movie *I Know Why the Caged Bird Sings*.

Angelou wrote several volumes of poetry, including *Just Give Me a Cool Drink of Water 'fore I Diiie* (1971), which was nominated for the Pulitzer Prize; *Oh Pray My Wings Are Gonna Fit Me Well* (1975); *And Still I Rise* (1978); *I Shall Not Be Moved* (1990); and *Phenomenal Woman: Four Poems Celebrating Women* (1994). She received a Tony Award nomination for her role as Mrs. Keckley in *Look Away* in 1973 and an Emmy nomination for her role as Nyo Boto in the televised *Roots* miniseries in 1977. She appeared in the film *How to Make an American Quilt* (1995) and directed *Down in the Delta* (1998). She was appointed to the Bicentennial Commission by President Gerald Ford and to the Commission of International Women's Year by President Jimmy Carter, and recited her poem "On the Pulse of Morning" at the inauguration of President Bill Clinton, for which she won a Grammy Award for Best Spoken Word Album in 1994. She was the Reynolds professor of American Studies at Wake Forest University in Winston-Salem, North Carolina, where she received a lifetime appointment in 1981. In 2002, she was elected to the National Women's Hall of Fame. She received honorary degrees from several universities. In 2013, Angelou received an honorary National Book Award (the Literarian Award) for her many contributions to American letters (Dilworth). Angelou died in her Winston-Salem home on May 28, 2014.

Lindsey Renuard

See also: Black Arts Movement; Feminism/Black Feminism.

Resources

Maya Angelou: *All God's Children Need Traveling Shoes* (New York: Random House, 1986); *And Still I Rise* (New York: Random House, 1978); *Gather Together in My Name* (New York: Random House, 1975); The Heart of a Woman (New York: Random House, 1981); *I Know Why the Caged Bird Sings* (New York: Random House, 1969); *I Shall Not Be Moved* (New York: Random House, 1990); *Just Give Me a Cool Drink of Water 'fore I Diiie* (New York: Random House, 1971); *Oh Pray My Wings Are Gonna Fit Me Well* (New York: Random House, 1975); *Phenomenal Woman: Four Poems Celebrating Women* (New York: Random House, 1994); *Singin' and Swingin' and Gettin' Merry Like Christmas* (New York: Random House, 1976); *A Song Flung Up to Heaven* (New York: Random House, 2002); Joanne M. Braxton, *Black Women Writing Autobiography: A Tradition Within a Tradition* (Philadelphia: Temple University Press, 1989); Darlene Dilworth, "Toni Morrison Honors Maya Angelou at National Book Awards," *Adweek* (Nov. 20, 2013): https://www.adweek.com/galleycat/toni-morrison-honors-maya-angelou-at-the-national-book-awards/81257.

Autobiography

As the etymological roots of the word (auto/self, bios/life, and *graphe*/writing) indicate, autobiography is the art and practice of writing the story of one's own life. An autobiography is a written or spoken narrative in which an individual tells the story of how he or she came over time to be an independent, often original, agent.

In *The Oxford Companion to African American Literature*, William L. Andrews, arguably the preeminent scholar of African American autobiography, explains that during its evolutionary phase, African American autobiography "held and continues to hold a position of priority, if not preeminence, among the narrative traditions of black America . . . [and] has testified since the late eighteenth century to the commitment of people of color to realize the promise of their American birthright and to articulate their achievements as individuals and as persons of African descent" (Andrews and Bassard, "Autobiography," 34).

Briton Hammon's spiritual autobiography, *Narrative of the Uncommon Sufferings, and Surprizing Deliverance of Briton Hammon, a Negro Man*, published in Boston, Massachusetts, in 1760, was the first work by a Black author published in North America. It is also a good example of the journey/quest motif and the theme of atonement. In 1747, Hammon left his Boston employer and sailed to Jamaica. His narrative describes his kidnapping, his imprisonment, and, finally, a reunion with his master more than ten years later. Other important autobiographies of this era include those by James Gronniosaw and Venture Smith.

It was almost fifty years after the publication of Hammon's Narrative, according to Andrews, before African American autobiographers began to prove to readers that they were best qualified to tell their own stories. From these beginnings until the proclamation of full emancipation in 1865, Black American autobiography evolved into a complex "oratorical" mode springing from narratives of ex-slaves who spoke on the antislavery lecture circuit (Andrews,

To Tell a Free Story, 1; Emmanuel Nelson, ed., *African American Autobiographers*).

Between 1760, the year of the first African American autobiography, and 1831, the year of the Nat Turner insurrection, narratives written by former slaves seemed less concerned with slavery itself as a primary topic and concentrated more on issues of self-fulfillment and spiritual growth. Notable African American spiritual autobiographies include those by John Marrant, Sojourner Truth, George White, Richard Allen, Zilpha Elaw, Lucy A. Delaney, Elizabeth (also known as Old Elizabeth), Jarena Lee, and John Jea (Nelson).

Andrews argues that perhaps more than any other form of literary discourse, autobiography has been chosen by African Americans to articulate ideals of selfhood integral to an African American sense of identity, both individual and communal. More important, "autobiography has helped African Americans bear witness to an evolving tradition of liberated and empowered individuality" (Andrews and Bassard, "Autobiography," 34).

Besides providing a forum for sociopolitical and cultural concerns, African American autobiography established a tradition of powerful personal writing. Early African American autobiography influenced writing by Black American writers from William Wells Brown to Charles W. Chesnutt, from W.E.B. Du Bois to Richard Wright, Ralph Ellison, and James Baldwin, as well as Frances E. W. Harper, Pauline Hopkins, Zora Neale Hurston, Margaret Walker, and Toni Morrison.

Andrews, in *African American Autobiography*, concludes that African Americans had been dictating and writing first-person accounts of their lives for almost a century before the first Black American novel appeared in 1853: "It is significant that this novel, William Wells Brown's *Clotel*, was subtitled *A Narrative of Slave Life in the United States* and was written by a man who had made his initial literary fame as a fugitive slave autobiographer. Ever since, the history of African American narrative has been informed by a call-and-response relationship between autobiography and its successor, the novel" (Andrews, *African American Autobiography*, 1). From this perspective, then, one genre, the novel, can be said to have grown out of another genre, autobiography, in African American literature.

Many themes arise in the evolution of the African American autobiography. In *To Tell a Free Story*, Andrews identifies several "organizing principles and moral issues" that were also popular in White autobiographical genres. He cites "the captivity narrative, the conversion account, the criminal confession, the spiritual autobiography, and the journal of ministerial labors" (Andrews, *To Tell a Free Story*, 38). In *The Oxford Companion to African American Literature*, however, Andrews uses two controlling categories, "Secular Autobiography" (34) and "Spiritual Autobiography" (37), to help organize the potentially endless list of themes and moral and political issues (Andrews and Bassard, "Autobiography"). The best-known secular autobiographies were written by fugitives who documented the brutality of slavery.

The most effective narratives focused as much on the individual as on the institution of slavery, placing special emphasis on how slaves escaped and/or fought against brutality. Classic autobiographies of this kind include Frederick Douglass's *Narrative of the Life of Frederick Douglass, an American Slave* (1845), William Wells Brown's *Narrative of William Wells Brown, a Fugitive Slave* (1847), and Harriet Jacobs's

Incidents in the Life of a Slave Girl (1861). William and Ellen Craft, Solomon Northup, Henry Bibb, Mary Prince, and Moses Roper also wrote autobiographies that fall into the "secular" category.

After emancipation, African Americans, led by Booker T. Washington (*Up from Slavery*, 1901), continued the autobiographical tradition. In the first part of the twentieth century, W.E.B. Du Bois, Zora Neale Hurston, Langston Hughes, and Richard Wright produced important autobiographical writing. Wright's *Black Boy* is considered a classic midcentury African American autobiography. Since World War II, autobiography in the hands of individuals as different as Malcolm X, Ned Cobb, James Baldwin, Amiri Baraka, Samuel Delany, Angela Davis, Claude Brown, and Audre Lorde has taken on a wide spectrum of topics, including sexuality, religion, class, illness, and the Black family. Maya Angelou and John Edgar Wideman have produced prize-winning autobiographies, confirming the continuing literary vitality of African American first-person narrative. Even more recently, Anne Moody, Patrice Gaines, Itabari Njeri, Janet McDonald, Nathan McCall, Gloria Wade-Gayles, and Lorene Cary have produced acclaimed autobiographies, continuing the tradition that began over two centuries earlier. In 2007, Barack Obama, a U.S. Senator who was later elected to two terms as U.S. President, published the best-selling *Dreams of My Father: A Story of Race and Inheritance*, and in 2018, former first lady Michelle Obama published the partly autobiographical book, *Becoming*, to wide popular and critical acclaim. In 2015, Ta-Nehisi Coates, a writer for the *Atlantic*, published a highly acclaimed and widely read autobiography addressed to his son, *Between the World and Me*; among other things, the book describes Coates's upbringing in Baltimore and the ways in which he was both accepted and challenged at Howard University in Washington, DC.

John Greer Hall

See also: Baldwin, James; Coates, Ta-Nehisi; Craft, William and Ellen Smith Craft; Douglass, Frederick; Hughes, Langston; Hurston, Zora Neale; Jacobs, Harriet Ann; Malcolm X; Slave Narrative; Washington, Booker T.; Wright, Richard.

Resources

Frederick Luis Aldama, "Re-Visioning African American Autobiography," *MFS: Modern Fiction Studies* 46, no. 4 (Winter 2000), 1004–1007; William L. Andrews, *To Tell a Free Story: The First Century of Afro-American Autobiography, 1760–1865* (Urbana: University of Illinois Press, 1988); William L. Andrews, ed., *African American Autobiography: A Collection of Critical Essays* (Englewood Cliffs, NJ: Prentice-Hall, 1993); William L. Andrews and Katherine Clay Bassard, "Autobiography," in *The Oxford Companion to African American Literature*, ed. William L. Andrews, Francis Smith Foster, and Trudier Harris (New York: Oxford University Press, 1997), 34–39; Maya Angelou, *I Know Why the Caged Bird Sings* (New York: Bantam, 1983); James Baldwin, *Collected Essays* (New York: Library of America, 1998); Jonathan Bradford Brennan, "Speaking Cross Boundaries: A Nineteenth-Century African/Native American Autobiography," *A/B: Auto/Biography Studies,* 7, no. 2 (Fall 1992), 219–238; William Wells Brown: *Clotel; or, The President's Daughter*, ed. Hilton Als (New York: Modern Library, 2001), also in *Three Classic African-American Novels,* ed. William Andrews et al. (New York: Signet, 1990); *Narrative of William Wells Brown, a Fugitive Slave, Written by Himself* (Boston: American Anti-Slavery Society, 1847); Lorene Cary, *Black Ice* (New York: Knopf, 1991); Ta-Nehisi Coates, *Between the*

World and Me (New York: Spiegel and Grau, 2015); Frederick Douglass, *Narrative of the Life of Frederick Douglass, an American Slave, Written by Himself* (New York: W. W. Norton, 1997); Patrice Gaines, *Laughing in the Dark: From Colored Girl to Woman of Color—A Journey from Prison to Power* (New York: Crown, 1994); Henry Louis Gates Jr., and William Andrews, eds., *Slave Narratives* (New York: Library of America, 2000); James Albert Ukawsaw Gronniosaw, *A Narrative of the Most Remarkable Particulars in the Life of James Albert Ukawsaw Gronniosaw, an African Prince,* ed. W. Shirley (Bath, UK: S. Hazzard, 1770); Calvin L. Hall, *African American Journalists: Autobiography as Memoir and Manifesto* (Lanham, Maryland: Scarecrow Press, 2009); Briton Hammon, *A Narrative of the Uncommon Sufferings, and Surprizing Deliverance of Briton Hammon, a Negro Man* (Boston: Green & Russell, 1760); Langston Hughes: *The Big Sea* (New York: Knopf, 1940); *I Wonder as I Wander* (New York: Rinehart, 1956); Zora Neale Hurston, *Dust Tracks on a Road: An Autobiography* (New York: Harper Perennial, 1996); Harriet A. Jacobs, *Incidents in the Life of a Slave Girl, Written by Herself* (Cambridge, MA: Harvard University Press, 1987); George E. Kent, "Maya Angelou's *I Know Why the Caged Bird Sings* and Black Autobiographical Tradition," in *African American Autobiography: A Collection of Critical Essays,* ed. William L. Andrews (Englewood Cliffs, NJ: Prentice-Hall, 1993); Eric D. Lamore, editor, *Reading African American Autobiography: 21st Century Contexts and Criticism* (Madison: University of Wisconsin Press, 2017; Jeff Loeb, "MIA: African American Autobiography of the Vietnam War," *African American Review* 31, no. 1 (Spring 1997), 105–123; Audre Lorde, *The Cancer Journals* (San Francisco: Aunt Lute Books, 1997); Malcolm X, *The Autobiography of Malcolm X,* written with Alex Haley (New York: Ballantine, 1987); R. Baxter Miller, "The Rewritten Self in African American Autobiography," in *Alternative Identities: The Self in Literature, History, Theory,* ed. Linda Marie Brooks (New York: Garland, 1995), 87–104; Emmanuel S. Nelson, ed., *African American Autobiographers: A Sourcebook* (Westport, CT: Greenwood Press, 2002); Itabari Njeri, *Every Good-bye Ain't Gone* (New York: Vintage, 1991); Barack Obama, *Dreams of My Father: A Story of Race and Inheritance* (New York: Crown Publishers, 2007); Michelle Obama, *Becoming* (New York: Crown/Random House, 2018); Crispin Sartwell, *Act Like You Know: African American Autobiography and White Identity* (Chicago: University of Chicago Press, 1998); Johnnie M. Stover, "Nineteenth-Century African American Women's Autobiography as Social Discourse: The Example of Harriet Ann Jacobs," *College English* 66, no. 2 (Nov. 2003), 133–154; Booker T. Washington, *Up from Slavery,* ed. William L. Andrews (New York: Oxford University Press, 1995); John Edgar Wideman, *Brothers and Keepers* (New York: Vintage, 1995); Roland L. Williams Jr., *African American Autobiography and the Quest for Freedom* (Westport, CT: Greenwood Press, 2000); Richard Wright, *Black Boy* (New York: Perennial Classics, 1998).

B

Baldwin, James (1924–1987)

Novelist, essayist, playwright, poet, and activist. James Baldwin was one of the most influential and widely respected voices in American literature of the twentieth century, the heir to W.E.B. Du Bois's intellectual fervor and Richard Wright's anger, and the predecessor of Toni Morrison's challenging aesthetics. Baldwin was born in Harlem, New York, on August 2, 1924, the oldest of nine children. His mother, Emma Berdis Jones, married his stepfather, the preacher David Baldwin. One of Baldwin's public-school teachers in Harlem was Countee Cullen. James never knew his biological father, and his relationship with his stepfather was antagonistic. Yet James became a preacher when he turned fourteen, having undergone a religious conversion similar to the one that John Grimes, the protagonist of Baldwin's first novel, *Go Tell It on the Mountain* (1953), experiences. He describes this experience in *The Fire Next Time* (1963). Before he was twenty, Baldwin had left the church, and this painful decision is reflected in many of his works.

Baldwin's writing career began after he graduated from high school in 1942. He reviewed books, and in 1948, he published his first essay and his first short story, "Previous Condition," about the torment of a young actor who leaves Harlem and is evicted from an apartment in a White neighborhood, leaving him with nowhere to go. Reacting to similar instances of racist persecution, Baldwin left for Paris soon thereafter, the first of many periods of exile.

Paris gave Baldwin the opportunity to confront a number of pasts that related to his own identity. As he describes in "Encounter on the Seine" (1950), his African past exists in Paris in the form of Frenchmen of African descent and Algerian immigrants. Baldwin discovers his kinship with these people who are connected to him by the color of his skin, yet the French Africans are different because of their status as colonial subjects rather than as American tourists or expatriates. "Encounter on the Seine" demonstrates Baldwin's awareness of the complex connection between race and his identity. The murderous anger he felt toward American racists could only tear him apart or land him in jail, so he left his native country. He would come to realize in Paris that racism was going to follow him. He went from Paris to a village in Switzerland, where he completed his first novel.

Go Tell It on the Mountain, a coming-of-age story of fourteen-year-old John Grimes, also explores the stories of John's aunt, stepfather, mother, and biological father. The middle section of the book, the stories of John's parents and aunt, broadens the scope of the novel to include the struggles of African Americans who left their homes in the early twentieth century. John's story takes place on his fourteenth birthday. Like Baldwin, who underwent a violent conversion experience at the age of fourteen, John is surprised to find himself on the "threshing floor" in front of the altar of his church. Also like Baldwin, who went to Paris partially to escape the racial persecution of his home country, John attempts to escape the filth and low station of his home. But dirt follows John just as racism followed Baldwin. John attempts to transcend his circumstances in solitude, first by mounting a hill in Central Park, then by entering a movie theater. In both cases he is attracted to fame and wealth, the very sins that his stepfather Gabriel denounces from the pulpit. John's individual identity quest is diverted by guilt over his obligations to family. He reenters Gabriel's church and, fulfilling everyone's expectations that he will become a minister to compensate for his brother's misbehavior, he prepares himself for conversion. John's journey continues in Baldwin's 1955 play *The Amen Corner*. In this play, David Alexander is caught between the ways of the church, represented by his mother, who is a pastor, and the ways of the world, represented by his father, who is a jazz musician. In contrast to John Grimes, David runs off to explore himself, not through religion but through art.

Whereas in *Go Tell It on the Mountain*, the sexual attraction between male characters is suggested subtly, Baldwin's second novel, *Giovanni's Room* (1956), addresses the subject of homosexuality in such a direct way that it shocked publishers and readers alike. Although homosexuality is not incidental in *Giovanni's Room*, the novel is really about something broader: the refusal to accept oneself, which leads to the impossibility of loving another. Though he acknowledged his own bisexuality, Baldwin spent much of his career arguing with labels and would never accept being called "gay." Yet *Giovanni's Room* is widely considered Baldwin's "gay novel," perhaps because it was so unusual in 1956 to read fiction about homosexual experiences described so candidly, and perhaps because the narrator David's homosexual experiences pointedly frame the dilemma of the novel. In contrast

to his other novels, *Giovanni's Room* is not about race relations or racism: David is White. Baldwin did not want to overburden the book's central message with too many issues.

Baldwin again attempted to create a deeply affecting psychological narrative about facing reality and about the responsibility of the individual to care for others in his most famous short story, "Sonny's Blues" (1957), published the year after *Giovanni's Room* appeared. The narrator of "Sonny's Blues" attempts to lead an upright, middle-class existence in order to avoid suffering. Just as Giovanni causes David to see life from another point of view, so the narrator's brother, Sonny, causes him to revise his own safe viewpoint. Because of the healing power of music, "Sonny's Blues" ends in transcendence rather than tragedy.

Baldwin's message took on a more political and racially charged context during the turbulent 1960s. The Civil Rights Movement had begun, and it needed guidance. Baldwin returned from Europe and journeyed to the South to witness firsthand how the promise of America was failing and to provide hope for its renewal. His essays in *Nobody Knows My Name* (1961) and *The Fire Next Time* (1963) gained him fame as the rising star in the American literary scene, and he was invited to the White House to meet President John Kennedy and Attorney General Robert Kennedy, who consulted him on American race relations. The long essay "Down at the Cross," from *The Fire Next Time*, is considered by many to be Baldwin's best work: a combination of reportage, personal history, and historic commentary that provides an important perspective and offers a vision of the anger exploding throughout America. From this point on, the tone of his essays became apocalyptic, and Baldwin's increasing militancy can be seen in the last short story he published, "Going to Meet the Man" (1965), which gave the title to his only collection of stories. "Going to Meet the Man" is a vicious story filtered through the viewpoint of a racist White sheriff who as a youth had witnessed the lynching and castration of a Black man and is permanently damaged as a result.

Baldwin's perspective changed as a result of his political involvement in the South in the early 1960s. His 1964 play *Blues for Mister Charlie* coincided with the onset of the Black Arts Movement. Inspired by the infamous 1955 murder of Emmett Till, *Blues for Mister Charlie* illustrates the connection Baldwin perceived between racial violence and sexual mythology. It also dramatizes the possibilities for violent or nonviolent reactions to racial injustice. Richard Henry, who is murdered at the outset of the play, had given a gun to his father, Meridian, and although Meridian does not fire it in the third act, he is carrying it under his Bible at the play's conclusion, as if to signal the potential danger to come. Baldwin's novels *Another Country* (1962) and *Tell Me How Long the Train's Been Gone* (1968) are notable departures. They are sprawling narratives that range over time and space in a way that his earlier works do not. Baldwin's readers had to revise their preconceived notions of Baldwin if they were to follow these challenging books. Many readers were not willing to do so, and although *Another Country* remains one of Baldwin's greatest literary achievements in terms of its daring experimentation and its engagement with human despair, American identity, and the complexity of sexual and racial relationships. It begins with the final, desperate days of Rufus Scott, a despondent Black New Yorker who has been emotionally damaged and marginalized by

society. He has no outlet for the bitterness and poison that fill him, though he attempts to take them out on Leona, a Southern White woman. When he realizes the futility of this attempt either to love or to hate, Rufus feels that he has no alternative but to commit suicide. The bulk of the novel concerns the way Rufus's friends and family continue their lives in the aftermath of the tragedy.

Like *Another Country*, *Tell Me How Long the Train's Been Gone* explores nearly all of the themes associated with Baldwin's work: the conflicted role of the artist, the tense relationship between brothers, the church's oppression, the difficulty of self-acceptance, and the failure of contemporary America to deal with its race problems. The novel is the story of Leo Proudhammer, a stage and film actor who suffers a heart attack and who uses his convalescence to reflect upon his life. Weary of his role as a spokesman, Baldwin was clearly projecting a side of himself in the character of Leo. Leo helps himself recuperate by telling his story, making himself vulnerable in a way actors typically do not. From the public's perspective, his story is the classic rags-to-riches tale, made more poignant because he grew up poor and Black. In the novel's final pages, a White character holds Leo up as an example of how anyone of any race can succeed in America. At the same time, a militant Black character named Christopher presents a persuasive case for the type of righteous anger evident in groups such as the Black Panther Party in the late 1960s. Like *Blues for Mister Charlie*, this novel ends with the potential for future violence, yet it does not endorse violence as the solution to America's racial strife.

The anger that characterizes the play and two novels Baldwin published in the 1960s can be seen in his essays of the same period, which also tended to be longer and more ambitious than his earlier efforts. To be Black during that decade invariably meant that one was asked to choose between two distinct forces: the radical militancy associated with Malcolm X and the Black Muslims, and the peaceful nonviolence associated with Martin Luther King Jr. As someone who resisted labels and never stayed in America long, Baldwin found himself left behind or left out of the debates that he had contributed to so frequently in the early 1960s. In Baldwin's celebrated essay on Elijam Mohammed, "Down at the Cross" (1962), he had already distanced himself from the Black Muslims, though not from Malcolm X. His book-length essay *No Name in the Street* (1972) was a comprehensive attempt to come to terms with the turbulence of race relations in contemporary America. In this ambitious and wide-ranging essay, he tried to demonstrate his anger in the aftermath of the assassinations of Medgar Evers, Malcolm X, and King.

No Name in the Street ends on a typical Baldwinian note of prophecy: "I think black people have always felt this about America, and Americans, and have always seen, spinning above the thoughtless American head, the shape of the wrath to come" (195). This wrath derives at least partially from one of the most pervasive injustices in contemporary America, the systematic police brutality and wrongful imprisonment that defined African American experience in the post–Civil Rights era. Baldwin addressed this situation in *If Beale Street Could Talk* (1974), a novel markedly different from Baldwin's earlier work in terms of its vernacular voice. Tish Rivers, the novel's narrator, is a streetwise nineteen-year-old Black girl, a character type less prominent in Baldwin's previous novels (with the

exception of Ida in *Another Country*). Tish and her family seek to prove the innocence of her boyfriend, Fonny, who has been wrongfully charged with rape. The situation is urgent, for she is carrying Fonny's baby. Baldwin turns his attention to injustice on the street in this novel, which is another blues story, as the title indicates. *If Beale Street Could Talk* was adapted to the screen, under the same title, in 2018 (Jenkins).

Baldwin's health was beginning to deteriorate when his final novel, *Just Above My Head* (1979), was published. *Just Above My Head* has a huge cast of characters and covers the range of Baldwin's travels, from New York City to Paris to the American South. Readers are introduced to characters who are confused by their sexual attractions in the face of society's taboos. As in *Beale Street*, Baldwin sees a tremendous need for strong, functional families as supports for the individual. Among all of these familiar Baldwin motifs is the central struggle of Hall, the narrator, who is a witness to his brother's life.

Baldwin published his collected poems in a slim volume titled *Jimmy's Blues*, which appeared first in England in 1983. The poems, written at various times throughout his life, are distilled versions of the blues theme that he had been trying to communicate all along, and the themes of blindness, invisibility, the burden of the witness, and the difficulties of loving are once again evident. His last work, *The Evidence of Things Not Seen* (1985), was similarly neglected and is similarly important, a counterpart to his most famous essay, "Down at the Cross," and an exploration of the post–Civil Rights South paralleling his earlier explorations in *Nobody Knows My Name*. During this trip south, Baldwin was investigating a series of child murders that began in

Atlanta, Georgia, in 1979. He ended up writing about the murders as evidence of something more widespread in America: the racism, lack of faith, and lack of vision that plagues our nation and prevents its dream.

Baldwin died in southern France in 1987 from cancer of the esophagus. His death was marked by a tremendous celebration of his life at the Cathedral of St. John the Divine in New York, and celebrations thereafter have focused on his literary achievements and his wisdom. There has been a resurgence in recent years of criticism about Baldwin's life and writing; five books of criticism and one biography have been published on his writings since the mid-1990s. Toward the end of his life, Baldwin wrote a long letter to his literary agent outlining a proposed book about Black leaders Medgar Evers, Malcolm X, and Martin Luther King Jr., all assassinated in the 1960s and all of whom Baldwin new well. Although the book, provisionally titled "Remember This House," never materialized, in 2017, Raoul Peck produced a feature-length documentary film that reconstructs Baldwin's project: *I Am Not Your Negro*. It is narrated by Samuel L. Jackson and features archival footage of the three men and of Harry Belafonte, Bob Dylan, Ray Charles, and Robert F. Kennedy, among others. The film received wide critical acclaim and drew many new readers to Baldwin's works (Als, Woubshet). Although there is always healthy debate over what Baldwin should be remembered for, there is no doubt that he will be remembered as one of the most important American writers of the latter twentieth century.

D. Quentin Miller

See also: Autobiography; Essay; Gay Literature; Protest Literature.

Resources

Primary Sources: James Baldwin: *The Amen Corner* (New York: Dial, 1968; first produced 1955); *Another Country* (New York: Dial, 1962); *Blues for Mister Charlie* (New York: Dial, 1964); *The Evidence of Things Not Seen* (New York: Holt, Rinehart, and Winston, 1985); *The Fire Next Time* (New York: Dial, 1963); *Giovanni's Room* (New York: Dial, 1956); *Go Tell It on the Mountain* (New York: Knopf, 1953); *Going to Meet the Man* (New York: Dial, 1965); *If Beale Street Could Talk* (New York: Dial, 1974); *James Baldwin: Collected Essays*, ed. Toni Morrison (New York: Library of America, 1998); *James Baldwin: Early Novels and Stories*, ed. Toni Morrison (New York: Library of America, 1998); *Jimmy's Blues* (London: Michael Joseph, 1983); *Just Above My Head* (New York: Dial, 1979); *No Name in the Street* (New York: Dial, 1972); *Nobody Knows My Name* (New York: Dial, 1961); *Notes of a Native Son* (Boston: Beacon, 1955); *The Price of the Ticket: Collected Nonfiction 1948–1985* (New York: St. Martin's Press, 1985); *Tell Me How Long the Train's Been Gone* (New York: Dial, 1968); Jenkins, Barry, writer and director, *If Beale Street Could Talk* (Annapurna Pictures, 2018).

Secondary Sources: Hilton Als, "Capturing James Baldwin's Legacy Onscreen," *The New Yorker*, Feb. 13 and 20, 2017: https://www.newyorker.com/magazine/2017/02/13/capturing-james-baldwins-legacy-onscreen (accessed 2018); Katherine L. Balfour, *The Evidence of Things Not Said: James Baldwin and the Promise of American Democracy* (Ithaca, NY: Cornell University Press, 2001); Harold Bloom, ed., *James Baldwin* (New York: Chelsea House, 1986); Donald Bogle, "A Look at the Movies by Baldwin," *Freedomways* 16, no. 2 (Spring 1976), 103–108 (review of *The Devil Finds Work*); James Campbell, *Talking at the Gates: A Life of James Baldwin* (Berkeley: University of California Press, 2002); Trudier Harris, *Black Women in the Fiction of James Baldwin* (New York: Cambridge University Press, 1996); Trudier Harris, ed., *New Essays on "Go Tell It on the*

Mountain" (New York: Cambridge University Press, 1996); David Leeming, *James Baldwin* (New York: Knopf, 1994); Dwight A. McBride, ed., *James Baldwin Now* (New York: New York University Press, 1999); D. Quentin Miller, ed., *Reviewing James Baldwin: Things Not Seen* (Philadelphia: Temple University Press, 2000); Raoul Peck, director, *I Am Not Your Negro* (documentary film), produced by ARTE France, Independent Lens, and others, 2017; Horace A. Porter, *Stealing the Fire: The Art and Protest of James Baldwin* (Middletown, CT: Wesleyan University Press, 1989); Lynn Orilla Scott, *Witness to the Journey: James Baldwin's Later Fiction* (East Lansing: Michigan State University Press, 2002); Fred L. Standley and Nancy V. Burt, eds., *Critical Essays on James Baldwin* (Boston: G. K. Hall, 1988); Fred L. Standley and Louis H. Pratt, eds., *Conversations with James Baldwin* (Jackson: University Press of Mississippi, 1989); W. J. Weatherby, *James Baldwin: Artist on Fire* (New York: D. I. Fine, 1989); Dagmawi Woubshet, "The Imperfect Power of *I Am Not Your Negro*," *The Atlantic*, Feb. 8, 2017: https://www.theatlantic.com/entertainment/archive/2017/02/i-am-not-your-negro-review/515976/ (accessed 2018).

Baraka, Amiri (1934–2014)

Poet, playwright, essayist, editor, novelist, and political activist. Baraka is a controversial and prolific writer who has transformed his name, philosophy, and political stance throughout his career, yet has maintained a consistently rebellious and contentious tone, never relenting in his attacks on the status quo. He first changed his name from LeRoy to LeRoi Jones and then began using the Islamic name Imamu Amiri Baraka (1968) before finally using just Amiri Baraka (1974). From his early involvement in the Beat Movement, he went on to become a leading figure in Black Nationalism and the

Black Arts Movement, and is now most often regarded as having been a spokesperson for Third World Marxism. Baraka has been accused by some critics of unevenness in the quality of his work, of being racist, and of sacrificing aesthetics to his leftist political views; others see him as an authentic voice of and leader for African Americans and as one whose innovations and wide-ranging talents marked him as among the greatest African American authors, comparable in influence with W.E.B. Du Bois and Richard Wright.

Baraka was born Everett Leroy Jones in Newark, New Jersey, to Coyette "Coit" LeRoy Jones, a postal supervisor, and Anna Lois Jones, a social worker. After graduating from high school with honors in 1951, he attended Rutgers University on a scholarship, then transferred to Howard University in 1952. At Howard, he changed the spelling of his name to LeRoi. After dropping out of Howard University (1954), Baraka joined the Air Force (what he calls the "Error Farce" in his *Autobiography*), from which he received an undesirable discharge (1957). He settled in Greenwich Village, where he met and married a Jewish woman, Hettie Cohen (1958). Baraka and his wife (who took the name Hettie Jones) published the Beat literary journal *Yugen*, and he interacted with and was influenced by such authors as Allen Ginsberg, Charles Olson, and Frank O'Hara.

In 1960, following the Cuban revolution, Baraka traveled to Cuba with a group of African American authors and intellectuals and met Fidel Castro and a group of Latin American intellectuals. Baraka's essay "Cuba Libre" is based on these meetings and is divided into two sections: "What I Brought to the Revolution" and "What I Brought Back Here." In 1961, he published his first collection of poems, *Preface to a*

Twenty Volume Suicide Note. In it, according to one critic, Baraka "probes into the realms of autobiography and identity, high art and avant-gardist artists, Black music, American popular culture, and the heroes and anti-heroes of the Western world" (Sollors, 37). Baraka later wrote *Blues People: Negro Music in White America* (1963), a nonfiction book in which he discusses jazz and blues as expressions of African American social history; he also published a second collection of poetry, *The Dead Lecturer* (1964). During this period, Baraka further developed his dramatic technique by writing such plays as *The Slave* (1964) and *Dutchman* (1964), an absurdist drama focusing on racial stereotyping and identity. *Dutchman* is about Clay, a well-dressed young Black man who is taunted by Lula, a flirtatious White woman, for acting White while they are riding together on the subway. When the incessant taunting enrages Clay, Lula stabs him to death. *Dutchman,* which received an Obie for the best Off-Broadway production, greatly enhanced Baraka's visibility and reputation.

In 1965, the year Malcolm X was assassinated, Baraka divorced Hettie and moved to Harlem, New York, where he started the short-lived Black Arts Repertory Theatre/School, beginning a period during which he focused on Black Nationalism, Black arts, and other African American issues, and increasingly began to use Black English in his writing. Baraka then returned to Newark, where, in 1966, he married an African American woman, Sylvia Robinson (now Amina Baraka); founded Jihad Productions (1966), which published the works of such African American authors as Ben Caldwell, Yusef Iman, and Clarence Reed; and founded Spirit House (1967), an African American community theater and center for arts and culture. He also became active in politics,

Black Nationalism, and the Nation of Islam, even helping arrange a national Black Power conference (1967). During the 1967 race riots in Newark, Baraka was arrested and convicted of unlawfully carrying firearms and resisting arrest, but his conviction was overturned on appeal. Baraka was also instrumental in electing Kenneth Gibson, Newark's first African American mayor (1970) and one of the first African American mayors of a major U.S. city; in organizing the Congress of African People (1970), a national Pan-African organization; and in arranging the National Black Political Convention (1972), which met in Gary, Indiana.

By 1974, Baraka was shifting his focus from Black Nationalism and Islam to Third World Marxism and had dropped the title Imamu (Swahili for spiritual leader) from his name. In his poetry collection *Hard Facts* (1976), Baraka's focus is on class struggles, and he is highly critical of the African American middle class and many African American authors and intellectuals, such as Nikki Giovanni, for selling out to White ideals. He also wrote several plays, including *The Motion of History* (1977), *What Was the Relationship of the Lone Ranger to the Means of Production* (1979), and *Dim'Cracker Party Convention* (1980). For two decades (1980–2000), Baraka was a professor of African Studies at the State University of New York at Stony Brook while continuing his prolific writing career, penning plays, essays, and poetry, including *Wise, Why's, Y's* (1996), an epic poem in which Baraka uses the narrative persona of a griot (an African storyteller) to discuss the history of oppression and struggle of African Americans.

Baraka was named poet laureate of New Jersey by Governor James E. McGreevey, but just one month after he became poet laureate (2002), Baraka was asked to resign after an outcry following a public reading of his "Somebody Blew Up America" (2001), a poem about the 9/11 terrorist attacks. Baraka was accused of anti-Semitism, primarily on the basis of the lines "Who knew the World Trade Center was gonna get bombed / Who told 4000 Israeli workers at the Twin Towers / To stay home that day / Why did Sharon stay away?" Ultimately, since there was no way to rescind the award and Baraka refused to give it up, the position of poet laureate was abolished in New Jersey (2003), effectively stripping Baraka of the title before his term was completed.

In 2009, Baraka published a collection of his essays about blues music and jazz: *Digging the Afro-American Soul of American Classical Music*. The work assesses the music of famous jazz musicians Max Roach, Miles Davis, Charlie Parker, and John Coltrane but also investigates the music of lesser-known figures.

A *New York Times* obituary of Baraka observed that both Baraka's "champions and detractors agreed that at his finest he was a powerful voice on the printed page, a riveting orator in person and an enduring presence on the international literary scene whom—whether one loved or hated him—it was seldom possible to ignore" (Fox).

David Carrell

See also: Black Arts Movement; Blues Poetry; Drama; Jazz in Literature; Postmodernism.

Resources

Primary Sources: Amiri Baraka: *The Autobiography of LeRoi Jones* (New York: Freundlich Books, 1984; repr. Chicago: Lawrence Hill Books, 1997); *Digging the Afro-American Soul of American Classic Music* (Berkeley: University of California Press, 2009); *The LeRoi Jones/Amiri Baraka Reader*, ed. William J. Harris (New York: Thunder's Mouth, 1991); *Selected Plays and Prose of Amiri Baraka/ LeRoi Jones* (New York: William Morrow, 1979); *Somebody Blew Up America and Other Poems* (Albany, NY: House of Nehesi, 2004); *S.O.S.: Poems 1961–2013* (New York: Grove Press, 2016); *Transbluescency: The Selected Poems of Amiri Baraka/LeRoi Jones (1961–1995)*, ed. Paul Vangelisi (St. Paul, MN: Marsilio, 1995); *Wise, Why's, Y's: The Griot's Tale* (Chicago: Third World Press, 1995); LeRoi Jones, *Blues People: Negro Music in White America* (New York: William Morrow, 1963).

Secondary Sources: Bob Bernotas, *Amiri Baraka: Poet and Playwright*, ed. Nathan I. Huggins (New York: Chelsea House, 1991); Cecil Brown, "About LeRoi Jones," *Evergreen Review* 75 (Feb. 1970), 65–70; Ralph Ellison, "The Blues," *New York Times Review of Books*, Feb. 6, 1964, pp. 5–7; Margalit Fox, "Amiri Baraka, Polarizing Poet and Playwright, Dies at 79," *New York Times*, Jan. 9, 2014: https://www.nytimes.com/2014/01/10/arts/amiri-baraka-polarizing-poet-and-playwright-dies-at-79.html (accessed 2018); Suzy Hansen, "Amiri Baraka Stands by His Words," *Salon.com, October 18, 2002*; William J. Harris, "The Transformed Poem," in *Poetry and Poetics of Amiri Baraka: The Jazz Aesthetic* (Columbia: University of Missouri Press, 1985), 91–121; Theodore Hudson, *From LeRoi Jones to Amiri Baraka: The Literary Works* (Durham, NC: Duke University Press, 1973); Werner Sollors, *Amiri Baraka/LeRoi Jones: The Quest for a "Populist Modernism"* (New York: Columbia University Press, 1978); Jerry Gafio Watts, *Amiri Baraka: The Politics and Art of a Black Intellectual* (New York: New York University Press, 2001).

Black Arts Movement (1960–1970)

The Black Arts Movement grew out of the rebellion of the 1960s and cannot be separated from the political and social upheavals of the time. The creative component of the Black Power movement, this artistic revolution was shaped by a Black Nationalist agenda as the artists fought for social justice and Black empowerment. While the Black Power movement, the foundation of this creative collaborative, focused on the political and social directions that African Americans should take in their demand for liberation, the Black Arts Movement simultaneously defined the direction and purpose of the creative arts, especially literature. In "The Black Arts Movement," Larry Neal, one of the literary theorists of the period, delineates the objectives of the movement and explains its vision: "The Black Arts Movement is radically opposed to any concept of the artist that alienates him from his community. Black Art is the aesthetic and spiritual sister of the Black Power concept. As such, it envisions an art that speaks directly to the needs and aspirations of Black America. In order to perform this task, the Black Arts Movement proposes a radical reordering of the western cultural aesthetic. It proposes a separate symbolism, mythology, critique, and iconology" (Neal, 2039). As part of the nationalist thrust of the 1960s, the Black Arts writers looked at their art as inseparable from the people and, therefore, turned their attention to the community. While Black Power sought to redirect the social, political, and economic goals for African American people, the Black Arts Movement worked for a radical change in what art should be and do.

As far back as the 1920s, Langston Hughes noted in his essay, "The Negro Artist and the Racial Mountain," "We younger Negro artists who create now intend to express our individual dark-skinned selves without fear or shame . . . We know we are beautiful" (36). In his 1937 essay "Blueprint for Negro Writing," Richard Wright asserted that the writer should function as an agent of change, and in order to do so, it was necessary to develop and use a "complex consciousness" (1407). Both Hughes and Wright were prophetic as they discussed the roles of the African American writer in presenting a certain vision of African American life and experiences.

The Black Arts writers wanted to take the positions of Hughes and Wright to another level as they sought to incorporate nationalism into their art. Although marginalized by many Blacks and most Whites, the Black Arts writers created an aesthetic that was their own. In "Toward a Black Aesthetic" (1968), Hoyt Fuller comments on his Chicago organization, the Organization of Black American Culture, and its definition of the Black aesthetic: "In the writers' workshop sponsored by the group, the writers are deliberately striving to invest their work with the distinctive styles and rhythms and colors of the ghetto, with those peculiar qualities which, for example, characterize the music of a John Coltrane or a Charlie Parker or a Ray Charles" (1858). The Black Arts writers realized that rather than looking outside themselves to find material appeasing to White critics, who would relegate the Black writer to oblivion anyway, they would turn to their community for its cultural resources.

The Black Arts writers believed that since their art drew on the resources of the community, they would make it political, purposeful, and dedicated to the people. No longer were they concerned about reaching a White audience or appealing to the artistic sensibilities of the European. Committed to a literature by the people, about the people, and in the interests of the people, they wanted their material accessible to the average person in the community. To that end, they participated in community readings, workshops, forums, and council gatherings, and held creative writing contests for interested people in the community. Even theater, an artistic venue usually prohibitive to many people, found an eager young audience with their minds and hearts ripe for this new Black consciousness.

In their duty and dedication to the audience, and their rebellious approach to creativity, the artists believed their work should be instructional and consciousness-raising. With a commitment to the people's liberation, they worked with the themes of the Black Power movement—Black is beautiful, Black pride, Black self-identification, revolution, Black Nationalism, art as a tool of liberation, racism, praise of cultural icons such as Malcolm X and Martin Luther King Jr., attacks against Blacks who emulated bourgeois White values, and, of course, the purpose of art. Imamu Amiri Baraka, a key figure in the development of the Black Arts movement, writes in his poem "Black Art" (1969), "We want 'poems that kill.' / Assassin poems, Poems that shoot / guns," declaring that if art does not destroy and rebuild, it has no purpose. He concludes the poem thus: "We want a black poem. And a Black World. Let the world be a Black Poem And Let All Black People Speak This Poem Silently Or LOUD" (*Selected Poetry*, 106–107).

Poetry was the main genre of Black Arts writing. Largely influenced by Black Nationalism and the Black Power rhetoric of some of the more vocal activists, it flourished in anthologies, broadsides, pamphlets, and books in community bookstores, workshops, and forums, at conferences, and on street corners. Many young people— activists, revolutionaries-in-the-making, artists, Black Power sympathizers, even White radicals—were content to listen to poets delivering their work against a background of conga drums. Of course, not all the poets acquired name recognition, but seeking celebrity status and recognition were considered European, and therefore discouraged. The Black Arts poets wanted a revolution.

Nikki Giovanni, another key figure of the Black Arts Movement, notes in her poem "For Saundra" (1968) that this was not a time for poetry writing, but for revolution, and that "maybe [she] shouldn't write at all / but clean [her] gun and check [her] kerosene supply" (*Selected Poems*, 59). Although there were signs that the revolution would occur in the streets, the poets believed the prerequisite for a transformation in the streets was a transformation of the mind. Haki Madhubuti (formerly Don L. Lee) in "a poem to complement other poems" (1969), writes, "change change your change change change / your / mind n—" (2096).

As much as the Black Arts writers called for a revolution of the mind as the prerequisite to a revolution in the streets, there were also other important themes in their poetry. For example, some writers wanted to celebrate Black people—other artists, people in the community, political icons, and historical figures, among others. Baraka, Carolyn Rodgers, and Haki are among the poets who wrote poems celebrating Malcolm X and his legacy to Black nationhood. In "Beautiful Black Men" (1968), Nikki Giovanni pays tribute to the ordinary Black man on the streets, doing ordinary things. She also mentions some of the R&B performers who were popular during the 1960s—"jerry butler, wilson pickett, the impressions / temptations, mighty mighty sly" (*Selected Poems*, 54). The writers who reclaimed and celebrated the genius of John Coltrane include Sonia Sanchez, A. B. Spellman, Carolyn Rodgers, Michael Harper, Jayne Cortez, and Larry Neal.

Perhaps the most dominant theme in Black Arts poetry was the beauty and goodness of Blackness. Created to raise the level of Black awareness among the people and teach them to love themselves, many poems romanticized and glorified Blackness, presenting a vision of it as transformative, inspiring, and celebratory. Mari Evans's poem "I Am a Black Woman" (1964) looks at herself, the Black woman, as the embodiment of history, strength, and fortitude (Baraka and Baraka, 105–106). There was no question that many of the Black Arts writers believed that Black self-definition meant loving everything black, blackening those things that weren't already black, and believing in the possibility of a Black world. Developing a Black consciousness, however, did not occur without a process of reeducation and transformation. Typical of the rhetoric of the times, the Black Arts writers were critical of those who continued to embrace European values. Baraka addressed the self-hatred of the Black man who emulated middle-class Whites in his 1969 poem "Black Bourgeoisie." A similar theme emerged in his "Poem for Half White College Students" (1969), in which the poet questions the self-definition of those preoccupied with European values. Anytime the poets referred to "colored" or "negro," they were usually making a pejorative comment about identity and self-definition, and rating each other's level of Blackness. Many of the Black Arts poets believed that it was their responsibility, both politically and artistically, to change the way Black people looked at themselves.

While the Black Arts writers worked assiduously to educate the people to a liberating way of thinking about themselves, they were also working to develop their own style based on their own culture. No longer bound by the European standards of "good" art nor concerned about moving into the American literary mainstream, the Black Arts writers looked to their own life

and experiences for the metaphors, similes, symbols, and other literary devices, and found the Black world rich with resources. Carolyn Rodgers, for example, uses the rich cultural language of African American women in her poem "For Sistuhs Wearin' Straight Hair" (1969). Her references to "edges" and "kitchen" and hair that "was not supposed to *go back* home" (2126) are strong examples of the Black vernacular. In valuing their own experiences, the writers were experimental and often innovative in form, as illustrated in Sonia Sanchez's poem "a chant for young / brothers & sisters" (1970). With demonstrated emphasis on the spoken word, the poem makes interesting use of the performance nature of Black speech.

Also characteristic of the style of Black Arts poetry was the use of popular street language, profanity, signification, references to Black music (particularly jazz and R&B), and the interconnection of form and theme. Although some of these stylistic practices were not necessarily new, the Black Arts writers aggressively stretched these techniques to the limits as they revolted against Western concepts of art. Redefining art, what it is and what it should do, the writers were the creative practitioners of the Black Power ideology.

While most discussions of Black Arts literature focused on poetry, since there were literally hundreds of poets, drama, fiction, and other narrative forms were also important areas of revolutionary expression. Drama was especially defining during the 1960s in that it presented Blacks and Whites in situations new to the theatergoing audience. This theater meant recognizing the enemy, making sure he reaps death and destruction so that a new value system, a new world, a new Black people can emerge heroically. In his 1969 essay "The Revolutionary Theatre,"

Baraka delineated the standards for this art form. "The Revolutionary Theatre should force change," he writes. "It should be change . . . must EXPOSE!" (*Selected Plays and Prose*, 130).

Other playwrights of the Black Arts era include Alice Childress, Sonia Sanchez, Ed Bullins, Ted Shine, Adrienne Kennedy, and lesser-known names, but Baraka was clearly the spiritual leader and the most productive. Among his many plays, the most celebrated was *The Dutchman* (1964), which deals with a Black middle-class man who is murdered by the White woman he meets on the subway. This play and the others in the trilogy, *The Toilet* and *The Slave*, are striking examples of Baraka's vision of Black theater as an agent of social change.

There were other forms of literature that had a major impact on the Black Arts Movement. *The Autobiography of Malcolm X* (1965) was a defining work for the Black Power movement. Prior to its publication, Malcolm X's nationalist agenda helped shape the political platform of the Black Power movement. Another important book, Eldridge Cleaver's *Soul on Ice* (1967) presented the author's pent-up anger and aggression against an oppressive society. Because Cleaver was a member of the Black Panther Party, his widely read book became an important philosophical tool for the Black Power movement as much for its expressions of rage as in spite of it.

Like other genres, fiction tended to lurk in the literary shadows of poetry during the Black Arts Movement. Nevertheless, there were writers whose novels and short stories today prompt us to look again at the breadth and depth of the movement. While not as rebellious as the younger poets, and still somewhat influenced by European aesthetics, writers such as John O. Killens, Margaret Walker, Paule Marshall, William Melvin Kelley, and a few others contributed to the 1960s. However, John A. Williams's novel *The Man Who Cried I Am* (1967) and the fiction in *Black Fire: An Anthology of Afro-American Writing* (1968), edited by Baraka and Larry Neal, are good examples of more revolutionary contributions to the movement.

These young writers of the Black Arts Movement created a literature of liberation. Often militant in tone, sometimes angry, sometimes filled with rage, they distanced themselves from European aesthetics and drew on their own resources. With emphasis on Black language, Black music, the Black spoken-word tradition, and Black performance techniques, these Black Arts writers helped nurture the Black Power movement. The Black aesthetic, the literary directive emerging from the Black Arts Movement, provided future artists the freedom to explore and use their own cultural resources.

In the early-to-mid-1970s, the Black Arts Movement increasingly lost its momentum. Suffering from governmental interference, the activists' exclusivity and essentialism, and an intellectual and social burnout from efforts to make the rhetoric real, the Black Arts Movement could not sustain itself. However, readers today still look to the 1960s as a time when a Black world seemed possible, and in the twenty-first century, the Movement continues to draw interest from critics and scholars.

Angelene J. Hall

See also: Angelou, Maya; Baraka, Amiri; Blues Poetry; Free Verse; Giovanni, Nikki; Jordan, June; Madhubuti, Haki R. (Don Luther Lee); Protest Literature; Sanchez, Sonia; Shange, Ntozake; Vernacular.

Resources

Amiri Baraka: *Selected Plays and Prose of Amiri Baraka/LeRoi Jones* (New York: Morrow, 1979); *Selected Poetry of Amiri Baraka/LeRoi Jones* (New York: Morrow, 1979); Amiri Baraka (LeRoi Jones) and Amina Baraka, *Confirmation: An Anthology of African American Women* (New York: Quill, 1983); Hoyt Fuller, "Toward a Black Aesthetic" (1968), in *The Norton Anthology of African American Literature*, 2nd ed., Henry Louis Gates Jr. and Nellie Y. McKay, gen. eds. (New York: W. W. Norton, 2004), 1853–1859; Addison Gayle, *The Black Aesthetic* (Garden City, NY: Doubleday, 1971); Nikki Giovanni, *The Selected Poems of Nikki Giovanni* (New York: Morrow, 1996); Langston Hughes, "The Negro Artist and the Racial Mountain" (1926), in *The Collected Works of Langston Hughes*, vol. 9, ed. Christopher De Santis (Columbia: University of Missouri Press, 2002), 31–36; LeRoi Jones (Amiri Baraka) and Larry Neal, eds., *Black Fire: An Anthology of Afro-American Writings* (New York: Morrow, 1968); Haki Madhubuti, "a poem to complement other poems" (1969), in *The Norton Anthology of African American Literature*, 2nd ed., Henry Louis Gates Jr. and Nellie Y. McKay, gen. eds. (New York: W. W. Norton, 2004), 2094–2096; Larry Neal, "The Black Arts Movement" (1968), in *The Norton Anthology of African American Literature*, 2nd ed., Henry Louis Gates Jr. and Nellie Y. McKay, gen. eds. (New York: W. W. Norton, 2004), 2039–2050; Keith D. Leonard, "Love in the Black Arts Movement: The Other American Exceptionalism," *Callaloo* 36, no. 3 (2013), 618–624; Daniel Punday, "The Black Arts Movement and the Genealogy of Multimedia," *New Literary History* 37, no. 4 (2006), 777–794; Carolyn Rodgers, "For Sistuhs Wearin' Straight Hair" (1969), in *The Norton Anthology of African American Literature*, 2nd ed., Henry Louis Gates Jr. and Nellie Y. McKay, gen. eds. (New York: W. W. Norton, 2004), 2126; Mike Sell, "Blackface and the Black Arts Movement," *TDR: The Drama Review* 57, no. 2 (2013), 143–162; Richard Wright, "Blueprint for Negro Writing" (1937), in *The Norton Anthology of African American Literature*, 2nd ed., Henry Louis Gates Jr. and Nellie Y. McKay, gen. eds. (New York: W. W. Norton, 2004), 1403–1410.

Blues Poetry

The term "blues poetry" can refer either to the sometimes highly poetic lyrics of blues performers and composers or to poetry written by authors who have employed some aspect or aspects of the oral blues tradition, lyrically or musically, in generating their own poetic works. In either case, a familiarity with the characteristics of the blues tradition with regard to subject matter, lyric and music structures, performance techniques, and the functions of the work as a means of entertainment, education, connection to the spirit and values of the community, and a kind of therapeutic release helps readers better understand the important network of ideas that is conjured when a creative artist evokes the blues. Since the emergence of the blues into popular culture in the 1920s, poets such as Langston Hughes, Sterling Brown, Melvin Tolson, Robert Hayden, Gwendolyn Brooks, Margaret Walker, James Baldwin, Amiri Baraka, Sonia Sanchez, Ishmael Reed, Sterling Plumpp, Sherley Anne Williams, Al Young, Etheridge Knight, and Jayne Cortez, among many others, have experimented with ways to demonstrate the centrality of the blues tradition to their aesthetics and creativity, and to their sense of the nature of the world and of the art they have created to describe, criticize, celebrate, and improve it. With the influence of the blues on other musical genres, such as rhythm and blues, rock and roll, heavy metal, pop, and hip-hop, and the popular resurgence of blues into mainstream American culture in television, film, commercials, blues clubs, and a burgeoning blues recording industry, the influence of the blues is certain to continue and expand in the twenty-first century.

On the one hand, the roots of the blues are in West African artistic aesthetics as reflected in the nature and function of music in that society. Such elements as call-and-response patterns, syncopation (placing an accent slightly before or after the measured beat), blue notes, and growling and buzzing inflections are all found in both African music and the blues, as is an orientation toward making the music, which is part of daily life rather than a separate element of it, reflect the needs, concerns, and values of the community through the individual voice. On the other hand, the blues did not come into existence until the enforced contact of enslaved Africans with elements of European music in America. After the African elements previously enumerated helped develop distinctive African American genres such as work songs, field hollers, and spirituals, the stage was set for the blues to emerge in the 1880s. The blues seem to have arisen, then, as a result of the historical experiences of the first generation of Blacks born outside of slavery coming to their majority in a world that was different from the slave world of the plantations. No longer enslaved, though experiencing many of the attitudes and restrictions endured by their slave forebears, the new generation had a greater ability to move about, seeking better times, and an expanded set of choices with regard to personal relationships—both common subjects in blues songs. By joining African aesthetic components with European elements, such as stanza patterns (especially a modified version of the ballad stanza that was a precursor to the most common blues lyric pattern) and English

language, the blues arose to provide an artistic outlet for post–Reconstruction African Americans. By the time the blues were first recorded by African Americans, beginning with Mamie Smith in 1920, there were a number of strong individual blues personalities and regional blues styles that demonstrated the remarkable possibilities for the innovation that has continued to be a hallmark of the blues up to the present day.

Despite the notion that the blues is a limited genre, and thus might have a limited set of characteristics to contribute to poetry, the blues are, in fact, quite diverse in musical structures and stanza patterns. The most common musical pattern in the blues consists of a stanza that is roughly twelve bars or measures (the metrical division of a musical composition) long, built around a musical progression that uses a I–IV–V chord pattern, and employing a division into roughly three equal parts, each of which contains a "line" or thought. However, there are also recorded examples of eight- and sixteen-bar blues as well as other variations, especially in the vaudeville blues tradition. Lyrically, various stanza patterns are evident as well. For the twelve-bar blues, there can be one line repeated approximately three times (AAA), as in Tommy Johnson's "Lonesome Blues"; a line sung, repeated, and then completed by a different line with an end rhyme (AAB), as in Gwendolyn Brooks's "Queen of the Blues"; a line sung, and answered by a different line with end rhyme that is then repeated (ABB), commonly used for the blues, as in "See See Rider," and employed by Langston Hughes in his play *Don't You Want to Be Free?*; a line sung followed by a different line with end rhyme answering it in the first four bars, followed by a repeating refrain from stanza to stanza (AB refrain), employed in "Jim Jackson's Kansas City Blues" and in

Hughes's lyric "Tired as I Can Be"; three different lines with end rhyme (ABC), as in Lonnie Johnson's "Trust Your Husband" and Hughes's "Only Woman Blues"; and a number of other variations, such as Sterling Brown's use of the blues ballad stanza in "Strange Legacies." The eight-, sixteen-, and other bar variations present a variety of lyric options as well. By far the most common form is the twelve-bar AAB pattern, but other patterns occur with fair frequency.

In performance, individual artists have the freedom to shorten or extend the length of musical stanzas (as, for example, Charley Patton does in "Pony Blues") or alter the lyric pattern (as King Solomon Hill does in "The Gone Dead Train," which mixes AB and AAB stanzas). The point is that, formally, the blues offer the performer and the poet a set of standard forms to use, representing a passing on of tradition from one generation to another, which have not been worn out because they are flexible enough to encompass variations and idiosyncrasies of performance that may extend a twelve-bar pattern to 13 ½ bars without any worry or strain. Thus, the frequent rigidity of formal literature is replaced in blues poetry by spontaneous, improvisatory flexibility that suggests either resistance to externally imposed European poetic standards or a more "natural" adherence to the standards of the oral tradition. The implication is that the oral tradition is a viable vehicle for poetic sentiments that could be appreciated by society in general, not just the "folk," and that even those who may have associated themselves with mainstream American mass culture, such as the literate African American middle and upper classes, should not lose sight of the value of oral culture.

Of course, the use of formal elements and the relative freedom of oral performance

from the blues tradition are not the only ways the blues are manifested in blues poetry. Some poems use the word "blues" in the title or body of the text without using the blues form, as Derek Walcott did in "Blues." There may be references to real or fictional blues singers, as in Bessie Smith tributes such as Alvin Aubert's "Bessie" and Robert Hayden's "Homage to the Empress of the Blues," or recorded blues songs, as in Sherley Anne Williams's "Any Woman's Blues." We may come across terms or ideas that are in some ways associated with blues culture, such as the use of Crow Jane in some poems by Amiri Baraka; riders, jelly rolls, and such sexual euphemisms; or references to relentless travel in Baraka's poem "Blues People."

Steven C. Tracy

See also: Baraka, Amiri; Hughes, Langston.

Resources
Houston Baker, *Blues, Ideology, and Afro-American Literature* (Chicago: University of Chicago Press, 1984); Sterling Brown, "The Blues as Folk Poetry," in *Folk-Say*, vol. 2, ed. B. A. Botkin (Norman: University of Oklahoma Press, 1930); Samuel Charters, *The Poetry of the Blues* (New York: Oak, 1963); Sascha Feinstein, *Jazz Poetry: From the 1920s to the Present* (Westport, CT: Greenwood Press, 1997); Paul Garon, *Blues and the Poetic Spirit* (London: Eddison, 1975); Stephen Henderson, *Understanding the New Black Poetry* (New York: William Morrow, 1973); Dick Lourie, "Poetry and the Blues," *Journal of Popular Music Studies* 13, no. 1 (March 2001), 111–115; Paul Oliver, *Blues Fell This Morning: Meaning in the Blues*, 2nd ed. (Cambridge: Cambridge University Press, 1990); Richard Rankin Russell, "Down in the Delta: Tallahatchie County Mississippi, and Langston Hughes's Blues Poetry about Emmett Till," *Five Points: A Journal of Literature and Art* 16, no. 2 (Winter, 2015), 146(18); Steven C. Tracy, *Langston Hughes*

and the Blues (Urbana: University of Illinois Press, 1988); Steven C. Tracy, ed.: *A Historical Guide to Langston Hughes* (New York: Oxford University Press, 2004); *Write Me a Few of Your Lines: A Blues Reader* (Amherst: University of Massachusetts Press, 1999); Sherley A. Williams, "The Blues Roots of Contemporary Afro-American Poetry," in *Chant of Saints: A Gathering of Afro-American Literature, Art, and Scholarship*, ed. Michael S. Harper and Robert B. Stepto (Urbana: University of Illinois Press, 1979), 123–135.

Bontemps, Arna (1902–1973)

Poet, novelist, children's author, and editor. Bontemps was a major figure in the Harlem Renaissance who, as a librarian and editor, made vital contributions to the preservation of African American culture. His children's books are groundbreaking expressions of pride in Black history and tradition.

Arnaud Wendell Bontemps was born on October 13, 1902, in Alexandria, Louisiana. His father, Paul Bismark Bontemps, was a bricklayer, and his mother, Marie Pembroke, a schoolteacher. Increasing racial tension in Alexandria caused Paul to move the family to Los Angeles, California, when Arna was three years old. In Los Angeles, Paul encouraged his family to assimilate as much as possible into White society. The family left the Catholic Church and became Seventh-Day Adventists. There were conflicts, however, with Bontemps's Uncle Buddy, who embodied the family's Southern Black heritage. Paul did not want the Bontemps children looking up to Buddy as a role model. Throughout his life, Bontemps resisted his father's insistence upon assimilation and embraced his African American heritage (Jones, *Renaissance Man*).

Bontemps graduated from Pacific Union College (an Adventist school) in 1923 and began working in the U.S. Postal Service in Los Angeles. In 1924, he used connections within the Seventh-Day Adventist Church to secure a teaching position at the Harlem Academy, an Adventist school in New York City. Harlem was the center of Black culture in America at the time. Arna began associating with many writers and artists who would form the nucleus of the Harlem Renaissance. In that year, he formed what would be a lifelong association and friendship with Langston Hughes.

Throughout the 1920s, Bontemps wrote in many genres and had success publishing poetry and short stories in magazines and journals. His poems won numerous prizes; two of his best-known poems are "The Day-Breakers" and "Golgotha Is a Mountain" (Lewis). He also worked on a novel, *Chariot in the Sky*, which went unpublished until 1951. In 1931, however, he published *God Sends Sunday*, a novel based to some extent on his Uncle Buddy. The novel formed the basis for his later collaboration with Countee Cullen on the play *St. Louis Woman*. In 1926, Bontemps married Alberta Johnson, a former student at Harlem Academy.

As the Great Depression gripped America, Bontemps, like many of Harlem's brightest stars, moved away from the city to find employment, securing a teaching position at Oakwood Junior College, an Adventist school in Huntsville, Alabama. The return to the South was a pivotal event for Bontemps. He felt more in touch with his own cultural heritage, but he was also confronted with the hatred of racism in a way that he had never experienced in Los Angeles or New York. While in Alabama, Bontemps collaborated with Langston

Hughes on *Popo and Fifina*, a children's book. It depicts events in the lives of two children in Haiti, as their family moves to a new village in hopes of earning a better living. The story was praised for its simplicity and stylistic charm. Other children's books followed quickly, including *You Can't Pet a Possum*, in 1934. All of Bontemps juvenile works are admired for the positive image they present to African American children.

In 1934, Bontemps parted company with Oakwood after a conflict over books about civil rights he had in his own collection. He returned to Los Angeles to do research for a book. Published in 1936, *Black Thunder* is Bontemps's most highly regarded novel. A work of historical fiction, it describes an unsuccessful slave revolt in Virginia led by Gabriel Prosser in 1800. A recent study has interpreted both the novel's folklore motifs and its relationship to Southern American literature and to Modernism (Leroy-Frazier).

The late 1930s and early 1940s were a busy time for Bontemps. After writing *Black Thunder*, he moved to Chicago, Illinois, and began teaching at the Shiloh Academy. He held this position until 1938, when he received a Rosenwald fellowship to finance travel in the Caribbean. He returned from these travels, continued his graduate studies in English at the University of Chicago, worked as a writer for the Works Progress Administration, and published more books for children and adults. *Drums at Dusk*, another historical novel, appeared in 1939 to less enthusiastic reviews than those received by *Black Thunder*. It recounts events of the Haitian slave revolt of 1791. *The Fast Sooner Hound* appeared in 1942. It was the first of many children's books done in collaboration with Jack Conroy. In 1941, Bontemps also worked as the ghostwriter

(credited as the editor) on W. C. Handy's *Father of the Blues: An Autobiography* and published *Golden Slippers: An Anthology of Negro Poetry for Young Readers.*

Although Bontemps completed all his coursework for a PhD in English at the University of Chicago, he never took his comprehensive examinations or wrote a dissertation. Instead, he enrolled in the library science program at Chicago. He completed a master's degree in this program in 1943 and was hired as head librarian at Fisk University in Nashville, Tennessee. The Fisk position offered another opportunity to return to his native South, and it proved to be a profitable relationship. Bontemps remained at Fisk for twenty years and became the preeminent authority in the United States on Black librarianship and African American bibliography.

Throughout his Fisk years, Bontemps produced many successful children's books and edited a number of significant anthologies of African American literature. His *Story of the Negro* (1948) was a Newbery honored book (runner-up to the Newbery Medal winner *King of the Wind* by Marguerite Henry). *The Poetry of the Negro, 1746–1949: An Anthology* (1949), edited in collaboration with Langston Hughes, was one of the most important compilations of Black poetry up to that time, comparable in stature with the anthology James Weldon Johnson had published in 1922. Hughes and Bontemps also collaborated on *The Book of Negro Folklore* in 1958. The lifelong friendship between Bontemps and Hughes was extraordinary; selected letters between the two were published in 1980.

Bontemps's other important anthologies included *American Negro Poetry* (1963) and *Great Slave Narratives* (1969). His many histories, such as *100 Years of Negro*

Freedom (1961), and biographies (primarily for children) were also well received.

Bontemps worked in many genres throughout his life, but his work as a librarian and children's author made the most lasting contributions to African American literature. His children's books demonstrated that there was a market for works that celebrated the heritage of Black America. As a librarian, he showed that African American works were important documents in the cultural heritage of the United States, worthy of being collected, edited, and anthologized. The understanding and enjoyment of African American literature would be much less substantial without his contributions.

Steven R. Harris

See also: Children's Literature; Harlem Renaissance.

Resources

Primary Sources: Arna Bontemps: *Black Thunder* (New York: Macmillan, 1936); *Drums at Dusk* (New York: Macmillan, 1939); *The Fast Sooner Hound*, with Jack Conroy (Boston: Houghton Mifflin, 1942); *Father of the Blues: An Autobiography by W. C. Handy* (New York: Macmillan, 1941), as ghostwriter; *Frederick Douglass: Slave, Fighter, Freeman* (New York: Knopf, 1959); *Free at Last: The Life of Frederick Douglass* (New York: Dodd, Mead, 1971); *God Sends Sunday* (New York: Harcourt, Brace, 1931); *100 Years of Negro Freedom* (New York: Dodd, Mead, 1961); *Lonesome Boy* (Boston: Houghton Mifflin, 1955); *The Old South: "A Summer Tragedy" and Other Stories of the Thirties* (New York: Dodd, Mead, 1973); *Popo and Fifina, Children of Haiti*, with Langston Hughes (New York: Macmillan, 1932); *Sam Patch, the High, Wide, & Handsome Jumper*, with Jack Conroy (Boston: Houghton Mifflin, 1951); *The Story of*

George Washington Carver (New York: Grosset & Dunlap, 1954); *Story of the Negro* (New York: Knopf, 1948; enl. ed., 1955); *Young Booker: Booker T. Washington's Early Days* (New York: Dodd, Mead, 1972); Arna Bontemps, ed.: *The Book of Negro Folklore*, with Langston Hughes (New York: Dodd, Mead, 1958); *Golden Slippers: An Anthology of Negro Poetry for Young Readers* (New York: Harper & Row, 1941); *Great Slave Narratives* (Boston: Beacon, 1969); *The Harlem Renaissance Remembered: Essays* (New York: Dodd, Mead, 1972); *The Poetry of the Negro, 1746–1949*, with Langston Hughes (Garden City, NY: Doubleday, 1949), rev. as *The Poetry of the Negro, 1746–1970* (Garden City, NY: Doubleday, 1970).

Secondary Sources: Robert E. Fleming, *James Weldon Johnson and Arna Wendell Bontemps: A Reference Guide* (Boston: G. K. Hall, 1978); Kirkland C. Jones: "Arna Bontemps," in *Dictionary of Literary Biography,* vol. 51, *Afro-American Writers from the Harlem Renaissance to 1940*, ed. Trudier Harris and Thadious M. Davis (Detroit: Gale Research, 1987), 10–21; *Renaissance Man from Louisiana: A Biography of Arna Wendell Bontemps* (Westport, CT: Greenwood Press, 1992); Nancy Kang, "Manchild in the Compromised Land: Intertextuality and Arna Bontemps's 'Lonesome Boy,'" *MELUS: Multi-Ethnic Literature of the U.S.* 39, no. 4 (2014), 114–139; Jill Leroy-Frazier, "Othered Southern Modernism: Arna Bontemps's *Black Thunder*," *The Mississippi Quarterly* 63, no. 1/2 (Winter 2010), 3–29; David Levering Lewis, ed., *The Portable Harlem Renaissance Reader* (New York: Viking, 1994), 224–226; Christine Montgomery, "Pendulum Time, Collective Freedom, and Rethinking the Neo-Slave Narrative in Arna Bontemps's *Black Thunder: Gabriel's Revolt: Virginia, 1800*," *MELUS: Multi-Ethnic Literature of the U.S.* 41, no. 4 (2016), 140–165; Charles H. Nichols, ed., *Arna Bontemps–Langston Hughes Letters, 1925–1967* (New York: Dodd, Mead, 1980).

Brooks, Gwendolyn (1917–2000)

Poet. Gwendolyn Brooks ranks among the greatest American poets of all time. Few have equaled her brilliant range in both traditional and innovative uses of the sonnet and ballad forms as well as in the use of African American vernacular. From her first volume, *A Street in Bronzeville* (1945), she explored the questions of human meaning in the postwar world. Later, she sought to answer, within epic poetry (*Annie Allen*, 1949), whether the consequent rift in human alienation could ever be closed. Finally, she concluded that the great visionary, whether an imagined Langston Hughes (*Selected Poems*, 1963) or an urban tenant in a decaying apartment building (*In the Mecca*, 1968), represents a potential for human health in moral and social dimensions. While her images are often Eurocentric—especially those before 1967—her ironic and coy tone is distinctly African American. She places Western art forms in a Black folk perspective so as to authenticate poetics through African American experience (Miller, "Gwendolyn Brooks," 1164).

Brooks walked a tightrope of negotiation between the beauty of artistic forms and the human self interpreting them. She voiced the hurt and triumph of the common people. Hence, she created a poetic art that helped free such people from an easy acceptance of social limits. Her earlier verse helped save the Euro-American tradition of poetry that often ignores the way the poor are human, and her later verse helped usher in a new era of new Black poets and Black aesthetics (*see* Black Arts Movement).

Brooks was born in Topeka, Kansas, on June 7, 1917, to Keziah Corinne Wims Brooks and David Anderson Brooks. As early as first grade, the dark-skinned girl began to recognize distinctions based on color, gender, and class. She lacked athletic skills and many social graces as well as straight hair. For her, the writing of poetry became a positive antidote to peer rejection. Supported in these efforts by her parents, she wrote many poems about the triumph of beauty and order in the world, but discrimination based on race–gender–class would become the focus of her later poetry.

Early on, Brooks was influenced by English and American romantic poets such as William Wordsworth, John Keats, William Cullen Bryant, and Henry Wadsworth Longfellow. In 1930, at age thirteen, she wrote "Eventide" for *American Childhood* magazine; four years later, she began to write poetry for a variety column, "Lights and Shadows," in the *Chicago Defender*. She graduated in 1934 from the integrated Englewood High School in Topeka and, by 1935, was well on her way in writing the traditional forms of poetry. Influenced by Sara Teasdale, she focused primarily on love as a subject and occasionally treated a theme of racial pride. Briefly, she corresponded with James Weldon Johnson, a Harlem Renaissance poet, fiction writer, and editor. Her mother had taken her to meet Johnson and hear him lecture in 1933. The same year, Langston Hughes encouraged Brooks at one of his readings to continue writing, surprising her by taking time after a performance to read some of her poems. By the late 1930s, Brooks had published seventy-five poems in the *Chicago Defender*.

After graduating from Wilson Junior College (today Kennedy-King) in 1936, Brooks read the works of such modern poets as T. S. Eliot, Ezra Pound, and e. e. cummings. Five years later, she began to study at Chicago's South Side Community Art Center with Inez Cunningham Stark, a White socialite who was a reader for *Poetry* magazine. Brooks did odd jobs and even worked as a typist. Others who studied at the Center were Henry Blakely, Brooks's future husband; William Couch, scholar of African American drama; Margaret Taylor Goss Burroughs, curator of African history in a Chicago museum; and Margaret Danner, a fine poet. Many of the poems Brooks wrote in 1941 and 1942 appeared in her initial volume, *A Street in Bronzeville* (1945).

With "Gay Chaps at the Bar" (1944) and "The Progress" (1945), Brooks won the prize awarded by the Midwestern Writers Conference. Both of the pieces rival some by W. H. Auden as the most accomplished war poems in the twentieth century. At first, Brooks tried to publish her early poetry through Emily Morrison at Alfred A. Knopf, but finally she gathered together nineteen pieces, mainly about African Americans, and sent them to Harper. *A Street in Bronzeville*, which was published in August 1945, received a good review from Paul Engle in the *Chicago Tribune Book Review*. It was Engle, in fact, who had helped secure prizes for Brooks at the Northwestern University Annual Writers Conference that year.

For Brooks, the 1940s was a decade of rising fame. In 1945, she received the Mademoiselle Merit Award as one of the ten outstanding women of the year. In 1946 and 1947, she was awarded Guggenheim fellowships. In 1949, she won the Eunice Tietjens Memorial Prize from *Poetry* for several pieces that would appear in *Annie Allen* (1949). As a testimony to the quality of the volume, she was awarded the 1950 Pulitzer Prize, the first time it was presented to an African American. During the 1950s, she wrote reviews for the *New York Times*, *Negro Digest*, and the *New York Herald Tribune*. She also wrote personal articles such as "How I Told My Child About Race" and "Why Negro Women Leave Home."

During the next decade, Brooks developed her commitment to nurturing young students. From 1963 to 1969, she led a poetry workshop at Columbia College in Chicago and taught at Elmhurst College in Elmhurst, Illinois. About then, she completed stints as the Rennebohm Professor of English at the University of Wisconsin at Madison and distinguished professor of the arts at the City College of New York. Though in many ways she informally began to retreat from the academic world, in 1971 she helped establish the Illinois Poet Laureate Awards to promote creative writing.

With a startling development in stylistic complexity from 1945 to 1949, and with an abrupt shift in explicit ideology from 1967 on, Brooks's poetry has retained technical excellence. Particularly riveting is the ironic distance through which she achieves a pervasiveness of historical suffering. As early as *A Street in Bronzeville* (1945), Brooks accomplished startling shifts of tense as well as shimmering perceptions about memory, writing "The Mother," for example, a classic poem about abortion. In 1975, Brooks told a literary critic that she would never again write some of the apologetic lines in *Annie Allen* (1949) that beg Whites to accept that she was human (Kent). In *Maud Martha* (1953), an autobiographical novel in poetic sketches, she tells the story of a young Black girl who grows into complete womanhood. In a version written for Herbert Hill's anthology *Soon One Morning* (1963), Brooks produced what would become a revision published as "The Life of Lincoln West" in *Family Pictures* (1970). Brooks's *Bean*

Eaters (1960) contained explicitly social verse. In one of her poems, a White mother–narrator agonizes over the lynching in 1955 of Emmett Till, a fourteen-year-old Chicagoan. In "The Chicago Defender Sends a Man to Little Rock," a Northern Black narrator travels to Arkansas in 1957 to witness the uproar over school integration, only to discover that those in the mob "are like people everywhere." And in "Negro Hero" and "The Progress," Brooks continues to reveal historical irony. In her poetic world, evil is endemic to human existence. Hence, all people must eschew a barbarism that threatens human life.

In the mid-1950s, Brooks was sent by the Illinois Employment Service to work as a secretary for Dr. G. N. French, the manager of a large slum known as the Mecca Building. After exploiting the tenants by selling them useless trinkets and charms, he was eventually murdered. In 1962, Brooks wrote to her Harper's editor about plans to complete a 2,000-line poem on the subject. At about the same time, she completed poems about Medgar Evers and Malcolm X, martyrs of the 1960s Civil Rights Movement, as commemorated in *Mecca* (1968) and *The World of Gwendolyn Brooks* (1971). *Report from Part One* (1972), with prefaces by Don L. Lee (Haki Madhubuti) and George E. Kent, details the events that helped shape her epic vision. Besides many details about her family life, the autobiography represents, through fragmented sketches, her supposedly magical transformation from a conservative "Negro" in 1945 into a proud Black woman in 1967, following the Fisk University Writers Conference. "First Fight/Then Fiddle" (*Annie Allen*, 1949) even today remains a dazzling poem about the way military power underlies the development of European pictorial

and verbal art from the Augustan age of the first century through the Crusades of the Middle Ages.

Especially during the last third of the twentieth century, Brooks earned worldwide acclaim. Though the center of her personal renaissance was certainly African, her reach extended into the Soviet bloc. In the summer of 1971, she traveled alone to the East African nations of Kenya and Tanzania, and in the summer of 1974, with her husband to the West African cities of Accra and Kumasi, Ghana. In viewing the slave castle at Emina—and quite likely the infamous Door of No Return through which Africans were forced as slaves to the Americas—she rounded out her own life's quest in the African diaspora.

Brooks's beautifully polished sonnets, historical ballads, and highly inflected free verse—including works resonant and delightful with the urban idiom of "We Real Cool"—have clearly won the approval of literary history. In 1970, she began, with the brief *Family Pictures*, a steady stream of eight to ten little pamphlets that appeared during the next twenty-one years. Appointed by Librarian of Congress Daniel Boorstin as consultant in poetry to the Library of Congress in 1985, she received support from John Broderick, the assistant librarian (Brooks, *Report from Part Two*). The first female writer to be accorded such a distinction, she delivered her final lecture of the position on May 5, 1986. Later, the consultancy would develop into the office of poet laureate, the first of which would be Robert Penn Warren. Brooks became one of the most celebrated American women poets in the twentieth century. And she is one of the finest writers, regardless of race or gender. Through her election to the National Institute of Arts and Letters (as the first African American woman) in 1976, she more than capably filled a racial divide that had persisted since the induction of W.E.B. Du Bois in 1943 (Melhem, 157).

In 1989, Brooks was awarded the Frost Medal of the Poetry Society of America, and in 1990, she was the first American to receive the Society of Literature Award from the University of Thessalonica in Athens. In 1994, she received the medal of the National Book Foundation for Distinguished Contribution to American Letters. Selected as the Jefferson lecturer by the National Endowment for the Humanities in 1994—"the highest honor the federal government bestows for intellectual achievement in the humanities"—Brooks received more than seventy honorary doctorates during her lifetime. "An Old Black Woman, Homeless and Indistinct" (*Drum Voices Review*, Fall/Winter 1992–1993) encapsulates her poetic quest: "Folks used to say, 'That child is going far.'"

Many aims informed the rich complexity of Brooks's wide-ranging poetics. Though she claimed in the last third of her life to write poetry worthy of the tavern—and sometimes she actually did so—much of her early and late craft reveals a keen eye for poetic form, a penchant for profundity. By the time of her death in Chicago, on December 3, 2000, she had become one of the greatest modern poets. A book of newer criticism and interpretation of her work appeared in 2010 (Mickle).

R. Baxter Miller

See also: Epic Poetry/The Long Poem; Feminism/Black Feminism; Lyric Poetry.

Resources

Primary Works: Gwendolyn Brooks: *Aloneness* (Detroit: Broadside Press, 1971); *Annie Allen* (New York: Harper, 1949); *The Bean Eaters* (New York: Harper, 1960); *Beckonings* (Detroit: Broadside Press, 1975); *Blacks* (Chicago: Third World Press, 1987); *A Broadside Treasury* (Detroit: Broadside Press, 1971); *Children Coming Home* (Chicago: David Co., 1991); *Family Pictures* (Detroit: Broadside Press, 1970); *In Montgomery, and Other Poems* (Chicago: Third World Press, 2003); *In the Mecca: Poems* (New York: Harper & Row, 1968); *Maud Martha* (New York: Harper, 1953); *Report from Part One* (Detroit: Broadside Press, 1972); *Report from Part Two* (Chicago: Third World Press, 1996); *Riot* (Detroit: Broadside Press, 1969); *Selected Poems* (New York: Harper & Row, 1963); *To Disembark* (Chicago: Third World Press, 1981); *The World of Gwendolyn Brooks* (New York: Harper & Row, 1971); Gwendolyn Brooks, ed., *Jump Bad: A New Chicago Anthology* (Detroit: Broadside Press, 1971).

Secondary Sources: Jacqueline K. Bryant, ed., *Gwendolyn Brooks' "Maud Martha": A Critical Collection* (Chicago: Third World Press, 2002); Arthur P. Davis, "The Black and Tan Motif in the Poetry of Gwendolyn Brooks," *CLAJ* 6 (1962), 90–97; Joanne V. Gabbin, "Blooming in the Whirlwind: The Early Poetry of Gwendolyn Brooks," in *The Furious Flowering of African American Poetry*, ed. Joanne V. Gabbin (Charlottesville: University Press of Virginia, 1999), 252–273; Melba Joyce, "The Cultural Activism of Margaret Danner, Margaret Burroughs, Gwendolyn Brooks, and Margaret Walker During the Black Arts Movement," *Revista Canaria de Estudios Ingleses* 37 (1998), 55–67; George E. Kent, *A Life of Gwendolyn Brooks* (Lexington: University Press of Kentucky, 1990); Haki R. Madhubuti, *Say That the River Turns: The Impact of Gwendolyn Brooks* (Chicago: Third World Press, 1987); D. H. Melhem, *Gwendolyn Brooks: Poetry and the Heroic Voice* (Lexington: University Press of Kentucky, 1987); Mildred Mickle, ed., *Gwendolyn Brooks: Critical Insights* (Salem, Oregon: Salem Press, 2010); R. Baxter Miller: "Gwendolyn Brooks," in *Call and Response: The Riverside Anthology of African American Literature*, ed. Patricia Liggins Hill et al.

(Boston: Houghton Mifflin, 1998); *Langston Hughes and Gwendolyn Brooks: A Reference Guide* (Boston: G. K. Hall, 1978); R. Baxter Miller, ed.: *Black American Literature and Humanism* (Lexington: University Press of Kentucky, 1981); *Black American Poets Between Worlds, 1940–1960* (Knoxville: University of Tennessee Press, 1986); Maria Mootry and Gary Smith, eds., *A Life Distilled: Gwendolyn Brooks, Her Poetry and Fiction* (Urbana: University of Illinois Press, 1987); Stephen Caldwell Wright, *On Gwendolyn Brooks: Reliant Contemplation* (Ann Arbor: University of Michigan Press, 1996).

Butler, Octavia E. (1947–2006)

Science-fiction writer. In her lifetime, Butler was arguably the only Black female science-fiction writer with a national reputation and is, with Samuel R. Delany, one of the two best-known African American writers of science fiction. Her work often features Black protagonists and often explores issues of class, race, and feminism. Butler published more than a dozen novels and one collection of short stories, and her writing has won many awards.

Born in Pasadena, California, in 1947, Butler was raised by her mother, to whom she attributes her early love of reading (*Bloodchild and Other Stories*, 125, 128–129). When she was about ten, the film *Devil Girl from Mars* convinced her she could write better stories. She has been writing science fiction ever since. By age thirteen she was mailing manuscripts to publishers. After high school, she attended Pasadena City College, California State University at Los Angeles, and the University of California at Los Angeles, but her real immersion in writing came in 1970 when she began attending writing workshops (such as the Clarion Science Fiction Writers Workshop); at these, she received encouragement and support from practicing science-fiction writers, most notably Theodore Sturgeon.

Butler's big break came in 1976 with the publication of *Patternmaster*. Over the following years, this book became part of her Patternist series, which includes *Mind of My Mind* (1977), *Survivor* (1978), *Wild Seed* (1980), and *Clay's Ark* (1984). The series describes the evolution of a culture founded and ruled by powerful telepaths. *Wild Seed*, the first in the story line, opens in Africa in the 1600s and describes the enslavement and breeding of people with psychic powers, a process that continues for generations as psychics are sought out and brought into what becomes called "the pattern"—a society of people mentally linked to each other. Each novel in the series examines a phase in the history of the telepathic culture that evolves. Although only *Wild Seed* makes explicit connections to the American culture of slavery, the series as a whole examines issues of enslavement and the effects of unchecked power. In 1979, Butler published *Kindred*, her work that most explicitly focuses on slavery in the United States. The protagonist, a young Black woman named Dana, is forced to travel from the 1970s back in time to Maryland in the 1830s in order to save the lives of a young Black woman and her White master, who will become Dana's great-great-grandparents, if they live long enough. The story explores the psychology of enslavement and the legacy bequeathed to Black Americans by their nation's long acceptance of a legalized slave economy.

In the mid-1980s, Butler won two Hugo Awards—for the short story "Speech Sounds" (1984) and the novella "Bloodchild" (1985). Both were included in her 1995 collection *Bloodchild and Other*

Stories. "Bloodchild," which Butler calls her "pregnant man story," also won Nebula and Locus awards.

Despite the acclaim she has received for her short stories, Butler considered herself primarily a novelist, and she returned to this genre in the late 1980s with the trilogy *Dawn* (1987), *Adulthood Rites* (1988), and *Imago* (1989). Called her Xenogenesis series, these works explore the resistance of Earth's few surviving human beings to their saviors—a tentacled, three-sexed alien species who nurture the human beings they rescued from Earth's holocaust back to health. The alien Oankali put these survivors in stasis while they spend years patiently restoring an Earth all but dead from human nuclear wars and planet-threatening practices. They eventually bring the remnant of the human race out of stasis and offer to return them to Earth—the price they demand is that all future offspring be products of interbreeding between the two species, thus providing the aliens with the genetic diversity needed for their own survival. In 2000, the trilogy was published in a single volume, *Lilith's Brood.*

Butler began a new series with the publication of *Parable of the Sower* (1993) and *Parable of the Talents* (1998). These books follow the fortunes of Lauren Olamina, a young Black woman who leads a small, ethnically diverse group of people determined to survive the horrific times in which they live. The first novel opens in California in 2024 and depicts a United States on its last legs, beset by drought; famine; disease; the rise of drug-crazed gangs; the collapse of the economy; the breakdown of national communication, education, and security networks; the secession of Alaska from the Union; and the near collapse of the federal government. In this world, communities wall themselves in for protection, water costs more than food, fuel-run vehicles are seldom seen, technology-based items are abandoned when they break, and literacy is an increasingly rare accomplishment. When her walled community is razed by invaders, Lauren flees north with a small group of survivors in search of safety and self-sufficiency. She gradually converts her fellow survivors to Earthseed, a religion she has conceived to provide the hope and vision needed for the human race to reverse its descent. Earthseed recognizes Change as the only god, preaches that every person must learn to shape this god in responsible ways, and says that the destiny of the human race lies among the stars.

Lauren's story continues in *Parable of the Talents*, when conditions in the United States are at their nadir. But conditions gradually improve, and Earthseed's message spreads throughout a country desperate for direction and hope. This novel follows Lauren's rise to leadership of a large religious movement and her daughter's struggles with feelings of abandonment after her separation from her family and resentment of her famous mother.

The collection *Bloodchild and Other Stories* contains five short stories followed by two "Afterwords." In the first, "Positive Obsession," Butler explains how she came to be a writer despite being told that Blacks couldn't earn their livings by writing. Her love of reading and her passion for putting words onto paper made her persevere. Success came slowly: after selling her first two short stories (only one of which made it into print), she was unable to sell anything else for five years. The second essay, "Furor Scribendi," offers advice to would-be writers.

Butler's last novel, *Fledgling* (2005), is a highly original vampire narrative set in the Pacific Northwest and California. In 2006,

Butler died after falling in her home in Lake Forest Park, near Seattle, Washington (Fox). Her papers, including manuscripts, correspondence, and working materials, are held by the Huntington Library in Pasadena, California.

Butler won many prestigious awards in her career. The most significant of these recognitions came in 1995 when she received a coveted "genius grant" from the MacArthur Foundation.

Butler's reputation rests, in part, on the important role she has played in providing high-quality science fiction featuring Black protagonists (often women). Butler, a self-proclaimed feminist, was one of the first writers to create strong female African American characters in the science-fiction genre. Her fiction also highlights themes that reflect African American issues. For instance, she often explores the subject of enslavement. In the Patternist series, telepathy becomes a means to enslave others. In the Parable series, weakened governments, collapsed economies, and privatization of police and medical services lead to a resurgence of "debt labor"—a term that Lauren points out is another way to say "slavery." In *Parable of the Sower*, her book set closest to current times, she shows us just how quickly and thoroughly civil rights for minority peoples could erode. Butler's works also tend to incorporate issues involving prejudice and its consequences. Human beings' intense prejudice against the kindly but repulsive-looking Oankali of her Xenogenesis series makes many choose species extinction over interspecies breeding. *Kindred* looks at the prejudice behind and perpetuated by the legalization of slavery in the United States.

Butler's importance, then, comes from both her themes and her adding a strong African American presence to the science-fiction genre. Her works remind readers that racial prejudice takes many forms and is a threat to species survival; she points out how compelling the temptation is to use extreme power to enslave others; and she illustrates the fragility of the advances we have made in creating a society more committed to racial equality. Butler's strong African American protagonists—many female—fill a void in earlier science-fiction offerings, which tend to offer only a token representation of Blacks. Her commercial success helped break the color barrier in one of our most popular fiction genres.

Grace McEntee

See also: Horror Fiction.

Resources

Octavia Butler, *Bloodchild and Other Stories* (New York: Four Walls Eight Windows, 1995); *Kindred* (Boston: Beacon Press, 1998); *Lilith's Brood* (includes *Dawn, Adulthood Rites,* and *Imago,* together known as the Xenogenesis Trilogy; New York: Grand Central Publishing, 2000); *Parable of the Sower* [1993] (New York: Warner Books, 1995); *Parable of the Talents* (New York: Seven Stories Press, 1998); Robert Crossley, "Introduction," in Octavia Butler, *Kindred* (Boston: Beacon Press, 1988), ix–xxii; Margalit Fox, "Octavia E. Butler, Science Fiction Writer, Dies at 58," *New York Times,* March 5, 2006: https://www.nytimes.com/2006/03/01/books /octavia-e-butler-science-fiction-writer-dies -at-58.html (accessed 2019); Ayana Jamieson and Moya Bailey, "Mining the Archive of Octavia E. Butler," *Verso: the Blog of the Huntington Library, Art Collection, and Botanical,* June 22, 2017: http://huntington blogs.org/2017/06/mining-the-archive-of -octavia-e-butler/ (accessed 2019); Gardens Michele Osherow, "The Dawn of a New Lilith: Revisionary Mythmaking in Women's Science Fiction," *National Women's Studies Association Journal* 12, no. 1 (2000), 68–83; Catherine S. Ramirez, "Cyborg Feminism:

The Science Fiction of Octavia Butler and Gloria Anzaldua," in *Reload: Rethinking Women + Cyberculture*, ed. Mary Flanagan and Austin Booth (Cambridge, MA: MIT Press, 2002); Charles H. Rowell, "An Interview with Octavia E. Butler," *Callaloo* 20, no. 1 (1997), 47–66; Gregory E. Rutledge, "Futurist Fiction & Fantasy: The Racial Establishment," *Callaloo* 24, no. 1 (2001), 236–252; Ruth Salvaggio, "Octavia Butler and the Black Science-Fiction Heroine," *Black American Literature Forum* 18, no. 2 (1984), 78–81; Peter G. Stillman, "Dystopian Critiques, Utopian Possibilities, and Human Purposes in Octavia Butler's Parables," *Utopian Studies* 14 (2003), 15–35.

C

Chesnutt, Charles Waddell (1858–1932)

Short-story writer and novelist. Widely regarded as one of the most influential African American writers of the late nineteenth and early twentieth centuries, Charles W. Chesnutt voiced the experiences and concerns of mixed-race, middle-class African Americans as well as those of the working-class Blacks of the rural South. His stated objective was "not so much the elevation of the colored people as the elevation of the whites" (Broadhead, 139). In other words, he believed that greater social equality for African Americans could be accomplished by a reformation of White social perceptions. Chesnutt envisioned himself as a writer from a young age, and though he earned substantial (if sporadic) critical praise as well as unprecedented acceptance from a White-controlled publishing industry, he would never become successful enough to support himself by his writing alone. Late-twentieth-century criticism, however, has recognized Chesnutt as a significant contributor to the development of African American short fiction, an innovator of novel forms, an enabler of the Harlem Renaissance of the 1920s, and a figure of indisputable importance in the canon of American literature.

Born in Cleveland, Ohio, in 1858, Chesnutt was the son of free, mixed-race African Americans who were both illegitimate children of White fathers. In 1866, the family moved to Fayetteville, North Carolina, where Charles's father established a grocery store. Chesnutt worked in the store and attended school until 1871, when the death of his mother forced him to seek full-time employment. At the age of fourteen, he began working as a teacher, and, by 1880, he was principal of a Fayetteville normal school for Blacks. In these years, he spent much of his free time studying European literary classics. In 1878, Chesnutt married and began establishing a family, but these professional and domestic responsibilities were unable to quell the literary ambitions of his youth, and he resigned from the normal school in 1883 to pursue a life of letters. By 1887, he had moved his family back to Cleveland, passed the Ohio bar examination, and established his own court reporting business. Chesnutt also began to hone his talents as a writer, publishing short sketches with the S. S. McClure newspaper organization throughout the late 1880s. This gained him the attention and friendship of George Washington Cable, a prominent figure on the Southern literary scene, and through this connection he began writing essays for the Open Letter Club, a group that sought solutions for the socioeconomic difficulties of the postwar South.

Chesnutt's first major success as a writer occurred when "The Goophered Grapevine" (1887) was accepted for publication by *The Atlantic Monthly*. On the surface, this short story seems to operate in the tradition of Southern plantation fiction popularized by Joel Chandler Harris and Thomas Nelson Page, as it featured an ex-slave storyteller named Uncle Julius McAdoo, a trickster figure similar to the storyteller of

Harris's Uncle Remus tales. Chesnutt manipulated this convention, however, to contradict the typically romanticized view of Southern plantation life and to introduce elements of Black folk culture, such as conjuration lore and hoodoo beliefs. The *Atlantic Monthly* printed two more of Chesnutt's Uncle Julius stories over the next two years, and, in 1898, the prestigious Houghton Mifflin publishing house in Boston, Massachusetts, agreed to publish several of the stories as a collection. The following year, this collection was issued under the title *The Conjure Woman* (1899). Considered as a whole, these stories represent one of the first literary validations of the African American plantation experience by an African American author, and they did much to debunk the mythology of a plantation-era golden age and the notion that former slaves yearned in any way for its revival.

Promising sales and a favorable critical reception prompted Houghton Mifflin to publish a second collection of stories. *The Wife of His Youth and Other Stories of the Color Line* (1899) represented a different direction in Chesnutt's writing, but one that was much closer to his own lived experience. Chesnutt had published a story in *The Independent* titled "The Sheriff's Children" (1889), which proved to be the seed of a major literary theme in his career. Eight more stories dealing with similar topics were written over the next decade, including the title story of the collection, which appeared in the *Atlantic Monthly* just months before the publication of *The Conjure Woman*. These stories addressed such sensitive social issues as segregation, racial violence in the era of Reconstruction, and, predominantly, the repercussions and complications of miscegenation. Chesnutt sought to express in these tales the conflicts and the dehumanization inherent in the mixed-race African American's search for identity along the color line, the ethnically ambiguous intersection between White and Black.

Several contemporary literary figures, William Dean Howells among them, heralded *The Wife of His Youth* as a triumph of realist fiction. The critical reception and the public's reaction were decidedly less enthusiastic, but this did not prevent Chesnutt from turning his energy completely to writing. Having established a name for himself, he felt he would be able to compensate for irregular sales by taking on the odd literary job. Small, Maynard, and Company of Boston, for instance, commissioned him to write a high school–level biography of Frederick Douglass (1899), which appeared in the Beacon Biographies series. In late 1899, Chesnutt closed the doors of his business and submitted to Houghton Mifflin a novel-length version of an unpublished short story that had originally been titled "Rena Walden." In March 1900, the novel was published as *The House Behind the Cedars*. Again taking up the theme of miscegenation, the novel portrays the social and psychological tribulations of a mulatto heroine, Rena Walden, as she attempts to pass as White in order to attain a level of prosperity that is forbidden to her as a woman of mixed race. In keeping with Chesnutt's general literary objective, *The House Behind the Cedars* questioned a White-dominated society that offered promises of the American dream but enforced an unspoken racial caste system that imposed limits on an individual's ability to succeed.

The House Behind the Cedars was well received by critics as a sensible depiction of a legitimate social problem. The sales, however, were moderate at best. Still, Houghton Mifflin was confident enough in Chesnutt to solicit another novel, which he readily provided. This second novel, *The Marrow of Tradition* (1901), is a fictionalized rendering of the Wilmington, North Carolina, massacre of 1898, in which several Blacks were killed during a White supremacist uprising. The book extends Chesnutt's exploration of the color line, depicting the tense interactions between an aristocratic White family and a mixed-race family who have both been drawn into the town's violent events. The novel's characterizations, along with its intricate scheme of subplots, allow it to comment on a variety of Southern cultural issues from a variety of perspectives and mark it as Chesnutt's most complex work. Sales and reviews were disappointing, however, and Chesnutt was faced with the reality of his family's needs. In 1902, he resumed his court stenography business.

Writing on the side, Chesnutt produced *The Colonel's Dream* (1905), the last novel of his to be published in his lifetime. Though this novel deals with race issues, Chesnutt attempted to secure the empathy of White readers by using a White protagonist, Col. Henry French, an ex-Confederate officer who returns to his Southern homeland after acquiring substantial wealth in the North. He attempts to alleviate the socioeconomic depression he finds there, but the depravity and unwillingness of the community, along with unchecked acts of racial violence, convince him of the futility of his efforts. In a larger sense, the novel can be read as an expression of Chesnutt's own sense of failure in his efforts to change White attitudes. Chesnutt continued to work as an essayist and activist until his death in 1932.

Chesnutt's impact on the development of African American literature was unquestionably deep. He has come to be regarded as the initiator of the first truly definable African American short-story tradition, and the inclusiveness of Black perspectives present in his works prompted the NAACP to present him with Spingarn Medal in 1928. His entry into the White publishing world set an irrevocable precedent, and his tireless efforts to expose the social conventions that bolstered racial disharmony paved a road upon which the New Negro authors were able to step forward. Ironically, Chesnutt united briefly with W.E.B. Du Bois and William Stanley Braithwaite in the late 1920s to criticize the experimentations of the Harlem Renaissance. In his essay "Post-Bellum—Pre-Harlem" (1931), however, he expressed a realization that he belonged to a bygone era and that the continued progression of the African American literary voice was positive evidence of the strength and resonance it had achieved in American culture.

In 2009, a volume of essays reappraising Chesnutt's writing and influence was published (Izzo and Orban).

Lewis T. LeNaire

See also: Novel.

Resources

William L. Andrews, *The Literary Career of Charles W. Chesnutt* (Baton Rouge: Louisiana State University Press, 1980); Bernard W. Bell, *The Afro-American Novel and Its Tradition* (Amherst: University of Massachusetts Press, 1987); Robert Bone, *Down Home: Origins of the Afro-American Short Story* (New York: Columbia University Press, 1975); Richard Brodhead, ed., *The Journals of Charles W. Chesnutt* (Durham, NC: Duke University Press, 1993); Charles Waddell Chesnutt: *The Colonel's Dream* (New York: Doubleday, Page, 1905); *The Conjure Woman* (Boston: Houghton Mifflin, 1899); *The House Behind the Cedars* (Boston: Houghton Mifflin, 1900); *Mandy Oxendine*, ed. Charles

Hackenberry (Urbana: University of Illinois Press, 1997); *The Marrow of Tradition* (Boston: Houghton Mifflin, 1901); *The Wife of His Youth and Other Stories of the Color Line* (Boston: Houghton Mifflin, 1899); Helen Chesnutt, *Charles W. Chesnutt: Pioneer of the Color Line* (Chapel Hill: University of North Carolina Press, 1993); J. Noel Heermance, *Charles W. Chesnutt: America's First Great Black Novelist* (Hamden, CT: Archon, 1974); David Garrett Izzo and Maria Orban, eds., *Charles Chesnutt Reappraised: Essays on the First Major African American Fiction Writer* (Jefferson, NC: McFarland & Co., 2009); Frances Richardson Keller, *An American Crusade: The Life of Charles Waddell Chesnutt* (Provo, UT: Brigham Young University Press, 1978); Ernestine Williams Pickens, *Charles W. Chesnutt and the Progressive Movement* (New York: Pace University Press, 1994); Sylvia Lyons Render, *Charles W. Chesnutt* (Boston: Twayne, 1980); Eric Sundquist, *To Wake the Nations: Race in the Making of American Literature* (Cambridge, MA: Harvard University Press, 1993); Henry B. Wonham, *Charles W. Chesnutt: A Study of the Short Fiction* (New York: Twayne, 1998).

Children's Literature

Although children have always enjoyed and used narratives, oral and written, for their entertainment, children's literature emerged as a distinct and independent form only in the late eighteenth century. The genre encompasses a wide range of work, including acknowledged classics of world literature, picture books and easy-to-read stories, poetry, novels, and short fiction, as well as lullabies, fairy tales, fables, folk songs, and folk narratives from oral traditions. Children's literature as a broad category blossomed in England and the United States in the nineteenth century. Since the 1960s, the genre has been studied and taught as two distinct but overlapping categories: children's literature meant for preschool and elementary school children, and young-adult literature designed for readers approximately ten to eighteen years of age. However, preadolescents often read young-adult titles, and adults often enjoy picture books. Just as the boundaries between children's and young-adult literatures are blurred, so are the features that constitute African American literature for young people. Historically, when writing about African American children's literature, most critics tended to dwell on literature by White American authors and illustrators that represents African Americans. These critics assumed that African American children's literature is a matter of audience rather than authorship. However, African American children's literature as a category more accurately describes a body of work for children and young adults produced by African American authors and illustrators and appreciated by a multiethnic audience from many age groups.

The late nineteenth century, often referred to as the golden age of children's literature, witnessed a profusion of books designed specifically for a young audience. Despite their abundance, however, these works represented only a portion of the literate youth in America. There were few depictions of African American children in textbooks, periodicals, stories, and poems, and very few of the depictions that did exist were unbiased or avoided stereotypes. African American children would have been exposed mainly to racist stories such as Helen Bannerman's *The Story of Little Black Sambo* (1899), which was reprinted frequently into the 1930s. As late as 1920, the prevailing popular magazine for children, *St. Nicholas* (1873–1945), featured a poem titled "Ten Little N——." These texts reinforced popular racist sentiment toward

African Americans and perpetuated the ignorance of the White community, the children of which were offered no other literary portrayal of their Black counterparts. Further, *Little Black Sambo* and literature like it threatened to devastate a slowly growing sense of self-worth among a new generation of African Americans.

However, African Americans began to publish for children during the so-called golden age and thereby present an alternative tradition of literature for young people. Beginning in 1887, Mrs. A. E. (Amelia) Johnson, an African American, printed a number of religious tracts for children, including an eight-page magazine, *Joy*. She later published novels, including *Clarence and Corinne; or, God's Way* (1890), which, for whatever reasons, largely featured White characters. Also published in the early era of African American children's literature, Paul Laurence Dunbar's *Little Brown Baby* (1895) is a seminal text in the genre. A collection of Dialect Poetry that celebrates African American folk culture, *Little Brown Baby* is neither didactic nor religious. Intending to delight his young readers, Dunbar depicts African American people and culture in a positive light. Other early pieces have only recently been recovered, among them Leila A. Pendleton's *An Alphabet for Negro Children* (date unknown).

After the turn of the century, this alternative tradition of children's literature expanded with the development of an educated African American middle class that both demanded and could financially support such an endeavor. Readers containing poetry, essays, short stories, folklore, and artwork became available, such as Silas X. Floyd's *Floyd's Flowers, or Duty and Beauty for Colored Children* (1905). W.E.B. Du Bois's visionary magazine *The Brownies' Book* offered African American

children an alternative to *St. Nicholas*. Recognizing the urgent need for characters that Black children could respect and emulate, Du Bois, the only Black founder of the NAACP and the editor of that organization's magazine, *The Crisis*, experimented with "Children's Numbers," an annual children's issue of *The Crisis*. These issues were so successful that in 1920, Du Bois, along with business manager Augustus Granville Dill and literary editor Jessie Redmon Fauset, established a new magazine aimed specifically at children aged six to sixteen. Incorporating a variety of popular forms, such as fiction, folktales and fairy tales, poetry, drama, biography, and photography and illustrations by African American artists, *The Brownies' Book* offered nonreligious, nondidactic entertainment that attempted to infuse Black youth with a sense of self-worth and impress upon them the importance of education. The result was often too idealistic in its portrayal of childhood and American society. *The Brownies' Book* effectively inspired self-esteem, confidence, and racial pride.

Du Bois and Dill also published two biographies for children, Elizabeth Ross Haynes's *Unsung Heroes* (1921) and Julia Henderson's *A Child's Story of Dunbar* (1913), thereby pioneering another important form of African American children's literature. Haynes published twenty-two biographies, and many of them introduced children to African Americans rarely depicted in their school texts, figures who are now well known, including Frederick Douglass and Harriet Tubman.

Known best for their writing for adults, Langston Hughes and Arna Bontemps also created large bodies of work for children. Hughes's *The Dream Keeper* (1932) is a classic collection of poetry for children, and his *Black Misery* (1969) remains a popular children's book. His nonfiction titles, among them *The First Book of Jazz* (1955), the *First Book of the West Indies* (1956), and *The First Book of Negroes* (1952), made important contributions, and several have been reprinted. Bontemps also created an extensive body of work, including biography, fiction, and poetry, that helped African American children's literature gain widespread acceptance. The poetry anthology Bontemps edited, *Golden Slippers* (1941), includes poetry by such respected authors as Dunbar, Countee Cullen, Claude McKay, Langston Hughes, and James Weldon Johnson. Through this and other anthologies, his novels, and his biographies, Bontemps offered children many positive African American role models. In novels such as *You Can't Pet a Possum* (1934) and *Lonesome Boy* (1955), he celebrates African American folk culture and language patterns. One of his collaborations with Hughes, *Popo and Fifina* (1932), remains popular with children. Further, Bontemps's work has gained wide popularity in part because of its literary quality and in part because he offers authentic portrayals of African Americans engaged in daily activities.

While publishers seemed to shy away from African American fiction for children through the 1940s and early 1950s, several African American writers, among them Hughes, Shirley Graham, and Carter G. Woodson, followed Bontemps in publishing biographies of notable African Americans. Woodson, a noted scholar, writer, and educator, worked toward a new kind of pedagogy that was unfettered by racist ideology, offered new purposes and goals, and used new texts in order to educate African American youth in critical thinking and commitment to the advancement of their race. As the founder of the Associated Press, Woodson achieved many of his objectives; he

published a significant number of collections of poetry and folklore, readers, biographies, and histories.

Like Woodson, librarians, classroom teachers, and postsecondary educators and administrators have worked to ensure that African American children's literature flourishes and reaches an audience. In 1939, the librarian Mary McLeod Bethune argued that "the ideals, character and attitudes of races are born within the minds of children; most prejudices are born with youth and it is our duty to see that the great researchers of Negro History are placed in the language and story of the child" (10). When Augusta Baker started work as a young librarian in the Harlem branch of the New York City Public Library, she found few children's books portraying Black people in a realistic manner. During the next thirty-seven years, Baker corrected this situation, not only by adding appropriate books to the library's collections but also by meeting with authors and publishers to get more African American stories written. She also edited anthologies of African American literature for young readers. A renowned storyteller, Baker started the James Weldon Johnson Memorial Collection in 1939. To promote the project, she met with a number of children's authors, publishers, and editors. By the time the bibliography of the collection was published under the title *Books About Negro Life for Children* (1961), Baker had assembled hundreds of titles. In 1953, she became the first Black librarian to hold an administrative position in the New York Public Library, and, by 1961, she was in charge of children's policies and programs in all eighty-two branches.

Baker's influence spread beyond the library itself: she involved schools and community groups, was a consultant for the television program *Sesame Street*, moderated television and radio programs, and taught courses on storytelling and children's literature. Following Baker, African American members of the American Library Association became concerned that African American children's literature was not being recognized for its artistry and range. In 1969, Glyndon Greer, with the support of Mabel McKissack, established the Coretta Scott King Award for African American authors and illustrators of books for children. It has been the mechanism through which several African American writers and artists have gained professional and public recognition. Also in the late 1960s, the Council on Interracial Books for Children began holding contests in order to identify and support promising young artists. Their first winner, Kristin Hunter Lattany's *The Soul Brothers and Sister Lou* (1968), sold over a million copies.

With such encouragement from educators and librarians, and with the 1954 Supreme Court decision to desegregate schools, African American children's literature became an established and expanding tradition that reflected contemporary social and cultural consciousness. Some of these texts offered an integrationist approach to racial difference and the problems of bigotry. The work of Bontemps's later contemporaries—Jesse Jackson's *Call Me Charley* (1945) and Lorenz Bell Graham's *South Town* (1958) and *North Town* (1965)—are some of the many books about African American experiences written for children of all races. These novels tried to instill in all children a social conscience that afforded awareness and tolerance of racial difference without taking into account social and cultural difference. This "social conscience" literature promoting an ideology of assimilation and integration quickly gave way to African American children's literature that is more

culturally conscious. Rudine Sims describes culturally conscious children's literature as "books that reflect, with varying degrees of success, the social and cultural traditions associated with growing up Black in the United States" (49).

Since the late 1960s, African American children's literature has most often been "culturally conscious," its focus on African American perspective and setting. Since the mid-1970s, dozens of African American writers have gained wide popularity through works that present the range of African American experiences. They offer historically accurate portrayals of African American lives and a tradition of resistance to racism and discrimination. They provide aesthetic experience, and they entertain and educate even as they engender racial pride. These books cover multiple forms and genres and are joined by magazines, such as *Ebony Jr.* (1973–1985), which offered positive representations of African Americans in art and literature and provided a forum for young writers to publish their work, and *Footsteps*, which has been published since 1999, and has included reprints of Jacob Lawrence's work, an interview with baseball great Hank Aaron, and articles on celebrities such as Ossie Davis. Today, African American children's literature includes illustrated texts for young children that offer a visual schema that will inform identity formation, and texts for older readers that provide rich literary material for exploring the issues and dilemmas of human experience as perceived by the young.

No literary genre is more dependent on illustrations than literature for children, and African American children's literature is particularly reliant on the ability of illustrations to depict African Americans as individuals with a rich and diverse culture.

While children are especially sensitive to illustrations, illustrated texts are read by a wide audience, and it is important that African Americans and their culture and history be accurately depicted. Picture-book author Eloise Greenfield recognizes the importance of illustrations by stipulating in her book contracts that her work be illustrated by African American artists. Books such as artist Tom Feelings's *The Middle Passage* (1995) rely on pictures alone to tell a story. *The Middle Passage*, which relates the painful story of Africans taken across the Atlantic Ocean and sold into slavery in the Americas, is one of many picture books that make clear the African roots of African American culture and identity. Ashley Bryan's linocut illustrations for his four volumes of African folktales; Muriel Feelings's Swahili abcedarium and counting book, *Jambo Means Hello* (1974) and *Moja Means One* (1971), illustrated by Tom Feelings; Leo and Diane Dillon's illustrations for Verna Aardema's editions of African fables, such as *Why Mosquitoes Buzz in People's Ears* (1975); and John Steptoe's African Cinderella story, *Mufaro's Beautiful Daughters* (1987), are other notable examples of texts based in African culture and history. The last three of these were the first three texts by African American illustrators to win Caldecott Medals.

African motifs, particularly patterns and colors of cloth, appear in many picture books that tell African American stories. For example, kente cloth is the predominant pattern of Carole Byard's illustrations in Phil Mendez's *The Black Snowman* (1989), African masks and sculptures inform Byard's work in Camille Yarbrough's *Cornrows* (1979), and Faith Ringgold's African-inspired quilts and tankas (fabric sculptures) are predominant in her *Tar Beach* (1991) and *Dinner at Aunt Connie's House* (1993).

In this latter book, Ringgold relies on the African American history that informs many picture books, as her young protagonist imagines historical figures such as Harriet Tubman and Mary McLeod Bethune coming to dinner with her extended family. Ashley Bryan's illustrated collections of African American spirituals, *I'm Going to Sing* (1976) and *Walk Together Children* (2 vols., 1974, 1982), and Brian Pinkney's illustrations for Patricia McKissack's collection of African American folktales, *The Dark Thirty* (1992), are other notable examples.

Illustrated collections of African American poetry are also important in this genre, such as Romare Bearden's collages of poems by Langston Hughes in *The Block* (1995), Ashley Bryan's illustrated collection of Hughes's nativity poems in *Carol of the Brown King* (1998), and the many titles by Arnold Adoff, among them *All the Colors of the Race* (1982), illustrated by Steptoe. Illustrated books provide young children, and readers of all ages, with positive images of African Americans and the rich diversity of their history and culture and offer a literary experience that can aid in the understanding and interpretation of life experiences.

African American literature for young adults plays important educational and cultural roles. The adolescent years are a period for dealing with issues of discrimination, prejudice, and cultural differences because adolescents often perceive themselves as a "culture" apart from the mainstream. Authors of young-adult fiction who deal with themes of diversity in race, religion, feminist criticism, or class can touch young readers in a profound way. Since the 1960s, African American young-adult fiction has grown into a vast body of work that has achieved recognition and popularity among wide audiences. Again, themes and genres are diverse. These writers offer stories of the inner city and rural America, such as Walter Dean Myers's stories about Harlem in *Fallen Angels* (1988) or June Jordan's urban landscape in *His Own Where* (1971), and Mildred D. Taylor's continuing saga of the Logans, set in rural Mississippi. African American young-adult writers set their fiction in the past, the present, and the future, such as Julius Lester's slave narrative *To Be a Slave* (1968), Virginia Hamilton's realistic novel *M. C. Higgins, the Great* (1974), or Octavia Butler's futuristic fantasy *The Parable of the Sower* (1993). These writers deal with themes about and alongside racism, such as Rosa Guy's exploration of a lesbian relationship between two Black teenagers in *Ruby* (1976); Sharon Bell Mathis's *Listen for the Fig Tree* (1974), about the experience of a blind girl, or Joyce Carol Thomas's short stories representing the African American teenager in the midst of various ethnic groups in *A Gathering of Flowers* (1990). Further, poets and novelists who write mainly for adults are widely read by young adults and are taught in their classrooms, among them Maya Angelou, Alice Walker, Toni Cade Bambara, Lorraine Hansberry, James Baldwin, Lucille Clifton, and Zora Neale Hurston.

Now more than a century old, African American children's literature performs essential functions in the growth and development of its readers, and its benefits go far past simply making visible in texts for children the formerly absent African American, or countering negative portrayals of African Americans with positive ones. Generally, it enables them to define themselves in terms of their cultural heritage as well as their national heritage. Both text and illustration develop the young reader's self-perception, comprehension of the world and personal experience, and ability to form relationships with others.

In 2010, Jonda C. McNair published the results of a systematic survey aimed at reflecting a consensus about which books for children and young adults by African American authors deserve to be considered classics (McNair). In 2015, McNair and Wanda Brooks published a study of how hair is represented in children's books (McNair and Brooks). In 2019, Ibi Aanu Zoboi edited a collection of new short stories for young adults entitled *Black Enough: Stories of Being Young and Black in America*.

Roxanne Harde

See also: Bontemps, Arna; Hughes, Langston.

Resources

Primary Sources: Verna Aardema, *Why Mosquitoes Buzz in People's Ears: An African Folktale*, illus. Leo and Diane Dillon (New York: Dial Press, 1975); Arnold Adoff, *All the Colors of the Race*, illus. John Steptoe (New York: Lothrop, Lee & Shepard, 1982); Helen Bannerman, *The Story of Little Black Sambo* (New York: F. A. Stokes, 1899); Arna Bontemps: *Lonesome Boy* (Boston: Houghton Mifflin, 1955); *You Can't Pet a Possum* (New York: Morrow, 1934); Arna Bontemps, ed., *Golden Slippers: An Anthology of Negro Poetry for Young Readers* (New York: Harper & Row, 1941); Ashley Bryan: *I'm Going to Sing: African American Spirituals* (New York: Atheneum, 1976); *Lion and the Ostrich Chicks, and Other African Folk Tales* (New York: Atheneum, 1986); *The Ox of the Wonderful Horns, and Other African Folktales* (New York: Atheneum, 1971); *Walk Together, Children: Black American Spirituals*, 2 vols. (New York: Atheneum, 1974–1982); Octavia Butler, *The Parable of the Sower* (New York: Four Walls Eight Windows, 1993); Paul Laurence Dunbar, *Little Brown Baby* (1895; repr. New York: Dodd, Mead, 1940); Muriel Swahili Feelings: *Jambo Means Hello*, illus. Tom

Feelings (New York: Dial, 1974); *Moja Means One*, illus. Tom Feelings (New York: Dial, 1971); Tom Feelings, *The Middle Passage: White Ships, Black Cargo* (New York: Dial, 1995); Silas X. Floyd, *Floyd's Flowers, or Duty and Beauty for Colored Children* (Atlanta: Hertl, Jenkins, 1905); Lorenz Bell Graham: *North Town* (New York: Crowell, 1965); *South Town* (Chicago: Follett, 1958); Eloise Greenfield, *Africa Dream*, illus. Carole Byard (New York: John Day, 1977); Rosa Guy, *Ruby* (New York: Viking, 1976); Virginia Hamilton, *M. C. Higgins, the Great* (New York: Macmillan, 1974); Elizabeth Ross Haynes, *Unsung Heroes* (New York: Dubois and Dill, 1921); Julia Henderson, *A Child's Story of Dunbar* (Chicago: Conkey, 1913, 1921); Langston Hughes: *Black Misery* (New York: P. S. Eriksson, 1969); *The Block*, illus. Romare Bearden (New York: Viking, 1995); *Carol of the Brown King*, illus. Ashley Bryan (New York: Atheneum, 1998); *The Dream Keeper* (New York: Knopf, 1932); *The First Book of Jazz* (New York: Franklin Watts, 1955); *The First Book of Negroes* (New York: Franklin Watts, 1952); *The First Book of Rhythms* (New York: Franklin Watts, 1954); *The First Book of the West Indies* (New York: Franklin Watts, 1956); Langston Hughes and Arna Bontemps, *Popo and Fifina: Children of Haiti* (New York: Macmillan, 1932); Jesse Jackson, *Call Me Charley* (New York: Harper & Bros., 1945); A. E. Johnson, *Clarence and Corinne; or, God's Way* (Philadelphia: American Baptist Publication Society, 1890); June Jordan, *His Own Where* (New York: Crowell, 1971); Kristin Hunter Lattany, *The Soul Brothers and Sister Lou* (New York: Scribner's, 1968); Julius Lester, *To Be a Slave*, illus. Tom Feelings (New York: Dial, 1968); Sharon Bell Mathis, *Listen for the Fig Tree* (New York: Viking, 1974); Patricia McKissack, *The Dark Thirty*, illus. Brian Pinkney (New York: Knopf, 1992); Phil Mendez, *The Black Snowman*, illus. Carole Byard (New York: Scholastic, 1989); Walter Dean Myers, *Fallen Angels* (Austin, TX: Holt, Rinehart and Winston, 1988); Leila A. Pendleton, *An Alphabet for Negro Children* (publisher and date unknown); Faith Ringgold: *Dinner at Aunt Connie's House* (New York: Hyperion, 1993); *Tar Beach* (New York: Crown, 1991); John Steptoe, *Mufaro's Beautiful Daughters* (New York: Lothrop, Lee & Shephard, 1987); Joyce Carol Thomas, *A Gathering of Flowers* (New York: Harper & Row, 1990); Camille Yarbrough, *Cornrows*, illus. Carole Byard (New York: Coward, McCann and Geoghegan, 1979); Ibi Aanu Zoboi, ed., *Black Enough: Stories of Being Young and Black in America* (New York: Balzer & Bray/HarperCollins, 2019).

Secondary Sources: Augusta Baker, "The Changing Image of the Black in Children's Literature," *Horn Book* 51 (Feb. 1975), 79–88; Mary McLeod Bethune, "The Adaptation of the History of the Negro to the Capacity of the Child," *Journal of Negro History* 24 (Jan. 1939), 9–13; Rudine Sims Bishop: "Reflections on the Development of African American Children's Literature," *Journal of Children's Literature* 38, no. 2 (2012), 5–13; *Shadow and Substance: Afro-American Experience in Contemporary Children's Fiction* (Urbana, IL: National Council of Teachers of English, 1982); Arna Bontemps, "Special Collections of Negroana," *Library Quarterly* 14 (July 1944), 187–206; Violet J. Harris, "African American Children's Literature: The First One Hundred Years," *Journal of Negro Education* 59, no. 4 (1990), 540–555; Dianne Johnson-Feelings, ed., *The Best of The Brownies' Book* (New York: Oxford University Press, 1996); Jonda C. McNair, "Classic African American Children's Literature," *The Reading Teacher* (Newark, NJ), 64, no. 2, (October 2010), 96–105; Jonda C. McNair and Wanda Brooks, "'Combing' Through Representations of Black Girls' Hair in African American Children's Literature Eleanor," *Children's Literature in Education* 46, no. 3 (2015), 296–307; Weakley Nolen, "The Colored Child in Contemporary Literature," *Horn Book* 18, no. 5 (1942), 348–355; Carole A. Park, "Goodbye, Black Sambo: Black Writers Forge New Images in Children's Literature," *Ebony* (November 1972), 60–70; Jacque Roethler, "Reading in Color:

Children's Book Illustrations and Identity Formation for Black Children in the United States," *African American Review* 32, no. 1 (1998), 95–105; Charlemae Rollins, "Promoting Racial Understanding Through Books," *Negro American Literature Forum* 2 (1968), 71–76; Barbara Rollock, *Black Authors and Illustrators of Children's Books* (New York: Garland, 1988); Nancy Tolson, "Making Books Available: The Role of Early Libraries, Librarians, and Booksellers in the Promotion of African American Children's Literature," *African American Review* 32, no. 1 (1998), 9–16.

Clifton, Lucille (1936–2010)

Poet and children's author. Along with her accomplishments as a poet, Clifton is known for her work in bringing cultural diversity to children's literature. Born Thelma Louise Sayles on June 27, 1936, in Depew, New York, Clifton is the child of Samuel and Thelma Sayles, who were both laborers. Her father worked in the steel mills. Her mother was a laundress but wrote poetry for her own enjoyment (Moody, 157). Clifton's mother recited poetry to her, and her father was an avid storyteller, a griot who taught his children the history of their ancestors and those ancestors' journeys to America (Hatch and Strickland, 60). Although neither parent had been formally educated, both encouraged Clifton to attempt whatever she wanted to do, even though her father was against the idea of her mother trying to publish her own work (Glaser, 313–314).

Clifton attended Howard University on a drama scholarship; there she met Sterling A. Brown, A. B. Spellman, LeRoi Jones (a.k.a. Amiri Baraka), and Chloe Wofford (now known as Toni Morrison) and acted in the first performance of James Baldwin's play *The Amen Corner* (Draper, 458). She left Howard to attend Fredonia State Teachers College. She met her husband, Fred James Clifton, during that time.

Clifton worked for the U.S. Department of Education as a literature assistant for the Central Atlantic Regional Educational Laboratory from 1969 to 1971 ("Lucille Clifton," 56). Clifton noted that the position involved locating books to be used in schools. As she described it, "I had to find books that had characters in them that looked like my children, which is why I started writing children's books" (Davis, 1060). Clifton asserted that "American children's literature ought to mirror American children" (Davis, 1061). Clifton wrote a number of children's books, many of which feature a boy named Everett Anderson who experiences a number of life events, such as a new stepparent and death of a relative. One of the books in this series won the Coretta Scott King Award in 1984.

Although she did not complete her college degree because she became engrossed in her writing and "forgot to study," education remained important to her (Draper, 458). She received honorary doctorates from Colby College, the University of Maryland, Towson State University, Washington College, and Albright College ("Lucille Clifton," 57), and held several visiting professorships. She was distinguished professor of humanities at St. Mary's College of Maryland since 1991 ("Lucille Clifton," 56). A well-received teacher of poetry and creative writing, she had interesting experiences while teaching, including an occasion at Duke University when her students did not know who Paul Robeson was. In telling the story, Clifton said, "Well, I thought, 'Okay, he's dead,' but when they said they had never heard of Julian Bond," she became more concerned, and made it her practice to "teach about the things people don't know about" (Davis, 1061). In her own experiences growing up, Clifton said she became a "nosy kind of curious person" when she realized that teachers were "only going to teach me what they thought I could learn or what they wished me to know" (Davis, 1064).

In her 1976 work *Generations*, Clifton wrote about her family history. Each segment is written in the first person, giving an individual voice to each particular ancestor (Moody, 157). The collection has received greater critical attention in recent years for its narrative structure, her use of lines from Walt Whitman's "Song of Myself" as epigraphs for each segment, and its importance not just for African Americans, but as American genealogy, history, and literature (Holladay; Wall; Whitley). Among the ancestors who tell their stories are her great-great-grandmother, Caroline Sale Donald, born in 1822 or 1823, who was taken from Dahomey to New Orleans as a slave (Peppers, 57; Moody, 157). During and after her time in slavery, Caroline was a strong woman who was viewed as a leader among her community. Caroline's daughter Lucille, who was the first Black woman legally hanged in Virginia (for killing the White man who was the father of her son) is also given a voice in *Generations* (Peppers, 57). The poems in *An Ordinary Woman* (1974) also feature the lives of Caroline and other family members, based upon the stories that Clifton's father told her.

Clifton's earlier works are often associated with the Black Arts Movement, which promoted the arts as a means to overcome racism and oppression (Draper, 458). Her subsequent works, as one critic put it, were "a poetry not of race but of revelation, in the manner of Denise Levertov" (Cooper, 94). Many of her poems deal with politics; some, for example, concern events in Soweto, South Africa; Nagasaki, Japan; Kent State; and Gettysburg. Other poems deal with religion, in both Eastern and Western traditions. Her works of family history previously mentioned are also remarkable; many of her writings are elegies or poems of mourning for dead friends and family members, particularly for her mother, who died at age forty-four. Clifton's poetry has been nominated for the Pulitzer Prize three times; she has also been nominated for the National Book Award. Clifton was poet laureate of Maryland from 1974 to 1985 and received three National Endowment for the Arts awards. She received a number of awards and prizes, including induction into the National Literature Hall of Fame for African American Writers in 1998 and a Lila Wallace Readers Digest Award in 1999. Her poem, "They Thought the Field Was Wasting" appeared in *Poetry* magazine in the year of her death, 2010. *The Collected Poems of Lucille Clifton* was published in 2012 with a foreword by Nobel Prize–winning writer Toni Morrison.

Writing for Clifton is about bearing witness and being connected to the world intellectually and emotionally. When asked why she continues to write, Clifton replied that "writing is a way of continuing to hope" and "a way of remembering" that she is not alone (Glaser, 311).

Elizabeth Blakesley Lindsay

See also: Feminism/Black Feminism.

Resources
Primary Works: Lucille Clifton: *The Black BC's* (New York: Dutton, 1970); *Blessing the Boats: New and Selected Poems 1988–2000* (Brockport, NY: BOA Editions, 2000); *The Collected Poems of Lucille Clifton*, ed. Kevin Young and Michael S. Glaser, with a foreword

by Toni Morrison (Rochester, NY: BOA Editions, 2012); *Everett Anderson's Goodbye* (New York: Holt, Rinehart and Winston, 1983); *Everett Anderson's 1-2-3* (New York: Holt, Rinehart and Winston, 1977); *Everett Anderson's Year* (New York: Holt, Rinehart and Winston, 1974); *Generations* (New York: Random House, 1976); *Good News About the Earth: New Poems* (New York: Random House, 1972); *Good Times: Poems* (New York: Random House, 1969); *Good Woman: Poems and a Memoir, 1969–1980* (Brockport, NY: BOA Editions, 1987); *An Ordinary Woman* (New York: Random House, 1974); *Quilting: Poems, 1987–1990* (Brockport, NY: BOA Editions, 1991); *Some of the Days of Everett Anderson* (New York: Holt, Rinehart and Winston, 1970); *Sonora Beautiful* (New York: Dutton, 1981); *The Terrible Stories: Poems* (Brockport, NY: BOA Editions, 1996); "They Thought the Field Was Wasting," *Poetry* 196, no. 2 (May 2010); *Three Wishes* (New York: Viking, 1976); *The Times They Used to Be* (New York: Holt, Rinehart and Winston, 1974); *Two-Headed Woman* (Amherst: University of Massachusetts Press, 1980).

Secondary Works: Jane Todd Cooper, "Lucille Clifton," in *The Oxford Companion to Twentieth-Century Poetry in English*, ed. Ian Hamilton (New York: Oxford University Press, 1994), 94–95; Eisa Davis, "Lucille Clifton and Sonia Sanchez: A Conversation," *Callaloo* 25, no. 4 (2002), 1038–1074; Michael S. Glaser, "I'd Like Not to Be a Stranger in the World: A Conversation/Interview with Lucille Clifton," *Antioch Review* 58, no. 3 (2000), 310–328; Shari Dorantes Hatch and Michael R. Strickland, eds., *African-American Writers: A Dictionary*, ed. Shanti Dorantes Hatch and Michael R. Strickland (Santa Barbara, CA: ABC-CLIO, 2000); Sylvia Henneberg: "Fat Liberation in the First World: Lucille Clifton and the New Body," *Women's Studies* 47, no. 1 (2 January 2018), 60–79; "Lucille Clifton," in *Black Literature Criticism*, ed. James P. Draper (Detroit: Gale, 1992), 458–469; "Lucille Clifton," in *Contemporary Authors*, new rev. ser., vol. 97 (Detroit: Gale, 2001), 56–62; Jocelyn K. Moody, "Lucille Clifton," in *The Oxford Companion to African American Literature*, ed. William L. Andrews, Frances Smith Foster, and Trudier Harris (New York: Oxford University Press, 1997), 157–158; Wallace R. Peppers, "Lucille Clifton," in *Dictionary of Literary Biography*, vol. 41, *Afro-American Poets Since 1955* (Detroit: Gale, 1985), 55–60.

Coates, Ta-Nehisi (1975–)

Journalist, essayist, memoirist, comic book writer, and professor. Coates was born and grew up in Baltimore, Maryland. His mother was a teacher who encouraged his writing, and his father, a member of the Black Panthers in the 1970s, founded a publishing firm, Black Classics Press. Coates graduated from Howard University in Washington, DC.

As a journalist, he has worked for the *Washington City Paper*, the *Village Voice*, the *Philadelphia Weekly*, and the *Atlantic*. He became a staff columnist for the *Atlantic*.

Both his first book, *The Beautiful Struggle: A Father, Two Sons, and an Unlikely Road to Manhood* (2008), and his second, *Between the World and Me: Notes on the First 150 Years in America* (2015), concern in part his having grown up in Baltimore, but it was the second book that earned Coates widespread critical acclaim and popularity. Part of the book describes the chronic difficulties faced by African Americans in Baltimore and in the United States generally because of racism, White supremacy, poverty, and violence. The book also describes experiences at Howard University that gave him a sense of belonging but also challenged him intellectually. It also ponders American history in general.

Coates has also written two landmark essays. "The Case for Reparations" (2014) analyzes the extent to which enormous wealth was created by means of slave labor, and it asserts that African Americans are owed both moral and financial reparations. "Fear of a Black President" (2013) analyzes the White backlash against the presidency of Barack Obama. That presidency and the overreaction to it also comprise topics of his third book, *We Were Eight Years in Power* (2017).

Coates also writes the *Black Panther* series for Marvel Comics, the first book appearing in 2016, drawn by Brian Stelfreeze and Chris Sprouse. The series formed the basis for the enormously popular film *Black Panther* (2018), directed by Ryan Coogler.

Coates has been a frequent guest on radio and television programs, and he was awarded a prestigious fellowship from the MacArthur Foundation. A visiting professor at the Massachusetts Institute of Technology in 2012–2014, Coates has also taught at the City University of New York and New York University.

Hans A. Ostrom

See also: Autobiography; Essay.

Resources

Ta-Nehisi Coates: *The Beautiful Struggle: A Father, Two Sons, and an Unlikely Road to Manhood* (New York: Spiegel and Grau, 2008); *Between the World and Me: Notes on the First 150 Years in America* (New York: Spiegel and Grau, 2015); "The Case for Reparations," *The Atlantic* (June 2014), https://www.theatlantic.com/magazine/archive/2014/06/the-case-for-reparations/361631/: (accessed 2019); "Fear of a Black President," *The Atlantic* (September 2012), https://www.theatlantic.com/magazine/archive/2012/09/fear-of-a-black-president/309064/: (accessed 2019); *Were Eight Years in Power* (New York: One World, 2017); Ta-Nehisi Coates and Stan Lee, *Black Panther: A Nation Under Our Feet* (Books I, II, and III), illus. Brian Stelfreeze and Chris Sprouse (New York: Marvel Comics, 2017); Ryan Coogler, director, *Black Panther* (feature film) (2018); Stacey Gibson, "Sourcing the Imagination: Ta-Nehisi Coates's Work as a Praxis of Decolonization," *English Journal* 106, no. 4 (March 2017), 54–59; William Voegeli, "Beyond hope? Beyond change? (Ta-Nehisi Coates's *Between the World and Me*)," *Claremont Review of Books* 15, no. 4 (Fall 2015), 12(7).

Cooper, Anna Julia Haywood (1858/1859–1964)

Essayist and lecturer. An activist and pioneer in education, Cooper devoted her life to scholarship and the improvement of conditions for African Americans, particularly women. Born in 1858 or 1859 in Raleigh, North Carolina, to Hannah Stanley, a slave, and George Washington Haywood, her White owner, Cooper early demonstrated her intellect, tutoring fellow students at St. Augustine's Normal and Collegiate Institute when she was only nine. In 1877, she married George A. C. Cooper, who died unexpectedly in 1879.

Shortly thereafter, Cooper enrolled at Oberlin College, where she took the "gentlemen's courses" and earned a BA and an MA in mathematics. As principal at the "M" Street School (later known as Dunbar High School) in Washington, DC, Cooper's support of a rigorous academic curriculum angered officials of the school system, who revoked her principalship when she refused to implement Booker T. Washington's vocational model of education. Cooper chaired the Language Department at Lincoln Institute in Jefferson City, Missouri, from 1906 until 1910, returned to "M" Street as a Latin teacher in 1910, and, in 1929, became president of Frelinghuysen University, an evening school for working people. She remained with this institution, despite its loss of accreditation, until it closed in the 1950s.

Cooper's studies reflected her belief that education must be varied and challenging. In the summer of 1911, she began studying at the Guilde Internationale in Paris; in 1925, when she was sixty-six, she became the fourth-known African American woman to earn a doctorate when the Sorbonne (University of Paris) awarded her the degree. Cooper completed two dissertations—*Le Pèlerinage de Charlemagne: Voyage à Jérusalem et à Constantinople* (1925), a translation of a medieval tale, and *L'Attitude de la France à l'Égard de l'Esclavage Pendant la Révolution* (1925), a historical study of French racial attitudes. As the work of an African American who had herself been a slave, *L'Attitude* (published in English as *Slavery and the French Revolutionists*) is a significant text. Although concerned with French slavery on both sides of the Atlantic, it situates slavery within a global and historical framework and suggests that slavery everywhere could have been abolished if there had been a will to do so.

Cooper's other major work, a collection of essays titled *A Voice from the South, by a Black Woman of the South* (1892), addresses social issues from a Black female's perspective, insisting that even though they are generally denied access to higher education, African American women are the key to improving social conditions for their race. She cites as evidence her own experiences at St. Augustine and Oberlin, where males with only "a floating intention to study" were encouraged, while females had to struggle "against positive discouragements." As to the race problem, Cooper suggests that the solution lies in the hands of God and will be resolved when America becomes more concerned with capabilities than with color. While acknowledging that the African American experience has encouraged oratory, Cooper argues for a written African American literary tradition crafted by African Americans. She describes African American folklore as a "native growth" that "could claim the attention and charm the ear of the outside world" and wishes for a "painter-poet" to depict "a black man honestly and appreciatively" and "the white man, occasionally, as seen from the Negro's standpoint."

Cooper's extensive activist career expounded her theme of uplift for African American women. It began in 1886 with "Womanhood: A Vital Element in the Regeneration and Progress of a Race," a presentation at the Convocation of Clergy of the Protestant Episcopal Church, and included such important addresses as "The Needs and Status of Black Women" (Congress of Representative Women, 1893) and "The Negro Problem in America" (first Pan-African Conference in London, 1900). Cooper helped found the Colored Women's League (1892) and the Colored Women's YWCA in Washington (1905). She was the only woman elected to the prestigious American Negro Academy and was active in numerous organizations. Cooper's later works include *Legislative Measures Concerning Slavery in the United States* (1942), *Equality of Races and the Democratic Movement* (1945), *The Life and Writings of the Grimké Family* (1951), and an autobiography, *The Third Step* (ca. 1950). Her long life validated her commitment to social and intellectual equality, her feminist stance, and her racial pride.

Gloria A. Shearin

See also: Feminism/Black Feminism.

Resources

Karen Baker-Fletcher, *A Singing Something: Womanist Reflections on Anna Julia Cooper* (New York: Crossroad Publishing, 1994); Anna Julia Cooper: *Slavery and the French Revolution*, trans. Frances Richardson Keller (Lewiston, NY: Mellen, 1988); *A Voice from the South, by a Black Woman of the South* (1892; New York: Oxford University Press, 1988); Leona C. Gable, *From Slavery to the Sorbonne and Beyond: The Life and Writings of Anna J. Cooper* (Northampton, MA: Dept. of History, Smith College, 1982); Beverly Guy-Sheftall, "Black Feminist Studies: The Case of Anna Julia Cooper," *African American Review* 43, no. 1 (2009), 11–15; Larese C. Hubbard, "When and Where I Enter: Anna Julia Cooper, Afrocentric Theory, and Africana Studies," *Journal of Black Studies* 40, no. 2 (November 1, 2009), 283–295; Karen A. Johnson, *Uplifting the Women and the Race: The Educational Philosophies and Social Activism of Anna Julia Cooper and Nannie Helen Burroughs* (New York: Garland, 2000); Charles Lemert and Esme Bhan, eds., *The Voice of Anna Julia Cooper* (Lanham, MD: Rowman & Littlefield, 1998); Shirley Wilson Logan, ed., *With Pen and Voice: A Critical Anthology of Nineteenth-Century African-American Women* (Carbondale: Southern Illinois University Press, 1995); Vivian M. May, *Anna Julia Cooper, Visionary Black Feminist: a Critical Introduction* (New York: Routledge, 2007).

Craft, William (1824–1900) and Ellen Smith Craft (1826–1891)

Abolitionists and activists. Important figures in the abolitionist movement, the Crafts are most famous today for their slave narrative *Running a Thousand Miles for Freedom; or, the Escape of William and Ellen Craft from Slavery* (1860).

Both were born into slavery in Georgia. William's parents' names are unknown. He may have been the slave of George W. Craft, of Bibb County, Georgia. William gained a rudimentary knowledge of carpentry before he and his sister Sarah were mortgaged in 1841 and eventually sold. His new master, a slaveholder living in Macon, Georgia, allowed him to work for hire as a carpenter/cabinetmaker and keep some of his earnings.

Ellen was born in Clinton, Georgia, to a slave named Maria and her master, Maj. James Smith. Her extremely cruel mistress, Eliza Smith, gave Ellen to her namesake daughter (and Ellen's half sister) on the daughter's marriage to wealthy speculator Robert Collins in 1837. The younger Eliza seems to have been kinder, and Ellen became both a personal servant and a seamstress in her household. Collins kept a home in Macon, and, while there, Ellen met William around 1842. They married in 1846 but recognized that they ran continuous risk of separation. Given this and the violence both had experienced in slavery, they planned to escape. In late 1848, they obtained passes for the Christmas holidays, and, on December 21, 1848, the couple left Macon.

Their escape became one of the most celebrated in the abolitionist movement. The light-skinned Ellen dressed as an invalid planter (with poultices on her face and spectacles hiding her eyes) and kept her right arm in a sling so that she, being illiterate, would not have to sign her name. The darker-skinned William posed as her valet. Using funds William had saved, "Mr. William Johnson" and his "slave" traveled to Savannah, Charleston, and eventually Baltimore, Maryland, before arriving in Philadelphia, Pennsylvania, on Christmas Day. In rich irony, they met a friend of Ellen's former master who did not see through her disguise, planters' daughters who were attracted to the soft-spoken and sickly "Mr. Johnson," and Southerners who were consistently concerned that abolitionists might "make off" with William.

In Philadelphia, Robert Purvis and William Still, who would later recount their story in *The Underground Rail Road* (1872), aided them, as did Quakers in the area. William Wells Brown, who would also invoke the Crafts in his writing (in *Clotel; or, The President's Daughter* [1853]), accompanied them to Boston, Massachusetts, a few weeks later. There, the Crafts became important figures at antislavery events. Brown and the Crafts began lecturing together as early as 1849; generally, the more experienced Brown would begin and, after telling his story, introduce William, who would speak and, on most occasions, introduce Ellen. Initially, contemporary historians questioned how active Ellen's role in such lectures was, but recent research shows that she spoke more often than initially assumed (McCaskill).

Abolitionist Theodore Parker performed a marriage ceremony for the Crafts on November 7, 1850. Already harassed by the passage of the Fugitive Slave Law, though, they decided to go to Great Britain when agents of their master successfully appealed to President Millard Fillmore to help secure their capture.

The Crafts were already recognized as celebrities among British abolitionists. Befriended by, among others, Lady Byron, the Crafts lived, studied, and taught at the experimental Ockham School before moving to London. There, Brown and the Crafts continued to lecture; prints of Ellen in her disguise became popular souvenirs. Active in the formation of the London Emancipation Society, they published their narrative on the eve of the American Civil War.

Arguably more fragmented than most slave narratives, it appeared too late to have significant impact on the U.S. abolitionist movement. Still, it is regularly read today because of the richness of the Crafts' escape story, which has been adapted by writers ranging from Thomas Wentworth Higginson to Georgia Douglas Johnson. While the narrative is told in William's voice, some contemporary critics have begun to assert that Ellen may have made some contributions to its writing. Both William and Ellen contributed to the abolitionist press.

Active in a variety of reform causes, the Crafts evinced a growing interest in Africa during this period; eventually, William made two trips to Dahomey as an agent for the African Aid Society. During their time in Britain, they had five children: Charles, Brougham, William, Ellen, and Alfred; in 1865, Ellen, with the aid of British friends, brought her mother to live in London.

In London, the Crafts appeared at the Great Exhibition at the Crystal Palace beside American Hiram Powers's sculpture of a Greek slave. They were joined by William Wells Brown, a former fugitive slave and an author. Lisa Merrill's 2012 article on the topic explores the problematic issues connected to racism, exploitation, and uses of visual rhetoric (Merrill).

The Crafts returned to the United States in 1869 and, after a stay in Boston, moved to South Carolina. While historians have claimed that only two or three of their children accompanied them, evidence shows that at least four of the children settled and raised families in the United States. Using the principles they learned at Ockham, the Crafts bought a plantation close to the Georgia line called Hickory Hill and opened an industrial school for African Americans in the area. Racist "night riders" burned the school down within a year, and the Crafts moved to Savannah, where their sons Charles and Brougham worked as rental agents. The elder Crafts reportedly incurred substantial losses when an attempt at running a boardinghouse failed in 1871, but they saved enough money to buy another plantation—Woodville, in Bryan County, Georgia—where they again set up a school.

Ellen seems to have managed both the school and the farm, while William divided his time between fund-raising (often in the North) and participating in local Republican politics; he was a candidate for the Georgia State Senate in 1874. They were able to maintain the school—and a working farm—for several years, but eventually financial problems and the opposition of Whites in the area forced the school's closure in or soon after 1878. While William attempted to keep the farm going, Ellen moved to Charleston, where she lived with her daughter, who had married a physician named William Demos Crum (an advocate of Booker T. Washington's ideas who served as collector of the port of Charleston and, later, Minister to Liberia). Eventually, William joined his wife in Charleston. When she died, she reportedly was buried under her favorite oak tree at Woodville; William continued to live with their daughter until his death.

Eric Gardner

See also: Slave Narrative.

Resources

R. J. M. Blackett, *Beating Against the Barriers: Biographical Essays in Nineteenth-Century Afro-American History* (Baton Rouge: Louisiana State University Press, 1986); Barbara McCaskill: "Introduction," in *Running a Thousand Miles for Freedom* (Athens: University of Georgia Press, 1999); "The Profits and the Perils of Partnership in the 'Thrilling' Saga of William and Ellen Craft," *Multi-Ethnic Literature of the United States* 38, no. 1 (2013), 76–97; Lisa Merrill, "Exhibiting Race 'Under the World's Huge Glass Case': William and Ellen Craft and William Wells Brown at the Great Exhibition in Crystal Palace, London, 1851," *Slavery & Abolition* 33, no. 2 (June 2012), 321–336 [includes 2 Black and White Photographs]; Dorothy Sterling, *Black Foremothers: Three Lives* (New York: Feminist Press of CUNY, 1988).

Crafts, Hannah (1830?–?)

Fugitive slave and novelist. In April 2002, Henry Louis Gates Jr. published Hannah Crafts's novel *The Bondwoman's Narrative* to acclaim and controversy. Almost as fascinating as the author's identity and the novel's provenance is Gates's purchase of the previously unpublished manuscript at the Swann Galleries' auction of "Printed and Manuscript African-Americana" in New York City for $8,000 two years earlier. The manuscript had been in the library of the noted Howard University librarian and historian Dorothy Porter Wesley. Gates then embarked on a diligent and long-from-completed search for Crafts's identity; Wesley had surmised she was Black and a fugitive slave. If this proves to be true, *The Bondwoman's Narrative* is "a major discovery, possibly the first novel written by a Black woman and definitely the first novel written by a woman who had been a slave" (Gates, xii). Indeed, Gates argues that the authentication of Crafts's narrative and identity would be of "great historical importance: to be able to study a manuscript written by a black woman or man, unedited . . . would help a new generation of scholars to gain access to the mind of a slave in an unmediated fashion heretofore not possible" (Gates, xxxiii).

At issue in determining Crafts's identity is the degree to which the *Narrative* is a purely fictionalized slave narrative or a thinly disguised autobiography (the protagonist's name is Hannah). Proceeding under the assumption that the narrative is at least partly autobiographical, Gates searched through census records and databases trying to locate Hannah Crafts. So far, he has identified several possible candidates but has been unable to secure many hard facts. Crafts probably was born in Virginia, circa 1830, and was a slave on plantations in Virginia and North Carolina. She was likely purchased by John Hill Wheeler (a Wheeler is also mentioned in the novel) in 1855. Based on expert manuscript historians' investigations, Crafts's use of polysyllabic words, coupled with frequent misspellings, suggests she was self-educated and may have had access to Wheeler's sizable library (Gates, xxxiii). She most likely escaped to freedom in the North between March 21 and May 4, 1857 (Gates, lvi). Since she was a fugitive slave and subject to the provisions of the Fugitive Slave Act, Gates guesses Crafts may have settled in a free Black community in New Jersey as Hannah Vincent, married to a Methodist clergyman (lxi–lxiii).

The Bondwoman's Narrative relates the story of a young educated house slave who escapes to freedom in the North with her mistress, who has been passing and has just been betrayed by the appropriately named Mr. Trappe. Like Harriet Wilson's *Our Nig*, Crafts's *The Bondwoman's Narrative* combines the conventions of several genres, including spiritual narratives, slave narratives, gothic novels, and sentimental novels (Gates, xxi). It is one of the earliest narratives to chronicle the tension between house slaves and field slaves. Also significant,

according to Gates, is Crafts's resistance to using distinctive racial markers to identify her characters, instead suggesting racial identity by context (Gates, xxiv–xxv). Her plot device of switching a "mulatto" and White child at birth presages Mark Twain's use of the device in *Pudd'nhead Wilson*. It is not clear why Crafts failed to publish her novel. Gates argues that publishing in the nineteenth century was especially difficult for African American women and that Crafts may have wanted to conceal her identity if she was passing in the North. She also may not have wanted the veracity of her story challenged. In any case, scholars' interest in *The Bondwoman's Narrative* is considerable, as demonstrated in a new collection of twenty-seven essays edited by Gates and Hollis Robbins covering the novel's place in the canon and the literary marketplace, its relationship to African American gothic literature, and the search for her identity.

Rebecca R. Saulsbury

See also: Slave Narrative.

Resources

Martha J. Cutter, "Skinship: Dialectical Passing Plots in Hannah Crafts' *The Bondwoman's Narrative*," *American Literary Realism* 46, no. 2 (January 1, 2014), 116–136; Henry Louis Gates Jr., "Introduction," in *The Bondwoman's Narrative* (New York: Warner Books, 2002), ix–lxxiv; Henry Louis Gates Jr. and Hollis Robbins, eds., *In Search of Hannah Crafts: Critical Essays on The Bondwoman's Narrative* (New York: Basic/Civitas Books, 2004); Roselyne M. Jua, "Circles of Freedom and Maturation in Hannah Crafts' *The Bondwoman's Narrative*," *Journal of Black Studies* 40, no. 2 (November 1, 2009), 310–326; Rebecca Soares, "Literary Graftings: Hannah Crafts's *The Bondwoman's* Narrative and the Nineteenth-Century Transatlantic Reader

[2010 VanArsdel Prize Winner]," *Victorian Periodicals Review* 44, no. 1 (2011), 1–23.

Crime and Mystery Fiction

Fashioned in the nineteenth century out of gothic literary forms, sensationalistic journalism, and discourses of scientific rationalism by the American writer Edgar Allan Poe, the English novelist Sir Arthur Conan Doyle, and others, crime and mystery writing seeks to sort out the tangle of modern social relations by way of recognizable narrative conventions and an especially clever and determined protagonist. The rise of crime fiction has also been connected to urbanization and industrialization, to the growth of psychology, and to the ever-increasing influence of science, among other social forces (Kalikoff; Thomas). Ultimately, crime fiction came to feature three primary kinds of detectives: the amateur, the independent professional (private investigator), and the police detective employed by a city or state (Mansfield-Kelley and Marchino). Themes of detection and intrigue have preoccupied African American novelists since the turn of the twentieth century, but it was not until the early to mid-twentieth century that Black writers took up crime mystery as a precise mode of genre writing. Contemporary African American crime novelists have moved beyond the genre's historically White, masculinist, and sometimes patently racist imaginaries to constitute a rich tradition of Black literary critique on questions of culture, justice, and the law.

As the critics Frankie Y. Bailey, Maureen T. Reddy, and Stephen F. Soitos have extensively and instructively documented, the hard-boiled crime fiction made popular by early twentieth-century American writers such as Dashiell Hammett and Raymond Chandler feature non-White characters—Blacks, "Mexicans," Asians—in stereotyped roles that alternate among domestic servants, obsequious hired hands, "taboo women," and shifty buffoons. Chandler is even self-reflexive about such stereotypes; for example, in *Farewell, My Lovely* (1940), he has a police detective admit that a homicide involving a Black victim is much less important than one involving a White person, and Chandler's detective, Philip Marlowe, becomes interested in a murder in spite of the fact that the victim is Black. These characterizations should not be surprising, however, given the ideological valences of hard-boiled crime fiction. The development of the genre between the 1920s and 1940s, through a variety of pulps (a term that refers to inexpensive, widely circulating magazines) but particularly in the magazine *Black Mask*, popularized the all-important persona of the detective protagonist as a quick-witted and determined White man, a maverick who lives and plays by his own rules. Hammett's Sam Spade and Chandler's Marlowe work outside or barely within the bounds of the law in order to solve their cases. This narrative gesture grants them a certain mobility of social positioning in performing the duties of the police more effectively than the police themselves. It also infuses the detectives with a rugged individualism that serves as a device of compensatory masculine heroism in the midst of feminizing bureaucracy, consumerism, and mass culture. Scholars have pointed out the historical irony of this individualist fantasy being packaged and distributed through the very institutions of modern society it deemed stultifying. Whether ironic or not, Spade and Marlowe remain larger-than-life icons of White heterosexual masculinity, whose crime-solving capacities are unmarked by race, feminist criticism, or sexual difference.

In her study of hard-boiled crime fiction's fascination with racial tropes, *Traces, Codes, and Clues* (2003), Reddy argues that the detective protagonist's typically first-person narrative voice is both the primary agent of racist ideology in the genre and the primary target for critical revision by non-White and female mystery writers. She notes,

> The centrality of voice distinguishes the hard-boiled from the classical detective story [by Poe or Doyle] and I think is the element that most attracts writers interested in challenging hard-boiled racial and sexual codes—because the voice is everything. To change the voice, to let the Other speak, is to transform the genre by replacing the traditional central consciousness with another that does not share the ideology or the racial (or sexual or gender) identity around which the genre formed. (9)

Soitos's path-breaking genealogy of African American crime fiction, outlined in *The Blues Detective* (1996), seems to confirm this thesis. Black writers have generally given non-White "Others" fuller "speaking" or agential roles in their detective stories, but they have done so mainly in the process of articulating alternate narrative consciousnesses whose relation to the law is already conditioned by racial discrimination and gender exclusion. One might say, then, that the history of African American crime fiction has been the history of radical deconstruction and then reconstruction of this popular genre's most alluring

and entertaining element, the detective protagonist.

The earliest prototypes of African American crime fiction are serial novels: Pauline E. Hopkins's *Hagar's Daughter*, published in the *Colored American* magazine in 1901–1902, and John E. Bruce's *The Black Sleuth*, published in *McGirt's* magazine in 1907–1909. These texts have more in common with the classical detective story than with the hard-boiled tradition, which had yet to come into existence. Still, Hopkins and Bruce construct narratives that go a long way in displacing stereotypes about Black intellectual and cultural inferiority that were circulating at the time. The central conceit of intrigue in *Hagar's Daughter* is racial passing. The buildup of suspense in this tragic saga about racial prejudice in antebellum and postbellum society rests upon Hagar and her daughter Jewel's capacity to pass as White members of aristocratic families. Despite the sprawling narrative, the mystery of the Enson, Sumner, and Bowen families' bloodlines is neatly left to be sorted out by Detective Henson; his Black assistant, Henry Smith; and, most notably, Venus Johnson, a Black maid who uses her intuition and connections in the Black community to locate the kidnapped Jewel. Technically a minor character in the novel, Venus becomes the crux of narrative resolution, thanks to her keen and attentive participation in the case.

The Black Sleuth is notable for its Yoruba protagonist, Sadipe Okukenu, and the narrative's internationalist scope, with scenes set in Africa, the United States, and England. In the employ of the private International Detective Agency, Sadipe is charged with recovering American Capt. George De Forrest's African diamond, which was stolen from him by White robbers. Combining sharp intellect with playful masquerade, Sadipe tracks down the bandits by putting on a repertoire of "blackface" disguises that conceal his true identity. Here Bruce invokes stereotypes about the African persona in order to use them parodically against the perpetrators of those stereotypes, including the decidedly supremacist Captain De Forrest. This critical inversion of racist thought and practice is common among Sadipe, his brother Mojola, and their father, the elder Okukenu. In its emphasis on the family's collective pride and resistance to White domination, the novel is one of the most fascinating precursors to the Pan-Africanist ideals of Black Nationalism in the 1960s. In terms of the emergence of African American crime fiction, *The Black Sleuth* shares with *Hagar's Daughter* the early counterdiscursive portrayal of Blacks thinking critically and creatively in solving problems to which White characters are largely color-blind.

A product of the Harlem Renaissance, Rudolph Fisher's *The Conjure-Man Dies* (1932) is the first Black detective novel originally published in book form. According to Soitos, Fisher's story takes up the country-house mystery mode made famous by Agatha Christie and the locked-room mystery-mode characteristic of Poe's "The Murders in the Rue Morgue" (1841). The seven suspects in the murder of Harlem, New York, conjure man N'Gana Frimbo are "confined to one locale," and "red herrings are scattered through the text" (101, 102). It is up to two African American detectives— Perry Dart of the New York Police Department and amateur sleuth John Archer, a physician by trade—to piece together the suspects' testimonies and analyze their motives for wanting N'Gana dead. The intimate setting of this jigsaw puzzle of a mystery ultimately points to marital infidelity as the primary motive for N'Gana's eventual murder, "eventual" because his body is not the one that turns up at the beginning of the tale. Aside from its entertaining narrative qualities, *The Conjure-Man Dies* establishes in Dart and Archer the paradigmatic Black male crime-solving duo: the streetwise, pragmatic, and physically intimidating Dart complementing the lighter-complexioned abstract thinker Archer, and vice versa.

Undoubtedly, the preeminent African American crime writer of the twentieth century was Chester Himes. With the benefit of hard-boiled hindsight and the capital to support his writing for a living, Himes was the first African American to pen a full series of crime novels, all of which are set in Harlem and feature the memorable partnering of police detectives, Grave Digger Jones and Coffin Ed Johnson. Interestingly, Himes was living in Paris, France, by 1953, and so it was Marcel Duhamel, editor of the publisher Gallimard's "Série Noire" and translator of Himes's novel *If He Hollers Let Him Go* (1945), who invited him to write detective stories on commission. Thus, most of the eight novels that constitute the Harlem series were written in Europe explicitly for future translation into French: *For Love of Imabelle* (1957), retitled *A Rage in Harlem* (1965); *The Crazy Kill* (1959); *The Real Cool Killers* (1959); *All Shot Up* (1960); *Big Gold Dream* (1960); *Cotton Comes to Harlem* (1965); *The Heat's On* (1966); and *Blind Man with a Pistol* (1969). Grave Digger and Coffin Ed are a striking pair; though the former tends to be the more reasonable of the two, they both regularly flout standard police procedure to extract information from witnesses and informants. Yet despite the pair's bullying practices and identification with a mostly White police force, the people of Harlem look up to Grave Digger and Coffin Ed as protectors of their neighborhood and, indeed, racial community. Himes's detectives may be mavericks, but their actions, even when extravagantly violent, are almost always rooted in sympathy for the common folk, the real victims of particular acts of crime as well as of structural state racism in the form of police brutality and urban blight. In the trenchant satire *Cotton Comes to Harlem*, Grave Digger and Coffin Ed almost single-handedly foil Rev. Deke O'Malley's scheme to swindle Harlemites out of their life savings after they sign up for his back-to-Africa steamship cruise.

Ishmael Reed's *Mumbo Jumbo* (1972) and *The Last Days of Louisiana Red* (1974) signal African American postmodernism's somewhat limited engagement with the genre. It is difficult to situate Reed's work within the crime fiction tradition because his story lines defy most narrative conventions and generic categories. But his "Hoo-Doo" detective Papa LaBas might be said to explode the Eurocentric valences of Spade's and Marlowe's characters in the carnivalesque way he unearths the mysteries of Black social and cultural being. At stake in these mysteries is the course of global history itself: whether it will recognize the life-giving properties of creolization or deny them through the clash of Western and non-Western civilizations. LaBas is a sleuth of hybrid origins, then, and Reed's hyper-referential prose saturates his plots with a fullness of detail that questions the stylistic economy of most other modes of crime writing.

In the 1990s, a number of African American male crime novelists flourished in the wake of the Terry McMillan–led renaissance of Black popular writing in the United States. Robert O. Greer, Gar Anthony Haywood, Hugh Holton, and Blair S. Walker are notable examples. But Walter Mosley has

easily been the most celebrated Black crime and mystery writer since Himes's Harlem series ended in 1969. The first African American to become president of the influential Mystery Writers of America (1995), Mosley has created a series of detective novels set in Los Angeles, California, and featuring the working-class private eye Ezekiel "Easy" Rawlins: *Devil in a Blue Dress* (1990), *Red Death* (1991), *White Butterfly* (1992), *Black Betty* (1994), *A Little Yellow Dog* (1996), *Gone Fishin'* (1997), *Bad Boy Brawly Brown* (2002), and *Little Scarlet* (2004); *Six Easy Pieces* (2003) is a collection of Easy Rawlins stories. In post–World War II Los Angeles, amid abstract promises of racial progress and upward mobility, Easy struggles not only as a sleuth prone to errors in judgment but also as a divorced single father of two adopted kids. But insofar as these struggles are characteristic of the Black community in this city and of this era more generally, the reader is able to imagine Easy's immersion in his work as a matter-of-fact way of life. *Devil in a Blue Dress* is the most compelling of Mosley's narratives; in it, he revisits Hopkins's trope of passing by way of the mysterious and seductive Daphne Monet and deliberately rewrites the opening scene of Chandler's *Farewell, My Lovely*, one might say, from the previously degraded Black character's point of view. Amazingly, while developing the essential narrative thread of his Easy Rawlins mysteries, Mosley has found the time to initiate another series set in Los Angeles, this one focused on U.S. Army veteran Fearless Jones, who is much more of an unpredictable loose cannon than Easy. The two novels in this emerging series are *Fearless Jones* (2001) and *Fear Itself* (2003).

In recent years, however, African American women have come to problematize the hard-boiled Harlem and Los Angeles imaginaries of Himes and Mosley, not because their writing is lacking but because their writing is so adept at continuing to stifle or degrade female characters in the genre. At the core of Black feminist crime fiction is a radically different conception of the roles and functions of the detective protagonist. Eleanor Taylor Bland's trailblazing Marti MacAlister series—*Dead Time* (1992), *Slow Burn* (1993), *Gone Quiet* (1994), and *Done Wrong* (1995), to name only the first four volumes—is set in Lincoln Prairie, Illinois, a suburb of Chicago, Illinois, where the veteran investigator tackles cases that are shrugged off by the police department because they involve the socially disadvantaged, including endangered children and the mentally ill. Barbara Neely's remarkable Blanche White series—*Blanche on the Lam* (1992), *Blanche among the Talented Tenth* (1994), *Blanche Cleans Up* (1998), and *Blanche Passes Go* (2001)—is set in Farleigh (Raleigh), North Carolina, and Boston, Massachusetts, where a domestic-turned-sleuth keeps her ear to the ground to solve murders in aristocratic Southern and New England families. With sharp wit and penetrating insight, Neely has Blanche uncover more than secret plots; she also addresses issues from class and color politics to sexual violence and rape. In a similar vein, Valerie Wilson Wesley's Tamara Hayle is a Newark, New Jersey, private eye and single mother whose relation to her clients is always mediated by concerns about her immediate family and the surrounding Black community. Crucially, although Marti, Blanche, and Tamara share with Easy a fundamental connection with Black working-class concerns, the women detectives are persistently reminded of their feminist criticism and sexual difference in ways that Easy, even as a single father, cannot

experience. Other well-known Black female detectives include Nikki Baker's Virginia Kelly, Charlotte Carter's Nanette Hayes, Grace F. Edwards's Mali Anderson, Pamela Thomas-Graham's Veronica "Nikki" Chase, and Paula L. Woods's Charlotte Justice. These characters, among others, count cops, professors, journalists, and business-women among their ranks, and they highlight the extent to which successful Black females utilize their professional expertise to solve crime cases.

As these contemporary examples demonstrate, African American crime fiction continues to develop in new and unexpected ways as more and more publishers distribute this type of popular literature. Black women writers have critiqued the patriarchal and sexist elements of both the hard-boiled and the Black male crime traditions in order to tease out the most progressive potential of the genre's appeal. Furthermore, African American crime fiction's narrative strategy of situating "law and order" within social structures of dominance has influenced revisionary cultural production in a variety of media, from blaxploitation cinema and gangsta rap to the ghetto realism of Donald Goines and Iceberg Slim, and the Prison Literature of Eldridge Cleaver and Angela Y. Davis. In this regard, the genre merits further attention by literary and cultural critics who continue to labor to produce responses to the seemingly indefinite criminalization of the Black underclass and young, urban Black males in particular. Rather than posit "real world" policy solutions to this procedure of state control, authors such as Mosley, Neely, and Wesley offer ways to reimagine the precise history of racial discrimination within dominant conceptions of justice and the law. Their literary output also suggests that changing these conceptions requires not an absolute ideal of narrative consciousness but a narrator who is himself or herself grounded in family and community, the trials and struggles of everyday Black life.

In 2018, a librarian at the Los Angeles Public Library published an annotated list (with titles of books) of Black crime and mystery authors that includes Karen Grigsby Bates, Frankie Y. Bailey, Eleanor Taylor Bland, Kyra Davis, Rachel Howzell Hall, Attica Locke, Glenville Lovell, and Penny Mickelbury, as well as authors previously mentioned.

Kinohi Nishikawa

See also: Fisher, Rudolph John Chauncey.

Resources

Primary Sources: Nikki Baker, *The Lavender House Murder* (New York: Naiad Press, 1992); Eleanor Taylor Bland: *Dead Time* (New York: St. Martin's Press, 1992); *Done Wrong* (New York: St. Martin's Press, 1995); *Gone Quiet* (New York: Signet, 1994); *Slow Burn* (New York: St. Martin's Press, 1993); John Edward Bruce, *The Black Sleuth* (Boston: Northeastern University Press, 2002); Charlotte Carter, *Walking Bones* (London: Serpent's Tale, 2002); Raymond Chandler, *Farewell, My Lovely* (1940; repr. New York: Vintage, 1988); Grace F. Edwards, *The Viaduct* (New York: Doubleday, 2003); Rudolph Fisher, *The Conjure-Man Dies: A Mystery Tale of Dark Harlem* (Ann Arbor: University of Michigan Press, 1992); Gar Anthony Haywood, *Bad News Travels Fast* (New York: Putnam, 1995); Chester Himes: *All Shot Up* (1960; repr. New York: Thunder's Mouth Press, 1996); *Big Gold Dream* (London: Chatham Bookseller, 1960); *Blind Man with a Pistol* (1969; repr. New York: Vintage, 1989); *Cotton Comes to Harlem* (1965; repr. New York: Vintage, 1988); *The Crazy Kill* (1959; repr. New York: Vintage, 1989); *For Love of Imabelle* (1957; repr. London: Chatham

Bookseller, 1973); *The Heat's On* (1966; repr. New York: Vintage, 1988); *If He Hollers Let Him Go* (1945; repr. New York: Thunder's Mouth Press, 2002); *The Real Cool Killers* (1959; repr. New York: Vintage, 1989); Hugh Holton, *The Thin Black Line* (New York: St. Martin's Press, 2005); Pauline E. Hopkins, *The Magazine Novels of Pauline Hopkins* (New York: Oxford University Press, 1987); Walter Mosley: *Bad Boy Brawly Brown* (Boston: Little, Brown, 2002); *Black Betty* (New York: W. W. Norton, 1994); *Devil in a Blue Dress* (New York: W. W. Norton, 1990); *Fear Itself* (Boston: Little, Brown, 2003); *Fearless Jones* (Boston: Little, Brown, 2001); *Gone Fishin'* (Washington, DC: Black Classic Press, 1997); *Little Scarlet* (Boston: Little, Brown, 2004); *A Little Yellow Dog* (New York: W. W. Norton, 1996); *Red Death* (New York: W. W. Norton, 1991); *Six Easy Pieces* (New York: Atria, 2003); *White Butterfly* (New York: W. W. Norton, 1992); Barbara Neely: *Blanche among the Talented Tenth* (New York: St. Martin's Press, 1994); *Blanche Cleans Up* (New York: Penguin, 1998); *Blanche on the Lam* (New York: St. Martin's Press, 1992); *Blanche Passes Go* (New York: Penguin, 2001); Ishmael Reed: *The Last Days of Louisiana Red* (New York: Random House, 1974); *Mumbo Jumbo* (1972; repr. New York: Scribner's, 1996); Pamela Taylor-Graham, *Orange Crush: An Ivy League Mystery* (New York: Simon and Schuster, 2004); Blair S. Walker, *Up Jumped the Devil* (New York: William Morrow, 1997); Paula L. Woods, *Dirty Laundry* (New York: One World/Ballantine, 2003).

Secondary Sources: Frankie Y. Bailey, *Out of the Woodpile: Black Characters in Crime and Detective Fiction* (Westport, CT: Greenwood Press, 1991); Eleanor Taylor Bland, ed., *Shades of Black: Crime and Mystery Stories by African-American Authors* (New York: Berkley, 2004); Michel Fabre and Robert E. Skinner, eds., *Conversations with Chester Himes* (Jackson: University Press of Mississippi, 1995); Adrienne Johnson Gosselin, ed., *Multicultural Detective Fiction: Murder from the "Other" Side* (New York: Garland, 1999); Janice B.,

"African American Mystery Writers and Their African American Detectives," Los Angeles Public Library Blog, February 26, 2018: https://www.lapl.org/collections-resources/blogs/lapl/african-american-mystery-writers-and-their-african-american (accessed 2019); Beth Kalikoff, *Murder and Moral Decay in Victorian Popular Literature* (Ann Arbor: UMI Research Press, 1986); Kathleen Gregory Klein, ed., *Diversity and Detective Fiction* (Bowling Green, OH: Bowling Green State University Popular Press, 1999); Helen Lock, *A Case of Mis-Taken Identity: Detective Undercurrents in Recent African American Fiction* (New York: Peter Lang, 1994); Deane Mansfield-Kelley and Lois A. Marchino, eds., *The Longman Anthology of Detective Fiction* (New York: Pearson-Longman, 2005); Maureen T. Reddy, *Traces, Codes, and Clues: Reading Race in Crime Fiction* (New Brunswick, NJ: Rutgers University Press, 2003); Charles L. P. Silet, ed., *The Critical Response to Chester Himes* (Westport, CT: Greenwood Press, 1999); Robert E. Skinner, *Two Guns from Harlem: The Detective Fiction of Chester Himes* (Bowling Green, OH: Bowling Green State University Popular Press, 1989); Stephen F. Soitos, *The Blues Detective: A Study of African American Detective Fiction* (Amherst: University of Massachusetts Press, 1996); Ronald R. Thomas, *Detective Fiction and the Rise of Forensic Science* (Cambridge: Cambridge University Press, 1999); Charles E. Wilson Jr., *Walter Mosley: A Critical Companion* (Westport, CT: Greenwood Press, 2003); Paula L. Woods, ed., *Spooks, Spies, and Private Eyes: Black Mystery, Crime, and Suspense Fiction of the Twentieth Century* (New York: Doubleday, 1995).

Cullen, Countee (1903–1946)

Poet, novelist, and teacher. Apart from an obligatory inclusion in Harlem Renaissance anthologies, relatively little attention is paid today to Countee Cullen, who was one of the most celebrated young Harlem Renaissance stars, the movement's poet laureate, and an extremely accomplished writer of formal verse. Personal information extant about him is somewhat confusing. Starting with his place of birth and continuing with his childhood, Cullen's personal life seems shrouded in mystery. For instance, it remains unclear exactly where Cullen was born on May 30, 1903—Kentucky; Baltimore, Maryland; or New York City—he gave different information at various times during his career. Cullen, who was adopted by Rev. Frederick Asbury Cullen and his wife in 1914 or 1918, apparently had an unhappy childhood and was highly sensitive regarding his personal life. He was still in high school when he entered the limelight by winning a citywide poetry contest, but he quickly realized the significance of a public image. Consequently, it seems, he invented an "appropriate" family background: claiming to be born in New York, he could uphold the fiction that he was the Cullens' natural son. To some extent, the poet laureate Cullen was thus a public construct.

Cullen's resolve to cover up blemishes in his personal history indicates the extent to which he was willing to guard his reputation and the importance he attributed to his public image. He focused on a literary career and sought a leading position among the "Talented Tenth," the educated African American elite. Cullen worked hard to attain the academic merits required and succeeded. He excelled in his studies of English and French at New York University, received numerous awards, graduated Phi Beta Kappa, and went on to receive an MA from Harvard in 1926. At the same time, the young poet successfully followed his literary ambitions. His poems were published in all the leading magazines from *Vanity Fair* to *The Bookman*, *Opportunity*, and *The Crisis*; his works were recited in Harlem's churches; he was invited to poetry readings; and his first volume of poetry, *Color*, was published in 1925 while Cullen was still in graduate school. At the age of twenty-two, Cullen had already taken a major career step—he was a Harlem Renaissance star, a celebrity whose every accomplishment was followed by the media and whose works were critically appraised. It seemed only natural that Cullen's career flourished further during the 1920s. Within a span of five years, he not only published the tale *The Ballad of the Brown Girl* (1927) and two more poetry volumes, *Copper Sun* (1927) and *The Black Christ* (1929), but also his poems were included in Alain Locke's *The New Negro* (1925); further, he edited a volume of young Renaissance writers' works (*Caroling Dusk*, 1927) and, from December 1926 to September 1928, contributed a monthly literary column, "The Dark Tower," to *Opportunity*, one of the best-known African American journals of the era. In addition, Cullen won several literary awards and prestigious fellowships, including a Guggenheim Fellowship (1928).

Among the large group of young writers and artists who gathered in Harlem, New York, in the early-to-mid-1920s, Cullen stood out. Within the New Negro movement, he represented an "old-school" writer whose choice of a strict, formal Romanticism and adherence to traditional measures and rhymes separated him from, for instance, Langston Hughes, who experimented with form and created his popular blues poetry. Whereas many younger Renaissance writers celebrated blackness, intending to, as Hughes put it, "express [their] individual dark-skinned selves without fear or shame," Cullen declared that he

was a "POET and not NEGRO POET" and bemoaned in "Yet Do I Marvel" (1925) the seeming irony of a God who decided to "make a poet black and bid him sing." (The poem remains one of the most accomplished sonnets in English.) Some scholars of the Harlem Renaissance resist dealing with the extremely popular but at the same time curiously old-fashioned poet, who seems out of place in an era generally identified more with raunchy blues songs than with decorous Romanticism.

Many of the younger Renaissance writers were highly critical of Cullen. An artistic gulf separated them—a fact that was demonstrated in the publication of the provocative journal *Fire!!* (1926), to which Cullen contributed the strictly metered sonnet "From the Dark Tower," which contrasted harshly with the majority of other contributions, such as tales about prostitution (Wallace Thurman's "Cordelia the Crude") and homoerotic fantasies (Richard Bruce Nugent's "Smoke, Lilies, and Jade").

While many of the younger writers of the Harlem Renaissance—the "N—atti," a satiric term made popular by Wallace Thurman and Zora Neale Hurston—rebelled against the Renaissance establishment, represented by figures such as W.E.B. Du Bois and Alain Locke, Cullen proved a model Renaissance artist who willingly accepted what could be termed a "burden of representation"—the responsibility of African American artists as interpreters and representatives of the whole "race." When the N—atti thus proclaimed their artistic freedom, Cullen admonished them that "whether they relish the situation or not, Negroes should be concerned with making good impressions." He was willing and able to contribute fully to the aim of the Harlem Renaissance as defined by its leaders: the artistic creation of new and "representative" (meaning positive) images of African Americans was to convince White Americans of Black Americans' equality and to end racial discrimination. Unsurprisingly, Cullen, following in the footsteps of his literary idols John Keats, Alfred Tennyson, and A. E. Housman, was highly acclaimed by genteel critics and Renaissance leaders alike.

In order to attain and then keep this prominent and respected position within the Harlem Renaissance, Cullen continued to work hard to present an acceptable public persona. Far more significant at the time than a dubious family background, Cullen's same-sex desire could have provided a significant obstacle on the path to fame and popular approval. Describing himself as "Puritanical" in taste, the conservative Cullen felt unable to follow, for instance, the path traveled by the openly gay bohemian writer and artist Richard Bruce Nugent. Instead, Cullen opted for a strenuous division of his private and public sexual personas. He thus publicly presented himself as a shy yet clearly heterosexual young man. One can conclude from his private correspondence that his interest in women mainly rested on their representative function as potential wives. In 1928, he married Nina Yolande Du Bois, the daughter of the leading African American intellectual. The public display of heterosexual bliss was extravagant—1,300 invited guests and numerous spectators were at the ceremony—yet the marriage did not endure. On his "honeymoon," Cullen was accompanied not by his wife but by his intimate friend Harold Jackman, a young, attractive bisexual African American teacher who belonged to the Harlem Renaissance network. By 1930, the unhappily married couple was divorced.

While some critics claim that there is no "proof" of Cullen's homosexuality, his intimate correspondence with Locke, a closeted gay Harlem Renaissance intellectual, clearly indicates Cullen's love interest in and sexual desire for men. Locke introduced the young man to a gay literary heritage and to a special type of gay discourse that fused terms from the Greek discourse of homosexuality such as "perfect friendship" with Whitmanesque expressions such as "camaraderie"—terms that one encounters in Cullen's poetry. Locke's interpretations of homosexuality as a "perfect friendship," as Cullen commented, "threw a noble and evident light on what [he] had begun to believe, because of what the world believes, ignoble and unnatural," thereby sparing him from internalizing homophobia. However, he still retained doubts and feared detection. But while Cullen exercised self-censorship even in his private correspondence, he did not exclude the topic of homosexuality from his literary works, in which his gay voice, ranging from somber depictions of same-sex love to the expression of hope, is audible to varying degrees. His preference for Romanticism served him well as a veil for references to same-sex love, yet sometimes Cullen proved more courageous, as in "Tableau" (1925), which was dedicated to Donald Duff, a White male lover of Cullen. Here, Cullen depicts a White boy and a Black boy who, walking arm in arm, publicly transgress racial and sexual boundaries.

Despite claims to the contrary by a number of Harlem Renaissance scholars who focus on Cullen's alleged unwillingness to discuss racial issues, Cullen masterfully blended a multitude of topics in his works, ranging from moods of desperation and gloom in poems such as "Saturday's Child" (1925) and "Suicide Chant" (1925) to hope and courage, as evident in "Tableau." While

Cullen refused to be viewed solely as a racial poet, he did not shy away from the topic either, as two of his most famous poems—"Heritage," in which the question "What is Africa to me?" is explored in sensuous detail, and "The Black Christ," in which Cullen transforms Christ into a deity suitable to the needs of African Americans—clearly show. Cullen's most successful works contain exquisite layerings of themes. He interweaves religion, paganism, love, desire, (homo)sexuality, and race, thereby appealing to overlapping audiences consisting of genteel critics who applauded his application of traditional poetic forms, a Black readership focusing on racial readings, and gay readers accustomed to the sounds of his specific gay voice.

In 1930, Cullen returned from a two-year stay in France that had been sponsored by a Guggenheim Fellowship. In France, Cullen had felt liberated, embracing an environment he perceived to be less racist and homophobic than the United States. After Cullen's return, his steep climb up the career ladder slowed perceptibly. It seems, in fact, that by the time he was twenty-six, Cullen's literary career had already passed its climax. The Harlem he encountered on his return had changed; the Great Depression had left its marks, calling in the end of a decade of splendor. It seems that Cullen adapted to this new sense of reality. The boy wonder had grown up, and Cullen the man now decided on a career as a public-school teacher in New York City and eventually gave marriage another try; in 1940, Cullen married Ida Roberson. Though this marriage lasted for the rest of his life, Cullen proved incapable of dedicating himself solely to a heterosexual relationship and was involved in a long-lasting secret love affair with the younger Edward Atkinson. Significantly, Cullen continued his literary efforts and started exploring different literary genres, writing *One Way to Heaven* (1932), a Harlem-based novel that barely received critical attention, juvenile fiction with *The Lost Zoo* (1940), and *My Lives and How I Lost Them* (1942), a choreo-musical with Owen Dodson, as well as dramatic adaptations of his own novel and Arna Bontemps's *God Sends Sunday*. Additionally, he published one more volume of verse—*The Medea and Some Poems* (1935), arguably the weakest of his poetry collections. His career was slowing down, and Cullen, who suffered from serious heart problems, seems to have sensed, if not his life's nearing end, at least his creative period's passing. In 1945, he started to prepare a collection of his poems, thereby determining his own literary heritage. He died on January 9, 1946, and thus did not live to see the publication of *On These I Stand* (1947).

Cullen's works remain outstanding examples of Harlem Renaissance writing, indicating the great variety of work produced during the era and the divergent ideologies of the writers and artists involved. In contrast to many of his younger colleagues, Cullen proved a fully committed Harlem Renaissance artist whose efforts to contribute to the aim of racial uplift and an end of racial discrimination were rewarded with praise by his readers who, as Dodson summarized, found in Cullen's poetry "all . . . dilemmas . . . the hurt pride, the indignation, the satirical thrusts, the agony of being black in America." In 2012, Charles Molesworth published a new biography of Cullen.

A. B. Christa Schwarz

See also: Gay Literature; Harlem Renaissance; Lyric Poetry.

Resources

Primary Sources: Countee Cullen: *Color* (New York: Harper & Bros., 1925); *Copper Sun* (New York: Harper & Bros., 1927); "Countee Cullen," in *Caroling Dusk: An Anthology of Verse by Negro Poets*, ed. Countee Cullen (New York: Harper & Bros., 1927), 179; "The Dark Tower," *Opportunity*, Mar. 1928, p. 90; *The Lost Zoo (A Rhyme for the Young, but Not Too Young)* (New York: Harper & Bros., 1940), published as by Christopher Cat and Countee Cullen; *The Medea and Some Poems* (New York: Harper & Bros., 1935); *My Lives and How I Lost Them* (New York: Harper & Bros., 1942), published as by Christopher Cat and Countee Cullen; *My Soul's High Song: The Collected Writings of Countee Cullen, Voice of the Harlem Renaissance*, ed. Gerald Early (New York: Doubleday, 1991); *On These I Stand: An Anthology of the Best Poems of Countee Cullen* (New York: Harper & Bros., 1947); *One Way to Heaven* (New York: Harper & Bros., 1932); Countee Cullen, ed., *Caroling Dusk: An Anthology of Verse by Negro Poets* (New York: Harper & Bros., 1927); Countee Cullen Papers, Amistad Research Center, Tulane University, New Orleans; Countee Cullen, letter to Harold Jackman (n.d.), Countee Cullen Papers, box 1, Beinecke Rare Book and Manuscript Library, Yale University.

Secondary Sources: Houston A. Baker Jr., *Afro-American Poetics: Revisions of Harlem and the Black Aesthetic* (Madison: University of Wisconsin Press, 1988); Nicholas Canaday Jr., "Major Themes in the Poetry of Countee Cullen," in *The Harlem Renaissance Remembered*, ed. Arna Bontemps (New York: Dodd, Mead, 1972), 103–125; Owen Dodson, "Countee Cullen (1903–1946)," *Phylon* 7 (1946), 20; Gerald Early: "Introduction," in *My Soul's High Song: The Collected Writings of Countee Cullen, Voice of the Harlem Renaissance*, ed. Early (New York: Doubleday, 1991), 3–73; "Three Notes Toward a Cultural Definition of the Harlem Renaissance," *Callaloo* 14 (1991), 136–149; Michel Fabre, *From Harlem to Paris: Black American Writers in France, 1840–1980* (Urbana: University of Illinois Press, 1991); Blanche E. Ferguson, *Countee Cullen and the Negro Renaissance* (New York: Dodd, Mead, 1966); Michael L. Lomax, "Countee Cullen: A Key to the Puzzle," in *The Harlem Renaissance Re-examined*, ed. Victor A. Kramer (New York: AMS, 1987), 213–222; Verner D. Mitchell, "To one not there: the Letters of Dorothy West and Countee Cullen, 1926–1945," *Langston Hughes Review* 24–25 (Winter–Fall 2010), 112(13); Charles Molesworth: *And Bid Him Sing: A Biography of Countée Cullen* (Chicago and London: University of Chicago Press, 2012); "Countee Cullen's Reputation: the Forms of Desire," *Transition: An International Review* 107, no. 1 (October 2011), 66(12); Hans Ostrom, "Countee Cullen: How Teaching Re-Writes the Genre of 'Writer,'" in *Genre and Writing: Issues, Arguments, Alternatives*, ed. Wendy Bishop and Hans Ostrom (Portsmouth, NH: Heinemann, 1997), 93–104; Margaret Perry, *A Bio-Bibliography of Countée P. Cullen, 1903–1946* (Westport, CT: Greenwood Press, 1971); Alden Reimonenq, "Countee Cullen's Uranian 'Soul Windows,'" in *Critical Essays: Gay and Lesbian Writers of Color*, ed. Emmanuel S. Nelson (New York: Haworth Press, 1993), 143–166; D. Dean Shackleford, "The Poetry of Countée Cullen," in *Masterpieces of African-American Literature*, ed. Frank N. Magill (New York: HarperCollins, 1992), 382–386; Alan Shucard, *Countee Cullen* (Boston: Twayne, 1984); Margaret Sperry, "Countee P. Cullen, Negro Boy Poet, Tells His Story," *Brooklyn Daily Eagle*, Feb. 10, 1924, n.p.; James W. Tuttleton, "Countee Cullen at 'The Heights,'" in *The Harlem Renaissance: Revaluations*, ed. Amritjit Singh, William S. Shiver, and Stanley Brodwin (New York: Garland, 1989), 101–137; Jean Wagner, *Black Poets of the United States: From Paul Laurence Dunbar to Langston Hughes*, trans. Kenneth Douglas (Urbana: University of Illinois Press, 1973).

D

Danticat, Edwidge (born 1969)

Writer and professor. Danticat was born in Port-au-Prince, Haiti. She moved to Brooklyn, New York, when she was twelve. Her writing often reflects on the life of the refugee/exiled immigrant. Her father immigrated to the United States for economic and political reasons in 1971, followed two years later by her mother. Raised by her aunt, and speaker of Kréyol until she moved to America to reunite with her parents, Danticat published her first English writings at age fourteen, including newspaper articles about her migration that inspired *Breath, Eyes, Memory* (1994). Her books, essays, and editorial work also reflect on this conundrum of identity for the Haitian national—torn between the country that defines her identity and the revolutionary movement that defines Haiti's place in the diaspora, she depicts the human striving for hope.

Danticat graduated with a degree in French literature from Barnard College and received her MFA from Brown University. Her short stories have appeared in twenty-five periodicals, and her books have been translated into Korean, Italian, German, French, Spanish, and Swedish. She is currently a visiting professor of creative writing at New York University and the University of Miami.

Danticat, who was the American Book Award winner for *The Farming of Bones* in 1999, and was National Book Award finalist for *Krik? Krak!* in 1995, also won the Fiction Award from *The Caribbean Writer* in 1994. In 1995, she won the Woman of Achievement Award and the Pushcart Short Story Prize. In 1996, Danticat received the Best Young American Novelist Award from GRANTA for *Breath, Eyes, Memory*, and, in 1999, she won the International Flaiano Prize for Literature for *Farming of Bones*.

In addition to *Farming of Bones*, *Krik? Krak!*, and *Breath, Eyes, Memory*, Danticat has written *After the Dance: A Walk Through Carnival in Jacmel, Haiti* (2002), and *Behind the Mountains* (2002, her first book for young readers). She has edited *The Butterfly's Way: Voices from the Haitian Dyaspora in the United States* (2001) and *The Beacon Best of 2000: Great Writing by Men and Women of All Colors and Cultures* (2000). *The Dew Breaker*, a novel that partly concerns torture, appeared in 2004.

Each of Danticat's works reflects on Haiti's bloody past and notes how the scars of the present are merely markers of memory for those Haitians who dealt with the dictatorships and revolutions that erupted in Haiti and the Dominican Republic in the 1930s. Hers is a postcolonial, feminist perspective with the issues of strained migration experiences, broken family life, suppressed human sexuality, and gender roles as main themes for her texts. She explores the relationship between mother and daughter in a deconstructionist fashion, keeping in mind the political underpinnings that sometimes play just under that characterization. Her personal experience plays a part in her politics as a writer and in her young female characters' inner lives. With a voice that bores into these young girls' psyches, Danticat's place as the writer is that of the eyewitness, using the Haitian tradition of storytelling as the medium through which to purge the experiences of those who suffered through the torture of living under siege.

Danticat's most recent book, *The Dew Breaker*, is written in vignettes that focus on the central character, Ka Bienaimé, and the macoute who is her father, named the "Dew Breaker" for his tendency to come early and strike swiftly in matters of torture and killing. Ka is a sculptress who captures in her art what she has learned of her father's experiences in prison—little knowing that her father was, in fact, a government-sanctioned torturer. The vignettes swing back to her father's past and forward through characters affected by torture and migration, coming to Ka's father's confession, and the place her mother has in this revelation. The book is a study in the temporality of trauma and the remorse of a man haunted by a past filled with the blood of others. Danticat based the novel on stories inspired by sightings in Brooklyn of a former leader of the Haitian paramilitary group that, in the early 1990s, terrorized and killed Jean-Bertrand Aristide supporters.

In *The Farming of Bones* Danticat focuses on the 1937 massacre in the Dominican Republic of Haitians commonly attributed to Generalissimo Rafael Leonidas Trujillo. Trujillo was the Dominican dictator widely praised initially for his reforms and economic stabilization of the Dominican Republic. He was trained as a member of the Dominican Republic National Guard by the United States and ultimately feared as an unruly killer and leader of that guard. The title of the book reflects doubly on the bones of those left in the cane fields following those massacres and the actual farming of those fields; in this way, she comments on the politics of the era in the context of those left to cope with the trauma of loss. Danticat uses the interwoven lives of two characters who might be seen as representatives of both sides of Hispaniola—Señora Valencia and Amabelle, who both view this time period through the lens of love and family.

Breath, Eyes, Memory is Danticat's most personal exploration of migration. Sophie, the main character, bears some resemblance in her experience to that of the author, insofar as separation of family and difficulty in adjustment to immigrant life are concerned. In this narrative, Danticat reflects on the body as a site of trauma, noting the experience of the childless mother in exile and the motherless child with whom she is reunited in the United States. Escape from psychological and physical harm is the theme of the storytelling present in this text through the matriarchal figures who influence Sophie's break with her and her mother's past, rooted in the act of rape. A product of rape, Sophie in some ways represents the Haitian diaspora.

Krik? Krak! is a collection of nine stories about life under Haiti's dictatorships. Highlighted is the terrorism of the Tonton Macoutes and the national psyche with regard to this as well as the issues unique to migration. Her first young reader's novel, *Behind the Mountains*, focuses on Haiti during election time and highlights the upheaval that forces migration. *After the Dance: A Walk Through Carnival in Jacmel* is Danticat's perspective on her first experience of carnival after years of being afraid to attend.

Brother, I'm Dying (2007) is an autobiography that explores Danticat's and her family's tremendous challenges in Haiti and the United States. *Create Dangerously: The Immigrant Artists at Work* (2010) is a nonfiction book based on a lecture Danticat gave at Princeton University in the Toni Morrison Lecture Series. *Claire of the Sea Light* (2013) is a novel that concerns a girl who goes missing in a small seaside town. *Untwine* (2015) is a novel for young adults about twin girls, Giselle and Isabelle Boyer, their family, and a terrible injury Giselle suffers. *Mama's Nightingale: A Story of Immigration and Separation* (2015) is an illustrated book for young children.

Elizabete Vasconcelos

See also: Feminism/Black Feminism.

Resources

Edwidge Danticat: *After the Dance: A Walk Through Carnival in Jacmel, Haiti* (New York: Crown Journeys, 2002); Edwidge Danticat, ed., *Beacon Best of 2000: Great Writing by Women and Men of All Colors and Cultures* (Boston: Beacon Press, 2000); *Behind the Mountains* (New York: Orchard Books, 2002); *Breath, Eyes, Memory* (New York: Soho Books, 1994); *Brother, I'm Dying* (New York: Knopf, 2007); *The Butterfly's Way: Voices from the Haitian Dyaspora in the United States* (New York: Soho Press, 2001); *Claire of the Sea Light* (New York: Knopf, 2013); *Create Dangerously: The Immigrant Artist at Work* (New York: Knopf, 2010); *The Dew Breaker* (New York: Knopf, 2004); *Farming of Bones* (New York: Vintage, 1998); *Krik? Krak!* (New York: Soho Books, 1995); *Mama's Nightingale: A Story of Immigration and Separation* [illustrated by Leslie Staub] (New York: Dial Press, 2015); Rebecca Fuchs, *Caribbeanness as a Global Phenomenon: Junot Díaz, Edwidge Danticat, and Cristina García* (Trier, Germany and Tempe, Arizona: Wissenschaftlicher Verlag Trier, copublished by Bilingual Press/Editorial Bilingüe, 2014); Maxine Lavon Montgomery, ed., *Conversations with Edwidge Danticat* (Jackson: University of Mississippi Press, 2017); Martin Munro, ed., *Edwidge Danticat: A Reader's Guide* (Charlottesville: University of Virginia Press, 2010).

Delany, Martin R. (1812–1885)

Author, editor, orator, and politician. Martin Robison Delany was born free in Charles Town, Virginia (now Charleston, West Virginia), to Pati and Samuel Delany, a free Black woman and her slave husband. In 1822, Delany's mother moved the family to Chambersburg, Pennsylvania, fleeing Virginia authorities who had threatened to imprison her for teaching her children how to read and write. In 1823, after purchasing his own freedom, Delany's father joined the family in Pennsylvania. At the age of nineteen, Delany walked the 150 miles from Chambersburg to Pittsburgh, Pennsylvania, where he attended Lewis Woodson's school at Bethel African Methodist Church. After five years of schooling, Delany began studying medicine with Dr. Andrew M. McDowell, eventually setting up his own medical practice as a "cupper, lecher [*sic*], and bleeder" in 1836. Delany's early years in Pittsburgh were marked by his participation in a number of societies and organizations dedicated to the abolition of slavery and the elevation of the African American masses. He founded the Theban Literary Society in 1832 and the Young Men's Literary and Moral Reform Society of Pittsburgh in 1837. Delany also helped organize the State Convention of the Colored Freedmen of Pennsylvania in 1841. His years in Pittsburgh were also marked by the first of his many travels, nationally and internationally. In 1836, he attended a Black conference in New York City, and, in 1839, he traveled through Texas and the Southwest, scouting possible locations for Black settlement.

In March 1843, Delany married Catherine A. Richards. They had eleven children, seven of whom survived into adulthood. All the sons were named after prominent African American leaders and revolutionaries: Toussaint L'Ouverture (founder of Haiti and Black military hero), Charles Lenox Redmond (abolitionist), Alexander Dumas (author), Saint Cyprian (the sanctified Christian bishop), Faustin Soulouque (emperor of Haiti), and Ramses Placido (the ruler of ancient Egypt, and the poet and martyred hero of Cuba). They named their one daughter, born in 1864, Ethiopia Halle Amelia for the land of Delany's ancestors.

The 1840s marked Delany's entry into publishing, first in 1843 as the editor of *The Mystery*, one of Pittsburgh's African American Newspapers, and in 1847 as coeditor of *The North Star*, the newspaper of Frederick Douglass. As coeditor of *The North Star*, Delany became subject to Douglass's influence and spent much of 1848 touring the Midwest delivering antislavery lectures, visiting free Black communities, and soliciting subscriptions. In 1849, Delany ended his association with Douglass, retired as coeditor of *The North Star*, and returned to Pittsburgh to resume his medical practice close to his family. He attended Harvard Medical School during the fall of 1850, but he was expelled following petitions from White medical school students to Dean Oliver Wendell Holmes. Delany returned to publishing in 1856 as contributing editor to the *Provincial Freeman* of Chatham, Ontario, Canada, and again in 1875 as editor for several months of the *Charleston Independent*.

In the 1850s, Delany pursued two closely related facets of his life: his own literary production as an author of fiction and nonfiction and his interest in Africa. In 1852, Delany published *The Condition, Elevation, Emigration, and Destiny of the Colored People of the United States*. This was followed in 1853 by *The Origin and Objects of Ancient Freemasonry*, a work derived from Delany's own participation in Prince Hall Freemasonry and augmented by his desire to see African American traditions of Freemasonry regarded as authentic. In 1859, while Delany traveled to Liberia to meet with other members of the Niger Valley Exploring Party (experiences chronicled in *Official Report of the Niger Valley Exploring Party*, 1861), portions of his serialized novel *Blake; or, The Huts of America* appeared in *The Anglo-African Magazine* from January to July 1859. Although the magazine continued to publish after that time, no more installments of Delany's novel appeared. Probably the installments were delayed by the onset of the Civil War. The entire novel was not printed until the fall of 1861. *The Weekly Anglo-African* ran a complete version of *Blake* in consecutive weekly installments from November 26, 1861, until around May 24, 1862; the novel likely contains six chapters that remain missing, although they probably were published in the first four issues of *The Weekly Anglo-African* in May 1862. The novel follows the slave Henry Holland, who has escaped from Colonel Franks's Southern plantation after sending his son north to Canada. Henry spends the bulk of the novel wandering around the South, disguised, visiting with slaves on various plantations, inquiring as to their treatment there, and meeting with the most trustworthy and reputable of them. He talks of his plans for a general slave rebellion and mentions a two-year time frame. The first part of the novel ends with Henry successfully escorting the remaining slaves from the Frankses' farm to the safety of Canada. In the second part of the novel, Henry is hired out to some Whites heading to Cuba. There, he continues to visit slaves, gathering information about their status. Before departing, he meets his cousin, the Cuban poet Placido. The slaves throughout Cuba begin their planned revolt, but the government steps in and stops their plans. In the remainder of the novel, Blake sails on a slaver for Africa, with the intention of seizing the boat at sea, but instead does nothing, and the novel ends in its current incomplete state, without the threatened slave revolt across the Americas. Though incomplete, *Blake* remains significant for its imagining of an organized slave rebellion and its promise of retribution for the evils of slavery.

In addition to his editorial work and literary production, Delany is best remembered as a nascent Black Nationalist and budding politician. During the Civil War, he recruited Black troops for the Union Army, eventually meeting with President Lincoln and becoming the first commissioned Black major in the Union Army in February 1863. Following the Civil War, Delany worked with the Freedmen's Bureau in the South to guarantee the rights of recently emancipated African Americans. His involvement in politics continued as he sought, among other things, appointment as the first Black minister to the Republic of Liberia. Delany's last decade was occupied with African resettlement plans. He worked with the Liberian Exodus Joint Stock Steam Ship Company in 1877. When their ship, the *Azor*, sailed from South Carolina and Georgia to Africa in 1878, the company was consumed by debt. Delany worked unsuccessfully to raise funds to save the ship from being sold at auction. Before his death in 1885, Delany campaigned for Virginia Republican congressional candidate John F. Dezendorf, unsuccessfully sought a civil service appointment in Washington, DC, and worked for a Boston, Massachusetts, firm as its agent to South America.

Matthew R. Davis

See also: Protest Literature.

Resources

Tunde Adeleke, "'Much Learning Makes Men Mad': Classical Education and Black Empowerment in Martin R. Delany's Philosophy of Education," *Journal of Thought* 49, no. 1/2 (Spring/Summer 2015), 3–26, 90; Martin R. Delany: *Blake; or the Huts of America*, intro. Floyd J. Miller (Boston: Beacon Press, 1970); *The Condition, Elevation, Emigration, and Destiny of the Colored People of the United States* (Philadelphia: Martin R. Delany [self-published], 1852); *Official Report of the Niger Valley Exploring Party* (New York: T. Hamilton, 1861); *The Origin and Objects of Ancient Freemasonry; Its Introduction into the United States, and Legitimacy among Colored Men*, 2nd ed. (Xenia, OH: A. D. Delany, 1904); Cyril E. Griffith, *The African Dream: Martin R. Delany and the Emergence of Pan-African Thought* (University Park: Pennsylvania State University Press, 1975); John C. Havard, "Mary Peabody Mann's *Juanita* and Martin R. Delany's *Blake*: Cuba, Urban Slavery, and the Construction of Nation," *College Literature* 43, no. 3 (Summer 2016), 509(35); Mandy A. Reid, "Utopia Is in the Blood: The Bodily Utopias of Martin R. Delany and Pauline Hopkins," *Utopian Studies* 22, no. 1 (January 1, 2011), 91–103; Frank A. Rollin, *Life and Public Services of Martin R. Delany* (New York: Arno Press, 1969); Dorothy Sterling, *The Making of an Afro-American: Martin Robison Delany, 1812–1885* (Garden City, NY: Doubleday, 1971); Victor Ullman, *Martin R. Delany: The Beginnings of Black Nationalism* (Boston: Beacon Press, 1971).

Delany, Samuel R. (1942–)

Writer and professor. Delany is a prolific science fiction writer, memoirist, self-described "pornographer," literary critic, and social commentator. Since the publication in 1962 of his first book, *The Jewels of Aptor*, he has published numerous novels, short stories, essays, interviews, cultural commentary, and memoirs. What is most remarkable about this prolific output is its consistent quality, wide range, and continual development. Despite his numerous works in other genres, Delany has always strongly identified himself as a science fiction writer. But his work has always pushed at and expanded the boundaries and conventions of the field, constantly seeking out new forms, ideas, and themes. Indeed, his work has become more challenging and complex, and in some ways more difficult, over the course of his career.

Delany has also been an important figure in opening up the once almost exclusively White male world of science fiction to minority voices, both by being one of the first Black science fiction writers and by writing about the experiences of non-White characters of all hues and backgrounds, of women, and of gay and bisexual characters. Almost none of his protagonists are heterosexual White men, but the racial identity of his characters is not made an issue in his books. He creates worlds in which race as we understand it is not a significant category, and thus implicitly critiques our society's obsession with race and racial categorization. Delany has been a trailblazer for such later Black writers as Octavia E. Butler and Stephen Emery Barnes, who have used science fiction as an arena in which to explore racial questions in a speculative and imaginative manner.

Samuel Ray Delany Jr. was born in 1942 and raised in Harlem, New York's Black middle class. His position as both marginal (as a Black man and a gay man) and privileged (in the economic and social opportunities available to him) is a major influence on his work. Delany graduated from the prestigious Bronx High School of Science and attended the City College of New York, though he did not take a degree. He has traveled and lived in Europe and Turkey, and for many years made his living as a writer. Since 1988, he has been a professor at the University of Massachusetts at Amherst, the State University of New York at Buffalo, and currently at Temple University. However, he still makes his permanent home in his native New York City, to which he has a great attachment and about which he has written powerfully and evocatively, most recently in his book-length essay *Times Square Red, Times Square Blue* (1999).

The power of language to shape human reality has been a strong theme of Delany's work since the beginning of his career. Much of his later work explicitly refers to literary and cultural theorists such as Roland Barthes, Jacques Derrida, and Michel Foucault, who sought to reveal and undo assumptions about language and communication. For such theorists, language is not a passive tool but an active social force. But Delany's work has always demonstrated a strong literary and linguistic awareness and even self-consciousness, both in its style and in its subject matter. He has always been fascinated by language's influence on the way we perceive and conceive of the world and ourselves. This may be related to his dyslexia, which he has said heightened his sense of the material reality of language. *Babel-17* (1966) centers on the efforts of a poet to crack what is believed to be a military code used by an alien race with which Earth is at war. What she finally discovers is that this code is in fact a highly exact and analytical language that has no word for *I* and thus no concept of individual identity. The novel examines the capacity of culture and language not only to control the way people see the world but also to determine who they are as persons.

Dhalgren (1974), which is simultaneously Delany's most "difficult" and his most popular novel, is about the efforts of a nameless bisexual amnesiac to find his identity in the course of his wanderings through a postapocalyptic American city. He can find such an identity only by constructing one, and one of the ways he does so is through writing. By the end of the book (whose final phrase loops back to its opening words), the reader is left with the strong implication that the protagonist has written the novel that we have just finished reading about him. The novel is an enactment of the ways in which we create ourselves through our language and our ideas about ourselves. Delany had earlier explored this idea of self-creation through self-narration in *The Einstein Intersection* (1967), a retelling of the ancient Greek myth of the poet Orpheus set in the far distant future. In the original myth, Orpheus descends into the underworld to bring his dead wife back to life by the power of his song, only to lose her again because of his own doubts. Delany's protagonist is a member of an alien race that has come to earth long after humanity has departed. These aliens live out human myths and stories in an attempt to understand what it meant to be human, trying to make sense of the world they have inherited. By the end of his quest, the protagonist realizes that he and his people must create their own stories, rather than live out secondhand versions of someone else's. He must be a new Orpheus, one who no longer sings the dead songs. Thus, the novel is also an allegory about the power of art to create new realities.

Delany's work argues against the notion of a single, unified human nature. Instead, it celebrates difference, exploring the wide range of human possibilities that different languages and cultures can produce. However, Delany's work also delves into the complications and difficulties (up to and including war) that can result from such differences, especially when they are not acknowledged or recognized. His novel *Stars in My Pocket Like Grains of Sand* (1984) is largely about a clash of cultures, the conflict of incompatible assumptions about the universe and about people—including who and what (in a universe occupied by many different intelligent species) get to be defined as "people." In this book, the conflict between a social ideal based on exclusion and hierarchy and an ideal based on inclusion and free choice ends almost with the destruction of a planet. The implication is that differences, even or especially the most radical differences, must be accepted if humanity is to survive, let alone thrive. On a smaller scale, the antihero of *Trouble on Triton* (originally published in 1976 under the title *Triton*) makes himself and those around him miserable because he cannot reconcile his rigid, sexist ideas of the ways in which people should live and think with the variety and openness of his utopian society.

Delany's celebration of difference particularly focuses on the celebration of sexual difference. Many of his protagonists are women, and most of his male protagonists are gay or bisexual. The exploration of sexuality is central to Delany's work. In his fiction, he not only presents universes in which homosexuality is completely accepted and women are fully equal members of society, but he also presents universes in which our familiar sexual categories do not apply. In his Nebula Award-winning short story "Aye, and Gomorrah" (1967), those people who are physically capable of deep space travel are neither male nor female, and are eagerly sought after as sexual partners. In *Trouble on Triton*, it is as easy to change one's gender or one's sexual orientation as it is to change one's hair color.

Delany further explores the various ways and means of sexuality in the four-volume "Return to Nevèrÿon" series: *Tales of Nevèrÿon* (1979), *Neveryóna* (1983), *Flight from Nevèrÿon* (1985), and *Return to Nevèrÿon* (originally published in 1987 under the title *The Bridge of Lost Desire*). Rather than being set in the future, these books are set in the distant past, in a world in which the rulers are dark-skinned and the barbarian lower classes are blonde and blue-eyed. These books are a deliberate revision of the sword and sorcery genre of which the Conan the Barbarian series is the most famous example. In them, Delany investigates the complex and contradictory realities of such a fantasized primitive world, examining the development of civilization in order to uncover the historical roots of our own culture. Among the topics these ambitious books address are the origins and development of language, the family, sexuality, gender roles, private property, commerce, social hierarchy, and the interconnections of sex and power and of language and power. Slavery is a major theme of the series, with clear references to American history. The protagonist of the series is a former slave who rises to power and abolishes slavery. He is also a gay man whose sexual desires are all sadomasochistic, based on submission and domination. This is an example of the difficulty of separating sexuality and power in a hierarchical society in which, like our own, not all people are equal or equally free: slavery is both a sociopolitical phenomenon and a state of mind. But by making a mutually consenting game out of the power some people exercise over others, Delany's protagonist is able to defuse it to an extent, and to create pleasure out of pain. In the third book of the series, Delany makes explicit the parallels between the ancient world he has created and our contemporary world by juxtaposing a plague that affects only homosexuals in his fictional world with the AIDS epidemic in 1980s New York City. In so doing, he directly addresses questions of homophobia and social stigma.

As is confirmed by his many awards, Delany has gained recognition and acclaim not only in the science fiction but also in literary theory, Gay Literature, and Lesbian Literature. Despite controversies regarding the intellectual and stylistic challenges of some of his work, and the graphic sexual content of novels such as *The Mad Man* (1994) and *Hogg* (1998), his reputation as an important writer and thinker is secure and growing. In 2006, Delany published the nonfiction book, *About Writing: Seven Essays, Four Letters, and Five Interviews*, and, in 2017, *In Search of Silence: The Journals of Samuel R. Delany, Volume I, 1957–1969*, edited by Kenneth R. James, was published. A single-volume hardback edition of the *Fall of the Towers* trilogy was published in 2018. In 2013, Delany received the Damon Knight Memorial Grand Master Award from the Science Fiction Writers Association.

Reginald Shepherd

See also: Gay Literature.

Resources

Primary Sources: Samuel R. Delany: *About Writing: Seven Essays, Four Letters, and Five Interviews* (Middletown, CT: Wesleyan University Press, 2006); *Atlantis: Three Tales*

(Middletown, CT: Wesleyan University Press, 1995); *Aye, and Gomorrah* (New York: Vintage, 2003); *Babel-17* (Boston: Gregg Press, 1966); *The Ballad of Beta-2* (Boston: Gregg Press, 1965); *The Bridge of Lost Desire* (New York: Arbor House, 1987) (reprinted as *Return to Nevèrÿon*); *The Complete Nebula Award-Winning Fiction* (New York: Bantam, 1986); *Dhalgren* (Boston: Gregg Press, 1974); *Distant Stars* (New York: Ultramarine, 1981); *Driftglass* (Garden City, NY: Doubleday, 1971); *The Einstein Intersection* (London: Gallancz, 1967); *Empire: A Visual Novel* (New York: Berkeley, 1978); *Empire Star* (Boston: Gregg Press, 1966); *The Fall of the Towers* (trilogy: *Out of the Dead City*, *The Towers of Toron*, and *City of a Thousand Suns*) (Boston: Gregg Press, 1970; Lakewood, CO: Centipede Press, 2018); *Flight from Nevèrÿon* (Middletown, CT: Wesleyan University Press, 1994); *Hogg* (New York: Talman, 1995); *The Jewels of Aptor* (London: Gallancz, 1962); *The Mad Man* (New York: Richard Kasak Books, 1994); *Neveryóna* (New York: Bantam, 1983); *Nova* (New York: Doubleday, 1968); *Search of Silence: The Journals of Samuel R. Delany, Volume I, 1957–1969*, ed. Kenneth R. James (Middletown, CT: Wesleyan University Press, 2017); *Stars in My Pocket Like Grains of Sand* (New York: Bantam/Dell, 1984); *Tales of Nevèrÿon* (New York: Bantam, 1979); *They Fly at Ciron* (New York: St. Martin's Press, 1993); *The Tides of Lust* (New York: Lancer Books, 1973) (reprinted as *Equinox*); *Triton* (New York: Bantam, 1976) (reprinted as *Trouble on Triton*). Nonfiction: *The American Shore* (Elizabethtown, NY: Dragon Press, 1978); *Bread and Wine* (New York: Juno Books, 1999); *Heavenly Breakfast* (New York: Bantam, 1979); *The Jewel-Hinged Jaw* (New York: Ultramarine, 1977); *Longer Views: Extended Essays* (Middletown, CT: Wesleyan University Press, 1996); *The Motion of Light in Water* (New York: Masquerade Books, 1988); *1984: Selected Letters* (Middletown, CT: Wesleyan University Press, 2000); *Shorter Views* (Middletown, CT: Wesleyan University Press, 2000); *Silent Interviews* (Middletown, CT: Wesleyan University Press, 1994);

Starboard Wine (New York: Ultramarine, 1984); *The Straits of Messina* (New York: Serconia Press, 1989); *Times Square Red, Times Square Blue* (New York: New York University Press, 1999).

Secondary Sources: Anonymous, "'Samuel R. Delany' [report on the Damon Knight Memorial Grand Master Award], 15 Feb. 2014, p. 77; Douglas Barbour, *Worlds Out of Words: The SF Novels of Samuel R. Delany* (Frome, UK: Bran's Head Books, 1979); Richard Bleiler, ed., *Science Fiction Writers: Critical Studies of the Major Authors from the Early Nineteenth Century to the Present Day*, 2nd ed. (New York: Scribner's, 1998); Damien Broderick, *Reading by Starlight: Postmodern Science Fiction* (New York: Routledge, 1995); Robert Elliott Fox, *Conscientious Sorcerers: The Black Postmodernist Fiction of Leroi Jones/Amiri Baraka, Ishmael Reed, and Samuel R. Delany* (Westport, CT: Greenwood Press, 1987); Seth McEvoy, *Samuel R. Delany* (New York: Ungar, 1984); Christian Ravela, "'Turning Out Possessive Individualism': Freedom and Belonging in Samuel R. Delany's *The Mad Man*," *Modern Fiction Studies* 62, no. 1 (Spring 2016), 92–114, 189; James Sallis, ed., *Ash of Stars: On the Writing of Samuel R. Delany* (Jackson: University Press of Mississippi, 1996); George Edgar Slusser, *The Delany Intersection: Samuel R. Delany Considered as a Writer of Semi-Precious Words* (San Bernardino, CA: Borgo, 1977); Jane Branham Weedman, *Samuel R. Delany* (Mercer Island, WA: Starmont House, 1982).

Dialect Poetry

Written in what are known as "nonstandard" forms of English, African American dialect poetry has a long and controversial history. Some of the earliest examples of African American vernacular literature presented in lyric form can be found in songs from the slavery era, such as in the recurring phrase "Coming for to carry me home" in the spiritual "Swing Low, Sweet Chariot" or in the lines "We bake de bread / Dey gib us de crust" from a secular song exposing the injustices of slavery rather than expressing a hope for release. By contrast, the first published African American poets—Phillis Wheatley is an example—employed a lofty Standard English and wrote in traditional forms of English poetry. It was not until the later 1800s that Black dialect (real or invented) was used regularly in poetry by White and Black Americans. African American poets at first adopted and modified the White poetic traditions for representing Black dialect in verse, only to move away from the use of dialect around 1920 and later. Black vernacular English has regained much of its status and popularity in African American poetry since the 1960s.

After the Civil War, dialect poetry began to enjoy widespread and enthusiastic acceptance in part because of the growing demand for literary realism and local color writing. Most dialect poetry in this period was written by White authors who were generally less concerned with presenting authentic Black speech patterns than with creating specific moods or atmospheres in their works. In what is now commonly called the plantation tradition, White authors used invented Black dialects to paint a nostalgic picture of a rapidly disappearing way of life, a change signaled by the decline of plantation culture and an increase of schooling among Blacks in the South. Examples of the plantation tradition in verse include poems by Irwin Russell and Sidney Lanier and minstrel songs by Stephen Collins Foster. A few White poets have used Black dialect for other purposes. John Greenleaf Whittier's poem "At Port Royal" (1862) includes an effort to render Black dialect in the service

of abolitionism, for instance, and the White literary avant-garde incorporated Black dialect in their poems well into the twentieth century, as evidenced in Vachel Lindsay's "Congo: A Study of the Negro Race" (1914) and John Berryman's *The Dream Songs* (1964). In prose, Joel Chandler Harris, a White writer, used Black dialect in his Uncle Remus tales.

When White writers use Black dialect, questions about authenticity, stereotyping, and cultural appropriation may arise (see Gubar and Jones in Resources at the end of this entry). Also, linguists now understand African American English as a linguistic entity with its own features, so that effectively replicating it in literature requires a significant understanding of and experience with how individuals and groups actually deploy the language over times (see Green in Resources).

An early instance of Black vernacular used by an African American poet in the era of Reconstruction is Frances E. W. Harper's *Sketches of Southern Life* (1872), which includes six poems narrated by Aunt Chloe and presents both the autobiography of a former slave and an oral history of the eras of slavery and Reconstruction. The speech in these poems sounds more genuine than the dialect used by a number of other Black poets—such as Daniel Webster Davis, James Edwin Campbell, and James D. Corrothers—whose poems often appeared in White publications and adhered to the conventions of the plantation tradition. Two of the most notable late nineteenth-century poets writing in this tradition are Paul Laurence Dunbar and James Weldon Johnson. Dunbar mixed Standard English and dialect poems in *Majors and Minors* (1895) and his best-selling volume *Lyrics of Lowly Life* (1896); in the introduction to the latter work, the influential White critic William Dean Howells praised the dialect poems above the others in the volume, although Dunbar had little direct contact with rural speakers of Black dialect, learning what he knew secondhand from his parents, and was influenced primarily by White American and British poets such as Poe, Longfellow, Tennyson, Shelley, and Shakespeare. Dunbar nonetheless succeeded in producing some of the most sophisticated and musical of the dialect poems written in this period. Fearing he would be remembered only as a writer of dialect poetry, he expressed remorse that his most serious poetry had not received the same attention and praise as his dialect poetry, which he disparaged in "The Poet" (1903) as "a jingle in a broken tongue."

Dunbar has been criticized as a supporter of negative racial stereotypes, but he was by all accounts a positive influence on subsequent generations of Black poets. Langston Hughes gave him thoughtful attention in his essay "The Negro Artist and the Racial Mountain" (1926), as did Sterling A. Brown in his study *Negro Poetry and Drama* (1937). Subsequent generations of Black poets have located in Dunbar the beginnings of an authentic Black voice in American poetry; he has been the subject of a number of studies since the later 1960s, and his collection of poems was reissued in 1967 and, in expanded form, in 1993. The poetry of Johnson, Dunbar's contemporary and close friend, similarly included pieces written in strongly inflected Black dialect, such as "Sence You Went Away" (1900), alongside others in spoken Black English, such as "The Creation" (1920), or in elevated forms of Standard English, such as "Lift Ev'ry Voice and Sing" (1921).

By the early 1920s, the tide was turning against dialect poetry. In his preface to *The Book of American Negro Poetry* (1922), James Weldon Johnson characterized the African American vernacular as a softened, and thus more musical, form of English, and commented positively on the dialect poetry of Claude McKay, John W. Holloway, James Edwin Campbell, and Daniel Webster Davis, yet Johnson ultimately rejected this artistic mode as fundamentally limited to the expression of humor and pathos. The problem for Johnson lay not in the dialect itself but in its seemingly inextricable ties to the long-standing plantation tradition of White authors using invented Black speech to present romanticized accounts of the slavery-era South. Countee Cullen echoed this judgment in his preface to the poetry anthology *Caroling Dusk* (1927), characterizing dialect poetry as a "fast-dying medium" that had offered only a limited range of poetic expression and had mostly been the province of White poets.

The minstrel and plantation traditions had indeed burdened the literary use of Black dialect with racial stereotyping. By the 1920s, Claude McKay had moved away from his poems in Jamaican English, as presented in his two early collections *Songs of Jamaica* (1912) and *Constab Ballads* (1912), and toward the loftier forms and language of traditional English poetry, particularly the sonnet. Several other of the most significant writers of the Harlem Renaissance, however, purposefully and effectively used Black dialect verse in their works. Zora Neale Hurston included examples of song lyrics and poems employing the Black vernacular in her essay "Characteristics of Negro Expression" (1934) as well as in her collection *Mules and Men* (1935) and her autobiographical *Dust Tracks on a Road* (1942), and Jean Toomer incorporated African American dialect into his prose poems in *Cane* (1923). More extensive use of Black vernacular was made by Langston Hughes and Sterling A. Brown, both of whom demonstrated a strong interest in the spoken language of working-class African Americans.

Hughes's poetry was strongly influenced by Dunbar and frequently made innovative use of dialect alongside African American musical traditions, including the blues. For example, Hughes's first collection of poetry, *The Weary Blues* (1926), contains a number of poems written in Black dialect and structured according to the three-line blues stanza. Brown's poetry offers an even more complete fusion of artistic and popular concerns; for example, the title poem of *Southern Road* (1932) combines the work song, blues form, and Black dialect to tell the powerful story of a man convicted of murder and sentenced to work on a chain gang. Engagement with this compelling poetry by Brown and Hughes prompted Johnson to reevaluate his statements on the limitations of dialect and to publish a new preface to the 1931 edition of *The Book of American Negro Poetry*, in which he praised the use of "genuine folk stuff" and the representation of "the common, racy, living, authentic speech of the Negro."

Hughes, in particular, was a strong influence on two prominent African American poets of the 1940s, Margaret Walker and Gwendolyn Brooks. Walker's poem "Poppa Chicken," appearing in *For My People* (1942), strongly resembles the vernacular poems by Hughes. Brooks's early poems, by contrast, reflect Hughes's humor and melodies but not his use of dialect. In 1967, the year of Hughes's death, Brooks met Imamu Amiri Baraka and other young, engaged writers of the Black Arts Movement at a writers' conference; only after this meeting did she begin to blend urban Black dialect with the language of traditional poetry, as evidenced in her poem "The Third Sermon on the Warpland" (1969) and elsewhere.

Hoyt Fuller's "Toward a Black Aesthetic" (1968), an important manifesto of the Black Arts Movement, called for a new Black Poetry that was relevant and revolutionary in both content and style. In keeping with this new aesthetic, Black English permeates the poetry from this period and is frequently presented alongside (although not always clearly distinguishable from) the many other ways of speaking in contemporary American culture. Baraka's words in *Preface to a Twenty Volume Suicide Note* (1961) and subsequent volumes bridge the gap between the Beats and the Blacks; Etheridge Knight's *Poems from Prison* (1968) speak in the various voices of America's street, drug, and prison cultures; and Gil Scott-Heron's recorded poem "The Revolution Will Not Be Televised" (1970) opposes the chatter of White media culture with a call for militancy in the Black vernacular. In comparison, a number of the poems by Black women writers who regularly employ Black vernacular in their work—such as Sonia Sanchez's "Summer Words of a Sistuh Addict" (1966), Nikki Giovanni's "Beautiful Black Men" (1968), and Carolyn M. Rodgers's "Jesus Was Crucified" (1969)—often present a voice that is more unified and intimate but no less capable of recording conflict, resistance, and resilience.

The poems written after the waning of the Black Arts Movement in the mid-1970s are too numerous and too varied to allow for a full account of the uses of Black English, even if one arbitrarily excludes spoken word poetry and rap lyrics from the discussion. In any case, the use of Black vernacular English is found in much contemporary poetry, and important critical studies in recent years—such as Aldon Lynn Nielsen's *Black Chant: Languages of African-American Postmodernism* (1997) and Fahamisha Patricia Brown's *Performing the Word: African American Poetry as Vernacular Culture* (1999), have maintained that the spoken (rather than the written) word has long been the base unit of African American poetry. (*See* Folklore; Performance Poetry)

James B. Kelley

See also: Dunbar, Paul Laurence; Hughes, Langston; Terry [Prince], Lucy; Vernacular.

Resources

John Berryman, *The Dream Songs* (New York: Farrar, Straus and Giroux, 1969); Fahamisha Patricia Brown, *Performing the Word: African American Poetry as Vernacular Culture* (New Brunswick, NJ: Rutgers University Press, 1999); Sterling A. Brown, *Southern Road* (New York: Harcourt, Brace, 1932); Countee Cullen, ed., *Caroling Dusk* (New York: Harper & Bros., 1927); Paul Laurence Dunbar, *The Complete Poems of Paul Laurence Dunbar* (New York: Dodd, Mead, 1913); Rachel Blau DuPlessis, *Genders, Races, and Religious Cultures in Modern American Poetries, 1908–1934* (New York: Cambridge University Press, 2001); Lisa J. Green, *African American English: A Linguistic Introduction* (New York and Cambridge: Cambridge University Press, 2002); Susan Gubar, *Racechanges: White Skin, Black Face in American Culture* (New York: Oxford University Press, 1997); Gavin Roger Jones, *Strange Talk: The Politics of Dialect Literature in Gilded Age America* (Berkeley: University of California Press, 1999); Langston Hughes, *The Weary Blues* (New York: Knopf, 1926); Vachel Lindsay, *Collected Poems* (New York: Macmillan, 1925); Claude McKay, *The Dialect Poetry of Claude McKay* (Salem, NH: Ayers, 1987); Aldon Lynn Nielsen: *Black Chant: Languages of African-American Postmodernism* (New York:

Cambridge University Press, 1997); *Reading Race: White American Poets and the Racial Discourse in the Twentieth Century* (Athens: University of Georgia Press, 1988); Michael North, *The Dialect of Modernism: Race, Language, and Twentieth-Century Literature* (New York: Oxford University Press, 1998); Hans Ostrom, "Audience," "Black Dialect," and "Poetics," in his *A Langston Hughes Encyclopedia* (Westport, CT: Greenwood Press, 2002), 12–14, 38–40, 306–308; Steven C. Tracy, *Langston Hughes and the Blues* (Urbana: University of Illinois Press, 1988).

Douglass, Frederick (1818–1895)

Abolitionist, orator, author, editor, and politician. Frederick Bailey (he later changed his name) was born to a slave named Harriet Bailey and an unknown White man in February 1818 at Tuckahoe, near the town of Easton, in Talbot County, Maryland. Reared on the plantation of Col. Edward Lloyd, young Frederick Douglass was the property of Capt. Aaron Anthony, the plantation's manager. Having grown up not knowing the identity of his father and having lost his mother (who was sold) near the age of seven, Douglass grew up committed to battling slavery, the institution that had deprived him of a father and taken away his mother. Douglass's early years appear to have been relatively free from physical abuse, and his favored status as an intelligent and tractable young man led to his selection, in 1825, to become a servant in the Baltimore, Maryland, home of Hugh and Sophia Auld, relatives of his master. In the Auld home, Douglass received rudimentary education in reading and writing from Sophia Auld, until Hugh discovered her teaching and put a stop to the practice. One of Douglass's first acts of rebellion against the dictates of slavery, famously recounted in his autobiographies, was to learn to read and write despite prohibitions to the contrary. As he wrote in his *Narrative* of 1845, hearing that he was barred from furthering his literacy made him see "the pathway from slavery to freedom." Douglass's literacy would become one of his strongest assets later in life, as he was able to convey the horrors of slavery passionately and articulately in his orations, autobiographies, a novella, and countless editorials and articles in support of the anti-slavery cause.

Following a dispute between Hugh Auld and his brother Thomas, Douglass returned to Maryland as the slave of Thomas Auld, who subsequently hired Douglass out to the notorious Edward Covey, a "slave-breaker." It was under Covey's supervision that Douglass first personally experienced the brutality of the slave system, finding himself subject to frequent and unprovoked physical beatings at the hands of his overseer. Following six months of abuse, Douglass, then sixteen years old, fought back, in a famous scene recounted in his *Narrative*. In his recollection of the fight, Douglass discusses the impact of his resistance, which not only kept him from further beatings by Covey for the remainder of the year he spent with him but also "rekindled the few expiring embers of freedom, and revived within me a sense of my own manhood. It recalled the departed self-confidence, and inspired me again with a determination to be free" (115). Buoyed by this desire, Douglass made a first, and unsuccessful, attempt to escape from slavery in 1836 as he was being sent back to Baltimore to reside with Hugh and Sophia Auld.

From 1836 to 1838, Douglass learned the caulking trade in the Baltimore shipyards, hiring himself out independently to shipbuilders and returning a prearranged portion of his earnings each week to Hugh Auld. By taking on additional work and negotiating higher wages, Douglass was able to set aside a small portion of his earnings each week. This money later helped him achieve his freedom. On September 3, 1838, Douglass, disguised as a free Black merchant sailor and aided by Anna Murray, took a train from Baltimore to New York City. From New York, he headed to New Bedford, Massachusetts, where he married Anna and selected Douglass as his new last name.

In the years following, Douglass became a regular presence as an articulate and impassioned speaker for the abolitionist movement against the horrors of slavery. Less than three years following his escape, Douglass was working full-time as a lecturer. During this period, he befriended the noted abolitionist William Lloyd Garrison. The most important document to emerge out of Douglass's collaboration with Garrison was Douglass's *Narrative of the Life of Frederick Douglass, an American Slave* (1845), which he wrote at the urging of Garrison, who published and distributed the book. Released in June 1845 under the aegis of the American Anti-Slavery Society, and subsidized by the Massachusetts Anti-Slavery Society, the *Narrative* sold remarkably well: 4,500 copies in the first five months and 30,000 over the next five years. The success of the *Narrative* propelled Douglass to international celebrity as a speaker against slavery. The *Narrative* was considered so incendiary and inflammatory that Douglass was sent to England as a speaker immediately following its publication, in response to worries that his former master would seek his capture. In anticipation of the publication of his narrative, Douglass sailed to Liverpool, England, on August 16, 1845, to embark upon a lecture tour and to stay clear of those intent on capturing him and returning him to slavery. His success as a speaker and agitator for American abolition during his sojourn in England earned him friends, influence, and investors willing to assist Douglass in the purchase of his freedom from his former master and in the establishment of his own newspaper, *The North Star.*

Shortly after the publication of Douglass's *Narrative*, Douglass and Garrison began a planned two-month speaking tour of Ohio and New York. While the tour was largely successful—speaking to large crowds and converting many to the causes of free soil and immediatism—Garrison paid a price for his efforts. In late September, after speaking to crowds at three large meetings in one day in Cleveland, he collapsed from exhaustion. Unable to continue and confined to bed, Garrison left Douglass to continue their engagements in New York, and he traveled alone to Syracuse and Buffalo. When he was finally well enough to return home to Boston, Massachusetts, at the end of October, Garrison expressed only one complaint about the experience that had left him near death, far from family and friends—that throughout his convalescence, he had heard nothing from Douglass, and was disappointed to hear secondhand that Douglass was continuing with plans to start a newspaper of his own.

The possibility of Douglass's beginning his own newspaper had first been broached when Douglass returned from his trip to England. British supporters had raised money and negotiated for the purchase of Douglass's freedom in a complicated transaction that required the transfer of Douglass's ownership from Hugh Auld to his brother. These supporters had also offered Douglass more than $2,000 in the form of an annuity, which would free Douglass

from wage earning and give him ample opportunity to promulgate the abolitionist cause. Douglass politely declined the offer, arguing that he was too young to be "superannuated" and suggesting instead that the money be used for the purchase of a printing press and equipment for a Black-run newspaper. Upon Douglass's return to the United States in 1847, he brought news of the gift from British supporters and asked the American Anti-Slavery Society for its support of another newspaper. The leadership of the American Anti-Slavery Society argued that other antislavery newspapers had been started in his absence, that a Black-run newspaper would reinforce the color distinction, and that Garrison's *The Liberator* was itself having difficulty in retaining Black subscribers. The leadership persuaded Douglass to lay aside the venture for the time being. However, when he ultimately decided to begin his own paper, and word reached Garrison, the effort marked the first of many disagreements that would drive the two men further and further apart.

While the founding of Douglass's own newspaper—*The North Star*—in 1847 was instrumental in driving a wedge between Douglass and Garrison, it was not in itself the cause of trouble between the two, but rather a symptom of a larger disagreement developing out of Douglass's sense of his own position within the movement. According to Douglass's biographer William S. McFeely, Douglass "decided to begin his own newspaper . . . to find his own voice." Others have also described Douglass's dissatisfaction with his position relative to Garrisonian abolition in these terms: given that Douglass himself was educated and articulate, he became increasingly frustrated the more he imagined that he was valuable to abolitionists merely as a symbol or a figure, and not as someone with his own ideas and agenda. According to James L. Gray, "William Lloyd Garrison and other abolitionists wanted [Douglass] to appear on the platform to show his whip-scarred back while they talked about the evils of slavery, but Douglass soon decided that he should denounce slavery as well as describe it and become analyst as well as example" (39). In addition to the sense that he was valued more for his physicality than for his opinions, Douglass expressed dissatisfaction with the manner in which he felt himself to be taken as the basis of Garrison's speeches and writing. The establishment of his own newspaper gave him ample opportunity to speak for himself and denounce the wrongs of slavery rather than merely serve as a symbol to an abolitionist cause, a cause he felt was increasingly limiting his ability to voice his own opinions. Douglass continued to publish *The North Star*—later retitled *Frederick Douglass's Paper*—through 1863, contributing nearly all of its content.

In 1853, Douglass published a novella, *The Heroic Slave*, his sole work of fiction. It was written in response to a scheme hatched in 1852 by Julia Griffiths of the Rochester Ladies' Anti-Slavery Society to raise funds for the cause. She asked celebrities to submit antislavery statements that were to be printed along with a facsimile of the author's signature. The entire collection was to be entitled *Autographs for Freedom*. The two-volume collection included assorted entries by individuals such as Harriet Beecher Stowe, John Greenleaf Whittier, and William Henry Steward. Most of these entries were brief, but Douglass's contribution was a sixty-five-page novella that Douglass biographer William S. McFeely has described as a "curious mirror of his *Narrative of the Life of Frederick Douglass*." Douglass's novella fictionalizes the successful 1841 slave revolt led by Madison Washington aboard the American ship *Creole* while it was en route from Virginia to New Orleans, Louisiana. After wresting control of the ship from their captors, Washington and his fellow slaves directed the ship to Nassau, where they gained their freedom. Filtered through the remembrances and recollections of both a sailor aboard the *Creole* and Washington's abolitionist friend, Mr. Listwell, Madison Washington emerges as a heroic figure of epic proportions. *The Heroic Slave* is therefore significant not just for being Douglass's sole work of fiction but also for the manner in which the novella imagines the violent overthrow of slavery through armed resistance. The novella thus presents a more radical stance concerning resistance than Douglass ever took in his multiple autobiographies or in his many speeches and articles.

Douglass's second autobiography, *My Bondage and My Freedom*, appeared in 1855. In some ways an enlarged and expanded version of the 1845 *Narrative*, *My Bondage and My Freedom* also reflected on Douglass's years of freedom and painted a more arresting picture of slavery's evils. The first half of the work, "Life as a Slave," recounts many of the scenes that had so moved readers of his first autobiography—his fight with Edward Covey, the beating of his aunt Esther, and his acquisition of literacy. The second half, "Life as a Freeman," entered new territory. Here Douglass recounted his rising prominence within the abolitionist movement and his decision to go his own way in order to achieve his own voice. Douglass indicates that "it did not entirely satisfy me to *narrate* wrongs; I felt like *denouncing* them" (361–362). He would go on to write one more account of his life, *Life and Times of Frederick Douglass* (1881; revised and expanded in 1892). While these later autobiographies offer significant insights into the life and mind of Frederick Douglass, his first autobiography remains the most significant of these works, marking his emergence as an articulate and thoughtful voice against slavery with national importance.

Following the outbreak of the Civil War in 1861, Douglass became increasingly involved in politics, all the while continuing publication of his papers and speaking tours. Douglass lobbied President Abraham Lincoln to let African Americans fight in the Union ranks; later, in 1863, he published an address in *Douglass's Monthly* urging African Americans to enlist in the Union Army. His efforts in lobbying the president and encouraging African Americans toward service were instrumental in the establishment of the Fifty-fourth and Fifty-fifth Massachusetts Regiments of colored soldiers. In 1866, Douglass urged President Andrew Johnson to grant suffrage to newly freed African Americans. In 1871, he visited Santo Domingo as part of a commission tasked with determining the country's attitude toward annexation by the United States. These efforts, combined with Douglass's national stature and continued allegiance and service to the Republican Party, led to a number of political appointments, many of which were firsts for any African American. In 1874, he was named president of the Freedmen's Bureau Bank. In 1877, he was appointed federal marshal and recorder of deeds for Washington, DC, a post he held until 1881. In 1889, he was named consul to Haiti and, in 1893, chargé d'affaires for the Dominican Republic. In 1893, Douglass attended the World's Columbian Exposition in Chicago, Illinois, a world's fair held to commemorate the 400th anniversary of Columbus's arrival in the New World. At the exposition, Douglass, along with Ida B.

Wells-Barnett, circulated a pamphlet, *The Reason Why the Colored American Is Not in the World's Columbian Exposition*, which protested the exclusion of African Americans from displays highlighting America's progress over the past four centuries. Douglass and Wells-Barnett also objected to the limitation of African Americans' presence to ethnographic displays and the tawdry entertainments of the Midway Plaissance.

Douglass died of a heart attack February 20, 1895, at his home at Cedar Hill, Washington, DC. He is buried alongside his wife and daughter in Mount Hope Cemetery in Rochester, New York, where he lived during much of his life. Douglass's importance to American literature and culture is difficult to overstate. His 1845 *Narrative* stands as one of the finest examples of the Slave Narrative genre and is a testament to Douglass's eloquence and persuasiveness as he combated slavery in particular and racial discrimination in general. Many of the twentieth century's notable African American authors, particularly those writing within the autobiographical tradition, owe a debt to Douglass and his writings (*see* Autobiography). These authors include Booker T. Washington, W.E.B. Du Bois, James Weldon Johnson, Ralph Ellison, and James Baldwin, among many others. While Douglass is best remembered for his efforts to end slavery and to better the situation of African Americans, he was also a passionate voice for the equal rights of women, participating in the 1848 Seneca Falls Convention along with Elizabeth Cady Stanton and Susan B. Anthony to advocate equal rights for women. In fact, Douglass's last public act before his death was to deliver a rousing address at a rally for women's rights.

Matthew R. Davis

See also: Autobiography; Protest Literature; Slave Narrative.

Resources

Nolan Bennett, "To Narrate and Denounce: Frederick Douglass and the Politics of Personal Narrative," *Political Theory* 44, no. 2 (April 2016), 240–264; Bernard Boxill, "Frederick Douglass's Patriotism," *The Journal of Ethics* 13, no. 4 (2009), 301–317; Frederick Douglass: *The Heroic Slave*, in *Three Classic African-American Novels*, ed. Williams L. Andrews (New York: Mentor, 1990); *My Bondage and My Freedom*, ed. John David Smith (New York: Penguin, 2003); *Narrative of the Life of Frederick Douglass, an American Slave: Written by Himself*, ed. John W. Blassingame, John R. McKivigan, Peter P. Hinks, and Gerald Fulkerson (New Haven, CT: Yale University Press, 2001); James L. Gray, "Culture, Gender, and the Slave Narrative," *Proteus* 7, no. 1 (Spring 1990), 37–42; Nathan Irvin Huggins, *Slave and Citizen: The Life of Frederick Douglass* (Boston: Little, Brown, 1980); Gregory P. Lampe, *Frederick Douglass: Freedom's Voice, 1818–1845* (East Lansing: Michigan State University Press, 1998); Waldo E. Martin Jr., *The Mind of Frederick Douglass* (Chapel Hill: University of North Carolina Press, 1984); William S. McFeely, *Frederick Douglass* (New York: W. W. Norton, 1991); Daniel A. Morris, "Liberated from the Liberator: Frederick Douglass and Garrisonian Political Theology," *Political Theology* 18, no. 5 (July 4, 2017), 423–440; Omedi Ochieng, "A Ruthless Critique of Everything Existing: Frederick Douglass and the Architectonic of African American Radicalism," *Western Journal of Communication* 75, no. 2 (March 17, 2011), 168–184; Dickson J. Preston, *Young Frederick Douglass: The Maryland Years* (Baltimore: Johns Hopkins University Press, 1980); Benjamin Quarles, *Frederick Douglass* (Englewood Cliffs, NJ: Prentice-Hall, 1968); Eric J. Sundquist, ed., *Frederick Douglass: New Literary and Historical Essays* (Cambridge: Cambridge University Press, 1990); Booker T. Washington, *Frederick Douglass* (Philadelphia: George W. Jacobs, 1907).

Dove, Rita (1952–)

Poet, novelist, short-story writer, dramatist, and professor. Although a versatile writer, Dove is chiefly known for her poetry. Her poems started to appear in major periodicals in the early 1970s. In just over a decade, she became one of the most celebrated poets of her generation with her Pulitzer-winning collection *Thomas and Beulah* (1986). From 1993 to 1995, she was the youngest Poet Laureate of the United States, and she is also the only African American to date to win that honor. Dove's poetry has been widely praised for its technical sophistication as well as its accessibility. Critics have noted her innovative imagery, her well-controlled syntactic structure, and the complexity and range of her subject matter. In terms of her literary ancestry, Dove has been compared with Emily Dickinson, Robert Frost, Langston Hughes, Zora Neale Hurston, and Gwendolyn Brooks, to name just a few. While Dove's central focus is on her African American heritage and her identity as a woman, she endeavors to speak to the broadest possible spectrum of the reading public. She states, "Obviously, as a black woman, I am concerned with race . . . But certainly not every poem of mine mentions the fact of being black. They are poems about humanity, and sometimes humanity happens to be black. I cannot run from, I *won't* run from any kind of truth" (Kastor, B2). Currently Commonwealth professor of English at the University of Virginia, Dove continues to lead a productive career as a poet.

Rita Frances Dove was born in Akron, Ohio, on August 28, 1952, to Elvira

Elizabeth Hord and Ray Dove, who encouraged their daughter's academic and artistic pursuits. As a young girl, Dove showed a propensity for reading and writing. But she did not realize the full significance of writing in her life until the eleventh grade, when an English teacher took her to a book-signing event featuring the poet John Ciardi. From there, a path in literature opened up in front of the aspiring young Dove. In 1970, Dove enrolled at Miami University in Ohio as a presidential scholar and studied English literature with a secondary focus on German language and literature. She graduated summa cum laude in 1973 and went on to study modern European literature at the University of Tübingen in Germany as a Fulbright scholar. Dove earned an MFA in 1977 from the University of Iowa's Writers' Workshop and married Fred Viebahn, a German novelist, in 1979.

After two early chapbooks (*Ten Poems* in 1977 and *Only Dark Spot in the Sky* in 1980), Dove's first full-length collection, *The Yellow House on the Corner*, appeared in 1980. Based on her master's thesis at Iowa, this collection clearly shows Dove's poetic vision: although deeply affected by such contemporary African American poets as Haki Madhubuti (Don L. Lee) and Gwendolyn Brooks, Dove strives to move beyond the Black Arts Movement toward a broader vision of humanity. In this volume, surrealist expressions (often cast in the context of dreams) contrast with slave narratives grounded in specific experiences of individuals or historical events. This interest in narrative led to her next collection, *Mandolin* (1982), another chapbook that features a seven-poem sequence that, a few years later, was incorporated into her masterpiece, *Thomas and Beulah* (1986). *Museum* (1983) represents an important stage of development in Dove's career in

that it breaks out from the largely autobiographical nature of her previous work. With a broad social, cultural, and historical perspective, *Museum* explores issues of cultural heritage, the dissemination of knowledge, and historical memory. In poems as wide-ranging in time and space as "Tou Wan Speaks to Her Husband, Liu Sheng," "Catherine of Alexandria," and "Parsley," Dove highlights her interest in presenting history and culture from her perspective as a woman as well as an African American.

Thomas and Beulah, the most critically acclaimed collection of Dove's work, recreates family history against a backdrop of significant social events from the 1920s to the 1960s. The forty-four-poem volume is divided into two parts: "Mandolin" and "Canary in Bloom." "Mandolin," which more than triples the original version of seven poems, recounts in fictionalized form the experiences of Dove's maternal grandfather, Thomas Hord, who moved from his native Tennessee to Akron, Ohio, in 1921. Thomas, an expert mandolin player, is haunted all his life by the loss of his dear friend at the start of his journey north ("The Event"). Even his marriage to Beulah and their family life cannot completely assuage his remorse and pain ("Nothing Down"); he dies alone in his car, unable to get his medication ("Thomas at the Wheel"). "Canary in Bloom" commemorates Dove's maternal grandmother, who died in 1969, and had its genesis in a poem titled "Dusting," which first appeared in *Museum*. According to Dove, at first she did not envision parallel stories about her grandparents in *Thomas and Beulah*, which started out as her account of the story her grandmother told about her grandfather. "Then this poem 'Dusting' appeared, really out of nowhere. I didn't realize that this was Thomas's wife saying 'I want to talk. And you can't do his side without doing my side'" (Kitchen and Rubin, 236). The result is a life balanced between the weight of domesticity ("Daystar") and the yearning for love ("Recovery" and "Company").

Dove's later collections of poetry, including *Grace Notes* (1989), *Mother Love* (1995), and *On the Bus with Rosa Parks* (1999), continue to consolidate her reputation as one of America's leading poets today. (A selection from her previous published work appeared as *Selected Poems* in 1993.) *Grace Notes* is more personal than any of her earlier work; she allows the reader glimpses of her new role as a mother and of her career as an academic. Section three deals primarily with maternal life, including breast-feeding ("Pastoral") and changes in her body brought on by childbirth ("Genetic Expedition"). "After Reading *Mickey in the Night Kitchen* for the Third Time Before Bed" is a mother's candid lesson in sex education to her three-year-old daughter. In *Mother Love*, Dove continues the maternal theme but adapts the sonnet, a form traditionally devoted to romantic idealizations, to portray the tension between mother and daughter through a reworking of the classic myth of Demeter and Persephone. *On the Bus with Rosa Parks* returns to personal and social history, beginning with a section depicting African American life titled "Cameos," set in the 1920s through the 1940s, and closing with the title section that commemorates the civil rights pioneer. As Dove notes, the collection's title is a phrase uttered by her daughter in reference to the fact that they were riding on the same bus with Mrs. Parks during a conference in 1995 (91).

American Smooth: Poems (2004) engages a variety of topics, including African Americans who served in World War I and jazz.

Sonata Mulattica: Poems (2009) is based in fact and explores the life of George Polgreen Bridgetower, a mixed-race violinist who travels to Vienna to meet composer Ludwig Van Beethoven, who dedicates a sonata to Bridgetower but later revokes the dedication.

In 2011, an anthology edited by Dove was published: *The Penguin Anthology of Twentieth-Century American Poetry* (see Teicher in Secondary Sources at the end of this entry).

Just as Dove resists any preconceived notion of what her poetry ought to be like, so she does not restrict herself to one mode of literary expression. In 1985, her first collection of short stories, *Fifth Sunday*, appeared. It consists of eight stories and concerns young, often female characters who find themselves in conflict with social conventions. As Dove explains, the stories in this book "feature individuals who are trying to be recognized in a world that loves to pigeonhole and forget" (Rubin and Kitchen, 13). Dove's 1992 novel, *Through the Ivory Gate*, is motivated by a similar impulse. Virginia King, a young Black college graduate not unlike Dove herself, returns to her native Akron, Ohio, where she feels alienated from her family and romantic love. In an interview, Dove discussed the difficulty of moving from poetry to fiction (Ostrom). In 1994, Dove published a verse play, *The Darker Face of the Earth*, which reworks the classic tragedy of *Oedipus the King*. Dove's play follows the classic model in its plot of mistaken identity and incest, but her story is set on a South Carolina plantation where slavery and miscegenation are the key factors for the identity confusion.

Dove has taught at Arizona State University and the University of Virginia.

Wenxin Li

See also: Lyric Poetry.

Resources

Primary Sources: *American Smooth* (New York: W.W. Norton, 2004); *The Darker Face of the Earth: A Verse Play* (Brownsville, OR: Story Line, 1994); *Fifth Sunday* (Lexington: University of Kentucky Press, 1985); *Grace Notes* (New York: W. W. Norton, 1989); *Mandolin* (Athens, OH: Ohio Review, 1982); *Mother Love* (New York: W. W. Norton, 1995); *Museum* (Pittsburgh, PA: Carnegie-Mellon University Press, 1983); *On the Bus with Rosa Parks* (New York: W. W. Norton, 1999); *The Only Dark Spot in the Sky* (Phoenix, AZ: Porch, 1980); [editor] *The Penguin Anthology of Twentieth Century American Poetry* (New York: Penguin, 2001); *Selected Poems* (New York: Pantheon, 1993); *Sonata Mulattica* (New York: W.W. Norton, 2009); *Ten Poems* (Lisbon, IA: Penumbra, 1977); *Thomas and Beulah* (Pittsburgh, PA: Carnegie-Mellon University Press, 1986); *Through the Ivory Gate* (New York: Pantheon, 1992); *The Yellow House on the Corner* (Pittsburgh, PA: Carnegie-Mellon University Press, 1980).

Secondary Sources: Grace Cavalieri, "Rita Dove: An Interview," *American Poetry Review* 24, no. 2 (1995), 11–16; Susan Davis, "Entering the World Through Language," in *Conversations with Rita Dove*, ed. Earl G. Ingersoll (Jackson: University Press of Mississippi, 2003), 38–52; Peter Erickson, "'Othello's Back': *Othello* as Mock Tragedy in Rita Dove's *Sonata Mulattica*," *Journal of Narrative Theory* 41, no. 3 (2011), 362–377; Akasha Hull, "Review of *Selected Poems*," *Women's Review of Books* 11, no. 8 (1994), 6–7; Elizabeth Kastor, "The Poet, the Biographer, and the Pulitzer Glow," *Washington Post*, Apr. 17, 1987, pp. B1–B2; John Keene, "Rita Dove's *The Darker Face of the Earth*: An Introductory Note," *Callaloo* 17, no. 2 (1994), 371–373; Judith Kitchen and Stan Sanvel Rubin, "A Conversation with Rita Dove," *Black American Literature Forum* 20, no. 3 (1986), 227–240; Adele S. Newson, "Review of *On the Bus with Rosa Parks*," *World Literature Today* 74, no. 1 (2000), 165–166; Hans Ostrom, "Interview with Rita Dove/Review of *Through the Ivory Gate*," *Soundlife* (Sunday suppl.), *Tacoma News Tribune*, Nov. 29, 1992, p. 11; Stan Sanvel Rubin and Judith Kitchen, "Riding That Current as Far as It'll Take You," in *Conversations with Rita Dove*, ed. Earl G. Ingersoll (Jackson: University Press of Mississippi, 2003), 3–14; Reena Sastri, "Rita Dove's Poetic Expeditions," *Twentieth Century Literature* 58, no. 1 (April 1, 2012), 90–116; Claire Schwartz, "An Interview with Rita Dove," *The Virginia Quarterly Review* 92, no. 1 (Winter 2016), 164–171; John Shoptaw, "Review of *Thomas and Beulah*," *Black American Literature Forum* 21, no. 3 (1987), 335–341; "Twentieth-Century Demeter," *The New Yorker*, May 15, 1995, pp. 90–92; Craig Morgan Teicher, "PW talks with Rita Dove: Shaking up the Canon" [interview], *Publishers Weekly* 258, no. 38 (September 19, 2011), 38(1); Helen Vendler, "Identity Markers," *Callaloo* 17, no. 2 (1994), 381–399.

Drama

The consensus is that African American drama, or literature for the stage, essentially begins with William Wells Brown, who usually is also identified as the first African American novelist. Brown wrote two plays, *Experience; or, How to Give a Northern Man a Backbone* (1956) and *The Escape; Or, A Leap for Freedom* (1857). The former is linked to concerns of the abolitionist movement, of which Brown was a part; the play's protagonist is a minister from the North who supports slavery but who is, as fate would have it, sold into slavery himself, whereupon he changes his view of the institution. As one might guess, the latter play, *The Escape*, concerns an escape from slavery and draws on conventions of slave narratives, which often feature dramatic tales of fleeing slavery. As early as the 1820s, a writer now known as Mr. Brown (his first name is disputed) created a play titled *The Drama of King Shotaway*, which was produced in New York City in 1923. The play concerns a rebellion on the Caribbean Island of St. Vincent. (Brown was a native of the West Indies and a former sailor.) In addition to *The Drama of King Shotaway*, there were also performative, dramatic elements in much African American folklore and in African American folk music, such as work songs, which sometimes featured a dramatic "call and response" element. Also, the form of stage entertainment known as Minstrelsy featured dramatic sketches and skits as well as short melodramatic performances. Nonetheless, William Wells Brown is viewed as the first African American to become a bona fide dramatist.

Later in the nineteenth century, Pauline E. Hopkins wrote the play *Peculiar Sam; or, the Underground Railroad*, a drama combining music with historical elements based on the Underground Railroad. It was first staged in Boston, Massachusetts, in 1880.

Among the important signposts in the progress of African American drama is the play *Rachel*, by Angelina Weld Grimké; it was arguably the first widely successful, genuinely popular play by an African American playwright and performed by African Americans; it was first produced in 1916, in Washington, DC, and it dramatized the impact of lynching on an African American family. Although Paul Laurence Dunbar is known chiefly for his poetry, he also wrote plays, including the one-act *Winter Roses* (1899), a love story. Just after the turn of the century, Joseph Seamon Cotter Sr. wrote *Caleb, The Degenerate* (1903), which Peterson and others see as dramatizing "the industrial education and work philosophy of Booker T. Washington" (Peterson, "Drama," 229).

Between the era of Hopkins, Grimké, Cotter, and Dunbar and the era of the Harlem Renaissance, African American drama continued to grow slowly but steadily. W.E.B. Du Bois wrote and produced *The Star of Ethiopia* in 1913, and Mary ("Mamie") Powell Burrill, a Washington, DC, writer, published *They That Sit in Darkness* and *Aftermath* in 1919; the former concerns birth control, and the latter concerns an African American soldier who had served in World War I. Two of the most prolific playwrights of this era were Willis Richardson and Randolph Edmonds. Richardson's *The Chip Woman's Fortune* (1923) is considered the first dramatic play by an African American to be produced on Broadway. Richardson wrote dozens of other plays and also edited anthologies of African American drama. Edmonds is known for his numerous one-act plays, which were collected in such volumes as *Shades and Shadows* (1930) and *Six Plays for a Negro Theatre* (1934). Richardson and Edmonds are especially important figures because playwriting was their main focus, whereas some earlier writers, including Du Bois and Dunbar, wrote drama only occasionally. Additionally, Richardson made African American drama more visible by means of his anthologies, and Edmonds, a professor, taught playwriting and established theater companies affiliated with colleges. Thus both men helped expand the audience for African American drama.

The Harlem Renaissance in particular, and the decades of the 1920s and 1930s generally, were crucial to African American drama, which took a great leap forward then, especially with regard to the volume and quality of plays created and the variety of dramatic forms in which African

American writers worked. Harlem, New York, became an active site for theater; the magazines *The Crisis* and *Opportunity* offered awards for playwriting; and playwriting was among the arts that Du Bois, Alain Locke, and other "architects" of the Harlem Renaissance supported as part of a larger plan to cultivate the Talented Tenth. The musical play/revue *Shuffle Along*, by Noble Sissle and Eubie Blake, debuted in 1921, starring Josephine Baker and Paul Robeson. It took Broadway by storm and became a symbol of the Roaring Twenties. Writers connected with the Harlem Renaissance who wrote plays include Garland Anderson, Frank Wilson, Wallace Thurman, Georgia Douglas Johnson, John F. Matheus, and Eulalie Spence. Zora Neale Hurston's play *Color Struck* was published in the magazine *Fire!!* (1926). In Washington, DC, May Miller was beginning what was to become a prolific career as both playwright and poet; she received encouragement from Willis Richardson, Mary Burrill, and others. Her plays include *Scratches* (1929) and *Stragglers in the Dust* (1930). She also edited the anthology *Negro History in Thirteen Plays* (1934) with Richardson.

In 1930, Langston Hughes and Zora Neale Hurston began a promising but ill-fated collaboration on a musical and comedic play, *Mule Bone*, which drew on Hurston's short story "Bone of Contention" and, like the short story, was set in rural Florida. Unfortunately, an irreparable quarrel occurred, springing in part from their different relationships to a patron of the arts, Charlotte Osgood Mason, and in part from a personality conflict. In any event, they abandoned the collaboration even though they had made considerable progress on the manuscript, and *Mule Bone* was not produced until 1991, long after both

writers had died and legal issues had been sorted out. *Mule Bone* debuted on Broadway in February 1991, with music composed by Taj Mahal, who set some of Hughes's poetry to music for the production. The play was also published in 1991, accompanied by a full account of the controversy in 1930.

After the *Mule Bone* collaboration disintegrated, Hughes wrote the tragic play *Mulatto* in 1931. Four years later, while he was traveling in Mexico, a theatrical agent produced the play in upstate New York, drew interest from investors, and arranged for the play to be produced on Broadway, all unknown to Hughes (Ostrom, 260–261). Producer Martin Jones rewrote the third act, making it more melodramatic, without Hughes's permission. The play opened on Broadway on October 24, 1935, but met with harsh reviews. It was later restored to its original form and published in *Five Plays by Langston Hughes* (1963). Hughes's short story "Father and Son," included in the collection *The Ways of White Folks* (1934), uses the same characters and conflict as those in *Mulatto*.

In 1938, Hughes helped establish the avant-garde Harlem Suitcase Theatre at 317 West 125th Street in Harlem (Ostrom, 154). Actors, writers, and others associated with the group included Louise Thompson, Mary Savage, Grace Johnson, Dorothy Peterson, Toy Harper, Alta Douglas, Gwendolyn Bennett, Waring Cuney, Dorothy Maynor, and Robert Earl Jones (the father of James Earl Jones, who became a renowned theater and motion picture actor). Among the plays produced by the Harlem Suitcase Theatre was Hughes's *Don't You Want to Be Free?*

Although Hughes is known primarily as a poet, he produced many kinds of drama over the course of his career. In 1932, he published the one-act play *Scottsboro*

Limited, which concerned the Scottsboro Boys, and, in 1938, he wrote *Angelo Herndon Jones*, which concerned the arrest and trial of labor activist Angelo Herndon in Atlanta, Georgia. Hughes's comedic plays include *Little Ham* (1936) and *When the Jack Hollers* (1936), written with Arna Bontemps. His musical plays include *Tambourines to Glory* (1963); *Simply Heavenly* (1959), which is based on a character from his short fiction, Jesse B. Simple; and *Black Nativity: A Christmas Song Play* (1961), which is still produced frequently. With Elmer Rice and Kurt Weill, he collaborated on the opera *Street Scene* (1946), based on Rice's play of that title. He collaborated with Jan Meyerowitz on two operas—*The Barrier* (1950, based on Hughes's play *Mulatto*), and *Esther* (1957), based on the biblical character—as well as the oratorio *Five Foolish Virgins* (1954) and the Easter cantata *The Glory Around His Head* (1955). With William Grant Still, Hughes collaborated on the opera *Troubled Island* (1938), set in Haiti and based on Hughes's play of the same title. With James P. Johnson, composer of the famous 1920s song "Charleston," Hughes collaborated on a blues opera, *De Organizer* (1940). Other plays by Hughes include *Soul Gone Home* (1937), *The Road* (1935), *Jericho-Jim Crow* (1963), *The Sun Do Move* (1942), *Prodigal Son* (1965), and *Front Porch* (1938).

In addition to the energy supplied by the Harlem Renaissance, the Federal Theatre Project (FTP), one of the New Deal programs of Franklin D. Roosevelt's administration, also gave a boost to African American drama in the 1930s, and its creative energy carried into the 1940s (Fraden). Directed by Hallie Flanagan, the FTP included several subgroups known as Negro Units, which were devoted to developing African American drama. Abram Hill, Willis Richardson, Georgia Douglas Johnson, Richard Wright, Frank Wilson, Theodore Ward, Theodore Browne, Hughes Allison, Owen Dodson, and Rose McClendon were among those involved, in varying degrees, with the FTP, which also sponsored the famous production of an African American version of Shakespeare's *Macbeth*, produced and directed by John Houseman and Orson Welles. (Welles and Houseman also produced a stage version of Richard Wright's novel *Native Son* on Broadway in 1941.) Negro units existed in every region of the United States and in cities such as New York; Seattle, Washington; Cleveland, Ohio; Chicago, Illinois; Indianapolis, Indiana; and Atlanta. An archive of the FTP is held in the library at George Mason University.

In addition to Hughes, playwrights active in the 1950s included Alice Childress, Ossie Davis, and Loften Mitchell, who later wrote an important critical book (*Black Drama*, 1967). Arguably the two most important African American plays of the decade were James Baldwin's *Amen Corner* (1955), concerning a Black female minister in Harlem, and Lorraine Hansberry's *A Raisin in the Sun* (1959), a realistic drama about a Black family that takes its title from a poem ("Harlem") by Langston Hughes. With *A Raisin in the Sun*, Hansberry became the first African American female playwright to have a play produced on Broadway and also created one of the most significant, widely produced, and critically acclaimed works of American drama in the twentieth century. Her achievement symbolized how far African American theater had come in 100 years.

The Black Arts Movement of the 1960s ushered in the next great era of African American drama. Probably the most influential figure in Black theater in the 1960s was LeRoi Jones, later known as Amiri Baraka. His plays, which include *Dutchman* (1964), *The Slave* (1964), and *The Toilet* (1964), are unvarnished, provocative dramatizations of racism, race relations, class conflict, and intersections between sexuality and race. Baraka also founded the Black Arts Repertory Theatre/School, an influential drama group in Harlem. Adrienne Kennedy, Ed Bullins, Ben Caldwell, Ron Milner, Douglas Turner Ward, Vinnette Carroll, and Thomas Covington Dent are among the playwrights associated with this politically charged, artistically adventurous period of African American drama. As a playwright, teacher, and supporter of community theater, Rob Penny was an important figure in Pittsburgh, Pennsylvania, during this period.

In the latter third of the twentieth century, many important African American playwrights emerged. Charles Gordone won the Pulitzer Prize in drama in 1971 for his play *No Place to Be Somebody* (1969); he was the first African American playwright to win the Pulitzer in drama. Melvin Van Peebles, Phillip Hayes Dean, Richard Wesley, J. E. Franklin, Joseph A. Walker, Charles H. Fuller Jr., Samm-Art Williams, Jeff Stetson, and George C. Wolfe were among the other award-winning dramatists of this period. Ntozake Shange won critical acclaim with the enormously popular dramatic work, *for colored girls who have considered suicide/when the rainbow is enuf* (1975). Suzan Lori Parks has been another dynamic young voice in African American and American theater, winning the Pulitzer Prize in 2002 for her play *Topdog/Underdog* (2001). However, the most influential and widely acclaimed African American playwright of the period was August Wilson. Wilson's evocative, historically alert, and enormously innovative plays include

Ma Rainey's Black Bottom (1982), which won a Drama Critics Circle Award; *Fences* (1986), which won a Pulitzer Prize in 1987; and *The Piano Lesson* (1990). *Fences* was adapted into a motion picture in 2016.

By the time Shange, Parks, and Wilson had achieved their place of prominence in American theater, African American drama had come of age in every dramatic subgenre and theatrical venue, from musical plays and comedy to realistic drama, tragedy, and avant-garde theater, and from community theater and college drama programs to regional theater, Off-Broadway, Broadway, and the international stage.

More recent African American playwrights include the following: Branden Jacobs-Jenkins, whose plays include *Neighbors* and *Appropriate*; C. Rosalind Bell, whose plays include *The New Orleans Monologues* (2005), which concerns the aftermath of Hurricane Katrina in the summer 2005, and *1620 Bank Street* (2012), which explores the integration of a high school in the South in the 1970s; Joceylyn Bioh, whose plays include *School Girls; or the African Mean Girls Play* and *The Ladykiller's Love Story,* a musical; Tarell Alvin McCraney, who wrote *In Moonlight Black Boys Look Blue,* which is the basis for the motion picture, *Moonlight* (2016), and Antoinette Nwandu, whose plays include *Pass Over* and *Breach.* (see Cox in Resources at the end of this entry.)

Zell Miller's anthology, *Plays from the Boom Box Galaxy: Theater from the Hip-Hop Generation* appeared in 2009.

In 2011, Ted Shine and James V. Hatch edited *Black Theatre USA: Plays by African Americans From 1847 to 1938, Revised and Expanded Edition.*

In 2014, Broadway World highlighted the work of male Black playwrights Donald Allen II, Idris Goodwin, Glenn Gordon,

Eric Holmes, Glenn Nsangou, and Nathan Yungerberg (see BWW Newsdesk in Resources).

Hans A. Ostrom

See also: Baraka, Amiri; Grimké, Angelina Weld; Hansberry, Lorraine; Hughes, Langston; Hurston, Zora Neale; Parks, Suzan-Lori; Shange, Ntozake; Smith, Anna Deavere; Wilson, August.

Resources

Esther Spring Arata and Nicholas John Rotoli, *Black American Playwrights, 1800 to the Present: A Bibliography* (Metuchen, NJ: Scarecrow Press, 1976); BWW Newsdesk, "Six Black Male Playwrights to Be Featured in The New Black Fest's *Hands Up* This Fall," Broadway World, August 22, 2014: https://www.broadwayworld.com/article/Six-Black-Male-Playwrights-to-Be-Featured-in-The-New-Black-Fests-HANDS-UP-This-Fall-20140822 (accessed 2019); Gordon Cox, "Take Note: These Female Playwrights of Color Should Be on Your Radar," *Variety*, June 23, 2017: https://variety.com/2017/legit/news/kilroys-list-2017-female-playwrights-of-color-1202474906/ (accessed 2019); Thadious M. Davis and Trudier Harris, eds., *Dictionary of Literary Biography*, vol. 38, *Afro American Writers After 1955: Dramatists and Prose Writers* (Detroit: Gale, 1985); Harry J. Elam, *Taking It to the Streets: The Social Protest Theater of Luis Valdez and Amiri Baraka* (Ann Arbor: University of Michigan Press, 1997); Harry J. Elam and Robert Alexander, eds., *Colored Contradictions: An Anthology of Contemporary African-American Plays* (New York: Plume, 1996); Harry J. Elam and David Krasner, eds., *African American Performance and Theater History: A Critical Reader* (New York: Oxford University Press, 2001); Federal Theatre Project materials [archive], George Mason University Library, Washington, DC, http://www.gmu.edu/library/specialcollections/federal.html; Ann M. Fox, "A Different Integration: Race and Disability in Early-Twentieth-Century African American Drama by Women," *Legacy: A Journal of American Women Writers* 30, no. 1 (January 1, 2013), 151–171; Rena Fraden, *Blueprints for a Black Federal Theatre, 1935–1939* (Cambridge: Cambridge University Press, 1994); Christy Gavin, ed., *African American Women Playwrights: A Research Guide* (New York: Garland, 1999); Anita Gonzalez, "Diversifying African American Drama," *Theatre* 19, no. 1 (2009), 59–66; Christine Rauchfuss Gray, *Willis Richardson, Forgotten Pioneer of African-American Drama* (Westport, CT: Greenwood Press, 1999); Samuel A. Hay, *African American Theatre: An Historical and Critical Analysis* (Cambridge: Cambridge University Press, 1994); Trudier Harris, *Reading Contemporary African American Drama: Fragments of History, Fragments of Self* (New York: Peter Lang, 2007); Errol G. Hill and James V. Hatch, *A History of African American Theatre* (Cambridge: Cambridge University Press, 2003); Langston Hughes: *The Collected Works of Langston Hughes*, ed. Arnold Rampersad, 16 vols. (Columbia: University of Missouri Press, 2001–2004), esp. vols. 5 and 6; *Five Plays by Langston Hughes*, ed. Webster Smalley (Bloomington: Indiana University Press, 1963); Zora Neale Hurston and Langston Hughes, *Mule Bone: A Comedy of Negro Life*, ed. George Houston Bass and Henry Louis Gates Jr. (New York: HarperPerennial, 1991); David Krasner, *A Beautiful Pageant: African American Theatre, Drama, and Performance in the Harlem Renaissance, 1910–1927* (New York: Palgrave Macmillan, 2002); Taj Mahal, *Mule Bone: Music Composed and Performed by Taj Mahal/Lyrics by Langston Hughes* [compact disc] (Santa Monica, CA: Grammavision/Rhino Records, 1991); Patrick Maley, "What Is and What Aint: *Topdog/Underdog* [by Suzan-Lori Parks] and the American Hustle," *Modern Drama* 56, no. 2 (Summer 2013), 186–205; Zell Miller, *Plays from the Boom Box Galaxy: Theater from the Hip-Hop Generation* (New York: Theatre Communications Group, 2009); Loften Mitchell, *Black Drama: The*

Story of the American Negro in the Theatre (New York: Hawthorn Books, 1967); Hans Ostrom, *A Langston Hughes Encyclopedia* (Westport, CT: Greenwood Press, 2002); Bernard L. Peterson: *A Century of Musicals in Black and White: An Encyclopedia of Musical Stage Works by, About, or Involving African Americans* (Westport, CT: Greenwood Press, 1993); *Contemporary Black American Playwrights and Their Plays: A Biographical Directory and Dramatic Index* (Westport, CT: Greenwood Press, 1988); "Drama," in *The Oxford Companion to African American Literature*, ed. William L. Andrews, Frances Smith Foster, and Trudier Harris (New York: Oxford University Press, 1997), 228–234; *Early Black American Playwrights and Dramatic Writers* (Westport, CT: Greenwood Press, 1990); Charlie Reilly, ed., *Conversations with Amiri Baraka* (Jackson: University Press of Mississippi, 1994); Willis Richardson and May Miller, eds., *Negro History in Thirteen Plays* (Washington, DC: Associated Publishers, 1935); Audrey Seraphin, "10 Contemporary Black Playwrights You Should Know," *ArtsBoston*, February 6, 2018: http://artsboston.org/2018/02/06/10-contemporary-black-playwrights-you-should- know/ (accessed 2019); Ted Shine and James V. Hatch, *Black Theatre USA: Plays by African Americans From 1847 to 1938, Revised and Expanded Edition* (New York: Free Press, 2011); Allen L. Woll, *Dictionary of the Black Theatre: Broadway, Off-Broadway, and Selected Harlem Theatre* (Westport, CT: Greenwood Press, 1983).

Du Bois, W.E.B. (1868–1963)

Scholar, activist, author, and editor. Renowned for his work as an activist and scholar, William Edward Burghardt Du Bois (usually pronounced *do-boyz*, as opposed to the French pronunciation) wrote with prophetic passion and published in a wide range of genres. Fully aware that his words affected readers emotionally as well as intellectually, Du Bois drew upon the duality of his personal experiences as a Black writer raised in an Episcopalian family in rural Great Barrington, Massachusetts, to create works that explore the question of what it means "to be black and to be an American." His *The Souls of Black Folk* (1903) reveals the tragedy of the Black experience in America and has been said by some to be to Black literature what *The Adventures of Huckleberry Finn* is to the canon of Anglo-American literature. In 1933, James Weldon Johnson wrote that the impact of *Souls* was "greater upon and within the Negro race than any other single book published in this country since *Uncle Tom's Cabin*." The concept of "double consciousness" articulated in the book remains a potent idea in Black Studies (see Adell and Pittman in Resources at the end of this entry). It concerns the extent to which, because of historical and social circumstances, African Americans are virtually forced to be conscious of themselves as individuals but simultaneously and constantly as Black Americans, thereby being "doubly conscious" in ways White Americans rarely experience.

Du Bois, the first Black to graduate from Harvard University with a PhD, completed his dissertation, *The Suppression of the African Slave Trade to the United States of America, 1638–1870*, in 1895. He also studied abroad in Berlin, Germany. With *The Souls of Black Folk* he began to develop the distinctive voice that would later define him as an outspoken activist and as the leader of the National Association for the Advancement of Colored People (NAACP). Du Bois was the only Black man elected to the board of directors of the NAACP when it was founded, in 1910; among other duties as director of research and publications, he would edit and write for the organization's magazine, *The Crisis*.

Du Bois had already founded and edited the monthly journal *Horizon* (1907–1910) as part of the Niagara Movement, which had been organized from a meeting in 1905 of twenty-nine Black leaders to protest for Black civil and political rights. As editor of *The Crisis*, during the Harlem Renaissance, Du Bois sought to publish works of literature that were set in Black life but not so directly propagandistic that they ignored the principles of art. Under Du Bois's leadership, *The Crisis* became the primary vehicle in the nation for literary art and criticism written by Black Americans, a position it maintained until *Opportunity: A Journal of Negro Life* began publication in 1923. Among many intellectuals, editors, and writers responsible for the Harlem Renaissance, Du Bois was arguably the most influential figure, articulating views about the New Negro and the Talented Tenth, cultivating support for the arts and developing personal relationships with writers including Langston Hughes, Countee Cullen, and Jessie Redmon Fauset. (Cullen was married briefly to Du Bois's daughter, Yolanda.) In this era especially, Du Bois's assertive political stance was often perceived to be in contrast to that of Booker T. Washington, who tended to emphasize economic self-reliance over political activism.

A prolific writer, Du Bois wrote the short story "The Coming of John"; a biography, *John Brown* (1909); and poems including "A Litany of Atlanta," "A Hymn to the People," "Christ of the Andes," "The Prayer of the Bantu," and "The Prayers of the God," most of which were first published in *Horizon*. His novels, *The Quest of the Silver Fleece* (1911) and *Dark Princess: A Romance* (1928), are written in the drawing-room vernacular of Black America's intelligentsia, to which Du Bois belonged.

Du Bois's political views evolved considerably. At first he aspired chiefly to be an academic, taking a position at Atlanta University. He subsequently left academia to become more of an activist and leader, and he believed that African Americans could exert more control over their fate in the United States by pursuing education and changing the perception of Black Americans through the arts. At that time he thought a vanguard of educated African Americans could lead the way—hence the "Talented Tenth" concept. As Jim Crow laws (segregation) and lynching continued in the South, however, and as economic opportunities for Blacks remained paltry, even after African Americans served nobly in the Great War (World War I), Du Bois began to doubt his approach and explored other avenues. Although Du Bois felt that his writings and political activism could change the fate of Black America, he later became disillusioned with America. In 1961, he joined the Communist Party and moved to Accra, Ghana, where he obtained citizenship, and died on August 27, 1963, on the eve of the civil rights march on Washington, DC.

Du Bois's other writings include *The Philadelphia Negro* (1899), a sociological study; *The Star of Ethiopia* (1913); *The Negro* (1915); an open letter to President Woodrow Wilson (1916); essays in *The Crisis* on Blacks in the war in Europe (1919); *Dark Water: Voices from Within the Veil* (1920); *The Brownies' Book* (1920), a magazine for Black children; *The Gift of Black Folks: The Negroes in the Making of America* (1924); "A Lunatic or Traitor" (1924); "The Negro Mind Reaches Out" (1925); *Black Reconstruction* (1935); a weekly column in the *Pittsburgh Courier* (1936–1938); *Black Folk Then and Now* (1939); *Dusk of*

Dawn (1940); columns for the *Chicago Defender* (1945–1948); *Encyclopedia of the Negro and Democracy: Colonies and Peace* (1945); *The World and Africa* (1947); *The Ordeal of the Mansart* (1957); and *Black Flame* (1957). He began work on the *Encyclopedia Africana* project in 1961.

David Levering Lewis published a Pulitzer Prize-winning biography of Du Bois in 2009 (Lewis).

Imelda Hunt

See also: Harlem Renaissance; Protest Literature; Spirituals.

Resources

Sandra Adell, *Double-Consciousness/Double Bind: Theoretical Issues in Twentieth-Century Black Literature* (Urbana: Illinois University Press, 1994); Williams L. Andrews, ed., *Critical Essays on W.E.B. Du Bois* (Boston: G. K. Hall, 1985); Herbert Aptheker, *The Literary Legacy of W.E.B. Du Bois* (White Plains, NY: Kraus International, 1989); Houston A. Baker Jr., "The Black Man of Culture: W.E.B. Du Bois and 'The Souls of Black Folk,'" in Baker's *Long Black Song* (Charlottesville: University Press of Virginia, 1972); Keith Byerman, *Seizing the Word: History, Art, and the Self in the Work of W.E.B. Du Bois* (Athens: University of Georgia Press, 1994); W.E.B. Du Bois: *Black Reconstruction* (New York: Harcourt, Brace, 1935); *Dark Princess: A Romance* (New York: Harcourt, Brace, 1928); *Dusk of Dawn: An Essay Toward an Autobiography of a Race Concept* (New York: Harcourt, Brace, & Co, 1940); *The Negro* (New York: Holt, 1915); *The Ordeal of Mansart* (New York: Mainstream Publishers, 1957); *The Philadelphia Negro: A Social Study* (Philadelphia: University of Pennsylvania Press, 1899); *The Quest of the Silver Fleece: A Novel* (Chicago: A. C. McClurg, 1911); *The Souls of Black Folk* (Chicago: A. C. McClurg, 1903); *The World and Africa* (New York: Viking, 1947); Gerald Early, ed., *Lure and Loathing: Essays on Race, Identity, and the Ambivalence of Assimilation* (New York: Allen Lane, 1993); Robert Gooding-Williams, *In the Shadow of Du Bois: Afro-Modern Political Thought in America* (Cambridge, MA: Harvard University Press, 2009); Gerald Horne and Mary Young, *W.E.B. Du Bois: An Encyclopedia* (Westport, CT: Greenwood Press, 2001); Levering Lewis, *W.E.B. Du Bois: a Biography 1868–1963* (New York: Holt, 2009); Dale Peterson, "Notes from the Underworld: Dostoyevsky, Du Bois, and the Discovery of Ethnic Soul," *Massachusetts Review* 35 (Summer 1994), 225–247; John P. Pittman, "Double Consciousness," *Stanford Encyclopedia of Philosophy* [digital], March 21, 2016: https://plato.stanford.edu/entries/double-consciousness/ (accessed 2019); Arnold Rampersad, *The Art and Imagination of W.E.B. Du Bois* (New York: Schocken, 1990).

Dunbar, Paul Laurence (1872–1906)

Poet, essayist, fiction writer, playwright, and songwriter. Paul Laurence Dunbar was the first African American poet to gain national acclaim before the Harlem Renaissance. He was born in Dayton, Ohio, to former Kentucky slaves, Matilda and Joshua Dunbar. His father escaped slavery by fleeing to freedom in Canada, then returned to the United States and joined the Massachusetts 55th Regiment and the 5th Massachusetts Colored Cavalry during the Civil War. Matilda, a widow with two sons, was freed after the Civil War. During Dunbar's childhood years, his father told him plantation stories, and his mother recited poetry to him. Although Dunbar himself had not been enslaved, he interacted with the last generation of African Americans who were slaves. This early influence shaped his renowned Southern plantation Negro dialect poems. At age six he composed his first poem (Cunningham, 10). In developing his own poetic voice, Dunbar read the works of Oliver Wendell Holmes, Henry Wadsworth Longfellow, John Keats, and Alfred Lord Tennyson. His mother supported Dunbar throughout his writing career and ensured that he received his education, despite the family's poverty. The only African American student at Dayton Central High, Dunbar excelled in academics and extracurricular activities. He served as editor of the school's newspaper, was president of the Literary Society, and was a member of the debating team. He and a classmate, Orville Wright, edited a short-lived community Black newspaper, the *Dayton Tattler*.

After he graduated from high school in 1891, racial discrimination prevented Dunbar from attending college. He took a job in Dayton's Callahan Building as an elevator operator. When he wasn't running the elevator, he wrote poetry. He also published essays in local newspapers and magazines. Dunbar became locally known after James Newton Mathews invited him to recite his poetry at the Western Association of Writers yearly meeting in Dayton. Financial backing from Mathews allowed Dunbar to publish his first book of poetry, *Oak and Ivy*, in 1893. Also that year, he attended the World's Columbian Exposition, worked as a clerk for the Haitian Pavilion, and met Frederick Douglass. Douglass referred to Dunbar as "one of the sweetest songsters his race has produced of whom I hope great things" (Cunningham, 105).

In 1895, Dunbar moved to Toledo, Ohio, with the help of a psychiatrist, Dr. H. A. Tobey, and a lawyer, Charles Thatcher, both fans of his work. They arranged opportunities for Dunbar to recite his poems publicly, and they financially backed his second book, *Majors and Minors* (1896). The "majors" were Dunbar's poems written in Standard English verse, while his "minors" were poems written in Southern plantation Negro dialect. "*Majors and Minors* [became] the most notable collection of poems ever issued by a Negro in the United States" (Brawley, 40). During this time, Dunbar began corresponding with Alice Ruth Moore, a light-skinned teacher and writer from New Orleans, Louisiana. In 1897, he traveled to London on a poetry recitation tour. Upon returning to the United States, he married Alice and worked as a reading room assistant in the Library of Congress until 1898. However, Dunbar's health declined, possibly because of exposure to dust while working in the library. He developed tuberculosis and drank alcohol to try to cure it. From 1898 to 1900, he collaborated with Will Cook on Black musical plays. He separated from Alice in 1902 and continued to write until his death in 1906.

A versatile writer, Dunbar published short stories, novels, theatrical contributions, song lyrics, and articles. His novels include *Folks from Dixie* (1898), *Sport of the Gods* (1902), *The Strength of Gideon & Other Stories* (1900), and *The Fanatics* (1901). His theatrical contributions include *Clorindy, or the Origin of the Cakewalk* (1898) and *In Dahomey: A Negro Musical Comedy* (1902). An edition of his *Complete Stories* was published in 2005.

Dunbar wrote two kinds of poetry. In one he replicated African American vernacular or Black dialect; these poems, many of them comic, were especially popular with White readers (see Harrell and Nurhussein in Resources at the end of this entry). In the other he wrote in Standard English; many of these poems have joined the canon of lyric poetry in English. "We Wear the Mask," perhaps his most famous poem, is widely reprinted in anthologies and concerns African Americans' need to present a "mask" to the dominant White culture so as to survive. "The Haunted Oak" is a powerful poem about lynching.

It was rare during this time for a Black writer to achieve notoriety in such mainstream magazines as the *Saturday Evening Post*, *Harper's Weekly*, and *The Atlantic Monthly*. Dunbar marked a place in African American history by being the first Black author to be read by Blacks and Whites before the Harlem Renaissance. Prominent White author and literary critic William Dean Howells praised *Majors and Minors* in an 1896 book review in *Harper's Weekly*. Although this review propelled Dunbar into national recognition, his work, specifically the dialect pieces, garnered both acclaim and criticism. Blacks accused him of conceding to racist ideals in his dialect pieces (Harrell, Nurhussein). He often struggled between being a martyr for the African American plight and being accepted by White audiences. His reputation as a writer in the tradition of lyric poetry in English, however, has overtaken his reputation as a dialect poet.

Shawntaye M. Scott

See also: Dialect Poetry; Lyric Poetry; Vernacular.

Resources

Primary Sources: Paul Laurence Dunbar: *Clorindy, or the Origin of the Cakewalk*, music by Will Marion Cook and lyrics by Paul Laurence Dunbar (New York: Witmark Music, 1898); *The Collected Poetry of Paul Laurence Dunbar*, ed. Joanne Braxton (Charlottesville: University Press of Virginia, 1993); *The Complete Stories of Paul Laurenced Dunbar*, ed. Gene Andrew Jarrett and Thomas Lewis Morgan (Athens, OH: Ohio University Press, 2005); *Dream Lovers: An Operatic Romance*, with music by Samuel Coleridge-Taylor (London: Boosey, 1898); *Folks from Dixie* (New York: Dodd, Mead, 1898); *In His Own Voice: The Dramatic and Other Uncollected Works of Paul Laurence Dunbar*, ed. Herbert Woodward Martin and Ronald Primeau (Athens: Ohio University Press, 2002); *Lyrics of Love and Laughter* (New York: Dodd, Mead, 1903); *Lyrics of Lowly Life* (New York: Dodd, Mead, 1896); *Lyrics of Sunshine and Shadow* (New York: Dodd, Mead, 1905); *Lyrics of the Hearthside* (New York: Dodd, Mead, 1899); *Majors and Minors* (Toledo, OH: Hadley & Hadley, 1895); *Oak and Ivy* (Dayton, OH: United Brethren Publishing House, 1893); *Poems of Cabin and Field* (New York: Dodd, Mead, 1899); *The Sport of the Gods* (New York: Dodd, Mead, 1902); *When Malindy Sings* (New York: Dodd, Mead, 1903).

Secondary Sources: Elizabeth Alexander, "Dunbar Lives!," *African American Review* 41, no. 2 (Summer 2007), 395–401; Marcellus Blount, "Paul Laurence Dunbar and the African American Elegy," *African American Review* 41, no. 2 (Summer 2007), 239–246; Robert Bone, *Down Home: A History of Afro-American Short Fiction from Its Beginnings to the End of the Harlem Renaissance* (New York: Putnam's, 1975); Benjamin G. Brawley, *Paul Laurence Dunbar: Poet of His People* (Chapel Hill: University of North Carolina Press, 1936); Virginia Cunningham, *Paul Laurence Dunbar and His Song* (New York: Dodd, Mead, 1947); Christopher C. DeSantis, "The Dangerous Marrow of Southern Tradition: Charles W. Chesnutt, Paul Laurence Dunbar, and the Paternalist Ethos at the Turn of the Century," *Southern Quarterly* 38 (Winter 2000), 79–97; Michele Elam, "Dunbar's Children," *African American Review* 41, no. 2 (Summer 2007), 259(10); Willie J. Harrell, *We Wear the Mask: Paul Laurence Dunbar and the Politics of Representative Reality* (Kent, OH: Kent State University Press, 2010); James Weldon Johnson, *The Book of American Negro Poetry* (New York: Harcourt, Brace, 1922; rev. ed., 1931); Carol S. Loranger, "The Outcast Poetics of Paul Laurence Dunbar and Edwin Arlington

Robinson," *Studies in American Naturalism* 10, no. 2 (2016), 133–149; Jay Martin, ed., *A Singer in the Dawn: Reinterpretations of Paul Laurence Dunbar* (New York: Dodd, Mead, 1975); Nadia Nurhussein, "'On Flow'ry Beds of Ease': Paul Laurence Dunbar and the Cultivation of Dialect Poetry in the *Century*," *American Periodicals: A Journal of History & Criticism* 20, no. 1 (2010), 46–67; William M. Ramsey, "Dunbar's Dixie," *Southern Literary Journal* 32 (1999), 30–45; J. Saunders Redding, *To Make a Poet Black* (Chapel Hill: University of North Carolina Press, 1939); Peter Revell, *Paul Laurence Dunbar* (Boston: Twayne, 1979); Jean Wagner, *Black Poets of the United States, from Paul Laurence Dunbar to Langston Hughes* (Urbana: University of Illinois Press, 1973); Lida Keck Wiggins, *The Life and Works of Paul Laurence Dunbar* (Naperville, IL: J. L. Nichols, 1907).

E

Elaw, Zilpha (ca. 1790–1873)

Preacher and autobiographer. Elaw was born free near Philadelphia, Pennsylvania. Her original surname is not known. Her *Memoirs of the Life, Religious Experience, and Ministerial Travels and Labours of Mrs. Zilpha Elaw, an American Female of Colour* (1845) recounts her pious upbringing in the free state of Pennsylvania. Having lost her mother at twelve, she was placed by her father with the Mitchell family, Quakers who exposed Elaw to their quiet, inner religion. Unused to their form of worship, Elaw fell to sin but was later converted following a dream where the angel Gabriel announced the coming of the Day of Judgment, which forced her to realize that she was unprepared to meet and be judged by God. Attempting to find God, Elaw prayed, and in the midst of singing, she had a vision of Jesus, whose "very looks spoke, and said 'Thy prayer is accepted, I own thy name.'" Her memoir was reprinted in an anthology edited by William Andrews (1986).

In 1808, Elaw joined a Methodist group and converted. In 1810, she met Joseph Elaw, a fellow Christian, married him, and moved to Burlington, New Jersey. Two years later, she gave birth to her daughter. Her husband died in 1823, leaving Elaw to work as a domestic in order to raise their daughter. In 1828, Elaw began her itinerant ministry, later traveling south at personal risk, for as a free Black person, she could have been arrested and sold into slavery, and as a woman preaching to slaves, she was a threat to the cultural and economic institution of oppression. In 1840, she traveled to London, England, where she preached for five years while writing her *Memoirs*, which were published in 1845 and which allude to a desire to return to the United States. Unfortunately, nothing further is known of Elaw following that publication. (*See* Autobiography.)

Pamela Ralston

See also: Autobiography.

Resources

William Andrews, ed., *Sisters of the Spirit: Three Black Women's Autobiographies of the Nineteenth Century* (Bloomington: Indiana University Press, 1986); Kimberly Blockett, "Disrupting Print: Emigration, the Press, and Narrative Subjectivity in the British Preaching and Writing of Zilpha Elaw, 1840–1860s," *MELUS: Multi-Ethnic Literature of the United States* 40, no. 3 (2015), 94–109; Rosetta Renae Haynes, *Radical Spiritual Motherhood: Autobiography and Empowerment in Nineteenth-Century African American Women* (Baton Rouge: Louisiana State University Press, 2011); Sue E. Houchins, ed., *Spiritual Narratives* (New York: Oxford University Press, 1988); Jocelyn Moody, *Sentimental Confessions: Spiritual Narratives of Nineteenth-Century African American Women* (Athens: University of Georgia Press, 2001); Mitzy Smith, "'Unbossed and Unbought': Zilpha Elaw and Old Elizabeth and a Political Discourse of Origins," *Black Theology* 9, no. 3 (June 22, 2011), 287–311.

Ellison, Ralph (1914–1994)

Novelist and essayist. Ralph Ellison is best known for his novel *Invisible Man* (1952), one of the most enduring, ambitious, and important American novels. He was born on March 1, 1914, in Oklahoma City, Oklahoma. He studied classical music at Tuskegee Institute in Alabama from 1933 to 1936, but failed to complete his degree because of financial difficulties. He started his writing career in New York City, beginning with a review published in 1937 in *New Challenge*, a journal edited by Richard Wright. He published a number of short stories in the early 1940s prior to his masterwork, *Invisible Man*, which won the National Book Award in 1953. Although he published two collections of essays during his lifetime—*Shadow and Act* (1964) and *Going to the Territory* (1986)—he never managed to complete a second novel, much to the disappointment of the American public who waited eagerly, in vain, for a follow-up to *Invisible Man*. Ellison spent his life composing an enormous work that he never completed. Much of the manuscript for it was destroyed in a fire in 1967, but it is generally agreed that he was simply unable to produce something that would match the power of his first novel. A version of his work-in-progress was published posthumously as *Juneteenth* (1999), to poor reviews.

Published at the beginning of the Civil Rights Movement, *Invisible Man* contains elements of protest, especially as it reflects on the meaning of the Harlem, New York, race riots of the 1930s and 1940s. Yet the more revolutionary Black activists of the 1960s criticized the novel because the narrator refuses to participate fully in those riots. Even the literary critic Irving Howe criticized Ellison for not taking a clear political stand in his works, and for not writing the kind of protest novel that Richard Wright had written, such as *Native Son*. In his essay "The World and the Jug," Ellison defends himself vigorously against Howe's attack, arguing essentially that ideology should not be the driving force behind fiction. Militant activists of the 1960s interpreted the fate of *Invisible Man*'s protagonist–narrator—exile in a hole—as a sign of his cowardice, or as escape from confrontation. Defenders of the novel and Ellison himself saw the narrator as an individualist and a victim of a fate that seems beyond his control. Virtually everything that happens to him in the novel stems from the fact that he was born Black in a world that refuses to recognize him as an individual. His quest to discover his identity cannot be separated from his race, and the injustice of that situation is precisely what sets the narrator in motion and eventually propels him into the hole where he writes the novel. Invisible Man would not be able to tell his story without first reflecting on his experiences, many of which are based on humiliation, abuse, and the loss of self-control.

Invisible Man is a novel of ideas, as surreal as it is emotionally gripping. Like those of a dream, the details of the narrative are clearly symbolic, and the reader is encouraged to figure out what everything means, even though the narrator seems unable to do so. The famous Battle Royal scene, for instance, or the scenes in Liberty Paints and in the hospital afterward are clearly allegorical. They represent some version of America where White men hold the power and Black men who work for them are both invisible and blind. As the narrator describes such scenes, he plays to the reader's confusion. Though he is composing his narration from his well-lit hole in the ground, he brings readers into the perspective of his younger, naïve self, asking them to share his mystification and refusing to interpret the world he describes.

Marking the beginning of his dreamlike journey is an actual dream of his grandfather, an ambiguous figure who seemed mad on his deathbed as he offered contradictory advice to the next generation. In the dream, this ex-slave mocks the narrator and gives him a prophetic note that reads, "Keep this n—boy running." This written message appears after a watershed moment in the narrator's life: he has received a scholarship to the local Black college after subjecting himself to humiliation and physical abuse at the Battle Royal. There are, in fact, a number of incidents in the novel in which the narrator's identity is controlled by written messages from powerful men: the letters he carries from the college administrator, Bledsoe, to prospective employers in New York, for instance, or the name given to him by Brother Jack when he joins the Brotherhood. He is blind to these messages because he only slowly learns the meaning of his grandfather's dream: that he will keep running until he takes charge of his own destiny.

Part of the narrator's problem is that he does not recognize the nature of power until he has been destroyed by it. Another part is that he too readily accepts the version of success projected by the dominant culture. He is drawn to money and fame and feels that college is the only way to achieve them. At the same time, he disdains the authentic Black folk history that has partially formed him. The event that ruins his college career demonstrates this division: he is ordered to drive Mr. Norton, a rich, White trustee, to meet Jim Trueblood, a poor, Black sharecropper. Trueblood narrates the story of how he unconsciously impregnated his daughter while Norton listens, fascinated,

and the narrator grows distraught at Norton's reaction and at Trueblood's existence, which is a source of shame for the narrator. The forces of Black folk culture and of White power contend throughout the novel, and the narrator is often caught between them and eventually thrust out by them, just as in the Battle Royal.

The individual and the group constitute another pair of antagonistic forces in *Invisible Man*. The pressures to conform to the vision of the college are at war with the narrator's understanding of his own free will. He gets in trouble for following Mr. Norton's orders even though he thought he was doing what was expected of him. Bledsoe, the college president, tries to convince the narrator that if he is to have any power at all, he must make decisions according to his own free will while hiding the fact that he has made these decisions. Ironically, Bledsoe undercuts this advice by sabotaging the narrator's progress when he arrives in New York. The same tension is felt when the narrator joins the Brotherhood and is trained to make speeches for their cause. At certain moments during his speeches, his emotions pour out of him, and the Brotherhood—a Communist organization that relies on precision, science, and history rather than the emotions of an individual—reprimands him and takes away what little power he has.

One memorable speech occurs in a large stadium when the narrator falters, recovers, then screams to the audience, "Look at me!" He confesses that a transformation is occurring right there on the stage: "I feel, I feel suddenly that I have become *more human*" (*Invisible Man*, 345–346). The development of his understanding of what it means to be human constitutes the novel's progress, but the movement of the novel is more like a downward spiral than a straight line. In the prologue, he describes history as a boomerang that will hit you in the head if you are not careful, and his life reflects a similar pattern. After the stadium speech, most of the members of the Brotherhood denounce him for his recklessness, his inattention to history, and his individualistic disregard of the good of the group. Like Bledsoe, they take away the power he has developed by preventing him from making speeches in Harlem. Yet he defies them in a funeral speech following the death of his only friend, Brother Tod Clifton.

Clifton's death provides a challenge for the reader as well as the narrator because he has left his position in the seemingly benevolent Brotherhood to sell racist icons—paper Sambo dolls—on the streets. Not only has he become a two-bit hustler, but he has chosen to peddle an object that the narrator considers an "obscenity." Clifton's downward spiral is mystifying, and the narrator recalls how Clifton, confronted by the militant Black activist Ras the Exhorter, suggests that men are tempted to plunge outside history. The narrator, of course, plunges outside history into his hole, so even though he is troubled by Clifton's decision to make money at the expense of the dignity of his race, he chooses to focus on Clifton's humanity in the funeral speech. There is much at stake here, for the narrator comes to realize that history has already left out men like himself and like Clifton, that they are invisible from history's point of view. Clifton surrenders to the condition of invisibility, which is a tragic refusal because he has the opportunity, like Louis Armstrong in the prologue and like the narrator in his writing of the book, to turn that invisibility into art. Despite Clifton's failure, the narrator insists on preserving his friend's dignity after his death by recognizing his essential humanity despite his flaws.

The Brotherhood again condemns the narrator for eschewing their party line, and he is finally able to recognize the hypocrisy of the organization and the contradictions of his role within it. Yet he has nowhere to go, which has been his condition throughout the novel. He tries to return to Harlem, but its streets are now a chaos of riots and madness. Disguising himself in sunglasses, he is mistaken for a man named Rinehart, who is revealed to be a protean trickster figure, a preacher, lover, and con man rolled into one. The narrator realizes that becoming Rinehart could benefit him, but he discards the disguise because he realizes that he is not Rinehart: adopting another's identity is not the solution. He is left with the fragments of the facets of his own identity that have been handed to him, and that he has carried around in his briefcase throughout the book, including a bank in the form of a racist depiction of Black people, one of the Sambo dolls Clifton had sold, the name that the Brotherhood gave him, and his scholarship to college. After falling into a hole during the riots, he destroys these items and, through the process of telling his story, begins to discover who he has really been all along.

The self-reliance that the narrator slowly develops is reminiscent of the great American thinkers of the nineteenth century, including Ellison's namesake, Ralph Waldo Emerson. Upon accepting the National Book Award for *Invisible Man*, Ellison highlighted his admiration for American literary tradition: "If I were asked in all seriousness just what I considered to be the chief significance of *Invisible Man* as a fiction, I would reply: Its experimental attitude, and its attempt to return to the mood of personal moral responsibility for democracy which typified the best of our nineteenth-century fiction" (*Shadow*, 102). One of the novel's epigraphs is from Melville's *Benito Cereno*, a work about the failure of this personal moral responsibility with regard to Black people. *Invisible Man*'s strength derives partly from Ellison's understanding of this American literary tradition, coupled with the fact that the African American perspective within it had been underrepresented before the 1950s. The first section of Ellison's essay collection *Shadow and Act* develops this theme as it delves into literary history of the nineteenth and twentieth centuries, scrutinizing individual writers such as Mark Twain, Stephen Crane, and Richard Wright. The second section in this collection focuses on music, and Ellison's perspective on jazz and blues is as clear and as valuable as his perspective on literature is. Many critics have detailed the connection between music and *Invisible Man*, a novel that reveals a deep knowledge of the blues and its folklore and that is structured as a kind of theme-and-variation with a good deal of jazzlike improvisation along the way.

Shadow and Act did not fully placate Ellison's readers, who continued to look for another novel. Interviewers consistently asked Ellison about his progress, and he methodically deflected them. His short fiction, originally published before *Invisible Man*, was also sparse, yet it was collected posthumously and published under the title *"Flying Home" and Other Stories* (1996). Although it contains some masterpieces, including the title story and "King of the Bingo Game" (1944), this collection is generally viewed in relation to *Invisible Man*. The power of Ellison's stories is not lessened by their scope, though: they are as emotionally intense as his grand work and, in some cases, more honest because they are less ambitious. The story "Mister Toussan" (1941) involves the interplay between

history, folklore, and storytelling, but it does not shoulder the burden felt by *Invisible Man* to say something enormous about this interplay.

Ellison's essays, collected in *Going to the Territory* (1986) as well as in *Shadow and Act*, also are frequently seen as potential insights into *Invisible Man*, yet they have merit apart from the novel. Like its predecessor, the latter collection of essays focuses on literature and music, but there is an even greater sense of history in them as well as insightful pronouncements on American government. Ellison also published fragments of what would become *Juneteenth* in his lifetime, but by all accounts the work was chaotic and unfinished despite his four decades of work on it. Ellison's literary executor, John Callahan, pieced together some of these fragments and published them as *Juneteenth* in 1999; the critical reception was hostile, both to the work and to Callahan's attempts to make a coherent story. It is a story of Reverend Hickman and Senator Sunraider, known as "Bliss" as a child. Bliss had been abandoned as a child, following his White mother's false accusation of rape against Hickman's brother. Bliss's transformation into a race-baiting politician and Hickman's continued protection of him despite this act continues, in a way, Invisible Man's realization at Tod Clifton's funeral: racism is part of the American fabric, but forgiveness and healing are possible. The fact that this message is not fully developed in *Juneteenth* does not detract from its power.

Ellison's stature as a public figure and an academic are noteworthy, especially in light of the fact that both he and his famous protagonist did not complete college. In addition to being the first African American to receive the National Book Award, Ellison was the recipient of the Rockefeller

Foundation Award and the Prix de Rome fellowship, the Medal of Freedom, and the Chevalier de l'Ordre des Arts et Lettres. He held fellowships and distinguished professorships at the University of Chicago, Rutgers, Yale, and New York University, and received honorary doctorates from many other universities. Far from invisible, he was recognized as one of the great writers of his time despite his relatively small body of published work, and his great novel will continue to make him visible throughout the imaginable future.

D. Quentin Miller

See also: Novel; Postmodernism.

Resources

Primary Sources: Ralph Ellison: *The Collected Essays of Ralph Ellison*, ed. John F. Callahan (New York: Modern Library, 1995); *"Flying Home" and Other Stories*, ed. John F. Callahan (New York: Random House, 1996); *Going to the Territory* (New York: Random House, 1986); *Invisible Man* (New York: Random House, 1952); *Juneteenth: A Novel*, ed. John F. Callahan (New York: Random House, 1999); *Living with Music: Ralph Ellison's Jazz Writings*, ed. Robert G. O'Meally (New York: Modern Library, 2001); *Shadow and Act* (New York: Random House, 1964).

Secondary Sources: Kimberly W. Benston, ed., *Speaking for You: The Vision of Ralph Ellison* (Washington, DC: Howard University Press, 1987); Harold Bloom, ed., *Ralph Ellison* (New York: Chelsea House, 1986); Robert Bone, *The Negro Novel in America* (New Haven, CT: Yale University Press, 1958); Mark Busby, *Ralph Ellison* (Boston: Twayne, 1991); Robert J. Butler, ed., *The Critical Response to Ralph Ellison* (Westport, CT: Greenwood Press, 2000); Cynthia Dobbs, "Mapping Black Movement, Containing Black Laughter: Ralph Ellison's New York Essays," *American Quarterly* 68, no. 4 (2016), 907–929; Ronald Gottesman, comp., *Studies in "Invisible Man"* (Columbus, OH: Charles E. Merrill, 1971); Maryemma Graham and Amritjit Singh, eds., *Conversations with Ralph Ellison* (Jackson: University Press of Mississippi, 1995); John Hersey, ed., *Ralph Ellison: A Collection of Critical Essays* (Englewood Cliffs, NJ: Prentice-Hall, 1974); Lawrence Jackson, *Ralph Ellison: Emergence of Genius* (New York: John Wiley, 2002); Kerry McSweeney, *Invisible Man: Race and Identity* (Boston: Twayne, 1988); Alan Nadel, *Invisible Criticism: Ralph Ellison and the American Canon* (Iowa City: University of Iowa Press, 1988); Robert G. O'Meally, *The Craft of Ralph Ellison* (Cambridge, MA: Harvard University Press, 1980); Robert G. O'Meally, ed., *New Essays on "Invisible Man"* (Cambridge: Cambridge University Press, 1988); Horace A. Porter, *Jazz Country: Ralph Ellison in America* (Iowa City: University of Iowa Press, 2001); John M. Reilly, ed., *Twentieth Century Interpretations of "Invisible Man"* (Englewood Cliffs, NJ: Prentice-Hall, 1970); Edith Schor, *Visible Ellison: A Study of Ralph Ellison's Fiction* (Westport, CT: Greenwood Press, 1993); Eric J. Sundquist, "'We dreamed a dream': Ralph Ellison, Martin Luther King, Jr. & Barack Obama," *Daedalus* 140, no. 1 (January 1, 2011), 108–124; Jerry Gafio Watts, *Heroism and the Black Intellectual: Ralph Ellison, Politics, and Afro-American Intellectual Life* (Chapel Hill: University of North Carolina Press, 1994).

Epic Poetry/The Long Poem

An epic poem is a long narrative in verse. Historically, epic poems have taken heroes, heroines, gods, or God as their subject; epics often tell stories of wars or quests of great importance, focusing on civilizations or ways of life in profound crisis. Constituting a Western literary tradition stretching from the *Iliad* and the *Odyssey* (ca. 800 BCE) through Edmund Spenser's *The Faerie Queene* (1590–1596) and John

Milton's *Paradise Lost* (1674), no other literary genre has enjoyed the status of the epic poem.

The genealogy of the modern African American long poem, of which Carolivia Herron has given a noteworthy outline, reached its first milestone with John Boyd's *The Vision*, published in England in 1835, and with the work of James Monroe Whitfield. In *America and Other Poems* (1853), Whitfield offers two long poems—"America" and "How Long?"—which exemplify the political utility of the genre by presenting a strongly abolitionist perspective. "America," written in iambic tetrameter, takes as its subject American hypocrisy, democracy, and slavery; "How Long?" is an extended reflection on the reasons why Black people are still enslaved. In the work of James Madison Bell, the genre's inherent polemical elements emerge with a vociferous argument for and against "American values," including freedom. Bell's long poems include a poem on emancipation (1862), "The Day and the War" (1864), a poem on the death of Lincoln (1865), "Valedictory on Leaving San Francisco" (1866), and "The Progress of Liberty" (1866), on the end of the Civil War.

The end of the nineteenth century and the beginning of the twentieth witnessed the publication of the three longest poems ever written by African Americans. Two of these poems were written by Albery Allson Whitman. Whitman's *Not a Man, and Yet a Man* (1877), which includes more than 5,000 couplet verses, concerns the exploits of a Black slave. Whitman also wrote *An Idyl of the South* (1901), an epic poem in two parts; composed entirely in ottava rima, it narrates stories of the South in the style of Tennyson. The third long poem is Robert E. Ford's 8,600-word *Brown Chapel, a Story in Verse* (1905).

Other African Americans who contributed to the genre of long poem include James Ephraim McGirt, George Marion McClellan, George Hannibal Temple, George Reginald Margetson, Edward Smyth Jones, Fenton Johnson, and Maurice N. Corbett. James Weldon Johnson included works by McClellan and Margetson in his anthology *The Book of American Negro Poetry* (1922).

McGirt wrote three epics in the pastoral and military styles of the Latin poet Virgil, including *Avenging the Maine* (1899). McClellan's intricate long poem "The Legend of Tannhauser and Elizabeth," based on Richard Wagner's opera *Tannhäuser* and published in *The Path of Dreams* (1916), is often described as the most accomplished work of nineteenth-century African American narrative epic (Bruce).

Temple wrote *The Epic of Columbus's Bell* (1900), which describes how a bell on Columbus's ship became the centerpiece of an African American church in New Jersey. Johnson self-published the long poem *Visions of the Dusk* in 1915. Corbett wrote *The Harp of Ethiopia* (1914).

In 1904, Frances Ellen Watkins Harper published *Moses: A Story of the Nile*, a poem in blank verse akin to that of Milton, and with a similar focus on biblical themes. The narrative suggests how a gifted African American can further the achievements of the race by making contributions to American democracy, technology, and education. Harper's distinctly irregular blank verse represents a significant stylistic innovation.

Harlem Renaissance poet Countee Cullen, best known for his lyric poetry, wrote the long poems "Shroud of Color," "Heritage," and "The Black Christ." Cullen's contemporaries Melvin B. Tolson, Jean Toomer, and Langston Hughes also wrote long poems. Sterling Brown wrote

"Odyssey of Big Boy," which, although it is a poem of less than 400 words, places the narrator, Big Boy, a working-class African American who has toiled and traveled during his whole adult life, against the backdrop of Homer's *Odyssey*. Tolson won the National Poetry Contest at the American Negro Exposition in Chicago, Illinois, for his long poem "Dark Symphony" (1940). In this poem, which employs musical tempos, Negro spirituals, and biographical sketches of great Blacks in world history, Tolson praises the achievements of his race while celebrating the New Negro. In 1953, Tolson published his *Libretto for the Republic of Liberia*, and *Harlem Gallery: Book I, The Curator* in 1965. In *Libretto*, Tolson draws upon Hart Crane's *The Bridge* (1930) to tell a multilingual history of Liberia that is divided into sections with titles drawn from the notes of an ascending scale (do, re, mi, etc.). In *Harlem Gallery*, Tolson initiates what was to have been a multivolume epic narrative of a Black man in America, but he died before he could complete the epic. Toomer, who is best known for his novel *Cane* (1923), also wrote the long poem "Blue Meridian" (1936).

Langston Hughes's *Montage of a Dream Deferred* (1951) is arguably the most famous African American long poem. Drawing on the blues, scat singing, and jazz, but also using traditional forms such as the ballad, Hughes expresses his vision of Harlem, New York, and, indirectly, of African Americans. Many of the poems within the poem are spoken by different imagined citizens of Harlem, giving the long poem a dramatic quality. In 1961, Hughes published the long poem *Ask Your Mama: 12 Moods for Jazz*.

Gwendolyn Brooks's *Annie Allen* (1949) is a formal mock epic with all the standard epic devices and is reminiscent of Alexander Pope's *The Rape of the Lock* (1714) (see Jimoh in Resources at the end of this entry). Playfully known as "The Anniad"—echoing *The Aeniad*, the celebrated epic poem in Latin by Virgil—*Annie Allen* deals with serious issues such as the doubly subservient position of Black women vis-à-vis Black men and their White oppressors. Brooks pursues her inquiry into the social and spiritual position of Black women in contemporary America in her poem *In the Mecca* (1968), which concerns Mrs. Sallie, who lives in the run-down Mecca Building in Chicago and is searching for her missing daughter, Pepita. On her quest, she encounters an array of urban characters who are generally optimistic about the future of African Americans. Ultimately, however, this bright sense of the future becomes bleak for Mrs. Sallie when she discovers that her daughter has been murdered by one of the poverty-stricken residents of the Mecca.

More recent examples of the African American long poem include *Black Anima* (1973), by N. J. Loftis, which describes from both Black and White perspectives a trip into the hell of historical slavery. Jay Wright published the long poem *The Double Invention of Komo* in 1980. He modeled his poem on ancient African rituals such as the Komo initiation rite among the Bambara. The poem celebrates both the pluralism and the unity of African Americans. Amiri Baraka published the book-length poem, *Wise, Why's, Y's: The Griot's Song* in 1995 (see Schultz's article on the poem in Resources). More recently, Harryette Mullen has worked in longer poetic forms (*Sleeping with the Dictionary*, 2002). Kathy Lou Schultz published a book-length study of modern African American long poems in 2013. In 2014, Claudia Rankine published *Citizen: An American Lyric*, which, despite its title, constitutes a book-length blending of poetry and prose. It confronts issues connected with the Black Lives Matter movement (see Chan in Resources). The book won the National Book Award in 2014.

Antony Adolf

See also: Baraka, Amiri; Brooks, Gwendolyn; Hayden, Robert; Hughes, Langston.

Resources

Amiri Baraka, *Wise, Why's, Y's: The Griot's Song* (Chicago: Third World Press, 1995); Margaret Beissinger, Jane Tylus, and Susanne Wofford, eds., *Epic Traditions in the Contemporary World: The Poetics of Community* (Berkeley: University of California Press, 1999); James Madison Bell, *The Poetical Works of James Madison Bell* (Lansing, MI: Wynkoop, Hallenback, Crawford, 1901); Carol Blackshire-Belay, ed., *Language and Literature in the African American Imagination* (Westport, CT: Greenwood Press, 1992); *Gwendolyn Brooks: Annie Allen* (New York: Harper, 1949); *In the Mecca* (New York: Harper & Row, 1968); Sterling Brown, "Odyssey of Big Boy," *The Collected Poems of Sterling A. Brown*, ed. Michael S. Harper (Evanston, IL: Triquarterly Books, 1996); Dickson D. Bruce, "George Marion McClellan," in *Dictionary of Literary Biography*, vol. 50, *Afro-American Writers Before the Harlem Renaissance*, ed. Trudier Harris (Detroit: Gale, 1986), 206–212; Mary-Jean Chan, "Towards a Poetics of Racial Trauma: Lyric Hybridity in Claudia Rankine's *Citizen*," *Journal of American Studies* 52, no. 1 (February 2018), 137–163; Frances Ellen Watkins Harper, *Poems* (Philadelphia: Ferguson, 1898); Carolivia Herron, "Early African American Poetry," in *The Columbia History of American Poetry*, ed. Jay Parini and Brett C. Miller (New York: Columbia University Press, 1993), 31–35; *Langston Hughes: Ask Your Mama: 12 Moods for Jazz* (New York: Knopf, 1961); *Montage of a Dream Deferred* (New York: Holt, 1951); A. Yemisi Jimoh, *Double Consciousness, Modernism, and* Womanist Themes in Gwendolyn Brooks's *The Anniad* Fenton Johnson, *Visions of the Dusk* (New York: Fenton Johnson, 1915); James Weldon Johnson, *The Book of American Negro Poetry* (New York: Harcourt, Brace, 1922); N. J. Loftis, *Black Anima* (New York: Liveright, 1973); George Marion McClellan, *The Path of Dreams* (1916; repr. Freeport, NY: Books for Libraries, 1971); *Poems* (Nashville, TN: A.M.E. Publishing, 1895); Hiram Kelly Moderwell, "The Epic of the Black Man," *The New Republic*, September 1917, 154–155; Harryette Mullen, *Sleeping with the Dictionary* (Berkeley: University of California Press, 2002); Claudia Rankine, *Citizen: An American Lyric* (New York: Harper Perennial, 2014); Kathy Schultz, "Amiri Baraka's *Wise Why's Y's*: Lineages of the Afro-Modernist Epic," *Journal of Modern Literature* 35, no. 3 (Spring 2012), 25–50, 201; Kathy Lou Schultz, *The Afro-Modernist Epic and Literary History: Tolson, Hughes, Baraka* (New York: Palgrave MacMillan, 2013); Melvin B. Tolson, *Harlem Gallery and Other Poems*, ed. Raymond Nelson (Charlottesville: University Press of Virginia, 1999); *Libretto for the Republic of Liberia* (New York: Twayne, 1953); James Monroe Whitfield, *Poems* (Buffalo, NY: Leavit, 1853); Albery Allson Whitman: *An Idyl of the South* (New York: Metaphysical Publishing, 1901); *Not a Man, and Yet a Man* (1877; repr. Upper Saddle River, NJ: Literature House, 1970); Jay Wright, *The Double Invention of Komo* (Austin: University of Texas Press, 1980).

Equiano, Olaudah (1745–1797)

Writer. African-born author of *The Interesting Narrative of the Life of Olaudah Equiano; or, Gustavus Vassa, the African* (1789), Equiano is an important figure of both multiple literary genres and of abolitionism. An Ibo born in Isseke in present-day Nigeria, Equiano begins his narrative with a discussion of Ibo society and his kidnapping into European slavery at age eleven. There is some inconclusive evidence that he was born in South Carolina, but even if this proves true, his *Narrative* remains a foundational work of the African American literary tradition (see Boyce in Resources below). For it sets out most of the arguments against slavery and racism that African Americans have developed during the two centuries since its publication Equiano's *Narrative* holds prominent places in such genres as the Slave Narrative, abolitionist literature, travel writing, autobiography, and spiritual/Christian literature.

Equiano's *Narrative* opens by quoting Isaiah, which situates Equiano's work in the biblical tradition of social criticism, the jeremiad. By the end of the first (of twelve) chapters, Equiano has discussed not only Christianity but also geography, anthropology, judicature, comparative cultural analysis, gender studies, race theory, economics, a comparison of slaveries, African religion, and historical theories on the Jewish diaspora. In addition to its diversity of topics, Equiano's *Narrative* recounts the author's travels in Africa, the Caribbean, Mesoamerica, the United States, Europe, Turkey, and even the Arctic. This not only provides an exciting read but also counters the traditional Western triumvirate of travel–knowledge–power associated with "White" men.

Three particularly important themes of the African American tradition in Equiano are the middle passage, the preference for death over slavery (famously dramatized by Toni Morrison in *Beloved*, 1987) and, perhaps most important, the theme of the "talking book." When Equiano acknowledges his great desire to "talk to the books" like a European, he acknowledges knowledge and linguistic fluency as a means to power, a paramount theme of African American

literature and arts that recurs from Frederick Douglass through Malcolm X to rap artists.

Equiano's *Narrative* shows the author imbued with high educational expectations before his capture. Although Equiano admires European culture, he depicts his native Ibo society as essentially equal to, and in some ways superior to, European society. Thus, when Equiano overcomes multiple injustices to buy himself out of slavery, start a business, join a North Pole expedition, accept a British government appointment to commissary, and even write and publish a book, the implicit argument is not that Africans are merely improvable specimens when exposed to European culture but that Equiano's successes are manifestations of his African heritage.

After publication of *Interesting Narrative*, Equiano married an Englishwoman, Susan Cullen. Before his death, Equiano's *Narrative* had gone through eight English editions and had been translated into Dutch, Russian, and French. Equiano remains one of the most widely read of all African authors, and his work appears in many anthologies of American literature.

Kevin M. Hickey

See also: Slave Narrative.

Resources

Robert J. Allison, "Introduction," in *The Interesting Narrative of the Life of Olaudah Equiano* (Boston: Bedford Books, 1995); Nell Boyce, "Out of Africa?: New Questions About the Origins of a Seminal Slave Narrative," *U.S. News & World Report*, February 10, 2003, pp. 54–55; Angelo Costanzo, *Surprising Narrative: Olaudah Equiano and the Beginnings of Black Autobiography* (Westport, CT: Greenwood Press, 1987); Emily Donaldson Field, "'Excepting himself': Olaudah Equiano, Native Americans, and the

Civilizing Mission," *MELUS: Multi-Ethnic Literature of the United States* 34, no. 4 (Winter 2009), 15(24); Rebecka Rutledge Fisher: "The Poetics of Belonging in the Age of Enlightenment Spiritual Metaphors of Being in Olaudah Equiano's *Interesting Narrative*," *Early American Studies: An Interdisciplinary Journal* 11, no. 1 (2013), 72–97; *Habitations of the Veil: Metaphor and the Poetics of Black Being in African American Literature* (Albany, NY: State University of New York Press, 2014); Andrew Kopec, "Collective Commerce and the Problem of Autobiography in Olaudah Equiano's *Narrative*," *The Eighteenth Century* 54, no. 4 (2013), 461–478; Geraldine Murphy, "Olaudah Equiano, Accidental Tourist," *Eighteenth-Century Studies* 27, no. 4 (Summer 1994), 551; Ross J. Pudaloff, "No Change Without Purchase: Olaudah Equiano and the Economies of Self and Market," *Early American Literature* 40, no. 3 (2005), 499–527.

Essay

Prose form based in the European tradition of writing by Michel de Montaigne, Francis Bacon, Blaise Pascal, Charles Lamb, William Hazlitt, Leigh Hunt, and Virginia Woolf. The American essay tradition is shaped by the writings of Thomas Paine, Ralph Waldo Emerson, Henry David Thoreau, and E. B. White. Many critics of the essay identify the writings of Montaigne as one important origin of the modern essay, which is based in the birth of the modern individual and the rise of secularism. The essay is well suited for explorations of specific locations, times, events, and pressing social questions. For example, Montaigne wrote about such diverse topics as the European discovery of the American continents in his essay "Of the Caniballes" (1580), the experience of reading philosophical traditions in "Of Books" (1580), and the worldly human body in "Of Cripples" (1588) and "Of Physiognomy" (1588).

The essay is a highly diverse prose genre marked by flexibility, digression, and openness. It often features meditations on personal experience that question common knowledge or philosophical traditions. Essayists often "speak" in the first person to offer a personal account of familiar experiences or ideas. Essays are also often composed of personal anecdotes, observations, and references to or direct quotation of other writers and well-known figures. Consequently, the essay is often considered an occasional or ephemeral form that must make the particular universal if the individual essay is to survive beyond the immediacy of its chronological or geographical context. In terms of tone and direction, the essay is marked by a digressive, provisional, sometimes wandering speaker seeking innovative ideas, experiences, and ways of viewing common questions or problems. Some locate the essay's exploratory nature in the rise of empiricism and discovery in the writings of scientist–philosophers such as Francis Bacon and New World explorers such as Christopher Columbus. Others turn to the essay as the most formless of prose genres, an open arena that is able to question received knowledge and to renounce dogma by seeking out the evidence of new experience or data. Audience is also a key component of the form, insofar as readers are invited to share in recounted personal experience or observations and since many essayists directly address a particular audience that might be incorporated into the essay itself. In the African American essay tradition, the form often also serves as a vehicle for direct engagement with political and cultural events, thereby bearing affinity to other rhetorical traditions and socially engaged forms such as sermons, protest novels, and political speeches.

The African American essay has played a central role in shaping national debates about racism, African American literary traditions, and the limits of American democratic systems for authors and intellectuals, who often hold positions of cultural power as race spokespersons. A significant proportion of African American novelists, dramatists, and poets are also essayists. Important African American essayists include Booker T. Washington, Anna Julia Haywood Cooper, W.E.B. Du Bois, James Weldon Johnson, Langston Hughes, Zora Neale Hurston, Richard Wright, Ralph Ellison, James Baldwin, Alice Walker, Audre Lorde, June Jordan, Gerald Early, Patricia J. Williams, and Stanley Crouch. These writers' essays are often valued in literary, cultural, and political traditions as much as, or more than, their poetry, fiction, and drama.

The most famous and influential early African American essays are Anna Julia Cooper's long meditation *A Voice from the South* (1892), Booker T. Washington's political essays "The Awakening of the Negro" (1896) and "Signs of Progress Among the Negroes" (1900), and W.E.B. Du Bois's collection of historical, sociological, and literary essays, *The Souls of Black Folk* (1903). These formative essays shaped the genre as an important venue for African American intellectuals' political commentary and analysis of the meanings of race, class, gender, and freedom in America. In their essays, Washington, Cooper, and Du Bois seek to represent the concerns of African Americans generally to an American public and to articulate a program for future race relations in America after Reconstruction. Washington underscored the importance of

basic education and hard work within African American communities that he would fully outline in his autobiography *Up from Slavery* (1901). Cooper emphasized the importance of giving voice to the countless Black women who were largely overlooked in dominant political conversations about race, the South, and the challenges of Reconstruction. Du Bois outlined a philosophy of racial uplift that included investment in the higher education and leadership of a "talented tenth" to represent the general African American population. As these early essayists demonstrated, the African American essay as a form provides the flexibility in speaking position and subject matter by which Cooper, Washington, and Du Bois were able to draw from both particular personal experiences and general experiences of members of the entire race as well as to address both a White and a Black audience in America, sometimes separately and sometimes simultaneously.

During the literary movement known as the Harlem Renaissance, the essay provided a venue for debates about the role of literature and African American artists' multiple responsibilities to art, to politics, and to representations of African American culture and experience. Langston Hughes's "The Negro Artist and the Racial Mountain" (1925) is a central document on the role of race and writing from the Harlem Renaissance. It was written as a kind of response to an essay, "The Negro-Art Hokum," by George Schuyler, but also stands alone as an important statement about aesthetics. Since then, nearly all African American writers have had to respond in some way to what James Weldon Johnson called "The Dilemma of the Negro Author" (1928), and the essay is often where African American authors debate the dilemma. Some look to the question of the racial composition of intended and actual audiences, such as in "Our Literary Audience" (1930), by Sterling A. Brown, which argued for the crucial role played by great audiences—both White and Black—in making great art, and sixty years later Stan West compared the role of the Black writer to that of a tightrope walker among a racially divided audience in "Tip-Toeing on the Tight Rope: A Personal Essay on Black Writer Ambivalence" (1998). Other writers have responded to Johnson's dilemma by considering what role and form African American fiction should take. Richard Wright laid out a "Blue Print for Negro Writing" (1937) by arguing that African American writers must recognize and use the political messages of art, while Addison Gayle Jr. argued for a specifically Black aesthetic in African American fiction in his essays that provided the theoretical grounding of the Black Arts Movement, including especially "Cultural Strangulation: Black Literature and the White Aesthetic" (1971).

The essay has also served as a key site for authors to create or refuse literary lineages. Wallace Thurman traced and evaluated the literary history of African Americans before the Harlem Renaissance by condemning previous writers for working within White literary traditions in his essays "Negro Artists and the Negro" (1927) and "Negro Poets and Their Poetry" (1928). Alain Locke provided the de facto manifesto for the Harlem Renaissance by arguing that writers must consciously create a new, specifically African American cultural tradition in his opening essay, "The New Negro" (1925), for the collection of the same name. Ralph Ellison was a key figure in redrawing American literary histories across and outside racial lines in his essay collections *Shadow and Act* (1964) and *Going to the Territory* (1986),

especially in the essays "Twentieth-Century Fiction and the Black Mask of Humanity" (1953), "Change the Joke and Slip the Yoke" (1963), and "The Novel as a Function of American Democracy" (1967). Within a specifically African American literary tradition, James Baldwin criticized the representational choices of his literary forefather Richard Wright as Baldwin staked out his own literary territory in his essay collection *Notes of a Native Son* (1955), most notably in his famous essay "Everybody's Protest Novel."

Regarding a specifically female literary tradition, Alice Walker's "Searching for Zora," (1975), originally published in the feminist magazine *Ms.*, was an important catalyst for projects to rescue literary foremothers, such as Zora Neale Hurston, from obscurity. In the essay, Walker recounts her quest to locate and buy a gravestone for Hurston's unmarked grave, a fate that Walker saw as emblematic of the African American woman writer. Walker also reexamined Southern literary histories at large to claim Flannery O'Connor as her literary foremother, and she included both essays in her bestselling collection *In Search of Our Mothers' Gardens* (1983). Toni Cade Bambara also participated in the creation of a woman-centered literary and cultural tradition in her groundbreaking collection *The Black Woman* (1970), considered the first major Black feminist publication, which brought together essays as well as short stories and poems, by African American women. June Jordan's *Civil Wars* (1981) is recognized as the first major collection of essays by an African American woman.

Many African American essayists were very conscious of their roles as race spokespersons. In response, many essayists borrowed from the ethnographic study genre, and consequently reflected and criticized contemporary ideas about race and anthropology. Pauline E. Hopkins augmented her romance fiction with the essay "The Dark Races of the Twentieth Century" (1905), an early examination of potential kinship based on race in the aftermath of the failures of Reconstruction to create a unified America and amid growing U.S. imperialism. The best-known, and most debated, use of ethnographic techniques is in the nonfiction of Zora Neale Hurston. In addition to her folkloric study *Mules and Men* (1935), Hurston penned many essays about African American folklore and culture, most notably "Characteristics of Negro Expression" (1930), informed by her training as an anthropologist by Franz Boaz at Barnard College.

Many African American writers have used the essay as a means of publicly exploring the complex cultural terrain of important African American cities, neighborhoods, and communities. Paul Laurence Dunbar and Langston Hughes both wrote essays about Washington, DC, in order to explore the myth and reality of middle-class and upper-class African American society. James Weldon Johnson, Wallace Thurman, Langston Hughes, and Arna Bontemps wrote essays specifically about Harlem, New York, during the Harlem Renaissance. James Baldwin examined his experiences in the city of Paris, France, as a means of contrasting African American living conditions and ideas about race both in the urban North and the segregated South in his essay collections *Notes of a Native Son* (1955) and *Nobody Knows My Name* (1961). Similarly, LeRoi Jones wrote about politics and life in Cuba to contrast the American political scene in his essay "Cuba Libre" (1961). (*See* Baraka, Amiri.)

The essay has served as a key site for writers to bring African American experiences and perspectives to major political questions of the day. James Baldwin's best-selling *The Fire Next Time* (1963) helped bring the moral challenge of the Civil Rights Movement to a national audience concerned about racial violence and the rise of the Nation of Islam and Black Nationalism. One of the first paid publications for the young Alice Walker was her essay "The Civil Rights Movement: What Good Was It?" (1967), which won a contest in the *American Scholar*. The essay has brought popular novelists into the realm of public debate—for instance, Chester B. Himes's sardonic call to action in response to segregation during World War II in "Negro Martyrs Are Needed" (1943)—and it has brought political activists into conversation with Black artists and traditions, as in Angela Y. Davis's "Billie Holiday's 'Strange Fruit': Musical and Social Consciousness" (1988), which joined a distinguished tradition of essays on Black music as well as Davis's own widely read essays of political theory in *Women, Race, and Class* (1981). African American intellectuals and academics have come to national prominence by using the essay form to bring personal experience and historical grounding to current topics of fierce public debate, such as legal scholar Patricia J. Williams's critiques of the Clarence Thomas–Anita Hill senate confirmation controversy in "A Rare Case Study of Muleheadedness and Men," and her critiques of multiculturalism and the fate of the Civil Rights Movement in her best-selling essay collection *The Alchemy of Race and Rights* (1991).

The essay has proven to be a central genre for African American journalistic enterprises and examinations of popular culture. Many African American writers gained a public name by writing for Black-identified magazines such as *Callaloo*, W.E.B. Du Bois's *The Crisis, Opportunity, Obsidian, Phylon*, and *Sojourner*, or for popular magazines designed for an African American audience, such as *Essence, Ebony*, and *Jet*. Toni Cade Bambara introduced readers of *Essence* to the folk character M'Dear in her essay "Beauty Is Just Care . . . Like Ugly Is Just Carelessness," which advocated "brainwashing" as a folk remedy for the racist messages permeating popular culture, within a magazine heavily packed with advertisements for Black beauty products. On the other hand, Langston Hughes's later career included regular contributions to the African American newspaper the *Chicago Defender*, both in the form of his Jesse B. Simple tales and of essays, and June Jordan wrote a regular essay column for *The Progressive*, a leftist magazine advocating peace and justice, both internationally and domestically. Many of James Baldwin's essays were commissioned by journalistic publications, most notably his essays about desegregation in the South, such as "Fly in the Buttermilk" (1958), which appeared in *Harper's Magazine*, and about life in Harlem and downtown Manhattan during that same period, which he contrasted in "Fifth Avenue, Uptown: A Letter from Harlem" (1960) and "East River, Downtown: Postscript to a Letter from Harlem" (1961), first published in the *New York Times Magazine* and *Esquire*, respectively. During the rise of Third World nationalism and the Black diaspora, journalistic essays proved a particularly important means for African Americans to become familiar with the everyday lives and struggles of Black people around the globe. Angela Davis and Amiri Baraka wrote many political essays in this vein. June Jordan reported from politically volatile countries for various magazines and collected her writings in *On Call: Political Essays* (1985), including her contribution to the growing antiapartheid movement in America with her essay "South Africa: Bringing It All Back Home" (1981), first published in the *New York Times*.

In addition to the European roots of the essay as a genre, it is important to note that African American essayists also draw from rhetorical and generic traditions specific to the African American experience. In addition to generally recognized American masters of the form—Ralph Waldo Emerson, Henry David Thoreau, Henry James, and E. B. White—African American essayists draw from a distinguished rhetorical tradition of African American orators, including Frederick Douglass, Henry Highland Garnet, David Walker, and Sojourner Truth. While the essay as a form is marked by its ability to forge a subjective speaking voice, the African American oratory tradition provides essayists with the rhetorical tools to address immediate audiences, often divided along racial lines. The abolitionist oratory tradition especially provides a tradition in which African Americans forged a public voice by claiming and critiquing widely held American beliefs about freedom, independence, and autonomy. African American essayists also draw from a robust Black church tradition, which lends a polemical tone to many essays. Some have discussed the essay as a print version of spaces of public debate, such as a Black pulpit used to launch accusations at its audience (Early, 1993, x), or as a passionate feminist dialogue between women from different backgrounds (Joeres, and Mittman, 1993, 156). The importance of oratorical prowess in contemporary African American essays is evidenced in the writings of Cornel West and Michael Eric Dyson, academics and essayists also well known as public speakers and influenced by the poetics of oral forms, such as hip-hop in Dyson's essays in particular.

Brian J. Norman

See also: Baldwin, James; Baraka, Amiri; Coates, Ta-Nehisi; Douglass, Frederick; Du Bois, W.E.B.; Ellison, Ralph; Hughes, Langston; Reed, Ishmael; Schuyler, George Samuel; Simms, Renee Elizabeth; West, Cornel.

Resources

Primary Sources: James Baldwin: *The Fire Next Time* (New York: Dell, 1963); *Notes of a Native Son* (Boston: Beacon Press, 1955); Amiri Baraka, *Home: Social Essays* (New York: Morrow, 1966); Ta-Nehisi Coates, *Between the World and Me* (New York: Spiegel & Grau, 2015); Anna Julia Cooper, *A Voice from the South: By a Black Woman of the South* (1892; repr. New York: Oxford University Press, 1988); Angela Y. Davis et al., *If They Come in the Morning: Voices of Resistance* (New York: Third Press, 1971); W.E.B. Du Bois, *The Souls of Black Folk* (Chicago: A. C. McClurg, 1903); Ralph Ellison, *Shadow and Act* (New York: Random House, 1964); Langston Hughes: *Good Morning Revolution: Uncollected Writings of Social Protest by Langston Hughes*, ed. Faith Berry (Seacaucus, NJ: Carol Publishing Group, 1992); *Langston Hughes and the Chicago Defender: Essays on Race, Politics, and Culture: 1942–1962*, ed. Christopher C. De Santis (Urbana: University of Illinois Press, 1995); "The Negro Artist and the Racial Mountain," *Nation* 23 (1926), 692–694; Zora Neale Hurston, "Characteristics of Negro Expression," in *Negro: An Anthology*, ed. Nancy Cunard (London: Wishart, 1934), 39–46; June Jordan, *Some of Us Did Not Die: New and Selected Essays* (New York: Basic/Civitas Books, 2002); Audre Lorde, *Sister Outsider* (Freedom, CA: Crossing Press, 1984); Alice Walker, *In Search of Our Mothers' Gardens* (Trumansburg, NY: Crossing Press, 1984); Richard Wright, "Blueprint for Negro Writing," *New Challenge* 2 (Fall 1937), 58–65.

Secondary Sources: T. W. Adorno, "The Essay as Form" (Frankfurt Am Main: Suhrkamp Verlag, 1958), trans. Bob Hullot-Kentor and Frederic Will, *New German Critique* 32 (1984), 151–171; Wendy Bishop and Hans Ostrom, eds., *Genre and Writing: Issues, Arguments, Alternatives* (Portsmouth, NH: Boynton-Cook/Heineman, 1997); Alexander J. Butrym, ed., *Essays on the Essay: Redefining the Genre* (Athens: University of Georgia Press, 1989); Emma Cleary, "'Here Be Dragons': The Tyranny of the Cityscape in James Baldwin's Intimate Cartographies," *James Baldwin Review* 1 (September 1, 2015), 10–15; Gerald Early: *Speech and Power*, vol. 1, *The African-American Essay and Its Cultural Content from Polemics to Pulpit* (Hopewell, NJ: Ecco Press, 1992); *Speech and Power*, vol. 2, *The African-American Essay and Its Cultural Content from Polemics to Pulpit* (Hopewell, NJ: Ecco Press, 1993); Ruth-Ellen Boetcher Joeres and Elizabeth Mittman, eds., *The Politics of the Essay: Feminist Perspectives* (Bloomington: Indiana University Press, 1993); Cristina Kirklighter, *Traversing the Democratic Borders of the Essay* (Albany: State University of New York Press, 2002); Philip Lopate, *The Art of the Personal Essay: An Anthology from the Classical Era to the Present* (New York: Anchor, 1994); Peter Mack, "Rhetoric and the Essay," *Rhetoric Society Quarterly* 23, no. 2 (Spring 1993), 41–49.

E-Zines, E-News, E-Journals, and E-Collections

The zine world has been evolving since its beginnings in the late 1970s. A zine was originally defined as a not-for-profit newspaper or magazine that was published, written, and distributed by an individual. Often expressing alternative or radical viewpoints, print zines were part of the underground press of the era. The advent of the internet gave birth to the e-zine, and as technology became more sophisticated many e-zines adopted a glossier, more commercial face. Both zines and e-zines can be difficult to track because they appear at the whim of the creator and often are published for just a few issues.

As web publishing has boomed, the meaning of e-zine has broadened to include any newspaper, magazine, or journal that is free or partly free via the internet. Although these often disappear or become available only by paid subscription, a few titles have shown staying power. *Black Press USA* identifies itself "your independent source of news for the African American community," offers news and opinion, and is written exclusively by African American journalists. Updated daily, it links to a growing number of newspapers throughout the country that are members of the *BlackUSA Network*, including the *Amsterdam News*, the *Birmingham Times*, and the *Seattle Median*. Blackvoices.com is a weekly, with a Black international perspective on news, commentaries, and culture, and has published since 1996. SeeingBlack.com, the "funky, alternative site for Black reviews, opinion & voice," emphasizes arts and entertainment, including book and film reviews, and has appeared since 2001. The current issue is free, and back issues are available for purchase. Black Collegian Online (http://black-collegian .com) is "the career site for students and professionals of color," and provides information on jobs, employers, graduate school, and related issues. Selected articles are available back to 1997.

North Star: A Journal of African-American Religious History is a free peer-reviewed journal from Vassar College that is published twice a year in association with the Afro-American Religious History section of the American Academy of Religion. All articles are available online back to 1997. *Freedom Journal*, the first African American–owned and –operated journal, has achieved e-zine status. Published between 1827 and 1829, all its issues are available through the Wisconsin Historical Society website.

Some libraries subscribe to commercial databases that offer Black literature collections. *Ethnic NewsWatch* provides full text of minority newspapers, magazines, and journals. It includes more than sixty African American and Caribbean titles, such as *Research in African Literatures* and *Black Child*. *JSTOR* offers archival issues for seven Black journals, including *African American Review*, *Black American Literature Forum*, and *Callaloo*. The *African-American Poetry 1760–1900* database and the *Database of Twentieth-Century African-American Poetry* from Chadwyck-Healey provide full text for thousands of poems. The *Black Drama* database is available from Alexander Street Press and has the full text of 1,200 plays from 1850 to the present, about a quarter of them previously unpublished. It includes the complete works of leading playwrights such as Amiri Baraka and Ed Bullins.

Maureen A. Kelly

See also: Research Resources: Electronic Works; Research Sources: Reference Works.

Resources

African American Newspapers and Periodicals (2003), http://www.wisconsinhistory.org /libraryarchives/aanp/; *Black Press USA*, http://www.blackpressusa.com; *Black Voices .com*, http://new.blackvoices.com; *North Star*, Vassar College (Spring 2004), http://northstar .vassar.edu; Bryon Anderson, "Bibliographic and Web Tools for Alternative Publications," *Counterpoise* 12, no. 4 (Fall 2008), 64–67; Anonymous, "Top 10 Black Magazines And Ezines To Follow In 2019," *Feedspot*, January 23, 2019: https://blog.feedspot.com/black_ma gazines/ (accessed 2019); Taylor Bryant, "10 Black-Run Zines To Get Familiar With," *Nylon*, February 27, 2017: https://nylon.com /articles/black-zines (accessed 2019); Suzanne A. Vega Garcia, *Recommended African American Websites Diversity & Ethnic Studies*, Iowa State University (August 6, 2002), http://www.public.iastate.edu/~savega /afr_amer.htm.

F

Fauset, Jessie Redmon
(1882–1961)

Novelist, poet, essayist, journalist, editor, and teacher. Fauset was born in Camden County, New Jersey, the youngest of seven children of Rev. Redmon Fauset and Annie Seamon Fauset. Both of her parents were well educated and literary, and her experience of a relatively elite African American literary culture is a major theme of her writing. Jessie Fauset grew up in Philadelphia, Pennsylvania, and attended the city's public schools. On the basis of her excellent academic record, she was admitted to Cornell University in 1901. Fauset received her BA in classical and modern languages in 1905 and was the first African American woman to be elected to the prestigious honor society Phi Beta Kappa. In 1919, she earned her master's degree at the University of Pennsylvania. During 1925–1926, Fauset traveled in Europe and spent six months studying French at the Sorbonne and at the Alliance Française in Paris, France.

Fauset wrote numerous essays, poems, and short stories from the 1910s to the early 1930s, publishing in various periodicals as well as in anthologies. At the beginning of the Harlem Renaissance, she moved to New York City and worked for *The Crisis*, the official publication of the National Association for the Advancement of Colored People (NAACP), then edited by W.E.B. Du Bois; she soon became its literary editor, a position she held for seven years (1919–1926). An important novelist herself, Fauset is more often remembered for discovering and publishing young writers, including Countee Cullen, Nella Larsen, Jean Toomer, Claude McKay, and Langston Hughes, who described Fauset as one of "the three people who midwifed the so-called New Negro Literature into being" (*The Big Sea*, 113).

Fauset's contributions to *The Crisis* were valuable and diverse, and included biographical sketches, essays on drama, articles, reviews, poems, short stories, essays, and translations of French West Indian poems. In addition, her innovative editorial work changed the face of *The Crisis* and fostered the New Negro Renaissance, now known as the Harlem Renaissance. She published the work of Countee Cullen, Langston Hughes, and many other Black writers from the era. In 1920 and 1921, Fauset was a writer and an editor for *Brownies' Book*, a short-lived monthly magazine, created by Du Bois, for African American children. She and her sister made the apartment they shared in Harlem, New York, into a gathering place for the African American intellectuals and their friends to gather and discuss art and politics.

Fauset left *The Crisis* in 1926 to find a job that would allow her more time for writing. During this time, she traveled, lectured, and wrote poems. In 1927, she married Herbert E. Harris; they had no children. Fauset could not make a living from writing, however, and discrimination prevented her from working in a New York publishing house. She therefore turned to teaching and continued writing.

Between 1924 and 1933, Fauset produced four full-length novels exploring issues of identity and race, class and gender differences. These novels focus on the careers, courtships, and marriages of the Black professional class and offer sentimental resolutions to the complex problems they raise. *There Is Confusion* (1924) was the first published novel by a Black woman to explore the theme of "color"; arguably her best novel, *Plum Bun*, was published in 1929; and her third, *The Chinaberry Tree*, appeared in 1931. Her final work, *Comedy, American Style* (1933), became her best-known novel; it traces the Black female protagonist, Olivia Carey, who hates being Black while her son and her husband are proud of their African American cultural heritage. Fauset's best-known essay, "The Gift of Laughter" (1925), analyzes the Black comic character in American drama. Among her best-known poems are "La Vie C'est la Vie," "Noblesse Oblige," "Christmas Eve in France," and "Rondeau." William Stanley Braithwaite, in *Opportunity* (January 1934), called Fauset "the potential Jane Austen of Negro Literature."

During the 1960s and 1970s, some critics charged that Fauset's work did not deal with the broader African American community, but critics today admire her portraits of African Americans and her literary influence, and one critic has characterized her feminism as "pragmatic" (Phipps). After her husband's death, in 1958, she left New Jersey for Philadelphia and lived with her stepbrother, Earl Huff, until her death from heart disease in 1961.

Truong Le

See also: Harlem Renaissance; Novel.

Resources

Jessie Redmon Fauset: *The Chinaberry Tree: A Novel of American Life* (1931; repr. New York: G. K. Hall, 1995); *Comedy: American Style* (1933; repr. New York: G. K. Hall, 1994); *The Gift of Laughter* (1925; repr. New York: Atheneum, 1992); *Plum Bun: A Novel Without a Moral* (1929; repr. Boston: Beacon Press, 1990); *There Is Confusion* (1924; repr. Boston: Northeastern University Press, 1989); Willie J. Harrell, "'I Am on the Coloured Side': The Rhetoric of Passing in Jessie Redmon Fauset's *Plum Bun: A Novel Without a Moral*," *College Language Association Journal*, 52, no. 2 (December 1, 2008): 187–208; Shari Dorantes Hatch, "Jessie Redmon Fauset," in *African American Writers: A Dictionary*, ed. Shari Dorantes Hatch and Michael R. Strickland (Santa Barbara, CA: ABC-CLIO, 2000), 114; Langston Hughes, *The Big Sea: An Autobiography* (New York: Knopf, 1940); Susan Levison, "Performance and the 'Strange Place' of Jessie Redmon Fauset's There Is Confusion," *Modern Fiction Studies* 46, no. 4 (December 1, 2000), 825–848; Michelle Phillips, "The Children of Double Consciousness: From *The Souls of Black Folk* to the *Brownies' Book PMLA*." *Publications of the Modern Language Association of America* 128, no. 3 (May 2013), 590; G. Phipps, "'The Deliberate Introduction of Beauty and Pleasure': Femininity and Black Feminist Pragmatism in Jessie Redmon Fauset's *Plum Bun*," *African American Review* 49, no. 3 (2016), 227–240; Erin A. Smith, "Jessie Redmon Fauset," in *African American Lives*, ed. Henry Louis Gates Jr. and Evelyn Brooks Higginbotham (New York: Oxford University Press, 2004), 293–294; Susan Tomlinson, "Vision to Visionary: The New Negro Woman as Cultural Worker in Jessie Redmon Fauset's *Plum Bun*," *Legacy* 19, no. 1 (2002), 90–97; Cheryl A. Wall: "Jessie Redmon Fauset," in *Encyclopedia of African-American Culture and History*, vol. 2, ed. Jack Salzman, David Lionel Smith, and Cornel West (New York: Macmillan Library Reference, 1996), 939–940; *Women of the Harlem Renaissance* (Bloomington: Indiana University Press, 1995).

Feminism/Black Feminism

Liberation movement focused on Black women. Black feminism is a political, artistic, and social movement that recognizes and resists the oppression experienced in the lives of Black women, an oppression involving racism and sexism as well as issues of social class. Elements of feminism have coexisted intimately with African American literature from the origins of that literature. Beginning with the oral tradition during American slavery and the work of one of the earliest published Black writers in the United States—Phillis Wheatley, a slave who published *Poems on Various Subjects, Religious and Moral* in 1773—Black women have consistently produced culture and art that critiques sexism and racism in American life. In recent years, due to the rapid growth of scholarship by and about Black women, some scholars make a distinction between "Black feminism," which for many now encompasses research on Black women across the world, and "womanism," a term coined by the American feminist writer Alice Walker.

While acknowledging the significant contributions to Black life and arts and to feminism by African American women in the nineteenth century and earlier, most scholars date the development of contemporary Black feminism to the early 1970s and to frustrations experienced by African American women in the Civil Rights Movement and Women's Liberation movement. In stressing that Black feminism has been in effect in the United States as long as African and African American women have been here, historians are recognizing a fundamental tenet of Black feminism: that Black women have created a long-standing and unique tradition of struggle, in art, politics, and other cultural venues, for survival and empowerment. These are the many named and unnamed "foremothers" of the contemporary Black feminist movement that emerged in the 1970s in the United States and has subsequently evolved into a global movement for rights of women of color and for an end to all racial, class, and gender oppression.

A significant figure in the origins of Black feminism, known as much through legend as through fact, is Sojourner Truth, whose renowned "Ain't I a Woman?" speech, delivered at an 1851 Akron, Ohio, women's suffrage convention, was a defiant rebuttal to the prominent definitions of women as the "weaker sex" and of slaves as "less than human." Truth traveled as a preacher and lecturer for abolition and women's rights and published *The Narrative of Sojourner Truth* in 1850 ("Sojourner Truth"). Her famous speech serves as a touchstone of Black feminism, and it is the title phrase for the first of many works by contemporary the Black feminist cultural critic bell hooks, *Ain't I a Woman: Black Women and Feminism* (1981).

Many other women, especially in the nineteenth century, made contributions to Black feminism by recognizing that race and sex interact in the lives of Black women in such a way that speaking from one perspective or the other does not recognize the total picture of Black female existence in the United States, another idea central to Black feminism. According to the critic Hazel V. Carby, Ida B. Wells-Barnett, Anna Julia Haywood Cooper, and Pauline E. Hopkins all wrote and spoke about the "double jeopardy" of the social position of the Black female. Working in African American churches and in the women's clubs movement, Wells, Cooper, Hopkins, and many others encouraged and empowered Black women to work for racial uplift as well as for their rightful place at the table of American politics. Cooper, who was born a slave in 1858, wrote *A Voice from the South, by a Black Woman of the South* in 1892, which is considered by many to be the "wellspring of modern Black feminist thought" ("Anna Julia Cooper").

Other significant contributors to Black feminism are Frances Ellen Watkins Harper, Alice Moore Dunbar-Nelson, and Zora Neale Hurston, to name just a few. While all three were creative writers, Harper and Dunbar-Nelson were also active in the suffrage and temperance movements, and Hurston was a leading talent of the Harlem Renaissance who also did important anthropological work preserving Afro-Caribbean and African American cultural heritage and folk traditions. She wrote many creative and scholarly works, including *Their Eyes Were Watching God* (1937). Contemporary African American feminists, particularly Alice Walker, in her collection *In Search of Our Mothers' Gardens* (1983), have reclaimed Hurston's work and significance as a foremother. These brief descriptions only imply the breadth and scope of African American women's contributions to struggles for the liberation of women and people of color in the United States prior to the feminist movements of the 1970s. The novels of Jessie Redmon Fauset, also a Harlem Renaissance writer, explore convergences between conflicts of race and those of gender. Her novels include *There Is Confusion* (1924) and *Plum Bun* (1929).

Contemporary Black feminism/womanism emerged in the United States in the late 1970s from Black women's experiences in the Civil Rights and Women's Liberation movements, specifically from frustrations with White feminists and male Black activists. Many Black feminists, among them

bell hooks, Beverly Guy-Sheftall, Audre Lorde, Patricia Hill Collins, and Angela Y. Davis, add critiques of classism and sometimes heterosexism, voicing another tenet of Black feminism: that race, class, gender, and other categories of identity exist in a complex web of power that is manifested in the lived experiences of Black women. This principle has led to serious and extended critiques in contemporary Black feminist writing of the cultural institutions that carry out the social control of Black women.

In their groundbreaking history, analysis, and resource guide to Black Women's Studies, *All the Women Are White, All the Blacks Are Men, But Some of Us Are Brave: Black Women's Studies*, Gloria T. Hull, Patricia Bell Scott, and Barbara Smith provide accounts of key moments in the progression of Black feminist thought. In the spring of 1973, a group of politically active Black women gathered to discuss the relationship of Black women to the women's movement, resulting in the formation of the short-lived, but significant, National Black Feminist Organization. Michele Wallace noted in "A Black Feminist's Search for Sisterhood" that during that period she started a Black feminist consciousness-raising group. Wallace's sense of the Black man's hostility to empowered Black women and her concerns about racism in parts of the feminist movement led her to conclude in 1974 that, despite the presence of Black feminists such as Eleanor Holmes Norton, Florynce Kennedy, Faith Ringgold, Shirley Chisholm, and Alice Walker, there was no separate Black women's movement. Wallace voiced her hopes for a "multicultural women's movement" (Hull et al., 2), which some consider a foreshadowing of the current global Black feminist movement.

Two essays written in the 1970s placed Black women's literary culture at the center of Black feminist inquiry. Alice Walker's 1974 essay, "In Search of Our Mothers' Gardens," asked, "What did it mean for a black woman to be an artist in our grand-mothers' time? In our great-grandmothers' day?" Her answer—"It is a question with an answer cruel enough to stop the blood" (*In Search*, 233)—laid bare the agonizing real-ity of living in a culture that not only deval-ued the art of Black women but actually punished learning. Walker has continued to produce creative and critical writing about Black women from a feminist perspective, including the Pulitzer Prize–winning novel *The Color Purple* (1982) and recent writing about female genital mutilation, including *Possessing the Secret of Joy* (1992). Bar-bara Smith's groundbreaking essay, "Toward a Black Feminist Criticism," published in July 1977, claimed she was "attempting something unprecedented, something dangerous" in writing about "Black women writers from a feminist per-spective and about Black lesbian writers from any perspective at all. These things have not been done" (Hull et al., 157). In her discussion, Smith calls for "a viable, auton-omous Black feminist movement in this country" (158). Smith claims that the prob-lem in the Black Arts Movement and femi-nist movement was that they did not focus clearly on Black women; their theories did not have the experience, perceptions, and ideas of Black women at their centers. Smith called for a Black feminist criticism that would begin with a "primary commitment to exploring how both sexual and racial pol-itics and Black and female identity are inex-tricable elements in Black women's writings," and that would acknowledge Black women's writing as an "identifiable literary tradition" (163). Smith's call for Black feminist critics to be consistently vigilant in connecting their work to the "political situation of all Black women" (164) closely followed the growing impera-tive that Black feminist thought focus on the realities of life for Black women.

Another significant moment in the early public life of Black feminism was in April 1977, when the Combahee River Collective, a group of Black feminists in Boston, Mas-sachusetts, who had been meeting since 1974, released a statement that addressed the issues and practices of contemporary Black feminism and provided a narrative of the "herstory" of their organization. Signifi-cantly, like many Black feminists, this group placed high emphasis on both the his-tory of African American women and their day-to-day struggles.

Based on their experiences up to the 1970s, probably neither Walker nor Smith would have predicted the renaissance of Black women's literary productions of the 1970s and 1980s or the volume of subse-quent critical attention the literature gener-ated. The explosion of fiction by Black women writers, many of whom identified as feminists, began around 1970 with the pub-lication of Toni Morrison's and Alice Walk-er's first novels, *The Bluest Eye* and *The Third Life of Grange Copeland*, respec-tively, and includes Maya Angelou's *I Know Why the Caged Bird Sings* and Toni Cade Bambara's collection *The Black Woman: An Anthology*. Other watershed works include three extremely influential collections of fiction and poetry: Mary Helen Washing-ton's *Black-Eyed Susans* (1975); Cherríe Moraga's and Gloria Anzaldúa's *This Bridge Called My Back: Writings by Radi-cal Women of Color* (1981); and Barbara Smith's *Home Girls: A Black Feminist Anthology* (1983). This short list excludes a great number of individual works and lesser-known anthologies produced during this period. By 1985 the critic Hortense J.

Spillers wrote in *Conjuring: Black Women, Fiction, and Literary Tradition* (1985) that "the community of Black women writing in the United States now can be regarded as a vivid new fact of national life" (245). The growth of fiction by Black women created a significant enough stir in academic and literary circles that the well-known African-American critic Henry Louis Gates Jr. said in 1990:

> The black women's literary movement, it seems safe to say, already has taken its place as a distinct period in Afro-American literary history, and could very well prove to be one of the most productive and sustained. Certainly it has features that make it anomalous in black literary history. (3)

From the 1980s on, there has been an enormous proliferation not just of literary criticism about the creative writing of Black women, but of Black feminist academic writing in general, as Black feminists have been researching and writing in nearly every academic discipline, producing a body of information, analysis, and interpretation spanning the experiences of Black women not just in contemporary and historical America, but around the globe.

A significant development in Black feminism in the 1990s was the growth of the "third wave" of the American feminist movement, which had a concurrent and connected Black/multicultural/global component. The third wave includes creative and critical writing that focuses on young women of color, including works by Rebecca Walker and Joan Morgan and the anthology *Colonize This!* (2002). While the impact of "third wave" and "hip-hop" feminism on Black culture and the feminist movement remains to be seen, the creative and critical writing that has emerged from young Black feminists is marked by a continuing commitment to Black women's historical struggles and an acknowledgment of the complexity of definitions of identity in twenty-first-century multicultural America and beyond. As young feminists influence literary and popular culture, their contributions will certainly draw on the tenets that have sustained Black feminism throughout the years.

Sharon L. Barnes

See also: Angelou, Maya; Cooper, Anna Julia Haywood; Gay, Roxane; Giovanni, Nikki; Hurston, Zora Neale; Jacobs, Harriet Ann; Jordan, June; Lorde, Audre; Morrison, Toni; Naylor, Gloria; Perkins-Valdez, Dolen; Sanchez, Sonia; Simms, Renee; Truth, Sojourner; Walker, Alice.

Resources

Lisa M. Anderson, *Black Feminism in Contemporary Drama* (Urbana: University of Illinois Press, 2008); Lindsey Andres, "Black Feminism's Minor Empiricism: Hurston, Combahee, and the Experience of Evidence," *Catalyst: Feminism, Theory, Technoscience* 1, no. 1 (2015); Joanne Braxton and Andrée Nicola McLaughlin, eds., *Wild Women in the Whirlwind: Afra-American Culture and the Contemporary Literary Renaissance* (New Brunswick, NJ: Rutgers University Press, 1990); Hazel V. Carby, *Reconstructing Womanhood: The Emergence of the Afro-American Novelist* (New York: Oxford University Press, 1987); Barbara Christian, *Black Feminist Criticism: Perspectives on Black Women Writers* (New York: Pergamon, 1985); Patricia Hill Collins, *Black Feminist Thought: Knowledge, Consciousness, and the Politics of Empowerment* (Boston: Unwin Hyman, 1990), 230; Combahee River Collective, "Combahee River Collective Statement," https://combaheerivercollective.weebly.com/the-combahee-river-collective-statement.html (accessed 2019); Angela Davis, *Women,*

Race, and Class (New York: Random House, 1981); Mari Evans, ed., *Black Women Writers (1950–1980): A Critical Evaluation* (Garden City, NY: Anchor/Doubleday, 1984); Henry Louis Gates Jr., "Introduction," in *Reading Black Reading Feminist: A Critical Anthology*, ed. Henry Louis Gates Jr. (New York: Meridian, 1990), 1–17; Beverly Guy-Sheftall, ed., *Words of Fire: An Anthology of African American Feminist Thought* (New York: New Press, 1995); Daisy Hernández and Bushra Rehman, eds., *Colonize This! Young Women of Color on Today's Feminism* (New York: Seal, 2002); bell hooks: *Ain't I a Woman: Black Women and Feminism* (Boston: South End Press, 1981); *Feminist Theory from Margin to Center* (Boston: South End Press, 1984); *Talking Back: Thinking Feminist, Thinking Black* (Boston: South End Press, 1989); Gloria T. Hull, Patricia Bell Scott, and Barbara Smith, eds., *All the Women Are White, All the Blacks Are Men, But Some of Us Are Brave: Black Women's Studies* (Old Westbury, NY: Feminist Press, 1982); Audre Lorde, *Sister Outsider* (Trumansburg, NY: Crossing Press, 1984); Heidi Safia Mirza, "Decolonizing Higher Education: Black Feminism and the Intersectionality of Race and Gender," *Journal of Feminist Scholarship* 7/8 (May 1, 2015), 1–12; Cherríe Moraga and Gloria Anzaldúa, eds., *This Bridge Called My Back: Writings by Radical Women of Color*, 3rd ed. (Berkeley, CA: Third Woman Press, 2001); Marjorie Pryse and Hortense J. Spillers, eds., *Conjuring: Black Women, Fiction, and Literary Tradition* (Bloomington: Indiana University Press, 1985); Barbara Smith, ed., *Home Girls: A Black Feminist Anthology* (New York: Kitchen Table: Women of Color Press, 1983); Alice Walker, *In Search of Our Mothers' Gardens: Womanist Prose* (San Diego, CA: Harcourt Brace Jovanovich, 1983); Michele Wallace, *Black Macho and the Myth of the Superwoman* (New York: Dial, 1979); Mary Helen Washington, ed., *Black-Eyed Susans and Midnight Birds: Stories by and About Black Women* (New York: Anchor, 1975; repr. 1990).

Fisher, Rudolph John Chauncey (1897–1934)

Novelist, short-story writer, and medical doctor. Fisher is known chiefly as a novelist now but also was one of the most multitalented intellectuals of his generation. Born on May 9, 1897, in Washington, DC, and reared mainly in Providence, Rhode Island, he arrived in Harlem, New York, in the mid-1920s—just in time to become a major protagonist of the Harlem Renaissance. Fisher's versatility—he became known as the "writer–doctor"—set him apart from the rest of the Renaissance crowd. After graduating with a BA, an MA, and numerous awards from Brown University, where he excelled in both biology and English, Fisher studied at Howard University Medical School. By then, he had already displayed his artistic talent, touring the eastern seaboard with the singer Paul Robeson, whom he accompanied on the piano. Only toward the end of his studies did Fisher achieve his artistic breakthrough: his first short story, "The City of Refuge," was published in *The Atlantic Monthly* in 1925. From then on, Fisher blended a literary and a medical career, establishing a practice as a radiologist and gaining recognition as one of the Harlem Renaissance's most popular writers.

"The City of Refuge" caught the attention of Walter White, a leading Harlem Renaissance figure, who urged Fisher to move to New York because he believed he "[had] very real ability as a writer." Carl Van Vechten, a major White literary figure and sponsor of the Harlem Renaissance, also counted Fisher among "the most promising" of the younger Renaissance writers—a judgment shared by the leading Harlem Renaissance intellectual Alain Locke, as is evident in his inclusion of two stories by Fisher in his definitive Harlem Renaissance volume, *The New Negro* (1925). A first prize for Fisher's tale of intraracial color discrimination, "High Yaller," in *Opportunity*'s literary contest followed in 1926. While the older Renaissance establishment's literary taste rarely matched that of the majority of younger Renaissance members, they agreed at least initially in their assessment of Fisher and his work: Wallace Thurman deemed Fisher's "The City of Refuge" to be "one of the best short stories of Negro life ever written," and Langston Hughes in retrospect described Fisher as the "wittiest of these New Negroes of Harlem."

Fisher's early stories already display the trademarks of his fiction: a witty, predominantly humorous style, a mastery of African American dialect, and a focus on the "Negro metropolis," Harlem. Throughout his literary career, Fisher proved to be a keen observer of the Harlem scene who steered clear of propagandist efforts and fashionable exoticist trends. Instead, as is evident in his essay "The Caucasian Storms Harlem" (1927), he was highly critical of the faddish excesses of Harlem's development into New York's entertainment center. In his fictional work, Fisher focused on the daily experiences of African Americans in their new and complex urban environment, particularly highlighting intraracial color and class conflicts, and depicting Harlem and its inhabitants critically yet affectionately.

Migrants were among Fisher's favorite protagonists. In stories such as "The City of Refuge," "The Promised Land" (1927), and "Miss Cynthie" (1933), Fisher dramatizes the effects of the movement of thousands of African Americans from the South to the North, the ensuing disruption of social ties, and the clashes between newly arrived Southerners and Northern inhabitants. In "The City of Refuge," for instance, readers are introduced to the protagonist King Solomon Gillis, who fled the South for fear of being lynched and who is overwhelmed when he reaches Harlem. Here, he observes a miraculous reversal of prevalent racial power relations: in Harlem, African Americans form the majority while Whites are outsiders. The harsh reality of life in Harlem quickly catches up with Gillis; yet, although in the end he has to submit to the force of law and is arrested, he is satisfied because the police officer in charge is Black, proving his first impression of Harlem: Blacks are in power.

In 2012, a previously unpublished short story, "The Shadow of White," was published (see Fisher/Rothenberg in Resources) and takes its place beside Fisher's other migrant stories. It concerns an African American child who travels north with his father to Harlem, facing difficult circumstances. A White man has given him the cruel nickname, "Smut." The story had been submitted to *Survey Graphic* magazine and accepted for publication, but it was not published.

The Harlem life Fisher portrays is tough, violent, and ruled by capitalism. A recurrent theme is the lack of harmony and compassion—in Fisher's fiction a result of African Americans' adaptation to urban life. This grim effect is evident in "The Promised Land," which depicts the estrangement between two brothers who migrated to Harlem. In the "Negro capital," they are forced to submit to the survival of the fittest, a system distinguishing between those who quickly adapt to strenuous city life and prosper and those who lag behind. In the end, the weaker man is defeated: he is killed by his brother. But in Fisher's tales, not all hope is lost. In "Miss Cynthie"

(1933), the transition from tradition to modernity is depicted as a difficult yet manageable process demanding sensitivity and understanding from old and young, Southerners and Northerners. When Miss Cynthie, a Southern grandmother, visits her grandson, a successful Harlem entertainer, for the first time, a clash of values and traditions ensues. Yet music proves the binding link between old and young. Black cultural heritage is thus shown to be a valuable good—not only for White spectators but also within the Black community that it can reunite.

Fisher's success extended beyond the African American community with its major publishing outlets *The Crisis* and *Opportunity*. Many of his works were printed in journals such as *The Atlantic Monthly* and *McClure's Magazine*. Fisher's awareness of the demands of his White readership is reflected in his writing: "The Promised Land," for instance, contains an explanation of the term "rent party," which would have required no further elaboration for a Black audience. Reminiscent of Van Vechten's provocative novel *N— Heaven* (1926), Fisher's novel *The Walls of Jericho* (1928) contained "An Introduction to Contemporary Harlemese," a glossary that made his work more accessible to White readers unfamiliar with Harlem slang expressions.

Fisher's stories were highly popular and earned him positive reviews from Black and White critics alike. It may have been exactly this appeal to White audiences that provoked W.E.B. Du Bois's criticism of *The Walls of Jericho*, a novel that satirically contrasts working-class life in Harlem with that of the higher classes. Du Bois claimed that Fisher did not write "of Negroes like his mother, his sister and his wife . . . The glimpses of better-class Negroes which he gives us are poor,

ineffective make-believes." Viewing the Harlem Renaissance as an opportunity to replace stereotypical images of African Americans, Du Bois and other Black intellectuals were highly sensitive concerning the subject material chosen by Renaissance artists, favoring "moral" and middle-class Black characters. But Fisher opted for a bottom-up approach, focusing on the fundamental transformations occurring particularly among working-class Harlemites and on Harlem's vibrant entertainment world.

Unsurprisingly, Thurman, the leader of the "N—atti" group that rebelled against their elders' more conservative views, gladly defended Fisher. Yet Fisher refused to join the N—atti's ranks and resisted being claimed or co-opted by any Renaissance faction. While he was a prolific contributor to the Harlem Renaissance, Fisher at the same time stood somewhat apart. In contrast to most Renaissance protagonists, the well-liked and handsome Fisher was happily married and had a son, leading a lifestyle that differed decisively from the chaos characterizing many of his literary colleagues' lives. Following his parallel medical and literary ambitions, Fisher retained a measure of independence from the Harlem Renaissance.

Befitting this special status, Fisher dared to explore a literary genre heretofore left almost untouched by African American writers: detective fiction. There had been some earlier ventures—for instance, a serialized tale by Pauline E. Hopkins (1901–1902)—but Fisher's *The Conjure-Man Dies* (1932) was the first classic detective story published in book form that featured Black protagonists in an urban environment. By creating a tale revolving around the mysterious death of a voodoo priest in Harlem, Fisher took a literary risk. Detective fiction, "invented" by Edgar Allan Poe in the 1840s, was generally not regarded as a serious genre and was predominantly confined to pulp magazines or newspapers. Fisher's courage was rewarded with mainly positive reviews. His mystery tale experienced a revival as a comic stage adaptation in Harlem's Lafayette Theatre in 1936. With *The Conjure-Man Dies* and his last published story "John Archer's Nose" (1935), Fisher helped establish a tradition of Black detection that was taken up by writers such as Chester Himes and Ishmael Reed, and later by Barbara Neely and Walter Mosley. His detective fiction is, however, frequently excluded from scholarly discussions—a fact that seems to indicate the unease with which the genre of crime fiction was and still is treated by some scholars.

It seems that Fisher's medical ambitions eventually proved fatal. On December 26, 1934, he died of intestinal cancer that may have been caused by overexposure to radiation. Fisher left a number of unpublished works and outlines for ambitious future projects. In Harlem Renaissance scholarship, he has not received much attention because many scholars assess his writings as light entertainment, lacking the seriousness necessary to describe African Americans' existence. Fisher's popularity during the Harlem Renaissance, however, indicates his works' relevance for White and Black audiences who appreciated his vivid capturing of life in 1920s Harlem. (*See* Crime and Mystery Fiction.)

A. B. Christa Schwarz

See also: Crime and Mystery Fiction; Harlem Renaissance; Novel.

Resources

Primary Sources: Rudolph Fisher: "The Caucasian Storms Harlem," *American Mercury* 11 (1927), 393–398; *The City of Refuge: The Collected Stories of Rudolph Fisher*, ed. John McCluskey Jr. (Columbia: University of Missouri Press, 1987); *The Conjure-Man Dies* (New York: Covicie, Friede, 1932); *The Walls of Jericho* (New York: Knopf, 1928); Rudolph Fisher and Molly Anne Rothenberg, "Rudolph Fisher's Missing Story 'The Shadow of White': A Study in the Transformation of Race Consciousness," *PMLA: Publications of the Modern Language Association* 127, no. 3 (May 2012), 617–625; Pauline E. Hopkins (pseud. Sarah A. Allen), "Hagar's Daughter: A Story of Southern Caste Prejudice," serialized in *Colored American Magazine*, Mar. 1901–Mar. 1902; Langston Hughes, *The Big Sea: An Autobiography* (1940; repr. New York: Hill and Wang, 1993); Wallace Thurman, "High, Low, Past and Present," *Harlem* 1 (1928), 31–35; Carl Van Vechten, *"Keep A-Inchin' Along": Selected Writings of Carl Van Vechten About Black Art and Letters*, ed. Bruce Kellner (Westport, CT: Greenwood Press, 1979); Walter White, letter to Rudolph Fisher, Feb. 14, 1925, Walter White Papers, NAACP Collection, Library of Congress, Washington, DC.

Secondary Sources: Jervis Anderson, *Harlem: The Great Black Way, 1900–1950* (London: Orbis, 1982); Harish Chander, "Rudolph Fisher (1897–1934)," in *African American Authors, 1745–1945: A Bio-Bibliographical Critical Sourcebook*, ed. Emmanuel S. Nelson (Westport, CT: Greenwood Press, 2000), 161–169; Leonard J. Deutsch, "Rudolph Fisher's Unpublished Manuscripts: Description and Commentary," *Obsidian* 6 (1980), 82–98; Adrienne Johnson Gosselin, "The World Would Do Better to Ask Why is Frimbo Sherlock Holmes?: Investigating Liminality in Rudolph Fisher's The Conjure-Man Dies," *African American Review* 32, no. 4 (December 1, 1998), 607–619; Oliver Louis Henry, "Rudolph Fisher: An Evaluation," *The Crisis*, July 1971, 149–154; Nathan Irvin Huggins, *Voices from the Harlem Renaissance* (London: Oxford University Press, 1971); David Levering Lewis, *When Harlem Was in Vogue* (New York: Knopf, 1981); John McCluskey

Jr., "Introduction," in *The City of Refuge: The Collected Stories of Rudolph Fisher*, ed. McCluskey (Columbia: University of Missouri Press, 1987), xi–xxxix; Vincent McHugh, "The Left Hand of Rudolph Fisher," *Providence Journal*, March 5, 1930, p. 13; Emad Mermotahari, "Harlemite, Detective, African?: The Many Selves of Rudolph Fisher's *Conjure-Man Dies*," *Callaloo* 36, no. 2 (2013), 268–278; Hans Ostrom, "Rudolph Fisher," in *American writers a Collection of Literary Biographies—Supplement XIX David Budbill to Bruce Weigl*, ed. Jay Parini (Farmington Hills, MI: Thomson Gale, 2010); Margaret Perry, "The Brief Life and Art of Rudolph Fisher," in *The Short Fiction of Rudolph Fisher*, ed. Perry (Westport, CT: Greenwood Press, 1987), 1–20; Calvin H. Sinnette, "Rudolph Fisher: Harlem Renaissance Physician–Writer," *Pharos* 53 (1990), 27–30; Stephen F. Soitos, *The Blues Detective: A Study of African American Detective Fiction* (Amherst: University of Massachusetts Press, 1996); Eleanor Q. Tignor, "The Short Fiction of Rudolph Fisher," *Langston Hughes Review* 1 (1982), 18–24.

Folklore

Folklore consists of the traditional beliefs, customs, stories, and practices that are passed down through generations of a community.

Folklore has been a vital force in African American literature. Abrams defines "folklore" as a "collective name applied to sayings, verbal compositions, and social rituals that have been handed down solely, or at least primarily, by word of mouth and by example rather than in written form" (70). From the first writings to the most recent ones, images, terms, concepts, and narrative forms have been transferred from folk culture to African American literature. Among the earliest links between oral and written culture are folklore and folktales that found their way into print by various means and that now appear in widely available collections and anthologies (e.g., Abrahams; Courlander; Dance; Young). African American poets, including Langston Hughes, Countee Cullen, and Paul Laurence Dunbar, have used folklore extensively; with Arna Bontemps, Hughes edited a collection of folklore. Playwrights, too, have drawn on the folklore reservoir, including Randolph S. Edmonds, Lorraine Hansberry, and Ntozake Shange. Essayists, including Audre Lorde, Cornel West, and bell hooks, make frequent allusions to folk idioms and icons. Arguably, however, one sees the most extensive and sustained use of folklore in African American literature in the social worlds represented in fiction.

Many accomplished fiction writers—including James Baldwin, Toni Cade Bambara, Charles Waddell Chesnutt, Alice Childress, Ernest J. Gaines, Ralph Ellison, Zora Neale Hurston, James Weldon Johnson, Toni Morrison, Ishmael Reed, Alice Walker, Margaret Walker, and Richard Wright—incorporate folkloric elements in substantive ways within their literary works (Thomas). As Ted Olson points out, black magic, the "badman" figure (Bryant), the blues, conjuring, sermons, trickster figures, legendary heroes (such as John Henry), superstitions, and lore surrounding voodoo are among the elements of folklore that these and other writers have used (Olson, 286).

As Abrams's definition suggests, folklore includes songs, stories, proverbs, parables, riddles, and sayings. African American folklore also includes ancestral understandings culturally transmitted through traditional beliefs, myths, tales, and language practices of African American people, whether that transmission takes place orally, observationally, or through writing about such lore. Much of this transmission has taken place in legends, tales, and stories as well as in rituals that include narrative elements.

Recent analysts of African American folktales have interpreted the form's functions variously (Dundes; Gates; Levine). Some see tales as vehicles for self-affirmation, social protest, and/or psychological release. Others see folktales as reiterating, inculcating, and complementing cultural values, although many would warn against interpreting tales too literally. For instance, many scholars believe that animal tales and the paradigms those tales provide had their origin in substitutions of animal names for specific people's names. A literal approach, then, could mask important subtextual meanings of such texts (Gates).

Many present-day readers' notions about African American storytelling traditions have been filtered through the work of Joel Chandler Harris, whose *Uncle Remus: His Songs and His Sayings* (1880), came to represent—and in many instances misrepresent—African American storytelling traditions. Harris claimed he was recording these stories in their original and unadulterated form. His language proves revealing, though, for when he refers to other people and their cultures as "simple" or "picturesque," he trivializes them and exposes a condescending attitude. While he may not consciously have set out to impose his own attitudes about African Americans on the folktales, he was not self-conscious about the implications of a White observer presenting African American culture to a White audience.

In terms of assessing the influence of folklore on African American literature, the works of Zora Neale Hurston, and in particular her tales collected in *Mules and Men*, offer one illuminating, representative case study and an important contrast to *Uncle Remus*. Although Hurston may be best known for her fiction, including such book-length fiction as *Their Eyes Were Watching God*, she was also a formally trained and published collector of African American folklore. Hurston's education took her to Columbia University and Barnard College, where she found a mentor in the noted anthropologist Franz Boas. In the preface to *Mules and Men*, Boas suggests that in the past, White interest in African American folklore, including Harris's interest, had been both halfhearted and biased.

It is difficult to fully appreciate the social world Hurston depicts so richly in the folklore she collected unless one is familiar with the traditions of boasting, playing with the dozens (a practice of ritualized, playful insult), and storytelling to which it corresponds and pays tribute. For example, Hurston uses dialect extensively in both her folklore and her fiction, and readers new to her work may wonder why she "misspells" words so extensively. She misspells words chiefly to represent the sound of spoken language and, figuratively, to let African Americans speak for themselves and to recapture the flavor of such oral traditions as boasting and storytelling.

Toni Cade Bambara also stresses the power of folklore, pointing out how fables and parables (short, instructive tales) enabled storytellers, both in Africa and in American slavery, to encode meanings even within conventional narrative forms (Bambara). She discusses how this folkloristic technique of "talking back" to a cultural narrative is called signifying. The retold, revised, and sometimes reversed stories she then presents, including "The Three Little Panthers," show characters and storytellers signifying on familiar tales, in this case the traditional children's tale "The Three Little Pigs." In this retelling, three panthers move into a neighborhood where residents, responding to the differences they discern in the newcomers, seek to eradicate those distinctions. The story concludes with the panthers affirming rather than erasing their differences, and thus deflecting the host culture's normative expectations and intrusive need for conformity. The tale demonstrates how the panthers regard folk practices from attire to literature as integral to their communal and historical identity, and therefore decline to assume the practices of their new neighbors. Like Zora Neale Hurston and Alice Walker, Toni Cade Bambara recognized the importance of revisiting and interrogating the tales that surround and precede one's cultural position.

Elements derived from folklore also find expression within the domains of recent African American literary theory and criticism. In *The Signifying Monkey: A Theory of Afro-American Literary Criticism* (1988), for example, critic Henry Louis Gates Jr. uses the practice of signifying to characterize the way that African American literature contests the master narratives of American culture. Just as W.E.B. Du Bois argued that African American thought is characterized by "double consciousness," Gates suggests that African American literature is double-voiced because it speaks both to and beyond existing cultural scripts. In much the same way that Bambara's three panthers dare to talk back to the insistent voices that threaten their traditions, so signifying texts in African American literature challenge the assumptions behind traditional literary and cultural narratives that would silence or slight the ancestral knowledge of historically disenfranchised populations.

The history of African American literature and criticism is rich in works that refer to African American folklore, whether in terms of style, content, or message. In his life narrative, abolitionist and former slave Frederick Douglass wrote about an experience in which he was given a piece of root to carry in his pocket, a practice suggestive of a lucky charm that also makes specific reference to one's literal and figurative roots, as applied within cultural practices such as conjuring. While Douglass conveys skepticism about the root's magical qualities, that bit of root, tucked away in his pocket, makes the journey to freedom with Douglass. Like this root tucked away in a pocket, folklore (in the form of the language and lessons of a shared cultural past) has accompanied African American writers ever since. From Charles Waddell Chesnutt's *The Conjure Woman* and Ralph Ellison's *Invisible Man* to Toni Morrison's *Tar Baby* and Toni Cade Bambara's *The Salt Eaters*, tales and their tellers ground themselves in the soil of folk traditions. Whether reading Jean Toomer's *Cane* or Paule Marshall's *The Chosen Place, the Timeless People*, one has a clear sense that the collective past does not, and ought not to, pass away, but rather plays an important role in efforts to fight for and shape the future, on the page and in the lived world. An *Encyclopedia of African American Folklore* was published in 2006 (Prahlad).

Linda S. Watts

See also: Chesnutt, Charles Waddell; Hurston, Zora Neale; Reed, Ishmael; Trickster; Vernacular.

Resources

Roger D. Abrahams, ed., *African American Folktales: Stories from Black Traditions in the New World* (New York: Pantheon, 1999); M. H. Abrams, *A Glossary of Literary Terms*, 6th ed. (Fort Worth, TX: Harcourt Brace Jovanovich, 1993); Toni Cade Bambara, *Deep*

Sightings and Rescue Missions: Fiction, Essays, and Conversations, ed. Toni Morrison (New York: Pantheon, 1996); Jerry H. Bryant, *Born in a Mighty Bad Land: The Violent Man in African American Folklore and Fiction* (Bloomington: Indiana University Press, 2003); Keith Byerman, *Fingering the Jagged Grain: Tradition and Form in Recent Black Fiction* (Athens: University of Georgia Press, 1985); Harold Courlander, *A Treasury of Afro-American Folklore: The Oral Literature, Traditions, Recollections, Legends, Tales, Songs, Religious Beliefs, Customs, Sayings and Humor of Peoples of African American Descent in the Americas* (New York: Marlowe, 2002); Daryl Cumber Dance, "Can Trayvon Get a Witness? African American Folklore Elucidates the Trayvon Martin Case," *College Language Association Journal* 58, no. 3/4 (March 1, 2015), 147–153; Daryl Cumber Dance, ed., *From My People: 400 Years of African American Folklore* (New York: Norton, 2002); Alan Dundes, ed., *Mother Wit from the Laughing Barrel: Readings in the Interpretation of Afro-American Folklore* (Jackson: University Press of Mississippi, 1973); Henry Louis Gates, *The Signifying Monkey: A Theory of Afro-American Literary Criticism* (New York: Oxford University Press, 1988); Joel Chandler Harris, *Told by Uncle Remus: New Stories of the Old Plantation* (New York: Grosset and Dunlap, 1903); Langston Hughes and Arna Bontemps, eds., *The Book of Negro Folklore* (New York: Dodd, Mead, 1958); Lawrence W. Levine, *Black Culture and Black Consciousness: Afro-American Folk Thought from Slavery to Freedom* (New York: Oxford University Press, 1977); Mitch Nyawalo, "From 'Badman' to 'Gangsta': Double Consciousness and Authenticity, from African-American Folklore to Hip Hop," *Popular Music and Society* 36, no. 4 (September 2013), 460–475; Ted Olson, "Folklore," in *The Oxford Companion to African American Literature*, ed. William L. Andrews, Frances Smith Foster, and Trudier Harris (New York: Oxford University Press, 1997), 286–290; Anand Prahlad, ed., *The Greenwood Encyclopedia of African American Folklore* (Westport, CT: Greenwood Publishers, 2006); Marjorie Pryse and Hortense J. Spillers, eds., *Conjuring: Black Women, Fiction, and Literary Tradition* (Bloomington: Indiana University Press, 1985); H. Nigel Thomas, *From Folklore to Fiction: A Study of Folk Heroes and Rituals in the Black American Novel* (Westport, CT: Greenwood Press, 1988); Richard Alan Young and Judy Dockrey Young, eds., *African-American Folktales for Young Readers: Including Favorite Stories from African and African-American Storytellers* (Little Rock, AR: August House, 1993).

Formal Verse

Formal verse can be defined as poetry that closely follows European literary conventions in its line count and line structure or in its regular use of rhyme and meter. Formal verse thus includes at least three main groupings: (1) patterns between lines or within stanzas, such as the heroic couplet, terza rima, and quatrain; (2) general types of poems, such as the ballad and dramatic monologue; and (3) rigidly defined and complete poetic forms, such as the villanelle, sestina, and sonnet. The earliest African American poets wrote in traditional European verse forms. In the early twentieth century, however, Black poets and critics began to question the relevance and possible limitations of these traditional forms for Black poetic expression. By the middle of that century, many African American poets had moved away from formal verse toward free verse, an open form of poetry that enjoys widespread popularity to this day.

Early African American poetry demonstrates a strict adherence to the traditional meters, lines, and stanzaic patterns of European poetry or song. The earliest known literary work by a Black author, Lucy Terry's poem "Bars Fight" (1755), chronicles the fate of eight individuals during an Indian attack on August 25, 1746, and is written in iambic tetrameter with rhyming couplets. A second example is Jupiter Hammon's earliest known published poem, "An Evening Thought" (1760), which adopts the highly regular meter and alternating rhyme of the Protestant hymn. Like the hymn, Hammon's poem is written in four-line units (quatrains), with the first and third lines in iambic tetrameter and the second and fourth lines in iambic trimeter. Finally, much of Phillis Wheatley's poetry, including her most famous piece "On Being Brought from Africa to America" (1773), is written in heroic couplets (rhyming two-line units in iambic pentameter), a form that had been popularized by the early eighteenth-century English poet Alexander Pope.

Fewer in number are the slavery era works by Black poets that have overtly political content. Some poems parody the form and content of popular songs or hymns. James Monroe Whitfield's "America" (1853) mockingly echoes "America the Beautiful" and points out the country's failure to realize the ideals presented in that popular and patriotic hymn. Similarly, the appendix to Frederick Douglass's *Narrative of the Life of Frederick Douglass* (1845) contains a parody of the hymn "Heavenly Union" and indicts the hypocrisy of Christianity as practiced in the South. The formal but original verse of Frances E. W. Harper, such as "The Slave Mother" (1854) and "Bury Me in a Free Land" (1864), is often heralded as the origin of African American protest poetry. In comparison with these and later writers producing overtly political poems, the earliest African American poets have often been dismissed as purely derivative, echoing the

forms and voices of their masters. In the final decades of the twentieth century, however, critics have reconsidered the use and value of conventional forms in early African American poetry. In particular, Hammon, Wheatley, and others—including George Moses Horton—are now more highly esteemed for using conventional forms, to varying degrees, to present subtle expressions of protest and to bolster claims of racial equality.

From the era of Reconstruction through the end of the twentieth century, many African American poets continued to work in a wide range of traditional Western poetic forms. James Weldon Johnson's "O Black and Unknown Bards" (1908) is an ode, a song of praise written in a lofty style and usually addressed to a particular person or important abstract idea; Johnson's poem is addressed to the anonymous African American creators and performers of the spirituals that comforted and converted the slaves who listened to them. Similarly, Paul Laurence Dunbar's "The Colored Soldiers" (1895) follows the conventions of the epic, a chronicle of events (usually in war) presented in verse form; Dunbar's poem begins with an invocation to the muse, a convention of epic poetry since antiquity, and recounts the sacrifices and achievements of Black soldiers in the Civil War. (*See* Epic Poetry/The Long Poem.)

A wide range of formal poetry is represented in the works of African Americans collected in *The Poetry of the Negro 1746–1970*, an anthology edited by Langston Hughes and Arna Bontemps (1949; reprinted in expanded format in 1970). This anthology includes, especially among the later poets, examples of all three types of formal poetry: poems using regular patterns between lines or within stanzas, such as terza rima and the cinquain; general types of poems, such as the epigram and the ballad; and rigidly defined and complete poetic forms, such as the sonnet and villanelle.

Terza rima is a series of tercets, or three-line stanzas, in which the rhyme of one stanza is continued in the next stanza, with the outer lines of each following stanza rhyming with the middle line of the preceding stanza: *aba bcb cdc*, and so on. Terza rima is used famously in Dante's *Divine Comedy* but makes occasional appearance in African American poetry, as is the case in G. C. Oden's "A Private Letter to Brazil." George Marion McClellan's "The Feet of Judas," also included in the anthology, follows the equally rare model of the cinquain (or quintain), a five-line stanza with a regular rhyme scheme.

Among the many general types of poems represented in the anthology are the epigram, dramatic monologue, and ballad. The epigram, a cleverly condensed observation or turn of thought, was developed into a literary form in ancient Greece and Rome, and was cultivated in Europe by Voltaire, Schiller, and others during the seventeenth and eighteenth centuries. It is represented by Countee Cullen's "For a Lady I Know," which pokes fun at a privileged White woman who assumes that in heaven, too, she will be waited on by Black servants. Dramatic poetry (including the dramatic monologue) uses the direct speech of the characters involved to tell a story or portray a situation, and is represented by Langston Hughes's "Mother to Son." The ballad, by contrast, is a far longer poem that has its origins in folk songs and presents an account of some past event, usually heroic or romantic but almost always catastrophic. The story is related in the third person and emphasizes dialogue and action over description and character development. The

ballad form usually consists of alternating four- and three-stress lines, with simple and regular rhymes, and often includes a refrain. An example is what James Smethurst calls Margaret Walker's "folk poems" in *For My People* (1942), such as "Molly Means," a ballad included in the 1970 anthology that is traditional in its depiction of young lovers and supernatural forces, yet emphatically African American in its use of Black vernacular and Black folk magic, or "root work." Langston Hughes published numerous ballads, including twenty-five in which "ballad" was explicitly part of the poem's title (Ostrom).

Finally, the 1970 anthology includes a number of complete poetic forms, among them the sonnet and villanelle. The sonnet, a fourteen-line poem following one of several predetermined rhyme schemes, is particularly well represented. The anthology includes some of the most famous sonnets by Claude McKay ("If We Must Die"), Countee Cullen ("Yet Do I Marvel"), and Helene Johnson ("Sonnet to a Negro in Harlem"), as well as more recent and more experimental versions by Robert Hayden, Margaret Walker, and Gwendolyn Brooks. A book-length survey of African American sonnets was published in 2018 (see Müller in Resources).

A far less common form in Black poetry is the villanelle, a nineteen-line poetic form that consists of five tercets, rhymed *aba*, and a concluding quatrain, rhymed *abaa*, and reuses the first and third lines of the opening stanzas at predetermined points throughout the poem. Walter Adolphe Roberts's poem "Villanelle of Washington Square" exemplifies this form in the 1970 anthology.

African American poets have long had a contested relation to European literary conventions and forms. As early as the 1920s, one finds clearly formulated and partisan statements on both sides of the question of the relations between traditional European poetic forms and new African American poetry. In the foreword to his anthology *Caroling Dusk: An Anthology of Verse by Negro Poets* (1927), as in William Stanley Braithwaite's arguments from two decades earlier, Countee Cullen maintains that there should be no forced distinction between Black and White poets in America, since the obligation of both is to maintain and further the British poetic traditions. Cullen's emulation of John Keats earned him praise among many White readers but criticism among some Black intellectuals. Without calling out Cullen by name, Langston Hughes criticizes him in the essay "The Negro Artist and the Racial Mountain" (1926) for wanting "to write like a white poet" or, on a subconscious level, "to be a white poet" or "to be white." (That said, Hughes often used rhyming and set stanzas in his poetry.) Similarly, in his essay "Propaganda—or Poetry?" (1928), Alain Locke rejects a strict adherence to White European literary conventions; he develops a critical characterization of the average Black poet after World War I as "something of a traditionalist with regard to art, style and philosophy, with a little salient of racial radicalism jutting out front" and points to Claude McKay's sonnet "If We Must Die" as a case in point, finding (perhaps without justification) that the poem's strongly voiced opposition to racial oppression remains trapped within a form prescribed by the dominant White culture. Similar rejections of strict adherence to European poetic conventions can be found in Richard Wright's "Blueprint for Negro Writing" (1937) and in Hoyt Fuller's "Toward a Black Aesthetic" (1968), a manifesto of the Black Arts Movement. Wright argues that African American poetry up through the Harlem Renaissance was often formally sophisticated but rarely addressed Black readers, and Fuller characterizes the emerging poetry of the Black Arts era as one that rejects "the literary assumption that the style and language and the concerns of Shakespeare establish the appropriate limits and 'frame of reference' for black poetry and people" (1857).

Not all Black critics have dismissed the production of formal poetry by Black poets. In his study *Modernism and the Harlem Renaissance* (1987), Houston A. Baker Jr. has pointed to the strategic "mastery" and "deformation" of European forms within the African American literary tradition, and in "The Unreadable Black Body: 'Conventional' Poetic Form in the Harlem Renaissance" (1990), Amitai F. Avi-Ram has demonstrated that Black formal verse is not inherently more politically or socially conservative than free verse. Much of the recent criticism on African American poetry, however, has continued to move away from a discussion of traditional poetic forms. The essays in the collection *The Furious Flowering of African American Poetry* (1999) are a case in point; many of them focus on some aspect of the "vernacular matrix" of African American poetry. As a whole, this collection and other critical statements emphasize the central importance of African American oral traditions and maintain that these have always accompanied and informed the written word in works by Black poets.

Although free verse has displaced much of formal verse in African American poetry since the mid-1900s and much critical attention has shifted away from European forms toward Black vernacular forms, a number of significant contemporary African American poets insist on an attention to form. In the interviews recorded in D. H. Melhem's *Heroism in the New Black Poetry* (1990), for example, Dudley Randall discusses his systematic study of versification, and Sonia Sanchez explains how she has her poetry students write in fixed forms to develop both discipline and an attention to word choice so that their free verse, too, will be well crafted rather than "just go and sprawl" (Melham, 169).

James B. Kelley

See also: Brooks, Gwendolyn; Cullen, Countee; Dove, Rita; Dunbar, Paul Laurence; Hayden, Robert; Hughes, Langston; Lyric Poetry; Wheatley, Phillis.

Resources

Amitai F. Avi-Ram, "The Unreadable Black Body: 'Conventional' Poetic Form in the Harlem Renaissance," *Genders* 7 (Spring 1990), 32–46; Houston A. Baker Jr., *Modernism and the Harlem Renaissance* (Chicago: University of Chicago Press, 1987); Robert Beum and Karl Shapiro, *A Prosody Handbook* (Mineola, NY: Dover Books, 2006); Countee Cullen, ed., *Caroling Dusk: An Anthology of Verse by Negro Poets* (1927; repr. New York: Harper & Row, 1955); Hoyt Fuller, "Toward a Black Aesthetic" (1968), in *The Norton Anthology of African American Literature*, ed. Henry Louis Gates Jr. and Nellie Y. McKay, 2nd ed. (New York: Norton, 2004), 1853–1859; John Hollander, *Rhyme's Reason: A Guide to English Verse*, 4th ed. (New Haven: Yale University Press, 2014); Langston Hughes and Arna Bontemps, eds., *The Poetry of the Negro, 1746–1970* (Garden City, NY: Doubleday, 1970); Alain Locke, "Propaganda—or Poetry," in *The Critical Temper of Alain Locke: A Selection of His Essays on Art and Culture*, ed. Jeffrey C. Stewart (New York: Garland, 1983); D. H. Melhem, *Heroism in the New Black Poetry: Introductions and Interviews* (Lexington: University Press of Kentucky, 1990); Timo Müller, *The African American Sonnet: A Literary History* (Jackson: University of Mississippi Press, 2018); Hans Ostrom, *A Langston Hughes Encyclopedia* (Westport, CT: Greenwood Press, 2002), esp. "Ballad," 19–20, and "Poetics, Hughes's," 306–308; James Edward Smethurst, *The New Red Negro: The Literary Left and African American Poetry, 1930–1946* (New York: Oxford University Press, 1999); Margaret Walker, *For My People* (New Haven, CT: Yale University Press, 1942); Richard Wright, "Blueprint for Negro Writing" (1937), in *The Norton Anthology of African American Literature*, ed. Henry Louis Gates Jr. and Nellie Y. McKay, 2nd ed. (New York: Norton, 2004), 1403–1410.

Free Verse

In *Understanding the New Black Poetry* (1972), Stephen Henderson argues that African American poetry from its slavery era beginnings to the 1960s had been permeated by the theme of liberation. Particularly in the latter half of the twentieth century, this theme of liberation in poetry has often been coupled with a liberation in form, a move away from the fetters of rhyme and meter toward *vers libre*, free verse modeled on authentic and living speech. Ron Padgett writes,

> Free verse is just that—lines of poetry that are written without rules: no regular beat and no rhyme. The *vers libre* (French for "free verse") movement began in late nineteenth century Europe, especially in France. But unrhymed poetry without a regular rhythm had appeared in translations of the Bible, and one of the first great poets to use the form was Walt Whitman, an American. (85)

Free verse is unquestionably the most widely used form in modern poetry and is characterized by the absence of fixed metrical patterns, regular line lengths, or predictable rhyme schemes (*see* Formal Verse). The basic unit of free verse is the line or even the stanza, not the metric foot on which Western poetic conventions have been built. In the absence of traditional unifying devices, such as meter and rhyme, poems in free verse frequently repeat words, short phrases, or grammatical structures in order to reinforce the poem's unity. Nikki Giovanni is one of many twentieth-century African American poets to reject the constraints of conventional poetic forms and to write instead in free verse. Her poem "For Saundra" (1968), for example, begins with the speaker stating she will abstain from writing a poem that uses rhyme because "revolution doesn't lend / itself to be-bopping."

Arnold Rampersad (1979) credits W.E.B. Du Bois with being "the first black poet publicly to break with rhyme and blank verse in his most anthologized poem 'A Litany of Atlanta'" (53), published in 1906. Rampersad is correct in identifying Du Bois's poem as a very early instance of free verse in African American poetry. However, some of the most prominent African American poets writing in free verse in the twentieth century—including Langston Hughes, Margaret Walker, Amiri Baraka, and June Jordan—have identified not Du Bois but late-nineteenth-and early-twentieth-century White poets as their models, particularly Walt Whitman, Carl Sandburg, and William Carlos Williams. One of Hughes's earliest and best-known poems, "The Negro Speaks of Rivers," reflects the tone of Whitman and Sandburg especially. Regardless of its origins, free verse has come to be the dominant medium of modern African American poetry. In the course of its development, African American free verse has also drawn heavily from Black vernacular traditions, particularly of the religious sermon and of various types of African American music, including spirituals, blues, and jazz.

Fenton Johnson's poetry from the opening decades of the twentieth century draws on the forms of the spirituals, and James Weldon Johnson's poems collected in *God's Trombones* (1927) use the sermon as a model. Other poets found flexible models for their poetry in more secular musical traditions. Sterling A. Brown includes the blues and work songs alongside the spirituals and at least one conventional poetic form, the ballad, in his first volume of poetry, *Southern Road* (1932). As the title of another first volume of poetry, *The Weary Blues* (1926), suggests, Langston Hughes likewise employed the three-line structure of the blues in some of his poetry, elsewhere using longer lines reminiscent of Walt Whitman or shorter lines recalling improvisational jazz pieces. Michelle Cliff's "Within the Veil" (1985) is a third and more recent example of the use of the blues stanza as an organizing element that does not prescribe line length or number of stresses per line. Tony Bolden argues that such blues-based poetry is "resistance poetry," revising the Black vernacular musical form in order to describe and respond to Black experiences "in styles that challenge conventional definitions of poetry" (37).

Particularly in the Black Arts Movement, free verse poetry became the primary artistic means of conveying a sense of directness, immediacy, and relevance to audiences (see Gayle in Resources). Perhaps all the major poets active in that period who are frequently read and anthologized today—including Amiri Baraka, Lucille Clifton, Nikki Giovanni, June Jordan, Audre Lorde, Michael S. Harper, Etheridge Knight, and Sonia Sanchez—have written substantial works in free verse, as have many later poets. At its best, free verse as a form is limitless in its possibilities. Alice Walker's "a woman is not a potted plant" (1991) demonstrates some of the strengths of the free verse form. The poem is held together only by sets of parallel grammatical constructions, none of which extends beyond a few lines, and this loose and changing form reflects and reinforces the liberating theme of the poem: a woman is not to be confined to the home and to live only to be caring and to be cared for by another. Rita Dove and Colleen McElroy also have written free verse that is distinctive, original, and compelling, as have Thomas Sayers Ellis, June Jordan, and Nicky Finney. At its worst, however, free verse can, and often does, lack distinctiveness. Written quickly and easily, it can be just as quickly and easily forgotten.

James B. Kelley

See also: Angelou, Maya; Baraka, Amiri; Black Arts Movement; Giovanni, Nikki; Jordan, June; Knight, Etheridge; Komunyakaa, Yusef; Lorde, Audre; Modernism; Rodgers, Carolyn Marie; Sanchez, Sonia.

Resources

Tony Bolden, *Afro-Blue: Improvisations in African American Poetry and Culture* (Urbana: University of Illinois Press, 2004); Addison Gayle, ed., *The Black Aesthetic* (Garden City, NY: Doubleday, 1971); Stephen Henderson, *Understanding the New Black Poetry: Black Speech and Black Music as Poetic References* (New York: Morrow, 1973); Ron Padgett, ed., *The Teachers & Writers Handbook of Poetic Forms* (New York: Teachers & Writers Collaborative, 1987), 85–86; Arnold Rampersad, "W.E.B. Du Bois as a Man of Literature," *American Literature* 51, no. 1 (March 1979), 50–68.

G

Gates, Henry Louis, Jr. (1950–)

Professor, editor, literary theorist and historian, and public intellectual. One of the most influential literary scholars of his time, Gates has successfully highlighted race and ethnicity not only in an American setting but also in a global one. Not only has he put forth compelling theoretical paradigms for the analysis of race and ethnicity in literature, but he has also advanced his arguments in contemporary social and political settings, published his views in both scholarly and nonacademic settings, and helped expand institutional settings for the study of African American literature and culture.

Gates was born and grew up in Keyser, West Virginia. After attending a small community college, he transferred to Yale University, where he received his BA in history in 1973. While he was an undergraduate, Gates traveled through fifteen countries in Africa, absorbing the diversity of African cultures that would later inform his work on both literature and history. With the assistance of fellowships from the Ford and Mellon foundations, Gates pursued graduate work at Cambridge University, under the guidance of the Nigerian writer Wole Soyinka, who convinced him to study literature. He received his MA in 1974 and his PhD in 1979, both from Cambridge. After returning to teach at Yale (1979), he joined the faculty at Cornell (1985–1990) and Duke (1991) universities before arriving at Harvard University in 1992. He is currently the W.E.B. Du Bois Professor of the Humanities, chair of the Department of African and African American Studies, and the director of the W.E.B. Du Bois Institute for African and African American Research. From such a position of prominence, Gates has been able to acquire considerable resources to study African American literature and culture both within and beyond the academic setting.

In the 1980s, Gates began to develop an argument that has shaped the bulk of his scholarly writing and multicultural theory. His contention was that African American literature, like texts that were regarded then as more "canonical" or mainstream, should be studied through a critical analysis of its particular textuality, utilizing terms not simply "provided by the master" (Gates, *"Race," Writing, and Difference*). In other words, African American literature should be studied on its own terms, in Gates's view. Instead of agreeing that African American literature merely serves to describe the experience of Blackness to a White readership, Gates argues that readers should utilize a range of critical tools—many rooted in African American traditions—to analyze the specific complex texture of African American works. (Joining Gates in the effort to change modes of criticism was literary theorist Houston A. Baker Jr., among others.)

Gates calls his particular theoretical concept "signifyin(g)," a term developed in his seminal theoretical texts *Figures in Black* (1987) and *The Signifying Monkey* (1988). Signifyin(g) is a concept that synthesizes the deconstructive literary theories at the vanguard of postmodern American scholarship with the indigenous African tradition of literary interpretation that Soyinka had taught Gates. His poststructuralist training leads him to see race as a category not simply forged by biology, but rather as a text that can be "*read* with painstaking care and suspicion" (*see* Poststructuralism). Gates's work with Soyinka informs this practice of reading race. The mythical trickster figure in the Yoruba culture of West Africa told stories about the present through the refashioning of stories from the past in often ironic, critical, humorous, and provocative ways. Gates calls this kind of improvisation and ironic refashioning "signifyin(g)," and he sees it at work in much African American literature. The spoken nature of this mode of storytelling traveled with African slaves to the Americas. African American texts for Gates are thus double-voiced, telling a familiar story and a radically new one at the same time, voicing both an invitation and an implicit critique. This vernacular tradition, Gates argues, is thus inflected in African American writing across history. He uses this framework to read the slave narratives of the eighteenth and nineteenth centuries, the poetry of Phillis Wheatley, Zora Neale Hurston's novel *Their Eyes Were Watching God* (1937), Ishmael Reed's novel *Mumbo Jumbo* (1972), and Alice Walker's novel *The Color Purple* (1982).

Gates's way of interpreting race and ethnic literature merges Euro-American practices of scholarship with the uniqueness of the African American experience. For many literary scholars, cultural theorists, and a wider public audience, this merging made Gates's ideas not just credible but useful.

Loose Canons: Notes on the Culture Wars (1992) put Gates at the center of the controversy concerning education and multiculturalism. In Gates's view, one task for teachers involved in teaching African American literature is to be aware of the political implications of teaching. Gates, therefore, was connecting ways of interpreting race and ethnicity with politically alert ways of teaching and learning. Those believing in the possibility and desirability of politically neutral teaching opposed Gates's ideas, as did those who did not agree with his ethnic-based mode of criticism.

Gates has not only helped reconceptualize the existing American literary canon, but he has also added to American literature by collecting and publishing manuscripts written by African Americans in the eighteenth and nineteenth centuries. One of his first pieces of scholarship was to establish Harriet O. Wilson's *Our Nig, or Sketches from the Life of a Free Black* (1859) as the first novel by an African American to be published in the United States. He has also clarified the life experience of the eighteenth-century poet Phillis Wheatley (*The Trials of Phillis Wheatley: America's First Black Poet and Encounters with the Founding Fathers*). In 2002, he published a manuscript by Hannah Crafts, dated about 1855 (*The Bondwoman's Narrative*).

Gates's position as an American public intellectual has allowed him to produce numerous other works with nonacademic audiences in mind. For example, in 2003, Gates and the Public Broadcasting Services produced an award-winning television miniseries investigating the wonders of the African world, from the ancient kingdoms of the Nile to the Swahili Coast. And in 1999, Gates and his colleague Kwame Anthony Appiah published *Africana*, an encyclopedic compendium of African and African American culture and history, a project an earlier African American public intellectual, W.E.B. Du Bois, spent much of his life conceptualizing. In 2004, Gates produced another television miniseries, *America Beyond the Color Line*.

On July 16, 2009, Gates was arrested in a case of mistaken identity for "breaking and entering" his own house in Cambridge Massachusetts. He spent several hours in jail before being released, and additional charges of "disorderly conduct" were dropped. The incident reflected broader issues connected to policing and race and the United States, and eventually Gates, President Barack Obama, and the arresting officer (Sergeant James Crowley) drank beverages together at the White House as a form of symbolic reconciliation (Goodnough; Ogletree). In 2010, Gates published *Faces of America: How 12 Extraordinary People Discovered Their Pasts*, and, in 2012, Gates began hosting *Finding Your Roots*, a program in which famous people discover, through DNA analysis, information about their ancestors. The program appeared on the Public Broadcasting Network (PBS) on American television. In 2013, Gates produced, wrote, and hosted *The African Americans: Many Rivers to Cross* (PBS), for which he won an Emmy Award Emmy Award for Outstanding Historical Program—Long Form and a Peabody Award. At this writing, Gates is Alphonse Fletcher University Professor and Director of the Hutchins Center for African & African American Research at Harvard University.

Keith Feldman

See also: Postmodernism; Slave Narrative; Trickster.

Resources

Primary Sources: Henry Louis Gates Jr.: *Colored People: A Memoir* (New York: Knopf, 1994); *Faces of America How 12 Extraordinary People Discovered Their Pasts* (New York: New York University Press, 2010); *Figures in Black: Words, Signs and the "Racial" Self* (New York: Oxford University Press, 1987); "Frederick Douglass's Camera Obscura: Representing the Antislave 'Clothed and in Their Own Form,'" *Critical Inquiry* 42, no. 1 (September 1, 2015), 31–60; *Loose Canons: Notes on the Culture Wars* (New York: Oxford University Press, 1992); *The Signifying Monkey: A Theory of Afro-American Literary Criticism* (New York: Oxford University Press, 1988); *Thirteen Ways of Looking at a Black Man* (New York: Random House, 1997); *The Trials of Phyllis Wheatley: America's First Black Poet and Encounters with the Founding Fathers* (New York: BasicCivitas, 2003); Henry Louis Gates Jr., ed.: *The Bondwoman's Narrative*, by Hannah Crafts (New York: Warner Books, 2002); *"Race," Writing and Difference* (Chicago: University of Chicago Press, 1987); Henry Louis Gates Jr. and Kwame Anthony Appiah, eds., *Africana: The Encyclopedia of the African and African American Experience* (New York: BasicCivitas, 1999); Henry Louis Gates Jr. and Nellie Y. McKay, eds., *The Norton Anthology of African American Literature* (New York: Norton, 1996); Henry Louis Gates Jr. and Cornel West, *The African-American Century: How Black Americans Have Shaped Our Country* (New York: Free Press, 2002).

Secondary Sources: Diana Fuss, "'Race' Under Erasure? Poststructuralist Afro-American Literary Theory," in her *Essentially Speaking: Feminism, Nature and Difference* (London: Routledge, 1989), 73–96; Amy Goodnough, "Harvard Professor Jailed; Officer Is Accused of Bias," New York Times, July 20, 2009: https://www.nytimes.com/2009/07/21/us/21gates.html (accessed 2019); Theodore O. Mason Jr., "Between the Populist and the Scientist: Ideology and Power in Recent Afro-American Literary Criticism; or, 'The Dozens' as Scholarship," *Callaloo* 11 (Summer 1988), 605–615; Charles J. Ogletree, *The Presumption of Guilt: the Arrest of Henry Louis Gates, Jr., and Race, Class, and Crime in America* (New York: Palgrave Macmillan,

2012); Miele Steele, "Metatheory and the Subject of Democracy in the Work of Ralph Ellison," *New Literary History* 27 (Summer 1996), 473–502; Robert M. Young, "The Linguistic Turn, Materialism, and Race: Toward an Aesthetic of Crisis," *Callaloo* 24, no. 4 (Winter 2001).

Gay, Roxane (1974–)

Novelist, short-story writer, memoirist, editor, comic book writer, and professor. Gay was born and grew up in Omaha, Nebraska, and her family is of Haitian origin. After attending Phillips Exeter Academy in New Hampshire, Gay attended Yale University but left before completing an undergraduate degree, earning one later at the University of Nebraska in Lincoln, where she also completed an MA in creative writing. She earned a PhD in rhetoric and technical communication at Michigan Technical University.

Gay's first collection of short stories, *Ayiti*, concentrates on the experiences of Haitians facing a variety of conflicts and struggles. It was first published by Artistically Declined Press in 2011 and reissued by Grove Atlantic Press in 2018. Grove Atlantic had published Gay's second collection, *Difficult Women*, in 2017. These stories feature women protagonists who do not necessarily fit the normative expectations of society. Gay's novel, *An Unclaimed State*, received a glowing critical response (Bass, Locke). The novel centers on the kidnapping for ransom of a young Haitian woman.

Bad Feminist (2014) is a collection of essays about literature, politics, and feminism as seen through the lens of Gay's personal experiences. Many of the essays are laced with humor. Gay's best known and most widely read book to date is *Hunger: A Memoir of (My) Body* (2017), which describes her own struggle with overconsumption and addresses issues of body-image, fear, and self-esteem.

Collaborating with writers Ta-Nehisi Coates and Yona Harvey, Gay wrote a comic book for the Marvel Comics Black Panther series: *Black Panther: The World of Wakanda* (2017), which won a GLAAD Media Award for Best Comic Book. Gay has also edited three anthologies: *Girl Crush: Women's Erotic Fantasies* (2010), *The Best American Stories 2018* and the collection of essays *Not That Bad: Dispatches from Rape Culture* (2018). Gay has taught at Eastern Illinois University, Purdue University, and Yale University.

Hans A. Ostrom

See also: Feminism/Black Feminism; Graphic Novels.

Resources

Holly Bass, "Captive Rites," (review of *An Untamed State*) *New York Times*, May 9, 2014: https://www.nytimes.com/2014/05/11/books/review/an-untamed-state-by-roxane-gay.html (accessed 2019); Ta-Nehisi Coates, Roxane Gay, and Yona Harvey, *Black Panther: The World of Wakanda,* illus. Alitha E. Martinez and Robert Poggi (New York: Marvel Comics, 2017); Roxane Gay, *Ayiti* (Oregon: Artistically Declined Press, 2011; New York: Grove Press, 2018); *Bad Feminist* (New York: Harper Perennial, 2014); *Difficult Women* (New York: Grove Atlantic Press, 2017); *Hunger: A Memoir of (My) Body* (New York: Harper, 2017); "The Price of Black Ambition," *The Virginia Quarterly Review* 90, no. 4 (Fall 2014), 54–59; Roxane Gay, ed., *Best American Short Stories 2018* (New York: Houghton Mifflin, 2018); *Girl Crush: Women's Erotic Fantasies* (Jersey City, NJ: Cleis Press, 2010); *Not That Bad: Dispatches from Rape Culture* (New York: Harper, 2018). Attica Locke, "*An Untamed State* by Roxane

Gay: Review—'an unflinching portrayal of sexual and spiritual violence,'" *The Guardian*, January 7, 2015: https://www.theguardian.com/books/2015/jan/07/an-untamed-state-roxane-gay-review-novel (accessed 2019); Amber Moore, "Famished: On finishing *Hunger* by Roxane Gay," *Journal of International Women's Studies* 19, no. 2 (January 2018), 269–270.

Gay Literature

Gay literature, as envisioned and written by African Americans, speaks to the desire to represent the self in its totality. Most of this literature addresses the complex, multivalent intersection between the Black identity and the gay identity. The majority of Black authors who write gay literature choose to do so because they know it is disingenuous, if not impossible, to disentangle one's "Blackness" from one's "gayness." Both identities live within the individual and inform that individual's outlook and life choices. Gay literature by African Americans is notable because it illuminates the unique experiences of the Black gay subject, and there is no foregrounding of one identity—Black or gay—over the other in this literature. The two coalesce, resulting in a more accurate, multifaceted representation of the Black gay individual.

Traces of Black gay experience have been embedded in African American literature since African Americans began putting pen to paper centuries ago. Some critics have discovered gay threads in some of the earliest texts written by African Americans, for instance, in slave narratives. Charles Clifton, for example, in *The Greatest Taboo* identifies and examines gay underpinnings in Olaudah Equiano's eighteenth-century autobiography. Other critics locate the beginnings of an African American gay literary tradition in the Harlem Renaissance—particularly in works by Langston Hughes, Countee Cullen, Richard Bruce Nugent, and Wallace Thurman. Such conceptions are easily contested, because most authors of slave narratives, as well as most Harlem Renaissance writers, neither considered nor positioned themselves as gay, although Nugent published a short story in which an openly gay relationship is represented ("Smoke, Lilies, and Jade," in *Fire!!* magazine). The feature film *Brother to Brother* (2005) is based loosely on Nugent's life and contains flashbacks in which Harlem Renaissance figures are depicted as openly gay.

Although self-identifying as gay is not a prerequisite for writing gay literature, the absence of this self-identification may reinforce the cultural silence and marginalization that precluded Black gay individuals from sharing their experiences in the first place. Much of what might be considered an early Black gay literary tradition is written in a coded fashion designed to draw attention to Black gay characters without shedding any light on the author's own sexuality, gay or not.

James Baldwin was, arguably, the first Black author to claim a gay identity. In addition to claiming this identity, Baldwin infused gay sensibilities into several of his better-known texts, such as *Giovanni's Room* (1956) and *Just Above My Head* (1979), his last novel. One reason Baldwin may have been able to address Black gay sexuality is the cultural cachet he possessed as an author and a critic. Although individuals writing gay literature always run the risk of incensing the masses, resulting in the further demonization of gay literature and those who write it, Baldwin enjoyed a measure of success as a writer that allowed him to avoid the aspersions that might have been cast on lesser-known and less-esteemed authors who addressed gay sexuality in their writings.

Samuel R. Delany, who began writing around the same time as Baldwin, also incorporates gay issues into his texts. Delany writes in the science fiction genre, locating his gay subjects elsewhere in space and time, away from "here." The fact that Delany fashions so many of his subjects as gay bears witness to his sustained engagement with issues of gay subjectivity. As an openly gay Black author, Delany continues to include gay subjects in his texts. One of his more recent works, *Times Square Red, Times Square Blue* (1999), received a Lambda Literary Award for Gay Men's Studies.

Authors such as Baldwin and Delany helped pave the way for other writers to address Black gay experience. The texts that followed Baldwin's *Just Above My Head* and Delany's earlier works were written largely in response to the AIDS crisis. Indeed, Black gay literature includes some of the most harrowing and provocative critical responses to Auto-Immune Disorder Syndrome (AIDS). Writers such as Melvin Dixon, Essex Hemphill, and Joseph Beam offered valuable commentary on the experience of Black gay individuals during the first decade of the AIDS pandemic. This emphasis is all the more valuable given the fact that mainstream culture, in the early years of the pandemic, generally envisioned individuals living with AIDS exclusively as White gay men. It is important, therefore, to consider the seminal Black gay anthologies *In the Life* (1986) and *Brother to Brother* (1991) in order to gauge how Black authors situated themselves within the culture of AIDS. Many of these authors were writing about the disease from which they would

ultimately die, a trend that continues virtually unabated; almost a quarter of the contributors to the most recently published anthology of Black gay authors, *Freedom in This Village* (2005), died from AIDS.

The AIDS crisis of the late twentieth century inspired a legion of Black gay writers, as it also inspired White gay collectives such as the Violet Quill and individual authors such as Larry Kramer and Paul Monette. Previously, Black gay writers had been concerned primarily with shedding light on their efforts to survive cultural stigma and marginalization based on their homosexuality. AIDS changed the focus from surviving oppression to survival in general. These authors, and by extension their readers, resolved to combat what Melvin Dixon has termed the "chilling threat of erasure" (201), by which individuals are removed not only from the physical space but from the cultural narrative and history as well.

Although efforts to represent the Black gay response to AIDS continue intermittently, Black gay literature shifted focus in the early-to-mid-1990s with the rise of best-selling authors such as E. Lynn Harris and James Earl Hardy. Harris struck a nerve with his depictions of Black gay and bisexual subjectivity in mainstream (i.e., heterosexual) Black communities. Perhaps more than any other Black gay author, including James Baldwin, Harris has achieved a popular acclaim that shows no sign of tapering off. Although not as commercially successful as Harris, James Earl Hardy has experienced a string of successes with his *B-Boy Blues* series of novels. Both Harris and Hardy indicate the future of gay literature by Black gay authors, particularly in the ways they introduce new considerations to the literature. Harris, for example, imbricates a class consciousness in his novels that does not appear as often in other Black gay texts, while Hardy includes numerous instances of sociolinguistic code-shifting in his texts in order to lend verisimilitude to his characters.

Chris Bell

See also: Baldwin, James; Delany, Samuel R.; Hemphill, Essex; Lesbian Literature; Nugent, Richard Bruce.

Resources

James Baldwin: *Giovanni's Room* (1956; New York: Delta, 2000); *Just Above My Head* (1979; New York: Delta, 2000); Joseph Beam, ed., *In the Life: A Black Gay Anthology* (Boston: Alyson, 1986); Devin W. Carbado et al., eds., *Black Like Us: A Century of Lesbian, Gay, and Bisexual African American Fiction* (San Francisco: Cleis Press, 2002); Delroy Constantine-Simms, *The Greatest Taboo: Homosexuality in Black Communities* (Los Angeles: Alyson, 2001); Samuel R. Delany, *Times Square Red, Times Square Blue* (1999; New York: New York University Press, 2001); Melvin Dixon, "I'll Be Somewhere Listening for My Name," in *Sojourner: Black Gay Voices in the Age of AIDS*, ed. B. Michael Hunter (New York: Other Countries, 1993), 199–203; Olaudah Equiano, *The Interesting Narrative of the Life of Olaudah Equiano, or Gustavus Vassa the African*, ed. Henry Louis Gates Jr. (New York: Signet, 2002); Rodney Evans, writer and director, *Brother to Brother* (New York: Miasma Films (Firm);C-Hundred Film Corp.; Intrinsic Value Films.; Wolfe Video, 2005); E. Lynn Harris, ed., *Freedom in This Village: Black Gay Men's Writing, 1969 to the Present* (New York: Carroll and Graf, 2005); Essex Hemphill, ed., *Brother to Brother: New Writings by Black Gay Men* (Boston: Alyson, 1991); E. Patrick Johnson, ed., *No Tea, No Shade: New Writings in Black Queer Studies* (Durham: Duke University Press, 2016); Kevin McGruder, "To Be Heard in Print: Black Gay Writers in 1980s New York," *Obsidian III* 6, no. 1 (April 1, 2005), 49–65; Bruce Morrow and Charles H. Rowell, eds., *Shade: An Anthology of Fiction by Gay Men of African Descent* (New York: Avon, 1996); Robert Reid-Pharr, *Black Gay Man: Essays* (New York: New York University Press, 2001); Roger Sneed, "Like Fire Shut Up in Our Bones: Religion and Spirituality in Black Gay Men's Literature," *Black Theology* 6, no. 2 (December 6, 2008), 241–261; Kai Wright, "Documenting a Black Gay and Lesbian Literary Canon," *Black Issues Book Review* 6, no. 4 (July/August 2004), 39.

Giovanni, Nikki (1943–)

Poet, essayist, children's writer, and professor. Nikki Giovanni is one of the most prolific and widely read poets to spring from the Black Arts Movement of the 1960s. Her work exemplifies the ethnic pride and social engagement found in other expressions of Black Power at the end of the Civil Rights Movement. Her continued success as a poet, however, owes itself to an adaptive style that is both conversational and musical. A poet of the people, Giovanni has always had great popular appeal, if not close critical attention. Critics have alternately praised her work as warm and unaffected or castigated it as trivial, sentimental, and bitter. Few have attempted to understand the relationship between the overtly political and the deeply personal within her work.

Born Yolande Cornelia Giovanni Jr. on June 7, 1943, in Knoxville, Tennessee, to Jones and Yolande Giovanni, Nikki grew up in Cincinnati, Ohio, but frequently returned to Knoxville to spend time with her maternal grandparents. She graduated from high school there in 1960. Her grandmother, Emma Louvenia Watson, was a powerful influence on Giovanni's attitudes and figures prominently in many of her poems and essays.

Giovanni entered Fisk University in Nashville, Tennessee, at the age of seventeen, but her attitudes were often in conflict with the strict university administration. She was dismissed from school at the end of her first semester, in part because of an unauthorized visit to her grandparents in Knoxville during the Thanksgiving holiday. She spent the years 1961–1963 living with her parents in Cincinnati, working odd jobs, and taking courses at the University of Cincinnati. In 1964, she returned to Fisk and became engaged in campus literary and political activities. She abandoned her earlier conservative politics and took up more progressive views. She edited the student literary magazine, *Élan*, and helped reestablish a chapter of the Student Nonviolent Coordinating Committee. Giovanni completed a BA degree in history at Fisk in 1967. She then moved back to Cincinnati to be near her parents. There, she immersed herself in reading and writing poetry.

In Cincinnati, Giovanni met H. Rap Brown and other leaders of the Black Arts Movement and then organized a Black Arts Festival for the city. Later that year, with assistance from the Ford Foundation, she moved to Delaware and enrolled in the University of Pennsylvania School of Social Work. In 1968, she privately published *Black Feeling, Black Talk* and dropped out of graduate school to pursue a career in writing. With a National Endowment for the Arts grant, she moved to New York City. Her second book of poetry, *Black Judgement*, was published later the same year. In 1969, she gave birth to a son, Thomas Watson Giovanni. A year after the birth of her son, she formed her own publishing company, NikTom Limited, to publish the works of Black female poets.

Throughout the 1970s, Giovanni published a prodigious volume of poetry and became one of the most recognized artists in the country. She gave frequent public readings and lectures, appeared on television and radio, and released several sound recordings, which further served to make her a poet of the people. The spoken word album she released in 1971, *Truth Is on Its Way*, became a best seller. In 1971, Giovanni also published a book of poems for children dedicated to her son, *Spin a Soft Black Song*. She would return to children's literature repeatedly in the future, primarily as a means of giving positive images and a sense of pride to African American children.

Giovanni held instructor and professorial positions at several universities: Queens College (1968), Rutgers University (1968–1972), Ohio State University (1984–1985), and Mount St. Joseph's College (1985–1987). In 1987, Giovanni accepted a position as visiting professor of English at Virginia Tech in Blacksburg. She was given permanent, tenured status at Virginia Tech in 1989.

Giovanni's earliest works *Black Feeling, Black Talk*, and *Black Judgement* (published together in a single volume in 1970) are often seen as expressions of an angry and militant Black consciousness. "The True Import of Present Dialogue, Black vs. Negro" (from *Black Feeling, Black Talk*), says of African Americans, "We ain't got to prove we can die / We got to prove we can kill."

Her subsequent works are usually considered to be a retreat from this early revolutionary stance toward a more private poeticism. But even in her earliest work, the revolutionary and the private live side by side. "The Great Pax Whitie" (*Black Judgement*), considered one of Giovanni's most militant expressions of Black pride, asks in a recurring refrain whether White America has any shame, and answers itself, "nah, they ain't got no shame." The very birth of America, in this poem, is a genesis of genocide. Yet this expression appears immediately after "Nikki-Rosa," a poem of intense personal sentiment and well-crafted childhood nostalgia. Within "Nikki-Rosa," anger and joy form two sides of one coin. The narrator of the poem (Giovanni) hopes that no White person will ever write about her. The happiness alluded to in "Nikki-Rosa" is poignantly described a few pages later in "Knoxville, Tennessee," with a remembered childhood of picnicking, gospel music in church, and familial warmth.

Giovanni's works in the early 1970s, *Re:Creation* (1970), *Gemini*, an autobiography (1971), and *My House* (1972) continue to address questions about equality and justice, but they also embrace a more personal aesthetic, one that takes precedence over political action. In "Revolutionary Dreams," the narrator talks about former dreams of militancy, but comes to embrace the revolutionary personally. Many of the poems in *Re:Creation* abandon angry invective for biting humor and irony. "No Reservations" plays off a double or perhaps triple meaning for the word "reservation." The narrator leads the reader to realize that one cannot make "reservations" to attend the revolution at one's convenience. Neither can one *have* reservations about taking part. Finally, she warns, "there will be reservations only if we fail."

My House (1972) again exhibits moments of personal introspection, coupled with comments about public events. The book is divided into sections titled "The Rooms Inside" and "The Rooms Outside," the sections forming an exchange between the poet's personal and public selves. The "inside" poems make observations about relationships, family members, and childhood memories. The "outside" poems comment with quiet rage on events such as the use of napalm in Vietnam, the actions of Richard Nixon, and the dealings of the FBI.

Cotton Candy on a Rainy Day (1978) deals poignantly with the failures of the revolution. As in many of Giovanni's collections from the later 1970s, there is a great emphasis on the music of the poetry. Many critics, however, complain that the structure of Giovanni's poetry never quite reaches a level of distinction to equal the content of her work, or that the sense and meaning are sacrificed to musicality. In *Those Who Ride the Night Winds* (1983) Giovanni seems to give up poetic form altogether in favor of startling bits of phrase linked together by ellipses in a staccato manner that is neither prose nor prose poem.

In addition to poetry, Giovanni has published several notable volumes of nonfiction. These are primarily collections of magazine articles, reviews, and occasional pieces. Of these, *Gemini* (1971) gives the most insightful look into Giovanni's psyche, development as a writer, and political engagement. It includes a number of nostalgic essays on her relationship with her grandparents and the sadness she felt when their social order was disturbed by urban development in Knoxville. *Sacred Cows . . . and Other Edibles* (1988) employs a much more biting sense of humor and irony. *Racism 101* (1994) contains remembrances of Giovanni's experiences growing up in Cincinnati and attending Fisk University. It also comments at length on such important Black leaders as Malcolm X and W.E.B. Du Bois. The state of higher education in America comes under severe scrutiny in several essays.

Giovanni continues to produce poetry with a unique and enduring style, wedding intimacy and activism into a single musical voice. Our understanding of her work was enhanced by the publication of *The Selected*

Poems of Nikki Giovanni (1996) and *The Collected Poetry of Nikki Giovanni* (2003). The latter, unfortunately, excludes her children's poetry and the new work published in *Love Poems* (1997), *Blues: For All the Changes. New Poems* (1999), and *Quilting the Black-eyed Pea: Poems and Not Quite Poems* (2002). *The Prosaic Soul of Nikki Giovanni* (2003) brings together most of her published nonfiction. *Chasing Utopia: A Hybrid*, which is a short collection of mixed-genre work, was published in 2013. *A Good Cry: What We Learn From Tears and Laughter* (a book of poems) appeared in 2017, and the children's illustrated book, *I Am Loved*, was published in 2018. The reading public recognizes Giovanni as a distinctive poetic persona, a lively consciousness and conscience for Americans of all ethnicities. In time, Nikki Giovanni might receive critical attention that is the equal of her popular readership.

In April 2007, a mass shooting occurred at Virginia Technical University, where Giovanni was a professor. At a large memorial gathering on April 16, 2007, Giovanni read a poem, "We Are Virginia Tech," after which she led those assembled in a stirring chant, which provided a remarkable moment of reconciliation and encouragement that attracted widespread media attention (Bernstein, in Secondary Sources).

Steven R. Harris

See also: Black Arts Movement; Feminism/Black Feminism; Free Verse.

Resources

Primary Sources: Nikki Giovanni: *Black Feeling, Black Talk* (1968; repr. Detroit: Broadside Press, 1970); *Black Feeling, Black Talk, Black Judgement* (New York: Morrow, 1970); *Black Judgement* (Detroit: Broadside Press, 1968); *Blues: For All the Changes. New Poems* (New York: Morrow, 1999); *The Collected Poetry of Nikki Giovanni, 1968–1998* (New York: Morrow, 2003); *Cotton Candy on a Rainy Day* (New York: Morrow, 1978); *Chasing Utopia: A Hybrid* (New York: William Morrow, 2013); *A Dialogue: James Baldwin and Nikki Giovanni* (Philadelphia: Lippincott, 1973); *Ego-Tripping and Other Poems for Young People* (New York: Lawrence Hill, 1973); *Gemini: An Extended Autobiographical Statement on My First Twenty-Five Years of Being a Black Poet* (Indianapolis, IN: Bobbs-Merrill, 1971); *The Genie in the Jar* (New York: Henry Holt, 1998); *A Good Cry: What We Learn From Tears and Laughter* (New York: William Morrow, 2017); *I Am Loved* [children's book], illus. Ashley Bryan (New York: Atheneum, 2018); *Knoxville, Tennessee* (New York: Scholastic, 1994); *Love Poems* (New York: Morrow, 1997); *My House: Poems* (New York: Morrow, 1972); *A Poetic Equation: Conversations Between Nikki Giovanni and Margaret Walker* (Washington, DC: Howard University Press, 1974); *The Prosaic Soul of Nikki Giovanni* (New York: Perennial, 2003); *Quilting the Black-Eyed Pea: Poems and Not Quite Poems* (New York: Morrow, 2002); *Racism 101* (New York: Morrow, 1994); *Re:Creation* (Detroit: Broadside Press, 1970); *Sacred Cows . . . and Other Edibles* (New York: Morrow, 1988); *The Selected Poems of Nikki Giovanni* (New York: Morrow, 1996); *Shimmy Shimmy Shimmy Like My Sister Kate: Looking at the Harlem Renaissance Through Poems* (New York: Henry Holt, 1996); *Spin a Soft Black Song: Poems for Children* (New York: Hill & Wang, 1971); *The Sun Is So Quiet* (New York: Henry Holt, 1996); *Those Who Ride the Night Winds* (New York: Morrow, 1983); *Vacation Time: Poems for Children* (New York: Morrow, 1980); *The Women and the Men* (New York: Morrow, 1975); Nikki Giovanni, ed.: *Grand Fathers: Reminiscences, Poems, Recipes and Photos of the Keepers of Our Traditions* (New York: Henry Holt, 1999); *Grand Mothers: Poems, Reminiscences, and Short Stories about the*

Keepers of Our Traditions (New York: Henry Holt, 1994).

Secondary Sources: Robin M. Bernstein, "Utopian Movements: Nikki Giovanni and the Convocation Following the Virginia Tech Massacre," *African American Review* 45, no. 3: 341–353; Carrington Bonner, "An Interview with Nikki Giovanni," *African American Review* 50, no. 4 (2017), 715–716; Anna M. Esquivel, "'Isn't This Counterrevolutionary?': Discourse and Silence in the Erotic Poetry of Nikki Giovanni, Kalamu ya Salaam, and Etheridge Knight," *African American Review* 47, no. 4 (Winter 2014); Virginia C. Fowler, *Nikki Giovanni* (New York: Twayne, 1992); *Nikki Giovanni: A Literary Biography* (Santa Barbara: Praeger, 2013); "A Nikki Giovanni Chronology," *Appalachian Heritage* 40, no. 4 (2012), 51–62; Virginia C. Fowler, ed., *Conversations with Nikki Giovanni* (Jackson: University Press of Mississippi, 1992); Trudier Harris, "Nikki Giovanni: Literary Survivor Across Centuries," *Appalachian Heritage* 40, no. 4 (2012), 34–47; Judith Pinkerton Josephson, *Nikki Giovanni, Poet of the People* (Berkeley Heights, NJ: Enslow, 2000).

Graphic Novels

These publications grew out of the comic book movement in the 1960s and came into being at the hands of writers who sought to use the comic book format to address more mainstream topics. There is some debate about who coined the term "graphic novel," but one of the first graphic novels, if not the first, was Will Eisner's *Contract with God*, published in 1978 (Arnold, Nov. 14, 2003, par. 2; Weiner, 17). Eisner, who began working in comics in 1936, has stated that he devised the term as a marketing technique to increase the chances that his comic book about working-class Jewish families during the Great Depression might be published (Arnold, Nov. 14, 2003, par. 2;

Weiner, 17). (Although the genre is called graphic *novels*, nonfiction, speeches, poems and short stories may be adapted to the form as well.)

The graphic novel has gained popularity since 1980 in a variety of geographic and topical areas. A Japanese form called *manga* is exceptionally popular. Art Spiegelman's *Maus* (1986), a Holocaust memoir that casts the Germans and Jews as cats and mice, respectively, is one of the best-known examples of a graphic novel. Graphic novels have embraced a wide array of subjects, including superhero stories, historical fiction, nonfiction topics, and memoirs. Several graphic novels have been adapted into feature films, including Daniel Clowes's *Ghost World*, Max Allan Collins and Richard Piers Raynner's *Road to Perdition*, and Harvey Pekar's *American Splendor*. Other highly regarded graphic novelists include Lynda Barry, Gilbert Hernandez, Chris Ware, and Neil Gaiman.

African American history is one of the topics tackled by graphic novelists. *Still I Rise*, by Roland Owen Laird and Elihu Bey, tells the history of African Americans in the United States, beginning in 1619. The book includes extensive historical information and chronicles the accomplishments and struggles of African Americans. The novelist Charles R. Johnson contributed the introduction, which includes information about African Americans' little-known contributions to the field of cartoons and comics. Ho Che Anderson has written a three-volume series of graphic novels about Martin Luther King Jr. The first volume tells of King's life through 1960, while the second and third volumes cover the rest of his life and the Civil Rights Movement in great detail. Cartoonist Aaron McGruder ("The Boondocks") and writer/director Reginald Hudlin recently teamed up to write *Birth of a Nation*, which portrays a secession movement in East St. Louis. The African American writer Jimmie L. Westley Jr. has begun a series of online graphic novels under the general title *Tribal Science*.

In 2014, Eureka Productions published a collection of twenty-two graphic versions of African American stories and poems by Paul Laurence Dunbar, W.E.B. Du Bois, Charles Chesnutt, Langston Hughes, Zora Neale Hurston, Jean Toomer, James Weldon Johnson, and others. Each story or poem has a different adapter and illustrator. These are a subset of its Modern Age Classics series, which publishes graphic versions of novels in the Western genre, H. G. Wells narratives, Bram Stoker vampire stories, Halloween classics, and more.

In 2006, Andrew Helfer and Randy DuBurke published *Malcolm X: A Graphic Biography*. In 2017, author and illustrator Bria Royal published a graphic novel centered on surviving manic depression: *Black Girl Mania: The Graphic Novel*. Other relatively recent African American graphic narratives include *Strange Fruit, Volume I: Uncelebrated Narratives from Black History*, by Joel Christian Gill (2014), *Run For It: Stories Of Slaves Who Fought For Their Freedom*, by Marco D'salete (2017), *Black, Volume I*, by Kwanza Osajyefo, Jamal Igle, Robin Riggs, Tim Smith, and Derwin Robinson (2017), *I Am Alfonso Jones*, by Tony Medina, Stacey Robinson, and John Jennings (2017), and an adaptation of Octavia Butler's 2003 novel, *Kindred,* by Damian Duffy and John Jennings (2017). (See also Anonymous and Cornog in Secondary Sources for access to more titles.)

Elizabeth Blakesley Lindsay

See also: Coates, Ta-Nehisi; Gay, Roxane.

Resources

Primary Sources: Ho Che Anderson: *King* (Seattle, WA: Fantagraphics, 1993); *King 2* (Seattle, WA: Fantagraphics, 2002); *King 3* (Seattle, WA: Fantagraphics, 2003); Octavia Butler, Damian Duffy, and John Jennings, *Kindred* (New York: Abrams ComicArts, 2017); Marco D'salete, *Run For It: Stories Of Slaves Who Fought For Their Freedom* (Seattle: Fantagraphics, 2017); Andrew Helfer and Randy DuBurke, *Malcolm X: A Graphic Biography* (New York: Hill and Wang, 2006); Joel Christian Hill (New Boston, NH: Strange Fruit Comics, 2014); Langston Hughes, et al., *African-American Classics (Graphic Classics, Vol. 22)* (Algonquin, IL: Eureka Productions, 2014); Roland Owen Laird and Elihu Bey, *Still I Rise: A Cartoon History of African Americans* (New York: Norton, 1997); Aaron McGruder and Reginald Hudlin, *Birth of a Nation* (New York: Crown, 2004); Tony Medina, et al., *I Am Alfonso Jones* (New York: Tu Books, 2017); Kwanza Osajyefo, et al., *Black Volume I* (Los Angeles: Black Mask Comics, 2017); Bria Royal, *Black Girl Mania: The Graphic Novel* (United States: CreateSpace, 2017); Jimmie L. Westley Jr., *Tribal Science*, online graphic novels in progress, http://www.geocities.com/~tribalscience/01page.html.

Secondary Sources: Anonymous, "Must-Have Graphic Novels in Time for Black History Month and Beyond: Diverse Voices & Viewpoints," *Library Journal* 143, no. 18 (November 1, 2018), 58(2); Andrew D. Arnold: "A Graphic Literature Library," *Time*, November 21, 2003, http://www.time.com/time/columnist/arnold/article/0,9565,-547796,00.html; "The Graphic Novel Silver Anniversary," *Time*, November 14, 2003, http://www.time.com/time/columnist/arnold/article/0,9565,542579,00.html; Jan Baetens, ed., *The Graphic Novel* (Louvain, Belgium: Leuven University Press, 2001); Martha Cornog, "Diverse Heroes, New Series: Fourteen Graphic Novels for February, Black History Month," *Library Journal,* November 15, 2015, 140, no. 19 (November 15, 2015), 71(2);

"Superheroes & Heroic Struggles: Eighteen Graphic Novels for February, Black History Month," *Library Journal* 141, no. 19 (November 15, 2016), 70(4); Scott McCloud, *Understanding Comics* (New York: HarperPerennial, 2004); Roger Sabin, *Comics, Comix & Graphic Novels: A History of Comic Art* (London: Phaidon, 1996); Stephen Weiner, *Faster Than a Speeding Bullet: The Rise of the Graphic Novel* (New York: NBM, 2003); Deborah Elizabeth Whaley, *Black Women in Sequence: Re-inking Comics, Graphic Novels, and Anime* (Seattle and London: University of Washington Press, 2016).

Grimké, Angelina Weld (1880–1958)

Playwright, poet, and short-story writer. Grimké is most noted as the author of the first significant play by a Black female and, more recently, as the author of early poems with lesbian themes. Her play *Rachel* (1916) stands out as a classic among numerous antilynching dramas that found popularity during the Harlem Renaissance.

Angelina Weld Grimké was a member of the famous biracial Grimké family of South Carolina. She was born in Boston, Massachusetts, on February 27, 1880, to Archibald Henry Grimké, a Harvard-trained lawyer, and Sarah Stanley, a White woman. Archibald Grimké was the grandson of Henry Grimké, a South Carolina plantation owner, and a slave woman, Nancy Weston. His aunts were the famous abolitionists Sarah Moore Grimké and Angelina Emily Grimké Weld, after whom Angelina Weld Grimké was named. Angelina was raised principally by her father after he and her mother separated in 1883. She was educated in some of the best schools in the country, including the Fairmount School in Hyde Park, Massachusetts, the Carleton Academy in Minnesota, the Cushing Academy in Massachusetts, and the Boston Normal School of Gymnastics. Beginning shortly after her graduation in 1902, Grimké taught school in Washington, DC; from 1916 until 1926, she was on the faculty of the famous Dunbar High School in Washington. In 1930, after the death of her father, whom she nursed during an extended illness, she moved to New York City where she lived in relative obscurity until her death in 1958.

Grimké's play *Rachel* (1920) was a highly popular drama that had successful runs in Washington, Harlem, New York, and Cambridge, Massachusetts. As a work of drama, it shows the far-reaching and implacable negative effects of race prejudice as much as it foregrounds the heinousness of lynching. The Loving family has left the South for a new life of safety and progress in the North after the lynching of Mr. Loving and his stepson, George. Regardless of how much distance they try to put between themselves and the despicable, cowardly act, the Lovings—Rachel, her mother, and her brother Tom—continue to suffer from the effects of the color prejudice manifested in education, employment, and social standing. Rachel is the most severely affected, vowing never to marry or to bring into the world a Black child who must live in fear for his life at the hands of would-be lynchers. Grimké's play is a damning indictment of lynching and the ever-present White prejudice that promotes it.

Grimké wrote a second antilynching play, *Mara*, which remains unpublished and unproduced. In addition, much of her fiction focused on lynching. Notable in this genre is the short story "Goldie," which was based substantially on an actual lynching that occurred in Georgia in 1918. Although less successful, these works are no less searing in their denunciation of lynching.

Although Grimké's poems date back to her girlhood, many of them were never published. Others, however, appeared in a number of anthologies of the period, including Countee Cullen's *Caroling Dusk* (1927). A number of her poems were published in *Opportunity*; although she collected her poems later in life, they were never published together. Recent biographers such as Gloria Hull have noted that many of Grimké's poems were love poems written to women, while others were lyrical poems that focused on nature. Although Grimké produced high-quality work, she could not sustain her writing thematically or in tone beyond the Harlem Renaissance. Her work is available now in an anthology edited by Patton and Honey.

Warren J. Carson

See also: Drama; Harlem Renaissance.

Resources

Stephen H. Browne, *Angelina Grimké: Rhetoric, Identity, and the Radical Imagination* (East Lansing: Michigan State University Press, 1999); Angelina Weld Grimké, *Rachel* (London: Oberon Books, 2014); Carolivia Herron, ed., *Selected Works of Angelina Weld Grimké* (New York: Oxford University Press, 1991); Gloria Hull, *Color, Sex, and Poetry: Three Women Writers of the Harlem Renaissance* (Bloomington: Indiana University Press, 1987); Gerda Lerner, *The Grimké Sisters from South Carolina: Pioneers for Women's Rights and Abolition* [revised and expanded edition] (Durham: University of North Carolina Press, 2012); Venetria K. Patton and Maureen Honey, eds., *Double-Take: A Revisionist Harlem Renaissance Anthology* (New Brunswick, NJ: Rutgers University Press, 2001); Kathy A. Perkins and Judith L. Stephens, eds., *Strange Fruit: Plays on Lynching by American Women* (Bloomington: Indiana University Press, 1998); Lorraine Roses and Ruth Randolph, eds., *Harlem's Glory: Black Women Writing, 1900–1950* (Cambridge, MA: Harvard University Press, 1996).

H

Hansberry, Lorraine (1930–1965)

Playwright, screenwriter, journalist, essayist, and short-story writer. With her classic play *A Raisin in the Sun* (*Raisin*), Hansberry became the first African American woman to have a play on Broadway and the first African American playwright to enjoy a successful run in New York City's central theater district. Though most noted for her prize-winning *Raisin* (New York Drama Critics Circle Award 1959), she was a prolific author in several fields and part of a new generation of African American playwrights whose literary activities contributed to the struggle for civil rights.

Born in Chicago, Illinois, to Carl Augustus and Nannie Perry Hansberry, Lorraine grew up wealthy, her father having made a considerable fortune in real estate. Still, the family's economic status did not protect it from the institutionalized racial segregation of the times. In 1938, they were threatened, terrorized, and finally forced to vacate by court order when they attempted to occupy a home in an officially White neighborhood. Despite a successful appeal to the Supreme Court, her father sought to relocate the family to Mexico, having become bitter toward race relations in the United States. This effort was cut short by his death in 1945.

Hansberry studied at the University of Wisconsin at Madison (UWM) in 1948. Though a predominantly White institution, UWM had a number of racially progressive educators. In 1950, she withdrew without graduating. Her brief college career provided a foundation for Hansberry's activism.

She was the first Black student in her dormitory, served in the presidential campaign of Progressive Party candidate Henry Wallace (the 1948 counter to Strom Thurmond's pro-segregation States' Rights bid), and was the 1949 campus president of the Young Progressives of America. After college, she moved to Harlem, New York.

As a consequence of her 1952 appointment as associate editor of the Black newspaper *Freedom*, Hansberry interacted with such major political and artistic figures as the newspaper's founder, Paul Robeson; its editor, Louis Burnham; and Langston Hughes and W.E.B. Du Bois. Her first theatrical production was a spectacle celebrating the newspaper's anniversary. Her time at *Freedom* helped shaped many of the themes of her major dramas. Hansberry's ex-husband, in his introduction to Hansberry's "last plays," mentions books such as Du Bois's *Black Folk: Then and Now* and Jomo Kenyatta's *Facing Mount Kenya* among her readings (37). This interest in the broad scope of the African diaspora resulted in a number of articles on both African American and African national politics and society. Others, in their focus on reconciling Black America to Africa, discern a "call [on] Africans and diasporic blacks to develop the sense of belonging to a single cohesive family" (Effiong, 35) in *A Raisin in the Sun*.

While reporting on a protest at New York University, Hansberry met Robert Barron Nemiroff, a White student, whom she married the following year. Though they eventually divorced, Nemiroff proved a significant promoter of Hansberry's work, both before and after her untimely death. She left *Freedom* shortly thereafter, intending to focus on her writing. The couple struggled in various jobs during the early years of their marriage, and Hansberry's literary efforts were slowed. Fortunately, in 1956, her husband and a colleague, Burt D'Lugoff, wrote a popular song titled "Cindy, Oh Cindy," which provided adequate regular income for Hansberry to cease gainful employment. She spent the next three years writing and seeking production for the play that would make her famous.

A number of Hansberry's and her husband's friends and colleagues reviewed *Raisin* with interest. Among them was the music publisher Phil Rose, who later became its producer with David J. Cogan. But Broadway investors were generally disinclined to risk money on a "Negro play," and the only interested individual made demands for changes in the production team to which Hansberry was unwilling to submit. The producers opted to finance a series of out-of-town tryouts (in New Haven, Connecticut, Chicago, and Philadelphia, Pennsylvania). Strong audience responses and a sold-out run in Philadelphia encouraged their endeavors, and the show finally opened at New York's Ethel Barrymore Theatre on March 11, 1959. Lloyd Richards, the director, was the first Black director of a Broadway show since the 1920s. The original cast included such future notables as Ruby Dee, Lou Gosset, Claudia McNeil, Sydney Poitier, Diana Sands, and Glynn Turman. The play was an immediate success, running 538 performances and leading to a 1961 Columbia Pictures release starring nearly all the original cast members, as well as a Tony Award-winning musical, *Raisin* (1973).

Hansberry cited witnessing a production of Irish playwright Sean O'Casey's *Juno and the Paycock* as a transfiguring moment in her artistic development. Both *Raisin* and *Juno* share a quality of cultural specificity, a lens into the particular experiences of a social group. Yet both derive universal humanist themes from the local struggles of their communities. Consequently, the plot of *Raisin* marries Hansberry's early experiences with American economic injustice to a global African consciousness she had cultivated as a journalist, and weaves those themes through the public and private conflicts of a middle-class Black family, the Youngers. Hansberry borrowed the final title (originally *The Crystal Stair*) from a verse in the Langston Hughes poem "Harlem."

In its most elementary summary, *A Raisin in the Sun* depicts a conflict within a middle-class African American family over how they will spend a $10,000 inheritance, left by the family father. The matriarch, Lena Younger, intends to purchase a home in a White suburban neighborhood. Her son, Walter, wants to invest in a liquor store. After Lena makes the down payment on their new home, she gives the rest of the money to Walter with instructions to deposit it in the bank. Walter defies his mother and gives the remaining inheritance to his business partner, Willie Harris. The partner is revealed a grifter, and he disappears with the remainder of the family fortune. A representative of the Youngers' new neighborhood visits them; the White households have made an offer to buy the house from the Youngers in order to keep them out. Walter, lamenting his foolishness and concerned for the family's financial future, nearly accepts the offer. In the end, the Youngers decide to move into their new home. In the official refusal, Walter invokes his father's life of service, the family's many vocations, and their "pride," promising not to "join any protests" or cause any grief for their new neighbors but affirming their right to live in whatever home they can afford.

The assertion of individual economic rights, the emphasis on personal responsibility, and the avowal of the work ethic connect *Raisin* thematically to earlier important African American folk dramas and White problem plays. *Raisin* became a watershed event in theatrical representation, bringing to the mainstream Broadway theater a project begun in the 1920s with the Little Negro Theatre Movement and the Harlem Renaissance. At the same time, the play marries domestic values to an ideological conflict over Pan-Africanism through the relationship between Beneatha Younger, Walter's sister, and Asagai, a Nigerian intellectual. His pro-Africa platitudes collide with the anti-Africa Western assimilationism of George Murchison. Caught between them is Beneatha, who performs a traditional Yoruba welcome dance and contradicts George's cynicism with romantic claims about the Ashanti knowing surgery in antiquity, but later is hesitant to accept Asagai's invitation to wed and live in Nigeria (Effiong, 39–42).

Hansberry's original screenplay for the film version of the play sharpened its attack on segregation and called for more combative resistance to racism. Such changes were rejected; Asagai's substantive comparisons between African revolutions and African American struggles for civil rights were also deleted from the final script. In the end, the motion picture, though a critical success, was an enervated version of the stage play. The more aggressive side of Hansberry's work would not be silenced, however. Her last six years of life were characterized by increasingly radical advocacy in her dramatic, political, and journalistic efforts.

Hansberry delivered "The Negro Writer and His Roots" to the American Society of African Culture in New York, a speech in which she demanded that African American writers participate in intellectual and social progress for all humankind, vilifying exclusive attempts to reach only the middle classes or American citizens. Later, she publicly advocated violent defense against White attacks. Her 1960 television play, *The Drinking Gourd*, commissioned by NBC as the opening for a Civil War series, represented slavery as a system that victimized both Blacks and poor Whites. Deemed too controversial, NBC eventually abandoned the project. Her film adaptation of the Haitian novel *Masters of the Dew* by Jacques Roumain was also discontinued, this time for contract problems. She completed three other stage plays before her premature death in 1965 (though only one was produced in her lifetime): *The Sign in Sydney Brustein's Window*, *Les Blancs*, and *What Use Are Flowers?*

Less than three months before her death, Hansberry showcased her second major play, *The Sign in Sydney Brustein's Window*. It tells of a Jewish intellectual who, though previously detached from politics, becomes involved in a city reform candidate's election by hanging a sign in his window. In this comprehensive critique of the political spectrum, Brustein's politician proves to be connected to crime, a Black character proves to be a racist, and friends and family prove to be disloyal. Critical response was mixed and, despite the efforts of friends and several sympathetic fellow artists, the play closed the night of Hansberry's death (January 12, 1965). Many found it overwritten and depressing; others praised it as an honest and astute depiction of life's moral complexities.

Hansberry remained a diligent writer throughout a losing battle with cancer. She managed to drag herself from the hospital to deliver two crucial speeches in 1964, one for the United Negro College Fund's writing contest and another for a public debate titled "The Black Revolution and the White Backlash." In the latter, she admonished White liberal criticism of militant civil rights action. After her death, her ex-husband brought much of her work to the public, including a collection of her writings titled *To Be Young, Gifted, and Black* (after a comment in her speech to the UNCF), a number of posthumous stage productions, and *Les Blancs: The Collected Last Plays of Lorraine Hansberry* (1972).

Les Blancs stands as the first recorded play by an African American author to deal with armed resistance to African colonial rule. With its combination of realism and thematic expressionist techniques, Hansberry achieved in *Les Blancs* what would be a primary objective of the rising Black Arts Movement, a Black American aesthetic informed by native African ethics. A 1970 staging produced by Nemiroff at the Longacre Theatre in New York received mixed reviews. Many audiences were uncomfortable with its seeming defense of combative revolution when democratic evolution fails. *What Use Are Flowers?*, a study of the aftermath of a nuclear holocaust, has never had a Broadway production.

In the early 1980s, two fiction stories by Hansberry appeared in prominent magazines. In 1978, Woodie King Jr. released *The Black Theatre Movement: "A Raisin in the Sun" to the Present*, a documentary film based on over sixty interviews with artists and writers. More than two-thirds of those interviewed noted their debt to Hansberry's pioneering accomplishments. Her early death robbed America of innumerable contributions to literature, journalism, and the burgeoning Civil Rights Movement. But a 1988 television production of *Raisin*, starring Danny Glover and Esther Rolle, included the more radical, previously unused, scenes from Hansberry's film script, had the largest Black audience in public television history and proved the enduring social relevance of her work.

Ben Fisler

See also: Drama.

Resources

Primary Sources: Lorraine Hansberry: "All the Dark and Beautiful Warriors," *Village Voice*, August 16, 1983, pp. 1+; "The Black Revolution and the White Backlash," *National Guardian*, July 4, 1964, pp. 5–9; "The Buck Williams Tennessee Memorial Association," *Southern Exposure*, September–October 1984, 28–30; *Les Blancs: The Collected Last Plays of Lorraine Hansberry*, ed. Robert Nemiroff (New York: Random House, 1972); *Lorraine Hansberry Speaks Out: Art and the Black Revolution*, ed. Robert Nemiroff (audiocassette) (Caedmon Records, 1972); *The Movement: Documentary of a Struggle for Equality* (New York: Simon and Schuster, 1964); "On Summer," *Playbill*, June 27, 1960, pp. 3+; *Raisin* (New York: Samuel French, 1978); *A Raisin in the Sun*, dir. Bill Duke (American Playhouse, 1988); *A Raisin in the Sun*, dir. Daniel Petrie (Columbia Pictures, 1961); *A Raisin in the Sun: A Drama in Three Acts* (New York: Random House, 1959); *The Sign in Sydney Brustein's Window: A Drama in Three Acts* (New York: Samuel French, 1965); *To Be Young, Gifted, and Black: Lorraine Hansberry in Her Own Words*, ed. Robert Nemiroff (Englewood Cliffs, NJ: Prentice-Hall, 1969); *To Be Young, Gifted, and Black: Lorraine Hansberry in Her Own Words*, dir. Michael A. Schultz (Educational

Broadcasting Corp., 1972); "Willy Loman, Walter Lee Younger, and He Who Must Live," *Village Voice*, August 12, 1959, pp. 7–8.

Secondary Sources: Doris E. Abramson, *Negro Playwrights in the American Theatre, 1925–1959* (New York: Columbia University Press, 1969); *The Black Theatre Movement: "A Raisin in the Sun" to the Present*, dir. Woodie King Jr. (AM Video, 1978); Elizabeth Brown-Guillory, *Their Place on the Stage: Black Women Playwrights in America* (Westport, CT: Greenwood Press, 1988); Steven R. Carter, *Hansberry's Drama: Commitment amid Complexity* (Urbana: University of Illinois Press, 1991); Anne Cheney, *Lorraine Hansberry* (Boston: Twayne, 1984); Lynn Domina, *Understanding "A Raisin in the Sun": A Student Casebook to Issues, Sources, and Historical Documents* (Westport, CT: Greenwood Press, 1998); Philip Uko Effiong, *In Search of a Model for African American Drama: A Study of Selected Plays by Lorraine Hansberry, Amiri Baraka, and Ntozake Shange* (Lanham, MD: University Press of America, 2000); Christy Gavin, ed., *African American Women Playwrights: A Research Guide* (New York: Garland, 1999); John Cullen Gruesser, *Black on Black: Twentieth-Century African American Writing About Africa* (Lexington: University Press of Kentucky, 2000); James Haskins, *Black Theater in America* (New York: Thomas Y. Crowell, 1982); *Lorraine Hansberry: The Black Experience in the Creation of Drama*, dir. Ralph J. Tangney (Films for the Humanities, 1975); Robbie Lieberman, "'Measure Them Right': Lorraine Hansberry and the Struggle for Peace," *Science & Society* 75, no. 2 (April 2011), 206–235; Elizabeth C. Phillips, *The Works of Lorraine Hansberry: A Critical Commentary* (New York: Monarch Press, 1973); Jacques Roumain, *Masters of the Dew*, trans. Langston Hughes and Mercer Cook (New York: Reynal and Hitchcock, 1947); Yomna Saber, "Lorraine Hansberry: Defining the Line Between Integration and Assimilation," *Women's Studies* 39, no. 5 (June 22, 2010), 451–469; Catherine Scheader, *They Found a Way: Lorraine Hansberry* (Chicago: Children's Press, 1978); Sanford V. Sternlicht, *A Reader's Guide to Modern American Drama* (Syracuse, NY: Syracuse University Press, 2002); Margaret B. Wilkerson: "Lorraine Hansberry," *African American Writers* (New York: Scribner's, 1991), 147–158; "The Sighted Eyes and Feeling Heart of Lorraine Hansberry," *African American Review* 50, no. 4 (2017), 698–703.

Harlem Renaissance (ca. 1920–1932)

The Harlem Renaissance was the first cohesive literary and artistic movement in African American cultural history. Occasioned by the unprecedented numbers of Black people who moved to cities such as Washington, DC, Philadelphia, Pennsylvania, and New York (including Harlem and Brooklyn) during the Great Migration, the movement was then vitalized by Black and White visionaries such as W.E.B. Du Bois, Jessie Redmon Fauset, Langston Hughes, Alain Locke, and Carl Van Vechten, who believed that the arts would be an essential avenue for racial progress. While the Harlem Renaissance inspired, and was inspired by, African American arts generally, the following paragraphs will focus on its effects on African American literature, after a short discussion of the factors that gave rise to the movement.

In the 1890s, the years that commenced the era known as the Great Migration, African Americans found themselves grappling with a host of factors that were pushing them out of the South and pulling them toward the North. The "push" factors in the South included an increasing degree of racist repression and violence, natural disasters (both a boll weevil infestation and a drought), and a lack of viable job opportunities. The "pull" factors in the North—more freedom and better jobs, relatively speaking—made big cities look like places where Black people might have a fair chance at a future, particularly when the United States entered World War I in 1917, and scores of able-bodied White men joined the armed forces. By 1920, at least 300,000 African Americans had left the South and taken up residence in Northern industrial centers.

Life in the North came with its troubles. Some rural Black laborers discovered too late that they had been lured to urban centers in order to break strikes by White workers attempting to unionize. Meanwhile, Black people who had fled the escalating violence in the South saw the North erupt in flames as well. The summer of 1919 was known as the "Red Summer," and race riots broke out in Washington, DC; Chicago, Illinois; Charleston, South Carolina; Longview, Texas; and elsewhere. But even these dismal events could not keep African Americans from migrating North where the dream of self-determination seemed much more within reach.

Not only a year marked by violence, 1919 was also a period of triumph and optimism. "Here Comes My Daddy" was the song that accompanied 369th Infantry as it made its way through Harlem on February 17, 1919. This regiment of Black soldiers had been dubbed the "Hell Fighters," and the all-Black military band that preceded the Hell Fighters that day was led by Bill "Bojangles" Robinson. All of Harlem was celebrating not only the heroism and success of the World War I soldiers, which was formidable—they were the only American unit awarded the Croix de Guerre, after they spent 191 consecutive days in the trenches—but also the hope and sense of possibility embodied by the victorious men.

The music, dignity, and sense of selfhood evoked by the parade of returning soldiers directly gave way to hopes that an equitable cultural victory could be won by the art and artists of the Harlem Renaissance.

Some scholars argue that the term "Harlem Renaissance" is misleading. They hold that what took place during this period was not actually a renaissance, or rebirth, but another stage in the evolution of African American art that had begun with the inception of African presence in America. In addition, they point out that the cultural activity that characterizes the Harlem Renaissance was by no means limited to the two square miles at the northern end of New York, where Harlem is located. African American music, art, literature, and politics also thrived during these years in Chicago, Detroit, Michigan, Philadelphia, and Washington, DC, where Blacks settled in record numbers. Finally, it is important to recognize the creative interplay developing between African American, Caribbean, and African writers. Not only were African American writers in the 1920s reading the work of Blacks in other parts of the diaspora—and vice versa—but several Harlem Renaissance writers spent significant parts of their careers abroad and otherwise far away from Harlem.

Even though African American arts of the 1920s flourished all over the country and the world, Harlem was still unique as a city that spoke to Black hopes and dreams. "I'd rather be a lamppost in Harlem than Governor of Georgia," went a popular saying of the day. No city in the North captured the imagination of the Black migrant more fiercely than Harlem, which first was a Dutch settlement, then German, then Irish, then Jewish, and then Black, after a considerable real estate war and subsequent White flight out of Harlem neighborhoods.

The neighborhoods that comprised Harlem, known as the "Black Mecca," were not only famously elegant but also became home to some of the most diverse Black populations in the country. Laborers fresh from the South rubbed elbows with African Americans who had known wealth, independence, and social prestige in the North for generations. Immigrants from the West Indies and Africa encountered Black people with entirely different sensibilities and customs. Some of these subcultures blended harmoniously while others did so grudgingly, but all this mixing provided excellent fodder for African American artists determined to translate the cultural upheaval they saw around them into their art. In 1928, Harlem claimed 200,000 Black residents.

Black migrants mingled with African American natives of New York across cultural and class lines both outdoors—along the elegant avenues and broad sidewalks that characterized Harlem—and indoors—inside cabarets, buffet flats, speakeasies, and ballrooms that dominated nightlife in the city. The Harlem Renaissance flourished alongside the Jazz Age, an era that recalls the institutions that made it famous, such as the Cotton Club, which catered to Whites and featured Black entertainment. Nightclubs such as the Cotton Club, Connie's Inn, and Small's Paradise, which featured performers including Edward Kennedy "Duke" Ellington, Louis Armstrong, and Bessie Smith, brought White people—and their money—to Harlem in droves. White financial support was essential to the success of the Harlem Renaissance, but it also forced restraints on Black creative expression. In the case of Harlem nightlife, for instance, while White interest meant increased revenue in Harlem neighborhoods, it also meant that Black patrons had to sit in segregated, "Jim Crow" sections in

order to accommodate the downtown clientele, who wanted to watch Black people but not experience them as equals. "Rent parties," thrown ostensibly to raise rent money for the host, became important avenues for Blacks to congregate privately, away from the curious gazes of White people. However successful these parties were at giving Blacks in Harlem sanctuary from inquiring White eyes, they could not resolve the larger conundrum of White influence on the Harlem Renaissance, a phenomenon to which this essay will return.

While Harlem called to many, its appeal for African American writers was very specific. For Black people with literary ambitions, New York City was important because it had recently replaced Boston, Massachusetts, as the center of American publishing. New York and Harlem were also home to the most important social and political institutions of the Harlem Renaissance period: the National Association for the Advancement of Colored People (NAACP), the National Urban League, and the Universal Negro Improvement Association (UNIA). Each of these institutions had a distinct personality embodied both by the individuals most closely associated with it and the magazines and newspapers it produced. The NAACP had its most visible spokesperson in the scholar and novelist W.E.B. Du Bois, who edited *The Crisis*, the house organ of the NAACP. The National Urban League had educator and writer Charles Spurgeon Johnson, who edited its magazine, *Opportunity*. The UNIA was founded and led by Marcus Garvey, who also edited the organization's weekly newspaper, *Negro World*. These organizations and magazines were among several that were crucial during the Harlem Renaissance because of their dedication to social and political progress for Black people. In addition, the two magazines, in particular, were critical because of their commitment to the identification and development of African American literature and art. For most African American writers, getting a book published was the ultimate goal, but newspapers and magazines reached the broadest audiences and, because of this, constituted significant vehicles for cultural expression during the Harlem Renaissance.

This entry identifies 1924 as the initial year of the Harlem Renaissance period because of a party given in March of this year by Charles S. Johnson, editor of *Opportunity*. Johnson originally intended to throw this party as a way of honoring Jessie Fauset, literary editor of *The Crisis*, on the publication of her first novel, *There Is Confusion* (1924). In the end, 110 members of the New York literati, Black and White, attended the dinner, which was held at the Civic Club, the only elite club in Manhattan that welcomed both Black people and White women. Black and White editors, writers, and publishers addressed the crowd and referred to their common belief that a new era had begun for Black creativity.

After the dinner, Paul Kellogg, editor of the sociological periodical *Survey Graphic*, suggested to Charles S. Johnson that his magazine devote an entire issue to African American culture and that Johnson serve as editor of the volume. Johnson enlisted the philosopher Alain Locke to help him assemble the issue. In March 1925, a special edition of *Survey Graphic*, titled "Harlem: Mecca of the New Negro," was released. It was the most widely read issue in the magazine's history, selling 42,000 copies—more than twice its regular circulation. Months later, Alain Locke expanded this special edition into an arts anthology, *The New Negro* (1925), widely recognized as the first manifesto produced by the Harlem Renaissance. *The New Negro*, which featured portrait drawings as well as essays, poetry, and fiction, includes the work of most of the key figures of this movement, with the notable exception of Zora Neale Hurston.

Inspired by the success of his 1924 dinner, Charles S. Johnson decided that *Opportunity* would host a literary contest; prizes would be awarded in May 1925. The first announcement for the contest appeared in the August 1924 issue of *Opportunity*. Johnson titillated his readers by adding new names of influential Whites who would serve as judges in each issue. Ultimately, twenty-four respected White and Black editors, publishers, and artists served as contest judges in five categories: essays, short stories, poetry, drama, and personal experiences. The wife of Henry Goddard Leach, editor of *Forum* magazine, contributed the prize money, which totaled $470.

The awards ceremony, held in May 1925, was a resounding success; 316 people attended to witness such future luminaries as Sterling A. Brown, Roland Hayes, Edward Franklin Frazier, Zora Neale Hurston, Eric Walrond, Countee Cullen, and Langston Hughes accept their awards. Cullen and Hughes, who would always be rivals for hearts of Harlem's poetry lovers, dominated the poetry category. One of Hughes' signature poems, "The Weary Blues" (1925), took the first prize. At the end of the evening, Johnson announced that Casper Holstein, king of the Harlem numbers racket, would fund the second annual *Opportunity* contest.

Charles S. Johnson and *Opportunity* provided an impetus for the literary flowering of the Harlem Renaissance, but no magazine and no single figure meant more to this period than *The Crisis* and its editor, W.E.B. Du Bois. *The Crisis* also held literary contests, and Du Bois presided over the first, which was held in November 1925. *The Crisis* had an enormous circulation—95,000 at its peak in 1919—so to be published there was a sign of success, at least among the Black middle class. Nothing was published in *The Crisis* that did not meet Du Bois's exacting standards. Between 1919 and 1924, when he became deeply involved in the Pan-African Congress movement, Du Bois relied upon his literary editor at *The Crisis*, Jessie Redmon Fauset. These years were rich for African American writing, and Jessie Fauset's understanding of the literary contours of the Harlem Renaissance was reflected in the foresight she demonstrated by publishing writers such as Langston Hughes and Jean Toomer before other gatekeepers had even heard of them. Fauset left *The Crisis* in 1926. By that time she had made a substantial impact on the magazine and, by extension, the Harlem Renaissance. She would go on to write four novels of her own.

Du Bois had seen the coming of a Negro renaissance as early as 1920, when he had announced in the pages of *The Crisis* his belief in the importance of Black writers asserting authority over their own experience. For too long, he believed, Blacks had endured the ridicule of White artists who had risen to success by reducing African Americans to their most debased elements. Because art had the potential to liberate Black people from social bondage, Du Bois believed, it should be approached with gravity. In 1926, he wrote, famously, that he did not "care a damn" for any art that did not do the work of racial uplift. Because he was editor of *The Crisis*, his words carried weight.

The passion in Du Bois's words signals a larger tension that was at work in the Harlem Renaissance literary community by 1926. On one side were intellectuals such as Du Bois, who believed that Black art should serve as good propaganda for the race. On the other side were writers such as Langston Hughes and Wallace Thurman, who defended their right to represent the Negro as they pleased, in both positive and negative lights. Hughes wrote a 1926 essay for *The Nation*, "The Negro Artist and the Racial Mountain," which represented not only his personal philosophies about artistic freedom but also the philosophies of the "younger generation of Negro Artists," as Hughes christened them. Explicitly, "The Negro Artist" was a response to "The Negro Art-Hokum," a caustic essay by the satirist George S. Schuyler, also published in *The Nation* in 1926, who used his essay to lampoon the idea that an authentic Black art actually existed. In "The Negro Artist," Hughes staked his own position in the continuous debate about the meaning and purpose of Negro art. Both essays have been reprinted in the *Portable Harlem Renaissance Reader*.

These disparate aesthetic philosophies found concrete purpose in the scandal surrounding a single book, *N— Heaven*, and its singular author, Carl Van Vechten. When *N— Heaven* was published in 1926, Van Vechten, a novelist, cultural critic, and Negro arts enthusiast, had been a presence in the Harlem Renaissance since its inception. At the 1925 *Opportunity* awards dinner, he made a point of introducing himself to the evening's brightest star, Langston Hughes. Within three weeks of this meeting, Van Vechten had secured for Hughes a contract with Alfred A. Knopf for his first book of poetry, *The Weary Blues* (1926), and suggested the title for the volume, as well. Van Vechten would serve as a mentor to Hughes for the rest of his life. He would also come to serve as a champion of the work of Nella Larsen, whom he would also guide to publication at Knopf, as well as Zora Neale Hurston, who humorously deemed him a "Negrotarian." Van Vechten also rescued from obscurity the anonymously published *Autobiography of an Ex-Coloured Man* (1912) and reissued it in 1927 as a novel by James Weldon Johnson, the well-known African American political and cultural figure. Van Vechten was far from the only White person who championed the cause of Black arts during the Harlem Renaissance. Charlotte Mason, for instance, patron of Langston Hughes and Zora Neale Hurston, exercised power over the movement, albeit in her private, individual relationships with Hughes, Hurston, and Alain Locke, who introduced Mason to Hughes and Hurston, among others. There were other powerful White figures in the New Negro Movement, but none outdistanced Carl Van Vechten in his commitment to and impact on Black arts and letters.

Van Vechten called *N— Heaven* his most serious novel, and it was the only novel he would publish about African American life and culture. When the book came out, he was already the author of four novels that had, collectively, made him a celebrity and the book a best seller. In addition, he had published numerous articles in mainstream publications, such as *Vanity Fair*, extolling the virtues of spirituals and the blues, arguing for their recognition as authentic American art forms. Still, Van Vechten had concerns about how African Americans, not his primary readership heretofore, would react to his representation of Harlem life. In order to address these concerns, he anonymously composed a questionnaire for *The Crisis*, "The Negro in Art: How Shall He Be Portrayed?" in 1926. Answers to this questionnaire were solicited from a racially diverse group of literary figures from all

corners of the American literary world, and then published in *The Crisis* over a period of several months. Six months later, *N— Heaven* was published.

Du Bois hated the book and published a scathing review in *The Crisis*, advising readers to dispose of it. Hughes defended the book in newspaper articles and even in his 1940 autobiography, *The Big Sea*. The opposing viewpoints held by these two were matched by reviews that were equally extreme. Both loved and hated, *N— Heaven* went through nine printings in its first four months, selling more copies than any other Harlem Renaissance novel.

In 1926, Van Vechten and his novel *N— Heaven* became handy symbolic means for some Black writers to announce their desire to break away from literary conventions that had, according to these writers, traditionally constrained the Black writer. The 1926 journal *Fire!!* became the clearest articulation of the aesthetic goals of this younger generation, which included Langston Hughes, Zora Neale Hurston, Richard Bruce Nugent, and Wallace Thurman. In *Fire!!*, conceived and edited by Wallace Thurman, these writers and their peers wrote about sex and Carl Van Vechten, among other topics, as a way of critiquing censorship and racial parochialism in literature. As much as the editors of *Fire!!* dreamed that their magazine would operate free of White support, such a goal proved unrealistic. An actual fire put an end to the journal, which published only one issue.

The Harlem Renaissance, a Black movement that was necessarily dependent on White support, was diminished by the Wall Street crash of 1929, and then effectively terminated by the Great Depression, even though significant numbers of its key figures continued to produce work well beyond these years. Some scholars believe the

Harlem Renaissance was compromised by the degree to which it relied upon White influence for its existence. Still, the New Negro Movement is unmatched as the first collective attempt by Black writers and artists to grapple with the complexity of their identity in the modern world.

Emily Bernard

See also: Cullen, Countee; Du Bois, W.E.B.; Fisher, Rudolph John Chauncey; Grimké, Angelina Weld; Hughes, Langston; Hurston, Zora Neale; Johnson, Georgia Douglas; Johnson, James Weldon; Larsen, Nella; McKay, Claude; Nugent, Richard Bruce; Schuyler, George Samuel; Toomer, Jean; Walrond, Eric Derwent.

Resources

Emily Bernard, *Carl Van Vechten and the Harlem Renaissance: A Portrait in Black and White* (New Haven: Yale University Press, 2012); George Chauncey, *Gay New York: Gender, Urban Culture, and the Making of the Gay Male World, 1890–1940* (New York: Basic Books, 1994); Jessie Redmon Fauset, *There Is Confusion* (New York: Boni & Liveright, 1924); Robert Hemenway, *Zora Neale Hurston: A Literary Biography* (Urbana: University of Illinois Press, 1977); Nathan Irvin Huggins, *Harlem Renaissance* (New York: Oxford University Press, 1971); Langston Hughes: *The Big Sea* (New York: Knopf, 1940); *The Weary Blues* (New York: Knopf, 1926); George Hutchinson, *The Harlem Renaissance in Black and White* (Cambridge, MA: Harvard University Press, 1995); James Weldon Johnson, *The Autobiography of an Ex-Coloured Man* (New York: Knopf, 1927); Bruce Kellner, ed., *The Harlem Renaissance: A Historical Dictionary for the Era* (New York: Methuen, 1987); David Levering Lewis: *The Portable Harlem Renaissance Reader* (New York: Viking, 1994); *When Harlem Was in Vogue* (New York: Knopf, 1981); Alain Locke, ed., *The New Negro* (New York: Atheneum, 1925); Adam McKible and Suzanne W. Churchill, "Introduction: In Conversation: The Harlem Renaissance and the New Modernist Studies," *Modernism/Modernity* 20, no. 3 (2013), 427–431; R. Baxter Miller, "Traces of Sport from the Harlem Renaissance: The Embedded Narrative," *College Language Association Journal*, 59, no. 2 (December 1, 2015), 131–145; Hans Ostrom, *A Langston Hughes Encyclopedia* (Westport: Greenwood Press, 2002); A. B. Christa Scharz, *Gay Voices of the Harlem Renaissance* (Bloomington: Indiana University Press, 2003); Michael Soto, ed., *Teaching the Harlem Renaissance: Course Design and Classroom Strategies* (New York: P. Lang, 2008); Carl Van Vechten, *N—Heaven* (New York: Knopf, 1926); Steven Watson, *The Harlem Renaissance: Hub of African-American Culture, 1920–1930* (New York: Pantheon, 1995).

Harper, Frances Ellen Watkins (1825–1911)

Poet, essayist, novelist, short-story writer, orator, and political activist. Born free in 1825 in Baltimore, Maryland, Frances Ellen Watkins Harper wrote ten poetry collections, four novels, the first published short story by an African American, and countless political essays that appeared in African American periodicals such as *Frederick Douglass's Paper*, the *New York Independent*, the *Weekly Anglo African*, *The Provincial Freeman*, and *The African Methodist Episcopal Church Review*. She also served on the editorial board of the *Anglo-African Magazine*, the first African American literary journal. Harper is considered an extremely important figure in nineteenth-century American and African American literature.

Orphaned at age three, Harper was raised by her aunt and uncle, Henrietta and William Watkins. William, an outspoken abolitionist orator, writer, educator, and church leader, influenced Frances, who became an educator, writer, activist, and reformer who worked with numerous organizations committed to social justice, including the National Council of Negro Women, the Women's Christian Temperance Union, and the American Equal Rights Association. Harper was friendly with individuals involved in the Underground Railroad, lived for a time in a station of the Railroad in Philadelphia, Pennsylvania, and therefore probably participated directly in ferrying fugitive slaves to freedom. Harper joined the State Anti-Slavery Society of Maine and began lecturing on the abolitionist circuit at age twenty-nine. She was well regarded as an orator, traveling the United States and Canada delivering speeches to audiences of women and men, Black and White. During the Reconstruction era, she advocated political enfranchisement for African Americans, an end to lynching, and education. In particular, Harper emphasized the importance of literacy for recently freed African Americans, and while her writing was read by Whites, her poetry, essays, and fiction were especially intended for Black readers. For example, she hoped her poems and fiction would be used as texts for freedmen's schools and Black Sunday schools. A feminist and radical Christian reformer, her activism included suffrage and temperance efforts, and she emphasized the essential role of American women in political and moral reform, criticizing White women's groups for their racism when they failed to include women of color in their ranks or their analysis of patriarchal oppression.

Like many nineteenth-century American women writers, Harper employed her poetry and fiction as a tool for reform work and political argumentation. Harper's poetry directly analyzes the effects of racism, classism, and sexism in America,

charting a path by which her readers can contribute to bringing about needed change. Her poetry collections are *Forest Leaves* (1845), *Poems on Miscellaneous Subjects* (1854; 2nd ed., 1857), *Moses: A Story of the Nile* (1869), *Poems* (1871; repr. 1895 as *Atlanta: Offering Poems*), *Sketches of Southern Life* (1872), *The Martyr of Alabama and Other Poems* (ca. 1894), *The Sparrow's Fall* (no date), and *Light Beyond the Darkness* (n.d.). The collections represent Harper's wide variety of theme and form. *Poems on Miscellaneous Subjects* introduces many themes Harper would later explore in essays, speeches, and fiction, such as religion, slavery, gender, temperance, and poverty, while the title poem of *Moses: A Story of the Nile* is over 700 lines long, written in blank verse, and tells Moses's tale from the perspective of his two mothers. In *Sketches*, Harper further develops the incorporation of Black dialect in her poetry (Boyd, 14). While much of Harper's poetry had been out of print, the publication of *A Brighter Coming Day* (1990), which includes Harper's letters, prose, poetry, and speeches, and *The Complete Poems of Frances E. W. Harper* (1988) has made her work available to contemporary readers. Harper scholars continue to search for a surviving manuscript of *Forest Leaves*, which remains unrecovered.

Harper's fiction has also only in recent decades been made available to today's readers. Her three serialized novels, *Minnie's Sacrifice* (1869), *Sowing and Reaping* (1876–1877), and *Trial and Triumph* (1888–1889), which appeared in *The Christian Recorder*, the journal of the African Methodist Episcopal Church, were recovered by Frances Smith Foster and republished in 1994. Harper's short story "The Two Offers" (1859) is believed the first short story published by an African American.

A character in Harper's last and best-known novel, *Iola Leroy* (1892), argues that novels can "inspire men and women with a deeper sense of justice and humanity" (262). In all her fiction, Harper sets out to achieve just that goal, creating characters whose decisions either warn readers of the risks of living an immoral life or inspire readers with the possibilities of a life lived true to justice and humanity. Within conventional constructs of women's sentimental fiction, such as courtship, marriage, and women's struggles, Harper's fiction engages political, social, and ideological issues of her day, including racial identity and ambiguity, passing, class struggles, Christian morality, equal rights for women, egalitarian marriages, racial uplift work, lynching, temperance, political corruption, education, and the psychological legacies of slavery.

In her treatment of Christian morality and the legacy of sexual oppression of Black women in America, Harper participates in a tradition influenced by Harriet Jacobs's Slave Narrative, *Incidents in the Life of a Slave Girl* (1846). Like Jacobs, Harper had to negotiate nineteenth-century rhetoric associating "true womanhood" with piety and purity in order to write of Black women's sexual violation during a time when it was not acceptable for women to speak openly about sex, yet to address such truths was a necessary risk by which Black women exposed the epidemic of White men's rape of Black women during and after slavery. Critic Melba Boyd also links Harper's "black abolitionist-feminist aesthetic" to the influence of the poet Sarah Forten (13). Reading Harper's work is crucial to a fuller understanding African American literature and the legacy of Black feminism in America. Her incorporation of political activism into art makes her a forerunner of the Black Arts Movement, and her combining of folk and formal language in poetry and fiction predicts Zora Neale Hurston's and Langston Hughes's writing. In her analysis of the intersections among racism, sexism, and classism, she lays the foundation for contemporary feminist theory by such women of color as Audre Lorde, Barbara Smith, Cherríe Moraga, and Gloria Anzaldúa.

Vanessa Holford Diana

See also: Novel.

Resources

Primary Sources: Frances Ellen Watkins Harper: *A Brighter Coming Day: A Frances Ellen Watkins Harper Reader*, ed. Frances Foster (New York: Feminist Press, 1990); *Complete Poems of Frances E.W. Harper*, ed. Maryemma Graham (New York: Oxford University Press, 1988); *Iola Leroy, or Shadows Uplifted* (1892; repr. New York: Oxford University Press, 1988); *Minnie's Sacrifice, Sowing and Reaping, Trial and Triumph: Three Rediscovered Novels by Frances E. W. Harper*, ed. Frances Smith Foster (Boston: Beacon Press, 1994); *Moses: A Story of the Nile*, 3rd ed. (Philadelphia: Frances Harper, 1889); *Poems* (Philadelphia: G. S. Ferguson, 1895, 1896, 1898, 1900; repr. Freeport, NY: Books for Libraries, 1970); *Poems on Miscellaneous Subjects* (1857; repr. Philadelphia: Rhistoric Publications, 1969); *Sketches of Southern Life* (Philadelphia: Merrihew and Son, 1872, 1873, 1887, 1888).

Secondary Sources: Elizabeth Ammons, *Conflicting Stories: American Women Writers at the Turn into the Twentieth Century* (New York: Oxford University Press, 1991); Michael Bennett, "Frances Ellen Watkins Sings the Body Electric," in *Recovering the Black Female Body: Self-Representations by African American Women*, ed. Michael Bennett and Vanessa Dickerson (New Brunswick, NJ: Rutgers University Press, 2001), 19–40; Lauren Berlant, "The Queen of America Goes to Washington City: Harriet Jacobs, Frances Harper, Anita Hill," *American Literature* 65, no. 3 (September 1993), 549–574; Melba

Joyce Boyd, *Discarded Legacy: Politics and Poetics in the Life of Frances E. W. Harper 1825–1911* (Detroit: Wayne State University Press, 1994); Hazel Carby, *Reconstructing Womanhood: The Emergence of the Afro-American Woman Novelist* (New York: Oxford University Press, 1987); James Christmann, "Raising Voices, Lifting Shadows: Competing Voice-Paradigms in Frances E. W. Harper's *Iola Leroy*," *African American Review* 34, no. 1 (Spring 2000), 5–18; Anne duCille, *The Coupling Convention: Sex, Text, and Tradition in Black Women's Fiction* (New York: Oxford University Press 1993); John Ernest, "From Mysteries to Histories: Cultural Pedagogy in Frances E. W. Harper's *Iola Leroy*," *American Literature* 64, no. 3, 497–518. Frances Smith Foster, "Gender, Genre and Vulgar Secularism: The Case of Frances Ellen Watkins Harper and the AME Press," in *Recovered Writers/Recovered Texts*, ed. Dolan Hubbard (Knoxville: University of Tennessee Press, 1997), 46–59; Farah Jasmine Griffin, "*Minnie's Sacrifice:* Frances Ellen Watkins Harper's Narrative of Citizenship," in *The Cambridge Companion to Nineteenth-Century American Women's Writing*, ed. Dale M. Bauer and Philip Gould (Cambridge: Cambridge University Press, 2001), 308–319; Phillip Brian Harper, "Private Affairs: Race, Sex, Property, and Person," *GLQ: A Journal of Lesbian and Gay Studies* 1, no. 2 (1994), 111–133; Larese Hubbard, "Frances Ellen Watkins Harper: A Proto-Africana Womanist," *Western Journal of Black Studies* 36, no. 1 (Spring 2012), 68–75; Debra Rosenthal, "Deracialized Discourse: Temperance and Racial Ambiguity in Harper's 'The Two Offers' and *Sowing and Reaping*," in *The Serpent in the Cup: Temperance in American Literature*, ed. David S. Reynolds and Debra Rosenthal (Amherst: University of Massachusetts Press, 1997), 153–164; Michael Stancliff, *Frances Ellen Watkins Harper: African American Reform Rhetoric and the Rise of a Modern Nation State* (New York: Routledge, 2011); Claudia Tate, *Domestic Allegories of Political Desire: The Black Heroine's Text at the Turn of the Century* (New York: Oxford University Press, 1992); Michelle Campbell Toohey, "'A Deeper Purpose' in the Serialized Novels of Frances Ellen Watkins Harper," in *"The Only Efficient Instrument": American Women Writers and the Periodical, 1837–1916*, ed. Aleta Feinsod Cane and Susan Alves (Iowa City: University of Iowa Press, 2001), 202–215.

Hayden, Robert (1913–1980)

Poet, professor, and Consultant in Poetry to the Library of Congress. Robert Hayden was born in Detroit, Michigan, in 1913 to Ruth Sheffey. His birth mother soon gave him up for adoption, although she would continue to be a presence in his childhood. Hayden's adoptive parents, William and Sue Hayden, were strict Baptists. William Hayden's religious beliefs and work ethic would play an important role in Robert's poetry. Hayden showed interest in writing at an early age, preferring books to sports. His early influences include Countee Cullen, Carl Sandburg, Edna St. Vincent, and Langston Hughes.

Hayden's poem "Africa" was published in 1931 in *Abbott's Monthly*, and a year later he enrolled at Detroit City College (now Wayne State University), where he majored in Spanish. During this time, he published poems in the *Detroit Collegian*, researched the Underground Railroad for the Federal Writers' Project, and twice received the Hopwood Award for poetry. In 1940, he published his first book of poems, *Heart-Shape in the Dust*. He began working on his MA at the University of Michigan in 1941. At Michigan, Hayden met W. H. Auden, whom he credited as a major influence on his work.

After graduating from the University of Michigan, Hayden taught at Fisk University in Nashville, Tennessee, from 1946 to 1969. Two important events during Hayden's tenure at Fisk solidified his place as a major American poet, bringing him the attention he desired and deserved, but in a way he could not have expected. On April 7, 1966, his *Ballad of Remembrance* received the Grand Prix de la Poésie at the World Festival of Negro Arts in Dakar, Senegal. The volume had been submitted by Dr. Rosey Pool, and the award validated Hayden's work. At the same time, however, Hayden was losing credibility on campus. The Black Writers' Conference at Fisk in April 1966 came during a period when students and writers wanted to see Black art take a decisively political stand. Hayden had not shied away from discussing his experiences as an African American in his work. Such poems as "Night, Death, Mississippi," "Homage to the Empress of the Blues," and "Middle Passage" are a few of those in *Ballad of Remembrance* that comment on the history, culture, and struggle of African Americans. Still, Hayden refused to be viewed or classified as a "Black poet." This placed him at a distance from his peers. Fisk placed its new writer-in-residence, John Oliver Killens, in charge of the conference. Hayden tried to defend his position but quickly become the target of criticism by other attendees, including the poet Melvin B. Tolson. The critic John Hatcher describes Hayden's view of his own work:

> Poetry to him was an art and he was a consummate poet. He dedicated himself to his art, and dedicated his art to mankind. Every spare minute of his life he devoted to the cause of becoming the best poet he was capable of becoming, and this is how he saw his usefulness as an individual, whether as a Black American,

as a Baha'i, or simply as a human being. He cherished civil rights, abhorred the war in Vietnam, detested injustice and small-mindedness wherever it occurred, yet his standards for his art were inviolable. (*From the Auroral Darkness*, 39–40)

Hayden maintained this stance as a poet for the rest of his life, whether it was popular or not. In 1970, he returned to the University of Michigan as the first African American member of the English faculty. In 1976, he was named Consultant in Poetry to the Library of Congress, a position that eventually became the nation's poet laureateship.

Hayden published several books of poetry while teaching: *The Lion and the Archer* (1948), *A Ballad of Remembrance* (1962), *Selected Poems* (1966), *Words in the Mourning Time* (1970), and *Angle of Ascent: New and Selected Poems* (1975). Race, religion, and childhood are central themes in Hayden's work. He joined the Baha'i faith in 1943, and later edited the Baha'i journal, *World Order*. His poem "Electrical Storm" deals with the issues of faith and education and the reconciliation of the two. The first stanza of the poem describes the strict religious views of his youth. The pious formerly "huddled under Jehovah's oldtime wrath" when the storms came (line 9), but the poem's narrator grows up and discovers the scientific explanation for thunderstorms: "pressure systems/colliding massive energies." At the end of the poem, his neighbors must keep the narrator from crossing dangerous electrical lines that have fallen in his yard during a rainstorm. The value of faith even in the face of rational, scientific explanations is questioned, and the poet recognizes that his higher learning cannot explain some things.

One of Hayden's best-known poems, "Those Winter Sundays," also reflects on his strict Baptist upbringing. Instead of science versus faith, however, this poem focuses on Hayden's relationship with his adoptive father. He comes to terms with his father's hard and sometimes cruel work ethic, learning that love can be "austere and lonely." As often is the case, Hayden's reflections on his childhood lead him away from easy definitions of right and wrong. He chooses to examine his subjects as real people and attempts to understand how their flaws make them human.

Hayden died in 1980. He never defined himself as exclusively or even primarily an African American poet, and he never understood the need for the distinction:

> There's a tendency today—more than a tendency, it's almost a conspiracy—to delimit poets, to restrict them to the political and the socially or racially conscious. To me, this indicates gross ignorance of the poet's true function as well as of the function and value of poetry as art. (King, 68)

Hayden wanted his work placed beside the rest of modern poetry, where it stands out as among the best.

Jeff Cleek

See also: Epic Poetry/The Long Poem; Formal Verse; Lyric Poetry.

Resources

Brian Conniff, "Answering 'The Waste Land': Robert Hayden and the Rise of the African American Poetic Sequence," *African American Review* 33, no. 3 (Fall 1999), 487; Tim Dejong, "'Nothing Human is Foreign': Polyphony and Recognition in the Poetry of Robert Hayden,'" *College Literature* 43, no. 3 (Summer 2016), 481–508; Benjamin Friendlander, "Robert Hayden's Epic of Community," *MELUS: Multi-Ethnic Literature of the U.S.* 23, no. 3 (1998), 129–143; Laurence Goldstein and Robert Chrisman, eds., *Robert Hayden: Essays on the Poetry* (Ann Arbor: University of Michigan Press, 2001); Michael S. Harper and Anthony Walton, eds., *The Vintage Book of African American Poetry* (New York: Vintage Books, 2000); John Hatcher, *From the Auroral Darkness: The Life and Poetry of Robert Hayden* (Oxford: G. Ronald, 1984); Robert Hayden: *Angle of Ascent: New and Selected Poems* (New York: Liveright, 1975); *A Ballad of Remembrance* (London: Paul Breman, 1962); *Collected Poems*, ed. Frederick Glaysher (New York: Liveright, 1985); *Heart-Shape in the Dust* (Detroit: Falcon Press, 1940); *The Night-Blooming Cereus*, 2nd ed. (London: Paul Breman, 1972); *Words in the Mourning Time* (New York: October House, 1970); Woodie King Jr., *The Forerunners: Black Poets in America* (Washington, DC: Howard University Press, 1981); Raphaël Lambert, "The Slave Trade as Memory and History: James A. Emanuel's 'The Middle Passage Blues' and Robert Hayden's 'Middle Passage,'" *African American Review* 47, no. 2/3 (July 1, 2014), 327–338; Jim Murphy, "'Here Only the Sea is Real': Robert Hayden's Postmodern Passages," *MELUS: Multi-Ethnic Literature of the U.S.* 27, no. 4 (2002), 107–127; Pontheolla T. Williams, *Robert Hayden: A Critical Analysis of His Poetry* (Champaign: University of Illinois Press, 1987).

Hayes, Terrance (1971–)

Poet and professor. Hayes was born and grew up in Columbia, South Carolina. Before earning an MFA in writing at the University of Pittsburgh, he earned a BA at Coker College.

Hayes has published seven books of poetry. His first, *Muscular Music*, was published in 1999 by Tia Chucha Press and reprinted in 2006 by Carnegie Mellon

University Press in 2006. The title aptly describes Hayes's complex style, as his poetry is at once robust and lyrical, accessible and cerebral. Many of his poems generate a strong, consistent voice but can also make startling shifts of scene, mood, and image. They draw on a wide range of knowledge, interests, and experience.

His other volumes of poetry have all been published by Penguin Books: *Hip Logic* (2002), *Wind in a Box* (2006), *Lighthead* (2010), *How to Be Drawn* (2015), and *American Sonnets for My Past and Future Assassin* (2018). The poems in *American Sonnets for My Past and Future Assassin* improvise on the sonnet form and display a dazzling inventiveness. For example, he fills "American Sonnet for the New Year" with adverbs ("increasingly," "forcefully," etc.) and creates a playful but powerful indirect commentary on both the condition of the nation and of language.

Among the periodicals his poems have appeared in are the *New Yorker, Ploughshares, Poetry,* and the *Kenyon Review.* His work has been widely and enthusiastically reviewed, and he was awarded one of the prestigious fellowships from the MacArthur Foundation. He was also appointed a Chancellor of the American Academy of Poets.

To Float in the Space Between: A Life and Work in Conversation With the Life and Work of Etheridge Knight (2018) is a book of nonfiction. It is based on lectures he gave in the Bagley Wright Series and meditates on poems by African American writer Etheridge Knight and discusses poetics, politics and poetry, and ancestry.

Hayes has taught at Carnegie Mellon University and New York University.

Hans A. Ostrom

See also: Free Verse.

Resources

Terrance Hayes: "American Sonnet for the New Year," *The New Yorker,* January 14, 2019: https://www.newyorker.com/magazine/2019/01/14/american-sonnet-for-the-new-year (accessed 2019); *American Sonnets for My Past and Future Assassin* (New York: Penguin Books, 2018); *Hip Logic* (New York: Penguin Books, 2002); *How to Be Drawn* (New York: Penguin Books, 2015); *Lighthead* (New York: Penguin Books, 2010); *To Float in the Space Between: A Life and Work in Conversation With the Life and Work of Etheridge Knight* (Seattle: Wave Books, 2018); *Wind in a Box* (New York: Penguin, 2006).

Hemphill, Essex (1957–1995)

Poet essayist, activist, and editor. Born in Chicago, Illinois, and raised in Washington, DC, Essex Hemphill was the leading Black gay poet of his generation and is widely regarded as one of the most important poets of the late twentieth century. His writing, editing, and political activity focused on the dual identities of being both Black and gay in the United States. Clearly influenced by Langston Hughes and James Baldwin, Hemphill's work may be linked to that of the contemporary poet–writer–activists Audre Lorde and Melvin Dixon through his insistence on breaking silence by privileging the knowledge and experiences of oppressed peoples, specifically of Black gays and lesbians.

After graduating from high school, Hemphill studied English at the University of Maryland and the University of the District of Columbia. At this time he proclaimed his gay identity and eschewed Black Nationalism, to which he had been attracted in his early twenties, because of its open homophobia and rigid insistence on maintaining traditional gender and sexual roles. He began publishing poetry and essays in important literary journals and magazines, among them *Callaloo*, *Black Scholar*, and *Essence*, and emerged as an important voice among Black gay and lesbian writers. The mid-1980s saw a flurry of publication for Hemphill. Two chapbooks, *Earth Life* (1985) and *Conditions* (1986), were privately printed. He contributed poems to *In the Life* (1986), a groundbreaking anthology of Black gay writings edited by Joseph Beam; they included "Isn't It Funny," "Better Days," "Cordon Negro," "Serious Moonlight," and "For My Own Protection." Hemphill's inclusion in this anthology began an important personal and literary friendship with Beam.

When Beam died of complications from AIDS in 1988, Hemphill assumed Beam's duties of collecting and editing manuscripts for another Black gay anthology, *Brother to Brother: New Writings by Black Gay Men* (1991), which won the American Library Association's Gay and Lesbian Book Award. The book's title page indicates the collaborative nature of the project, listing Hemphill as editor, Beam as the man who conceived and began work on the collection, and Beam's mother, Dorothy, as the project's manager. To this anthology, a welcome expansion on the ideas of breaking silence and expressing Black gay men's desires, fears, needs, and joys showcased first in *In the Life*, Hemphill contributed numerous pieces. Among these are the poems "Commitments," "The tomb of sorrow," and "When my brother fell," a moving tribute to Beam; an essay, "Undressing Icons"; and "*Looking for Langston*: An Interview with Isaac Julien." These last two pieces are concerned with Isaac Julien's film *Looking for Langston*, controversial because of its depiction of Langston Hughes as gay man. To this film, Hemphill

contributed poetry. Continuing to work with filmmakers, he appeared in Marlon Riggs's *Tongues Untied* and narrated a documentary on AIDS, *Out of the Shadows*.

Cleis Press published Hemphill's only major collection, *Ceremonies*, which contained both poetry and essays, in 1992. Hemphill is best known for this collection, which includes some of his earlier work, including poems from his chapbooks, and the work for which he is best remembered. Opening with a biographical and critical introduction by Charles S. Nero, *Ceremonies* is divided into seven sections. Poetry and essays alternate to produce the effect of Hemphill's total engagement with his subjects: Black gay men's desires and positions in White supremacist and heterosexist U.S. culture as well as the necessary pain and excitement that come with speaking the truth. Among the poems are "American Hero," "Black Machismo," "To Some Supposed Brothers," the explicit and famous "American Wedding," and "Heavy Breathing," which A. Boxwell calls Hemphill's "longest, most complex and deliberately provocative poem." In these poems, Hemphill is at his technical best and acutely conveys the need for a coming-to-voice of Black gay men. "Black Machismo" shatters the racist myth of Black males and large penis size as it incorporates social and personal history to understand stereotype. "To Some Supposed Brothers" admonishes those men who treat women as inferior objects to be used by those who are also oppressed—Black men. And "American Wedding" asserts the need for both physical and emotional love between Black men and promises that with every kiss between Black gay men, a new world comes (184). The essays in the collection also mark Hemphill as an important thinker and writer. "Does Your Momma Know About

Me?" tackles AIDS, Robert Mapplethorpe's racist images of Black men, and the need for family and community; "If Freud Had Been a Neurotic Colored Woman: Reading Dr. Frances Cress Welsing" challenges homophobic attitudes among Black heterosexuals and academics; and "Ceremonies," a painful personal essay, details the exile in which Hemphill found himself as a gay adolescent and the actions he took to feign normalcy in the midst of antigay rhetoric.

Throughout his career, Hemphill received many awards, including grants from the National Endowment for the Arts and the Washington, DC, Commission for the Arts, and the Gregory Kolovakos Award for AIDS Writing. After Hemphill's death of complications from AIDS on November 4, 1995, many Black gay and lesbian writers and activists paid tribute to him as a visionary poet and leader who made possible contemporary Black gay and lesbian writing and consciousness. (*See* Gay Literature.)

Bill Clem

See also: Gay Literature.

Resources

Darius Bost, "Loneliness: Black Gay Longing in the Work of Essex Hemphill," *Criticism* 59, no. 3 (July 1, 2017), 353–374; A. Boxwell: "'Where the Absence of Doo Wop Is Frightening': The Body Politic in Essex Hemphill's 'Heavy Breathing,'" paper given at the Conference on Contemporary Poetry: Poetry and the Public Sphere, Apr. 24–27, 1997, http://english.rutgers.edu/boxwell/htm; "Essex Hemphill," http://www.africanpubs.com; Martin B. Duberman, *Hold Tight Gently: Michael Callen, Essex Hemphill, and the Battlefield of AIDS* (New York: The New Press, 2014); Thomas Glave, "(Re-) Recalling Essex Hemphill: Words to Our Now," *Callaloo* 23, no. 1 (2000), 278–284; Essex Hemphill, *Ceremonies: Prose and Poetry* (New York: Plume, 1992); Essex Hemphill, ed., *Brother to Brother: New Writings by Black Gay Men*, conceived by Joseph Beam (Boston: Alyson, 1991); Charles S. Nero, "Fixing Ceremonies: An Introduction," in *Ceremonies: Poetry and Prose*, by Essex Hemphill (San Francisco: Cleis Press, 1992).

Hip-Hop

Hip-hop is a subculture, chiefly urban and initially created and defined by rap artists and their audience. Rap music involves a steady beat accompanied by the rhyming lyrics, often improvised, that are sung or spoken "over" the beat. The steady beat can be produced by a DJ, but it does not have to be. The term "hip-hop" can be used as either a noun or an adjective. Hip-hop has developed over time to include not only music but also new forms of literature and literary discourse, art, dance, and fashion. Nonetheless, rap is the foundation of hip-hop's culture, and therefore hip-hop is a direct product of the ethnic, historical, sociological, musical, and philosophical circumstances that spawned rap music. All the defining elements of hip-hop, despite their later international commercialization, remain expressions of urban experiences. These elements spring from ethnic and socioeconomic circumstances shared by African Americans and Latinos in the urban Northeast of the United States and, subsequently, in other urban centers, including Los Angeles, California; Detroit, Michigan; and Atlanta, Georgia.

Hip-hop culture began with the development of rap music in the South Bronx section of New York City in the mid-1970s. (The first *commercial* rap hit recording was "Rapper's Delight" by a group called the Sugar Hill Gang from New York, but rapping had been developing before this recording was made). Hip-hop often concerned itself (and continues to concern itself) with everyday life in the Bronx and other urban centers, with surviving in that environment, with violence and racism, and especially with how young African American men and women view their lives. Hip-hop was also associated early on with graffiti art, specific styles of dress, and break dancing. The term "hip-hop" seems first to have appeared in 1982 (*Oxford English Dictionary* online). Hip-hop culture has, however, constantly redefined itself, partly in response to the larger culture's views of it.

The Source: The Magazine of Hip-Hop Music, Culture, and Politics (*The Source*) was established in 1988 as a newsletter and later graduated to a full-color glossy publication, reflecting the expansion of the culture on which it reported. It was published originally for a hip-hop audience, but its readership became more diverse. Employing the language of both African American vernacular and Standard American English, the magazine communicates with and disseminates information to both a marginalized hip-hop community and mainstream readers. Other hip-hop magazines emerged in the late 1990s, including *XXL* and *Blaze*. These magazines do not simply cover the rap music industry but extend their coverage to include the culture and politics that surround the music, such as racism and discrimination, American politics and policy, African American literature, sports, and other items of specific interest to the hip-hop community. Additionally, hip-hop culture has turned rappers, such as Gil Scott-Herron, Sister Souljah, and KRS-One, and most recently, The Last Poets and DMX, into published writers, not just performers or recording artists.

Literature published in the Black Arts Movement has become popular among rappers and in hip-hop culture. One example is the work of Donald Goines. His work has reemerged, becoming popular among rappers and their audiences. Goines, one of the best examples of a literary resurgence spawned by hip-hop, used language adopted by rap lyricists, and his books have sold briskly since the 1980s, primarily because his name and titles are mentioned in rap lyrics by artists such as Grand Puba of Brand Nubian, Tupac Shakur, and Noreaga.

Because of its language, its subject matter, and its perspectives on sexuality, women, the police, and violence, hip-hop has, from the beginning, been controversial in mainstream society. However, its controversial nature has not prevented it from becoming popular. Because rap artists use the vernacular and because they work in the mass medium of recording, they have introduced the vernacular to a world audience, which in turn uses the language of the Black community in new ways, some of them commercial. One result of hip-hop's mass distribution is that the language of hip-hop appears in nonfiction works produced by scholars and journalists, including Michael Eric Dyson, Keith Gilyard, and Nelson George.

Dyson's *Open Mike: Reflections on Philosophy, Race, Sex, Culture, and Religion* (2002) is a compilation of his conversations with several interviewers on his ideas and thoughts concerning race, identity, and cultural studies. Dyson and some of his interviewers not only discuss hip-hop but also use its language in their verbal exchanges. In Dyson's attempt to bridge the gap between the academy and urban "street culture," his scholarship provides new avenues that potentially close gaps between academics and other members of mainstream culture (on the one hand) and members of the urban hip-hop community (on the other).

George's *Hip Hop America* (1998) examines not only rap music and hip-hop culture, which is now more than thirty years old, but also the politics and issues of commercialization connected to rap and hip-hop.

Gilyard uses the vernacular of hip-hop to address issues of pedagogy surrounding students' rights and language practices in American schools. In Gary Olson's *Rhetoric and Composition as Intellectual Work* (2002), Gilyard's article "Holdin' It Down: Students' Rights and Struggle over Language Diversity," discusses language, race, identity, and diversity in public schools.

With regard to another linguistic issue, hip-hop culture has generated new interest in the word "n—," especially how and why it is prominent in the language of hip-hop, and the complications of its usage among non-African American hip-hoppers. A Tribe Called Quest's lyric "Sucka N—," from their 1994 CD *Midnight Marauders*, claimed that the "youth say [n—] all over town" and that the term's negative connotations are removed by the new generation of African American hip-hoppers. Randall Kennedy's *N—: The Strange Career of a Troublesome Word* (2002) notes that there are different relationships to and understandings of the word among African Americans. Kennedy explains that, on the one hand, there are African Americans who believe the term "to be only and unalterably a debasing slur," while rappers, including Ice T, insist "upon being called a n—," similarly to the way Kennedy's "father declared [himself] a 'stone n—,' " which for the senior Kennedy "meant [to be] a Black man without pretensions," standing "unafraid," "loud," and "proud" (Kennedy, xvii).

Mainstream perceptions of hip-hop culture sometimes serve as the sceneries, verbal expressions, and social relations presented in new fiction by African American novelists, such as Eric Jerome Dickey, Zane, Omar Tyree, and E. Lynn Harris, as they seem to express mainstream assumptions regarding the culture. However, other writers, including Amiri Baraka, Sonya Sanchez, Nikki Giovanni, and Ursula Rucker, often write against mainstream perceptions while absorbing hip-hop's expressions and ideas. Another complicating factor connected to hip-hop is that the main consumers of rap music are young White males. African Americans and Hispanics consume less of the commercial music and concerts, yet they are responsible for almost all the creativity in hip-hop, including the art, music, dance, and literature.

Hip-hop's commercial refinement by an international audience ultimately creates a tension within the culture and the community out of which hip-hop emerges. Over time, a large segment of American's mainstream White youth has been integrated into the culture, bridging gaps of racism and classism, with rebellion against authority being one symbolic unifying element.

Hip-hop culture's appeal to mass audiences creates an environment similar to that of the blues, jazz, and rhythm and blues (R&B). It introduces the culture to outsiders, and in so doing subjects the culture to mimicry. However, because outsiders come to the culture armed with more capital than hip-hop's originators, and also with genuine interest, there exists the opportunity for such global success as that of rap artist Eminem. His success is arguably determined by sales rather than by longevity, street credibility, or appeal within the community of hip-hop.

The complex issues of commercialism, language, ethnicity, and so on inform Greg Tate's edited book, *Everything but the Burden: What White People Are Taking from Black Culture* (2003). From Robin D. G. Kelley's "Reds, Whites, and Blues Peoples" to Carl H. Rux's "Eminem: The New White Negro," Tate's book dedicates itself to examining the growth of hip-hop and the influence of White culture on hip-hop culture. Earlier, Del Jones had examined similar issues in *Culture Bandits II: Annihilation of Afrikan Images* (1993). The argument underlying Tate's and Jones's books is that hip-hop culture, like rap, blues, jazz, and R&B, was created out of a particular Black experience of racial and economic oppression. Although Whites can consume the culture, the argument goes on to claim they are by no means the main producers of it and will therefore appropriate it in ways that will create anxiety within hip-hop culture. A counterargument is that hip-hop has always been a multiracial, multicultural enterprise that does not negate or define what rap music represents. From this point of view, the "loss" of hip-hop culture to outsiders is unlikely.

In any event, as hip-hop has become more popular, even globally known, the gap between hip-hop culture and mainstream culture seems to shrink, even as responses to hip-hop culture become more complex and less easy to analyze.

The tags painted by graffiti artists constitute a fascinating form of literature or textual art. Just as Egyptian hieroglyphs inscribe a history transposed into texts, so graffiti art arguably inscribes the history of urban America, its politics and values, thoughts and notions. Historically used by activists to communicate political statements, urban graffiti reports events and can present local reactions to those events.

The 1992 case of Malice Green is one example. Green was a young African American man beaten to death by Detroit, Michigan, police officers Larry Nevers and Walter Budzyn. The mural of Green, painted by Bernie White with tag speed, inscribes the event on its actual site: 24th and West Warren in Detroit. The location of the work, White's muralist style, and his creative timetable (he completed the work soon after the murder) raised Green's killing to national prominence.

Former graffiti artists are now paid by cities. They produce well-crafted artwork covering large areas of space and reflecting Afrocentric and multicultural ideas. Some works stand several stories high. In Philadelphia, Pennsylvania, the Mural Arts Program (PMAP) and the Philadelphia Anti-Graffiti Network (PAGN) are two of the oldest programs that encourage and employ graffiti artist to paint murals, offering them not only monetary reward but also autonomy over the many of messages they convey. In essence, graffiti artists have transcended being labeled criminal. Michael White and Andrew "Zephyr" Witten, in *Style Master General: The Life of Graffiti Artist Dondi White* (2001), offer readers the history of Dondi White, one of the first graffiti artists to move his work from New York's subways into the city's galleries. As part of Sam Esses's program of 1980, Dondi began painting on canvas and, with KEL 139, he produced his finest work, not only for the subway but also for the gallery.

Hip-hop's continuous evolution has made the culture into an international enterprise, defying conventional barriers of race, class, gender, and nationality. Like most grassroots movements, significant parts of it remain underground, and arguably the most important creative work in hip-hop culture remains outside the mainstream. Through evolutions of language, art, and music, hip-hop culture will continue to move beyond its own early conventions, but it remains rooted in African American experiences, language, sense of resistance, and sense of independence.

Ellesia Ann Blaque

See also: Blues Poetry; Performance Poetry; Postmodernism; Rap; Vernacular.

Resources

Jim Fricke and Charlie Ahearn, eds., *Yes, Yes, Y'All: The Experience Music Project Oral History of Hip-Hop's First Decade* (Cambridge, MA: Da Capo Press, 2002); Nelson George, *Hip-Hop America* (New York: Penguin, 1998); Yusef Ja and Chuck D., *Fight the Power: Rap, Race, and Reality* (New York: Delta Books, 1988); Andre E. Johnson, ed., *Urban God Talk: Constructing a Hip Hop Spirituality* (Lanham, MD: Lexington Books, 2015); Del Jones, *Culture Bandits II: Annihilation of Afrikan Images* (Philadelphia: Hikeka Press, 1993); Randal Kennedy, *N—: The Strange Career of a Troublesome Word* (New York: Vintage Books, 2002); Alan Light, ed., *Vibe History of Hip Hop* (Los Angeles: Three Rivers Press, 1999); Glen Mannisto, "Detroit Renaissance Art," *Metro Times*, Nov. 16, 1992, late ed., pp. F1+; Eddie S. Meadows, *Blues, Funk, Rhythm and Blues, Soul, Hip Hop and Rap: A Research and Information Guide* (New York: Routledge, 2010); Richard J. Powell, *Black Art: A Cultural History*, 2nd ed. (London: Thames and Hudson, 2002); Tricia Rose, *Black Noise: Rap Music and Black Culture in Contemporary America* (Hanover, NH: Wesleyan University Press; published by University Press of New England, 1994); Greg Tate, ed., *Everything But the Burden: What White People Are Taking from Black Culture* (New York: Harlem Moon, 2003); A Tribe Called Quest, "Sucka N—," on *Midnight Marauders* (Jive, 1994); Saul Williams, *The Dead Emcee Scrolls: The Lost Teachings of Hip-Hop and Connected Writings* (New York: MTV books/ Pocket Books, 2006).

Horror Fiction

The primary intent of horror fiction is to frighten the reader by inducing feelings of terror and/or dread. This fear is often brought about by the evocation of a supernatural source or cause of the terror. The fear may also be of a psychological or emotional kind, however, and need not spring from a supernatural source. The work may also focus upon instilling a feeling of suspense rather than utter dread.

The supernatural element at work in much horror fiction is often a monster or another kind of strange being: werewolf, ghost, mummy, or vampire. Vampires especially have been a favorite topic for writers of horror fiction. These creatures are usually the undead corpses of human beings (sometimes they are animals). They are immortals brought back from the dead by the bite of another vampire. They must suck the blood of humans in order to survive. Since the publication of Bram Stoker's *Dracula* in 1897, vampires have been a staple of horror fiction.

The modern horror fiction novel has its origins in the Gothic Literature of the late eighteenth and early nineteenth centuries. In America, Edgar Allen Poe, with short stories such as "The Tell-Tale Heart," "The Masque of the Red Death," and "The Black Cat"; Henry James with his novel *The Turn of the Screw* (1898); and Ambrose Bierce were pioneers in the field. H. P. Lovecraft, who called his works "weird tales," was also an important figure in the foundation of modern horror.

Perhaps the three most important classic works of horror fiction were produced during the nineteenth century: Mary Shelley's *Frankenstein; Or, The Modern Prometheus* (1818), Robert Louis Stevenson's *The Strange Case of Dr. Jekyll and Mr. Hyde* (1886), and Bram Stoker's *Dracula* (1897). These three novels had an enormous impact on the works that followed and continue to do so today. Stoker's Count Dracula has become an archetypal symbol of the vampire. Numerous films and books have been made and written about these works.

It is not surprising that African Americans did not begin exploring the genre of horror fiction until relatively recently. For much of the nineteenth century, during the years of slavery, it was illegal to teach a slave to read or write. What we do have from this time period are folktales that often contain horrific elements such as ghosts. These stories were passed down orally and served as a way of transferring information, and tales with horrific elements were used as a way of frightening people into a proper way of acting, in essence "scaring them straight."

Slave narratives relating the daily sufferings of African Americans often contained horrific elements as well, although we certainly would not classify them as horror fiction as it is known today. Writers of slave narratives cataloged the injustices and often the daily terror of life as a slave, but they certainly began to pave the way for all African American writers, including the horror writers of today. In the twentieth century, we have tales of lynchings in the South, and beatings and murders during the Civil Rights Movement of the 1950s and 1960s—all frightening to the reader—but it is only during the later portion of the twentieth century that we begin to see African American writers producing works of horror in the modern sense.

The popularity of the gothic novel began to decline during the mid-nineteenth century, and by the beginning of the twentieth century, much horror fiction was published mainly in inexpensive "pulp" magazines prevalent during the time period between the two world wars. In 1923, a pulp devoted specifically to horror fiction was introduced. *Weird Tales* published works by H. P. Lovecraft and reprinted works by Poe. There was a decline in interest and popularity in the pulps, and most of them were out of business by the time of World War II. In the 1960s, the horror novel began to gain popularity again, due in part to the writer Ira Levin. In 1974, the publication of Stephen King's first novel, *Carrie*, ushered in a boom in the horror publishing industry.

Only in recent years has the genre of horror fiction begun to be explored by African American writers. Currently, the most popular African American writer working in the genre is Tananarive Due. Due began her writing career as a journalist with the *Miami Herald* and began her career as a novelist in 1995 with *The Between*, in which the protagonist, Hilton, attempts to deal with nightmares and the fear of his own death. Due shies from the label of "horror writer," instead saying that she wants to write stories about African Americans. In a 1998 interview with Lee Meadows she said that she "wanted to write the books [she] couldn't read," meaning stories with supernatural elements and about African Americans. *The Between* was followed in 1997 by *My Soul to Keep*, dealing with the love story of the immortal David, or Dawit, and the secret he has been keeping from his mortal wife, Jessica, an investigative reporter. This book became the first in the African Immortals series by Due that includes *The Living Blood* (2001), *Blood Colony* (2008), and *My Soul to Take* (2011). Due also wrote

The Good House (2004), her take on a haunted house story. She has also written a historical novel, *The Black Rose* (2000), and the memoir *Freedom in the Family: A Mother-Daughter Memoir of the Fight for Civil Rights* (2003), which she authored with her mother, Patricia Stevens Due.

L. A. Banks (the pseudonym of Leslie Esdaile Banks) is another prominent voice within the genre. Her Vampire Huntress series deals with an African American woman named Damali Richards who is a spoken-word artist as well as a powerful vampire huntress called a Neteru. The three novels in the series thus far are *Minion* (2004), *The Awakening* (2004), and *The Hunted* (2004).

Linda Addison was winner of the Bram Stoker Award for her collection of poems, *Consumed, Reduced to Beautiful Grey Ashes* (2001).In recent years, there have also been a few important anthologies of African Americans working in speculative/horror fiction. Sheree R. Thomas edited the popular speculative fiction collection *Dark Matter: A Century of Speculative Fiction from the African Diaspora* (2000) and *Dark Matter: Reading the Bones* (2004).Brandon Massey is the editor of the short-story collection *Dark Dreams* (2004), one of the few anthologies that have been published thus far dealing exclusively with horror fiction written by African Americans. He has also written two novels, *Thunderland* (2002) and *Dark Corner* (2004).

Victor LaValle has attracted critical acclaim for his novels, which contain significant elements of horror but also weave in elements of other genres, including fantasy. *The Ecstatic* (2002) centers on a man who struggles with mental illness and who is also a connoisseur of horror movies. *The Devil in Silver* (2012) is set in a hospital's psychiatric ward in Queens, New York. *The*

Ballad of Black Tom (2016) earned LaValle the Shirley Jackson Award and the British Fantasy Award. *Victor Lavalle's Destroyer*, a graphic novel illustrated by Dietrich Smith, is an adaptation of Mary Shelley's Frankenstein and addresses contemporary social issues in the United States. Other African American writers who have produced works of horror fiction in recent years are Robert Fleming, Christopher Chambers, and Chesya Burke.

Kinitra Dechaun Brooks's critical book, *Searching for Sycorax: Black Women's Hauntings of Contemporary Horror* (2018) studies elements of horror in works that do not strictly fit the genre, including ones by Gloria Naylor and Nalo Hopkinson. The book also examines African American folklore and feminist issues.

Lakiska Flippin

See also: Butler, Octavia E.; Morrison, Toni.

Resources

Primary Sources: Linda Addison, *Consumed, Reduced to Beautiful Grey Ashes* (New York: Space and Time, 2001); L. A. Banks: *The Awakening: A Vampire Huntress Legend* (New York: St. Martin's Griffin, 2004); *The Hunted: A Vampire Huntress Legend* (New York: St. Martin's Griffin, 2004); *Minion: A Vampire Huntress Legend* (New York: St. Martin's Press, 2004); Tananrive Due: *The Between* (New York: HarperCollins, 1995); *Blood Colony* (New York: Atria, 2008); *The Good House* (New York: Simon and Schuster, 2004); Interview with Lee Meadows, *Book Beat*, WPON (Detroit, Nov. 4, 1998); *The Living Blood* (New York: Pocket Books, 2001); *My Soul to Keep* (New York: HarperPrism, 1997); *My Soul to Take* (New York: Washington Square Books, 2011); Robert Fleming, *Havoc After Dark: Tales of Terror* (New York: Kensington, 2005); Victor LaValle: *The Ballad of Black Tom* (New York: Tor, 2016); *The Devil in Silver* (New York:

Spiegel and Grau, 2012); *The Ecstatic* (New York: Crown, 2002); *Victor LaValle's The Destroyer*, illus. Dietrich Smith (Los Angeles: BOOM Studios, 2018); Brandon Massey, *Thunderland* (New York: Dafina, 2002); Brandon Massey, ed., *Dark Dreams: A Collection of Horror and Suspense by Black Writers* (New York: Dafina, 2004); Mary Shelley, *Frankenstein; or, The Modern Prometheus* (London: Lackington, Hughes, Harding, Mavor & Jones, 1818); Robert Louis Stevenson, *The Strange Case of Dr. Jekyll and Mr. Hyde* (London: Longman's, Green, 1886); Bram Stoker, *Dracula* (Westminster, UK: Archibald Constable and Co., 1897); Sheree Thomas, ed.: *Dark Matter: A Century of Speculative Fiction from the African Diaspora* (New York: Warner Books, 2000); *Dark Matter: Reading the Bones* (New York: Warner Books, 2004).

Secondary Sources: Roger Abrahams, *African American Folktales: Stories from Black Traditions in the New World* (New York: Random House, 1985); Harold Bloom, ed.: *Classic Horror Writers* (New York: Chelsea House, 1994); *Modern Horror Writers* (New York: Chelsea House, 1994); Kinitra Dechaun Brooks, *Searching for Sycorax: Black Women's Hauntings of Contemporary Horror* (New Brunswick: Rutgers University Press, 2018); David Pringle, *St. James Guide to Horror, Ghost & Gothic Writers* (Detroit: St. James Press, 1998); Jack Sullivan, ed., *The Penguin Encyclopedia of Horror and the Supernatural* (New York: Viking 1986); Jeffrey Trachtenberg, "Literature From the Edge: Novelist's Obsessions: 'Mental Illness, Horror and Religion,'" *Wall Street Journal*, July 25, 2009, p.W.4.

Hughes, Langston (1901–1967)

Poet, short-story writer, playwright, novelist, essayist, librettist, and editor. Langston Hughes emerged as one of the greatest of all African American writers. He is known for bold innovations in the poetics of the dream and for preserving the historical memory of racial freedom. His deceptively simple language represents a spiritual power that infuses lyrical landscapes such as those of daybreak in Alabama. Through political retorts about the imperative of civil rights expressed within a continuum—the consciousness and conscience of the nation—he redefined "American." His poems, short stories, novels, dramas, translations, and seminal anthologies of works by others, spanning the period from the Harlem Renaissance of the 1920s to the Black Arts Movement's reorientations in the 1960s and 1970s, helped reshape the national identity. In the United States, he paved the way for the new female voices, including Margaret Abigail Walker, Gwendolyn Brooks, and especially Alice Walker. Internationally, he inspired francophone visionaries such as the Négritude poet Léopold Sédar Senghor and the Haitian novelist Jacques Roumain. Intrigued by Spanish as well as by English, German, and French—he was an easy hook for new languages and cultures—he found a kindred spirit in a Cuban, Nicolás Guillén, whose literary artistry has proved crucial to a twenty-first century renaissance in African Latino studies. Hence, Hughes was a writer for the homeland and the world. Perhaps most significantly, he was the unofficial poet laureate of the African American people, whose memory lives on in his poetry.

Between 1921 and 1967, Hughes became both famous and beloved. Even before he had helped young Blacks gain entry to the major periodicals and presses of the day, his experiments in literary blues and jazz were acclaimed. He worked to introduce new forms that encapsulated confidence and racial pride. In his fictional characters and technical mastery, he displayed social awareness. Hughes, a product of the African American and American 1920s, helped shape four subsequent decades of literary history. In addition to the decade of the 1920s—in which his innovative poetry of blues and jazz emerged—the 1930s marked his lasting insight into the class inequities of the United States. By the war decade of the 1940s, some of his finest lyrics had appeared as artistic relief for the racial lynching that was common at the time.

James Langston Hughes was born to Carrie Langston Hughes and James Nathaniel Hughes sometime in 1901 (in Joplin, Missouri, but "Langston" became his de facto first name early on. Hughes himself gave his official birthdate on February 1, 1902, and until 2018, that was his accepted birthdate in biographies and other material. But in 2018, poet Eric McHenry and scholar Denise Low discovered in old newspapers mentions of Hughes and his mother in 1901 (see Flood in Resources). (Missouri did not require registration of births at that time.)

Carrie's father, Charles Howard Langston, known as Langston, had moved to Kansas in search of greater racial and financial freedom. His penchant for the literary and his desire to transcend the farm and the grocery store in Lawrence, Kansas, were passed on to Hughes. Charles's brother, John Mercer Langston, the poet's great-uncle, contributed to the family's literary efforts by penning an autobiography, *From the Virginia Plantation to the National Capitol* (1894). The financially secure John Mercer Langston willed to his descendants a big house as well as stocks and bonds.

In 1907, Langston's mother took him with her to a library in Topeka, where he fell in love with books, in part because he was impressed that the library was publicly maintained. Through the double perspective of boy and man, he recalled: "Even before I was six books began to happen to me, so that after a while there came a time when I believed in books more than in people which, of course, was wrong" (*BS*, 26).

In July 1920, on the train to visit his father in Mexico, while crossing the Mississippi River to St. Louis, Missouri, Hughes wrote the short lyric "The Negro Speaks of Rivers" (*CP*, 23). Through the images of water and pyramid, the verse suggests the endurance of human spirituality from the time of ancient Egypt to the nineteenth and twentieth centuries. The muddy Mississippi made Hughes think of the roles in human history played by the Congo, the Niger, and the Nile, down the waters of which the early slaves once were sold. And he thought of Abraham Lincoln, who was moved to end slavery after he took a trip on a raft down the Mississippi River. The poem that emerged from a draft he first wrote on the back of an envelope in fifteen minutes has become Hughes's most anthologized poem (Roessel, "Process").

Hughes lived with his father, who had left Hughes and his mother some years before, in Mexico until September 1921. He agonized over his father's desire for him to attend a European university and his own preference to attend Columbia University in New York City. To escape, he went to bullfights in Mexico City almost every weekend. He was unsuccessful in writing about them, but he did write articles about Toluca and the Virgin of Guadalupe. *The Brownies' Book*, a magazine just begun by W.E.B. Du Bois's staff at *The Crisis*, published two poems by Hughes in the January 1921 issue, and *The Gold Piece*, his one-act play for children, in the July 1921 issue. Jessie Redmon Fauset, the literary editor, accepted one of his articles and the poem "The Negro Speaks of Rivers" for the June 1921 issue of *The Crisis*.

During the winter of 1923, Hughes wrote the poem that would give the title to his first volume of poetry. "The Weary Blues," about a piano player in Harlem, New York, captures the flavor of the nightlife, people, and folk forms that would become characteristic of the experimental writing of the Harlem Renaissance (Barksdale; Tracy).

Hughes's poetry during this period is youthfully romantic. "As I Grew Older" (*CP*, 93) blends reflection and nostalgia as the speaker, framed by light and shadow, seeks to rediscover his dream. In "Mexican Market Woman" (*CP*, 25), Hughes's narrator uses simile to create a dark mood of weariness and pain. And through the persona in "Troubled Woman" (*CP*, 42), the narrator portrays humanity bowed but unbroken. "Mother to Son" (*CP*, 30), a dramatic monologue, shows how dialect can be used with dignity. The image of the stair as a beacon of success inspires hope in the son. All the poems appeared in *The Weary Blues*, which was published in January 1926. Also in 1926, Hughes published the essay "The Negro Artist and the Racial Mountain" in *The Nation*; it is considered one of the main aesthetic statements of the Harlem Renaissance.

Hughes met Charlotte Mason (who liked to be known as "Godmother") on a weekend trip to New York in 1927. A friend introduced him to the elderly White lady, who delighted Hughes immediately and who, despite her age, was modern in her ideas about books. She became his literary patron, a title both disliked. She was also well acquainted with Alain Locke, an early supporter of Hughes, and Zora Neale Hurston. With her support, he began work on his first novel, which he envisioned as a portrait of a typical Black family in Kansas. The work, *Not Without Laughter*, which was accepted for publication and appeared in 1930, captures the folk flavor so vital to Hughes.

In the early winter of 1930, Hughes broke irreparably with Mason. Certainly, he had loved her kindness and generosity, including her sincere support for Black advancement and liberal causes. But the two of them disagreed on political philosophy and race. She believed that Blacks linked American Whites to the primitive life and should concern themselves only with building on their cultural foundations. Hughes rejected such a simplistic view of the role of Blacks in the modern world. Though he did not openly criticize her, he became psychosomatically ill following his final meeting with her.

Hughes's first volume of stories, *The Ways of White Folks* (1934), appeared during the Great Depression. An interface between history and fiction occurred on October 29, 1929, the day the stock market crashed, ending so many opportunities for publication and artistic performance that the New Negro Movement had created. In his first autobiography, *The Big Sea* (1940), Hughes, writing about Mrs. Mason, also refers obliquely to the fateful year of 1929–1930:

I cannot write here about the last half hour in the big bright drawing-room high above Park Avenue one morning, because when I think about it, even now, something happens in the pit of my stomach that makes me ill. That beautiful room, that had been so full of light and help and understanding for me, suddenly became like a trap closing in, faster and faster, the room darker and darker, until the light went out with a sudden crash in the dark. (*BS*, 325)

During his travels in Russia in 1932, Hughes had learned well the relationship between writing and mythmaking. The representative of a leading American newspaper had intentionally printed a story in New York claiming that the film company with which Hughes was traveling was stranded and starving in Moscow. When the filmmakers showed the reporter the clippings, he merely grinned. But Hughes praised the many positive changes in post–Revolution Russia that Americans were ignoring, particularly the open housing and the reduced persecution of Jews. Eventually. the poet figuratively turned away from Russia because he refused to live without jazz, which the Communists banned.

Determined to confront worldwide fascism and racism, Hughes returned to San Francisco, California, by way of Asia in 1933. His trip home demonstrates his headstrong personality. Though Westerners in Shanghai had warned him that the watermelons were tainted and potentially fatal there, he ate well, enjoyed the fruit, and lived to write the story. Warned to avoid the Chinese districts, he visited the areas and found the danger illusory. In Tokyo, the police interrogated, detained, and finally expelled him. In the Japanese press's inflated stories of Korean crimes, he read the pattern of racism so familiar to him in the United States. Aware that victims become victimizers in turn, he understood the Japanese debasement of the Chinese, and, on the way back to the United States, he warned that Japan was a fascist country.

In 1933 and 1934, Hughes retired temporarily from world politics. In Carmel, California, at Noel Sullivan's home "Ennesfree," he completed a series of short stories that were later included in *The Ways of White Folks*. There he became acquainted with the poet Robinson Jeffers and his wife, Una. He also wrote articles, including one on the liberation of women from the harems of Soviet Asia. Grateful to Sullivan for the time to write, Hughes worked from ten to twelve hours a day, producing at least one story or article every week and earning more money than he ever had. He sent most of his earnings to his mother, who was ill. Having broken with his father in 1922, Hughes learned, too late to attend the funeral, that his dad had died in Mexico on October 22, 1934. He traveled to Mexico and remained there from January to April 1935, during which time he read Cervantes's *Don Quixote*.

Shakespeare in Harlem (1942), Hughes's next book of poems, was well crafted. His *Fields of Wonder* (1947) appeared in a United States still full of racial strife but with a promise of social and artistic progress. However modern he was, Hughes would never abandon Black folk life for Western imagism. In *Montage of a Dream Deferred* (1951), his first book-length poem, dramatic and colloquial effects amplify his lyricism. Numerous projects in the writing of history and short fiction, such as *The First Book of Negroes* (1952) and *Simple Takes a Wife* (1953), drained his poetic energies. His style became more sophisticated. Through monologue and free verse, he stressed dramatic situations and mastered the apostrophe for blending content with form, fusing poetic narrative with sound effects.

By the time the book of stories *Laughing to Keep from Crying* was published in 1952, the color line had begun to fade. In 1953, Hughes was called to testify to the Senate subcommittee chaired by Joseph McCarthy, as part of its investigation into the purchase of books by subversive writers for American libraries abroad. Hughes read a statement about his own political views but did not discuss anyone else's (Ostrom, *Encyclopedia*, 239–240; Rampersad). For several years subsequently, Hughes received fewer offers to read his poems. He continued to hone his fiction. When *The Best of Simple* (1961) appeared, it presented a comic veneer and lightness that artfully concealed its complex symbolism. He had developed the character Jesse B. Simple in a column he began writing for the *Chicago Defender* in the 1940s, and he ultimately filled several volumes with the Simple stories (Harper). Another recurring comic, deceptively wise character in his writing is Madame Alberta K. Johnson, who appears in eighteen poems (Ostrom, *Encyclopedia*, 229–230).

In 1960, Hughes visited Paris, France, for the first time in twenty-two years; he had first visited the city and was employed there as a waiter after having worked on a transatlantic freighter in the 1920s. Subsequently, he would make many trips on cultural grants from the State Department—an irony indeed, since until 1959 he had been on the "security index" of the FBI's New York office. The year 1961 saw the publication of his crowning achievement, *Ask Your Mama* (1961), which expresses a satiric response to the rising anger of the 1960s. By the time of publication, Hughes had lived from one great movement of African American culture in the twentieth century—the Harlem Renaissance—to the second great one, the Black Arts Movement of the 1960s and 1970s.

Until four years before his death, Hughes avoided any controversy over what might now be called gay rights. By exploring the complexity of sexual orientation in "Blessed Assurance," a story about a boy singing in church, he reveals that a sacredness of God-given talent transcends sexual orientation. Despite the church audience's discomfort with a boy singer—especially the troubled father's anxiety—the uniqueness of the boy's voice compels the female audience to suspend their normal conformity to assumptions about gender. The girls, in other words, make an exception for his extremely high voice for a male and still appreciate the way he sings. Hughes's own sexuality has been a point of contention among scholars and critics.

Hughes was a writer of almost incredible versatility. He helped establish the Harlem Suitcase Theatre, was active in theatrical circles in Chicago, Illinois, and wrote numerous plays. With Elmer Rice and Kurt Weill, he collaborated on the opera *Street Scene* (1946); he worked with Jan Meyerowitz and William Grant Still on other operas. He also wrote gospel song-plays, including *Black Nativity: A Christmas Song Play* (1961), which is still regularly produced. He edited *The Best Short Stories by Negro Writers: An Anthology from 1899 to the Present* (1967) as well as *Poems from Black Africa* (1963). Several of his children's books are still in print at this writing. On one of them, *Popo and Fifina* (1932), he collaborated with his lifelong friend Arna Bontemps. With Zora Neale Hurston, he collaborated on the ill-fated dramatic project *Mule Bone*, which was not produced until long after both writers had died. With Clarence Muse, he wrote the screenplay for the motion picture *Way Down South* (1939). With Milton Meltzer, he collaborated on *A Pictorial History of the Negro in America* (1956) (Miller, *Art and Imagination* and *Langston Hughes and Gwendolyn Brooks*; Ostrom, *Encyclopedia*).

Langston Hughes was both sympathetic and prophetic in a variety of ways. The 1980s marked a timely renaissance in his reputation. A Langston Hughes study conference held in March 1981 at Joplin, Missouri, helped inspire the founding of the Langston Hughes Society in Baltimore, Maryland, on June 26 of the same year. After a joint meeting with the College

Language Association in April 1982, the Society became the first group focused on a Black author ever to become an affiliate of the Modern Language Association, in 1984. In the winter of 1983, at the City College of the City University of New York, Raymond Patterson directed "Langston Hughes: Art International Interdisciplinary Conference," one of the most satisfactory tributes ever paid to the author. Later, a public television production, *Voices and Visions*, included a program on Hughes and reaffirmed his place among the most celebrated national poets. Arnold Rampersad's authoritative two-volume biography of Hughes appeared in 1986 and 1988.

Hughes's impact on American literary history is clear. He introduced some of the most experimental forms of African American music into the poetics of the twentieth century. During the despair of the Great Depression, he presented many deceptively simple stories that would endure beyond his time. He proved, during the late 1940s, that lyricism would prosper, despite the despondency of history. Neither the pessimism of the Cold War nor the mainstream backlash to the Civil Rights Movement of the 1960s—satirized by him in his final volume, *The Panther and the Lash* (1967)—disillusioned him completely. He discerned a disturbing cycle of inhumanity within history, but not without laughter. A man for all seasons, he was especially a voice of the mid-twentieth century. His work embodied a measured declaration on behalf of a most optimistic future. Thus, his words outlived his own century. He read the vicissitudes of history, often revealing their implications to those who experienced them with him (Miller, "Brief," 61).

Today it would be an unpardonable neglect to discuss either the Jazz Age or the Harlem Renaissance without mention of Hughes. The year 2001 began a steady stream of eighteen volumes, *The Collected Works*, from the University of Missouri Press. The publication is one of the most momentous in African American literary history. By the turn of the twenty-first century, at least four cities—Joplin, Missouri; Lawrence, Kansas; Cleveland, Ohio; and New York City—claimed Hughes as an honored citizen. Cleveland kicked off the national celebration early in June when the Case Western Reserve Historical Society and the NAACP reminded the nation that he had spent his high school years there. Soon major conferences took place at Lincoln University in Pennsylvania, the site of his undergraduate years; Yale University; and the University of Kansas, so close to the home of Mary Langston, the poet's maternal grandmother.

Indeed, the Kansas conference was a watershed moment in Hughes research. Outside the auditorium were long lines of local protesters who were angry that Langston Hughes—who was nearly as guarded about his sexual orientation as he was about his perception of God—may have been a gay Black male.

Nonetheless, the approval of Hughes by hundreds of academics and creative writers was indisputable, as was his acceptance by the general public: a U.S. postage stamp honoring Hughes was unveiled at the conference during a reading of his works by the actor Danny Glover. Inside the building were hundreds of intelligent laypersons from all walks of life who reaffirmed the legacy of the writer. Today Hughes still has the power to arouse strong emotions in people of varying aesthetics and ideologies. Few have been indifferent to his persistent belief in human freedom. Gwendolyn Brooks said his vision would last "until the air is cured of its fever." He voiced a celebration of survival and beauty that outlived his century. His writings are for all time.

R. Baxter Miller

See also: Autobiography; Drama; Essay; Harlem Renaissance; Humor; Lyric Poetry; Modernism; Short Fiction; Vernacular.

Resources

Primary Sources: All the primary sources are now available in Langston Hughes, *The Collected Works*, 18 vols., ed. Arnold Rampersad (Columbia: University of Missouri Press, 2001–2004). In text citations, *BS* = *The Big Sea* and *CP* = *Collected Poems*.

Secondary Sources: Richard K. Barksdale, *Langston Hughes, the Poet and His Critics* (Chicago: American Library Association, 1977); Faith Berry, *Langston Hughes, Before and Beyond Harlem* (Westport, CT: L. Hill, 1983); Tish Dace, *Langston Hughes: The Contemporary Reviews* (New York: Cambridge University Press, 1997); Christopher C. De Santis, ed., *Langston Hughes and the Chicago Defender Essays on Race, Politics, and Culture, 1942–62* (Urbana: University of Illinois Press, 1995); Donald C. Dickinson, *A Bio-Bibliography of Langston Hughes, 1902–1967* (Hamden, CT: Archon Books, 1967); Susan Duffy, ed., *The Political Plays of Langston Hughes* (Carbondale: Southern Illinois University Press, 2000); James A. Emanuel, *Langston Hughes* (New York: Twayne, 1967); Allison Flood, "Langston Hughes 'Born a Year Before Accepted Date', Researcher Finds," *The Guardian,* August 10, 2018: https://www.theguardian.com/books/2018/aug/10/langston-hughes-born-a-year-before-accepted-date-poet (accessed 2019); Kristin Grogan, "Langston Hughes's Constructivist Poetics," *American Literature* 90, no. 3 (September 2018), 585; Donna Akiba Sullivan Harper, *Not So Simple: The "Simple" Stories by Langston Hughes* (Columbia: University of Missouri Press, 1995); Onwuchekwa Jemie, *Langston Hughes: An Introduction to the Poetry* (New York: Columbia University Press, 1976); Isaac Julien, *Looking for Langston* (experimental documentary) (New York: Waterbearer, 1999), VHS format; Peter Mandelik and Stanley Schatt, *A Concordance to the Poetry of Langston Hughes* (Detroit: Gale Research, 1975); Joseph McLaren: "Langston Hughes and Africa: From the Harlem Renaissance to the 1960s," in *Juxtapositions: The Harlem Renaissance and the Lost Generation*, ed. Loes Nas and Chandré Carstens (Cape Town, South Africa: University of Cape Town, 2000), 77–94; *Langston Hughes Folk Dramatist in the Protest Tradition, 1921–1943* (Westport, CT: Greenwood Press, 1997); Thomas A. Mikolyz, comp., *Langston Hughes: A Bio-Bibliography* (Westport, CT: Greenwood Press, 1990); R. Baxter Miller: *The Art and Imagination of Langston Hughes* (Lexington: University Press of Kentucky, 1989); "A Brief Biography," in *A Historical Guide to Langston Hughes*, ed. Steven C. Tracy (New York: Oxford University Press, 2004), 23–62; "Café de la Paix: Mapping the Harlem Renaissance," *South Atlantic Review* 65, no. 2 (2000), 73–94; *Langston Hughes and Gwendolyn Brooks: A Reference Guide* (Boston: G. K. Hall, 1978); R. Baxter Miller, ed., *Critical Insights: Langston Hughes* (Ipswich, MA: Salem Press, 2013); Edward J. Mullen, ed., *Critical Essays on Langston Hughes* (Boston: G. K. Hall, 1986); Ifeoma Nwanko, "Langston Hughes and the Translation of Nicolas Guillién's Afro-Cuban Culture and Language," *Langston Hughes Review* 16, no. 1–2 (2001–2002), 55–72; Therman B. O'Daniel, *Langston Hughes: Black Genius* (New York: Collier Books, 1971); Hans A. Ostrom: *Langston Hughes: A Study of the Short Fiction* (New York: Twayne, 1993); *A Langston Hughes Encyclopedia* (Westport, CT: Greenwood Press, 2002); Arnold Rampersad, *The Life of Langston Hughes*, 2 vols. (New York: Oxford University Press, 1986–1988); David Roessel: "The Letters of Langston Hughes and Ezra Pound," *Paideuma: A Journal Devoted to Ezra Pound Scholarship* 29, no. 1–2 (Spring/Fall 2000), 207–242; "Process of Revision and Hughes," in Hans Ostrom,

A Langston Hughes Encyclopedia (Westport, CT: Greenwood Press, 2002), 327–333; Steven C. Tracy, *Langston Hughes & the Blues* (Urbana: University of Illinois Press, 1988); C. James Trotman, ed.: *Langston Hughes: The Man, His Art, and His Continuing Influence* (New York: Garland, 1995); *Voices and Visions: Langston Hughes* (New York: Winstar Home Entertainment, 2002), VHS format; Jean Wagner, *Black Poets of the United States from Paul Laurence Dunbar to Langston Hughes,* trans. Kenneth Douglas (Urbana: University of Illinois Press, 1973); Jeff Westover, "Langston Hughes's Counterpublic Discourse," *Langston Hughes Review* 24–25 (Winter–Fall 2010), 2(18).

Humor

Humor in the African American tradition can be found in the vernacular speech, songs, folklore, and literature of and by Black Americans. African American humor reflects a mixture of cultural influences and forms, many whose origins can be traced to Europe and Africa.

Ostensibly, African American humor shares many forms with the Western tradition of comedy that spans from antiquity to the present day. According to J. A. Cuddon, Aristotle defines comedy as that which "deals in an amusing way with ordinary characters in rather everyday situations" (149). While many histories of the tradition of comedy in the West do not usually include the contributions of writers of African descent (with the exception of Jean Genet, a dramatist whose work *The Blacks* is often considered within the tradition of the theater of the absurd), forms of comedy, such as farce, satire, parody, and tall stories characteristic of the European tradition are unmistakably evident in African American humor. For example, plantation sayings and stories told by slaves that mimicked the speech, manners, and mores of their masters and mistresses contain elements of both parody and satire.

The origins of minstrelsy in the United States, beginning in the nineteenth century, can be traced back to minstrels who traveled throughout Europe during the thirteenth and fourteenth centuries, singing traditional stories (Cuddon). However, the use of racial stereotypes became the standard in American minstrel shows in the early 1820s after the success of Thomas D. Rice's blackface act and song "Jump Jim Crow." Jim Crow, the character in Rice's show who was played by a White performer who applied burnt cork makeup to blacken his face, set in place the "comic darkie" stereotype in American popular culture, one that caricatured Blacks as slow, childish, shiftless, happy-go-lucky, watermelon-eating, and, contradictorily, as John Lowe writes, "stupid but crafty, humble but scheming, cowardly but reckless, innocent but lascivious" (Lowe, "Humor," in *Oxford Companion to African American Literature,* 371). This stock character, as an object of Whites' derisive humor, helped perpetuate stereotypes of African Americans and found its way in the works of such nineteenth-century American writers as Harriet Beecher Stowe and Mark Twain.

African storytelling practices that were transported with slaves as they crossed the middle passage to the Americas influenced African American humor. According to Mel Watkins, African American humor can be traced to African griots, or storytellers, who traveled throughout western African singing traditional stories. Other elements of African American humor have their roots in Africa. Harold Courlander has traced and recorded the use of animal tales, such as Brer (or "Buh") Rabbit and Brer Fox, shared by many peoples of African descent throughout the Americas. Henry Louis Gates Jr. in *The Signifying Monkey*, locates the origin of the Signifying Monkey—a trickster figure similar to other animal characters such as Brer Rabbit and a central character and trope of the oral tradition, verbal play, and folklore of African Americans—in Esu-Elegbara, a trickster figure in Yoruba. What is characteristic of African American humor is its roots in "an oral tradition that esteemed dramatic colorful speech, imaginative storytelling, irony, and libelous verbal satire" (Watkins, xvii).

The reasons for and uses of humor by African Americans are several. During the nineteenth century, Blacks used humor as a way of coping with slavery and racism. The slaves' plantation sayings, rhymes, animal and trickster tales, riddles, and songs evince deliberate uses of irony that served to "free" the slave from his or her subservient position. Daryl Cumber Dance notes that "folk riddles" are the earliest known forms of folklore (Dance, *From My People*, 538).

The animal and trickster tales that slaves told featured a cast of weaker animal characters (Brer Rabbit, the Signifying Monkey) who always managed to outwit the stronger (Brer Fox, the Lion). The slaves no doubt identified with the cunning ways in which Brer Rabbit and the Signifying Monkey were able to "trick" Brer Fox and the Lion, respectively. As Jennifer Andrews notes, the trickster, as a purveyor of the comic element, offered "a way to cope with and laugh at the strictures of white American culture" Joel Chandler Harris published many of these tales in *Uncle Remus, His Songs and His Sayings* (1880) and was responsible for preserving these early examples of African American humor. Another early example of African American humor that draws on the tradition of

oral storytelling and pokes fun at the institution of slavery is Charles Waddell Chesnutt's *The Conjure Woman* (1899).

While minstrel shows of the nineteenth century made Blacks the butt of racist humor, many plantation stories appropriated the stereotypical "darkie" and imbued him with subtle wit. Among them are the "John and Ole Massa" tales, in which John, the slave, is cast as dim-witted and slow. However, as each tale unfolds, John, who is associated with the legendary High John de Conqueror (Watkins, 46), emerges as a trickster hero, deftly demonstrating mastery of Massa's language in a subtly dazzling display of verbal play, outwitting him each and every time.

The animal and trickster tales and other early forms reveal some of the aims of humor. The objects of African American humor are often Whites who occupy positions of power; some of the humor, however, is self-reflexive—as in the appropriation of the stereotypical "darkie" in the "John and Ole Massa" tales. Self-reflexive humor is most confusing to people outside the group, in that a negative stereotype is seemingly embraced and laughed at by members inside the group. This type of humor is called "corrective comedy" (*Encyclopedia of African American Culture*, 370). Corrective comedy is evidenced not only in early African American humor but also in later forms of the twentieth and twenty-first centuries.

After emancipation and into the early part of the twentieth century, African American humor transformed significantly as many Blacks moved from rural to urban and industrial centers in the Northeast and the Midwest. While influences of the folklore of the old, rural South were still part of modern African America, the new brand of humor reflected the milieu of urban America.

What is characteristic of modern African American humor is bolder and more audacious use of language and verbal play. Signifying, joning/joaning, cracking, specifying, and bookooing are just a few of the terms used to refer to a type of verbal sparring called "playing the dozens." Playing the dozens is a game of verbal one-upmanship in which the players attack each other with insults, most commonly scathing remarks about "yo' mama." According to Daryl Cumber Dance, while some scholars maintain that the labels mark differences between these verbal games, most practitioners do not recognize such distinctions (*From My People*, 539). Boasts, toasts and ballads were also part of the growing repertoire of forms of African American humor. One famous ballad is the "Sinking of the Titanic," which tells the tale of the only Black passenger, a man named Shine, of that ill-fated ship. Tales of the city reflected the activities there, from gambling and other vices to street preaching and faith healing.

Animal tales were still widely told and circulated; but the city gave birth to a new cast of characters, some of them bad Black men such as Stackolee and Jack Johnson. Stackolee, based on a real man who allegedly killed another man in St. Louis, Missouri, for stealing his white Stetson hat, epitomized the "bad Negro" and was the subject of many a ballad. Jack Johnson, the first Black heavyweight boxer to win the championship (1908), became a character in many a humorous tall tale because of his extravagant lifestyle and his blatant disregard for the illegality of interracial relationships. (He was allegedly refused passage on the *Titanic* because he was Black, and this ironic circumstance became the stuff of humorous folklore).

The twentieth century welcomed a growing corpus of literary works written by African Americans who incorporated these new forms of humor and took the opportunity to correct negative stereotypes of Blacks made popular in the previous century. The goals of the Harlem Renaissance, beginning in 1925, were most notably expressed in Alain Locke's seminal essay "The New Negro" (1925). Locke's call for revision of representations of the Negro in literature and art brought new challenges to modern writers in terms of how to depict African American humor. The use of dialect was a big concern in the new literature because it was reminiscent of the nineteenth-century caricatures of Black slaves. Harold Courlander questions the use of dialect in expressing "wit and humor" because these can be easily translated from one language (or culture) to another (Courlander, 259).

Many writers were, of course, divided on this issue. Zora Neale Hurston was criticized for her representation of Black speech in her writing. Nonetheless, Hurston's research on folklore and vernacular speech allowed her to produce memorable moments of parody and verbal play in her novel *Their Eyes Were Watching God* (1937). Other novels by Hurston that showcased her skillful blending of Black Southern folklore and elements of humor include *Jonah's Gourd Vine* (1934), *Moses, Man of the Mountain* (1939), and *Seraph on the Suwanee* (1948).

Langston Hughes, who was a contemporary and good friend of Hurston, was legendary in his own contributions to humorous literature by African American writers during this period. Hughes is most famous for the creation of Jesse B. Simple, an urban folk character noted for his hilarious solutions to, and "simple" but ironic wisdom regarding, an array of issues from race relations to house cleaning. Hughes's Simple stories, first published in the

Chicago Defender, were enormously popular. Hughes penned other humorous works—*Not Without Laughter* (1930) and *Tambourines to Glory* (1958), a novel that blends traditional folk culture and religion with jive and vice—and he edited *The Book of Negro Humor* in 1966 (Ostrom, 56).

Other Harlem, New York, writers produced work that incorporated Black vernacular humor, parody, and satire. These writers and their works are Rudolph John Chauncey Fisher and his comedic detective novel *The Conjure-Man Dies* (1932), Wallace Thurman and his ribald send-up of the Harlem Renaissance in *Infants of the Spring* (1930), George S. Schuyler and his lampoon of Blacks' and Whites' preoccupation with skin color in *Black No More* (1931), and Carl Van Vechten and his controversial satire on Harlem nightlife in *N— Heaven* (1926).

Much of the literature after World War II was steeped in Social Realism. However, humor in African American literature, while at times obscured by the social and political milieu of 1950s America and the push for civil rights, still thrived. Ralph Ellison gleaned elements from Southern Black folklore and rural and urban Black humor in writing *Invisible Man* (1952). Ellison played on the comedic traditions of "old" and "new" Negroes through his creation two trickster characters, Trueblood and Rineheart, in his novel.

Other notable examples of literature by Black writers that use elements of African American humor from the 1960s to the present day are Chester Himes and his comedic detective novel *Cotton Comes to Harlem* (1964), Alice Walker and her use of Black vernacular speech in *The Color Purple* (1982), Ishmael Reed in his novel that takes up a dizzying array of folk practices from hoodoo to signifying, *Mumbo Jumbo*

(1971), Ntozake Shange and her tale of women and magic in *Sassafrass, Cypress & Indigo* (1982), Toni Morrison in the tales, gossip, and jokes shared by the women in *Jazz* (1992), and Percival Everett in *Erasure* (2001), a tour de force play on the question of who is Black, in which he deftly combines elements of satire, parody and verbal play. Humor is also a significant element of rap, hip-hop, and performance poetry, and blues poetry also can be quite humorous.

Patricia E. Clark

See also: Chesnutt, Charles Waddell; Giovanni, Nikki; Hughes, Langston; Hurston, Zora Neale; Reed, Ishmael.

Resources

Jennifer Andrews, "Reading Toni Morrison's *Jazz*," *Canadian Review of American Studies* 29, no. 1 (1999), 87–107; William L. Andrews, Frances Smith Foster, and Trudier Harris, eds., *Oxford Companion to African American Literature* (New York: Oxford University Press, 1997); Paul Beatty, ed., *Hokum: An Anthology of African-American Humor* (New York: Bloomsbury, 2006); Arna Bontemps and Langston Hughes, eds., *Book of Negro Folklore* (New York: Dodd, Mead, 1958); Glenda Carpio, *Laughing Fit to Kill: Black Humor in the Fictions of Slavery* (Oxford and New York: Oxford University Press, 2006); Harold Courlander, *A Treasury of Afro-American Folklore* (New York: Marlowe, 1996); J. A. Cuddon, *A Dictionary of Literary Terms and Literary Theory*, 4th ed., rev. C. E. Preston (Malden, MA: Blackwell, 1998); Daryl Cumber Dance, *From My People: 400 Years of African American Folklore* (New York: Norton, 2002); Daryl Cumber Dance, ed., *Honey, Hush! An Anthology of African American Women's Humor* (New York: Norton, 1998); Alan Dundes, ed., *Mother Wit from the Laughing Barrel: Readings in the Interpretation of Afro-American Folklore* (Englewood Cliffs, NJ: Prentice-Hall, 1973); Henry Louis Gates Jr., *The*

Signifying Monkey (New York: Oxford University Press, 1998); "Jack Johnson and Titanic Song," *Folknet Discussion*, http://www.folknet.org/_disc3/000002e3.htm; Dexter B. Gordon, "Humor in African American Discourse: Speaking of Oppression," *Journal of Black Studies* 29, no. 2 (November 1998), 254–276; Langston Hughes, ed., *The Book of Negro Humor* (New York: Dodd, Mead, 1966); John Lowe, *Jump at the Sun: Zora Neale Hurston's Cosmic Comedy* (Urbana: University of Illinois Press, 1994); Hans Ostrom, *A Langston Hughes Encyclopedia* (Westport, CT: Greenwood Press, 2002); Mel Watkins, *African American Humor: The Best Black Comedy from Slavery to Today* (Chicago: Lawrence Hill, 2002).

Hurston, Zora Neale (1891–1960)

Novelist, short-story writer, playwright, folklorist, and anthropologist. Hurston is best known for novels and short stories that make use of the vernacular and display a rich, complex sense of rural African American life, particularly in the South. She was born in Notasulga, Alabama, on January 7, 1891, to John Hurston, a preacher and carpenter, and Lucy Potts Hurston, a retired schoolteacher. Hurston was the fifth of eight children. Shortly after her birth, the Hurstons moved to Eatonville, Florida, the first incorporated Black city in the United States, a city alive with opportunity. Whenever Hurston spoke of "home," she meant Eatonville.

Growing up in Eatonville profoundly shaped Hurston's worldview. As a child there, she attended the Robert Hungerford Normal and Industrial School, modeled after Booker T. Washington's Tuskegee Institute. At this school, her industry and intelligence won her the praise of White philanthropists, along with her fair share of books, which she read voraciously, and

clothes. Along with her formal education, Hurston learned the craft of storytelling by listening to the ribald stories told by men on the porch of Joe Clarke's store (*Dust Tracks on a Road*). Hurston used many of these stories in her later writings, particularly in her 1937 novel *Their Eyes Were Watching God*; in short stories, such as those collected in *Spunk* and *Sweat*; and in *Mule Bone*, the play she wrote with Langston Hughes.

Hurston's mother died on September 18, 1904, when Hurston was thirteen years old, and her death was a great blow. While Lucy Hurston always encouraged her daughter to "jump at de sun," John Hurston attempted to squelch Zora's bodacious spirit, believing that his daughter was heading to a world of trouble if she did not humble herself to supposed authority (Hemenway; Boyd). With the loss of her mother, Hurston found herself alone in a community that frowned upon her wild stories and her lively spirit.

John Hurston wasted little time in sending his daughter off to the Florida Baptist Academy in Jacksonville, Florida. Already motherless, Hurston essentially became fatherless as well. John Hurston stopped making the tuition payments at Florida Baptist, and as a result, Hurston was forced to scrub floors and perform other menial tasks to pay her way. Later, John Hurston put Hurston up for adoption, but there were no takers. She excelled academically her first year at Florida Baptist, but her return home after her first year was a failure.

Hurston was shocked to find that her father had remarried. For his new wife, he had chosen Mattie Moge, who was younger than his oldest son, and only six years older than Zora, who never got along with her new stepmother. Hurston caused a tremendous uproar over Lucy's featherbed, the bed Lucy had died on and upon which Mattie now slept, for Lucy had bequeathed the bed to her. The tensions in the home escalated to the point that John Hurston pulled a knife on his daughter, and Hurston left home (Hemenway; Boyd).

Hurston's dream of completing her formal education was put on hold as she worked menial jobs, fending off sexual and physical violence—as she learned all too soon, a Black teenage girl had few rights, if any, in a world run by White men. In 1912, she left Florida, living first with her brother Bob and his wife in the Black Bottom section of Nashville, Tennessee, and later in a middle-class neighborhood on Scott Street in Memphis, Tennessee. In 1914, Hurston returned to Jacksonville, and lived with her brother John before landing a job with a traveling Gilbert and Sullivan theater troupe.

With the troupe, Hurston worked as a wardrobe girl and a maid for the lead singer. She left the group when it reached Baltimore, Maryland, and began life anew. In September 1917, she enrolled in Morgan Academy, an elite all-Black prep school of what is now Morgan State University. To be eligible for Morgan, Hurston lied about her age, making herself ten years younger than she actually was. To pay her way through school, she worked in the home of Dr. Baldwin, a White clergyman and school trustee whose wife had a bad hip. In exchange for performing domestic chores, Hurston had all tuition waived, received room and board, gained access to a well-stocked library, earned a stipend of $2 a week, and was free to study during the day. At Morgan, she excelled in her English and history classes and, at times, taught the history classes (Hemenway).

In June 1918, Hurston withdrew from Morgan to pursue her dream of attending Howard University. She moved to Washington, DC, and, waiting tables at the exclusive Cosmos Club, earned the fees for Howard. When she went to enroll, however, Hurston learned that her work at Morgan was incomplete and did not qualify her for admission to Howard. Hurston attended Howard Academy, earning her high school diploma in May 1919. In the fall of that year, she began her undergraduate studies at Howard University, studying part-time from 1919 to 1923, while waiting tables and working as a manicurist in a barbershop.

An English major at Howard, Hurston worked with the philosopher Alain Locke, one of the framers of the Harlem Renaissance, and began her career as a writer in earnest. Hurston was a member of the Howard literary club, the Stylus, and in May 1921, she published her first poem, "O Night," and her first short story, "John Redding Goes to Sea," in its literary magazine, *The Stylus* (Hemenway; Boyd). Hurston's literary pursuits ranged off campus as well. She published two poems in Marcus Garvey's *Negro World*, the official organ for his Universal Negro Improvement Association, and attended the salons of the African American poet Georgia Douglas Johnson. At Johnson's literary salons, visitors included W.E.B. Du Bois and James Weldon Johnson, the writers Jean Toomer and Rudolph John Chauncey Fisher, and the poets Sterling A. Brown and Angelina Weld Grimké. During the fall of 1923, Hurston's last term at Howard, she excelled in what interested her and failed courses that did not. After the holiday break, she did not enroll for the spring term of 1924.

That year she published two short stories, "Drenched in Light" and "Spunk," in Charles Spurgeon Johnson's *Opportunity*. Her writing career off to an auspicious start, Hurston left Washington for New York City in 1925. In New York, she took her place among other writers and artists of the Harlem Renaissance. Her story "Spunk" was anthologized in Alain Locke's foundational anthology of the Harlem Renaissance, *The New Negro* (1925), and in May 1925, Hurston received two second-place prizes at the *Opportunity* awards dinner. At that awards dinner, among meeting prime movers of the Harlem Renaissance such as Langston Hughes, Countee Cullen, Fannie Hurst, and Carl Van Vechten, Hurston met Annie Nathan Meyer, a trustee of Barnard College who was impressed with Hurston's vivacity to the extent that, despite Hurston's less than impressive Howard transcript, she helped Hurston find scholarship money to attend Barnard College, beginning in the fall of 1926. During her first term at Barnard, Hurston worked as a secretary and chauffeur for the novelist Fannie Hurst. This position earned Hurston the esteem of some of her classmates as well as of Virginia C. Gildersleeve, the dean of Barnard College. Despite access to White literary circles, $12.50 a week, and clothes, Hurston did not keep the job but decided to wait tables and do housework for friends of Meyer.

The only Black student at Barnard, Hurston studied anthropology with Franz Boas and collaborated with Aaron Douglas, Wallace Thurman, and Langston Hughes on the avant-garde journal *Fire!!*, which was a kind of response to Locke's anthology and aimed to support and celebrate what the editors perceived to be fresher work by younger artists. African American art, Hurston believed, was defined through traditions such as oral history and folklore. As a result, Black art and culture, according to Hurston, were not necessarily obligated to respond to racist stereotypes. This belief forms one of the core principles of

Hurston's body of work in which the "White" world is at the margins, never asserting a dominant influence over the humanity of her Black characters.

In 1927, Hurston, with the support of a fellowship from the Association for the Study of Negro Life and History, published her first field report, "Cudjo's Own Story of the Last African Slaves," in the *Journal of Negro History*. That same year, she met Charlotte Osgood Mason, a White philanthropist whose interest had turned from the Southwest American Indians to the "New Negro" of Harlem, New York. Mason supported a range of Black artists, writers, and intellectuals, including Langston Hughes, and she insisted that those in her pay call her "Godmother." For this work, Hurston received a stipend of $200 a month, with the understanding that all the folklore she collected belonged to Mason.

In 1928, Hurston became the first African American to earn a BA from Barnard College. With Barnard degree in hand and Mason's monthly stipend in pocket, Hurston traveled the South, gathering stories and folklore that she would fashion into novels, plays, and academic papers. In 1931, she published a 100-page scholarly article, "Hoodoo in America," which concerned what is commonly known as voodoo, in the *Journal of American Folklore*. That same year she began collaborating with Langston Hughes on a play, *Mule Bone*, which was to move beyond the minstrel images of Black people on stage. For a variety of reasons, including different views toward Mrs. Mason, the relationship between Hughes and Hurston disintegrated and collaboration ceased on *Mule Bone*, which was not produced until 1991 (*Mule Bone*; Taj Mahal), long after both writers were dead. The controversy surrounding *Mule Bone* is recounted in detail in the 1991 edition as well as in Rampersad's biography of Hughes, Hemenway's and Boyd's biographies of Hurston, and Hughes's autobiography, *The Big Sea*.

The relationship between Hurston and Mason became increasingly frayed as they clashed over the idea of folklore ownership; for Hurston, African American folklore was not something that could be owned, only shared. She left Mason's payroll in 1932, and began folklore concerts at which she dramatized life in railroad camps, using folk and work songs. In May 1934, Hurston published her first novel, *Jonah's Gourd Vine*, which became a Book-of-the-Month Club selection. The 1934 recipient of a Julius Rosenwald fellowship, Hurston published *Mules and Men* the following year, the first book of African American folklore written by an African American. With two solid books to her credit, Hurston was awarded a Guggenheim Fellowship in March 1936 that took her to the West Indies to study obeah practices. In Haiti, she wrote her finest novel, *Their Eyes Were Watching God*, in seven weeks. In September 1937, Hurston returned to the United States and published *Their Eyes*. In that novel, the protagonist, Janie Mae Crawford, gains an independence of voice and attains an ideal, though short-lived, romantic love that Hurston herself never attained.

With a life filled with writing and traveling, Hurston was never married for long. Her 1927 marriage to Herbert Sheen, a medical student she met at Howard in 1921, was annulled in 1931, although they had separated four months after their wedding vows. In 1939, Hurston tried marriage again, this time with Works Progress Administration playground director Albert Price III, fifteen years her junior. After eight months, divorce papers were filed, and the divorce became official in 1943.

In 1938, the fieldwork Hurston had done in Haiti while on Guggenheim Fellowships was published as her second collection of folklore, *Tell My Horse*. In June 1939, Morgan State College awarded Hurston an honorary Doctor of Letters, and in November she published her second novel, *Moses, Man of the Mountain*, in which she explored the figure of Moses and African oral traditions. In November 1942, Hurston published her autobiographical memoir, *Dust Tracks on a Road*, her sixth book in eight years, and her greatest commercial success.

After this flood of writing, along with a range of short stories and essays, Hurston continued to write, but not at the same pace, publishing stories and articles in the *Saturday Review*, the *American Mercury*, and the *Negro Digest*. In fact, her stature as a writer began to wane, partly because Richard Wright's *Native Son* (1940) brought protest literature into vogue. Nevertheless, Hurston continued the work that was important to her. In May 1947, she traveled to British Honduras (now Belize) to study Central American Black communities. In March 1948, she returned to the United States, and in October published her last novel, *Seraph on the Suwanee*. That same year, she was falsely accused of molesting a ten-year-old boy, and the charges were dropped in March 1949 when Hurston turned over her passport, which proved she was in British Honduras at the time of the accusation.

In the winter of 1950, Hurston moved to Belle Glade, Florida, and throughout the 1950s, she worked as a substitute teacher and as a domestic worker, while contributing to local Florida newspapers. Her income was never steady, but she never asked relatives for help. Even after a stroke in early 1959, Hurston remained fiercely independent, while her condition worsened financially and physically. In October 1959,

Hurston was forced to enter the St. Lucie County Welfare Home, where she died on January 28, 1960 of "hypertensive heart disease" (Hemenway). She was at work on a biography of Herod the Great.

When Hurston died, none of her books was in print, although she was the most prolific Black woman writer in America. Buried in an unmarked grave in Fort Pierce's African American cemetery, Hurston's body lay in obscurity until August 1973, when Alice Walker found her unmarked grave and placed a tombstone on it. On this tombstone, Walker named Hurston a "genius of the South," a phrase from one of Jean Toomer's poems in *Cane*, and a phrase that situates Hurston as one of the preeminent writers of the Harlem Renaissance as well as a progenitor of Black women writers following in her wake. Since the publication of Walker's "Looking for Zora" in the March 1975 issue of *Ms.* magazine, Hurston has become a significant figure in the canon of American and African American literature, and her work has been widely republished.

Delano Greenidge-Copprue

See also: Autobiography; Drama; Feminism/ Black Feminism; Folklore; Harlem Renaissance; Novel; Short Fiction.

Resources

Primary Sources: Zora Neale Hurston: *Collected Plays*, ed. Jean Lee Cole and Charles Mitchell (New Brunswick, NJ: Rutgers University Press, 2008); *The Complete Stories* (New York: HarperCollins, 1995); *Dust Tracks on a Road* (1942; repr. New York: HarperPerennial, 1996); *Jonah's Gourd Vine* (1934; repr. New York: Perennial Library, 1990); *Moses, Man of the Mountain* (Philadelphia: Lippincott, 1939); *Mule Bone: A Comedy of Negro Life*, written with Langston Hughes, ed. George Houston Bass and Henry Louis Gates Jr. (New York: HarperPerennial, 1991); *Mules and Men* (1935; repr. New York: Perennial Library, 1990); *Seraph on the Suwanee* (New York: Scribner's, 1948); *Spunk: Selected Stories of Zora Neale Hurston* (San Francisco: Publishing Group West, 1997); *Sweat*, ed. Cheryl A. Wall (New Brunswick, NJ: Rutgers University Press, 1997); *Their Eyes Were Watching God* (1937; repr. New York: Perennial Library, 1990).

Secondary Sources: John Beaufort, "*Mule Bone* Debuts after 60 Years," *Christian Science Monitor*, February 26, 1991, p. 13; Katherine Biers, "Practices of Enchantment: The Theatre of Zora Neale Hurston," *TDR: The Drama Review* 59, no. 4 (2015), 67–82; Valerie Boyd, *Wrapped in Rainbows: The Life of Zora Neale Hurston* (New York: Scribner's, 2003); Robert Wayne Croft, *A Zora Neale Hurston Companion* (Westport, CT: Greenwood Press, 2002); Ayesha K. Hardison, "Crossing the Threshold: Zora Neale Hurston, Racial Performance, and *Seraph on the Suwanee*," *African American Review* 46, no. 2 (2013), 217–235; Robert E. Hemenway, *Zora Neale Hurston: A Literary Biography* (Urbana: University of Illinois Press, 1977); Karla Holloway, *The Character of the Word: The Texts of Zora Neale Hurston* (Westport, CT: Greenwood Press, 1987); Nathan Irvin Huggins, *Harlem Renaissance* (New York: Oxford University Press, 1971); Langston Hughes, *The Big Sea* (New York: Knopf, 1940); Sharon L. Jones, ed., *Critical Insights: Zora Neale Hurston* (Ipswich, MA: Salem Press, 2013); Carla Kaplan, ed., *Zora Neale Hurston: A Life in Letters* (New York: Doubleday, 2002); Carla Kaplan and Ralph E. Van Raaphorst Luker: "Hurston, Zora Neale," *American National Biography Online* (February 2000), http://www.anb.org//articles/16/16 -00817.html; "Hurston, Zora Neale," in *African American Women: A Biographical Dictionary*, ed. Dorothy Salem (New York: Garland, 1996); Hans Ostrom, "*Mule Bone: A Comedy of Negro Life*," in his *A Langston Hughes Encyclopedia* (Westport, CT: Greenwood Press, 2002), 261–262; Arnold Rampersad, *The Life of Langston Hughes*, vol. 1, *1902–1941* (New York: Oxford University

Press, 1986); Taj Mahal, *Mule Bone* (Santa Monica, CA: Grammavision/Rhino Records, 1991), compact disc; Wallace Thurman et al., eds., *FIRE!! A Quarterly Devoted to the Younger Negro Artists* (facsimile reproduction) (New York: Fire Press, 1985); Alice Walker, *In Search of Our Mothers' Gardens* (San Diego: Harcourt Brace Jovanovich, 1983); Cheryl A. Wall: "Hurston, Zora Neale," in *The Oxford Companion to African American Literature*, ed. William L. Andrews, Frances Smith Foster, and Trudier Harris (New York: Oxford University Press, 1997); *Women of the Harlem Renaissance* (Bloomington: Indiana University Press, 1995); Steven Watson, *The Harlem Renaissance: Hub of African-American Culture, 1920–1930* (New York: Pantheon Books, 1995).

J

Jacobs, Harriet Ann (1813–1897)

Ex-slave, author of a slave narrative, and activist on behalf of the emancipated Southern slaves. Jacobs's narrative, *Incidents in the Life of a Slave Girl: Written by Herself* (1861), marks a significant moment and turning point in nineteenth-century African American literature. As the literary critic William L. Andrews has stated, her book, along with the *Narrative* (1845) of Frederick Douglass, represents the apex of the slave narrative genre. It incorporates elements of early American literature such as the Indian captivity narrative, Prison Literature, the novel, the tragic mulatta tale, and the Puritan jeremiad, while simultaneously introducing crucial aspects of Southern slave culture—sermons, spirituals, folk traditions—to create a uniquely African American text.

Very few female ex-slaves in the eighteenth and nineteenth centuries possessed the funds, time, patronage, and facility to publish narratives of their lives in slavery. Even when they did, quite often they emulated Louisa Picquet or Silvia Dubois by dictating to or conducting interviews with White (usually male) editors, who then transcribed these accounts with considerable editorial license that served their own religious, political, or educational purposes. Fewer still were slave narratives such as *Running a Thousand Miles for Freedom; or, The Escape of William and Ellen Craft from Slavery* (1860), in which, as several critics have suggested, the married authors Ellen and William Craft collaborated, even though William's voice dominates. Some literary productions even masqueraded as female slaves' narratives when they had not been written by African Americans at all, such as the sensational *Autobiography of a Female Slave* (1857), penned by the White Kentucky slaveholder Martha Griffith Browne (Mattie Griffith), who had inherited and then liberated her "property," moved north, and befriended abolitionists before emigrating to Europe to revive her failing health.

Incidents in the Life of a Slave Girl therefore carries additional importance because it inserts a rare, first-person, ex-slave woman's voice into the African American literary tradition, thereby introducing a stunning and detailed examination of traumas that slave women exclusively experienced: rape, sexual harassment, the jealousies of the mistress, and forced couplings with other male slaves. With its written indictment of the "peculiar institution," Jacobs's book thus complements the public oral testimonies of Sojourner Truth, Maria W. Stewart, Frances Ellen Watkins Harper, Sarah Parker Remond, Harriet Tubman, Mary Webb, Ellen Craft, and other literate and unlettered African American women preaching and lecturing in the United States, England, and Europe before the Civil War. Jacobs's life, begun "among the lowly" Southern slaves (Stowe, title page to *Uncle Tom*) and completed in the nation's capital, where she died after working for the newly freed men and women, testifies to the personal and political collaborations that characterized antislavery activism, and later the movements for suffrage, the cessation of racial violence, and African Americans' economic and social enfranchisement.

Jacobs uses pseudonyms in her autobiography (she calls herself "Linda," for example) to protect vulnerable friends and families still living in the South. It is due to the exhaustive scholarship of the historian and literary critic Jean Fagan Yellin that we not only can authenticate Jacobs's story but also can identify the real men and women she fictionalizes. Jacobs was born in bondage in Edenton, North Carolina, to mulatto parents. Her father (Elijah) was an itinerant slave carpenter, and her mother (Delilah) also was a slave. She and her brother John enjoyed a sheltered and happy childhood until their mother died in 1819 and, at six years of age, she realized her status as a slave and began chores for her White mistress (Margaret Horniblow). Nevertheless, her owner was a kind one who defied the slave codes in order to instruct Jacobs in reading and writing, and she furthermore encouraged Jacobs's interest in Christianity, trained her to sew, and provided liberal time for her to visit with her principled and assertive free grandmother Martha (Molly Horniblow).

When her kind mistress died (Jacobs's father passed on shortly thereafter), Jacobs was bequeathed in 1825 to the three-year-old daughter of the Flints (Dr. James Norcom Jr. and his wife, Maria), who became her tormenters. Although her new master was a respected community member and pious churchgoer, out of public view he starved, whipped, and abused his slaves. In particular, he tortured the adolescent Jacobs with whispered sexual innuendoes and his persistent resolve to make her his mistress. Flint's jealous wife suspected her husband's attraction but, in the context of slavery,

where the adultery of slave masters and the rape of slave women was an everyday reality that polite society ignored, she took out her anger and frustration on Jacobs.

In a bid to gain control of her own body and to assert her will over that of her cruel master, Jacobs became the lover of a wealthy White man whom she calls Mr. Sands (Maj. Samuel Tredwell Sawyer), and they had two children, Ben (Joseph) and Ellen (Louisa). She then escaped the Flint household and hid in woods, swamps, and safe houses until finally returning to her free grandmother's attic, where she remained for the next seven years. With Jacobs's son and daughter now much at risk for sale by Dr. Flint (in slavery, the condition of a child followed that of the mother), Sands reneged on his promise to free them but arranged them to work for relatives up North. Meanwhile, Jacobs wrote letters to Dr. Flint as if her flight to freedom had succeeded.

When Jacobs fled her attic prison in 1842, she found work in New York City as a nanny in the household of the author Nathaniel Parker Willis and his wife, Cornelia, and reunited with her daughter, her brother (who had also escaped and become an abolitionist), and later her son, now a sailor. Flint's relatives, however, tracked her down and came north to reclaim her and her children with the support of the 1850 Fugitive Slave Law. Cornelia Willis ended this situation by initiating a fund-raising effort and eventually purchasing Jacobs's freedom.

Jacobs's letters about slavery in the *New York Tribune* caught the attention of the abolitionist press and galvanized her decision to write a full-fledged book. The activist Lydia Maria Child edited the manuscript on matters of grammar and style, and helped guide it through the publishing process. Jacobs's collaborations with Child and her book's explicit attempts to feminize the evils of slavery underscored the effectiveness of arguments linking the bondage of African American women to the legal, religious, and cultural mores restricting the lives of White middle-class wives and mothers. The publication of *Incidents* in British and American editions links it to Phillis Wheatley's *Poems on Various Subjects, Religious and Moral* (1773) and the autobiographies of such former slaves such as Douglass and William Wells Brown, as well as literary works by White abolitionists such as Stowe and John Greenleaf Whittier, to demonstrate the importance of transatlantic alliances in engineering the social reforms of the age. Finally, Jacobs established forms and themes for African American women's autobiography that would be emulated and transformed by late nineteenth-century memoirists such as Elizabeth Keckley, and that would resonate in the fiction of Toni Morrison, Sherley Anne Williams, Octavia E. Butler, and others giving voice in the twentieth century to the humanity of enslaved women.

In 2008, the papers of Harriet Jacobs and her family were published in two volumes (Yellin, et al.).

Barbara McCaskill

See also: Slave Narrative.

Resources

William L. Andrews, *To Tell a Free Story: The First Century of Afro-American Autobiography, 1760–1865* (Urbana: University of Illinois Press, 1986); Charles T. Davis and Henry Louis Gates Jr., eds., *The Slave's Narrative* (New York: Oxford University Press, 1985); Benjamin Fagan, "Harriet Jacobs and the Lessons of Rogue Reading," *Legacy: A Journal of American Women Writers* 33, no. 1 (2016), 19–21; Frances Smith Foster: *Witnessing Slavery: The Development of Ante-Bellum Slave Narratives* (Westport, CT: Greenwood Press, 1979); *Written by Herself: Literary Production by African American Women, 1746–1892* (Bloomington: Indiana University Press, 1993); Deborah M. Garfield and Rafia Zafar, eds., *Harriet Jacobs and Incidents in the Life of a Slave Girl: New Critical Essays* (New York: Cambridge University Press, 1996); James C. Hall, ed., *Approaches to Teaching Narrative of the Life of Frederick Douglass* (New York: Modern Language Association, 1999); Harriet Jacobs, *Incidents in the Life of a Slave Girl*, by Linda Brent (pseudonym), ed. L. Marie Child (New York: Harcourt Brace Jovanovich, 1973); Deborah E. McDowell and Arnold Rampersad, eds., *Slavery in the Literary Imagination* (Baltimore: Johns Hopkins University Press, 1989); John Sekora and Darwin T. Turner, eds., *The Art of Slave Narrative: Original Essays in Criticism and Theory* (Macomb: Western Illinois University Press, 1982); Caleb Smith, "Harriet Jacobs among the Militants: Transformations in Abolition's Public Sphere, 1859–61," *American Literature* 84, no. 4 (2012), 743; Harriet Beecher Stowe, *Uncle Tom's Cabin, or, Life Among the Lowly* (Boston: John P. Jewett, 1852); Jean Fagan Yellin, *Harriet Jacobs: A Life* (New York: BasicCivitas Books, 2004); Jean Fagan Yellin, editor, Joseph M. Thomas, executive editor, Kate Culkin, associate editor, and Scott Korb, associate editor, *Harriet Jacobs Family Papers* (Chapel Hill: University of North Carolina Press, 2008).

Jazz in Literature

As a label, "jazz" encompasses such a wide array of music and ideas that coming up with a suitable definition can be a daunting task. Certainly there is the music, including (sometimes overlapping categories, and overlapping figures such as Miles Davis) the following "schools": New Orleans (King Oliver, Louis Armstrong, Jelly Roll Morton), early New York and Chicago styles

(Fletcher Henderson, Earl Hines, Bix Beiderbecke), swing (Edward Kennedy "Duke" Ellington, William "Count" Basie, Billie Holiday, Ella Fitzgerald), big band (Gerald Wilson, Miles Davis-Gil Evans), bop (Charlie Parker, Dizzy Gillespie, Bud Powell), hard bop (Wes Montgomery, Clifford Brown, Art Blakey), West Coast/cool (Miles Davis, Chet Baker, Lennie Tristano), soul jazz (Cannonball Adderley, Jimmy Smith), free jazz (Ornette Coleman, Cecil Taylor, John Coltrane), fusion (Miles Davis, Tony Williams, Herbie Hancock), chamber jazz and third stream (Gunther Schuller, John Lewis), avant-garde (Anthony Braxton, John Zorn), Latin jazz (Machito, Tito Puente, Mongo Santamaria), smooth jazz (Al Jarreau, Anita Baker, Grover Washington), and neotraditional jazz (Wynton Marsalis, Marcus Roberts). These various styles, developed and practiced in various locations in sometimes overlapping time periods linked to modernization, migratory patterns, sociopolitical developments, and phonograph recording distribution and media airplay, include some of the most important and influential music made in the world in the twentieth century. They also reflect the importance accorded to improvisation and individual expression in jazz, emphasizing the primacy of finding one's own voice in a world that seeks to suppress it or deny it, or insist on uniform and undifferentiated expression. Certainly, as people continue to work within these various "schools" and attempt to develop new directions, jazz players doubtless will continue to make major contributions to the field of music.

Additionally, the term "jazz" is sometimes also used as an all-encompassing reference to African American music of the twentieth century, including the blues—which is often seen as a primary source for jazz—rhythm and blues, and soul music. This is because these African American musical genres have a variety of characteristics in common, such as strong rhythmic emphasis, syncopation, blue notes, and improvisation, and as such can be seen as distinctly related genres. In this sense, "jazz" can also be used to refer to the impulse to do in other media what jazz does in music, especially related to the important elements of improvisation, both individual and group, polyrhythmic and percussive emphases, and the quest for freedom that is frequently seen as a central element of jazz. In African American literature, some of the most important figures in the field—Langston Hughes, Sterling A. Brown, Claude McKay, Gwendolyn Brooks, Robert Hayden, Melvin Tolson, Richard Wright, Ralph Ellison, James Baldwin, Amiri Baraka, Angela Y. Davis, Larry Neal, Sonia Sanchez, Ntozake Shange, Michael S. Harper, and Toni Morrison among them—have added their voices to the chorus of jazz performers who have been so central to African American (and American) culture since its inception. (The list of non-African American writers who have employed jazz in their works—including Carl Sandburg, William Carlos Williams, F. Scott Fitzgerald, Carl Van Vechten, Robert Lowell, Allen Ginsberg, Jack Kerouac, John Clellon Holmes, Eudora Welty, Robert Creeley, Muriel Rukeyser, and many others—is equally long.)

Jazz music has distinct ties to the West African culture from which the bulk of the slaves brought to America in the North Atlantic slave trade were taken. Such elements as polyrhythms, call-and-response patterns, syncopation, blue notes, percussive performance techniques, and vocal and instrumental straining, growling, and buzzing effects are all traceable to West Africa, as is the idea that music serves an important communal function that is present in various aspects of everyday life. Alice Walker references this notion as reflected on American soil in her short story "Everyday Use," which portrays both the daily spiritual and practical uses of art, in this case quilting, in opposition to the notion of art for art's sake. The predominance of polyrhythms in individual musical performances may in fact reflect the notion that a community is made up of a variety of ideas, personalities, and styles that can nonetheless still coalesce into a unified whole. During the eighteenth and nineteenth centuries, these techniques and ideas were reflected in various African American musical genres such as spirituals and jubilees, work songs, field hollers, and game songs, all of which served important individual and communal functions in slavery and post–slavery societies.

In the post–Reconstruction era, ragtime (Scott Joplin, James Scott), blues, and eventually jazz began to emerge from the music of earlier eras to express the desires, aspirations, and frustrations, and to serve the needs, of new generations of African Americans confronting a Jim Crow "freedom" that offered some possibilities and progress, though they were frustrated by social and political manifestations of attitudes held over from slavery times. Somewhere around the turn of the twentieth century in New Orleans, Louisiana—a city with a long tradition of African American musical performance, such as performances at Congo Square beginning in 1817 and in the important red-light Storyville district in the early twentieth century—elements of the blues and ragtime genres began to merge with the techniques and instrumentation of Black and Creole brass bands, which blended African and European characteristics in bands such as those led by James Reese

Europe, to bring the music we know as jazz into existence.

Though the first jazz recordings were made by a White group—the Original Dixieland Jazz Band—in 1917, since its inception most of the important developments in jazz have come from musicians from the African American communities that created it, though there have been some talented and important White players (Bix Beiderbecke, Django Reinhardt, Lennie Tristano) as well. Thus, jazz has often served as a metaphor for indigenous Black creativity, technique, and style—for Black genius resistant in many ways to the domination of a European artistic aesthetic, though it is clear that jazz is not untouched by European components. Jazz's wild popularity in the 1920s—it gave the era its name, "The Jazz Age"—its mainstreaming in the 1930s with the dominance of swing and boogie-woogie, its capturing of the restless, frenetic pace of postwar, post-Hiroshima America, and its centrality in expressing the anger and spirituality of the Black aesthetic—all this reflects the expressive flexibility of jazz and its continued relevance to African American and American culture. By celebrating Black roots, Black culture, and the possibilities of the individual Black voice in relation to them, it has remained central not only as a musical form but also as a resource for African American artists in other media, especially literature.

How does the reader tell when the jazz influence is present in a work of literature? There can be some obvious hints. For example, the work may be called jazz, as in Bob Kaufman's "Bagel Shop Jazz," or "O-JAZZ-O War Memoir: Jazz, Don't Listen to It at Your Own Risk," or Toni Morrison's *Jazz*. It may refer to places where jazz is performed, as in Langston Hughes's "Jam Session," Thulani N. Davis's "CT at the

Five Spot," or Wanda Coleman's "In a Jazz Club He Comes on a Ghost." It may mention characteristics of jazz music, such as Langston Hughes's "Flatted Fifths" or Carolyn M. Rodgers's "We Dance like Ella Riffs." It may mention jazz performers, real (Michael S. Harper's "Dear John, Dear Coltrane" or Sarah Webster Fabio's "For Louis Armstrong, a Ju-Ju") or imagined (James Baldwin's "Sonny's Blues"). Just as the title of August Wilson's play *Ma Rainey's Black Bottom* refers also to a song recorded by Ma Rainey, so Al Young's "Body and Soul" and "Lester Leaps In" refer to two famous jazz vehicles, and Carolyn M. Rodgers's "Written for Love of an Ascension—Coltrane" references a John Coltrane composition. The work may refer to a type of jazz, such as Xam Wilson Cartiér's *Be-Bop, Re-Bop*. And the work may refer to or imply the etymology or meaning of jazz related to West Africa languages, sexual potency (as in Nella Larsen's *Quicksand*), or the dynamics of style. Of course, writers may combine the influence of jazz with other literary elements as well: Ralph Ellison combines elements of Modernism picked up from T. S. Eliot and James Joyce with the appreciation of Louis Armstrong in *Invisible Man*, and Ted Joans combines jazz and surrealism in poems such as "Jazz Me Surreally Do." All these ways make it obvious that the jazz tradition should serve as a context for understanding the work in which it is used and invite or force the reader to enter the jazz world in order to grasp the social, political, aesthetic, and spiritual implications and meanings of jazz, not only for the individual work but also for the reader, the culture, the country, and the world.

It can be difficult to pin down in concrete terms the variety of subtle ways that material from the oral tradition influences the written tradition, especially if the material is not verbal. There are, of course, singers in the jazz tradition, but instrumentalists have predominated. How, then, do nonverbal sounds influence the writing of words? The answer lies in the dominant characteristics of jazz with regard to aesthetic and technique. For example, the rhythms of various kinds of jazz (and other African American music), including the frequent use of polyrhythms (combining various rhythmic patterns), along with the employment of syncopation (playing before or after the normally accented beat) and rough or stretched intonations, can be reflected in the scat singing (Louis Armstrong, Ella Fitzgerald) and vocalese (Eddie Jefferson, Jon Hendricks) of jazz. These can in turn also influence the word rhythms, textures, and structures of the writer seeking to capture the spirit of those rhythms. Thus, when Ralph Ellison's character Peter Wheatstraw (partially based on blues singer William Bunch, known on records as Peetie Wheatstraw) introduces himself to Ellison's protagonist in *Invisible Man*, his highly rhythmic and syncopated folk speech captures the rhythms of African American vernacular music, and his highly colorful manner is compared to the sounds and/or movements of a bear, rooster, and a dog, all of which turn up in titles and lyrics in the jazz tradition, reflecting the sometimes rough-hewn quality of the music. Langston Hughes makes use of the "hip" language (daddy-o, jive, dig) and rhythms of jazz and blues in many of his poems, and structures his entire volume *Montage of a Dream Deferred* using the polyrhythms and syncopation of bop to unify his multipoem, multivoiced portrait of a complex, dynamic, shifting Harlem, New York, as a contemporary community in transition.

Additionally, both Ann Lane Petry's *The Street* and Toni Morrison's *Jazz* have been interpreted as using shifts in chronology, pacing, and emphasis or accent in a jazzlike way. Always looking for ways to reflect the unity and power of African American culture, Langston Hughes, in his experimental volume *Ask Your Mama*, combines elements of jazz, blues, gospel music, the dozens, and other African American musical materials to confront American society about its own rapacity and hypocrisy. The reader can even see in Amiri Baraka's stage direction in *Great Goodness of Life* a reflection of the value of the jazz performer in awakening African Americans to their plight and to strategies for resistance. A confused Court Royal, who is being interrogated by an unseen "voice of the judge," is described as "jerk[ing] his head like he's suddenly heard Albert Ayler," a free jazz musician whose highly original sound, manner of improvisation, and use of folk motifs in his work provide an example of the attempt of performers in the jazz tradition to shock people out of the Euro-conventional and move them to rethink their notions of what art, society, and life are and are supposed to be. This is, of course, a sound that can be frightening as well, as Larry Neal relates in *The Glorious Monster in the Bell of the Horn*, though it can also be warmly passionate and rewarding as well. It is also important to acknowledge that a variety of African American writers have embraced the importance of oral performance to their work, emphasizing not only readings of their work but also recording their work to musical accompaniment, beginning with Langston Hughes and encompassing recordings by authors such as Sterling A. Brown, Sarah Webster Fabio, Michael S. Harper, Amiri Baraka, and Ishmael Reed.

In the twentieth century, and into the twenty-first, jazz has been, and will continue to be, a major force as a musical genre. It exerts a powerful influence on writers who seek to connect to an indigenous African American art form that acknowledges the importance of African roots and the African American community; exalts originality of voice and idea, improvisation, and freedom of expression; and at its best exemplifies the concept of unity out of diversity (E Pluribus Unum) that confronts the failures of the American democratic experiment, providing a wellspring of possibilities. In language, tone, rhythm, structure, aesthetic, and philosophy, it offers alternatives to the writer of African American as well as American (and even world) literature (see the Czech writer Josef Škvorecky's "Eine Kleine Jazzmusik," for example). As outlined in important critical works such as Larry Neal's "Any Day Now: Black Art and Black Liberation," Ralph Ellison's writings on jazz, Sherley Anne Williams's "The Blues Roots of Contemporary Afro-American Poetry," Houston A. Baker Jr.'s *Blues, Ideology, and Afro-American Literature*, as well as Leroi Jones/Amiri Baraka's *Blues People* and *Black Music*—and evident in a great amount of African American literature produced from a multitude of perspectives of time, place, aesthetic, and philosophy—jazz is a major force in African American literature.

Steven C. Tracy

See also: Baraka, Amiri; Blues Poetry; Hughes, Langston; Jones, Gayl; Reed, Ishmael; Troupe, Quincy Thomas, Jr.

Resources
Primary Sources: Richard N. Albert, *From Blues to Bop: A Collection of Jazz Fiction* (Baton Rouge: Louisiana State University Press, 1990); Amiri Baraka, *New Music—New*

Poetry (India Navigation LP 1048); Marcela Breton, ed., *Hot and Cool: Jazz Short Stories* (New York: Plume, 1990); Jayne Cortez, *Taking the Blues Back Home* (PGD Verve LP 31918); Sascha Feinstein and Yusef Komunyakaa, eds.: *The Jazz Poetry Anthology*, vol. 1 (Bloomington: Indiana University Press, 1991); *The Second Set*, vol. 2 of *Jazz Poetry Anthology* (Bloomington: Indiana University Press, 1996); Langston Hughes, *The Weary Blues with Langston Hughes* (Verve CD 841 660-2); Ted Joans, *Jazz Poems* (S Press LP 451); Art Lange and Nathaniel Mackey, eds., *Moment's Notice: Jazz in Poetry and Prose* (Minneapolis, MN: Coffee House Press, 1993); Ishmael Reed, *Conjure* (American Clave LP 1006).

Secondary Sources: Michael Borshuk, *Swinging the Vernacular: Jazz and African American Modernist Literature* (New York: Routledge, 2006); Sascha Feinstein: *Bibliographic Guide to Jazz Poetry* (Westport, CT: Greenwood Press, 1998); *Jazz Poetry: From the 1920s to the Present* (Westport, CT: Greenwood Press, 1997); Jürgen Grandt, "Kinds of Blue: Toni Morrison, Hans Janowitz, and the Jazz Aesthetic," *African American Review* 38, no. 2 (Summer 2004), 303–322; William J. Harris, *The Poetry and Poetics of Amiri Baraka* (Columbia: University of Missouri Press, 1985); Michael Jarrett, *Drifting on a Read: Jazz as a Model for Writing* (Albany: State University of New York Press, 1999); A. Yemisi Jimoh, *Spiritual, Blues, and Jazz People in African American Fiction* (Knoxville: University of Tennessee Press, 2002); Graham Lock and David Murray, eds., *Thriving on a Riff: Jazz and Blues Influences in African American Literature and Film* (Oxford and New York: Oxford University Press, 2009); Robert G. O'Meally, ed.: *The Jazz Cadence of American Culture* (New York: Columbia University Press, 1998); *Living with Music: Ralph Ellison's Jazz Writings* (New York: Modern Library, 2001); Keren Omry, *Cross-rhythms: Jazz Aesthetics in African-American Literature* (New York and London: Continuum, 2008); Steve Pinkerton, "Ralph Ellison's Righteous Riffs: Jazz, Democracy, and the Sacred," *African American Review* 44, no. 1 (2011), 201–206; Alan J. Rice, "Finger Snapping to Train Dancing and Back Again: The Development of Jazz Style in African American Prose," *Yearbook of English Studies* 24 (1994), 105–116; Steven C. Tracy: "The Blues Novel," in *The Cambridge Companion to the African American Novel*, ed. Maryemma Graham (Cambridge: Cambridge University Press, 2004); *Langston Hughes and the Blues* (Urbana: University of Illinois Press, 1988); Steven C. Tracy, ed., *Write Me a Few of Your Lines: A Blues Reader* (Amherst: University of Massachusetts Press, 1999); Craig Hansen Werner, *Playing the Changes: From Afro-Modernism to the Jazz Impulse* (Urbana: University of Illinois Press, 1994); David Yaffe, *Fascinating Rhythm Reading Jazz in American Writing* (Princeton, NJ: Princeton University Press, 2006).

Johnson, Georgia Douglas (1886–1966)

Poet and playwright. A highly prolific poet, playwright, and short-story writer, Johnson is widely recognized as one of "the most productive artists of the Harlem Renaissance" and "one of the first African American female poets to achieve a national reputation" (Donlon, 23).

Born Georgia Blanche Douglas Camp on September 10, 1886, Johnson spent her childhood and adolescence in Rome, Georgia, and Atlanta, Georgia. The daughter of Laura Douglas and George Camp, she graduated from Atlanta University's Normal School in 1893. Following her graduation, Johnson accepted a teaching position in Marietta, Georgia, which she held until 1902, when she enrolled in the Oberlin Conservatory of Music and the Cleveland College of Music, where she studied composition, piano, and violin.

On September 28, 1903, she married Henry Lincoln Johnson, and, in 1910, the couple moved to 1461 S Street NW in Washington, DC. The house, where Johnson resided for more than fifty years, became home to "one of the greatest literary salons of the Harlem Renaissance" (Honey). Throughout much of the 1920s, Johnson hosted a weekly Saturday Nighters' Club, which was attended by such acclaimed writers of the New Negro Renaissance (later the Harlem Renaissance) as Jean Toomer, Langston Hughes, Angelina Weld Grimké, and Alice Moore Dunbar-Nelson.

Between 1926 and 1932, Johnson wrote "Homely Philosophy," a weekly newspaper column that was syndicated by twenty publications. During this same time, she gained attention for her dramatic work, writing one-act plays that were produced by little theater groups. *Blue Blood*, a play about the rape of Black women by White men, was produced by the Krigwa Players in 1926, and the following year earned an honorable mention in *Opportunity* magazine's contest. That same year, *Plumes*, a folk tragedy about Black funeral rites, won first prize in the contest. Although *Blue Blood* and *Plumes* are arguably Johnson's best-known plays, she also wrote several lynching plays—*Sunday Morning in the South* (1926), *Safe* (1929), and *Blue-Eyed Black Boy* (1930)—and two historical dramas about runaway slaves—*Frederick Douglass* (1935) and *William and Ellen Craft* (1935). A collection of her plays was published in 2006 (see *The Plays of Georgia Douglas Johnson* in Resources).

Despite her successes as a dramatist, Johnson is best known for her work as a poet. She published her first poems—"Gossamer," "Fame," and "My Little One"—in *The Crisis* magazine in 1916 and, over the course of her long and prolific career, wrote four volumes of poetry: *The Heart of a Woman* (1918), *Bronze* (1922), *An Autumn Love Cycle* (1928), and *Share My World* (1962).

"The Heart of a Woman," one of her best-known poems, was set to music by Florence Price.

Although quite prolific in the early part of her career, Johnson became less so after the death of her husband on September 10, 1925. With two sons, both of whom she put through college, and a household to support, Johnson accepted a job with the U.S. Department of Labor as commissioner of conciliation, which left her little time to pursue writing. Johnson's writing also was compromised by her inability to secure fellowship money. Still, during this time, she continued to produce a few poems, short stories (at times writing under the pseudonym Paul Tremain), plays, and her newspaper column.

In 1965, Johnson was awarded an honorary doctorate by Atlanta University. One year later, on May 14, 1966, she died of a stroke.

Heath A. Diehl

See also: Harlem Renaissance; Novel.

Resources

Addell Austin Anderson, "Georgia Douglas Johnson," in *American Playwrights, 1880–1945: A Research and Production Sourcebook*, ed. William W. Demastes (Westport, CT: Greenwood Press, 1995), 224–229; Jocelyn Hazelwood Donlon, "Georgia Douglas Johnson," in *Black Women in America*, vol. 1, ed. Darlene Clark Hine (Brooklyn, NY: Carlson, 1993), 640–642; Winona Fletcher, "Georgia Douglas Johnson," in *Dictionary of Literary Biography*, vol. 51, ed. Thadious Davis and Trudier Harris (Detroit: Gale Research, 1987), 153–164; Christy Gavin, ed.: *African-American Women Playwrights:*

A Research Guide (New York: Garland, 1999); "Georgia Douglas Johnson," in *The Black Renaissance in Washington, D.C.*, June 20, 2003, D.C. Library, http://www.dclibrary .org/blkren/bios/johnsongd.html; Maureen Honey, "Georgia Douglas Johnson's Life and Career," *Department of English: Modern American Poetry*, UIUC, Aug. 3, 2003, http://www.english.uiuc.edu/maps/poets/g_l /Douglas-johnson/life.htm; Georgia Douglas Johnson: *An Autumn Love Cycle* (New York: Harold Vinal, 1928); "Blue Blood," in *Fifty More Contemporary One-Act Plays*, ed. Frank Shay (New York: Appleton, 1938); "Blue-Eyed Black Boy," in *Wines in the Wilderness: Plays by African American Women from the Harlem Renaissance to the Present*, ed. Elizabeth Brown-Guillory (Westport, CT: Greenwood Press, 1990); *Bronze: A Book of Verse* (Boston: Brimmer, 1922); *The Heart of a Woman and Other Poems* (Boston: Cornhill, 1918); "Let Me Not Lose My Dream," "Old Black Men," "Black Woman," "The Heart of a Woman," and "I Want to Die While You Love Me," in *The Portable Harlem Renaissance Reader*, ed. David Levering Lewis (New York: Viking, 1994), 273–276; *The Plays of Georgia Douglas Johnson from the New Negro Renaissance to the Civil Rights Movement*, ed. Judith L. Stephens (Urbana: University of Illinois Press, 2006); "Plumes," in *Plays of Negro Life: A Source Book of Native American Drama*, ed. Alain Locke and Montgomery Gregory (New York: Harper and Brothers, 1927); "Safe," in *Wines in the Wilderness: Plays by African American Women from the Harlem Renaissance to the Present*, ed. Elizabeth Brown-Guillory (Westport, CT: Greenwood Press, 1990); *The Selected Works of Georgia Douglas Johnson*, with an introduction by Claudia Tate (New York: G. K. Hall, 1997); "A Sunday Morning in the South," in *Black Theatre, U.S.A.: Forty-five Plays by Black American Playwrights, 1847–1974*, ed. James V. Hatch and Ted Shine (New York: Free Press, 1974); Elizabeth McHenry, *Forgotten Readers: Recovering the Lost History of African American Literary Societies* (Durham, NC: Duke University Press, 2002); Florence Price, "The Heart of a Woman: Medium High Voice and Piano" [musical setting], ed. Rae Linda Brown (Fayetteville, AR: Classical Vocal Reprints, 2009); Yvonne Shafer, *American Women Playwrights, 1900–1950* (New York: Peter Lang, 1995); Judith L. Stephens, "Art, Activism, and Uncompromising Attitude in Georgia Douglas Johnson's Lynching Plays," *African American Review* 39, no. 1/2 (April 1, 2005), 87–102; Ann Trapasso, "Georgia Douglas Johnson," in *Notable Black American Women*, ed. Jessie Carney Smith, Book 1 (Detroit: Gale, 1992), 578–584.

Johnson, James Weldon (1871–1938)

Poet, novelist, essayist, editor, lyricist, teacher, diplomat, and civil rights leader. In the course of his life James Weldon Johnson was a teacher, a lyricist for a theatrical act, a school principal, an attorney, a newspaper editor and publisher, a diplomat, a poet and novelist, an executive of a civil rights organization, and a professor of literature. This astounding range of achievement was engendered by parents who were both freeborn before the Civil War, his father James in Virginia, his mother, Helen Dillet, of French and Haitian descent, in the Bahamas. James was the headwaiter at Jacksonville, Florida's, premier hotel; Helen was a teacher at the local school for African Americans. James William Johnson (he changed his middle name to Weldon in 1913) was born in Jacksonville on June 17, 1871. From his father young James seems to have learned confidence in his ability to succeed, while his mother taught him and his younger brother, John Rosemond, drawing, piano, and poetry.

When he was seventeen, Johnson spent the summer as secretary to Thomas Osmond

Summers, a White Jacksonville physician who provided him, he notes in his autobiography *Along This Way* (1933), with his "model of all that a man and a gentleman should be." Dr. Summers was a late Victorian nonconformist: a research scientist who worked for the public good, a sophisticated reader, a poet, an atheist, and an antiracist. He took Johnson to Washington, DC, and New York City, and they shared ship cabins and hotel rooms as equals. He fostered Johnson's intellectual and artistic development, recommending and discussing books and commenting on the young man's first poems. This influence seems to have set the seal on Johnson's lifelong dual focus on public service and the private pleasures of art.

Johnson graduated from Atlanta University in 1894, having long since determined to be a writer. At Atlanta University he also learned how to be a "race man"; the ethical question of how graduates would be "of service to the race" after graduation was a lively topic of discussion among students and faculty. Johnson's first job was as principal of the elementary school where his mother had taught; he soon added a secondary curriculum, developing the first high school for Blacks in the state of Florida. For a year he served the Stanton School while also developing and editing a daily newspaper, which folded in 1896. Johnson studied law privately and became the first African American to be admitted to the Florida bar. For several years he practiced law, ran the Stanton School and spent the summers in New York City, writing theater songs with his brother and Bob Cole. It was the heyday of ragtime. American popular culture was awash with authentic images and sounds related to African Americans and demeaning White minstrel show versions of them. Cole and Johnson Brothers (James never performed on stage) was a highly successful act. James found ways to make his lyrics, usually written in dialect, encompass authentic emotions and not merely repeat the stereotypes of Negro laziness, ignorance, and sensuality. His and his brother J. Rosemond's best work, in songs such as "The Congo Love Song" and "Under the Bamboo Tree," connect African American life to universal elements such as love, wistfulness, and verbal play. They saw themselves as refining and poeticizing the potent raw material of African American culture rather than recycling conventional situations and imagery from the minstrel tradition.

Johnson's best-known collaboration with his brother was in the creation of "Lift Every Voice and Sing." Composed for a Lincoln's Birthday celebration in Jacksonville in 1900, the song was widely distributed throughout the South and was later adopted as the unofficial anthem of the National Association for the Advancement of Colored People (NAACP) and for African Americans in general:

> *Lift every voice and sing, Till earth and heaven ring, Ring with harmonies of liberty. Let our rejoicing rise High as the listening skies, Let it resound loud as the rolling sea. Sing a song full of the faith that the dark past has taught us, Sing a song full of the hope that the present has brought us. Facing the rising sun of our new day begun, Let us march on till victory is won.*

Despite his personal agnosticism, Johnson was able to connect here with the African American masses' confidence in the future based on religious faith.

In 1902, Johnson resigned the principalship and moved permanently to New York City, where he continued to work in the theater. He wrote dialect verse in the manner of his friend Paul Laurence Dunbar as well as dramatic monologues influenced by Robert Browning and ballads reminiscent of Rudyard Kipling. When not traveling with the act, he took classes at Columbia University with Brander Matthews, a writer and theater scholar and, like Dr. Summers, a man free of virulent racial prejudice. Johnson was fluent in Spanish, and Matthews called upon this knowledge in their studies of European drama. Matthews became a friend and mentor who offered Johnson advice on his new project, a novel. Johnson left Cole and Johnson Brothers in 1905, took the diplomatic service exams, and, through the influence of Matthews and Booker T. Washington, was appointed U.S. consul in Puerto Cabello, Venezuela, in the summer of 1906. He worked on the novel here and completed it before his second posting, to Corinto, Nicaragua, in 1909, to which he brought his new wife, Grace Nail. *The Autobiography of an Ex-Colored Man* was published anonymously in 1912 because Johnson felt that the book would not be accepted if it were known that the author was not telling a personal life story.

Johnson's only novel is a masterpiece of irony. Narrated by its nameless subject, an African American pale enough to pass for White, the novel presents a complex version of the dilemma of middle-class African Americans: how to choose between communal, race-conscious public service and individual, assimilationist personal safety and comfort. The ex-colored man is the illegitimate son of a White Southerner and an almost White African American woman. Brought up in Connecticut, the narrator does not have a Black identity until it is forced on him at school. Thereafter, he struggles to overcome the stereotypes of identity that limit and shame him.

Although Johnson allows the narrator considerable psychological self-analysis,

the deepest narrative structure is the ex-colored man's unreliability. He presents his story in a voice of self-assurance, but the reader realizes that despite his measured, analytic tone, he does not really know himself. The reader arrives at different assessments of his actions than the narrator means to convey. The ex-colored man is, from earliest childhood, self-protective. He works hard to avoid emotional discomfort. In every situation that calls for him to assert his African American identity, to acknowledge his membership in the race (or take responsibility for not doing so), he takes the coward's self-protective way out. When his trunk and money are stolen on his way to Atlanta University, he does not register for college but takes a job in a cigar factory, where he learns about race, color caste, and social class. He concludes with characteristic selfishness:

> I can realize more fully than I could years ago that the position of the advanced element of the colored race is often very trying. They are the ones among the blacks who carry the entire weight of the race question; it worries the others very little. (p. 60)

When the cigar factory closes, the ex-colored man goes to New York City, where he learns to play ragtime piano in a nighttime world of drinking, gambling, interracial sexuality, and violence. He is befriended by a cultured White gentleman, a millionaire who takes him to Europe but who also functions as a demonic tempter, urging the narrator to abandon his efforts to be race conscious. This mentor, unlike Johnson's Dr. Summers, is self-absorbed and cynical. He sees the racial situation as an evil but a force "like the physical and chemical forces" that cannot be overcome.

The narrator does not accept the man's advice to stay in Europe but returns home, fearing that he will, as the tempter suggests, waste his life "amidst the poverty and ignorance, the hopeless struggle of the black people of the United States."

Back in Georgia, the ex-colored man studies Black folk expression but then witnesses a lynching and is shaken by the ferocity and brutality of the Whites and the impotence of the Blacks. He flees to New York, abandoning his plans to compose music based on folk themes, spirituals and ragtime, once again avoiding the psychological pain of identity. In New York, he decides on passing permanently, and is successful in business and in love, courting and marrying a White woman who keeps his secret even from their children. At the end it becomes clear that the ex-colored man has exhibited unconscious moral weakness in the face of every racial challenge. "The practical joke on society" that he announced at the beginning of the narrative has turned out to be a not very funny joke on him.

After leaving the consular service, Johnson returned to New York and began to write editorials for the *New York Age*, a weekly African American newspaper. His column dealt with foreign and domestic politics as well as culture and racial uplift. Johnson's commitment to racial improvement evidenced in these articles brought him to the attention of the fledgling NAACP (founded in 1909), which hired him as its field secretary in 1916. On the artistic front, Johnson translated the libretto of Spanish composer Enrique Granados's opera *Goyescas* for its Metropolitan opera premiere in 1915, and, in 1917, he published a collection of his poetry, *Fifty Years and Other Poems*.

Johnson's early poems—some written as far back as his college years—fall into three groups. One set is composed of poems such as the sonnet "Mother Night," belonging to the tradition of nineteenth-century Romantic and Victorian verse. These sonnets and ballads are conventional stuff, with themes of lost love, untimely death, and mawkish humor. A second group is made up of poems on racial themes. The best work in the collection, poems such as "The White Witch," "Brothers," and "O Black and Unknown Bards," makes effective use of traditional forms (sonnet, ghost ballad, dramatic dialogue, etc.). The third group is dialect poetry; most of them make use of the dramatic monologue form favored by Dunbar. Most are not as rich or as effectively humorous as Dunbar's best, though some—"An Explanation," for example—are acutely observed comments on African American speech practices and performance folkways.

In 1920, Johnson was promoted to secretary (chief executive officer) of the NAACP, a position he held until retirement in 1930. Using his skills as attorney, public speaker, and mediator, he effectively led the organization into the forefront on civil rights issues such as the campaign to enact federal legislation against lynching. Johnson was also active as a writer and editor during this opening decade of the Harlem Renaissance. In 1922, he published a landmark anthology, *The Book of American Negro Poetry*, including a long historical and critical introduction that praises African American poetic production as proof of African American intellectual equality; an important, significantly revised second edition appeared in 1931. With his brother, who had gone on to a distinguished career in music, Johnson published *The Book of American Negro Spirituals* in 1925 and a second volume in 1926. His preface to the first of these texts delineates Johnson's ideas about folk creativity; in *The Second Book of American Negro*

Spirituals he develops the ways the spirituals had helped change the image of African Americans from "beggar at the gates of the nation" to a powerful creative force.

Johnson's major work of this period is *God's Trombones: Seven Negro Sermons in Verse*, published in 1927, with illustrations by the noted Harlem Renaissance painter Aaron Douglas. Begun in 1917, these seven poems represent Johnson's maturation as a modern poet. The poems are dramatic monologues, minidramas reflecting Johnson's reading of Browning and his study with Matthews, but they are couched in Whitmanian free verse rather than in the tight, rhyming forms he had previously favored. Moreover, they capture the rhetorical creativity of African American preachers without recourse to dialect, and show the connections between religious emotion and the African American community's desire for political and social freedom.

Johnson's major artistic contribution to the Harlem Renaissance validated the Negro folk preacher as subject and as artist, refuting many popular culture images of an infantile Black Christianity. *God's Trombones* is loving and respectful of the performative power, vivid imagination, and verbal skill of the people's traditional leaders.

Johnson worked hard throughout the 1920s to promote the New Negro or Harlem Renaissance, and is considered one of its presiding spirits, along with W.E.B. Du Bois and Alain Locke. He wrote essays including "Race Prejudice and the Negro Artist" and "The Dilemma of the Negro Author" for mainstream magazines, bringing home the message that the new, brilliant African American art and literature proved the full and complete humanity of African Americans. In 1930, he published *Black Manhattan*, a history of New York that focused on the African American presence in the performing arts. In the latter part of the book, Johnson presented a memoir of his own time as a member of the theatrical world of turn-of-the-century New York, and concluded that Black artists in literature, art, and theater are "going far towards smashing the stereotypes" and "reshaping public sentiment and opinion." While the book pays little attention to the economic situation of the ordinary person in the city's growing ghettos, it is Johnson's broadest expansion of his ideas about how talented individuals can affect the development of the race.

Johnson retired from the NAACP in 1930, took a position teaching at Fisk University, and began work on his autobiography, which he published in 1933 as *Along This Way*. The book is thorough, comprehensive, and informative, but unemotional. Johnson presents himself as never expressing rage, anger, or misery; his life, as presented here, is entirely under his control. He suppresses a few items, such as his ties to the Booker T. Washington political machine and his early support for the 1915 American occupation of Haiti.

In 1934, now comfortably settled into a routine of teaching one term at Fisk and one term in the New York University School of Education, Johnson published *Negro Americans: What Now?* After reviewing the community's institutional strengths—the churches, fraternities, the Black press, and the NAACP—Johnson emphasizes education, both formal and informal, as a key to advancement of the race and offers advice on developing businesses, cracking unions, and maximizing the power of the Black vote. Turning from advice to inspiration, he offers a credo in defense of spiritual integrity:

I will not allow one prejudiced person or one million or one hundred million to blight my life. I will not let prejudice or any of its attendant humiliations and injustices bear me down to spiritual defeat. My inner life is mine, and I shall defend and maintain its integrity against all the powers of hell. (103)

Johnson's last book, *Saint Peter Relates an Incident* (1935), brought together that longish poem, published privately in 1930, with a few other new works and selected poems from *Fifty Years*. "St Peter Relates an Incident of the Resurrection Day" is one of Johnson's most amusing efforts, joining a Byronic verse pattern and mock heroic manner, a bit of African American folkloric "signifying" about the color of the Unknown Soldier and a traditional literary folk fantasy of heaven and the afterlife.

Just after his sixty-seventh birthday, Johnson died in an automobile accident while on vacation in Maine with his wife, who survived. A quintessential "race man," he had given his racial community a lifetime of service and found time to create, in the *Autobiography* and *God's Trombones*, some enduring literature.

Joseph T. Skerrett Jr.

See also: Harlem Renaissance; Novel.

Resources

Primary Sources: James Weldon Johnson: *Along This Way: The Autobiography of James Weldon Johnson* (New York: Viking, 1933); *The Autobiography of an Ex-Colored Man* (1912; New York: Knopf, 1927); *Black Manhattan* (1930; repr. New York: Da Capo, 1991); *Complete Poems*, ed. Sondra Kathryn Wilson (New York: Penguin, 2000); *The Essential Writings of James Weldon Johnson,* ed. Rudolph P. Byrd, (New York: Modern Library, 2008); *Fifty Years and Other Poems* (Boston: Cornhill, 1917); *God's Trombones: Seven Negro Sermons in Verse* (New York: Viking, 1927); *Saint Peter Relates an Incident* (New York: Viking, 1935); *Writings* (New York: Library of America, 2004); James Weldon Johnson, ed., *The Book of American Negro Poetry* (New York: Harcourt, Brace, 1922; rev. ed., New York: Harcourt Brace, 1931); *The Book of American Negro Spirituals* (New York: Viking, 1925); *The Books of American Negro Spirituals, Including the Book of American Negro Spirituals and The Second Book of Negro Spirituals* (New York: Da Capo Press, 1977), with John Rosamond Johnson.

Secondary Sources: Gregory Carr, "Top Brass: Theatricality, Themes, and Theology in James Weldon Johnson's *God's Trombones,*" *Theatre Symposium* 21 (2013), 54–58, 141–142; Anne Carroll, "Art, Literature, and the Harlem Renaissance: The Messages of *God's Trombones,*" *College Literature* 29, no. 3 (Summer 2002), 57–82; Robert E. Fleming, *James Weldon Johnson* (Boston: Twayne, 1987); Henry Louis Gates Jr. and Cornel West, *The African American Century: How Black Americans Have Shaped Our Country* (New York: Free Press, 2000); Richard Hardack, "The Tragic Immigrant: Duality, Hybridity and the Discovery of Blackness in Mark Twain and James Weldon Johnson," *ELH (English Literary History)* 82, no. 1 (2015), 211–249; Eugene Levy, *James Weldon Johnson: Black Leader, Black Voice* (Chicago: University of Chicago Press, 1973); Noelle Morrissette, *James Weldon Johnson's Modern Soundscapes* (Iowa City: University of Iowa Press, 2013); Timo Müller, "James Weldon Johnson and the Genteel Tradition," *The Arizona Quarterly* 69, no. 2 (Summer 2013), 85–102; Chris Mustazza, "James Weldon Johnson and the Speech Lab Recordings," *Oral Tradition* 30, no. 1 (March 1, 2016), 95–110; Louis Hill Pratt, "James Weldon Johnson (1871–1938)," in *African American Authors, 1745–1945: A Bio-Bibliographical Critical Sourcebook,* ed.

Emmanuel S. Nelson (Westport, CT: Green-wood Press, 2000), 297–305; Brian Russell Roberts, "Passing Into Diplomacy: U.S. Consul James Weldon Johnson and *The Autobiography of an Ex-Colored Man*," *MFS Modern Fiction Studies* 56, no. 2 (2010), 290–316; Cristina L. Ruotolo, "James Weldon Johnson and The Autobiography of an Ex-Colored Musician," *American Literature* 72, no. 2 (June 2000), 249–274; Jennifer L. Schulz, "Restaging the Racial Contract: James Weldon Johnson's Signatory Strategies," *American Literature* 74, no. 1 (March 2002), 31–58; Salim Washington, "Of Black Bards, Known and Unknown: Music as Racial Metaphor in James Weldon Johnson's *The Autobiography of an Ex-Colored Man*," *Callaloo* 25, no. 1 (Winter 2002), 233–256.

Jones, Gayl (1949–)

Fiction writer, poet, playwright, professor, and literary critic. Born in Lexington, Kentucky, Gayl Jones was creatively precocious, writing her first short story at the age of seven. Writing was a family affair: her grandmother, Amanda Wilson, wrote plays for church productions, and her mother, Lucille, was a fiction writer who wrote and read stories for her children. In a 1982 interview, Jones said that if her mother had not read to her as a child, she probably would never have thought of writing ("About My Work"). After high school, where her teachers described her as brilliant but painfully shy, Jones left the South to attend Connecticut College, where she earned a BA in English in 1971. By 1973, she had earned her MA in creative writing at Brown University, and she had seen her first play, *Chile Woman*, produced in 1974. In 1975, she earned her doctorate in creative writing at Brown and published *Corregidora*, her first novel. Jones's creative writing teacher, the poet Michael S. Harper, had given the

manuscript to Toni Morrison, who edited both it and Jones's second novel *Eva's Man* (1976) for Random House.

Beginning what has become a lifelong exploration of both the physical and the psychological scars of slavery, Jones employs a compelling narrator in *Corregidora* in the figure of blues singer Ursa Corregidora. Wrestling with the painful complexities of her marriage, Ursa testifies to the impact of slavery, and the impact of its sexual legacy, on three generations of females. Amid the brutality, Ursa works out a mode of healing. She seems driven, as one critic suggests, by the mantra "Tell your story, or the master's story stands" (Burns). With the publication of this novel, lauded by Darryl Pinckney in *The New Republic* as "a small, fiercely concentrated story, harsh and perfectly told," Jones was hailed as a major new literary talent by such writers as John Updike and James Baldwin.

Jones further explored her preoccupation with psychological obsession, contradiction, and trauma, and what she calls the "blues relationship" between the sexes, in *Eva's Man* (1987). This almost surreal work is told from the perspective of Eva Medina Canada, a victim of physical and sexual abuse, who ends up institutionalized for a disturbing act of murder and dismemberment by way of dental castration. Jones has described *Eva's Man* as "a horror story," "a kind of dream or nightmare" she felt compelled to transcribe. Jones's fascination with voices—with *how* things are said and not just with *what* is said—is paramount in all her works. Beyond the pervasive influence of the blues, she is especially drawn to writers whose narratives are somehow connected to the oral tradition, from Chaucer, Cervantes, Ernest Hemingway, Ralph Ellison, and James Joyce, to Margaret Laurence, Jean Toomer, Gabriel García

Márquez, Toni Morrison, and Zora Neale Hurston.

Jones was an assistant professor of English and Afro-American and African Studies at the University of Michigan from the late 1970s to the early 1980s, at which point she and her husband left the United States until 1988 because of legal problems. Her dramatic resignation from her post came by way of a letter addressed to the university, a copy of which was sent to President Ronald Reagan. The letter bluntly read, "I reject your lying, racist shit." During her years at Michigan, Jones published *White Rat* (1977), an eclectic medley of short stories, mostly set in rural Kentucky, that capture an African American vernacular, explore a variety of sexual issues and experiences, and address the politics of speech and silence. In Michigan, Jones also produced two volumes of poetry— and *Song for Anninho* (1981) and *The Hermit-Woman* (1983).

Despite her gift for writing stark, evocative poetry, Jones considers herself primarily a fiction writer whose poems are but "little fictions" that foreground character and action. *Song for Anninho* is a retrospectively told, haunting prose poem dedicated to Jones's husband, Robert Higgins. The politically active Higgins, a former student at the University of Michigan, later assumed her surname. In this poignant love story between Almeyda and Anninho, two escaped slaves in seventeenth-century Brazil, Jones successfully moves beyond the "blues relationships" of her earlier published fiction and crafts a vision of love as the ultimate healing agent for physical and psychic abuse. *The Hermit-Woman* is a series of poems that illustrate love's mixed potential of danger and a promise. *Xarque and Other Poems* followed in 1985, while Jones was living abroad. A sequel to *Song for Anninho*, *Xarque* is set in mid-eighteenth-century Brazil and fuses past and present in a narrative spoken by Almeyda's granddaughter, Euclida.

Liberating Voices: Oral Tradition in African American Literature (1991) is Jones's only book of literary criticism to date. It offers a theoretical examination of the relationship between the African American oral and literary traditions.

After a decade of living privately in Lexington, Kentucky, Jones published *The Healing* in 1998, a provocative meditation on healing as recounted from the unique perspective of Harlan Jane Eagleton, a larger-than-life former hairdresser, gambler, and rock-star manager-turned-faith healer. Advertised by Beacon Press as the book that convinced it to publish fiction for the first time in its 150-year history, *The Healing* was a finalist for the National Book Award. Its critical success was tragically overshadowed by the suicide that year of Jones's husband, Robert Higgins, during a police raid on their home (see Manso in Resources). The police were acting on a fifteen-year-old arrest warrant. During the raid, Jones was held in handcuffs but not arrested.

Mosquito (1999), her most sprawling work of fiction to date, was published the following year. This imaginative political novel follows African American truck driver Sojourner Jane Nadine Johnson, a.k.a. Mosquito, as she travels through the American Southwest involved with a new scheme designed to help illegal Mexican immigrants.

Since the publication of *Corregidora* in 1975, Jones's works have occasionally drawn negative criticism on two principal counts—their excessive graphic violence and their lack of "positive race images." The latter claim is based on her purportedly negative images of Black men and her sexualized descriptions of Black women. On both counts, Jones's works may be defended as realistically conveying, in the lives of both her male and female characters, the public and private impact of slavery in the Americas. While she has noted the difficulties in dealing with Black female sexuality and admits to feeling extremely "double conscious" when treating the subject, she has said she will not provide "positive race images" at the expense of imaginative reality (Rowell). Jones remains a reclusive resident of Lexington, Kentucky. She was inducted into the Kentucky Writers Hall of Fame in 2017 but chose not to attend the induction ceremony, at which writer Nikki Finney read from Jones's work (see Barron and Eblen in Resources). She rarely gives readings or interviews.

Carol Margaret Davison

See also: Jazz in Literature; Novel; Postmodernism.

Resources

Primary Sources: Gayl Jones: "About My Work," in *Black Women* Writers (1950–1980): A Critical Evaluation, ed. Mari Evans (Garden City, NY: Anchor Books, 1984), 233–235; *Chile Woman* (New Haven, CT: Schubert Playbook Series Volume 2, No. 5, 1974); *Corregidora* (Boston: Beacon Press, 1975); *Eva's Man* (Boston: Beacon Press, 1987); *The Healing* (Boston: Beacon Press, 1998); *The Hermit Woman* (Detroit: Lotus Press, 1983); *Liberating Voices: Oral Tradition in African American Literature* (Cambridge: Harvard University Press, 1991); *Mosquito* (Boston: Beacon Press, 1991); *Song for Anniho* (Boston: Beacon Press, 1981).

Secondary Sources: Michael Barron, "Will Gayl Jones Ever Publish Another Novel?," Melville House Books Blog, February 18, 2018: https://www.mhpbooks.com /books/ (accessed 2019); Bernard W. Bell,

"The Liberating Literary and African American Vernacular Voices of Gayl Jones," *Comparative Literature Studies* 36, no. 3 (1999), 247–258; Veronica Chambers, *The Healing* by Gayl Jones [book review], *Newsweek*, February 16, 1998; Casey Clabough, *Gayl Jones: The Language of Voice and Freedom in Her Writings* (Jefferson, NC: McFarland & Co., Publishers, 2008); Stelamaris Coser, *Bridging the Americas: The Literature of Paule Marshall, Toni Morrison, and Gayl Jones* (Philadelphia: Temple University Press, 1994); Carol Margaret Davison, "'Love 'em and Lynch 'em': The Castration Motif in Gayl Jones's *Eva's Man*," *African American Review* 29 (1995), 393–410; Tom Eblen, "Barbara Kingsolver, Gayl Jones among new inductees into Kentucky Writers Hall of Fame," *Lexington Herald Leader*, January 7, 2017: https:// www.kentucky.com/news/local/news-colu mns-blogs/tom-eblen/article125141184 .html (accessed 2019); Joanne Lipson Freed, "Gendered Narratives of Trauma and Revision in Gayl Jones's *Corregidora*," *African American Review* 44, no. 3 (October 1, 2011), 409–420; Peter Manso, "Chronicle of a Tragedy Foretold," *New York Times Magazine*, July 19, 1998: https://www.nytimes.com/1998 /07/19/magazine/chronicle-of-a-tragedy -foretold.html (accessed 2019); Keith B. Mitchell and Fiona Mills, eds., *After the Pain: Critical Essays on Gayl Jones* (New York: Peter Lang, 2006); Charles H. Rowell, "An Interview with Gayl Jones," *Callaloo* 5 (1982), 32–53; Jerry W. Ward Jr., "Escape from Trublem: The Fiction of Gayl Jones," *Callaloo* 5 (1982), 95–104.

Jordan, June (1936–2002)

Poet, activist, essayist, novelist, memoirist, playwright, and academic. Jordan, born in Harlem, New York, to West Indian immigrants, spent much of her early years in the impoverished Bedford-Stuyvesant section of Brooklyn, New York, and eventually settled in Berkeley, California. Her immigrant heritage and the multicultural communities in which she lived often served as the subject matter for her essays and other work on America and democracy. Jordan attended Barnard College from 1953 to 1955 and 1956 to 1957, earning a BA, as well as the University of Chicago (1955–1956). She taught at various universities, including the City University of New York, Connecticut College, and Sarah Lawrence College, before directing the poetry center and creative writing program while a tenured professor of English at the State University of New York at Stony Brook (1974–1985). In 1986 Jordan began lecturing in the University of California, Berkeley, English Department, and eventually became a professor of African American and Women's Studies. At Berkeley, Jordan developed her popular course "Poetry for the People," from which student poems were collected into an anthology in 1995. Jordan refused to segregate teaching, activism, writing, and living in her quest to develop a "people's poetry" and to make the American dream of pluralism and democracy a reality. Jordan's honors include a National Book Award nomination, grants from the Rockefeller Foundation and the National Endowment for the Arts, and a National Association of Black Journalists award. She is remembered as much for her writing as she is for her political commitments to valuing diversity in all its manifestations: nationality, sexuality, gender, language, race, geography, class, and ideology.

In her autobiography, Jordan recounts her father's abusive lessons that she must always be on guard both physically and mentally, teaching her that she must be a "soldier" ready to fight for her life in a world where even the safest spaces may hide danger. While she was growing up, Jordan's father engaged her in a rigorous program of memorizing long passages from the Bible as well as from canonical Western texts such as those of William Shakespeare and Edgar Allen Poe. Much of Jordan's creative work endeavors to offer a literary tradition where people of color are not marginalized by an all-White canon. Jordan became a poet at the age of seven when she composed lines on pavement around her neighborhood. In 1951, her sophomore year, Jordan transferred from prestigious Midwood High to the Northern School for Girls in Massachusetts (on a scholarship). At both schools, she was one of the first African Americans to attend. In her autobiography, Jordan reports, "I was the 'only' one . . . I felt outnumbered. I was surrounded by 'them.' And there was no 'we.' There was only 'me.' I didn't like it" (2002, 248–249). Her career is marked by attempts to build the diverse community she found lacking in many parts of the United States. In her third collection of essays, *Technical Difficulties: African-American Notes on the State of the Union* (1992), Jordan presents Park Slope, Brooklyn, as a model multiracial community. And in the essay "Waking Up in the Middle of Some American Dreams," she describes such a community as the true manifestation of American democracy. Jordan explains, "*Demos*, as in democratic, as in a democratic state, means people, not person" (1992, 19).

After leaving Brooklyn, Jordan married Michael Meyer in 1955, gave birth to her only son, Christopher David Meyer, in 1958, and divorced her husband in 1965. During this time Jordan also worked on a film chronicling urban Black life, collected fellow poets' work into anthologies, and researched a biography on the pioneering activist Fannie Lou Hamer (1972). Much of her early work was published alongside that of other African American women writers gaining recognition in the 1970s through the Black Arts Movement and an emergent feminist movement. Throughout her career, Jordan continued to direct much of her energy and work toward Black women, including poems and essays dedicated to her colleagues and foremothers Fannie Lou Hamer, Ntozake Shange, Alice Walker, and Phillis Wheatley.

Throughout her career, Jordan remained committed to placing African American experience and vernacular at the center of her work. Her most noted contribution to African American literature is her consistent advocacy and inventive use of Black English in her writing, teaching, and political debates. Jordan's first novel, *His Own Where* (1971), is written in the voice of a narrator speaking in Black English, a language common to the predominantly Black and immigrant Brooklyn neighborhood of her childhood. Jordan also wrote much of her poetry in Black English, especially her poems about the character DeLiza, as in "Sometimes DeLiza" from her collection *Naming Our Destiny* (1989): "Sometimes DeLiza / she forget about location / and she wondering what to do / to make she Black self / just a little more / conspicuous" (203). Along with James Baldwin and Amiri Baraka, in the 1970s through the 1990s, Jordan was a key public voice defending Black English as a viable language in the classroom and in society during fierce English-only and anti-affirmative action movements in the United States, especially in California. Over the course of her career, Jordan's prose, too, increasingly assumed the poetic and dialogic forms that reflected the actual speech of the immigrant and multicultural communities that her essays address.

Jordan's initial fame in the 1970s was also due in large part to emerging feminist movements that valued creative work for its ability to bring the diverse personal experiences of women into public arenas. Jordan's poetry in the 1970s is especially valued for a personal politics that places Black women's experiences at the center of political analysis. In "Poem about My Rights," from *Passion* (1980), Jordan directly connects the speaker's experience of rape with the invasion of Namibia by South Africa. Her efforts to value the experiences and voices of marginalized people earned her recognition as an important political voice as well as one of the most important African American women poets of the later twentieth century, especially with her much anthologized poems "What Would I Do White?," from *Things That I Do in the Dark* (1977), "1977: Poem for Miss Fannie Lou Hamer," from *Passion* (1980), and "From Sea to Shining Sea," from *Living Room* (1985). Jordan also published celebratory love poetry alongside her explicitly political poetry, especially in the later collections *Haruko: Love Poetry* (1994) and *Kissing God Goodbye* (1997).

Jordan's legacy as an intellectual is as important as her legacy as a poet. In 1981, Jordan became one of the first African American women to publish a book-length collection of essays. In *Civil Wars* (1981) and in her four subsequent essay collections and regular columns in *The Progressive*, Jordan helped define the category "political essays" by writing about key political events and controversies as an African American woman deeply committed to democracy, justice, and global solidarity. Just before her death, she published a retrospective collection of new and selected essays in *Some of Us Did Not Die* (2002). In her work, Jordan is always aware of her voice as a "Black spokesperson" addressing audiences divided along multiple lines including race, gender, and ideology (MacPhail). Jordan offers her audience "righteous rage" as a response to injustice in poems and essays about apartheid in Soweto, Nelson Mandela's imprisonment and freedom, U.S. activities in Nicaragua, Bernard Goetz's racially motivated violence, presidential policies that disproportionately impact poor people and people of color, anti-affirmative action referenda, and many other headline political events. Jordan's creative work is deeply grounded in her activism regarding civil rights, the Vietnam War, South African apartheid, Palestine, Nicaragua, Lebanon, the Gulf War, bisexual identity, and terrorism. At the same time that she celebrates the lofty goals of democracy, she rigorously seeks out and values the voices of displaced peoples. For Jordan, poetry was both a place of, and a means toward, justice. Like Richard Wright, Jordan conceives of poetry itself as a "blueprint" for activism, especially in her Poetry for the People project (Muller).

When Jordan died in 2002, after a long battle with cancer that began in the 1970s, her death was noted by a diverse range of writers, activists, students, and scholars. Rather than mourning, many marked Jordan's passing with tributes in which writers came together, often in long poetry readings like those from her course in "Poetry for the People," to continue her project of giving voice to the people—all people—and in making poetry a powerful agent of political protest and change. In her tribute to Jordan's activist poetics, Angela Y. Davis described Jordan's legacy thus: "There was always joy in her rage. Politics was her life; collective pain, as well as collective resistance, was always something she felt in a deeply personal way" (Davis, 1).

Brian J. Norman

See also: Black Arts Movement; Essay; Feminism/Black Feminism; Free Verse; Protest Literature.

Resources

Primary Sources: June Jordan: *Affirmative Acts: Political Essays* (New York: Anchor, 1998); *Civil Wars* (Boston: Beacon Press, 1981); *Dry Victories* (New York: Holt, Rinehart, and Winston, 1972); *Fannie Lou Hamer* (New York: Crowell, 1972); *Haruko: Love Poems* (New York: High Risk Books, 1994); *His Own Where* (New York: Crowell, 1971); *I Was Looking at the Ceiling and Then I Saw the Sky* (New York: Scribner's, 1995); *Kimako's Story* (Boston: Houghton Mifflin, 1981); *Kissing God Goodbye: Poems, 1991–1997* (New York: Anchor, 1997); *Living Room: New Poems* (New York: Thunder's Mouth, 1985); *Moving Towards Home: Political Essays* (London: Virago, 1989); *Naming Our Destiny: New and Selected Poems* (New York: Thunder's Mouth, 1989); *New Days: Poems of Exile and Return* (New York: Crowell, 1974); *New Life: New Room* (New York: Crowell, 1975); *On Call: Political Essays* (Boston: South End Press, 1985); *Passion: New Poems, 1977–1980* (Boston: Beacon Press, 1980); *Soldier: A Poet's Childhood* (New York: Basic Civitas Books, 2000); *Some Changes* (New York: Dutton, 1971); *Some of Us Did Not Die: New and Selected Essays of June Jordan* (New York: Basic Civitas Books, 2002); *Soulscript: Afro-American Poetry* (Garden City, NY: Doubleday, 1970); *Technical Difficulties: African-American Notes on the State of the Union* (New York: Pantheon, 1992); *Things That I Do in the Dark: Selected Poetry* (Boston: Beacon Press, 1977); *The Voice of the Children* (New York: Holt, Rinehart and Winston, 1970); *Who Look at Me* (New York: Crowell, 1969).

Secondary Sources: Rafael Campo, "Dialogue with Sun and Poet: In memory of June Jordan," *Callaloo* 26, no. 1 (Winter 2003), 124, 273; Carol Boyce Davies, *Black Women, Writing and Identity: Migrations of the Subject* (New York: Routledge, 1994); Angela Davis, "Tribute to June Jordan," *Meridians* 3, no. 2 (2003), 1–2; Peter Erickson, "Putting Her Life on the Line: The Poetry of June Jordan," *Hurricane Alice: A Feminist Quarterly* 7, no. 1–2 (Winter–Spring 1990), 4–5; Jewelle Gomez, "June Jordan: July 9, 1936–June 14, 2002," *Callaloo* 25, no. 3 (Summer 2002), 715–718; Agnes Moreland Jackson, "June Jordan," in instructor's guide to *Heath Anthology of American Literature*, Paul Lanter, ed., vol. 2, 4th ed. (Boston: Houghton Mifflin, 2002); Korina M. Jocson, "'Taking It to the Mic': Pedagogy of June Jordan's Poetry for the People and Partnership with an Urban High School," *English Education* 37, no. 2 (Summer 2002), 132–148; Scott MacPhail, "June Jordan and the New Black Intellectuals," *African American Review* 33, no. 1 (Spring 1999), 57–71. E. Ethelbert Miller, "Remembering June Jordan: There are times when a gentle rain falls, and I think of my friend, June Jordan," *Black Renaissance/Renaissance Noire* 16, no. 1 (Winter–Spring 2016), 50(10); Lauren Muller et al., eds., *June Jordan's Poetry for the People: A Revolutionary Blueprint* (New York: Routledge, 1995).

K

King, Martin Luther, Jr. (1929–1968)

Baptist minister, author, and civil rights activist. Martin Luther King Jr. was the most renowned leader of the Civil Rights Movement in the United States during the 1950s and 1960s. He is known for his eloquent speeches and sermons delivered in a style heavily influenced by prophetic books of the Old Testament. His doctrine of brotherly love and nonviolent, direct action against racism—inspired by the teachings of Jesus, Henry David Thoreau, Mohandas K. Gandhi, and liberal Protestant theologians—was crucial to winning full citizenship rights for Blacks as well as other groups of racial minorities.

King was born and raised in Sweet Auburn, a Black middle-class neighborhood in Atlanta, Georgia, on January 15, 1929. His father, Michael (later Martin Luther) King Sr. was pastor of the Ebenezer Baptist Church, a Black congregation founded by his maternal grandfather; his mother, Alberta Williams King, was the choir director of the church as well as a schoolteacher. King was educated at David T. Howard Elementary School, Atlanta University Laboratory School, and Booker T. Washington High School. After finishing his junior year at Booker T. Washington, King entered Morehouse College in Atlanta as a gifted student, earning his BA degree in sociology in 1948. While attending Morehouse, he was ordained as a Baptist minister. In the fall of the same year, King entered Crozer Theological Seminary in Chester, Pennsylvania, where he learned liberal Protestant theology and the Gandhian philosophy of nonviolence. After receiving a Bachelor of Divinity from Crozer in 1951, he began doctoral study in theology at Boston University. While living in Boston, Massachusetts, King met and married Coretta Scott, a Marion, Alabama, native and a student at the New England Conservatory of Music. The couple had four children. In 1954, a year before he received a PhD in systematic theology, King was installed as pastor of the Dexter Avenue Baptist Church in Montgomery, Alabama.

By the time King and his family settled in Montgomery, Southern Blacks were simmering with rage against racial discrimination. King first became involved in civil rights activism through the boycott of the Montgomery bus system by Blacks. The National Association for the Advancement of Colored People (NAACP) elected King the leader of the Montgomery Improvement Association (MIA), which carried out the bus boycott. In his first civil rights speech, delivered to 7,000 Blacks at Holt Street Baptist Church, King declared, "There comes a time when people get tired of being trampled over by the iron feet of oppression." He added, however, that the fight for racial equality would be carried out through nonviolent means. The yearlong boycott of city buses was met by harassment, arrests, attacks, and intimidation by the police and White supremacists; King's home was bombed on January 30, 1956. Finally, on November 13, the U.S. Supreme Court declared segregation of public buses uncon-stitutional; on December 21, the Montgom-ery buses were desegregated. The bus boycott represented the first large-scale use of nonviolent resistance against racial dis-crimination in American history, making King a national hero for the oppressed—a moral voice, seasoned with Christian love, fighting for social justice.

In January 1957, King and other Black leaders formed the Southern Christian Leadership Conference (SCLC), a ministe-rial organization aimed at coordinating local civil rights groups in the South. The SCLC was instrumental in pressuring the federal government and Congress to pass the Civil Rights Act and the Voting Rights Act. As the first president of the SCLC, King delivered hundreds of speeches and consulted with other civil rights leaders across the country. In 1957, he received the Spingarn Medal, awarded annually by the NAACP to a distinguished American Negro.

In 1960, King and his family relocated from Montgomery to Atlanta, where he took the associate pastorate at his father's church. Under King's leadership, the SCLC gave its support to hundreds of Blacks in Greensboro, North Carolina, who were holding sit-ins at lunch counters. Later that year, King and thirty-three young people were arrested at one such sit-in at an Atlanta department store. He was released from prison but only through the intervention of Democratic presidential candidate John F. Kennedy. King next supported, without much success, the 1961 Albany, Georgia, movement for voter registration, desegrega-tion of public places, and equal employ-ment opportunity, among other causes. Local Black groups rioted, defying King's plea to use peaceful means to end racial discrimination.

In April 1963, King led a large-scale civil rights campaign in Birmingham, an upris-ing featuring peaceful marches by thou-sands of Blacks. More than 4,000 demonstrators were put in jail. As 2,500 more youths marched through the streets, they were brutally suppressed by police who used fire hoses, German shepherds, tear gas, and clubs. King was arrested, jailed, and held in solitary confinement. On April 16, he wrote "Letter from Birming-ham Jail" to White ministers who had opposed his campaign. He contended that unjust laws were unworthy of obedience and that nonviolent, direct action was intended to "create such a crisis and foster such a tension that a community which has constantly refused to negotiate is forced to confront the issue." Police brutality, which bolstered the national outcry to end racial segregation in the South, led President Ken-nedy to propose an extensive civil rights bill in Congress. In August, King and other civil rights leaders orchestrated a march on Washington, DC—the largest civil rights protest in U.S. history—to draw national and international attention to racial prob-lems in the United States and pressure Con-gress to pass Kennedy's bill. It was at this march that King delivered the famous speech "I Have a Dream" to more than 200,000 civil rights supporters of various races who had gathered around the Lincoln Memorial. He addressed the crowd, "I have a dream that my four little children will one day live in a nation where they will not be judged by the color of their skin, but by the content of their character." (*See* Essay.)

The year 1964 saw the historic passage of the Civil Rights Act. Signed by President Lyndon B. Johnson, it outlawed segregation of public accommodations and guaranteed equal opportunity in employment, educa-tion, and federal programs. In the summer, the SCLC supported CORE (Congress of Racial Equality) in its massive voter registration campaign for the Freedom Summer. In the same year, King was received two honors. In January, he was chosen by *Time* magazine as Man of the Year, and in December, he received the Nobel Peace Prize for advancing racial justice in the United States.

Having seen the passage of the Civil Rights Acts, King devoted more time and attention to securing federal voting rights for Blacks. In February 1965, he was arrested and briefly jailed while leading, alongside John Lewis, a "stand-in" at the Dallas County Courthouse in Selma, Alabama. After a Black man named Jimmy Lee Jackson was killed by a state trooper, King led a protest march with hundreds of religious people including Catholic priests and nuns, Protestant clergymen, and rabbis. Police responded with nightsticks and tear gas, fatally injuring Rev. James Reeb. After "Bloody Sunday," the day when police brutality reached its peak, more than 3,000 protesters marched from Selma to Montgomery. With the state capitol building as backdrop, King delivered a speech to a crowd of more than 20,000 people. The violence in Selma forced President Lyndon B. Johnson to seek passage of the Voting Rights Act. Approved by Congress, it was signed into law on August 6. In 2014, a feature film, *Selma*, rekindled interest in the Selma protest and its aftermath.

King's stature as the most revered civil rights leader began to diminish as the nation became increasingly preoccupied with the Vietnam War. Starting in early January 1966, King openly opposed U.S. military action in Vietnam, which he maintained was dishonorable and morally unjustifiable. War expenditures, he believed, would be better used for alleviating the plight of poor Blacks. In his "Beyond Vietnam" speech, delivered at Riverside Church in New York City on April 4, King called the United States "the greatest purveyor of violence in the world today." His antiwar stance alienated many fellow civil rights leaders as well as government figures, including President Johnson and J. Edgar Hoover, head of the FBI.

King's stature also diminished as militant Black leaders, especially those in Northern cities, began to question the effectiveness of his nonviolent civil protests. Accusing him of being too cautious, they resorted to violence in protest against Black poverty in ghettoes. The August 1965 rioting in the Watts district of Los Angeles, California, served as a prime example. At the beginning of 1966, King launched a massive protest in Chicago, Illinois—the first major civil rights campaign outside the South. Marchers demanded abolition of racial discrimination in housing, employment, and schooling. King also established Operation Breadbasket to promote job opportunities for Blacks. Except for Operation Breadbasket, however, King's Chicago campaign resulted largely in unfulfilled promises.

On November 27, 1967, King announced the "Poor People's Campaign," a multiracial, nonviolent mass march to be held in Washington, DC. Its aim was to demand elimination of all forms of barriers to economic freedom for the impoverished. It also called for the funding of a $12-billion "Economic Bill of Rights." While organizing this campaign, King accepted a request by sanitation workers in Memphis, Tennessee, to support their strike. He flew to Memphis and delivered a speech, "I've Been to the Mountaintop," at Mason Temple on April 3, 1968. In this prophetic address, King compared himself to Moses, who led his people out of slavery in Egypt but was not allowed by God to enter Canaan. The following day, while standing on the balcony of the Lorraine Motel, he was assassinated by a sniper. More than 10,000 people gathered outside the Ebenezer Baptist Church in Atlanta, where his funeral was held. James Earl Ray, a White sanitation worker, was charged with the murder. He pleaded guilty on March 10, 1969, and was sentenced to ninety-nine years in prison.

During his life as a civil rights leader, King wrote five books elucidating his philosophy of nonviolent protest: *Stride Toward Freedom: The Montgomery Story* (1958), a memoir in which he recollected the Montgomery bus boycott and theorized nonviolent civil disobedience; *Strength to Love* (1963), a collection of sermons expounding on civil protests founded upon the principle of Christian charity; *Why We Can't Wait* (1964), in which he recounts the experiences in Birmingham and contends that all Americans are morally obligated to act to improve race relations; *Where Do We Go from Here: Chaos or Community?* (1967), containing his reflections on the future of the Civil Rights Movement; and *The Trumpet of Conscience* (1968), a collection of five speeches including "Youth and Action" and "Nonviolence and Social Change."

A towering symbol of peaceful resistance, King has become a legendary figure in modern American history. In 1977, he was posthumously awarded the Presidential Medal of Freedom for his nonviolent struggle for the rights of Blacks. In October 1980, the Martin Luther King Jr. National Historic Site was established in Atlanta, and, in 1983, Congress designated the third Monday in January, beginning in 1986, as a national holiday in honor of his birth. In 1996, Congress established the Selma-to-Montgomery National Historic Trail under the National Trails System Act.

In addition to all this, numerous streets, highways, and schools across the United States bear the name of King.

John J. Han

See also: Black Arts Movement; Malcolm X; Protest Literature.

Resources

John J. Ansbro, *Martin Luther King, Jr.* (Maryknoll, NY: Orbis, 1982); Lewis V. Baldwin, *There Is a Balm in Gilead: The Cultural Roots of Martin Luther King, Jr.* (Minneapolis, MN: Fortress Press, 1991); Taylor Branch, *Parting the Waters: America in the King Years 1954–1963* (New York: Simon and Schuster, 1988); Richard L. Deats, *Martin Luther King, Jr.* (New York: New City Press, 1999); Ava DuVernay, director, *Selma* (Pathé, Harpo Films, 2014); Marshall Frady, *Martin Luther King, Jr.* (New York: Penguin, 2002); David J. Garrow, *Bearing the Cross: Martin Luther King, Jr., and the Southern Christian Leadership Conference, 1955–1968* (New York: Morrow, 1986); Martin Luther King Jr., *Strength to Love* (New York: Harper & Row, 1963); *Stride Toward Freedom: The Montgomery Story* (New York: Harper & Row, 1958); *The Trumpet of Conscience* (New York: Harper & Row, 1968); *Where Do We Go from Here: Chaos or Community?* (New York: Harper & Row, 1967); *Why We Can't Wait* (New York: Harper & Row, 1964); Flip Schulke and Penelope O. McPhee, *King Remembered* (New York: Norton, 1986); Stephen B. Oates, *Let the Trumpet Sound: The Life of Martin Luther King, Jr.* (New York: Harper & Row, 1982).

Knight, Etheridge (1931–1991)

Poet, prisoner, "toast" maker, and teacher. Born in Corinth, Mississippi, Knight abandoned school by the ninth grade, joined the Army by the age of sixteen, and was discharged ten years later, when dependencies on alcohol and drugs led him to prison for the offense of purse snatching in 1960. While Knight gained notoriety for urban "toasts" (oral improvisations of poems and narratives rooted in nineteenth-century African storytelling traditions) long before his incarceration, it was not until he was serving time at the Indiana State Prison that he began his illustrious career as a "prison poet" (see Prison Literature). He was often visited by major literary figures such as Gwendolyn Brooks, and was supported by members of the Black Arts Movement, such as his first wife, Sonia Sanchez.

For eight years, Knight wrote poetry in prison. The release of his first published collection, *Poems from Prison* (1968), roughly coincided with his release from prison. The poem "The Idea of Ancestry" from that collection suggests that personal freedoms can prevail in the bleakest of circumstances. The book also includes poems that indict the American prison system, such as "For Freckle-Faced Gerald" and "Hard Rock Returns to Prison from the Hospital of the Criminal Insane." The latter is one of Knight's best-known poems. The character "Hard Rock" is presented as the one Black man in prison who stands up to oppression and racism. In the poem, prison administrators decide to perform a makeshift lobotomy on Hard Rock, and he is stripped of the strength, the identity, and the self-determination that characterized him. In this regard, the poem is comparable to Ken Kesey's *One Flew over the Cuckoo's Nest* (1962), in which the rebellious Randall Patrick McMurphy suffers the same fate as Hard Rock.

The publication of *Black Voices from Prison* (1970), an anthology he edited and contributed to, reinforced Knight's reputation as a political, even revolutionary, poet. His blues-inspired verse links him with major writers such as Richard Wright and Langston Hughes. The critic Frank Magill suggests that Knight's poetry reflects a practice common to African American literature—paying respect to elders and familial ancestors (Magill, 419). In addition to being compared to major literary figures such as Walt Whitman and Sterling A. Brown, Knight won the respect of his peers while holding teaching positions (from 1969 to 1972) at the University of Pittsburgh, the University of Hartford, and Lincoln University in Pennsylvania.

Knight continued to struggle with addictions, checking himself in and out of drug-dependency treatment centers, and going through a divorce with Sanchez. However, within a two-year span, Knight was remarried, awarded a National Endowment for the Arts grant (1972), nominated for the National Book Award and the Pulitzer Prize (1973), and awarded a Guggenheim Fellowship (1974). Along with Amiri Baraka and Haki Madhubuti, Knight, who successfully experimented with African-based rhythms, blues idioms, and jazz, was one of the most inspirational figures to join the Black Arts Movement. Knight's impulse to establish connections in social and literary communities would reveal itself in *Belly Song and Other Poems* (1973). Reflecting his belief that prison and family leave uniquely indelible marks, Knight's fourth major collection, *Born of a Woman* (1980), pays homage to the essential female figures in his life. By this time, Knight had divorced his second wife, Mary Ann McAnally, and was married to his third wife, Charlene Blackburn. A poem such as "The Stretching of the Belly" (dedicated to Blackburn) compares a woman's stretch marks to a man's battle scars. Many of the poems that appear in both *Belly Song* and *Born of a Woman* have been recognized by critics such as

Patricia L. Hill for resurrecting instrumental devices from the blues (Hill, 21). Citing Knight's "Hard Rock Returns to Prison from the Hospital for the Criminal Insane" as a quintessential example of prison poetry, H. Bruce Franklin states: "In the immediate background of contemporary Black prison poetry is the body of work songs developed by Black convicts on chain gangs and prison farms" (254).

Critics such as Hill and Franklin have also noted the ways that Knight's poetic works actively demonstrate the connection between slave songs, urban toasts, and contemporary rap music. Knight was an editor of the magazine *Motive* as well as a contributing editor for the journal *New Letters*. After winning the Shelley Memorial Award from the Poetry Society of America in 1985, Knight published his most comprehensive collection, *The Essential Etheridge Knight* (1986), which won the 1987 American Book Award. Knight earned his bachelor's degree in American poetry and criminal justice from Martin Center University in 1990. He died from lung cancer on March 10, 1991.

Stephen M. Steck

See also: Free Verse; Prison Literature.

Resources
Michael S. Collins, "The Antipanopticon of Etheridge Knight," *PMLA: Publications of the Modern Language Association PMLA* 123, no. 3 (May 1, 2008), 580–597; *Understanding Etheridge Knight* (Columbia: University of South Carolina Press, 2012); H. Bruce Franklin, *Prison Literature in America: The Victim as Criminal and Artist* (New York: Oxford University Press, 1989); Terrance Hayes, *To Float in the Space Between: a Life and Work in Conversation with the Life and Work of Etheridge Knight* (Seattle: Wave Books, 2018); Patricia L. Hill, "'Blues for a Mississippi Black Boy': Etheridge Knight's Craft in the Black Oral Tradition," *Mississippi Quarterly* 36, no. 1 (Winter 1982–1983), 21–34; Etheridge Knight: *Belly Song and Other Poems* (Detroit: Broadside Press, 1973); *Black Voices from Prison* (New York: Pathfinder Press, 1970); *Born of a Woman* (Boston: Houghton Mifflin, 1980); *The Essential Etheridge Knight* (Pittsburgh, PA: University of Pittsburgh Press, 1986); *Poems from Prison* (Detroit: Broadside Press, 1968); Frank N. Magill, "The Poetry of Etheridge Knight," in *Masterpieces of African-American Literature*, ed. Frank N. Magill (New York: HarperCollins, 1992), 419–422; Steven C. Tracy, "A MELUS Interview: Etheridge Knight," *Multi-Ethnic Literatures of the U.S.* 12, no. 2 (July 1, 1985), 7–23.

Komunyakaa, Yusef (1947–)

Poet and professor. Komunyakaa's poetry reflects his childhood in the racially charged rural South, reveals his enthusiasm for jazz and literature, and illustrates his experiences as a Black soldier in the Vietnam War. Komunyakaa was born and raised in Bogalusa, Louisiana, the youngest of five children. Born James Willie Brown, Komunyakaa legally reclaimed the name Komunyakaa, the surname of his grandparents, who arrived in the United States as stowaways on a ship from Trinidad (Hedges, B2). As a child, Komunyakaa was a self-described daydreamer, spending much of his time either outdoors observing nature or working with his father, a finishing carpenter, whom he describes as a "black Calvinist" and who believed that hard labor and endurance led to freedom (*Conversation with Toi Derricotte*). Komunyakaa credits his methodical work with his father as a poetic influence during his childhood. Other early influences, evident in his poetry, include jazz and blues, which resonated from his mother's wooden radio, and the

Bible, which he read twice through to absorb its rhythm (Conley).

Shortly after graduating from high school in 1965, Komunyakaa joined the military and was quickly sent to fight in the Vietnam War. While there, he was an information specialist and, later, editor of *The Southern Cross*, a military newspaper. After his tour of duty, Komunyakaa was awarded the Bronze Star and left the military. At this point in his life, Komunyakaa had written only one poem, a 100-stanza piece in honor of his high school graduating class. He wrote no poetry in Vietnam, though he took with him Hayden Carruth's *The Voice That Is Great Within Us* and Donald Allen's *The New American Poetry* (Lehman).

Upon returning to the United States, Komunyakaa pursued a bachelor's degree in English and sociology at the University of Colorado. While there, he took a creative writing class, and he has not stopped writing since. After graduating in 1975, Komunyakaa went on to Colorado State University, where he earned his MA in 1979, and then to the University of California at Irvine to pursue an MFA in creative writing, which he received in 1980. During this time, Komunyakaa published his first two books of poetry, *Dedications and Other Dark Horses* (1977) and *Lost in the Bonewheel Factory* (1979). Shortly after joining the faculty of the University of New Orleans, Komunyakaa caught the attention of reviewers by publishing *Copacetic* (1984), a collection of jazz-inspired pieces modeled after works by Langston Hughes and Amiri Baraka (Gwynn, 176).

From New Orleans, Louisiana, Komunyakaa traveled north to teach English at Indiana University from 1985 to 1996. While there, he produced some of his most memorable works, including *I Apologize for the Eyes in My Head* (1986), which alludes to his experiences in Vietnam and which won the San Francisco Poetry Center Award, and the critically acclaimed *Dien Cai Dau* (1988), "crazy" in Vietnamese, a full-blown resurrection of Komunyakaa's wartime experiences. *Magic City* (1992), which reflects on his childhood and early manhood, followed. Komunyakaa's *Neon Vernacular* (1993), a compilation of both new and old poetry, was awarded the Pulitzer Prize for poetry, the Kingsley Tufts Award for poetry, and the William Faulkner Prize in 1994.

In 1996, Komunyakaa left Indiana University and held one-year lectureships at the University of California and Washington University. Today, he is a professor of the Council of Humanities and Creative Writing at Princeton University. Since moving to the East Coast, Komunyakaa has published several more books of poems, including *Thieves of Paradise* (1998), *Talking Dirty to the Gods* (2000), *Pleasure Dome: New and Collected Poems, 1975–1999* (2001), and *Scandalize My Name* (2002). His most recent work, *Taboo: The Wishbone Trilogy, Part One* (2004), has been described as a "personalized interior mosaic of black history and culture" where myth meets reality (Muratori, 66).

Komunyakaa credits a variety of poets, writers, and genres for inspiring and influencing his works. The first poem he committed to memory was Edgar Allan Poe's "Annabel Lee." Other poetic influences include Robert Hayden, Elizabeth Bishop, James Weldon Johnson, Ralph Tennyson, Shakespeare, and the Harlem Renaissance writers (Lehman). Komunyakaa also studied T. S. Eliot, Ezra Pound, Paul Celan, Aimé Césarie, Baudelaire, the French Surrealists, Jean Toomer, Bob Kaufman, Helene Johnson, and Amiri Baraka (Conley). Komunyakaa urges aspiring writers not only to read great literary works, but to be well educated in other fields of knowledge, including science, psychology, anthropology, and history (Lehman).

He has continued to write prolifically in recent years, publishing several new collections: *Gilgamesh: A Verse Play* (2006), *Warhorses: Poems* (2008), *Chameleon Couch: Poems* (2011), *Testimony, A Tribute to Charlie Parker: With New and Selected Jazz Poems* (2013), and *The Emperor of Clocks* (2015). *Condition Red: Essays, Interviews, and Commentaries* appeared in 2017.

Julie Claggett

See also: Free Verse.

Resources

Primary Sources: Yusef Komunyakaa: *Chameleon Couch: Poems* (New York: Farrar, Straus, and Giroux, 2011); *Condition Red: Essays, Interviews, and Commentaries*, ed. Radiclani Clytus (Ann Arbor: University of Michigan Press, 2017); *Copacetic* (Middletown, CT: Wesleyan University Press, 1984); *The Emperor of Clocks: Poems* (New York: Farrar, Straus, & Giroux, 2015); *Gilgamesh: A Verse Play* (Middletown, CT: Wesleyan University Press, 2006); *I Apologize for the Eyes in My Head* (Middletown, CT: Wesleyan University Press, 1986); *Lost in the Bonewheel Factory* (Amherst, MA: Lynx House Press, 1979); *Magic City* (Middletown, CT: Wesleyan University Press, 1992); *Neon Vernacular: New and Selected Poems* (Middletown, CT: Wesleyan University Press, 1993); *Pleasure Dome: New and Collected Poems* (Middletown, CT: Wesleyan University Press, 2001); *Princeton University Creative Writing Program Faculty 1997–1998*, http://www.princeton.edu/-visarts/Yusef1.htm; *Taboo: The Wishbone Trilogy, Part One* (New York: Farrar, 2004); *Talking Dirty to the Gods* (New York: Farrar, Straus, and Giroux, 2000); *Testimony, A Tribute to Charlie Parker: With New and Selected Jazz Poems* (Middletown, CT: Wesleyan University Press, 2013); *Thieves of Paradise* (Middletown, CT: Wesleyan University Press, 1998); *Warhorses: Poems* (New York: Farrar, Straus, and Giroux, 2008).

Secondary Sources: William Baer, "Still negotiating with the images: An interview with Yusef Komunyakaa," *The Kenyon Review* 20, no. 3/4 (Summer 1998), 5–20; Radiclani Clytus, ed., Michael Collins, "Yusef Komunyakaa: A Bibliography," *Callaloo* 28, no. 3 (2005), 883–886; Susan Conley, "About Yusef Komunyakaa," *Ploughshares: The Literary Journal at Emerson College*, https://www.pshares.org/issues/spring-1997/about-yusef-komunyakaa-profile (May 4, 2005); Toi Derricotte, "Review of *Copacetic, I Apologize for the Eyes in My Head, Dien Cau Dau*, and *Neon Vernacular*, by Yusef Komunyakaa," *Kenyon Review* 15, no. 4 (1993), 217, 222; R. S. Gwynn, ed., *Dictionary of Literary Biography*, vol. 120, *American Poets Since World War II*, 3rd ser. (Detroit: Gale Research, 1992); Shirley A. James Hanshaw, ed., *Conversations with Yusef Komunyakaa* (Jackson: University Press of Mississippi, 2010); Chris Hedges, "A Poet of Suffering, Endurance and Healing," *New York Times*, July 8, 2004, metro ed., p. B2; David Lehman, "Interview with Yusef Komunyakaa" (Nov. 10, 1999), http://www.cortlandreview.com/features/millennium/index.html; Thomas F. Marvin, "Komunyakaa's FACING IT," *Explicator* 61, no. 4 (2003), 242–245; Fred Muratori, "Review of *Taboo: The Wishbone Trilogy, Part One*, by Yusef Komunyakaa," *Library Journal* (September 15, 2004), p. 66; Angela M. Salas, "Race, Human Empathy, and Negative Capability: The Poetry of Yusef Komunyakaa," *College Literature* 30, no. 4 (October 1, 2003), 32–53; Daniel Turner, "Dying Objects/Living Things: The Thingness of Poetry in Yusef Komunyakaa's *Talking Dirty to the Gods*," *Mosaic: a Journal for the Interdisciplinary Study of Literature* 45, no. 1 (March 2012), 137–154.

L

Larsen, Nella (1891–1964)

Novelist. Known for her work during the Harlem Renaissance, Larsen wrote about the politically charged subjects of racial identity and White privilege as well as the social roles and expectations for women in the 1920s. She obscured many of the details of her personal life, which may have been a statement about her privacy or the desire to move between both Black and White cultures. Born in Chicago, Illinois, to Mary Hanson Walker, who was Danish, and Peter Walker, who was of West Indian descent, Larsen would not know family life with her parents. Shortly after her birth, her parents separated and her mother married another Dane, Peter Larsen. Soon after Larsen's mother remarried, she gave birth to another daughter. Many scholars speculate that the young Nella may have had a difficult childhood and a tense relationship with her stepfather, since she was the only "non-White" member of her immediate family. This struggle to identify herself as either Black or White, and the social constrictions placed on African Americans, would become a recurring theme throughout her life and her writing.

Regardless of these tensions, Larsen received an excellent education. She attended public schools in Chicago until 1907, when her stepfather enrolled her in Fisk University Normal School. She then attended Fisk University in Nashville, Tennessee, from 1909 to 1910. Then she decided to finish her education in Denmark, and audited classes at the University of Copenhagen for two years. Upon returning to the United States, she attended nursing school at Lincoln Hospital in New York City. After graduating from nursing school, she spent a brief time at the Tuskegee Institute, helping to train other nurses and serving as head nurse at John Andrew Memorial Hospital. However, Larsen soon returned to New York, and from 1916 to 1921, she worked as a nurse for both Lincoln Hospital and the Department of Health. During this time, she met and married a physicist, Elmer S. Imes.

Shortly after her marriage, Nella Larsen Imes, as she was known, began making the acquaintance of men and women involved in the growing arts movement later known as the Harlem Renaissance. The well-educated Larsen had been interested in writing and began trying to publish her work. One of her particular interests was children's literature. Jessie Redmon Fauset, another significant female writer of the Harlem Renaissance, was the editor of *The Brownies' Book*, a children's magazine founded by Fauset with W.E.B. Du Bois and Augustus Dill. The magazine was created with the goal of reducing the stigma many African American children felt about being Black. Larsen became a published author for the first time in *The Brownies' Book* by writing two articles about Danish children's games.

As Larsen's interest in literature and the growing Harlem Renaissance increased, she decided to quit her job as a nurse. In 1921, she took a position at the public library in Harlem, New York, first working as a library assistant and eventually as the children's librarian. She also attended Columbia University to pursue a degree in library science. This immersion in the literary and arts community of Harlem fueled Larsen's desire to become a full-fledged writer. As she attended school, she immersed herself in writing and worked on several pieces of short fiction that were published under the pen name Allen Semi, which is Nella Imes spelled backward. She was also busy working on what would eventually become her first novel, *Quicksand*. She stayed at the library in Harlem until September 1926, when her first short story, "Correspondence," was published in *Opportunity*. She felt ready to pursue a full-time career in writing.

As the wife of a prominent physicist and with a love of literature and the arts, Larsen had the social prominence to become acquainted with many of the important writers of the Harlem Renaissance. She had already developed a relationship with Jessie Fauset in the early 1920s, and she also came to know Langston Hughes, Carl Van Vechten, and Jean Toomer, who shared her interest in writing about the often difficult situation of being caught between Black and White life and culture. Her association with some of these significant writers helped her land a publishing contract with Alfred A. Knopf, one of the most notable and influential publishers of the time.

In 1928, *Quicksand* was published to critical acclaim and won the bronze medal from the Harmon Foundation. *Quicksand*'s heroine is Helga Crane, a woman who struggles with her identity as the daughter of a Danish mother and a Black father, and is then raised by her mother and a cruel White stepfather. The intelligent, yet troubled, Helga moves to the South, teaching at an all-Black school, only to find that she feels out of place because of her fair complexion. She continues to move about in search of a place she can call home; her travels take her to Harlem and even Denmark. After what seems to be a nervous breakdown, she decides to marry a Black, Southern man whom she knew from her time as a teacher. Living in a rural Southern community and becoming a mother weighs down Helga and makes her feel as if she is sinking in quicksand. She falls deeper and deeper into a depression. Certainly, Helga Crane's story echoed many of Larsen's own experiences. However, the novel is more than autobiographical fiction, for it serves as a commentary on issues of race and the conventions of women's sexuality.

Larsen's second novel, *Passing* (1929), tackled many of the same issues as its predecessor. However, *Passing* dealt more specifically with the issues of race and the practice of passing. The novel follows the lives of its two main characters, Clare Kendry and Irene Redfield. As a light-skinned Black woman, Clare escapes poverty by successfully passing as a White woman. She marries a wealthy White man, who thinks she is White, and lives the life of a New York socialite. Clare's childhood friend, Irene, has married a successful Black doctor. When the friends reunite, Clare finds she is attracted to Irene's husband and pursues a relationship with him. Feeling threatened, Irene reveals the truth of Clare's racial heritage to her husband. In a climactic ending to the story, Clare falls out of a window before her husband can confront her about the truth. Having a much more dramatic storyline than *Quicksand*, *Passing* deals directly with the problematic practice of passing that many African American men and women felt pressured to do during this era. As a commentary on both the narrowness of the Black bourgeois and the sometimes shifting color line, Larsen's novel was politically and socially significant in both African American and White communities at the time of its publication.

The publications of *Quicksand* and *Passing* sealed Nella Larsen as a significant literary figure not only in the Harlem Renaissance but also in the first half of the twentieth century. As the first African American woman to win a Guggenheim Fellowship for creative writing, she was a critically acclaimed and celebrated writer. However, her career was cut short by scandal. In the same year she won the Guggenheim, she published the short story "Sanctuary" in *Forum* magazine. The story is about a man who seeks refuge at a friend's mother's house after shooting someone. As the story unfolds, the man comes to realize that the person he has shot is the friend whose mother has given him sanctuary. Although it was a powerful story, it was quickly compared with a story published in the early 1920s, and Larsen was accused of plagiarism. She was able to prove her innocence of such accusations and even published a follow-up essay in *Forum*, "The Author's Explanation." However, the public sting of the accusations all but ended her career. With the money from the Guggenheim, she tried to escape the humiliation caused by the allegations and traveled to Europe to work on her next novel. It was subsequently turned down by Knopf.

By 1933, Larsen began experiencing marital problems, and because of her notoriety, she suffered through a divorce that was sensationalized in the press, including rumors of infidelity and attempted suicide. After her divorce, Larsen kept to herself and desperately sought privacy. Using her full married name, she lived as Nella Larsen Imes, cutting off connections with her literary friends and ending her career as a writer. She returned to the nursing profession and lived and worked in obscurity in New York City until her death in 1964.

Melissa Hamilton Hayes

See also: Feminism/Black Feminism; Harlem Renaissance; Novel.

Resources

Hazel Carby, "The Quicksands of Representation," in her *Reconstructing Womanhood: The Emergence of the Afro-American Woman Novelist* (Oxford: Oxford University Press, 1987); Barbara Christian, *Black Women Novelists: The Development of a Tradition, 1892–1976* (Westport, CT: Greenwood Press, 1980); Thadious Davis, *Nella Larsen, Novelist of the Harlem Renaissance: A Woman's Life Unveiled* (Baton Rouge: Louisiana State University Press, 1994); George Hutchinson, *In Search of Nella Larsen: a Biography of the Color Line* (Cambridge, MA: Belknap Press of Harvard University, 2006); Press Nella Larsen: *The Complete Fiction of Nella Larsen*, ed. Charles R. Larson (New York: Anchor Books, 2001); *Quicksand* and *Passing*, ed. Deborah McDowell (New Brunswick, NJ: Rutgers University Press, 1986); Charles R. Larson, *Invisible Darkness: Jean Toomer and Nella Larsen* (Iowa City: University of Iowa Press, 1993); Jacquelyn McLendon, *The Politics of Color in the Fiction of Jessie Fauset and Nella Larsen* (Charlottesville: University Press of Virginia, 1995).

Lesbian Literature

African American lesbian literature changed the shape of American literary history by celebrating previously ignored writers as well as illuminating and resisting the triply oppressive intersection of racism, sexism, and homophobia silencing the voices of African American lesbians. Although the presence of lesbian themes appeared in late nineteenth- and early twentieth-century diaries and poems by writers such as Alice Moore Dunbar-Nelson and Angelina Weld Grimké, literary critics did not begin to pay serious attention to lesbian literature until the 1970s. As a result of the progress made by feminist and civil rights advocates in the 1960s, lesbian, feminist, and African American writers and scholars were better equipped to address the topic of lesbian literature and defend its importance in the 1970s. Additionally, the positive affirmation of African American culture and art provided by the Black Power movement and the Black Arts Movement influenced the emerging recognition of African American lesbian writers; at the same time, the lesbian tradition developed in reaction to the sexism and homophobia often associated with those movements.

Author and scholar Barbara Smith sounded the clarion call for the establishment of an African American women's tradition in her revolutionary essay "Toward a Black Feminist Criticism" (1977), originally published in the journal *Conditions*, a forum for the words of many other African American lesbian writers. In this often reprinted essay, Smith claimed, "All segments of the literary world—whether establishment, progressive, Black, female, or lesbian—do not know, or at least act as if they do not know, that Black women writers and Black lesbian writers exist" (157). Smith attributed the belated recognition of African American lesbian literature to the lack of interest, and to racism and homophobia on the part of both publishing houses and, ironically, those who would have seemed most likely to support lesbian writers: Euro-American feminists, lesbians, and "the Black community as well, which is at least as homophobic" (172).

In reaction, Smith advocated an approach that acknowledged the existence of an identifiable African American women's literary tradition. She encouraged her readers to recognize how this tradition defied both African American rights advocates and Euro-American feminists by refusing to prioritize either race or gender as a singular oppression to be fought. Instead, she argued that African American women's literature, and lesbian literature in particular, demonstrated how race and gender function in tandem as oppressive forces in mainstream America. To develop this thesis, Smith offered a controversial lesbian reading of Toni Morrison's *Sula*. Smith argued that the close bond between Sula and Nel, though never consummated sexually, could be read as a lesbian relationship if one considered lesbianism synonymous with the marginalization of women and their resistance to Euro-American and African American patriarchal power. In this regard, Smith expanded on the ideas of other African American lesbian critics such as Wilmette Brown. The continued questioning of what it means to be lesbian is one of the most significant contributions of African American lesbian literature.

Lesbian literature has gained increasing attention since the 1970s. Critics began to search for and explore often hidden references to same-sex desire in earlier works by African American women. In *Color, Sex and Poetry: Three Women Writers of the Harlem Renaissance* (1987), poet and critic Akasha [Gloria T.] Hull called attention to Angelina Weld Grimké's unpublished love poetry to other women and Alice Moore Dunbar Nelson's diary narration of her affair with Fay Johnson Robinson. Hull emphasized the fact that none of their lesbian-centered works were published during their lifetimes. Critics also reexplored the relationship between the characters Clare Kendry and Irene Redfield in Nella

Larsen's novel *Passing* (1929) as a representation of lesbian desire. Because the African American lesbian has historically been silenced or ignored by so many other social voices, the reclaiming of both unpublished and ignored texts has significantly corrected the American Literary Canon.

The 1970s likewise witnessed the publication of several landmark collections of poetry, fiction, and memoir. Writer and activist Pat Parker followed years of public poetry readings in support of lesbian women with her first collection, *Child of Myself* (1972), printed by the lesbian press she helped establish, Women's Press Collective. The poems in *Child of Myself* demonstrate the themes that characterize Parker's later work, such as race and class struggle, and lesbian resistance to compulsory heterosexuality. Stylistically, Parker made use of the African American vernacular and call-and-response traditions in her poetry to construct a bridge between lesbian experience and African American community.

The critic, author, and activist Audre Lorde published "Martha," her first poem to openly explore lesbian themes, in her second volume of poetry, *Cables to Rage* (1970), thereby launching one of the most extensive bodies of work to focus on African American lesbian themes as well as nature, place, family, cancer, feminism, and ethnic identity. Whereas Parker incorporated African American vernacular into her poetry, Lorde made use of female mythic figures from West African oral traditions to blend her voice with an international African women's tradition. In an interview with Charles Rowell published in *Callaloo* a year before her death, Lorde identified herself as "a Black, Lesbian, Feminist, warrior, poet, mother doing my work" (92). She inspired other African American women and lesbians to name themselves and create positive self-identities, and she expressed how her poetry and essays were not only encouragements of self-definition but also calls to social action: "I want my poems—I want all of my work—to engage, and to empower people to speak, to strengthen themselves into who they most want and need to be and then to act, to do what needs being done" (94). Lorde was an ardent lesbian rights activist who spoke at the first national march for Gay and Lesbian Liberation in Washington, DC, in 1979; she also cofounded Kitchen Table: Women of Color Press, which has since published important works by both heterosexual and homosexual women.

Lesbian fiction also made strides in the 1970s. Ann Allen Shockley published the first avowedly lesbian African American novel, *Loving Her* (1974), the story of a singer, Renay, who falls in love with an affluent Euro-American woman, leaves her abusive husband, and raises her daughter on her own. Aside from its revolutionary focus on same-sex desire, *Loving Her* confronted the controversial subjects of interracial relationships and parenting by homosexuals. Shockley was also the first African American woman to publish a short-story collection centered on lesbian characters: *The Black and White of It* (1980). In spite of reviewers, including other African American lesbians such as Jewelle Gomez, who labeled Shockley's later work as shallow, unliterary, or too preoccupied with Euro-American characters, her fiction significantly contributed to the African American lesbian tradition in a decade that also gave rise to the poetry and plays of June Jordan and the establishment of *Azalea,* a magazine for Third World lesbians. An edition of Jordan's *Collected Poems* appeared in 2005.

In the 1980s and 1990s, a number of new writers appeared in print and further diversified the stylistic, social, and political scope of lesbian literature. The poet, novelist, and critic Jewelle Gomez self-published her first collection of poems, *The Lipstick Papers* (1980). In her first novel, *The Gilda Stories* (1991), Gomez expanded the African American literary tradition of reinventing popular myths; she revised the classic vampire tale to explore 200 years of African American history from a lesbian perspective. In both *The Gilda Stories* and essays, Gomez has called attention to the creative possibilities of science fiction and fantasy genres. Cherry Muhanji's debut novel, *Her* (1990), explored the bonds between women and the homophobia of Detroit, Michigan, in the 1960s. The jazz-inspired anthems in the poetry of Cheryl Clarke and the interracial relationships at the center of Becky Birtha's fiction further evidence the diverse preoccupations and accomplishments of lesbian writers. In 1983, Anita Cornwell published the memoir *Black Lesbian in White America.*

These writers have identified themselves publicly as lesbians and addressed how their sexuality influences their poems, stories, and memoirs; however, many writers who do not identify as lesbians have also contributed to the body of lesbian literature. Alice Walker's portrayal of the love affair between Celie and Shug Avery in *The Color Purple* (1982) is arguably the most widely read account of an African American lesbian relationship. The love affair between Lorraine and Teresa is just one of the many complex experiences shared by the seven women characters of Gloria Naylor's *The Women of Brewster Place* (1982). In Ntozake Shange's novel *Sassafrass, Cypress and Indigo* (1982), Cypress dances with a lesbian collective and begins an affair with another dancer; as in Naylor's novel, Shange's story explores the relationship between lesbianism and many other issues affecting women, such as Black Nationalism, domestic abuse, and pregnancy.

In 2011, the African American transgender woman Toni Newman published the memoir *I Rise—The Transformation of Toni Newman,* and in 2012 Mia McKenzie published the novel *The Summer We Got Free,* which won the Lambda Literary Award for Debut Fiction in 2013. McKenzie is the creator, director, and editor-in-chief of BGD (BlackGirlsDangerous) Press in Oakland, California. Cheryl Clarke published the book of poetry *Living as a Lesbian* in 2014.

The African American lesbian literary tradition continues to thrive, and it has inspired numerous anthologies, journals, and writer's organizations. Many of these, such as *This Bridge Called My Back: Writings by Radical Women of Color* (1981), exhibit how lesbian writers have embraced a multicultural community and united to resist a host of economic, political, and social problems. Edited by Barbara Smith, *Home Girls: A Black Feminist Anthology* (1983) includes poems, fiction, and essays by lesbian authors including Audre Lorde, Angelina Weld Grimké, Julie Carter, and Donna Allegra. Other noteworthy anthologies include *Black Like Us: A Century of Lesbian, Gay, and Bisexual African American Fiction* (2002); *Afrekete: An Anthology of Black Lesbian Writing* (1995); and *Does Your Mama Know? An Anthology of Black Lesbian Coming Out Stories* (1997), published by the African American lesbian publisher Redbone Press. *Aché*, a journal for African American lesbians, publishes literature, political essays, and art. These anthologies and organizations demonstrate that African American lesbian literature continues to command recognition of and acceptance for lesbian voices in literature and society; however, it also searches for a safe, self-affirming, positive cultural space—a community of its own where women can know and love and support other women. Becky Birtha's poem "My Next Lover" demonstrates the realization of this hope as the speaker does not wish but rather declares, "My next lover will never give up on us" (140).

Laura A. Hoffer

See also: Gay, Roxane; Lorde, Audre; Walker, Alice.

Resources

Becky Birtha, *The Forbidden Poems* (Seattle, WA: Seal Press, 1991); Devon W. Carbado et al., eds., *Black Like Us: A Century of Lesbian, Gay, and Bisexual African American Fiction* (San Francisco: Cleis Press, 2002); Cheryl Clarke, *Living as a Lesbian* (New York: Mid-summer's Night Press, 2014); Anita Cornwell, *Black Lesbian in White America* (Tallahassee, FL: Naiad Press, 1983); Jewelle Gomez, *The Gilda Stories: A Novel* (Ithaca, NY: Firebrand Books, 1991); Gloria T. Hull, *Color, Sex, and Poetry: Three Women Writers of the Harlem Renaissance* (Bloomington: Indiana University Press, 1987); June Jordan, *Directed by Desire: The Collected Poems of June Jordan*, ed. Jan Heller Levi and Sara Miles (Port Townsend: Copper Canyon Press, 2005); Christopher S. Lewis, "Cultivating Black Lesbian Shamelessness: Alice Walker's *The Color Purple*," *Rocky Mountain Review* 66, no. 2 (2012), 167–184; Audre Lorde, *Cables to Rage* (Detroit: Broadside Press, 1970); Mia McKenzie, *The Summer We Got Free* (Oakland: BGD Black Girls Dangerous Press, 2012); Catherine E. McKinley and L. Joyce Delaney, eds., *Afrekete: An Anthology of Black Lesbian Writing* (New York: Anchor Books, 1995); Lisa C. Moore, ed., *Does Your Mama Know? An Anthology of Black Lesbian Coming Out Stories* (Decatur, GA: Redbone Press, 1998); Cherríe Moraga and Gloria Anzaldúa, eds., *This Bridge Called My Back: Writings by Radical Women of Color* (Watertown, MA: Persephone Press, 1981); Cherry Muhanji, *Her* (San Francisco: Aunt Lute Books, 1990); Gloria Naylor, *The Women of Brewster Place* (New York: Viking, 1982); Toni Newman, *I Rise–The Transformation of Toni Newman* (CreateSpace Publishing Platform, 2011); Pat Parker, *Child of Myself* (Oakland, CA: Women's Press Collective, 1972); Charles H. Rowell, "Above the Wind: An Interview with Audre Lorde," *Callaloo* 14, no. 1 (1991): 83–95; Ntozake Shange, *Sassafrass, Cypress and Indigo* (New York: St. Martin's Press, 1982); Barbara Smith, "Toward a Black Feminist Criticism," in *All the Women Are White, All the Blacks Are Men, but Some of Us Are Brave,* ed. Gloria T. Hull, Patricia Bell Scott, and Barbara Smith (Old Westbury, NY: Feminist Press, 1982); Alice Walker, *The Color Purple* (New York: Harcourt Brace Jovanovich, 1982).

Lorde, Audre (1934–1992)

Poet, essayist, activist, autobiographer, and nonfiction writer. Lorde is revered as one of the foremost African American women writers of the twentieth century. Her voluminous body of poetry, essays, and speeches; her theoretical foresight; and her riveting autobiographical writings have helped establish her reputation as one of the preeminent Black feminist thinkers and writers of our time. Self-described as a "black feminist lesbian mother warrior poet," Lorde continually refused to sever any one part of her identity from other aspects of her life that constituted her being and understanding of self. Her collective body of work makes clear that she was very committed to engaging issues surrounding racial, sexual, and class oppression. She was also determined to explore the meaning and treatment of difference in a society marred by prejudice and inequality. Many readers and writers have been inspired by her call to end oppressive silences and to seek justice and freedom for all members of society.

Lorde was born on February 18, 1934, in Harlem, New York, and grew up during the Great Depression. Her parents, Frederick Byron and Linda Belmar Lorde, were immigrants from Grenada who had planned to return to the West Indies until the Depression ended their hopes to do so. Audre Geraldine, the youngest of three daughters, was born tongue-tied and was considered legally blind because her nearsightedness was so acute. She learned how to talk as she learned how to read at the age of four. Even as a young child, Lorde developed a fascination with language and words, so much so that she often spoke in poetry. It became a preferred mode of communication for her, and when she was unable to find poems that adequately described or expressed her feelings, she began to write her own. As she indicated in an interview with longtime friend and writer Adrienne Rich, "When someone said to me, 'How do you feel?' or 'What do you think?' or asked another direct question, I would recite a poem, and somewhere in that poem would be the feeling, the vital piece of information. It might be a line. It might be an image. The poem was my response" (*Sister Outsider*, 82). Her first poem was published in the magazine *Seventeen* when she was just seventeen years old, though by that time she had been writing poetry for several years.

The young Audre attended Catholic grammar schools in Manhattan before entering Hunter High School, places where she often felt like an outsider. She went on to receive her BA degree from Hunter College in 1959 and a master's in library science from Columbia University in 1961.

Lorde supported herself as a student with jobs including medical clerk, factory worker, X-ray technician, social worker, and apprentice to a maker of stained-glass windows, experiences she details in her autobiographical writing. Following her graduation from Columbia, she was a librarian in New York public schools from 1961 through 1968. In 1962, Lorde married attorney Edward Ashley Rollins. They had two children, and divorced in 1970. Lorde became the head librarian at the Town School Library in New York City in 1966, and continued both her writing and her growing participation as an activist in the civil rights, antiwar, gay and lesbian, and feminist movements.

The year 1968 was an especially pivotal time for Lorde. She received a National Endowment for the Arts grant and became poet-in-residence at Tougaloo College in Mississippi. There she developed a real love for teaching and entered into relationships with other Black writers whom she had not experienced while participating in the Harlem Writers Guild, a writing group that made her feel as though she was tolerated rather than accepted as a writer. Her time at Tougaloo was also especially significant because it resulted in her meeting her longtime partner, Frances Clayton. Though she was there for only six weeks, her experiences in Mississippi were thus life-altering on many fronts. She realized that teaching and writing were vocations she not only wanted but needed to pursue; she shared an emotional connection with other writers and students for the first time, talking openly about poetry; she met someone who became her lifelong partner; and she received a copy of her first volume of poetry, *The First Cities*, published in 1968.

The First Cities, written on such themes as the nature of personal relationships and feelings, was the beginning of Lorde's very prolific published writing career. Her second volume of poetry, *Cables to Rage*, appeared in 1970 and focuses on such themes as love and parenting, the transcendence of birth, and the unfortunate reality of betrayal. Her third volume of poetry, *From a Land Where Other People Live* (1973), was nominated for a National Book Award. It signaled Lorde's growing exploration of oppression on a global scale even as it continued her investigation of the complexities of her identity; the nature of anger, love, and loneliness; and the importance of relationships.

Lorde's vision and voice as a poet continued to flourish in the wake of her first three publications. Her fourth volume of poetry, *New York Head Shop and Museum*, was released in 1974 and was followed by *Coal* in 1976, whose publication by Norton brought her a broader readership than she had previously experienced. Her most celebrated work, however, is likely her seventh volume of poetry, *The Black Unicorn* (1978), considered by many critics to be the literary masterpiece of her career as a writer. Its complex themes, surrounding motherhood, spirituality, pride, gender, and sexuality, emerge as she spans three centuries of the Black diaspora and seeks to reclaim African mythology. Her more recent poetry collections include *Chosen Poems, Old and New* (1982) and *Our Dead Behind Us* (1986). More than 300 of her poems have been brought together in *The Collected Poems of Audre Lorde* (1997), which offers its readers unparalleled access to her diverse body of poetry.

Though Lorde identified most with poetry as a writer, her presence in African American literature is certainly also marked by her prose, essays, speeches, and autobiographical writings. A frightening diagnosis of breast cancer led her to publish her first book-length prose collection, *The Cancer Journals*, in 1980. This moving and very personal text details her decision to undergo a mastectomy, her feelings surrounding (and refusal to wear) a prosthesis, her confrontation with death and her own mortality, the sustaining love of the women who surrounded her throughout her surgery and thereafter, and the power and rewards that can be found in what she terms "self-conscious living." It is a remarkable account of a woman openly confronting the silences surrounding an illness that affects millions of women across the globe, a woman who seeks to understand the implications of those silences more fully. As she puts it in the introduction to the text,

> I am a post-mastectomy woman who believes our feelings need voice in order to be recognized, respected, and of use. I do not wish my anger and pain and fear about cancer to fossilize into yet another silence, nor to rob me of whatever strength can lie at the core of this experience, openly acknowledged and examined. (7)

Lorde continued to write about issues surrounding cancer and her own battle with the illness in her 1988 collection *A Burst of Light*.

Lorde's prose writing continued with the publication of *Zami: A New Spelling of My Name* in 1982. Labeled a biomythography, this memoir draws from a combination of history, autobiography, poetry, and other creative elements to explore her childhood and upbringing, development as a writer, sexuality, and other pivotal moments and relationships in her life. Following the publication of *Zami*, many of Lorde's best-known essays and speeches were collected in *Sister Outsider* (1984). This collection reveals Lorde's unyielding exploration and examination of difference and the reactions that difference elicits, her belief that poetry is a necessity for women, her refusal to see herself apart from injustices that are experienced globally, and her ongoing investigations and theorizations of identity, sexuality, feminism, and oppression.

Lorde's accolades include two National Endowment for the Arts grants (1968 and 1981), two Creative Artists Public Service grants (1972 and 1976), a Broadside Poets Award (1975), an American Library Association Gay Caucus Book of the Year for *The Cancer Journals* (1981), a National Book Award for Prose (1989), a Borough of Manhattan President's Award for literary excellence (1987), and a Walt Whitman Citation of Merit as poet laureate of New York (1991). She was also cofounder, with Barbara Smith, of the Kitchen Table: Women of Color Press, and served as editor of the lesbian journal *Chrysalis*.

Lorde is likely best known, however, as a writer, speaker, and thinker who was deeply invested in the power and potential of words and who used her vision and talent in the service of creating a more just world. Her writing continues to be widely taught in college classrooms nationwide, especially those centered on the areas of gay and lesbian literature, Women's Studies, contemporary poetry, and studies of race. Indeed, as many of her avid readers are well aware, Lorde's words have continued to live on well after her death. (An edition of her collected and unpublished writing was published in 2009.) She was a writer who urged her readers to see themselves not only as agents in their own lives but also as social members who were connected to all others

and who had the power to foster or to work to eliminate social and political oppression. Her body of work continues to resound in those who share her commitment to and passion for justice and who also seek to acknowledge and better understand those experiences shrouded in silence.

Amanda Davis

See also: Feminism/Black Feminism; Lesbian Literature; Protest Literature.

Resources

Primary Sources: Audre Lorde: *Between Ourselves* (Point Reyes, CA: Eidolon Editions, 1976); *The Black Unicorn* (New York: Norton, 1978); *A Burst of Light: Essays* (Ithaca, NY: Firebrand, 1988); *Cables to Rage* (London: Paul Breman, 1970); *The Cancer Journals* (1980; repr. San Francisco: Aunt Lute, 1997); *Chosen Poems, Old and New* (New York: Norton, 1982); *Coal* (New York: Norton, 1976); *The Collected Poems of Audre Lorde* (New York: Norton, 1997); *The First Cities* (New York: Poets Press, 1968); *From a Land Where Other People Live* (Detroit: Broadside Press, 1973); *I Am your Sister: Black Women Organizing Across Sexualities* (New York: Kitchen Table—Women of Color Press, 1985); *I Am Your Sister: Collected and Unpublished Writings of Audre Lorde*, ed. Rudolph P. Byrd, Johnnetta B. Cole, and Beverly Guy-Sheftall (Oxford and New York: Oxford University Press, 2009); *The Marvelous Arithmetic of Distance: Poems 1987–1992* (New York: Norton, 1993); *Need: A Chorale for Black Woman Voices* (Latham, NY: Kitchen Table—Women of Color Press, 1990); *New York Head Shop and Museum* (Detroit: Broadside Press, 1974); *Our Dead Behind Us: Poems* (New York: Norton, 1986); *Sister Love: the letters of Audre Lorde and Pat Parker 1974–1989*, ed. Julie R. Enszer, (New York: A Midsummer Night's Press; Dover, FL: Sinister Wisdom Press, 2018); *Sister Outsider: Essays and Speeches* (Trumansburg, NY: Crossing Press, 1984); *Undersong:*

Chosen Poems Old and New (New York: Norton, 1992); *Uses of the Erotic: The Erotic as Power*, Out and Out Pamphlet no. 3 (New York: Out and Out Books, 1978); *Zami: A New Spelling of My Name* (Watertown, MA: Persephone Press, 1982).

Secondary Sources: Barbara Christian, *Black Feminist Criticism: Perspectives on Black Women Writers* (New York: Pergamon, 1985); Alexis DeVeaux, *Warrior Poet: A Biography of Audre Lorde* (New York: Norton, 2004); Gloria T. Hull, "Living on the Line: Audre Lorde and *Our Dead Behind Us*," in *Changing Our Own Words: Essays on Criticism, Theory, and Writing by Black Women*, ed. Cheryl A. Wall (New Brunswick, NJ: Rutgers University Press, 1989), 150–172; Robina Khalid, "Demilitarizing Disease: Ambivalent Warfare and Audre Lorde's *The Cancer Journals*," *African American Review* 42, no. 3/4 (Fall 2008), 697–714, 795; Emily Lordi, "Souls Intact: The Soul Performances of Audre Lorde, Aretha Franklin, and Nina Simone," *Women & Performance: a Journal of Feminist Theory* 26, no. 1 (January 2, 2016), 55–57; Suryia Nayak, *Race, Gender and the Activism of Black Feminist Theory: Working with Audre Lorde* (Hove, East Sussex: Routledge, 2015); Lester C. Olson, "Anger among Allies: Audre Lorde's 1981 Keynote Admonishing the National Women's Studies Association," *Quarterly Journal of Speech* 97, no. 3 (2011), 283–308; Claudia Tate, ed., *Black Women Writers at Work* (New York: Continuum, 1983).

Lyric Poetry

Considered the broadest category of poetry, a lyric is any relatively short poem that expresses the personal mood or perception of a single speaker, not necessarily the poet. (Originally the *lyric* poem was meant to be accompanied by a *lyre*, a stringed instrument.) Throughout its long history, African American literature has struggled creatively with such a categorization. Traditionally, lyric poetry (as opposed to dramatic or narrative/epic poetry) encompasses a wide variety of genres from the more common dramatic monologue, sonnet, villanelle, elegy, hymn, and ode to the aubade, haiku, and epithalamion (*see* Formal Verse). Due to the vernacular roots of African American literature, it might be argued that African American literature widens this category by including spirituals and gospel, work songs, blues poetry, and jazz poetics. With this emphasis on musicality in mind, much of the African American poetic tradition (particularly in the twentieth century) closely parallels the lyric's musical origins.

Still other African American poems further widen the lyric category by employing not a singular speaker ("I") but a communal speaker ("we"). Communal speakers appear in African American lyric poetry from Paul Laurence Dunbar's "We Wear the Mask" (1895) to Gwendolyn Brooks's "We Real Cool" (1960). Similarly, in many poems, Langston Hughes uses the pronoun "I" to stand for a group of people, as in "The Negro Speaks of Rivers," so the singular pronoun represents a collective persona in this case (Ostrom, 77–78). Moreover, in keeping with the signifying nature of African American literature, African American lyric poetry often invokes its own ancestry. Many African American poets refer explicitly to earlier African American historical figures, poets, or artists; this tradition appears in poems such as Robert Hayden's "A Letter from Phillis Wheatley" (1978), referring to one of the earliest known African American poets, and Jayne Cortez's "How Long Has Trane Been Gone" (1969), referring both to an early twentieth-century blues lyric and to the jazz musician John Coltrane. To gain a more varied sense of development and periodization in African

American poetry, readers might usefully consider the introductions to anthologies of African American poetry and literary criticism, such as those by James Weldon Johnson, Stephen Henderson, Michael S. Harper, and Anthony Walton.

Colonial and Antebellum Periods

Phillis Wheatley's *Poems on Various Subjects, Religious and Moral* (1773) was the first published volume of African American literature. Her collection includes hymns and odes dedicated to classical figures ("To Maecenas"). Some poems express admiration ("To S.M., a Young African Painter, on Seeing His Works"). Still other poems, dedicated to American figures, garnered the most contemporary recognition: "To His Excellency General Washington" and the elegy "On the Death of the Rev. Mr. George Whitefield." "On Being Brought from Africa to America" is a more personal meditation on slavery and the potential of Christian redemption. In subsequent critical debates the poem has been considered controversial for its heavy emphasis on Christian redemption of Wheatley's "sable race."

Recent interventions in African American literature have excavated other poets from this time period who often remain overlooked. These include George Moses Horton, Jupiter Hammon, Lucy Terry, and James Monroe Whitfield. Horton published three books of poetry: *The Hope of Liberty* (1829), *The Poetical Works of George M. Horton* (1845), and *Naked Genius* (1865). Like Wheatley's collection, Horton's collections contain very few references to slavery; the majority of these poems concern the more traditional lyric moods of grief and love as well as religion. However, some consider his slavery poems, such as "On Hearing of the Intention of a Gentleman to Purchase the Poet's Freedom" and "The Slave's Complaint," his best work. Hammon's "An Evening Thought" and "An Address to Miss Phillis Wheatly" rely on the psalmlike structure of early Methodist hymns. Terry's "Bars Fight" (ca. 1746, pub. 1855) is a ballad. The renown of Whitfield's collection *America and Other Poems* (1853) rests largely on the title poem, an ironic hymn to nationalism.

The Nineteenth Century

In the nineteenth century, African American poets gained a slightly broader audience and continued to work within traditional lyric forms. Frances Ellen Watkins Harper's prolific literary production spanned several decades and covered several genres, including novels, essays, and poetry. During the nineteenth century, she published at least eight collections of poetry; during the decade after emancipation alone, she published three collections of poetry. Among Harper's known surviving collections, she is best known for *Poems on Miscellaneous Subjects* (1854); by 1874, this collection had undergone twenty editions. With the notable exception of *Moses: A Story of the Nile* (1869), an epic written in free verse, Harper typically wrote in rhyming quatrains of varying meters. Many of her poems disputed slavery outright, making her one of the founders of protest thematics in African American literature. Her poem "Eliza Harris" (1853), a direct response to *Uncle Tom's Cabin*, earned her immediate recognition when *The Liberator* published it. In poems such as "The Slave Mother" (1854) and "Bury Me in a Free Land" (1864), Harper used keenly sentimental rhetoric and dramatic monologues in order to rally her audience to the abolitionist cause. Other poems, such as "Songs for the People" (1895) and "An Appeal to My Country Women" (1900), appeal to a wider American audience, specifying humanitarian reasons for common cause or sisterhood.

While Paul Laurence Dunbar also wrote in Standard English, using lyric forms such as the ode and the hymn, his reputation rested largely on his lyric dialect poetry such as "When Malindy Sings," and "A Negro Love Song." As a result of this reputation, detractors have critiqued his poetry for perpetuating the "happy Negro" stereotype initiated by Southern White writers, while other anthologists of American literature have simply ignored his contributions to American poetry by omitting his poetry altogether. Dunbar's defenders have answered these critiques by emphasizing the White appetite for dialect poetry and concurrent disdain for Negro-authored poetry in Standard English. They have also noted the nuanced irony of "We Wear the Mask" and Dunbar's incisive exploration of "why the caged bird sings" in "Sympathy." Dunbar published several major collections, including *Oak and Ivy* (1893), *Majors and Minors* (1895), and *Lyrics of Lowly Life* (1896), the title of which referred to Wordsworth's *Lyrical Ballads*.

Other poets of this period include Charlotte Forten Grimké, Angelina Weld Grimké, Alice Moore Dunbar-Nelson, Georgia Douglas Johnson, Benjamin Griffith Brawley, and William Stanley Braithwaite. A prominent literary critic, Braithwaite also published poetry, leaning toward traditional forms such as rhyming quatrains ("The Watchers") and the octave ("The House of Falling Leaves"). (*See* Narrative Poetry.)

New Negro Renaissance

The poetry of the New Negro Renaissance, also known as the Harlem Renaissance, reveals an upsurge in racial consciousness, a turn away from sentimental apology or self-pity, and an emphasis on ancestry and self-awareness. While African American poets continued to use lyric poetry, these forms were now often infused with unapologetic anger and purposeful irony. The most prominent example of this infusion is Claude McKay's collection *Harlem Shadows* (1922), generally thought to have inaugurated the Renaissance. McKay is particularly noted for using the sonnet as a form of protest. "If We Must Die" and "To The White Fiends" are two of McKay's famously militant sonnets. Countee Cullen's sonnet "Yet Do I Marvel" explores the ironic situation of the Black artist in a racist society. By contrast, Arna Bontemps's lyrics are known for their meditative, reflective qualities, often referring to reaping and sowing ("A Black Man Talks of Reaping") as a metaphor for the consequences of history.

Several poets of the Renaissance experimented with vernacular roots as well as "high poetic" forms. James Weldon Johnson's work exemplifies this combination. He wrote not only dialect poems ("Sence You Went Away,") but also the unofficial "Negro National Anthem" ("Lift Ev'ry Voice and Sing" [ca. 1900, pub. 1921]). His landmark anthology, *A Book of American Negro Poetry* (1922), includes his own poetry as well as an incisive introductory essay covering the aesthetics of Negro poetics. Jean Toomer's virtuoso novel *Cane* (1923) pays homage to Southern Negro culture and mourns the upheaval caused by the Great Migration. *Cane*'s modernist poetic experimentation includes not only prose and scripted dialogue but also prose poems ("Karintha") and lyric poems ("Evening Song," "Song of the Son"). In a similar vein, Countee Cullen's poem "Heritage" asks "What is Africa to me?"—Africa's significance to African Americans forcibly removed from Africa.

Realism, Modernism, Naturalism

Continuing in the vein of ancestral invocation, other poets focused specifically on exploring the vernacular tradition of spirituals, work songs, ballads, and blues. Though Langston Hughes's career was launched during the New Negro Renaissance, his career spans several decades and several literary periods. One of his signature poems, "The Negro Speaks of Rivers," meditates on the place of the Negro across centuries, continents, and civilizations. Like Hughes, Sterling A. Brown experimented with the vernacular, writing dialect and folk poems that problematized the humor and pathos commonly associated with dialect verse. Publishing, along with other criticism and anthologies, several collections of his own poetry, Brown is known for creating the hybrid "blues ballad." The similarly multitalented poet and professor Melvin B. Tolson incorporated the communal speaker and the stridency of protest poetry with the musical terms for classical symphonic movements (e.g., "Allegro Moderato") in his most anthologized poem, "Dark Symphony."

Drawing partly on the momentum gained from the Renaissance, a few poets continued to experiment with traditional and vernacular forms during and after World War II. In her collection *For My People* (1942), Margaret Abigail Walker used the folk ballad in poems such as "Molly Means" and "Poppa Chicken" as well as the sonnet. The collection's title poem, which won the Yale University Younger Poet's Award, is a Whitmanesque sermon-anthem to her Black audiences. Robert Hayden is known more for his historical poems, such as "Middle Passage" (considered a hybrid of the lyric and narrative). However, he also wrote ballads ("The Ballad of Nat Turner," "A Ballad of Remembrance") as well as introspective lyrics ("Those Winter Sundays," "A Plague of Starlings," "Ice Storm").

Though Gwendolyn Brooks won the Pulitzer Prize for her epic poem *Annie Allen* (1949), she also experimented with the elegy, sonnet, ballad, and lyric. In *A Street in Bronzeville* (1945), her sonnet sequence "Gay Chaps at the Bar" transforms the sonnet's traditional subject, love, into war (Pettis, 36). Throughout her long and distinguished career, Brooks signified on traditional poetic forms, yet also adapted the free verse stylings of the Black Aesthetic, or the Black Arts Movement.

The Black Arts Movement

Rather than depending on traditional lyric forms to be heard and accepted by a mainstream audience, as some of their poetic predecessors had, the poets of the Black Arts Movement celebrated innovative experimentation through free verse. They played with several elements, including spelling and phonetics, line breaks, and punctuation such as the slash to emphasize or create pauses. Yet several poets of the Black Arts Movement used and experimented with lyric forms as well. The title poem of Amiri Baraka's *Preface to a Twenty Volume Suicide Note* (1961) is a lyric of despair. Larry Neal's "For Our Women" (1968) celebrates the endurance and beauty of Black women. Etheridge Knight's poignant collection *Poems from Prison* (1968) includes lyric meditations on the effects of imprisonment and liberation on identity and ancestry. Nikki Giovanni's well-known lyrics of childhood, "Nikki-Rosa" (1968) and "Knoxville, Tennessee" (1968) appeared during this period. Haki R. Madhubuti (Don Lee)'s radically experimental poetics still retained the lyric's singular speaking voice in "a poem to complement other poems" (1969). Later, Black Arts performance poet Sonia Sanchez used the blues in *A Blues Book for Blue Black Magical Women* (1974), and love lyrics and haiku in her *Homegirls & Handgrenades* (1984). June Jordan's "Poem About My Rights" (1980) highlights her transnational political consciousness, reaching from France to South Africa. As the poem's speaker puts it, "I am the history of the rejection of who I am."

Lyric Poetry Since 1975

Lyric poets who have published since (roughly) 1975 have continued to work with traditional, vernacular, ancestral, and experimental strands from the earlier parts of the twentieth century. The multiracial poet Ai has published six collections of dramatic monologues, inhabiting the viewpoints of public figures such as Senator Joseph McCarthy, Robert Oppenheimer, and John F. Kennedy. Jayne Cortez's jazz poetics concern not only musicians ("How Long Has Trane Been Gone," "Jazz Fan Looks Back") but also her African roots ("Adupe"). Yusef Komunyakaa's extensive repertoire includes poems about his Vietnam military experience (*Dien Cai Dau* [1988]) as well as blues poems calling on past ancestry ("Trueblood Blues," referring to the character in *Invisible Man*, and "Elegy for Thelonious"). Harryette Mullen uses folk speech and quatrains in her collection *Muse & Drudge* (1995). Michael S. Harper's many accomplishments include blues elegies for jazz musicians, most notably in his collection *Dear John, Dear Coltrane* (1970) and "Last Affair: Bessie's Blues Song." Derek Walcott, winner of the 1992 Nobel Prize, writes lyrics across Caribbean, African, and African American traditions.

The lyrics of several contemporary Black female poets have involved and celebrated the Black female body. Many of Lucille Clifton's best-known lyrics celebrate the Black female body ("homage to my hips," "homage to my hair"); her later poems include elegies for historical figures ("powell march 1991," "4/30/92 for rodney king"). Colleen McElroy also explores issues related to the body in her spare, warmly ironic lyric poems. Audre Lorde was lesbian, Black, activist, feminist, poet, memoirist, and essayist, and throughout her career struggled with the pigeonholing that these labels created. Her lyric poetry ranges from protest litanies ("A Litany for Survival") and personal lyrics of motherhood ("Now That I Am Forever with Child") to metaphorical celebrations of Blackness ("Coal"). Rita Dove, the second African American to win the Pulitzer Prize, credits the Black Arts Movement for paving the way to her artistic freedom. Her collection *Mother Love* (1995) uses both Italian and Shakespearean forms of the sonnet but also transmutes these into another sonnet form altogether.

Though more known for their novels or memoirs, some writers have crossed genres into lyric poetry; Ishmael Reed's "Dualism," Sherley Anne Williams's "I Want Aretha to Set This to Music," and Maya Angelou's "Phenomenal Woman" and "Still I Rise" are prominent examples.

Finally, among the newer generation of African American poets, Elizabeth Alexander, Kevin Powell, Terrance Hayes, and Ras Baraka stand out as voices who expand on several strands of their African American poetic ancestry, including the lyric and the blues. Recent anthologies of new African American poetry are testament to the anthology's power to unearth new trends. *The Norton Anthology of African American*

Literature's inclusion of rap and hip-hop lyrics also points toward new directions in African American lyric poetry, and a further expansion of the definition of lyric poetry itself.

Tamiko Nimura

See also: Brooks, Gwendolyn; Cullen, Countee; Dove, Rita; Dunbar, Paul Laurence; Giovanni, Nikki; Hughes, Langston; Johnson, Georgia Douglas; Johnson, James Weldon; McKay, Claude; Rodgers, Carolyn Marie; Wheatley, Phillis.

Resources

Fahamisha Patricia Brown, *Performing the Word: African American Poetry as Vernacular Culture* (New Brunswick, NJ: Rutgers University Press, 1999); Mary-Jean Chan, "Towards a Poetics of Racial Trauma: Lyric Hybridity in Claudia Rankine's *Citizen*," *Journal of American Studies* 52, no. 1 (February 2018), 137–163; William W. Cook, "The Black Arts Poets," in *Columbia History of American Poetry*, ed. Jay Parini (New York: Columbia University Press, 1993), 674–706; Joanne V. Gabbin, "Poetry," in *The Oxford Companion to African American Literature*, ed. William Andrews, Frances Smith Foster, and Trudier Harris (New York: Oxford University Press, 1997); Joanne V. Gabbin, ed., *The Furious Flowering of African American Poetry* (Charlottesville: University Press of Virginia, 1999); Henry Louis Gates Jr., and Nellie Y. McKay, eds., *The Norton Anthology of African American Literature*, 2nd ed. (New York: Norton, 2004); Michael S. Harper and Anthony Walton, eds.: *Every Shut Eye Ain't Asleep: An Anthology of Poetry by African Americans Since 1945* (Boston: Little, Brown, 1994); "Introduction," in *The Vintage Book of African American Poetry: 200 Years of Vision, Struggle, Power, Beauty, and Triumph from 50 Outstanding Poets*, ed. Michael S. Harper and Anthony Walton (New York: Vintage, 2000), xxiii–xxxiii; Stephen E. Henderson, *Understanding the New Black Poetry: Black Speech and Black Music as Poetic References* (New York: Morrow, 1973); Carolivia Herron, "Early African American Poetry," in *Columbia History of American Poetry*, ed. Jay Parini (New York: Columbia University Press, 1993), 23–32; James Weldon Johnson, *The Book of American Negro Poetry* (New York: Harcourt, Brace, 1922); E. Ethelbert Miller, ed.: *Beyond the Frontier: African American Poetry for the 21st Century* (Baltimore: Black Classic Press, 2002); *In Search of Color Everywhere: A Collection of African-American Poetry* (New York: Stewart, Tabori, & Chang, 1994); Maria Muresan, "Dickinsonian Moments in African American Poetry: Unsettling the Map of the Lyric," *Women's Studies* 47, no. 3 (2018), 286; Aldon Nielsen, "'Purple Haze': Dunbar's Lyric Legacy," *African American Review* 41, no. 2 (Summer 2007), 283–288; Hans Ostrom, *A Langston Hughes Encyclopedia* (Westport, CT: Greenwood Press, 2002), esp. "Collective Persona," 77–78, and "Poetics," 306–308; Jay Parini, ed., *The Columbia History of American Poetry* (New York: Columbia University Press, 1993); Joyce Pettis, *African American Poets: Lives, Works, and Sources* (Westport, CT: Greenwood Press, 2002); Lauri Ramey, "The Theology of the Lyric Tradition in African American Spirituals," *Journal of the American Academy of Religion* 70, no. 2 (June 1, 2002), 347–363; Arnold Rampersad, "The Poetry of the Harlem Renaissance," in *Columbia History of American Poetry* (New York: Columbia University Press, 1993), 452–476.

M

Madhubuti, Haki R. (Don Luther Lee) (1942–)

Poet, essayist, professor, and publisher. Madhubuti started Third World Press (TWP) with the assistance of Carolyn M. Rodgers and Johari Amini on September 20, 1967. TWP was an influential publisher of literature during the Black Arts Movement. In 1969, Madhubuti and Safisha (who later became his wife) started the Institute of Positive Education/New Concept School, and, in 1998, the Betty Shabazz International Charter School. Madhubuti is the author of twenty-six books, Distinguished Professor at Chicago State University, and founder of the Gwendolyn Brooks Center for Black Literature and Creative Writing.

Madhubuti, whose original name was Don L. Lee, was born in Little Rock, Arkansas. He pursued undergraduate studies at several colleges in the Chicago, Illinois, area, and he also served in the U.S. Army from 1960 to 1963. He changed his name to Haki R. Madhubuti in the late 1960s. In 1984, he earned an MFA in writing from the University of Iowa. His stature in the Black Arts Movement is unsurpassed, and, since the 1960s, he has remained a prolific poet, essayist, and community activist.

Celebrating its thirty-seventh anniversary in 2004, TWP is the oldest and longest running Black publishing house in the United States. In 1967, in his small basement apartment near 63rd and Ada Streets on the South Side of Chicago, Madhubuti started TWP with a used mimeograph machine and $400 from a poetry reading.

TWP has supported the tenets of Black Power, a theme of 1960s activism and of Madhubuti's own poetry, from *Think Black* (1967) to *Tough Notes* (2002). In the 1960s, Madhubuti, refusing to compromise his artistry, struck out on his own, selling his work from coast to coast and establishing a substantial following without being published by major publishers.

As a poet, Madhubuti's first titles, *Think Black* and *Black Pride*, are representative of his whole corpus of writing. His poetry is original in its intensity, capturing the spirit and ethos of the 1960s. His entire body of poetry and nonfiction demonstrates the staying power of the Black Arts Movement. His early themes encouraged readers and listeners to destroy the word "n/Negro" and to adopt another racial classification. He was among the first writers to use the term "African American" in his work, as opposed to "Black" or "Negro." He is particularly adept at writing about Black maleness and how Black males should approach and appreciate Black women. In his poetry and essays, Madhubuti does not simply glorify Blacks. He also chides, plays the dozens with, signifies on, and rebukes what he considers negative behavior that hurts the collective community of African Americans.

Lita Hooper's biography of Madhubuti was published in 2007.

In 2009, Madhubuti published *Liberation Narratives: New and Collected Poems: 1966–2009,* and, in 2016, he published the nonfiction work, *Taking Bullets: Terrorism and Black Life in Twenty-first Century America Confronting White Nationalism,*

Supremacy, Privilege, Plutocracy and Oligarchy.

As a poet, a publisher, a professor, and a school founder, Madhubuti has embodied the values of the Black Arts Movement in a variety of ways.

Regina Jennings

See also: Black Arts Movement; Vernacular.

Resources

Lita Hooper, *Art of Work: the Art and Life of Haki R. Madhubuti* (Chicago: Third World Press, 2007); Regina Jennings: "Cheikh Anta Diop, Malcolm X, and Haki Madhubuti: Claiming and Containing Black Language and Institutions," *Journal of Black Studies* 33 (Fall 2002), 126–144; "The Malcolm X Vision in the Poetics of Haki Madhubuti: Issues of Meleness and Memory," unpublished manuscript; Haki R. Madhubuti: *Black Pride* (Chicago: Third World Press, 1968); *Claiming Earth: Race, Rage, Rape, Redemption: Blacks Seeking a Culture of Enlightened Empowerment* (Chicago: Third World Press, 1994); *Don't Cry, Scream* (Chicago: Third World Press, 1992); *Enemies: The Clash of Races* (Chicago: Third World Press, 1978); *Ground-Work: New and Selected Poems of Don L. Lee/Haki R. Madhubuti from 1966–1996* (Chicago: Third World Press, 1996); *Kwanzaa: A Progressive and Uplifting African American Holiday* (Chicago: Third World Press, 1985); *Liberation Narratives: New and Collected Poems: 1966–2009* (Chicago: Third World Press, 2009); *Run Toward Fear: New Poems and a Poet's Handbook* (Chicago: Third World Press, 2004); *Say That the River Turns: The Impact of Gwendolyn Brooks* (Chicago: Third World Press, 1987); *Taking Bullets: Terrorism and Black Life in Twenty-first Century America Confronting White Nationalism, Supremacy, Privilege, Plutocracy and Oligarchy* (Chicago: Third World Press, 1994); Telephone interview with Regina Jennings, February 2004; *Think Black* (Detroit: Broadside Press, 1967); Mary A. Mitchell, "Afrocentric Educators Practice What They Teach," *Chicago Sun Times*, September 14, 1997, p. 19; Patrick T. Reardon, "Poetic Justice: Success Hasn't Diminished Haki Madhubuti's Passion for the 'Struggle,'" *Chicago Tribune*, August 10, 2000, sec. 5.

Major, Clarence (1936–)

Novelist, poet, essayist, lexicographer, painter, and professor. Clarence Major is an important voice who established himself during the Black Arts Movement of the 1960s as an experimental writer and has created a prolific body of work since then. Born in Atlanta, Georgia, he moved to Chicago, Illinois, with his mother after his parents divorced, although he remained connected to the South through frequent visits to his father and relatives. He briefly attended the Art Institute of Chicago before joining the Air Force in 1955 and subsequently turning his primary artistic attentions to writing. In 1958, he founded his own journal, *Coercion*, which he published until 1961.

In 1969, Major edited an important anthology of poetry, *The New Black Poetry*, which brought together the work of writers developing a new Black aesthetic, such as Ishmael Reed, Nikki Giovanni, Sonia Sanchez, Don L. Lee (Haki R. Madhubuti), and LeRoi Jones (Amiri Baraka). Though the volume spoke of a new Black nationalist aesthetic, it drew freely from poems both more and less overt in their political content. The following year, Major published the first important collection of his own poems, *Swallow the Lake*, which drew from poems he had printed in two smaller Coercion Press books and from other poems he had written.

Despite his considerable reputation as a poet, it is as an experimental fiction writer that Major has had the most impact. In 1969,

Olympia Press, noted for supporting the work of Henry Miller and William S. Burroughs, brought out his first novel, *All-Night Visitors*. Unfortunately, the press cut roughly half the manuscript to emphasize the erotic content. As a result, the work was open to criticism of being a stereotypical portrayal of a Black man and a series of one-dimensional women. The larger themes regarding the main character, Eli, which get lost in a crush of images as he tries to comprehend the world around him, come through more clearly in the restored version (1998). Major's next novel, *NO* (1973), was a similarly fragmentary narrative of a young Black man; his third novel, *Reflex and Bone Structure* (1975), continued his experimentation with the fragmented narrative, but this time he comically played it against the form of a detective novel. However, the narrator assures the reader that he is extending reality, not simply describing it, and the novel ends with the narrator taking credit for the deaths of Cora and Dale, which the narrator concedes was no more than a device he himself set. *Emergency Exit* (1979) was Major's most experimental to date; the slender plot is about Allen Morris, a drug dealer who goes to visit his lover in Inlet, Connecticut. The novel carefully interrupts its narrative with such things as photographs, charts, some of Major's own paintings, dictionary definitions, and even, at one point, a page asking the reader, "how do you feel about it?"

Though Major continued writing in an experimental vein in *My Amputations* (1986), *Such Was the Season* (1987) marked a turn to more conventional narrative. A good deal of postmodern wit remains (one subplot involves a conspiracy to rig tomato prices), but at its core, this is a comic novel about one week in the life a Southern Black family matriarch, Annie Eliza, and her family. Similarly, though *Painted Turtle: Woman with Guitar* (1988) has an episodic construction, in contrast to his earlier works, this novel contains a more conventional narrative, though one still concerned with the nature of representation. Based on Major's extensive immersion in Zuni culture (as is his 1989 collection of poems, *Some Observations on a Stranger at Zuni in the Latter Part of the Century*), *Painted Turtle* tells the story of a Zuni woman who has been forced out of the tribe and now makes her living as a folksinger, singing in part about her Zuni background. Narrated by an American Indian who is trying to seduce Painted Turtle, the novel continues Major's reflections on the nature of narrative, while its focus away from the African American experience calls attention to the multicultural nature of his art.

This move toward more conventional but still impressionistic narrative continued eight years later in *Dirty Bird Blues* (1996), a blues novel about Manfred Banks, a blues musician in the 1950s who lives the life of a blues song. Likewise, though his 2003 novel, *One Flesh*, engages more plot threads than it ever cares to tie up, this story of an African American mixed-race artist and his love affair with a Chinese American poet returns Major to the concerns of multiculturalism and the problems of representation that he developed in his Zuni works.

Clarence Major has remained an important editorial presence in African American literature. In the 1990s, he published two anthologies, *Calling the Wind* (1993) and *The Garden Thrives* (1996), collections of, respectively, African American short fiction and African American poetry from the twentieth century. He also updated his earlier *Dictionary of Afro-American Slang* (1970) and expanded it, publishing it as

Juba to Jive: A Dictionary of African American Slang (1994). Published at a time when Ebonics was a controversial educational issue, *Juba to Jive* was a conscious attempt to document the vitality of African American English. Additionally, Major has maintained an active career as a teacher in higher education. He has held positions at the State University of New York at Binghamton, Temple University, Howard University, and Sarah Lawrence University, and currently is Professor Emeritus of English at the University of California at Davis.

In 1999, Major published an important collection of poems, *Configurations: New and Selected Poem, 1958–1998*, which culled poems from eight previous collections and added quite a few new ones. The poems concern painting, racism, sex, and travel, among an astonishing array of other topics. This collection allows the reader to chart Major's development as a writer but also to see how some issues remain constant concerns for him. The poem "On the Nature of Perspective," for instance, begins, "Sometimes there is a point / Without a point of view," which neatly summarizes the concern with subverting single-perspective narrative in his novel.

In 2016, Major published *Chicago Heat and Other Stories*, in 2018, he published *My Studio: Poems*, and, in 2019, he published *The Paintings and Drawings of Clarence Major*. Keith Eldon Byerman's biography of Major appeared in 2012.

Major's paintings have been exhibited at numerous galleries throughout the United States. In 2015, the Congressional Black Caucus gave Major the Lifetime Achievement Award in the Fine Arts.

Thomas J. Cassidy

See also: Postmodernism; Vernacular.

Resources

Primary Sources: Clarence Major: *Afterthoughts: Essays and Criticism* (Minneapolis, MN: Coffee House Press, 2000); *All-Night Visitors* (1969; repr. Boston: Northeastern University Press, 1998); *Chicago Heat and Other Stories* (Brattleboro, VT: Green Writers Press, 2016); *Configurations: New & Selected Poems 1958–1998* (Port Angeles, WA: Copper Canyon Press, 1998); *Dirty Bird Blues* (San Francisco: Mercury House, 1996); *Emergency Exit* (New York: Fiction Collective, 1979); *From Now On: New and Selected Poems, 1970–2015* (Athens: University of Georgia Press, 2015); *Fun and Games: Short Fictions* (Duluth, MN: Holy Cow, 1990); *Juba to Jive: A Dictionary of African-American Slang* (New York: Penguin, 1994); *My Amputations* (New York: Fiction Collective, 1986); *My Studio: Poems* (Baton Rouge: Louisiana State University Press, 2018); *NO* (New York: Emerson Hall, 1973); *Painted Turtle: Woman with Guitar* (Los Angeles: Sun and Moon, 1988); *The Paintings and Drawings of Clarence Major* (Jackson: University Press of Mississippi, 2019); *Reflex and Bone Structure* (New York: Fiction Collective, 1975); *Some Observations of a Stranger at Zuni in the Latter Part of the Century* (Los Angeles: Sun and Moon, 1989); *Such Was the Season* (San Francisco: Mercury House, 1987); *Trips: A Memoir* (Minneapolis, MN: Coffee House Press, 2001).

Secondary Sources: *African American Review* (spec. iss.) 28 (Spring 1994); Bernard W. Bell, *Clarence Major and His Art: Portraits of an African American Postmodernist* (Chapel Hill: University of North Carolina Press, 2001); Nancy Bunge, ed., *Conversations with Clarence Major* (Jackson: University Press of Mississippi, 2002); Keith Byerman, *Fingering the Jagged Grain: Tradition and Form in Recent Black Fictions* (Athens: University of Georgia Press, 1985); Keith Eldon Byerman, *The Art and Life of Clarence Major* (Athens: University of Georgia Press, 2012); Linda Furgerson Selzer, "Walt Whitman, Clarence Major, and Changing Thresholds of American Wonder," *Walt Whitman*

Quarterly Review 29, no. 4 (Spring, 2012), 159(12); Joe Weixlmann, "A Checklist of Books by Clarence Major," *African American Review* 28, no. 1 (Spring 1994), 139.

Malcolm X (1925–1965)

Political activist, religious leader, speech-writer, speaker, and memoirist. Born Malcolm Little in Omaha, Nebraska, Malcolm X was one of the most influential leaders of his time. His writings, speeches, and thinking continue to exert a powerful influence on Black politics today. He was one of eight children born to Baptist minister Earl Little and homemaker Louise Little. Because of his ardent support for Black Nationalist leader Marcus Garvey, Earl Little received death threats from White supremacist groups. These threats forced the Little family to relocate twice before Malcolm X's fourth birthday. In 1929, the Little home in Lansing, Michigan, burned to the ground. Two years later, the elder Little was found dead on the Lansing trolley tracks under suspicious circumstances. Although the police ruled both incidents as accidents, the Little family believed the White suprema-cist group The Black Legion was responsi-ble. This was only the beginning of the Little family's tragedies, however. As a result of the many stresses placed upon her by the loss of her husband and being the sole caretaker of a large brood of children, Malcolm X's mother had a mental collapse. She subsequently went into a mental institu-tion. The children were then parceled out to foster homes and orphanages, some of them ending up in White homes.

In spite of having a difficult early life, Little was an attractive, precocious child and an excellent student, working hard and participating in many school activities. He was also eager to please and inclined to overlook racist slights. However, a turning point came when, in speaking to a teacher, he expressed a desire to become a lawyer. The teacher, a White man, made a cruelly racist comment about how that goal was unrealistic. This comment caused Malcolm X to lose interest in his studies, and he sub-sequently dropped out of school. He moved around the Northeast and got involved in petty crimes. In 1946, he was arrested and convicted on burglary charges and was sen-tenced to ten years in prison.

While in prison, due to his brother's influence, Malcolm converted to the Black Muslim faith and began reading the Koran. A highly controversial religious group, the Nation of Islam professed a profound suspi-cion of Whites, tending to believe that the White man's world and Christian faith were inherently evil. They also instilled racial pride in Blacks, arguing for the tenets of Black Nationalism. It was at this time that Malcolm X changed his last name to "X," a common practice among Nation of Islam converts because they believed their family names to have originated with White slave owners.

While in prison, Malcolm X showed many leadership qualities, reading classics in the prison library and leading a prison debating team. After serving seven years of his ten-year sentence, he was paroled. He went to the headquarters of the Nation of Islam in Chicago, Illinois; met the group's leader, Elijah Muhammad; and became his devoted follower.

Brilliant, charismatic, and a spectacular, inflammatory orator, Malcolm X quickly rose through the ranks. He was soon appointed a minister and national spokes-man for the Nation of Islam. He helped establish new mosques in Detroit,

Michigan, and Harlem, New York, and used many forms of media to get the Nation of Islam's message across. Because of his drive and conviction, membership in the Nation of Islam swelled dramatically in the years 1952 to 1963. It was not long before his fame eclipsed that of his mentor, Elijah Mohammed.

Malcolm X was strongly opposed to Martin Luther King's belief in nonviolent action and peaceful protest. Instead, he believed violence was an option in cases involving self-protection. Furthermore, he soundly renounced both integration and notions of racial equality, calling instead for a separation of Blacks from mainstream society and emphasizing Black independence and self-sufficiency. In spite of his charisma and growing numbers of followers, his approach was rejected by many civil rights leaders. Furthermore, his bitter criticism of civil rights leaders who advocated integration alienated many of them, and some of them considered him to be a fanatic.

After remaining celibate as a single man according to the strict doctrines of Islam, Malcolm X married Betty Shabazz in 1958. In 1961, he founded *Muhammad Speaks*, the official publication of the Nation of Islam movement. Then the tensions between Malcolm X and Elijah Muhammad began to heighten, due to the former's enormous popularity and the revelation that Elijah Muhammad had been having affairs with numerous women in his organization and fathering children by some of them. This was an especially bitter blow to Malcolm X, who lived strictly according to the Muslim faith. He began to show more and more signs of independence from the Nation of Islam, clearly preferring, for example, active political engagement, although doing so was contrary to Elijah Muhammad's teachings. When Elijah Muhammad publicly

silenced Malcolm X after John F. Kennedy's assassination for saying that the president's "chickens had come home to roost," Malcolm X became even more alienated from Elijah Mohammed. Furthermore, he got wind of rumors that his spiritual mentor had been plotting to have him assassinated. Although it was impossible to know whether these rumors were true, Malcolm X decided to leave the Nation of Islam and begin his own sect. He also began employing bodyguards around the clock because he was receiving numerous death threats, just as his father had.

In 1964, Malcolm X founded the Moslem Mosque, Inc. He also made a life-transforming trip to Mecca at that time, which caused him to modify his views on the innate evil of Whites. As a result, he began espousing a doctrine of the brotherhood of man. In October of that year, he also reaffirmed his conversion to orthodox Islam. The death threats continued against him, however. His home was firebombed on February 14, 1965; and on February 21, 1965, Malcolm X, just thirty-nine years old, was assassinated at a speaking engagement at the Audubon Ballroom in New York City. The killers shot him fifteen times at close range. After a funeral with hundreds in attendance, he was buried in Ferncliff Cemetery in Hartsdale, New York. In March 1966, his three assassins, all members of the Nation of Islam, were convicted of first-degree murder.

Prior to his death, Malcolm X had collaborated with Alex Haley on his life story, *The Autobiography of Malcolm X* (1965). The memoir, based primarily on interviews Haley had done with Malcolm X, is now recognized as a classic of African American autobiography. It was widely distributed after his death and became a battle cry for civil rights for many Black youth. Given

Malcolm X's early loss of his parents, his poverty-stricken childhood, the enormous obstacles he overcame, and his radical change from hoodlum to religious and ideological leader, the book speaks to all Americans, regardless of race, because it depicts his growing awareness of the world around him and his need for self-respect and action. Largely because of renewed interest in this autobiography and because of Spike Lee's 1992 film *Malcolm X*, Malcolm X is now viewed as a man who stood on the principles of Black self-help, racial pride, and world brotherhood, instead of as a hate-filled fanatic. *The Autobiography of Malcolm X* is still widely read today, often taught in America's public schools, colleges, and universities. Manning Marable published his biography of Malcolm X in 2011: *Malcolm X: A Life of Reinvention*.

Stephanie Gordon

See also: Autobiography; Black Arts Movement; King, Martin Luther, Jr.; Protest Literature.

Resources

Roger Barr, *Malcolm X* (San Diego: Lucent, 1994); George Breitman, ed., *By Any Means Necessary: Speeches, Interview, and a Letter, by Malcolm X* (New York: Pathfinder Press, 1970); John Henrik Clarke, *Malcolm X: The Man and His Times* (Trenton, NJ: Africa World Press, 1990); Lisa M. Corrigan, "50 Years Later: Commemorating the Life and Death of Malcolm X," *Howard Journal of Communications* 28, no. 2 (April 3, 2017), 144–159; Louis A. DeCaro Jr., *On the Side of My People: A Religious Life of Malcolm X* (New York: New York University Press, 1996); Michael Eric Dyson, *Making Malcolm: The Myth and Meaning of Malcolm X* (New York: Oxford University Press, 1995); Michael Friedly, *Malcolm X: The Assassination* (New York: Ballantine, 1995); Peter Goldman, *The Death and Life of Malcolm X* (New York: Harper & Row, 1973); Malcolm X and Alex Haley, *The Autobiography of Malcolm X* (New York: Grove Press, 1965); Manning Marable, *Malcolm X: A Life of Reinvention* (New York: Viking, 2011); Bruce Perry, *Malcolm* (Barrytown, NY: Station Hill, 1991); William W. Sales Jr., *From Civil Rights to Black Liberation: Malcolm X and the Organization of Afro-American Unity* (Boston: South End, 1994); William Strickland, *Malcolm X: Make It Plain* (New York: Viking, 1994); Stephen Tuck, "Malcolm X's Visit to Oxford University: U.S. Civil Rights, Black Britain, and the Special Relationship on Race," *The American Historical Review* 118, no. 1 (February 2013), 76; Jed B. Tucker, "Malcolm X, the Prison Years: The Relentless Pursuit of Formal Education," *Journal of African American History* 102, no. 2 (April 1, 2017), 184–212; Eugene Victor Wolfenstein, *The Victims of Democracy: Malcolm X and the Black Revolution* (New York: Guilford, 1993).

McKay, Claude (1889–1948)

Poet, novelist, critic, and journalist. Throughout his life, Claude McKay was a man of many identities, some of them conflicting. Born to relatively well-off peasant parents in the small Jamaican village of Nairne Castle, he became a leading intellectual and writer, a world traveler, a Communist, and eventually a Catholic. While McKay has been criticized, both during his lifetime and after his death, for ideological inconsistency and opportunism, he is widely acknowledged to have been one of the foremost figures of the Harlem Renaissance as well as a touchstone figure for the West Indian Négritude movement.

McKay was educated according to the conventional British model. He read British literature in school, and his father complemented this education by teaching him about the Ashanti, an African people, some of whom later settled in Jamaica. In 1911, McKay moved from his small village to the city of Kingston, where he encountered a larger White population and more racism. For a short time, he took a job as a policeman, enforcing White colonial rule; he gave this up after coming to believe that he was serving as a tool of oppression against his fellow Blacks and natives.

McKay's first volumes of poetry were published while he was still a young man. In 1912, with the assistance of his friend and patron, the White English folklorist Walter Jekyll, McKay published *Songs from Jamaica* and *Constab Ballads*. The poems in these volumes were written in Jamaican dialect, which Jekyll encouraged McKay to develop as a literary voice. *Songs from Jamaica* shows an early sign of McKay's lifelong devotion to a rural, idyllic lifestyle, while *Constab Ballads* contrasts this peaceful, egalitarian life with the harsh, racist world he encountered in Kingston.

After the publication of his two volumes of poetry, McKay decided to study agriculture in the United States, at the Tuskegee Institute in Alabama. He later transferred to Kansas State College, then abandoned his studies completely in favor of a return to writing and a move to New York City. Harlem, New York, was fast becoming a thriving center of African American culture, and while McKay lived outside of its geographical perimeter, he was a key figure in the "New Negro" movement and the Harlem Renaissance. He took a position as editor of the radical Communist journal *The Liberator* and continued writing his own poetry. In 1919, *The Liberator* published McKay's poem "If We Must Die," which protested violence by White mobs against Black workers in major cities across the United States. The poem and the rallying cry it engendered propelled McKay to literary celebrity, alongside such writers as Langston Hughes, Countee Cullen, and Zora Neale Hurston.

Later, in 1919, McKay traveled to England, where he worked on Sylvia Pankhurst's Communist newspaper, *The Workers' Dreadnought*. He continued to publish his poetry in magazines, and in 1920 published another book of poems, *Spring in New Hampshire and Other Poems*. He returned to New York in 1921, after Pankhurst was jailed for her publication, and the next year published an expansion of *Spring*, retitled *Harlem Shadows*. His work with *The Liberator* resumed, and he published both political journalism and protest poems about the conditions of African American life in the United States.

Spring in New Hampshire and *Harlem Shadows* secured McKay's position as a major writer of the Harlem Renaissance, but did not halt his involvement in politics. In 1922, he traveled to the Soviet Union to attend the Fourth Congress of the Third International as a special delegate–observer. McKay's commitment to communism was already waning at this point; for years he had criticized American and European Communists for their failure to address race politics, and his experience in Moscow confirmed his belief that formal communism would not make race a high priority. He stayed in the Soviet Union for several months as a special guest of the government, traveling, speaking, and writing for Soviet publications but felt that his contributions were not taken seriously enough. He left the country in 1923, and later that year published the works he had written during this period in *The Negroes in America*.

Following his departure from the Soviet Union, McKay began a long period of international exile, during which he traveled in

Europe and Africa. He also turned to writing fiction, which enabled him to shed some of the constrained tone that his poetry had taken. His first novel, *Home to Harlem*, was published in 1928. It concerned the lives of working-class migrant Blacks in Harlem and emphasized a theme that McKay struck repeatedly in many of his writings: the inherent health, vitality, and dignity of Black people, contrasted with the enfeeblement of Whites corrupted by Western European and American culture. *Home to Harlem* was criticized by some Black readers for its failure to present socially stable, conventionally admirable Black characters, but it was a best seller and was praised by many reviewers, including Langston Hughes.

McKay's second novel, *Banjo: A Story Without a Plot* was published in 1929, and set in Marseilles, France. The main characters are Black immigrants from the United States and the West Indies, who live on the margins of society and show both a primal zeal for life and a keen awareness of the social injustices they face. The novel was open to criticisms of stereotyping, but McKay's defenders saw it as continuing to develop an argument he had always favored; namely, that Blacks enjoy superior strength, humor, and fortitude because of their closeness to the natural world, while Whites have sacrificed these qualities in the drive for industrialization and urbanization.

Banjo was followed in 1932 by *Gingertown*, a collection of short stories set in both Harlem and Jamaica. McKay's final work, and the one in which he is deemed to have achieved his fullest creative powers, is the novel *Banana Bottom*, published in 1933. Set in Jamaica during the period of McKay's childhood, it concerns a young Jamaican woman who is raised partly in England, and who then returns to Jamaica as an adult. The rural, pastoral life she rediscovers in Jamaica is presented as vastly preferable to the stuffy, misguided morality of England.

In the twenty-first century, the unpublished manuscript of a novel by McKay was rediscovered: *Amiable With Big Teeth*, published in 2017. The book centers on efforts by African American artists and leaders in Harlem to cultivate support for Ethiopia in the 1930s, after Italy had invaded that country. The novel also satirizes politics. It is considered a significant addition to Harlem Renaissance literature.

In 1944, suffering from ill health and poverty, McKay was baptized into the Roman Catholic Church in Chicago, Illinois. He had been an agnostic his entire life and, despite an early marriage, was openly bisexual; his conversion was one more surprise in a life of contradictions. McKay may have tired of this tumult; in the final year of his life, he wrote and published *My Green Hills of Jamaica* (1979), a memoir longing for the peaceful, uncomplicated country of his youth.

Karen Munro

See also: Harlem Renaissance; Lyric Poetry.

Resources

Primary Sources: Claude McKay: *Amiable with Big Teeth*, ed. Jean-Christophe Cloutier and Brent Hayes Edwards (New York: Penguin, 2017); *Banana Bottom* (New York: Harper & Bros., 1933); *Banjo: A Story Without a Plot* (New York: Harper & Bros., 1929); *Complete Poems*, ed. William J. Maxwell (Urbana: University of Illinois Press, 2004); *Gingertown* (New York: Harper & Bros., 1932); *Home to Harlem* (New York: Harper & Bros., 1928); *A Long Way from Home* (1937; repr. New York: Harcourt Brace Jovanovich, 1970); *Trial by Lynching: Stories About Negro Life in North America*, trans. Robert Winter, ed. A. L. McLeod (Mysore, India: Centre for Commonwealth Literature and Research, University of Mysore, 1977).

Secondary Sources: Wayne F. Cooper, "Claude McKay, 1890–1948," in *African American Writers*, ed. Valerie Smith, Lea Baechler, and A. Walton Litz (New York: Collier, 1993); Smita Das, "Subjecting Pleasure: Claude McKay's Narratives of Transracial Desire," *Journal of Black Studies* 44, no. 7 (October 2013), 706–724; David Goldweber, "Home at Last," *Commonweal* 126, no. 15 (1999), 11–13; Heather Hathaway, *Caribbean Waves: Relocating Claude McKay and Paule Marshall* (Bloomington: Indiana University Press, 1999); Winston James: "Becoming the People's Poet: Claude McKay's Jamaican Years, 1889–1912," *Small Axe* 13 (2003), 17–45; "New Light on Claude McKay: A Controversy, a Document, and a Resolution," *Black Renaissance* 2, no. 2 (1999), 98–106; Wolfgang Karrer, "Black Modernism: The Early Poetry of Jean Toomer and Claude McKay," in *Jean Toomer and the Harlem Renaissance*, ed. Geneviève Fabre and Michel Feith (New Brunswick, NJ: Rutgers University Press, 2001); Sarala Krishnamurthy, "Claude McKay," in *African American Authors, 1745–1945*, ed. Emmanuel S. Nelson (Westport, CT: Greenwood Press, 2000); Diane Masiello, "McKay, Claude," in *African-American Writers: A Dictionary*, ed. Shari Dorantes Hatch and Michael R. Strickland (Santa Barbara, CA: ABC-CLIO, 2000); Eric H. Newman, "Ephemeral Utopias: Queer Cruising, Literary Form, and Diasporic Imagination in Claude McKay's *Home to Harlem* and *Banjo*," *Callaloo* 38, no. 1 (Winter 2015); A. B. Christa Schwarz, "Claude McKay: 'Enfant Terrible' of the Negro Renaissance," in her *Gay Voices of the Harlem Renaissance* (Bloomington: Indiana University Press, 2003), 88–119; Tyrone Tillery, *Claude McKay: A Black Poet's Struggle for Identity* (Amherst: University of Massachusetts Press, 1992).

Modernism (ca. 1890–1940)

Artistic and literary movement. This loosely defined movement of the late nineteenth to middle twentieth centuries understood itself as a break with tradition that prized the "new." Modernism can be discussed in terms of what it reacted against socially—the rise of industry and mass production, commodification, the loss of tradition, secularity—or in terms of what it celebrated aesthetically—abstraction, obscurity, fragments, difficulty, experimentation, the unique, genius. The figures usually associated with Modernism were Europeans and Americans. That African American writers of the period have been excluded from discussions of Modernism owes more to scholarly parochialism than to a lack of substantive aesthetic affiliations between Black and White artists in the Modernist period.

To the extent that Modernism's diverse aesthetic strains can be reduced to a single defining practice, Ezra Pound's famous dictum "Make it new" serves as well as any. Since Modernism's most prominent writers were Europeans and Americans in conversation with European traditions, Black writers and critics initially found little to value in its promotion of works that were difficult, highly learned, experimental, and abstract. Many White Modernists explored and lamented what they considered the decay of Western civilization—depicting "the modern" as fragmentary, alienating, urban, and materialistic—and offered the purities of art for art's sake (*l'art pour l'art*) as a remedy for a civilization that had reduced people to machinelike consumers and severed their ties with tradition, offering them only advertisements, mass-produced goods, and world war in return. The "Lost Generation" (a term attributed to Gertrude Stein), as the White American Modernists were known, sought to find themselves in art.

Though scholars have more often than not considered African American literature of the period *in contrast* to Modernism, they have found many connections between African American visuals arts and Modernism. Modernist abstraction's most prominent advocate in the visual arts, Clement Greenberg, argued that painting was the abstract medium par excellence, which may in part explain the apparently greater interaction of Modernist ideas and forms with African American cultural production—in the reduction of the human form to the silhouette, for example, in the work of Aaron Douglas, who was part of the Harlem Renaissance. The Modernist vogue for the "primitive"—a term of condescension—led many notable European painters and sculptors to draw on African or pseudo-African forms, lending these a kind of cultural legitimacy that Black artists were able to re-appropriate as "folk" art forms. The faith that art offered a kind of secular salvation and an interest in folk, or untutored, art forms were significant points of commonality between White Modernists and those African American artists associated with the Harlem Renaissance: both groups believed in the salvific power of art, and both looked for inspiration to folk art, the supposedly greater authenticity of which distinguished it from the culture of mass production. Still, by paying little or no attention to Black artists of the period, the majority of Modernist critics have lent credence to the view that Modernism had nothing to do with African Americans.

The first work of African American literature widely understood to exhibit Modernist sensibilities is Jean Toomer's *Cane* (1923), which catapulted Toomer, briefly, to the forefront of Black letters. Defying generic classification, *Cane* consists of poetry, short stories, and one dramatic piece that are unified through common themes, such as the rootedness of Black folk life in the rural South; the Black migration to

Northern cities such as Washington, DC, and Chicago, Illinois; and the rise of a Black middle class alienated from its rural Southern roots. The loss of tradition and religion as guiding lights animates much Modernist work, as it does *Cane*, but Toomer soon sought a remedy to this loss not in art but in the mysticism of the Russian George Gurdjieff, with whom the Modernist writer Katherine Mansfield was also associated. Toomer also rejected the notion that he was a "Negro" artist, insisting instead that he was racially "American." Neither Toomer's later mysticism nor his refusal to identify himself as Negro endeared him to critics. His personal involvement in Black letters was thus short-lived, but *Cane*'s influence on a generation of African American writers was immediate and profound.

Inspired by the publication of *Cane*, the Harlem Renaissance's inventor was, in a sense, the philosopher Alain Locke, who edited the groundbreaking anthology *The New Negro* (1925). In his foreword to that volume, Locke urged that "the New Negro must be seen in the perspective of a New World, and especially of a New America" (xxv). In his focus on the "new" and his faith in artists as a redeeming avant-garde, Locke exemplified major Modernist values. He highlighted the value he placed on the arts by foregrounding the work of creative writers and cultural commentators in the book's first and longer section, which was followed by a section of sociological works. "In art and letters, instead of being wholly caricatured," Locke wrote, the New Negro "is being seriously portrayed and painted" (9). Locke has since been criticized by some for his allegedly naïve faith in art's ability to transform society, but he was joined in this faith by many of the foremost thinkers of his day.

Present, too, in Locke's formulations is the value of folk culture. In introducing *The*

New Negro, Locke wrote that "in the very heart of the folk-spirit are the essential forces" (xxv). Locke's validation of Black folk culture may at first glance seem surprising in so highly cultured and Europeanized a figure. On the contrary, though, folk forms constitute African America's most important and, indeed, quintessentially Modernist contribution to the cultural productions of the first half of the twentieth century. One need think only of the centrality of jazz—the originators of which were unschooled in the traditional sense—to what F. Scott Fitzgerald would label the Jazz Age, the 1920s, to begin to appreciate how integral African American folk culture was to the transatlantic movement we now call Modernism. As Ralph Ellison so aptly remarked, jazz is by definition both derivative from a folk tradition and dramatically new with each performance. Its artists remain for the most part local heroes, and it "finds its very life in an endless improvisation upon traditional materials" (*Shadow*, 234). Only recently have critics seriously begun to ask why "the Jazz Age" conjures images of White expatriate artists in Paris or Berlin but not of African American artists in Harlem, New York, or Kansas City, Missouri. Jazz and the other folk forms associated with Africans and African Americans were romantically misunderstood by many White Modernists to be atavistic. For Euro-Americans disillusioned with modernity's sordid commercialization and cold mass production, the folk or "primitive" forms of Africa and African America offered what they, heirs of Jean-Jacques Rousseau, understood as noble authenticity and warm sensuousness. Thus, primitivism constitutes a major strain of Modernism. As such, it acted as a double-edged sword for those African American artists who worked under its aegis. On one hand, thanks to their association with the "primitivist" works of

august European visual artists such as Man Ray and Pablo Picasso, "primitive" or folk forms were granted legitimacy as high art. On the other hand, such forms had the potential to consign African Americans to a lower stratum of humanity and facilitated Whites' condescension toward Black creativity.

Today, the notions of African primitivity expressed in such works of Euro-American Modernism as Sigmund Freud's treatise on theoretical psychology, *Totem and Taboo* (1918), and Eugene O'Neill's play *The Emperor Jones* (1921) are likely to strike readers as decidedly antique, even though they were part and parcel of the same trends that produced the Cubist cornerstone of Modernism, Picasso's *Demoiselles d'Avignon* (1907), as well as African American works such as Aaron Douglas's elegant illustrations for *The New Negro*; Richmond Barthé's astonishing sculpture *Feral Benga* (1935); and Zora Neale Hurston's detailed ethnography of Haiti, *Tell My Horse* (1938). Also, composer and orchestra leader Duke Ellington and composer James P. Johnson are now recognized as having contributed significantly to fusions of jazz and other forms of Modern music, as critic John Howland, among others, has discussed in *Ellington Uptown: Duke Ellington, James P. Johnson, and the Birth of Concert Jazz* (2009).

In fact, the paintings of William H. Johnson and Jacob Lawrence—arguably the most significant African American visual art of the period—clearly draw on one variety of "folk" style, the faux-naïf, or "false naïve," so called because its practitioner is in fact an educated painter. Johnson spent much of the Harlem Renaissance abroad, studying from 1926 to 1929 in Paris, France. When he returned to Harlem, he encountered the work of Lawrence and developed, in Richard J. Powell's words, his "own distillation of

European Post-Impressionism and African American folk culture" (Hayward Gallery, 92). His faux-naïf style is simple and apparently untutored, used to depict modern, urban scenes. Thus, while the style is folk, the Harlem depicted is one of rich and confusing urban immixture. As Paul Gilroy writes: "The city's growth created new Harlemites not only from the West Indies but from the South and other rural areas. That rich and volatile mixture yielded no pure, seamless, or spontaneous articulation of black America's world-historic, national spirit" (Hayward Gallery, 107). Johnson's work attempts to extract aesthetic order from Harlem's discontinuities. The faux-naïf style, in particular, offered Johnson a strategy for doing so, since it was not only amenable to depicting the lives of rural people newly urbanized but was also available as a respected, modern, European aesthetic.

It was not until the arrival of Ralph Ellison that Black letters would find its greatest advocate and practitioner of Modernist values. In the essays collected in *Shadow and Act* (1964), Ellison claimed all of European literature for the African American writer, noting that whereas artists cannot choose their biological heritage, they can and do choose their artistic heritage. His 1952 novel *Invisible Man* exemplified Ellison's claims. Drawing at once on the most "advanced" Modernist themes, such as alienation, and on traditional folk material, the novel displays a dazzling, encyclopedic knowledge of Western culture, not to mention a formal elegance of language and plot that few other novels can match. Ellison's judgment of Ernest Hemingway, however, illustrates his critical stance toward Modernism. Though Hemingway exerted a strong influence on Ellison, Ellison argued that Hemingway's work was so emotionally and formally detached that it "conditions

the reader to accept the less worthy values of society" (*Shadow*, 40). Ellison demanded that literature achieve exacting formal standards but also that it assume ethical responsibility. It was Ellison's view that too much Modernist literature abdicated its social responsibility in favor of an amoral formal experimentation. For Ellison, there was no contradiction in asserting "that the work of art is important in itself, that it is a social action in itself" (137).

Douglas Steward

See also: Harlem Renaissance; Hayden, Robert; Hughes, Langston; Toomer, Jean; Wright, Richard.

Resources

Houston Baker, *Turning South Again: Rethinking Modernism/Re-reading Booker T.* (Durham, NC: Duke University Press, 2001); Ralph Ellison: *Invisible Man* (New York: Random House, 1952); *Shadow and Act* (New York: Random House, 1964); Hayward Gallery, *Rhapsodies in Black: Art of the Harlem Renaissance* (Berkeley: University of California Press, 1997); Paul Gilroy, *The Black Atlantic: Modernity and Double Consciousness* (Cambridge, MA: Harvard University Press, 1993); Judy Grahn, *Really Reading Gertrude Stein* (Freedom, CA: Crossing Press, 1989); John Howland, *Ellington Uptown: Duke Ellington, James P. Johnson, and the Birth of Concert Jazz* (Ann Arbor: University of Michigan Press, 2009); Langston Hughes, *Montage of a Dream Deferred* (New York: Holt, 1951); George Hutchinson, *The Harlem Renaissance in Black and White* (London: Oxford University Press, 1996); Melissa Kemp, "African American Women Poets, the Harlem Renaissance, and: An Apology," *Callaloo* 36, no. 3 (Summer 2013), 789–801, 836; David Levering Lewis, *When Harlem Was in Vogue* (New York: Penguin, 1997); Alain Locke, ed., *The New Negro* (1925; repr. New York: Atheneum, 1992);

Adam McKible, "Seeing Complexity and Hearing Laughter in the Harlem Renaissance," *Modernism/Modernity*, 23, no. 4 (November 2016), 897–904; Michael Nowlin, "Race Literature, Modernism, and Normal Literature: James Weldon Johnson's Groundwork for an African American Literary Renaissance, 1912–20," *Modernism/Modernity* 20, no. 3 (September), 503–518; Hans Ostrom: "Modernism and Hughes," in his *A Langston Hughes Encyclopedia* (Westport, CT: Greenwood Press, 2002), 250–253; "The Ways of White Folks, Hughes, and Modernism," in his *Langston Hughes: A Study of the Short Fiction* (New York: Twayne, 1993), 5–8; Jean Toomer, *Cane* (1923; repr. New York: Norton, 1988).

Morrison, Toni (1931–2019)

Novelist, nonfiction writer, editor, and professor. Born Chloe Anthony Wofford in Lorain, Ohio, Morrison took the risk of abandoning a successful career in publishing to become a full-time novelist. It was a risk that paid off. She became the most prominent American novelist of her time, and she won the Nobel Prize for Literature in 1993. She was the first African American to earn this prestigious award. She was also the recipient of the National Book Critics' Circle Award for *Song of Solomon* (1977) and the Pulitzer Prize for *Beloved* (1987), two novels that have become contemporary classics. She became Robert F. Goheen Professor at Princeton University in 1988.

Morrison studied literature at Howard University, then earned an MA at Cornell University in 1955. She taught English at Texas Southern University for the next two years, then returned to teach at Howard, where she met and married a Jamaican architect named Harold Morrison. The marriage produced two sons but only lasted a few years. In 1964, she left her teaching post and divorced her husband. The recurrence of the subject of motherhood and the motif of flight in Morrison's work are arguably connected to this period of her life.

Morrison began as a textbook editor for Random House in New York City and soon became a senior editor there while beginning work on her first novel, *The Bluest Eye* (1970). Part of her legacy at Random House was to bring into prominence the writings of African American writers, notably Toni Cade Bambara and Angela Y. Davis, and her 1992 book, *Playing in the Dark: Whiteness and the Literary Imagination*, details her reflections on the

> validity or vulnerability of a certain set of assumptions conventionally accepted among literary historians and critics and circulated as 'knowledge.' This knowledge holds that traditional, canonical American literature is free of, uninformed, and unshaped by the four-hundred-year-old presence of, first, Africans and then African-Americans in the United States. (*Playing*, 4–5)

To say nothing of Morrison's influence on other writers, the power of her fiction alone has gone a long way toward reshaping the American literary canon as well as deepening the meaning of historical memory as it affects fiction.

Morrison's first novel, *The Bluest Eye*, begins with a meditation on infertility, on marigold seeds that will not grow, and on a perversion of fertility: the character Pecola Breedlove is carrying her father's child. The structure of the novel is based on the four seasons, beginning in the dying season of autumn and ending in summer, the season of ripeness. The novel's structure would seem to imply a cycle, but there is little hope for rebirth. Pecola is powerless to preserve her innocence or to shelter herself from violence; a character named Junior kills a cat and blames it on Pecola, and her father rapes her. These are not the only instances of physical or emotional abuse in the novel: a lodger named Mr. Henry molests Frieda, the narrator Claudia's sister, for instance, and the schoolchildren are constantly taunting each other. In many ways the novel traces the difficult journey from innocence into something more evil than mere experience. Young girls who cannot correctly pronounce "menstruating," let alone cope with its meaning, are sexually initiated by older men.

The members of the community in Morrison's second novel, *Sula* (1973), also need an outlet for their anguish, and they pour their troubles into a ritual called National Suicide Day, but they also dump their anguish onto the title character, Sula Peace. If innocence is stolen in *The Bluest Eye*, then it is outright murdered in *Sula*. Sula's grandmother Eva, for instance, burns her own son alive, and Sula throws young Chicken Little into the river, where he drowns. Just as National Suicide Day is a way for the community to face its fears of death and inadequacy, so these ritual murders are attempts to get rid of these fears.

Though Sula and Pecola are both dumping grounds for their communities, they are not the same type of character: Sula is a brash, defiant woman who follows her own rules and would never dream of being influenced by such a clichéd version of beauty as blue eyes. Sula is the creator of her own story. It is Nel, the less adventurous protagonist of the story, who is in danger of absorbing a dominant worldview; in fact, she tries to alter her nose in pursuit of a White standard of beauty before she meets Sula.

The densely packed novel is about the dissolution of Nel and Sula's relationship, anticipating a theme that recurs in Morrison's fiction: friendships and love relationships are difficult to sustain when one person is a nonconformist and other is a joiner. The residents of the Bottom—the ironic name of the community in *Sula*—are a powerful force because they have been given so little. Yet the residents' tendency to judge Sula and her mother for their sexual promiscuity weakens the community and indirectly leads to their destruction. Strong, independent women like Sula live on as powerful forces in nature: even after her death, Sula's memory continues to haunt Nel and causes her to regret the fact that she rejected her best friend.

The ironic suicide of so many members of the community at the end of *Sula* and the dissolution of the friendship between Sula and Nel both anticipate the themes of Morrison's next novel, *Song of Solomon*. Morrison's emphasis on history becomes even more pronounced in this novel: the context for *Sula* was partially the aftermath of World War I; the context for *Song of Solomon* is the struggle of the Civil Rights Movement in the 1960s. Yet the novel has often been praised less for its historical context than for its rendering of mythology in a contemporary context. Milkman Dead's quest for selfhood leads him to trace his personal history through a children's playground chant. His quest is to fly, something the suicidal insurance agent Robert Smith fails to do in the novel's opening scene, yet something that Milkman's legendary ancestors were able to do.

Morrison's first two novels contain an implicit critique of White standards of beauty and of the hypocritical adherence to conventional morality as a means of ostracizing a member of the community. *Song of Solomon* similarly critiques excessive materialism and selfishness, both espoused by Milkman's parents, Ruth and Macon Dead.

Ruth gives Milkman his unwanted name by nursing him too long, and Macon gives Milkman his twisted set of values by encouraging him to "own things. . . . Then you'll own yourself and other people too" (*Song*, 55). Milkman's aunt Pilate and his friend Guitar attempt, in very different ways, to rescue Milkman from the poisoned atmosphere of his home and to send him on a journey to discover who he is or could become. Guitar represents the political consciousness of the 1950s and early 1960s. Outraged by the murder of Emmett Till and by the insensitivity of a White mill owner after his father's death, Guitar seeks to avenge his race by joining a group, called the Seven Days, who are committed to murder a White person for every Black person who dies. He tries to awaken a similar animosity in Milkman, who has lived most of his life in self-gratifying bliss. Milkman cannot accept his friend's race-motivated, murderous rage; he gravitates toward the sensibility of Pilate, who guides him into a personal journey to connect him with his past. Through it all, Milkman's life is threatened by those he loves most: his cousin Hagar and his friend Guitar. "Everybody wants the life of a black man" (*Song*, 222), Guitar tells him, and the novel's ambiguous conclusion indicates that the challenge of forging a meaningful life is worth the risk of losing it.

It is clear that Morrison is challenging the mythology of folklore and fairy tales in her first three novels, and in that sense, her fourth novel, *Tar Baby* (1981), continues the themes of the first three. Nevertheless, it has received less critical attention than most of her other novels: critics seem unprepared to cope with *Tar Baby*'s blunt critique. Set on a Caribbean island, in Paris, and in the United States, this novel takes on postcolonial themes of domination and oppression with a deep consideration of global marketing as the context for the particular conflicts on the island. In this sense, it grows out of the greed and materialism associated with Macon Dead in *Song of Solomon*. Yet here White characters, not just their values, are brought into contact with Black characters. Jadine Childs is a version of Milkman and Pecola, someone who has been removed from the context of her racial background and who has sought a White version of beauty and security. Just as Milkman needs someone like Guitar to lift him out of his complacency, so Jadine needs Son, and although she initially disdains him for representing the opposite of what she considers "civilization," she develops a new consciousness as she grows to love him.

In Morrison's fifth and most celebrated novel, *Beloved*, the title character arrives from beyond the grave to awaken something similar in Sethe. All her novels up to this time feature characters who do not truly love themselves in the context of their racial and personal history, and Sethe is no exception. She has murdered her daughter in order to save her from a life of slavery, and her guilt over this act has caused her to loathe herself, and thus to be paralyzed, or to lead nothing better than a dead life. Beloved comes back from the grave to teach her to love again, and thus to embrace life, which is, as Pilate asserted in *Song of Solomon*, "precious."

Beloved is inspired partially by the true story of Margaret Garner, a slave caught in the process of escaping who murdered one of her children because she believed death preferable to slavery. Sethe has similarly killed the child named Beloved, and part of Morrison's genius in this novel is that she is able to imagine the pain that someone like Margaret Garner must have suffered to arrive at such an awful decision. Sethe was systematically dehumanized, as all slaves were, not only in physical ways—beatings and rape—but also in emotional ways, as she is the subject of a lesson imparted by Schoolteacher, a pseudoscientist who uses Sethe's body to argue for the inferiority of African Americans. Her murdering Beloved cannot be completely forgiven, but it can be better understood through the process of what she calls "rememory"—the attempt to make oneself whole through the reconstruction of the past. Her inability to love her daughter, Denver, or her lover, Paul D., is related to her inability to love herself or her tendency to blame herself for her awful act without sufficiently blaming the institution of slavery that drove her to it.

The three novels Morrison has published since *Beloved* have gained widespread respect but not the same degree of critical attention. *Jazz* (1992), like *Sula* and *Beloved*, is situated in history and focuses on a female pariah. All three of these novels involve murder and memory as well as the haunting presence of the past. The novel is less coherent than *Beloved*; Morrison seeks to challenge the reader in the way that technically advanced jazz music challenges the listener. There are motifs that recur, even a central story line involving Joe, the murdered Dorcas, and the woman named Violet who slashes the face of Dorcas's corpse at her funeral. Some of Morrison's familiar themes are contained in this story line, and the reader is encouraged to understand the intention behind Violet's act of scarification that recalls Sethe's murder of Beloved. More interesting than the novel's bewildering plot, though, is the way its narrator mimics jazz in print, calling to mind again the distinction between an oral or performed history and written or official history.

Morrison's next novel, *Paradise* (1998), is a similar whirlwind of narration with a plot that is in some ways less fascinating

than the way in which it is told. Her single published short story, "Recitatif" (1994), demonstrates the division between the two main characters, Twyla and Roberta, who were best friends in school but who grew apart partially because they became increasingly aware of their different racial backgrounds. We know that one character is White and one is Black, but it is never clear which is which. Morrison does something similar in *Paradise*, in which we know that one of the girls at the convent is White—we even know from the first sentence that "They shoot the white girl first." Yet we are never sure which girl is White. The implication in both of these works is that racial discrimination is real and divisive but also that the relationship between individual identity and racial identity is confusing, regardless of perspective. Morrison also forces the reader to question his or her own racial stereotypes. *Paradise* tells the story of a convent, a place where women can exist free from the pressures of contemporary society, on the margins of an all-Black town in Oklahoma. The violence that opens the novel and the irony of the title suggest that such notions of exclusion are not the best response to a long history of oppression.

The title of Morrison's novel *Love* (2003) is every bit as ironic as *Paradise*. At the very least, Morrison is trying to get her readers to reassess the meaning of notions such as love and paradise, which are too often confused with pleasantry. Love can be a violent force in Morrison's fiction, and it has the power to kill. This novel is another attempt to come to terms with the destructive or murderous passion that is part of love. Many of the motifs of this novel are familiar to Morrison's readers. At the novel's center is Bill Cosey, a wealthy patriarch who returns as a ghost to Junior and as a memory to Christine and Heed. These three women live in the same house, yet it is no convent, as in *Paradise*. Much animosity and jealousy center on the disputed fact of Bill Cosey's will, and we learn deep into the novel of Cosey's pedophilia. As usual, Morrison challenges her readers to think of what growth might be possible in such a barren landscape.

A Mercy (2008) is a historical novel featuring a Dutch trader, Jacob Vaark, who acquires a young slave woman as payment for a debt. Morrison's novel *Home* (2012) centers on an African American veteran of the Korean War as he returns to the United States to face racism once again. Morrison's most recent novel to date, *God Help the Child* (2015), concerns a beautiful young African American woman, Bride, Booker (whom she loves), and the mysterious Rain, a White child.

The Origin of Others (2017) is a nonfiction book based on lectures Morrison gave at Harvard University.

Morrison's landscapes are the product of a superb literary imagination focused intently on the legacy of post–Civil War history. And yet it would be reductive to regard her writing as historical or realistic fiction. Her novels are often fantastic, steeped in a rich knowledge of folklore and mythology, and her meaning is never obvious. More than anything, her command of language and her narrative innovation, no less than her subject matter, earned Morrison the reputation as an author who will endure the fluctuations of literary history.

D. Quentin Miller

See also: Essay; Feminism/Black Feminism; Novel; Postmodernism.

Resources

Primary Sources: Toni Morrison: *Beloved* (New York: Knopf, 1987); *The Bluest Eye* (New York: Knopf, 1970); *God Help the Child* (New York: Knopf, 2015); *Home* (New York: Knopf, 2012); *Jazz* (New York: Knopf, 1992); *Love* (New York: Knopf, 2003); *A Mercy* (New York: Knopf, 2008); *The Origin of Others* (Cambridge, MA: Harvard University Press, 2017); *Paradise* (New York: Knopf, 1997); *Playing in the Dark* (Cambridge, MA: Harvard University Press, 1992); *Solomon's Song* (New York: Knopf, 1977); *Sula* (New York: Knopf, 1973); *Tar Baby* (New York: Knopf, 1981).

Secondary Sources: Sture Allén, ed., *Nobel Lectures, Literature 1991–1995* (Singapore: World Scientific Publishing, 1997), 47–53; Patrick Bryce Bjork, *The Novels of Toni Morrison: The Search for Self and Place Within the Community* (New York: Peter Lang, 1992); Harold Bloom, ed., *Toni Morrison* (Broomall, PA: Chelsea House, 2000); Carolyn C. Denard, ed., *Toni Morrison: Conversations* (Jackson: University Press of Mississippi, 2008); Henry Louis Gates Jr. and Anthony Appiah, eds., *Toni Morrison: Critical Perspectives Past and Present* (New York: Amistad, 1993); Carol Kolmerten, Stephen M. Ross, and Judith Bryant Wittenberg, eds., *Unflinching Gaze: Morrison and Faulkner Re-envisioned* (Jackson: University Press of Mississippi, 1997); Nellie McKay, comp., *Critical Essays on Toni Morrison* (Boston: G. K. Hall, 1988); Philip Page, *Dangerous Freedom: Fusion and Fragmentation in Toni Morrison's Novels* (Jackson: University Press of Mississippi, 1995); Nancy J. Peterson, ed., *Toni Morrison: Critical and Theoretical Approaches* (Baltimore: Johns Hopkins University Press, 1997); Wilfred D. Samuels and Clenora Hudson-Weems, *Toni Morrison* (Boston: Twayne, 1990); Valerie Smith, ed., *New Essays on Song of Solomon* (Cambridge: Cambridge University Press, 1995); Justine Tally, ed., *The Cambridge Companion to Toni Morrison* (Cambridge: Cambridge University Press, 2007); Danille Taylor-Guthrie, ed., *Conversations with Toni Morrison* (Jackson: University Press of Mississippi, 1994).

N

Naylor, Gloria (1950–2016)

Novelist, playwright, and professor. Naylor was among the more highly regarded American novelists of the late twentieth and early twenty-first centuries. She was born in New York City to Southern parents, Roosevelt and Alberta McAlpin Naylor, who had moved north from Mississippi to secure better opportunities for their children. Naylor's mother was an avid reader who had been refused use of the public library in the South under the racist policies of segregation. Naylor received a BA in English from Brooklyn College of the City University of New York in 1981. Her writing career developed in the midst of her education. Naylor's first novel, *The Women of Brewster Place*, was published in 1982. Her second novel, *Linden Hills*, published in 1985, was the creative thesis in her MA program at Yale University; she completed her MA in 1983. Naylor's subsequent novels are *Mama Day* (1988) and *Bailey's Café* (1992).

Naylor's novels include a number of African American men as significant characters, but the focus is on the experiences of African American women. In this regard, Naylor's writing is influenced by African American women writers who rose to prominence in the 1970s, including Alice Walker and Toni Morrison, who, in turn, were influenced by both a popular rediscovery of the Harlem Renaissance and by literature and theory from the Black Arts Movement of the 1960s.

Although Naylor grew up in the North, her work has been identified as "inherently southern" because of how she pays "careful attention to the details of her characters' lives and in the painstaking meticulousness with which she draws the places where those fictional characters dwell" (Whitt, 5).

Naylor's novels draw upon a variety of literary traditions, including African American literature, folktales and the oral tradition, and classics of English and world literature. Some of the authors and texts that have influenced her work, as evidenced by allusions in the works, include Jean Toomer's *Cane*, Toni Morrison's *The Bluest Eye*, the poetry of Langston Hughes, Charles Waddell Chesnutt's *The Conjure Woman*, the folktales collected by Zora Neale Hurston, the Bible, Chaucer's *The Canterbury Tales*, Shakespeare's *The Tempest* and *A Midsummer Night's Dream*, and Dante's *Inferno*.

Her first novel, *The Women of Brewster Place*, is made up of seven stories concerning seven different African American women, all of whom live on the same dead-end street in an unnamed Northern city. The women who make up Brewster Place are Mattie Michael, Cora Lee, Ceil, Etta Mae Johnson, Kiswana Browne, Lorraine, and Theresa. Brewster Place is the end of the line for these characters and all the other residents. The novel culminates in the rape of Lorraine and in the literal and symbolic destruction of the brick wall that has shut off Brewster Place from the city and has separated the residents from success and fulfillment in life. *The Women of Brewster Place* was made into a television movie in 1989 and starred Oprah Winfrey.

The structure of Naylor's second novel, *Linden Hills*, to some degree mirrors the structure of Dante's *Inferno* (Ward). Luther Nedeed, the founder of Linden Hills, a wealthy Black subdivision in an unnamed city, established Linden Hills in 1820 on a hillside unwanted by Whites. The physical layout of Linden Hills corresponds to the circles of Dante's hell, and those who live there are understood to have made a deal with the devil.

The novel is linked to *The Women of Brewster Place* by the characters Kiswana Brown and Theresa (Lorraine's partner), who escaped from Linden Hills to Brewster Place. The wife of the fifth and current Luther Nedeed is Willa Prescott. Willa is the grandniece of Miranda Day, Mama Day of Naylor's later novel of the same name. Luther Nedeed has her locked in the basement because he deems their newborn son an abomination for having skin color that is too light. Their son dies during her imprisonment, and the action switches between Willa's grieving and the experiences of Willie and Lester, two young men who travel the "circles" of Linden Hills doing odd jobs. The novel argues that the residents of Linden Hills are damned because they have accepted the racist and materialist doctrine of the United States—one that claims Whiteness is superior to Blackness and money is everything.

Naylor's third novel, *Mama Day*, is set in the fictional Sea Island of Willow Springs, an island situated between but unclaimed by either South Carolina or Georgia. It is a magical place. This magic is felt by all the residents and is traced to Sapphira Wade, the powerful and mysterious ancestress of the island, of whom Miranda Day, the Mama Day of the title, is a direct descendant and thus has inherited her power. The legends of the island tell of Sapphira's power to wrest freedom for herself and all the slaves of Bascombe Wade. The novel opens in the second person ("you") and exhorts the reader to listen. The story is told in flashback and is framed as a conversation between Ophelia, Mama Day's grandniece, and Ophelia's husband, George. It is a dramatic story with grand themes of enduring love, unshakable faith, and worthy sacrifice, and is arguably Naylor's most optimistic novel.

The action of Naylor's fourth novel, *Bailey's Café*, is centered on the café and its surrounding neighborhood. "Bailey" and his wife Nadine run the café, and the novel itself is made up of stories concerning the inhabitants of and visitors to the neighborhood. In addition to the café, there is a boardinghouse (or bordello) run by Eve and a pawnshop run by Gabriel. There are seven stories of abuse and oppression experienced by women who visit the café or live at Eve's. In this novel, Naylor emphasizes music, with blues and jazz songs as a recurrent motif informing, for instance, the titles of chapters. *Bailey's Café* was adapted into a stage play and performed in Hartford, Connecticut, in 1994.

Naylor's next novel, *The Men of Brewster Place*, can be understood as an answer to criticism leveled at her and other contemporary African American women writers that positive Black male characters are missing from their work. Naylor revisits Brewster Place, this time telling the stories of seven men, most of whom are characters from her previous novel: Ben the janitor; Mattie's son, Basil; Etta Mae's seducer, Moreland T. Woods; the gang leader C. C. Baker; Ciel's husband, Eugene; the silent Brother Jerome; and Kiswana's boyfriend, Abshu. Their stories also tell of the loneliness, the despair, and the oppression these men endure. Abshu emerges from the ruins of these stories as the only one with hope for a better future.

Like many other contemporary novelists, Naylor not only wrote but also taught and lectured. Among the universities where she taught are New York University, Princeton, the University of Pennsylvania, Boston University, Brandeis, Cornell, and the University of Kent in Canterbury, England. She received an American Book Award in 1983, a National Endowment for the Arts fellowship in 1985, and a Guggenheim Fellowship in 1988. Naylor established One Way Productions in 1990, a multimedia production company.

Rachael Barnett

See also: Feminism/Black Feminism; Novel.

Resources

Primary Sources: Gloria Naylor: *Bailey's Café* (New York: Harcourt Brace Jovanovich, 1992); *Linden Hills* (1985; repr. New York: Penguin, 1995); *Mama Day* (1988; repr. New York: Vintage, 1989); *The Men of Brewster Place* (New York: Hyperion, 1998); *The Women of Brewster Place* (1982; repr. New York: Penguin, 1983).

Secondary Sources: Anonymous, "In Memoriam: Gloria Naylor, 1950–2016," *Women in Academia Report*, October 12, 2016; Paula Gallant Eckard, "The Entombed Maternal in Gloria Naylor's *Linden Hills*," *Callaloo* 35, no. 3 (2012), 795–809; Sharon Felton and Michelle C. Loris, eds., *The Critical Response to Gloria Naylor* (Westport, CT: Greenwood Press, 1997); Henry Louis Gates Jr. and K. A. Appiah eds., *Gloria Naylor: Critical Perspectives Past and Present* (New York: Amistad, 1993); Margot Anne Kelly, ed., *Gloria Naylor's Early Novels* (Gainesville: University of Florida Press, 1999); Maxine Lavon Montgomery, *The Fiction of Gloria Naylor Houses and Spaces of Resistance* (Knoxville: University of Tennessee Press, 2010); Shirley A. Stave ed., *Gloria Naylor: Strategy and Technique, Magic and Myth* (Newark: University of Delaware Press, 2001); Catherin C. Ward, "Gloria Naylor's *Linden Hills*: A Modern *Inferno*," *Contemporary Literature* 28, no. 1 (April 1, 1987), 67–81; Margaret Earley Whitt, *Understanding Gloria Naylor* (Columbia: University of South Carolina Press, 1997).

Novel

A long form of narrative fiction. Typically, the novel has focused on the realistic depiction of the specificity of individuals' lives, but it is an open form; therefore, novels may also use surrealistic techniques, elements of fantasy, or stream-of-consciousness. Novels may be written in such long-established categories as crime and mystery fiction and science fiction, and one highly popular contemporary category is the romance novel. The epistolary novel is a form many novelists have used for over 200 years. Coming-of-age fiction, also known as the *Bildungsroman*, constitutes a looser but nonetheless important category of the novel, one focused on the experiences described (how individuals mature in societies) rather than conventions of form.

The history of the African American novel can be usefully, if somewhat artificially, discussed in terms of several periods: antebellum; Reconstruction and its aftermath; the Harlem Renaissance; the era of the Civil Rights Movement; the Black Arts Movement; and post–1970. Conventions and traditions of the novel, however, cut across these periods. Throughout this history, which spans roughly 200 years, the African American novel has proved to be intimately connected to social changes, devoted to the analysis of the various life conditions African Americans and others experience, and engaged in the kinds of promotion of interests and ideas that storytelling uniquely enables. Novels by African American authors have been central to many Americans' understanding of the pursuit of liberty in this country.

The African American novel has its most immediate and nourishing roots in slave narratives. Indeed, slave narratives were sometimes accused by slavery's proponents and apologists of being fictions. Slave narratives depicted the lives of men and women who had endured and escaped slavery to tell their tales. The testimonial value of these narratives should be emphasized; they were used by former slaves and abolitionists to show African Americans' humanity and intelligence and, by contrast, the inhumanity and brutality of slavery. The most famous of these narratives—those by Olaudah Equiano, Frederick Douglass, William Wells Brown, and Harriet Jacobs—were written during slavery, but thousands more were recorded after its end. In giving narrative shape and sensual detail to the experiences and psychologies of former slaves, the narratives together constitute a dramatic historical record, a major indictment of the country's failure to live up to the ideals of its Constitution, and a rich tradition of African American storytelling.

Several conventions of the slave narrative influenced African American fiction, and the narratives' detailed, realistic, sometimes lengthy depictions of individuals' lives easily lent themselves to the novel. In fact, the influence was mutual. As Valerie Smith notes in her introduction to Harriet Jacobs's *Incidents in the Life of a Slave Girl* (1861), Jacobs drew on the conventions of the sentimental novel in order to tell a story of sexual vulnerability, a story that slave narratives by men offered her no way to tell (Jacobs, xxxi). Middle-class White women sympathetic to abolition and familiar with the sentimental novel were a primary audience for Jacobs's narrative. The sentimental novel's conventions, melded with those of the slave narrative, appealed to such women. Several novels were published during the antebellum period. The first of these was William Wells Brown's *Clotel; or, The President's Daughter*, published in England in 1853. The novel tells the story of Thomas Jefferson's much-rumored slave mistress and her daughter by Jefferson after he sold them. Because of its depiction of women in peril and its tragic end, Brown's novel, like Jacobs's slave narrative, owes something to the conventions of the sentimental and seduction novels. Other novels from the antebellum period include Martin R. Delany's *Blake* (1859) and Harriet E. Wilson's *Our Nig* (1859).

When slavery ended after the Civil War, novels continued the social work that slave narratives had begun. During this period, the South was first occupied by federal troops that enforced the end of slavery and ensured some progress in Southern Blacks' lives. Then, in 1877, the troops withdrew, allowing Southern states to institute Jim Crow laws that did much to reverse the gains that African Americans had made. In fact, the period of Reconstruction is the period in which the first Ku Klux Klan was active. (The second Klan was formed in 1915.)

Two novels may serve as examples of the trend over these years in modes of depicting America in Black novels. The first of these is Frances E. W. Harper's *Iola Leroy; or, Shadows Uplifted* (1892). Bridging the antebellum and postwar periods, Harper began her career as an abolitionist lecturer and drew in her novel on antebellum writers' model of literary moral purpose, exemplified most famously in Harriet Beecher Stowe's *Uncle Tom's Cabin* (1852), the novel that Abraham Lincoln only half-jokingly referred to as the book that "made" the Civil

War. Like Stowe's, Harper's reputation as an artist was not recognized by scholars of literature until recently. This lack of recognition derived largely from a dual prejudice in literary scholarship on the novel: with few exceptions, neither popular nor political works were considered eligible for the literary canon. *Iola Leroy* plays on the reader's heartstrings: when its heroine, living as a White woman, discovers that she is partially Black, she is enslaved and deprived of her inheritance by a villainous relative. By contrast with the heroine of a novel like *Clotel*, however, Iola is not a tragic figure, and this marks an important distinction. In the sentimental novel, a White heroine who has been thrown on her own resources but protected her virtue would end up married; in the seduction novel, any woman whose virtue has been compromised would end tragically. Iola receives a marriage proposal from a White doctor who knows about her race, but Harper does not allow her character the sentimental resolution. Instead, as with other novels of racial uplift that characterize the postwar era, *Iola Leroy* affirms the heroine's racial identity and devotes her to the advancement of the race. Iola leads a productive life as a teacher and race advocate; she becomes a "race" woman. In this respect, she epitomizes the novel, which does not scruple to interrupt its narrative with didactic passages that impress on the reader the importance and greater social relevance of events.

To a considerable degree, James Weldon Johnson's *The Autobiography of an Ex-Colored Man* (1912) undermined the "uplift" novel's emphasis on racial identity and literary moral purpose. In a sense, it separated literature from the imperative to inspire African Americans to greater heights and to persuade Whites of African Americans' worth. *The Autobiography*'s protagonist–narrator is born to a White father and a light-skinned Black mother. Raised in Connecticut as White, the narrator quickly displays a great facility with music and decides to go to a Black school in the South after he learns of his heritage. Having lost all his money, the narrator takes up menial employment and discovers a love of ragtime music. Eventually, he tours Europe thanks to the support of a White patron. (Although there are only hints in the novel, some critics have interpreted the relationship between the two men as romantic, a noteworthy early same-sex relationship in African American fiction.) Significantly, the narrator develops a compelling amalgam of classical European and ragtime music. Such an amalgam was in fact Johnson's own goal for literature: a blend of Black vernacular and "standard" language.

After some time, the narrator resolves to break with his patron and returns to the South and the roots of African American music, convinced that he is allowing his talent for African American musical forms to go to waste. In the South again, the narrator witnesses a lynching, which profoundly disturbs him. His reaction is not so much fear or anger, however; it is shame. The narrator is ashamed to be a member of a race that could with impunity be treated more cruelly than animals. Therefore, he resolves to pass as White and returns to New York City, where he enters the business world and builds a family. The novel closes with stunning psychological ambiguity, throwing into question the decision to pass. The narrator describes having heard Booker T. Washington speak, stealing the show from the other speakers through conviction and moral purpose. While the narrator expresses an urgent desire that his children never be branded as Black, the narrator also feels a sense of "longing for [his] mother's people" (210). Hearing Washington speak, the narrator recounts: "I feel small and selfish. I am an ordinarily successful white man who has made a little money. [Race leaders] are men who are making history and a race. . . . I cannot repress the thought that, after all, I have chosen the lesser part, that I have sold my birthright for a mess of pottage" (211).

Whereas Harper's protagonist, upon discovering that she is Black, takes up the task of racial uplift in the face of personal hardship, Johnson's narrator flees into the White world to escape his sense of shame. Harper's message was clearly more uplifting and urged readers, Black and White alike, to applaud African Americans' hard work if not to take it up themselves. But the tide was turning against the programmatic uplift novel, and Johnson's deft, subtle, psychological realism was the new wave. Thus Johnson's novel, which was republished in 1927, attracted much more attention than Harper's during the Harlem Renaissance. African American literature was moving toward refined literary styles that innovatively blended standard and African American language, fearlessly explored moral ambiguity, and developed realistic portrayals of Black America. *The Autobiography*'s realism was reinforced by the fact that it was first published anonymously, purporting to protect the identity of its passing narrator. Other important novels published during Reconstruction and its aftermath include Sutton E. Griggs's *Imperium in Imperio* (1899), Pauline Elizabeth Hopkins's *Magazine Novels*, and Charles Waddell Chesnutt's *House Behind the Cedars* (1900). Novels such as these trace the ground separating Harper's and Chestnutt's literary visions and foreshadow developments to come in the African American novel. Whereas Griggs's novel anticipated

developments of the 1940s and 1960s, when highly politicized and confrontational aesthetics were developed, Hopkins's novels drew on "the strategies and formulas of the sensational fiction of dime novels and magazines" (Carby, 145). Chesnutt's novel tells another version of the tragic mulatto story, in which the protagonist is able to live neither in the Black world nor in the White one and dies as a result; its heroine achieves a greater moral complexity than *Clotel*'s but does not undertake the work of racial uplift that *Iola Leroy*'s does.

The dramatic changes that took place in the African American novel during the period loosely designated as the Harlem Renaissance may be measured in part by the fact that one of its major inspirations, Jean Toomer's *Cane* (1923), bore little resemblance to a conventional novel but was instead a highly innovative, stylish novel-in-stories that also included poetry. Toomer's own term for his aesthetic was "poetic realism," which cast his work in contrast to the sentimental and romantic works of the antebellum and post–Civil War authors (Rusch). *Cane* does not have a unifying plot; instead, it is a lyrical blend of poems, short stories, and one dramatic piece. In Bernard W. Bell's words, it is "an incantational collection of thematically related writings" (97). The book explores themes such as African Americans' rootedness in a rural past and their rapid urbanization, the rise of a Black middle class, and a mystical vision of sexuality. Toomer's experimental forms, which placed an unprecedented premium on the aesthetic possibilities for Black literature, immediately struck readers as the herald of a new literary era. Though previous African American authors had, to be sure, developed distinctive styles and voices, authors of the Harlem Renaissance excelled at putting the mark of their individual style on their works as they experimented with fictional and poetic forms. As a result, it becomes more difficult to generalize about novelistic production during this period.

It is clear, however, that a sense of "newness" marks the period, as Alain Locke's volume *The New Negro* (1925) announced. In the opening essay of that volume, Locke declared a rupture with past modes of representation, especially those that drew on popular forms such as the sentimental novel that relied on stock characters: "In art and letters, instead of being wholly caricatured, [the New Negro] is being seriously portrayed and painted" (9). This new, serious representation was as interested in ambiguity, irony, and difficulty as antebellum and post–Civil War literature had been in clear, effective, and popular means of communicating messages about slavery and racial uplift. Following the work of Toomer and Johnson, Harlem Renaissance novels by men typically participate in a realistic aesthetic. Like Toomer, Claude McKay represented rural Black folk as rooted and stable, and their urban counterparts as struggling to adapt to materialism and industrialization; his *Home to Harlem* (1928) aroused controversy for its apparently primitivist view of Black rural origins. *Not Without Laughter* (1930), by Langston Hughes, is a coming-of-age novel set in the Midwest and counterbalances McKay's primitivist view of Black rural America. Arna Bontemps's work of historical fiction, *Black Thunder* (1936), like *Imperium in Imperio*, is a revolutionary tale, but Bontemps draws on an actual slave revolt, and the novel's debt to slave narratives is apparent. The title of Wallace Thurman's *The Blacker the Berry* (1929) ironically refers to the folk saying, "The blacker the berry, the sweeter the juice." Far from living out this saying, the novel's female protagonist encounters constant discrimination because of her dark skin and internalizes others' negative attitudes about her complexion.

A number of women novelists emerged during the Harlem Renaissance. Zora Neale Hurston, for instance, devoted herself not only to the fictional representation of strong, independent women who feared neither men nor their own sexuality but also to the anthropological study of African American and Haitian life, study that informed her portrayal of the Black South. Whereas depictions of women, often passing mulattoes, had been tightly constrained by the traditions of the sentimental and seduction novels, Hurston's *Their Eyes Were Watching God* (1937) tells the story of a Black woman at the center of several Black communities in Florida, describing these with the care of an anthropological eye. Hurston's protagonist survives first an abusive marriage and then a passionate affair with a younger man whom she must shoot after he contracts rabies. The novel closes as it opens, with the woman telling her story to a friend. Similarly ambitious in opening new possibilities for representing women were Jessie Redmon Fauset and Nella Larsen. Bell has called Hurston's work "folk romance," contrasting it with Fauset's and Larsen's, which he names "genteel realism." Like Hurston, Fauset and Larsen were concerned to address the limitations put on women, though the women are not always successful in overcoming such hurdles and are especially unsuccessful in Larsen's work. Unlike Hurston's, their settings were middle-class and urban. Fauset's *There Is Confusion* (1924) reverses tradition and attributes the mulatto's problems to his White blood. Fauset's *Plum Bun* (1929) is an intricate, somewhat underappreciated novel of passing set in Philadelphia,

Pennsylvania, and New York City. The Black woman narrator of Larsen's *Passing* (1929) subtly reveals a lesbian attraction to a woman who is passing, an attraction that ends in the other woman's death, perhaps at the hands of the narrator.

The Harlem Renaissance set new standards of literary quality for Black literature and produced an astonishing number of enduring novels in a relatively short period. In some cases, the success of the Harlem Renaissance has had the effect of obscuring the careers of writers whose work was in a popular mode or otherwise violated the expectations of readers.

Chester Himes, for instance, wrote a number of significant detective and prison novels that show America's seamier side (*see* Crime and Mystery Fiction; Prison Literature). His first novels present a tragic vision of how racism determines Black men's lives. *Cast the First Stone* (1952) was published in bowdlerized form because it did not conform to the hard-boiled template that was expected of Himes and because of its depiction of situational homosexuality and tenderness among men in prison; republished in Himes's original form as *Yesterday Will Make You Cry* (1998), the novel focuses on a White convict who struggles unsuccessfully to overcome his grim circumstances. In his promotion of a deterministic vision, Himes was in step with the most prominent Black writer of the 1930s and 1940s, Richard Wright. Wright's "Blueprint for Negro Writing" (1937), one of the most influential literary manifestos of the twentieth century, represented a return of the repressed propaganda tradition in Black letters, demanding a sociological focus on the confrontation between Black and White cultures and a rejection of modes of representation that might entertain rather than instruct. Whereas it could be argued

that many Harlem Renaissance writers were concerned primarily with aesthetic quality, Wright viewed their works as compromised by White patronage and middle-class values. Partly because of the influence of Wright's protest novel, brilliant work by women such as Hurston, whose novels did not conform to the model, were eclipsed for decades, only to be rediscovered in the 1970s. Wright's model is epitomized by *Native Son* (1940), in which the accidents of circumstance drive the protagonist, Bigger Thomas, to a tragic end. There is little to endear Bigger to the reader, and the novel's mechanistic plot clearly dooms him from the outset. However, after he is sentenced to death for murder, Bigger comes to a kind of psychological closure, understanding how his environment has determined who he is.

As the Civil Rights Movement began, Wright's preeminence as a novelist found challengers in James Baldwin and Ralph Ellison, both of whom appeared to reject Wright's didacticism and determinism. A former protégé of Wright, Ralph Ellison seemed to be more interested in the aesthetics of the novel than in producing protest literature. Arguably, however, the plot of *Invisible Man* (1952) is nearly as deterministic as Wright's. Nonetheless, the style and structure of the novel are extraordinary and original. Its unnamed narrator eventually comes to understand that he has a "socially responsible role to play" (Ellison, 581). At the end of the novel, he has yet to undertake such a role.

Baldwin's work launched additional challenges to Wright's preeminence. Perhaps his most admired novel, *Go Tell It on the Mountain* (1953), thoroughly eschewed Wright's sociological Black–White conflict in favor of a nuanced psychological exploration rendered in richly literary language that owed equal parts to the Black church and to Henry James. For Baldwin, the novel was an exercise in coming to terms with his sexuality and his relationships with his father and the church. Its protagonist finds a kind of secular salvation in suffering, and Baldwin would return to this theme frequently. Baldwin's modern adaptation of the Black church's oral traditions is perhaps his most enduring stylistic contribution to African American literature. *Giovanni's Room* (1956), set mainly in Paris, tells the story of a White American man who falls in love with an Italian man but ultimately is unable to love anyone. With *Another Country* (1962), which is set in New York City and concerns interracial relationships, among other things, Baldwin earned both critical and popular acclaim. His reputation as an essayist probably still overshadows his reputation as a novelist, and his later works of fiction are arguably as protest-oriented as Richard Wright's work.

As the Civil Rights Movement continued into the 1960s, the Black Arts Movement promoted an aesthetic to complement the greater militancy of the Black Power Movement. Reasserting politics as the most important dimension of literary production, some members of the movement rejected figures such as Ellison and Baldwin as assimilationists whose work was too invested in European literary models. Because their forms lent themselves to performance, poetry and drama are more characteristic of the Black Arts Movement's literary activism. However, novelists such as John Williams in *The Man Who Cried I Am* (1967) did represent African Americans successfully countering discrimination with strategic anger. The nonlinear narrative of Williams's novel underscores the historical determination of both collective and individual destinies. Other novelists of the period, such as Margaret Abigail Walker in *Jubilee* (1966) and Ernest James Gaines

in *The Autobiography of Miss Jane Pittman* (1971), included clear critiques of racism in their work while maintaining a focus on the individual voice and psychology. Walker's novel, which was based on the life of her grandmother, and Gaines's, which is told in the voice of a 110-year-old ex-slave, returned once again to the tradition of the slave narrative. Other supporters of the Black Arts Movement, such as John Edgar Wideman in *A Glance Away* (1967), did not strictly adhere to the movement's exclusive focus on African American politics.

The publication of Alice Walker's *The Third Life of Grange Copeland* and Toni Morrison's *The Bluest Eye* in 1970 marked a revival of interest in Black women's literature. Thanks to Morrison's position as a senior editor at Random House for a number of years and recovery work such as Walker's on Hurston, new novels by Black women and the republication of relatively unread works from previous decades permanently transformed the field of the African American novel. This transformation was not simply a restoration of gender parity; on the contrary, women novelists such as Morrison espoused an approach to storytelling that rejected anything like Wright's protest novel, which had usually foregrounded male characters and focused exclusively on Black communities in conflict with White communities. Instead, women novelists have encouraged fictional portrayals of Black families' and communities' interiors, leaving aside the violence of interracial conflict. Moreover, these novelists have confronted problems within the Black community, including spousal abuse, drawing criticism from those who prefer that art promote a positive, empowering image of African Americans. For instance, Morrison explores Black family dynamics, some of them dysfunctional, and Black women's internalization of White beauty standards in *The Bluest Eye*; in this exploration, her novel was anticipated by Gwendolyn Brooks's *Maud Martha* (1953), a novel about an ordinary Black woman that was long eclipsed by fiction about men with extraordinary experiences. The epistolary novel *The Color Purple* (1982), which also concerns issues of gender and women's self-determination, is Alice Walker's most critically acclaimed work. Other significant women novelists include Toni Cade Bambara, Gayl Jones, Paule Marshall, Terry McMillan, and Gloria Naylor. Jones's *Eva's Man* (1976) provoked controversy over its explicit sex and violence and excited readers with its experimental narrative style, which took the form of an unreliable female narrator. The novel's depiction of sexuality is bleak and violent; its protagonist is sent to prison after she kills and castrates a lover. It closes with the woman's cellmate making love to her, the novel's only moment of possible redemption.

Naylor's *The Women of Brewster Place* (1982), *Linden Hills* (1985), and *Mama Day* (1988) are subtle, inventive narratives that explore women's issues, questions of identity, and conflicts within both the African American working class and middle class. McMillan's novel *Waiting to Exhale* (1992) was critically acclaimed and also enormously popular; it was adapted to the screen, as were Walker's *The Color Purple* and Morrison's *Beloved*.

Today, the African American novel is richly informed by a variety of traditions and is breaking new ground in innovative forms and in genres such as science fiction, to which Samuel R. Delany in *Dhalgren* (1974) and Octavia E. Butler in *Patternmaster* (1976) have made important contributions. For both Delany and Butler, race remains a concern, but the conventions of science fiction allow them to address race in less literal and more conceptually creative ways than the traditional novel might. Walter Mosley and Barbara Neely, among others, have contributed original novels to the crime fiction genre. Writers such as James Earl Hardy, E. Lynn Harris, Randall Garrett Kenan, and Ann Allen Shockley have expanded the possibilities for gay and lesbian representation in the Black novel, ground that was first broken by James Baldwin and Nella Larsen (*see* Gay Literature; Lesbian Literature). In 1993, Toni Morrison became the first African American to win the Nobel Prize for Literature. Finally, the popular success of works by Baldwin, Walker, Morrison, McMillan, and Harris, among others, has meant that the African American novel now reaches a much larger audience than ever before without sacrificing any of its commitment to the representing African American experiences (Graham).

In the twenty-first century, African American novelists have continued to build upon these traditions while achieving the highest levels of critical and popular recognition. Edward Jones received the 2003 National Book Critics Circle Award for Fiction and the 2004 Pulitzer Prize in Fiction for *The Known World* (2003). Jesmyn Ward received the National Book Award for Fiction in 2011 for *Salvage the Bones* (2011) and again in 2017 for *Sing, Unburied, Sing* (2017), while Colson Whitehead received the 2016 National Book Award for Fiction and the 2017 Pulitzer Prize in Fiction for *The Underground Railroad*. During the same period, Hannah Crafts's *The Bondwoman's Narrative* (ca. 1853–1861), possibly the first novel written by an African American woman, was published for the first time (2002), expanding scholarly understanding of the history of the novel as a genre and of African American literature more generally.

Douglas Steward

See also: Baldwin, James; Bontemps, Arna; Butler, Octavia E.; Delany, Samuel R.; Du Bois, W.E.B.; Ellison, Ralph; Fisher, Rudolph John Chauncey; Harper, Frances Ellen Watkins; Hughes, Langston; Hurston, Zora Neale; Johnson, Georgia Douglas; Johnson, James Weldon; Jones, Gayl; Larsen, Nella; Major, Clarence; McKay, Claude; Morrison, Toni; Naylor, Gloria; Nugent, Richard Bruce; Perkins-Valdez, Dolen; Petry, Ann Lane; Realism; Reed, Ishmael; Schuyler, George Samuel; West, Dorothy; Wideman, John Edgar; Wright, Richard.

Resources

Primary Sources: James Baldwin, *Early Novels and Stories: Go Tell It on the Mountain, Giovanni's Room, Another Country, Going to Meet the Man* (New York: Library of America, 1998); Arna Bontemps, *Black Thunder* (1936; repr. Boston: Beacon, 1997); William Wells Brown, *Clotel; or, The President's Daughter: A Narrative of Slave Life in the United States* (1853; repr. New York: Collier, 1970); Octavia Butler, *Patternmaster* (New York: Warner, 1976); Charles W. Chesnutt, *The House Behind the Cedars* (1900; repr. New York: Collier, 1969); Hannah Crafts, *The Bondwoman's Narrative* (New York: Warner Books, 2002); Martin Delany, *Blake; or, The Huts of America* (1859; repr. Boston: Beacon, 1970); Samuel R. Delany, *Dhalgren* (1974; repr. Hanover, NH: Wesleyan University Press, 1996); Ralph Ellison, *Invisible Man* (New York: Vintage, 1952); Ernest Gaines, *The Autobiography of Miss Jane Pittman* (1971; repr. New York: Bantam, 1982); Sutton Griggs, *Imperium in Imperio: A Study of the Negro Race Problem* (1899; repr. Miami: Mnemosyne, 1969); Frances E. W. Harper, *Iola Leroy; or, Shadows Uplifted* (1892; repr. Boston: Beacon, 1987); Chester Himes: *Cotton Comes to Harlem* (New York: Putnam, 1965); *If He Hollers, Let Him Go* (New York: Doubleday, 1946); *Yesterday Will Make You Cry* (1953; repr. New York: Norton, 1998); Pauline E. Hopkins, *The Magazine Novels of Pauline E. Hopkins* (New York: Oxford University Press, 1988); Langston Hughes, *Not Without Laughter* (1930; repr. New York: Scribner's, 1995); Zora Neale Hurston, *Their Eyes Were Watching God* (Philadelphia: Lippincott, 1937); Harriet A. Jacobs, *Incidents in the Life of a Slave Girl, Written by Herself* (New York: Oxford University Press, 1988); James Weldon Johnson, *The Autobiography of an Ex-Colored Man* (1912; repr. New York: Vintage, 1927); Nella Larsen, *Quicksand and Passing* (2 novels), ed. Deborah E. McDowell (New Brunswick, NJ: Rutgers University Press, 1986); Alain Locke, ed., *The New Negro* (1925; repr. New York: Atheneum, 1992); Claude McKay, *Home to Harlem* (1928; repr. Boston: Northeastern University Press, 1987); Toni Morrison: *Beloved* (New York: Knopf, 1987); *The Bluest Eye* (New York: Plume, 1970); Gloria Naylor: *Linden Hills* (New York: Penguin, 1985); *Mama Day* (New York: Vintage, 1993); *The Women of Brewster Place* (New York: Penguin, 1982); Wallace Thurman, *The Blacker the Berry* (1929; repr. New York: Collier, 1970); Jean Toomer, *Cane* (1923; repr. New York: Norton, 1988); Alice Walker, *The Color Purple* (New York: Harcourt Brace Jovanovich, 1982); *The Third Life of Grange Copeland* (New York: Pocket, 1970); Margaret Walker, *Jubilee* (Boston: Houghton Mifflin, 1966); John Williams, *The Man Who Cried I Am* (Boston: Little, Brown, 1967); Harriet E. Wilson, *Our Nig; or, Sketches from the Life of a Free Black, in a Two-Story White House, North, Showing That Slavery's Shadows Fall Even There* (1859; repr. New York: Vintage, 1983); Richard Wright, *Early Works: Lawd Today!, Uncle Tom's Children, Native Son* (New York: Library of American, 1991).

Secondary Sources: Bernard W. Bell: *The Afro-American Novel and Its Tradition* (Amherst: University of Massachusetts Press, 1987); *The Contemporary African American Novel: Its Folk Roots and Modern Literary Branches* (Amherst: University of Massachusetts Press, 2004); Robert Bone, *The Negro Novel in America* (New Haven, CT: Yale University Press, 1958); Hazel V. Carby,

Reconstructing Womanhood: The Emergence of the Afro-American Woman Novelist (New York: Oxford University Press, 1987); Barbara Christian, *Black Women Novelists: The Development of a Tradition, 1892–1976* (Westport, CT: Greenwood Press, 1980); Emine Lâle Demirtürk, *The Twenty-First Century African American Novel and the Critique of Whiteness in Everyday Life: Blackness as Strategy for Social Change* (Lanham, MD: Lexington Books, 2016); Maryemma Graham, ed., *Cambridge Companion to the African American Novel* (Cambridge: Cambridge University Press, 2004); Lovalerie King and Linda F. Selzer, eds., *New Essays on the African American Novel: from Hurston and Ellison to Morrison and Whitehead* (New York: Palgrave Macmillan, 2008); Frederik L. Rusch, "Form, Function, and Creative Tension in *Cane*: Jean Toomer and the Need for the Avant-Garde," *MELUS* 17, no. 4 (Winter 1991–1992), 15–28; Robert B. Stepto, *From Behind the Veil: A Study of Afro-American Narrative*, 2nd ed. (Urbana: University of Illinois Press, 1991); Ian Watt, *The Rise of the Novel: Studies in Defoe, Richardson, and Fielding* (Berkeley: University of California Press, 1957); John Kevin Young, *Black Writers, White Publishers Marketplace Politics in Twentieth-Century African American Literature* (Jackson: University Press of Mississippi, 2006).

Nugent, Richard Bruce (1906–1987)

Writer and artist. Nugent is often referred to as little more than an eyewitness to the Harlem Renaissance, yet he played a far more significant role, contributing to the movement as a prolific writer and artist. In Washington, DC, where he was born on July 2, 1906, Nugent became a member of Georgia Douglas Johnson's artistic circle and befriended Langston Hughes. After settling in New York City in 1925, he was initiated into the Harlem Renaissance's inner circle and contributed his African-themed short story "Sahdji" to what was to become the "bible" of the Harlem Renaissance—Alain Locke's famous collection of Renaissance writing, *The New Negro* (1925).

While this could have been the starting point of a successful career involving critical appraisal and awards, Nugent opted for the bohemian life. Unusual for a Renaissance member, he displayed great interest in the contemporary White avant-garde and regularly visited Greenwich Village. His open display of homosexual interests contributed to his special position within the movement: Nugent could be described as having embraced a "queer" identity. As one of the youngest Renaissance members, he delighted in playing the part of the extravagant bohemian and was famous for his informal way of dressing and his outrageous manners. Befitting this bohemian lifestyle, Nugent always lacked financial stability. He depended on friends' generosity and spent some of the Harlem Renaissance years on the floor of Wallace Thurman's residence at 267 West 136th Street—which Thurman and others dubbed "N—atti Manor," a pun on "literati"—and was well known for outrageous partying (Lewis).

Nugent's creative process seemed to fit his chaotic environment. He wrote on paper bags and toilet paper, and occasionally, as was the case with the poem "Shadow"— eventually published in *Opportunity* in 1925—his work had to be retrieved from the trash can where it had been discarded, mistaken for garbage. Many of Nugent's artistic creations were similarly endangered because he often lost, destroyed, or gave away his drawings. This, however, does not mean that his contributions to the Harlem Renaissance were negligible. Apart from "Sahdji" and a number of poems, Nugent's fame during the

Harlem Renaissance rested on his extraordinary stream-of-consciousness tale "Smoke, Lilies and Jade," the first openly homoerotic story published by an African American, which appeared in the highly provocative magazine *Fire!!* (1926).

In Nugent's work, race often plays only an incidental role because his focus was on aesthetics. Appropriately, he favored a decadent style as established by artists such as Aubrey Beardsley, to which he added African motifs. His range of literary subject material was wide, reaching from African themes to his late 1920s Bible stories, the undated Japanese-themed novel *Geisha Man*, and *Gentleman Jigger*, Nugent's autobiographical account of the Harlem Renaissance. The latter was finally published in 2008 and concerns two African American brothers, one who passes for White and becomes a well-known poet, and the other who lives openly as a gay man in Harlem. Since Nugent frequently featured male same-sex attraction in his works, few of his creations were published during the Harlem Renaissance.

Nugent's contribution to African American culture went far beyond the creation of literature and works of art. For instance, he proved himself a talented actor in *Porgy* (1927–1930) and was involved in the Negro Ballet Company in the late 1940s. In 1952, Nugent married Grace Marr, who died in 1969. In the early 1970s, Nugent was discovered as an expert on the Harlem Renaissance and, in the early 1980s, as a source of information on gay history. A film clip featuring him is used in the stylish quasi-documentary film by Isaac Julien, *Looking for Langston* (1989). He died of congestive heart failure on May 27, 1987. In 2002, a collection of Nugent's works was published, finally enabling an appropriate appreciation of this artist and writer whose multifaceted literary

and artistic heritage had been unknown to the public for decades. In 2004, the film *Brother to Brother* featured a character based on Nugent, "Bruce." The film concerns Black homosexuality in contemporary times and during the Harlem Renaissance, moving back and forth in time. It is set in Harlem.

A. B. Christa Schwarz

See also: Gay Literature; Harlem Renaissance.

Resources

Primary Sources: Richard Bruce (pseudonym of Nugent): "Cavalier," in *Caroling Dusk: An Anthology of Verse by Negro Poets*, ed. Countee Cullen (New York: Harper & Bros., 1927), 205–206; "The Dark Tower," *Opportunity* (October 1927), 305–306; "Sahdji," in *The New Negro*, ed. Alain Locke (New York: Boni, 1925), 113–114; "Sahdji: An African Ballet," in *Plays of Negro Life: A Sourcebook of Native American Drama*, ed. Alain Locke (New York: Harper & Bros., 1927), 387–400; "Shadow," *Opportunity* (October 1925), 296; "Smoke, Lilies and Jade," *Fire!!* 1 (1926), 33–39; "What Price Glory in Uncle Tom's Cabin," *Harlem* (November 1928), 25–26; Jean Blackwell Hutson, interview with Richard Bruce Nugent, videotape (April 14, 1982), Schomburg Center for Research in Black Culture, New York City; Richard Bruce Nugent: "'. . . and More Gently Still': A Myth," *Trend: A Quarterly of the Seven Arts* 1 (1932), 53–54; *Gay Rebel of the Harlem Renaissance: Selections from the Work of Richard Bruce Nugent*, ed. Thomas H. Wirth (Durham, NC: Duke University Press, 2002); *Gentleman Jigger* (Cambridge, MA: Da Capo Press, 2008) "Lighting FIRE!!," insert to *Fire!!* (1926; Metuchen, NJ: Fire!!, 1982); "Marshall's: A Portrait," *Phylon* 5 (1944), 316–318; "My Love," *Palms* (October 1926), 20; Richard Bruce Nugent Papers, private collection of Thomas H. Wirth, Elizabeth, NJ; Thomas H. Wirth, interviews with Richard Bruce Nugent, tape recordings (June 19, 1983–Sept. 5, 1983), collections of Thomas H.

Wirth, Elizabeth, NJ, and Schomburg Center for Research in Black Culture, New York City.

Secondary Sources: J. Edgar Bauer, "On the Transgressiveness of Ambiguity: Richard Bruce Nugent and the Flow of Sexuality and Race," *Journal of Homosexuality* (February 25, 2015), 1021–1057; Jeremy Braddock, "The Scandal of a Black Ulysses: Wallace Thurman, Richard Bruce Nugent, and the Harlem Reception of Joyce," *ELH (English Literary History)* 84, no. 3 (Fall 2017), 741–763; Michael L. Cobb, "Insolent Racing, Rough Narrative: The Harlem Renaissance's Impolite Queers," *Callaloo* 23 (2000), 328–351; Rodney Evans, dir., *Brother to Brother* (Miasma, 2004); Eric Garber, "Richard Bruce Nugent," in *Afro-American Writers from the Harlem Renaissance to 1940*, ed. Trudier Harris and Thadious Davis (Detroit: Gale, 1987), 213–221; James V. Hatch, "An Interview with Bruce Nugent—Actor, Artist, Writer, Dancer," *Artists and Influences* 1 (1982), 81–104; Isaac Julien, dir., *Looking for Langston* (New York: Waterbearer Films, 1992); Jeff Kisseloff, *You Must Remember This: An Oral History of Manhattan from the 1890s to World War II* (San Diego: Harcourt Brace Jovanovich, 1989); David Levering Lewis, *When Harlem was in Vogue* (New York: Knopf, 1981); A. B. Christa Schwarz, *Gay Voices of the Harlem Renaissance* (Bloomington: Indiana University Press, 2003); Seth Clark Silberman: "Lighting the Harlem Renaissance Fire!!: Embodying Richard Bruce Nugent's Bohemian Politic," in *The Greatest Taboo: Homosexuality in Black Communities*, ed. Delroy Constantine-Simms (Los Angeles: Alyson, 2001), 254–273; "Looking for Richard Bruce Nugent and Wallace Henry Thurman: Reclaiming Black Male Same-Sexualities in the New Negro Movement," *In Process* 1 (1996), 53–73; Charles Michael Smith, "Bruce Nugent: Bohemian of the Harlem Renaissance," in *In the Life: A Black Gay Anthology*, ed. Joseph Beam (Boston: Alyson, 1986), 209–220; Thomas H. Wirth: "FIRE!! in Retrospect," insert to *Fire!!* (1926; Metuchen, NJ: Fire!!, 1982); "Introduction," in *Gay Rebel of the Harlem Renaissance: Selections from the Work of Richard Bruce Nugent*, ed. Thomas H. Wirth (Durham, NC: Duke University Press, 2002), 1–61.

P

Parks, Suzan-Lori (1963–)

Playwright and author. Suzan-Lori Parks, the daughter of a career military father, was born on May 10, 1963, in Fort Knox, Kentucky. Her family moved frequently throughout her childhood. By the time she enrolled in high school in Germany, where her father was stationed at the time, she had lived in six different states. Following high school, she attended Mount Holyoke College, where she studied with the celebrated novelist James Baldwin. After graduating from college in 1985, Parks studied playwriting at the Yale School of Drama.

Parks's professional playwriting career began in New York City. Her first play, *Imperceptible Mutabilities in the Third Kingdom*, premiered at BACA Downtown in Brooklyn, New York. Mel Gussow, the senior theater critic of the *New York Times*, attended the production and wrote the following of Parks:

Ms. Parks' heightened, dreamlike approach is occasionally reminiscent of Adrienne Kennedy and Ntozake Shange. . . . But there is sufficient evidence of the playwright's originality. . . . Ms. Parks' identity as an artist is clear. [S]he is earnest about making political points but has a playful sense of language and a self-effacing humor.

The play received the 1990 Obie Award for Best New American Play. Parks again won the Obie in 1996 for *Venus*, her play about the exhibition of Saartjie Baartman, the

"Hottentot Venus." Her next major play, *In the Blood*, was a Pulitzer Prize finalist in 2001. Parks has received a MacArthur Foundation "genius" award (2001) and was the recipient of the 2002 Pulitzer Prize for Drama for her play *Topdog/Underdog*. She also received the PEN's 2017 Master American Dramatist Award and the 2018 Steinberg Distinguished Playwright Award.

Parks's popularity as a playwright anchors itself in her unique style of writing. Inspired by the rhythms of jazz music, her plays have a poetic style that is reminiscent of the choreopoems of Ntozake Shange. This style informs the content of her plays, which, to date, can best be divided into history and realist plays. The former category includes *Imperceptible Mutabilities in the Third Kingdom* (1989), *The Death of the Last Black Man in the Whole Entire World* (1990), *Devotees in the Garden of Love* (1992), *The America Play* (1993), *Venus* (1996), *Fucking A* (2000), and *In the Blood* (2000). These plays center on the history and the stereotypes African Americans in the United States and abroad. *Topdog/Underdog* is Parks's first realistic play. A "living room drama," it chronicles the tense relationship between two brothers, Booth and Lincoln. In *The Book of Grace* (2010), Parks explores the aspirations, struggles, and family dynamics of a working woman in South Texas. *Father Comes Home from the Wars, Parts 1, 2 & 3* (2014), set during the Civil War, explores the effects of war and the complexities of homecoming as it echoes and revises classical Greek narratives; it was also a finalist for the Pulitzer Prize in Drama.

Parks's writing career extends beyond the stage. In 1995, film director Spike Lee enlisted the playwright to write the screenplay for his film *Girl 6*. More recently, she worked on the teleplay adaptation of Zora Neal Hurston's *Their Eyes Were Watching God* (2005). In addition, Parks wrote her first novel, *Getting Mother's Body*, in 2003. Throughout her writing career, she has maintained a close connection with American universities. During the years that *The America Play* and *Venus* were produced, she served as the resident playwright at the Yale School of Drama, where both plays premiered. Currently, she teaches at New York University's Tisch School of the Arts.

Harvey Young

See also: Drama; Performance Poetry; Postmodernism.

Resources

Steven Drukman, "Suzan-Lori Parks and Liz Diamond: Doo-a-diddly-dit-dit," *TDR—The Drama Review* 39, no. 3 (1995), 56–75; Harry J. Elam Jr. and Alice Rayner, "Unfinished Business: Reconfiguring History in Suzan-Lori Parks's 'The Death of the Last Black Man in the Whole Entire World,'" *Theatre Journal* 46, no. 4 (1994), 447–462; Mel Gussow, "Identity Loss in *Imperceptible Mutabilities*," *New York Times*, September 20, 1998, p. C24; Philip C. Kolin, ed., *Suzan-Lori Parks: Essays on the Plays and Other Works* (Jefferson, NC: McFarland, 2010); Philip C. Kolin and Harvey Young, eds., *Suzan-Lori Parks in Person: Interviews and Commentaries* (New York: Routledge, 2014); Suzan-Lori Parks: *The America Play, and Other Works* (New York: Theatre Communications Group, 1995); *The Book of Grace* (New York: Theatre Communication Group, 2016); *Father Comes Home from the Wars, Parts I, 2, and 3* (New York: Theatre Communications Group, 2015); *Getting Mother's Body* (New York: Random House, 2003); *Imperceptible Mutabilities in the Third Kingdom* (Los Angeles: Sun and Moon, 1989); *In the Blood* (New York: Dramatists Play Service, 2000); *Red Letter Plays* (New York: Theatre Communications Group, 2000); *TopDog/Underdog* (New York: Theatre Communications Group, 2001); *Venus: A Play* (New York: Theatre Communications Group, 1997); Alisa Solomon, "Signifying on the Signifyin': The Plays of Suzan-Lori Parks," *Theater* 21, no. 3 (1990), 73–80.

Performance Poetry

Performance poetry is the oral, and sometimes visual, presentation of poetry in front of a live audience. It is often a multimedia, or "intermedia," art form that explores the intersection of poetry with drama, music, dance, and visual arts, and it is a genre that is largely concerned with the relationship between the poet and his or her immediate audience. Performance poets break down boundaries between writer and reader, and between art and life, as well as the barriers between different art forms. By emphasizing the communicative relationship between the writer and the reader or listener, performance poets present a challenge to some concepts of literature and art. Performance poetry is bound to a tradition that is more concerned with process, possibility, improvisation, spontaneity, and community rather than with the finished text as an artifact of literature.

African American writers have been seminal to the promotion, development, and proliferation of performance poetry throughout America since the early 1930s. For example, Langston Hughes wrote poetry that was inextricably linked to the rhythms, music, and dialects of the Black community in Harlem, New York, and that was particularly suited to be read aloud. The same can be said of the poetry of Sterling A. Brown, one of Hughes's contemporaries. For Hughes, Brown, and many other African American writers after them, poetry was often connected to jazz music, Black spirituals, and blues. Today, performance poetry, or spoken word, is experiencing a significant renaissance that is largely due to its promotion and practice by African American writers and performers.

However, the performance of poetry is not a recent phenomenon. The oral tradition was particularly significant in early African societies, where ancestral stories traveled along ancient trade routes and migrated with different cultural groups throughout the continent and beyond. Some early African societies were known for "signifying" contests or word battles that involved something similar to a public poetry performance. In most of these societies, poetic narratives connected past to present to future and preceded written texts. The mnemonic devices of rhyme, repetition, and rhythm, often found in poetry, formed a way to keep these stories and cultural mythologies alive. In this way, literature was enlarged and cultural history preserved.

In terms of modern poetics, the connection between drama and poetry increased with artists from the Dada movement, who drew from drama, collage, comedy, and dance in an attempt to challenge the dominant paradigms regarding art and literature. African American writers became more noticeably interested in the oral presentation of poetry towards the middle of the twentieth century with poets such as Hughes, Brown, Claude McKay, and Countee Cullen—all poets of the Harlem Renaissance—who drew on the idiosyncrasies, music, speech, and day-to-day life of urban Blacks. Aimé Césaire, Léopold Sédar Senghor, and Léon Damas, who pioneered an international movement called Négritude, wrote poetry

that combined aspects from French surrealism with Black dialects to challenge dominant representations of African societies. Both groups insisted that oral poetry and written poetry that featured the vernacular were a more accurate model for Black writers worldwide and thus helped promote the performance of poetry by writers of African descent.

Charles Olson's *Projective Verse* (1959), which linked the poetic line to the breath and voice, sparked a renewed interest in the way poetry was read aloud. Shortly after its publication, a renaissance in the performance of poetry began. In the 1950s and 1960s, Beat poets such as Allen Ginsberg, Jack Kerouac, Anne Waldman, and Amiri Baraka performed their work from San Francisco, California, to New York City. Baraka, an African American poet then called LeRoi Jones, was decisive in calling attention to the rhythms and intonations inherent in Black dialect, and in connecting poetic language to jazz music. He is famous for performances from the 1960s to the present day, where he reads poetry alongside famous jazz musicians, such as bassist Reggie Workman and saxophonist David Murray. Baraka's essay "How You Sound??" (1960) expanded on Olson's arguments, and it suggested further that the sound and musicality of language are directly linked to content and subject matter. A contemporary of Baraka's, Dudley Randall, began the Broadside Press (1965), which published poems on broadsides and recorded Black poets reading their work.

Other important Black writers at this time, and in the 1970s, include a group of protest poets who are sometimes referred to as The Last Poets: Mutabaruka, Linton Kwesi Johnson, and Gil Scott-Heron. Scott-Heron's "sound poems," such as "The Revolution Will Not Be Televised" (1971) and "Whitey on the Moon" (1971), were accompanied with jazz and percussion riffs, and challenged dominant White cultural values. These poets and many of the African American poets at this time called attention to the poverty, inequality, and injustice resulting from racism and oppression in America. In the late 1970s, when rap and hip-hop were just beginning to find voice and rhythm in New York, Ntozake Shange experimented with a mixture of poetry, dance, and music in San Francisco bars and clubs. Shange's performances eventually moved to Broadway (1975), where she enjoyed a wide audience for several years. Like Heron and others, she was interested in issues of race and Color of Skin, but her monologues also explored gender and sexuality.

In the 1980s, Nathaniel Mackey drew on African rituals and jazz music, and in his essay "Sound and Sentiment, Sound and Symbol" (1985) he argued that the origins of poetic language are the same as the origins of music. Mackey's poetry often enacts jazz rhythms in what he calls a "post bebop" lyric, in which he attempts to challenge the stereotype of Black musicians as exclusively artists of spontaneity. (Bebop was a style of jazz that emerged in the United States after World War II.) In the same decade, rap bands such as Public Enemy, Run-DMC, and rappers including Tupac Shakur and Ice-T, brought a new focus and attention to the lyrics, message, and musicality of the day-to-day language spoken within the African American community. These rappers provided a very high-profile example of Black expression that included rage and frustration. They also pointed to existing racist conditions and conflicts within the Black community.

With regard to performance of the spoken word, therefore, a thread runs from the Harlem Renaissance through the Black Arts Movement, rap, and hip-hop to contemporary performance poetry and "spoken word." Poetry's connection to hip-hop and the development and proliferation of the "poetry slam," or performance poetry contests, reveals a strong subversion of and reaction to academic formalism, and a rejection of the poststructuralist attention to the written text. This recent surge in spoken word poetry, with its clear African American origins, demonstrates a keen awareness of a long history of racial and cultural oppression, as well as the suppression of colloquial speech and dialect. Spoken word undermines and rejects restrictions on language by focusing on the recitation and performance of poetry in front of an audience; in this way, it is connected as much to drama as it is to poetry.

With influences from Langston Hughes to contemporary poets, including Baraka and Mackey, the writers and performers from the Nuyorican Poets Café in New York and elsewhere in the country have changed contemporary definitions and expectations of poetry. The use of everyday speech, Black English, and Spanglish, and the incorporation of diverse dialects in spoken word, subvert dominant expectations of poetry. In their performances, these poets often take on inequality, gender inequity, class hierarchy, and sexual liberation. Spoken word poetry is filled with the rhythms, rhymes, and other sonic devices that are part of contemporary hip-hop. For spoken word, like earlier performance poetry, the relationship between the author and an audience becomes fundamental to the experience of "reading" a poem. The contemporary Black American writers Paul Beatty, Saul Williams, Tracie Morris, Jessica Care Moore, Soul Evans, and many others demonstrate the vitality and energy of this burgeoning movement.

Mark Tursi

See also: Baraka, Amiri; Black Arts Movement; Jazz in Literature; Shange, Ntozake.

Resources

Zoë Anglesey, ed., *Listen Up! Spoken Word Poetry* (New York: One World, 1999); Crystal Leigh Endlsey, "Performing Blackness: Spoken Word Poetry and Performance," *Transformations* 24, nos. 1–2 (2013–2014), 110–120; Gary Mex Glazner, ed., *Poetry Slam: The Competitive Art of Performance Poetry* (San Francisco: Manic D Press, 2000); Javon Johnson, *Killing Poetry: Blackness and the Making of Slam and Spoken Word Communities* (New Brunswick, NJ: Rutgers University Press, 2017); Monica Molarsky, "Word Fever," *American Theatre* 16, no. 9 (1999), 59–65; Kevin Powell, ed., *Step into a World: A Global Anthology of the New Black Literature* (New York: Wiley, 2000); Ellen Marcia Zweig, *Performance Poetry: Critical Approaches to Contemporary Intermedia* (Ann Arbor, MI: University of Michigan Press, 1980).

Perkins-Valdez, Dolen (1973–)

Novelist, short-story writer, and professor. Perkins-Valdez is the author of two novels, *Wench* (2010) and *Balm* (2015). She is a native of Memphis, Tennessee, and earned a BA from Harvard College, an MA in creative writing from the University of Memphis, and a PhD from George Mason University. She was also a postdoctoral fellow at the University of California, Los Angeles.

Wench is a historical novel that focuses on three African American slaves—Lizzie, Sweet, and Reenie—who during the summer are taken to a resort in Ohio where they are the mistresses of married White slave owners. Tawawa House at Tawawa Springs was in fact was a summer resort that, before the Civil War, functioned as described in the novel. In 1856, it became the site of the first historically Black private college in the United States, Wilberforce University.

Perkins-Valdez's second novel, *Balm,* also a historical work, is set in Chicago in the aftermath of the Civil War. The main characters are an African American root doctor, an African American maid and former slave, and a White woman who has inherited wealth from her deceased husband. All three struggle to rebuild their lives in a new place and era.

For a new republication of the slave narrative *Twelve Years a Slave*, by Solomon Northrup, Perkins-Valdez wrote an introduction. She has also written one for a new republication of *Behind the Scenes: Or, Thirty Years a Slave, and Four Years in the White House* by Elizabeth Keckley.

Perkins-Valdez's short stories have appeared in the *Kenyon Review* and *StoryQuarterly*, among other periodicals. She has taught at the University of Mary Washington, the University of Puget Sound, and American University, and she is also on the faculty of the Stonecoast Writers Conference in Maine.

Hans A. Ostrom

See also: Feminism/Black Feminism; Novel.

Resources

Trudier Harris, "'Does northern travel relieve slavery?': 'Vacations' in Dolen Perkins-Valdez's *Wench,*" *South Atlantic Review* 78, no. 3–4 (Summer 2013), 90(20); Dolen Perkins-Valdez: "'Atlanta's Shame': W.E.B. Du Bois and Carrie Williams Clifford Respond to the Atlanta Race Riot of 1906," *Studies in the Literary Imagination* 40, no. 2 (Fall 2007), 133(19); *Balm* (New York: Amistad, 2015); "Introduction" to *Behind the Scenes: Or, Thirty Years a Slave, and Four Years in the White House* by Elizabeth Keckley (Hillsborough, NC: Eno Publishers,

2016); "Introduction" to *Twelve Years a Slave*, by Solomon Northrup.

Petry, Ann Lane (1908–1997)

Author of novels, short stories, and juvenile fiction. By debunking stereotypes of race, class, and gender, Petry contributed significantly to the non-sentimental depiction of the socioeconomic plight of African Americans in the 1940s and 1950s and thereby paved the way for contemporary African American women's writing.

Born in 1908 in Old Saybrook, Connecticut, Ann Petry graduated from the Connecticut College of Pharmacy in New Haven in 1931 and then worked at her family's drugstores. After marrying George D. Petry in 1938, she moved to New York City, where she wrote for the *Amsterdam News*. She also took up painting, writing short fiction, and acting in the American Negro Theatre. Later, she honed her writing skills by editing the woman's page of *The People's Voice* and by participating in Mabel Louise Robinson's creative writing workshop at Columbia University. The $2,400 from a Houghton Mifflin Library Fellowship enabled her to finish her first novel, *The Street* (1946), the first book by a Black woman writer to sell over a million copies. Petry published two more novels, *Country Place* (1947) and *The Narrows* (1953), a collection of short stories titled *Miss Muriel and Other Stories* (1971), several adolescent books, nonfiction articles, and some poetry. Among the many honors she received are the Doctorate of Letters from Suffolk University (1983) and the University of Connecticut (1988), the Lifetime Achievement Award at the Fifth Annual Celebration of Black Writers Conference in Philadelphia, Pennsylvania (1989), and the Connecticut Arts Award from the Connecticut Commission of the Arts (1992) (Ervin, xii–xviii).

In *The Street*, Lutie Johnson's hopes spring from her first contact with Ben Franklin's *The Way to Wealth* philosophy at the home of her White employers in Lyme, Connecticut. Petry describes how creature comforts and consumer goods create artificial desires in Lutie, who naively believes that she will be able to escape the restrictions of her social position and provide her son Bub with a better life. She asserts that "anybody could be rich if he wanted to and worked hard enough and figured it out carefully enough" (43). Consequently, she strives to improve herself by taking night classes and studying for the civil service exam. Petry models Lutie's behavior upon Franklin's only to reveal that Lutie is mistaken in her belief that the American dream is accessible even to a poor Black woman.

The title of Petry's novel underscores the formative influences of New York's 116th Street on its inhabitants. On the first page of the novel, the wind whips Lutie around the street, blinding her so that she can barely make out the street signs. It heaps up the garbage and nearly freezes the blood in her veins. Merciless in the pursuit of those it can hurt, it is an elemental force, uncaring and brutal. Petry employs the wind as the symbol of a force that continually threatens to take hold of Lutie, attacks her physically, and dampens her spirits. The walls in her apartment seem to trap her. The fear of Jones, the janitor, who lusts after Lutie and eventually tempts her son to steal mail from the residents in the apartment building, coupled with the uncertainty of her future, compel her to seek escape at the Junto Bar and Grill. Petry's choice of name for this bar is noteworthy, considering that Ben Franklin's first men's club in Philadelphia was called the Junto and was to serve philanthropic purposes.

At the end of the novel, while sitting on the train that is to take her away from the scene of the murder she committed in order to get the money for a lawyer to plead Bub's case, Lutie draws intersecting circles on the windowpane. They seem to represent the vicious cycle from which she could not free herself. Remembering her schoolteacher's derogatory remarks, she begins to wonder why, indeed, she was ever taught to write when she was not given the chance to put her talents to good use.

Dismissed as an assimilationist novel by some critics because it features a group of White characters and does not overtly discuss racial issues, *Country Place* (1947) sets out to examine the hypocrisies of a small New England town. The narrative moves from Doc Fraser's first-person story to several third-person limited omniscient accounts, a method that allows Petry to investigate different points of view and illumine the "composite reality" of the community's identity (Holloday, 34). The otherwise traditional narrative unfolds in one week and is driven by the rise of a powerful storm. Doc Fraser, a sixty-five-year-old White druggist in Lennox, Connecticut, plays a unifying role reminiscent of George Willard's in Sherwood Anderson's *Winesburg, Ohio*. Assisted by the town gossip (the taxi driver Tom Walker, called Weasel), Fraser proposes to report accurately what happened to the townspeople, "this record of events contains, of course, something of life and something of death, for both are to be found in a country place" (5). The novel focuses on Johnnie Roane's brief return to Lennox after World War II and on his estranged wife, Glory, whose affair with Ed Barrell encourages Johnnie to move to New York and fulfill his dream of becoming a painter. Two minor plots concern the wealthy Mrs. Gramby's conflict with her greedy daughter-in-law and the decision by the servants Neola and Portulacca to get married.

Set mainly in a Black neighborhood in Monmouth, Connecticut, *The Narrows* (1953) involves a more obviously sociological investigation of racial matters, which led Bernard Bell to remark that the novel's theme is "that our lives are shaped as much by contingency as they are by time and place" (181). With its modernistic shifts in narrative perspective, some stream-of-consciousness passages, and interesting word coinages, this novel constitutes a new development in Petry's oeuvre. The novel creates complex relationships among carefully developed Black and White characters. The main character, the twenty-six-year-old African American Link (short for Lincoln) Williams, an orphan and Dartmouth history graduate, is the novel's linking character between Black and White and rich and poor. He works at the Last Chance bar owned by Bill Hood, who on and off, despite his mob connections, serves as his father figure and instills in him a pride in his ethnic heritage. Abbie Crunch, a staunch New England lady, is Link's adoptive mother. Because of his love for Camilla Treadway Sheffield, alias Camilo Williams, the rich White heiress to a munitions company fortune, Link is murdered at the end of the novel. Neither the two lovers nor the community knows how to deal with their interracial relationship (Holloway, 88). In his article "'Same Train Be Back Tomorrer': Ann Petry's *The Narrows* and the Repetition of History," Michael Barry observes that the novel questions "Western progress narratives" while sustaining hopes for moral improvement (143).

In addition to some uncollected short stories, Petry also published *Miss Muriel and Other Stories* (1971), the first short-story collection by an African American woman, including thirteen pieces. The title story calls attention to the pernicious consequences of stereotyping and prejudice experienced by both Black and White characters. Ruth's is the only Black family in the fictional Wheeling, New York. The child narrator befriends the elderly shoemaker Blemish, who develops a keen interest in Ruth's aunt Sophronia. When two Black suitors enter the scene, Blemish is run out of town and Ruth debates whether she would have found this White suitor acceptable for her aunt. "The New Mirror" features the same Black family and comments again on their feelings of alienation as the only "'admittedly' black family" in Wheeling (59). "Has Anybody Seen Miss Dora Dean?" employs the same first-person, middle-class narrator as the preceding two stories. However, as an adult she is more acutely aware of latent discriminations. In the course of the story, she is finally able to answer a question that has preoccupied her since childhood: Mr. Forbes, a butler, killed himself because he could no longer stand his servile position, his suicide implicitly devaluing the lives of all African Americans who struggled for a place in the community (Holloday, 106). "Doby's Gone" introduces Sue, whose imaginary friend disappears when she faces racist violence in school. In "Solo on the Drums," Kid James, a drummer whose wife has left him, puts all his emotions into his music. Petry creates an eerily expressionistic musical sequence in this piece reminiscent of similar elements in Ralph Ellison's work.

Petry also wrote children's books, such as *The Drugstore Cat* (1949) and *Legends of the Saints* (1970). Driven by a desire to debunk stereotypes of African Americans, she created, in *Tituba of Salem Village* (1964), a partly historical and partly fictional portrait of a young Barbadian slave woman who came to Salem Village with the family of the Reverend Samuel Paris. Petry sympathetically describes the heartbreak of leaving home and the daily drudgeries of making a living in the colonies, in a staunchly Puritan community where any sort of "otherness" raises suspicions of witchcraft. *Harriet Tubman, Conductor on the Underground Railroad* (1955) emphasizes Harriet Tubman's early years, her escape from slavery, and her return to Maryland to free hundreds of other slaves. Each of the fictionalized chapters ends with a short historical commentary. As Petry explained in interviews, these two novels include none of the uncertainties and questions of her adult novels because she meant to supply children with viable African American role models.

Contemporary literary criticism of Petry's work transcends naturalistic inquiries. While Heather Holloday describes Petry as a "neighborhood" novelist who emphasizes community and family and complex relationships (44) instead of rigid individualism, others have examined Petry as a New England writer or studied her anticipation of strong African American women characters. Recent articles have also illustrated the depth and versatility of Petry's work by drawing attention to new critical approaches springing from the theories of Michel Foucault and Sigmund Freud, from the critical perspective known as New Historicism, and strategies of interpretation connected to feminism.

Susanna Hoeness-Krupsaw

See also: Realism; Short Fiction.

Resources

Primary Sources: Ann Petry: *Country Place* (Chatham, NJ: Chatham Bookseller, 1947); *The Drugstore Cat* (New York: Crowell, 1949);

Harriet Tubman, Conductor on the Underground Railroad (1955; repr. New York: Pocket Books, 1971); *Legends of the Saints* (New York: Crowell, 1970); *Miss Muriel and Other Stories* (1971; repr. Boston: Beacon, 1989); *The Narrows* (1953; repr. Boston: Beacon Press, 1988); "The Novel as Social Criticism," in *The Writer's Book*, ed. Helen Hull (New York: Harper, 1950), 32–39; *The Street* (1946; repr. Boston: Beacon Press, 1974); *Tituba of Salem Village* (1964; repr. New York: Harper Trophy, 1991).

Secondary Sources: "Ann Petry," *Voices from the Gap*, http://voices.cla.umn.edu/newsite/authors/PETRYann.htm; Michael Barry, "'Same Train Be Back Tomorrer': Ann Petry's *The Narrows* and the Repetition of History," *MELUS* 24, no. 1 (1999), 141–160; Bernard W. Bell, *The Afro-American Novel and Its Tradition* (Amherst, MA: University of Massachusetts Press, 1987); Robert Bone, *The Negro Novel in America*, rev. ed. (New Haven, CT: Yale University Press, 1965); Keith Clark: "A Distaff Dream Deferred? Ann Petry and the Art of Subversion," *African American Review* 26, no. 3 (1992), 495–505; *The Radical Fiction of Ann Petry* (Baton Rouge, LA: Louisiana State University Press, 2013); Hazel Arnett Ervin, *Ann Petry: A Bio-Bibliography* (New York: G. K. Hall, 1993); Heather Hicks: "Rethinking Realism in Ann Petry's *The Street*," *MELUS* 27, no. 4 (2002), 89–96; "This Strange Communion: Surveillance and Spectatorship in Ann Petry's *The Street*," *African American Review* 37, no. 1 (2003), 21–38; Hilary Holladay, *Ann Petry* (New York: Twayne, 1996); Alex Lubin, ed., *Revising the Blueprint: Ann Petry and the Literary Left* (Jackson, MS: University Press of Mississippi, 2007); Julia Mickenberg, "Civil Rights, History, and the Left: Inventing the Juvenile Black Biography," *MELUS* 27, no. 2 (2002), 65–93; Elizabeth Petry, *At Home Inside: A Daughter's Tribute to Ann Petry* (Jackson, MS: University Press of Mississippi, 2009); Marjorie Pryse, "'Pattern Against the Sky': Deism and Motherhood in Ann Petry's *The Street*," in *Conjuring: Black Women, Fiction and Literary Tradition*, ed. Marjorie Pryse and Hortense Spillers (Bloomington, IN: Indiana University Press, 1985), 116–131; Cherene Sherrard-Johnson, "City Place/Country Place: Negotiating Class Geographies in Ann Petry's Writing," in *Black Harlem and the Jewish Lower East Side: Narratives Out of Time*, ed. Catherine Rottenberg (Albany, NY: State University of New York Press, 2013), 65–85; Mary Helen Washington, ed., *Invented Lives: Narratives of Black Women 1860–1960* (Garden City, NY: Anchor, 1987).

Poetics

Poetics is the study of poetry as a genre, and it encompasses theories of poetry, criticism, poets' statements about poetry, and traditions of technique, as well as poetic texts. Within the Western literary tradition, from Aristotle's *Poetics* (ca. 350 BCE) to Houston A. Baker Jr.'s *Afro-American Poetics* (1988) and Kevin Powell's anthology, *Step into a World: A Global Anthology of the New Black Literature* (2000), poetics has played a central role in shaping, directing, and interpreting literary tastes and trends. African Americans, whose poetic traditions run deep, have made significant, distinctive contributions to poetics at least since the eighteenth century, and their contributions to the field have become even more important since the beginning of the twentieth century.

The roots of African American poetics are not to be found on the North American continent, but rather in Africa. Just as in ancient Greece songs constituted an important form of poetry, so early African poetry consisted of chants. Poets, often taking the histories of tribes, places, and wars as their subjects, worked orally either by improvising their poems to cater to local tastes or by memorizing and reciting the same poem or variants of it from generation to generation, sometimes as court griots or bards (Southern and Wright).

Several myths about early African poetry can cause misunderstanding. First, African poetry is not composed of "rhythmic prose," as was commonly supposed until the end of the nineteenth century, but rather of discrete lines of short and long syllables with or without accents. At the same time, the important role that rhythm (and often music and dance) plays in these poems cannot be underestimated. Second, poetry from different regions in Africa does not necessarily form a homogeneous whole. In ancient as in modern times, African poetics has been inherently heterogeneous, drawing from many different languages (some estimates range upwards of 3,000) and many different styles on an enormous continent. Third, current knowledge of these early poems is limited, since only about 200 examples are extant, and little or no commentary has been handed down to us from the times in which these poems were written. As a result, it is impossible to advance definitive claims about early African poetry.

With the rise of colonialism, the history of African poetry in one sense comes to an end because colonialism affected African culture so broadly, disrupting literary practices and traditions. In another sense, the history of African poetry continued but underwent enormous changes and fused with literary histories outside of Africa. During the colonial period, African writers began to emigrate to foreign, often hostile countries, sometimes willingly but more often as slaves. They began using languages other than their native ones, chiefly English and French. As a result of this diaspora, African Americans shaped English to fit African poetics, and African poetics to fit Anglo-American contexts.

"Bars Fight," by Lucy Terry, is commonly thought to be the first poem written by a Black person in America, although it was not published until 1855. The poem, written in twenty-eight (another edition has thirty) lines of rhymed tetrameter couplets, may be understood as the inauguration of one vein of African American poetics, which uses traditional English poetic styles, such as ballads and sonnets, to give voice to a "Negro" perspective. A more famous poet in this formal vein is Phillis Wheatley, born in Senegal, who is generally considered to be the first major African American poet. At the age of thirteen, Wheatley composed "On Being Brought from Africa to America" (1768), and four years later she published her celebrated *A Poem by Phillis, a Negro Girl in Boston, on the Death of the Reverend George Whitefield*. Wheatley's most important work, *Poems on Various Subjects, Religious and Moral* (1773), was published in England, where Wheatley had moved for health reasons. This more formal vein of poetics was more commonly practiced by African Americans in the North than those in the South, in part because African American literacy was not prohibited as strictly in the North as it was in the South, although it was often difficult for newly freed slaves to become literate. Jupiter Hammon, who published the first known work of African American literature in 1760, and George Moses Horton, who is credited with being the first professional African American poet, may be grouped with Terry and Wheatley. Countee Cullen and Georgia Douglas Johnson, Harlem Renaissance writers, can also be placed in this formal, Anglo-American vein; both, for instance, worked comfortably in the sonnet form.

The other major vein of African American poetics springs from the mostly oral, song-oriented tradition that developed because of the circumstances of slavery. This vein is sometimes referred to as the vernacular tradition. After the Revolutionary War, literacy was legally denied to

Black slaves; Negro poetry, rather than being stifled by such laws, flourished in the South, though in different guises. It had its roots in orally transmitted field hollers, work songs, and spirituals. Paul Laurence Dunbar works with the vernacular extensively in *Lyrics of Lowly Life* (1893). The vernacular informs some of the innovations in rhythm and idiom provided by blues and jazz in the nineteenth and twentieth centuries, and it continues in the intricate rhyme schemes, sampling, street language, and layering of voices in contemporary Performance Poetry, including the work of Gil Scott-Heron, and in hip-hop. The vernacular vein of African American poetics is intimately linked to the history of African American music, though it is in no way limited to this context. During the pre–Civil War era, rhyming aphorisms were used to communicate common complaints as well as secret messages across work fields, such as "I wants a piece a hoecake I wants a piece o' bread. / Well, Ise so tired an' hongry dat Ise almos' dead" (Talley, 280). One of the most prominent features of the field holler, which was to be taken up by the blues later on, is the call–response structure, in which one person says a line and another person or group of people answer according to certain lyrical prescriptions. During the post–Civil War era, Christian spirituals became a vehicle of increasing importance for African American poetic expression. Often as subversive as they were spiritual, these songs had been used during the antebellum period as codes in the Underground Railroad as well as in devotional meetings that were actually planning sessions to help slaves escape to the North.

From the late nineteenth century to the interwar period, blues artists (including Bessie Smith), ragtime performers (including Scott Joplin), Dixieland musicians (such as King Oliver and Louis Armstrong), and bebop jazz artists (such as Charlie Parker) played an important part in shaping the poetic sensibilities of Black and White audiences across America. For example, Langston Hughes's first book of poems, *The Weary Blues* (1926), draws heavily on blues language, structure, and sensibility (Tracy; Ostrom). The poetry of Sterling A. Brown and Fenton Johnson shows similar influences (Henderson). Hughes's essay "The Negro Artist and the Racial Mountain," although chiefly concerned with encouraging African American writers to write about what they know, makes an indirect statement about the need for a poetics that celebrates African American culture, including the blues and colloquial expression.

In the early twentieth century, Modernism had an enormous impact on all literature, including African American poetics. Critics often refer to "High" and "Low" Modernism. High Modernist poets include Ezra Pound and T. S. Eliot, whose work is structurally complex, full of allusions to other literary texts, often multilingual, sometimes surrealistic, and concerned broadly with cultural decay. The African American writers Jean Toomer (whose novel *Cane* includes poetry) and Melvin B. Tolson are associated with High Modernism. Low Modernists include Carl Sandburg, William Carlos Williams, Robert Frost, and Langston Hughes; their work is more accessible than that of Eliot and Pound, more colloquial, more at ease with themes related to everyday life, less densely allusive, and aimed at a broader audience.

In the postwar or Cold War era, the Black Arts Movement significantly influenced African American poetics, encouraging African American poets to explore African American experiences, politics, history, and language as fully as possible (Gayle). Poets connected with the Black Arts Movement include Amiri Baraka, Haki R. Madhubuti, Gwendolyn Brooks, Carolyn M. Rodgers, Dudley Randall, Sonia Sanchez, and Etheridge Knight. After the Black Arts Movement, African American poetics seems both to have exploded and to have imploded. It has exploded in the sense that it has become part of an everyday, global culture, but it has imploded in the sense that African American poetics has become more self-consciously distinct. On the popular front, musical metamorphoses into the free jazz of Sun Ra, the disco funk of Grand Funk Railroad, and the early rap of the Sugar Hill Gang and Grand Master Flash and Furious Five brought about a concomitant change in poetic tastes, and it is easy to discern the combined influence of Black Arts poetics, jazz, and rap in contemporary performance poetry.

Although tracing two strains of African American poetics—the formal and the vernacular—can be useful, many poets participate in both strains. For example, Countee Cullen preferred to work in traditional forms of English poetry, but his poetry addresses fundamental concerns of African American people, and his diction is chiefly contemporary. Langston Hughes's poetry is squarely in the vernacular tradition, but Hughes often deploys rhyme schemes and imagery common to an Anglo-American tradition, and the range of diction he deploys is deceptively broad. The poetry of Rita Dove and Michael S. Harper, to take just two examples, blends aspects of the vernacular and formal strains to such an extent that sharp distinctions become more difficult to make.

Poetry is always changing dynamically both in form and in content, and therefore poetics, or the set of ideas about poetry, is also extremely dynamic. The role that African American poetics has played in American literature and aesthetics cannot be underestimated. It has brought elements from a long oral tradition to American poetry, it has adapted and improvised on Anglo-American verse forms, and it has injected a sense of political urgency and of linguistic freedom into African American literature and American literature in general.

Antony Adolf

See also: Black Arts Movement; Blues Poetry; Epic Poetry/The Long Poem; Formal Verse; Free Verse; Harlem Renaissance; Lyric Poetry.

Resources

Klaus Benesch, "Oral Narrative and Literary Text: Afro-American Folklore in *Their Eyes Were Watching God*," *Callaloo* 11 (1988): 627–635; Benjamin A. Botkin, ed., *Folk-Say*, vol. 1 (Norman, OK: University of Oklahoma Press, 1930), a periodical; Charles T. Davis and Henry Louis Gates Jr., eds., *The Slave's Narrative* (New York: Oxford University Press, 1985), esp. "Charles Chesnutt and the WPA Narratives: The Oral and Literate Roots of Afro-American Literature," 37–49; Brent Hayes Edwards, *Epistophies: Jazz and the Literary Imagination* (Cambridge, MA: Harvard University Press, 2017); Sascha Feinstein, *Jazz Poetry: From the 1920s to the Present* (Westport, CT: Greenwood Press, 1997); Karen J. Ford, "These Old Writing Paper Blues: The Blues Stanza and Literary Poetry," *College Literature* 24, no. 3 (1997), 84–97; Addison Gayle Jr., *The Black Aesthetic* (Garden City, NY: Doubleday, 1971); Stephen E. Henderson, "The Heavy Blues of Sterling Brown: A Study of Craft and Tradition," *Black American Literature Forum* 14 (1980), 32–44; James Weldon Johnson, with J. Rosamond Johnson, eds., *The Book of American Negro Spirituals* (New York: Viking, 1925; repr. New York: Da Capo Press, 1989); Marit J. MacArthur, "Monotony, the Churches of Poetry Reading, and Sound

Studies," *PMLA* 131, no. 1 (2016), 38–63, 239; Hans Ostrom, *A Langston Hughes Encyclopedia* (Westport, CT: Greenwood Press, 2002); Kevin Powell, ed., *Step into a World: A Global Anthology of the New Black Literature* (New York: Wiley, 2000); Alex Preminger and Terry V. F. Brogan, eds., *The New Princeton Encyclopedia of Poetry and Poetics* (Princeton, NJ: Princeton University Press, 1993); Eileen Southern and Josephine Wright, comps., *African-American Traditions in Song, Sermon, Tale, and Dance, 1600s–1920: An Annotated Bibliography of Literature, Collections, and Artworks* (Westport, CT: Greenwood Press, 1990); Pauline Turner Strong, *Captive Selves, Captivating Others: The Politics and Poetics of Colonial American Captivity Narratives* (Boulder, CO: Westview Press, 1999); Thomas W. Talley, *Negro Folk Rhymes: Wise and Otherwise* (New York: Macmillan, 1922); Steven Tracy, *Langston Hughes and the Blues* (Urbana, IL: University of Illinois Press, 1988); Jeffrey Allen Tucker, "Waking Up to the Sound," *American Literary History* 27, no. 3 (2015), 599–613; M. Lynn Weiss, *Gertrude Stein and Richard Wright: The Poetics and Politics of Modernism* (Jackson, MS: University Press of Mississippi, 1988).

Poetry

See: Angelou, Maya; Baraka, Amiri; Blues Poetry; Brooks, Gwendolyn; Cullen, Countee; Dialect Poetry; Dove, Rita; Dunbar, Paul Laurence; Epic Poetry/The Long Poem; Fauset, Jessie Redmon; Formal Verse; Free Verse; Giovanni, Nikki; Hughes, Langston; Johnson, Georgia Douglas; Johnson, James Weldon; Jordan, June; Knight, Etheridge; Komunyakaa, Yusef; Lorde, Audre; Lyric Poetry; Madhubuti, Haki R. (Don Luther Lee); McKay, Claude; Performance Poetry; Poetics; Rodgers, Carolyn Marie; Terry [Prince], Lucy; Troupe, Quincy Thomas, Jr.; Wheatley, Phillis.

Postmodernism

Literary movement and cultural and political aesthetic. Postmodernism is considered by many scholars to be more a practice than a methodology. It reacts first and foremost to the self-assured air of Modernism. Euro-American cultural Modernism emerged from the Enlightenment (1700s), which emphasized empiricism, material progress, rational thought and reason, ideals of organic and universal truth, and increasing democratization that invested heavily in (or took its shape from) ideologies of the nation-state. Postmodernism also refers loosely to the cultural era after World War II. For the African American tradition, the most significant event of the modern era was the trade in African slaves. The trade not only helped create the African diaspora and establish the permanent presence of Africans in the New World; it also powered Western economic systems and served as the impetus behind the solidification of doctrines of inequality founded on pseudoscientific theories of Black racial inferiority. Thus, as Stephen Jay Gould (1981) has pointed out, the apex of the modern ideological moment might be described as the historical intersection (in 1776) of Thomas Jefferson's Declaration of Independence, Adam Smith's *The Wealth of Nations*, and Johann Blumenbach's *On the Natural Varieties of Mankind*. Jefferson's work limned the ideals of an emerging nation; Smith's book detailed the finer points of individualist economics; and Blumenbach, through his schema of racial classification and his coining of the term "Caucasian" as a racial descriptor for persons of European descent, unwittingly set into motion a slew of racist doctrines. The social and intellectual economy of the time was strongly informed by the intersection of the ideas put forward in these three documents, yet eighteenth-century Black writers such as Olaudah Equiano and Quobna Cugoano did not hesitate to contest these notions and to present their own accounts of Black life in the modern era.

Cornel West and bell hooks are among the best-known African American theorists of the postmodern. While he makes little effort to differentiate between postmodernism as practice and postmodernity as period, West, in his essay "Black Culture and Postmodernism" (1989), places the movement on a historical continuum that begins in 1945. Emphasizing the fall of Europe and the rise of the United States as a military and economic power, the slow resurgence and opposition of former European colonies in Africa and the Caribbean are significant for West. He harshly criticizes postmodern icons such as Jean-François Lyotard and Jacques Derrida. Lyotard's analysis of the "postmodern condition" is, to West's mind, "rather parochial and provincial—that is, narrowly Eurocentric" (391). Derrida fares no better under West: he neglects to include "Third World peoples, women, gays, lesbians—as well as their relative political impotence in creatively transforming the legacy of the age of Europe" (391). Indeed, Michel Foucault and Jürgen Habermas (who is no fan of postmodernists such as Derrida) likewise draw criticism from West, each proffering analyses that have "remained inscribed within narrow disciplinary boundaries, insulated artistic practices, and vague formulations of men and women of letters" (392). What is needed, West argues, is a push toward a radical reconsideration of historical methodologies and periodizations, which may lead us forthrightly to "issues of politics and ideology" (392). West encourages theorists to pluralize, historicize, and contextualize the postmodernism debate.

hooks, in her widely read essay "Postmodern Blackness" (1990), appears to apply certain pragmatism in her view of postmodernism. That is, for her, postmodernism should serve as a foundation upon which and a space wherein Black intellectuals reaffirm their connections to the Black folk community, a locus wherein the various points and tenets of postmodernist thought—fragmentation, exile, and marginalization—converge and intersect. At this nodal point, hooks tells us, oppositional strategies of resistance, strategies informed by the historicity of the Black presence in America as well as the postmodern work of countercultural movements, can agitate in favor of the goal of Black liberation.

African American practitioners of the postmodern aesthetic have often gained attention through their use of literary devices that underscore a sense of fragmentation and that question the very possibility of representation. Black literary postmodernism turns away from the essentialist identity politics of the 1960s (practiced by the Black Arts school) and turns instead toward conceptions of identity that emphasize pluralism and contingency, double-coding and self-reflexivity. Ralph Ellison's *Invisible Man* (1952) is an early example of a novel that not only deals with the issues of selfhood and existence but also interrogates and subverts traditional ideas of the novel as form. The bibliography, necessarily selective, includes contemporary African American writers considered to be significantly "postmodern," including Toni Morrison, Ishmael Reed, Samuel R. Delany, and John Edgar Wideman. Cultural studies, Whiteness studies, and critical race theory are among the discourses that come under the Black postmodernist umbrella. All examine the construction and maintenance of social power, and because Blackness is often posited as the oppositional social value of Whiteness, the examination of White supremacy through the lens of postmodernism is absolutely necessary.

Rebecka Rychelle Rutledge

See also: Baraka, Amiri; Ellison, Ralph; Jones, Gayl; Major, Clarence; Morrison, Toni; Parks, Suzan-Lori; Reed, Ishmael; Shange, Ntozake; Simms, Renee Elizabeth; Wideman, John Edgar.

Resources

Sandra Adell, "The Crisis in Black American Literary Criticism and the Postmodern Cures of Houston A. Baker and Henry Louis Gates, Jr.," in her *Double-Consciousness/Double Bind: Theoretical Issues in Twentieth-Century Black Literature* (Urbana, IL: University of Illinois Press, 1994); Hans Bertens, *The Idea of the Postmodern: A History* (New York: Routledge, 1995); Preston Park Cooper, *Playing with Expectations: Postmodern Narrative Choices and the African American Novel* (New York: Peter Lang, 2015); Samuel Delany, *Stars in My Pockets like Grains of Sand* (New York: Bantam Books, 1984); Madhu Dubey: "Post-Postmodern Realism?" *Twentieth-Century Literature* 27, nos. 3–4 (2011), 364–371; *Signs and Cities: Black Literary Postmodernism* (Chicago: University of Chicago Press, 2003); Robert E. Fox, *Conscientious Sorcerers: The Black Postmodern Fiction of Leroi Jones Amiri Baraka, Ishmael Reed, and Samuel R. Delany* (Westport, CT: Greenwood Press, 1987); Stephen Jay Gould, *The Mismeasure of Man* (New York: Norton, 1981); Philip Brian Harper, *Framing the Margins: The Social Logic of Postmodern Culture* (New York: Oxford University Press, 1994); Ihab Hassan, *The Dismemberment of Orpheus: Toward a Postmodern Literature*, 2nd ed. (Madison, WI: University of Wisconsin Press, 1982); W. Lawrence Hogue, *Race, Modernity, Postmodernity: A Look at the History and the Literatures of People of Color Since the 1960s* (Albany, NY: State University of New York Press, 1996); bell hooks, "Postmodern Blackness" (1990), in *A Postmodern Reader*, ed. Joseph Natoli and Linda Hutcheon (Albany, NY: State University of New York Press, 1993); Linda Hutcheon, *A Poetics of Postmodernism: History, Theory, Fiction* (New York: Routledge, 1988); Fredric Jameson, *Postmodernism, or the Cultural Logic of Late Capitalism* (Durham, NC: Duke University Press, 1991); Jean-François Lyotard, *The Postmodern Condition: A Report on Knowledge*, trans. Geoff Bennington and Brian Massumi (1979; Minneapolis, MN: University of Minnesota Press, 1984); Brian McHale, *Postmodernist Fiction* (London: Metheun, 1987); Kobena Mercer, *Welcome to the Jungle: New Positions in Black Cultural Studies* (New York: Routledge, 1994); Toni Morrison: *Beloved* (New York: Knopf, 1987); *Paradise* (New York: Knopf, 1998); Ishmael Reed, *Mumbo Jumbo* (New York: Simon and Schuster, 1996); A. Timothy Spaulding, *Re-Forming the Past: History, the Fantastic, and the Postmodern Slave Narrative* (Columbus OH: Ohio State University Press, 2005); Cornel West: "Black Culture and Postmodernism," in *A Postmodern Reader*, ed. Joseph Natoli and Linda Hutcheon (Albany, NY: State University of New York Press, 1993), 390–397; *Prophetic Thought in Postmodern Times* (Monroe, ME: Common Courage Press, 1993); John Edgar Wideman, *Reuben* (New York: Henry Holt, 1987); Howard Winant, "Postmodern Racial Politics: Difference and Inequality," *Socialist Review* 20, no. 1 (1990), 121–147.

Poststructuralism

A type of literary and cultural criticism, poststructuralism may be described as a philosophy that attempts to disrupt our reliance on language as something that guarantees meaning. It is largely associated with Deconstruction as well as with psychoanalysis (as used by the critics Frantz Fanon,

Julia Kristeva, and others), French feminism, and cultural studies. Any understanding of poststructuralist thought must begin with the work of Jacques Derrida, whose 1966 lecture at Johns Hopkins University, "Structure, Sign and Play in the Discourse of the Human Sciences," and three books, *Of Grammatology, Speech and Phenomena,* and *Writing and Difference,* all published in 1967, precipitated the revolution against structuralism. Structuralist theory, predicated on the work of the Swiss linguist Ferdinand de Saussure, evolved from the formalism of the Prague School (led by the Russian linguist Roman Jakobson and the Viennese critic René Wellek) in the period between 1926 and 1948. Heavily influenced by the Moscow Linguistic Circle, the structuralists imagined the literary text to be a set of formal relations, a gestalt comprising multiple elements which, nonetheless, allowed for a unified whole. The term "structuralism," coined by Jakobson, refers not simply to a theory or a method but to a way of seeing the world, a weltanschauung that insists upon an organic concept of reality and knowledge. Specific elements of this whole were considered to be both present and absent—present to the extent that they appear before us, yet absent insofar as they necessarily constitute factors of a larger system which we cannot fully grasp, but of which each existing ingredient, including we ourselves, forms a part. Structuralism was interested in neither individuality nor history; instead, it was concerned with relationships of meaning.

Derrida's early works initiated the turn away from language as a full and adequate representation of meaning, a principle central to the structuralist project. The quest for absolute meaning had long been the goal of Western metaphysics, and language, as a major constituent of the meaning-making process, had preoccupied Western thinkers from the time of Plato and Aristotle. The Platonic theory of Forms denigrated writing as a degenerate and inadequate representation of speech, and the French structuralists of the 1950s (Claude Lévi-Strauss and Jacques Lacan being quite prominent among them) were only the latest group to carry forward a program insisting upon the absolute ability of language to convey full meaning. Derrida, in working to collapse the binary opposition between speech and writing, also worked to "deconstruct" the notion of transcendental Truth, which had, for quite some time, powered metaphysics.

Poststructuralism came to the United States largely through the Yale School, a collective of scholars at Yale University who, led by Paul de Man, translated the French texts of Derrida and introduced them to American scholars and students. African American theorists and critics soon became invested in poststructuralist theory. In working to dismantle the notion of absolute Truth, a Eurocentric concept, they worked vigorously to disable the idea of a normative discourse of self and identity which posited people of color as "Other," as the inferior term in Hegel's famous dialectic of master and slave in his *Phenomenology of Spirit* (1806–1807). Without doubt, African Americanists had not waited for the work of Derrida to inaugurate a radical discourse of opposition and deconstruction. Olaudah Equiano, in his 1789 *Narrative of the Life of Olaudah Equiano,* strove to demonstrate the contradictions and gaps inherent in universalist theories of national identity. W.E.B. Du Bois's idea of double consciousness, expounded at length in *The Souls of Black Folk* (1903), corrects Hegel's dialectic by insisting not only upon an account of the forces of history (including the legacies and realities of slavery, peonage, and Jim Crow) but also upon a theory of materialism that questioned the Enlightenment notion of Progress. Double consciousness read clearly is not a resignation to a sense of alienation in national life; rather, it is the recognition of a multiple self with multiple identities to be negotiated. Du Bois's double consciousness may be seen at work in the Martinican psychoanalyst Frantz Fanon's *Black Skin, White Masks* (1952), specifically in the widely read essay "The Fact of Blackness."

Du Bois's work is, arguably, foundational to contemporary Black poststructuralism in the United States. While the Black Arts Movement produced structuralist and formalist dicta on an authoritarian "Black English" and a "true Black Subject" during the 1960s, poststructuralist theorists such as Houston A. Baker Jr. made the shift away from Black structuralism. Baker, among his many projects, worked to link the cultural and social theory of Du Bois to language and experimental writing in the work of Ralph Ellison (who was both novelist and critic) in order to produce a poststructuralist theory of a blues idiom. Although Barbara Christian, the late doyenne of twentieth-century Black women's literary criticism, disparaged theory and called for a return to close readings in her essay "The Race for Theory" (1987), Mae Gwendolyn Henderson, in "Speaking in Tongues: Dialogics, Dialectics, and the Black Woman Writer's Literary Tradition" (1989), embraced poststructuralist theories of language by insisting upon the heteroglossic (or polyphonic) nature of Black women's writing.

Poststructuralism is viewed by many as a political method of reading texts and analyzing culture, and thus it serves as a vehicle through which to defer or even eclipse authoritarian Western discourse. The Frenchman Roland Barthes's announcement of the "Death of the Author" (1968) at the very historical moment of accession by Blacks to fuller social representation in the United States (including the passage of the 1964 Civil Rights Act and the establishment of Black Studies departments in colleges and universities in the late 1960s) alarmed many African Americanists. Likewise, poststructuralism's view of the fragmented and unstable subject at a time when Blacks were, in many arenas, laying powerful claim to full subjectivity has caused critics such as Joyce Anne Joyce to denounce poststructuralism and its cognate movement, postmodernism, as anti-humanist and as anathema to Black literature and culture. Nevertheless, poststructuralism's potential to defer the Western logic of identity and legitimation continues to attract numerous adherents and has contributed to the development of such intellectual enterprises as cultural studies, Whiteness studies, and critical race theory.

Rebecka Rychelle Rutledge

See also: Baraka, Amiri; Jones, Gayl; Major, Clarence; Morrison, Toni; Reed, Ishmael.

Resources

Michael Awkward, "Appropriative Gestures: Theory and Afro-American Literary Criticism," in *African American Literary Theory: A Reader*, ed. Winston Napier (New York: New York University Press, 2000), 331–338; Houston A. Baker Jr., "Belief, Theory, and Blues: Notes for a Post-Structuralist Criticism of Afro-American Literature," *African American Literary Theory*, pp. 224–241; Barbara Christian, "The Race for Theory," in *African American Literary Theory*, pp. 280–289; Frantz Fanon, *Black Skin, White Masks*, trans. Charles Lam Markmann (1952; New York: Grove Press, 1967); Henry Louis Gates Jr.: "'What's Love Got to Do with It?' Critical

Theory, Integrity, and the Black Idiom," *African American Literary Theory*, pp. 298–312; "Writing 'Race' and the Difference It Makes," in *"Race," Writing, and Difference*, ed. Henry Louis Gates Jr. (Chicago: University of Chicago Press, 1986); Mae G. Henderson, "Speaking in Tongues: Dialogics, Dialectics, and the Black Woman Writer's Literary Tradition," in *African American Literary Theory*, pp. 348–368; Joyce A. Joyce, "The Black Canon: Reconstructing Black American Literary Criticism," in *African American Literary Theory*, pp. 290–297; Deborah McDowell, "Black Feminist Thinking: The 'Practice' of Theory," in *African American Literary Theory*, pp. 557–579.

Prison Literature

Prison literature conveys both the hardships and the accomplishments of prisoners through their autobiographies, essays, fiction, letters, poetry, and plays. African American prison literature begins with the early plantation songs that collectively embody "the most poignant evidence of the continuity from pre–Civil War chattel slavery to the twentieth-century prison" (Franklin, 29). In the 1920s and 1930s, prison writers would reach larger audiences due in part to such liberal publications as *Esquire* and *American Mercury* magazine. Moreover, H. Bruce Franklin, one of the most important critics of prison literature, notes that as "the Depression made poverty and crime intrude more and more into everyday life, prison literature continued to gain a wider and more appreciative audience" (11). Works of prison-inspired literature by the ex-convict Chester Himes, *If He Hollers Let Him Go* (1945) and *Cast the First Stone* (1952), helped make him an important African American writer and also a pioneer of a new literary category, African American

hard-boiled detective fiction (*see* Crime and Mystery Fiction).

In the context of the racial tension of the 1950s and 1960s and the assassinations of Malcolm X in 1966 and Martin Luther King Jr. in 1968, prison literature by African Americans informed a wide variety of American audiences. In the 1970s and 1980s, notorious autobiographies by Angela Y. Davis—*Angela Davis: An Autobiography* (1974)—and Assata Shakur—*Assata* (1987)—served to condemn what such writers saw as an unfair prison system that was part of a larger industrial economic and social system. Such a critique had already been advanced by Malcolm X in *The Autobiography of Malcolm X* (1965). Referred to as "Satan" before his conversion to Islam while in prison, Malcolm X inspired many confinement narratives. "After the assassination [of Malcolm X]," writes Franklin, "prison writers acknowledged him as both their political and spiritual leader; he is conventionally compared to Moses, Jesus, even Allah" (148). Like Davis and Shakur, American prison writers tend to echo Malcolm X's insistence upon the dire need for alternative modes of discourse inside what they regard as America's overtly patriarchal facilities.

Pivotal works by radical political prisoners include those by Black Panthers George Lester Jackson (*Soledad Brother*, 1970, and *Blood in My Eye*, 1972) and Eldridge Cleaver (*Soul on Ice*, 1967, and *Soul on Fire*, 1978). Other important works of African American prison literature are: *Dopefiend* (1971), *Black Gangster* (1972), and *Daddy Cool* (1974) by Donald Goines; *Poems from Prison* (1968), *Born of a Woman* (1980), and *The Essential Etheridge Knight* (1986) by Etheridge Knight; and works by Iceberg Slim. Described by Holloway House as America's "most read"

African American author, Iceberg Slim (born Robert Beck) remains an innovator in prison writing and crime fiction. His works are *Trick Baby* (1967), *Pimp: The Story of My Life* (1969, with introductions by both Sapphire and Ice-T), *Mama Black Widow* (1969), *The Naked Soul of Iceberg Slim* (1971), *Long White Con* (1977), *Death Wish* (1977) and *Airtight Willie & Me* (1979). Slim's raw vernacular and streetwise style make him an important precursor to rap and hip-hop, but they also serve as examples for younger prison writers.

Franklin was largely responsible for bringing American prison writing into academic institutions with the publication of *The Victim as Criminal and Artist* (1978). However, throughout the 1970s and the 1980s, prison regulations prohibited many prison writers from publishing their work. In his 1998 anthology, Franklin alludes to both the 1977 "Son of Sam" law and Title 28 of the Code of Federal Regulations, Section 540.20(b), which states: "The inmate may not receive compensation or anything of value for correspondence with the news media" (15). After a number of prohibitive laws were finally deemed unconstitutional, new prison literature emerged in the 1990s. Works by ex-gang members such as Sanyika Shakur—*The Autobiography of an L.A. Gang Member* (1993)—and Stanley "Tookie" Williams—*Life in Prison* (1998)—blend Malcolm X's theoretical discourse and Iceberg Slim's flare for storytelling. Writers such as Shakur and Williams also resurrect many of the arguments put forth by radical 1960s prisoners such as Davis, Jackson, and Cleaver, particularly theories promoting "prisoner-of-war" status for African American prisoners.

Controversial prison writers have had to spend time in isolation cells and have experienced immediate transfers to remote facilities with no access to writing supplies (Chevigny, 99). Mumia Abu-Jamal, a cofounder of the Philadelphia chapter of the Black Panthers and a death row inmate since 1982, had all writing privileges taken away after the release of his compilation *Live from Death Row* (1995) (Franklin, 351). Jamal's major works of nonfiction—*Death Blossoms* (1997), *All Things Censored* (2000), and *Faith of Our Fathers* (2003)—have dealt with prison topics pertaining to isolation, sexuality, violence, and the power hierarchy. In *Prison Masculinities* (2001), an anthology of writing by both prisoners and prison experts, Jamal comments on the issue of celibacy inside prison walls and reveals the consequences of homosexuality being detected by prison officials, many of whom he characterizes as homophobic. As American prison writers continue to reaffirm, both convicts and officials tend to target prisoners who chronicle the experiences of homosexually active and HIV-positive prisoners. *ManRoot* magazine founder and prison writer Paul Mariah was determined to describe the constant struggles of gay prisoners in the 1960s. The publication of Dannie Martin's essay "AIDS: The View from a Prison Cell" (1986) was deemed an intentional violation of Title 28 (Franklin, 14).

Incarcerated female writers such as Diane Hamill Metzger, author of "Uncle Adam" (1985), and Susan Rosenberg, author of "Lee's Time" (1993), critique what they regard as the "phallocentric" perspectives of prison authorities (Chevigny, xxv). Like other minority writers, including the Latino writer Miguel Pinero, women prison writers accuse officials of manipulating prisoners' bodies through acts that range from physical abuse to intentional overcrowding. These writers confirm that "bodies of color" are particularly susceptible to abuse.

While captives with firsthand experiences have written nearly all the works of prison literature, an exception to the rule remains Michel Foucault's *Discipline and Punish: The Birth of the Prison* (1975). In describing strategies imposed by those atop prison hierarchies in numerous nations, the French theorist indirectly validates works by African American prison writers. Ted Conover's *Newjack* (2000), winner of the National Book Critics Circle Award for Nonfiction, is a critique of both prisoners and prison officials—specifically, those who live and work in New York State's Sing Sing Prison. Posing and working as a prison guard, Conover observed the same institutionalized acts of violence, mistreatment, and blatant racism that prison writers have been documenting since the first prison narratives appeared. Notable contributions such as Nathan C. Heard's *House of Slammers* (1983), Kim Wozencraft's *Notes from the Country Club* (1993), and Jimmy A. Lerner's *You Got Nothing Coming* (2002) further serve to highlight one of Foucault's most significant contentions, that invisible bodies can be "transformed" into state-owned commodities (136).

Stephen M. Steck

See also: Knight, Etheridge.

Resources

Lee Bernstein, "Prison Writers and the Black Arts Movement," in *New Thoughts on the Black Arts Movement*, ed. Lisa Gail Collins and Margo Natalie Crawford (New Brunswick, NJ: Rutgers University Press, 2006), 297–316; Bell Gale Chevigny, *Doing Time: Twenty-five Years of Prison Writing* (New York: Arcade, 1999); Michel Foucault, *Discipline & Punish: The Birth of the Prison* (New York: Pantheon, 1977); H. Bruce Franklin, *Prison Writing in 20th-Century America* (New York: Penguin, 1998); Tara T. Green, ed., *From the Plantation to the Prison: African-American Confinement Literature* (Macon, GA: Mercer University Press, 2008); Tiffany Ana Lopez, "Critical Witnessing in Latino/a and African American Prison Narratives," in *Prose and Cons: Essays on Prison Literature in the United States*, ed. D. Quintin Miller (Jefferson, NC: McFarland, 2005), 62–77; Patricia E. O'Connor, *Speaking of Crime: Narratives of Prisoners* (Lincoln, NE: University of Nebraska Press, 2000); Davu Seru, "A Manifesto on African American Prison Literature," *American Book Review* 36, no. 3 (2015), 6; Breea C. Willingham, "Black Women's Prison Narratives and the Intersection of Race, Gender, and Sexuality in U.S. Prisons," *Critical Survey* 23, no. 3 (2011), 55–66.

Protest Literature

Protest literature condemns what its authors perceive to be injustice and incites its audience to fight the same. From this perspective, much of African American literature, from its inception to the present, can arguably be called protest literature, in that it rejects the racist ideology that sustained slavery, segregation, racism, and oppression. Protest literature asserts the equality between Blacks and Whites, at times calling for militant action to effect the changes deemed necessary to ensure this equality.

The Slave Narrative was the first type of protest literature in African American letters. Having escaped from the South to the North, former slaves wrote about the physical and psychological cruelty of Southern slavery, the hunger for freedom, the difficult journey from bondage to freedom, and the moral urgency to abolish slavery. In his *Narrative of the Life of Frederick Douglass, an American Slave* (1845), Frederick Douglass eloquently describes the annihilation wrought by slavery upon the slave's body and spirit but also, following a well-established tradition in autobiographical writing, he traces a trajectory from a sense of denied humanity and identity within slavery to the recovery of freedom. His writing is a rhetorical tour de force that convincingly describes and condemns slavery in Christian America.

Slave narratives, then, condemned an unjust system that treated human beings as chattel and mere commodities, but they also denounced the hypocrisy of the young American republic, a nation that claimed to be Christian and yet embraced the brutal institution of slavery. For example, to shame those who supported or tolerated slavery, William Wells Brown, in his 1853 novel *Clotel; or, the President's Daughter*, uses irony and sarcasm, two central tropes in protest literature. Several episodes in the novel echo the famed satire of Jonathan Swift in "A Modest Proposal" (1729).

Harriet Ann Jacobs's *Incidents in the Life of a Slave Girl* (1861) is another example of narratives from the antebellum years that show the evils of slavery. It focuses on the female slave, who, in addition to the usual brutality, also has to endure continuous sexual harassment and the agony of not being able to fulfill the moral expectations placed on the nineteenth-century woman. Jacobs's is a remarkable example of a Black woman's condemnation of, and resistance to, the brutality of slavery.

After the slave narrative, literature associated with early manifestations of Black Nationalism is probably the most ideologically articulated form of protest in African American letters. Already in the antebellum period, Martin R. Delany and Alexander Crummell, among others, had articulated the reality that Africans in America shared the brutal experience of slavery, the common tie to motherland Africa, exclusion and alienation from the American society, the necessity of a united front to overcome the ravages of slavery and racism, and the possibility of creating a great nation on the African continent. The realization that the end of the Civil War did not make African Americans any more acceptable in American society led to new nationalist discourses. Post-Reconstruction writers such as Sutton E. Griggs, Pauline Elizabeth Hopkins, Frances Ellen Watkins Harper, Charles Waddell Chesnutt, and James Weldon Johnson used their fiction to ponder and sometimes unequivocally advocate cultural nationalism and political separation in the face of continuing oppression. The most vocal message of protest against the state of Post-Reconstruction race relations probably came from W.E.B. Du Bois, whose work, notably his *The Souls of Black Folk* (1903), forcefully protested legalized segregation and large-scale violence against African Americans. He argued that the Jim Crow laws in the South and the accommodationist approach of some Black leaders (especially Booker T. Washington) created a steady course of disenfranchising African Americans and perpetuating the supposed inferiority of Blacks.

The cultural, literary, and artistic flowering of the Harlem Renaissance expressed aesthetic views rooted in race consciousness and pride, and it countered old stereotypes by presenting the complexity of Black people in America and in the world. Writers and artists such as Alain Locke, Claude McKay, Langston Hughes, Countee Cullen, Louis Armstrong, Billie Holliday, and Zora Neale Hurston offered America new and original forms of expression rooted in the

African American experience, such as the blues, jazz, and African American folklore. This cultural display was an implicit protest against the inferior status that had been hitherto imposed on Black literary and artistic creativity by the dominant culture. In this period, Marcus Garvey reproved White oppression and racism and proclaimed the oneness and greatness of people of African descent. He promoted self-help, race consciousness, and pride as well as the liberation of the African continent from European colonial power. His ideology of Black nationalism called for the separation of the races as a way of protesting racism and oppression that had barred African Americans from total acceptance in the American society. Garvey led a Back-to-Africa Movement.

After the Harlem Renaissance, Langston Hughes produced politically alert work influenced greatly by socialist ideas. Many of the stories in his collection *The Ways of White Folks* (1934) implicitly protest how "some white folks," as Hughes puts it, treat African Americans, and he especially emphasizes themes of sexuality and class conflict. The poem "Dear Mr. President" (1943) protests the fact that while Black soldiers are fighting tyranny abroad, they must endure segregation within the American military (Ostrom). Much of Hughes's work in the 1930s and 1940s qualifies as protest literature (Berry).

The publication of Richard Wright's novel *Native Son* in 1940 was hailed as a blunt portrayal of race matters in America. Fittingly, the novel opens with an alarm clock, symbolically calling America to pay attention to what centuries of enslavement and racism have wrought on the life of Bigger Thomas, a young man who lives in the Black belt of South Side Chicago in a small, rat-infested apartment he shares with his mother and his two siblings. In the novel, Wright deploys naturalism, which combines the literary technique of focusing on realistic detail with a worldview that focuses on human beings as victims of social forces that they cannot control. Wright portrays Bigger as a person conditioned to kill and as one ultimately executed by the same environment that created his criminal behavior in the first place.

A contemporary of Wright's, Chester Himes, who is better known for his work in crime and mystery fiction, also produced novels in the protest literature category.

In spite of significant African American contribution to the war effort, the period following World War II failed, as other periods had failed, to bring social justice to African Americans. Out of this period emerged the Civil Rights Movement of the 1950s and 1960s. Fighting to end racial segregation and inequality between the races, the movement was spearheaded by diverse figures and movements, including Martin Luther King Jr., Malcolm X, the Black Arts Movement, and the Black Power movement.

Martin Luther King Jr.'s fight is probably best conveyed through his speech "I Have a Dream," delivered on August 26, 1963, at the Lincoln Memorial in Washington, DC. One century after the Emancipation Proclamation, African Americans had not seen an end to racial injustice. King envisaged a society that would reject racism and segregation, and embrace true Christian love, brotherhood, and mutual acceptance. Another leader of the movement, Malcolm X, proclaimed that African Americans were not really Americans but rather Africans who happened to be in America because America had never accepted them as full members of the society and instead repeatedly oppressed them. In a speech delivered in Cleveland, Ohio, on April 3, 1964, "The Ballot or the Bullet," Malcolm X proposed Black Nationalism as a remedy to White racism and oppression. He called for Black unity and argued the necessity for African Americans to elect politicians who would address their concerns and aspirations, appealed to African Americans to own and support businesses in their communities, and underscored the obligation to deal with social evils such as drugs, prostitution, and alcoholism that were destroying African American communities.

On the literary front, the Black Arts Movement (BAM) of the 1960s and early 1970s included much protest literature. Amiri Baraka, Larry Neal, Sonia Sanchez, and Nikki Giovanni, to name only a few writers of the period, promoted and practiced literary expression in the service of the Black community. The BAM aesthetic was probably best conveyed through an anthology edited by Baraka and Neal: *Black Fire: An Anthology of Afro-American Writing* (1968), and through Neal's essay "The Black Arts Movement" (1968). Contributors to the collection called for Black art and literature to reflect the needs of the Black community and promoted cultural nationalism. Baraka called the BAM writers "soldier poets," a term that reflected the nature of protest literature as a weapon against racism and oppression, and Neal described the BAM as "the aesthetic and spiritual sister of the Black Power concept" (62).

Even after the fading of the militant BAM ideology in the mid-1970s, there is still an underlying element of protest in African American literature. Arguably, because racism in some form or other continues to affect African Americans, many African American writers will, out of necessity, produce works that protest current social and political situations. At the same time, protest literature has always attracted the claim that it is propaganda or otherwise too explicitly political. Whether protest literature, or any artistic expression, is "political" or "too political" depends largely upon the definition of art and the belief about the function of art.

Aimable Twagilimana

See also: Baraka, Amiri; Delany, Martin R.; Douglass, Frederick; Du Bois, W.E.B.; Jordan, June; King, Martin Luther, Jr.; Lorde, Audre; Truth, Sojourner.

Resources

Amiri Baraka and Larry Neal, eds., *Black Fire: An Anthology of Afro-American Writing* (New York: Morrow, 1968); William Wells Brown, *Clotel; or, The President's Daughter: A Narrative of Slave Life in the United States* (1853; repr. New York: Carol Publishing Group, 1995); Frederick Douglass, *Narrative of the Life of Frederick Douglass, an American Slave, Written by Himself* (1845; repr. Boston: Bedford Books, 1993); Addison Gayle, *The Black Aesthetic* (Garden City, NY: Doubleday, 1971); Mollie Godfrey, "Sheep, Rats, and Jungle Beasts: Black Humanisms and the Protest Fiction Debate," *Arizona Quarterly* 74, no. 2 (2018), 39–62; Willie J. Harrell Jr., *Origins of the African American Jeremiad: The Rhetorical Strategies of Social Protest and Activism, 1760–1861* (Jefferson, NC: McFarland, 2011); Langston Hughes, *Good Morning, Revolution: Uncollected Social Protest Writings*, ed. Faith Berry (Secaucus, NJ: Carol, 1992); Harriet Jacobs, *Incidents in the Life of a Slave Girl, Written by Herself* (1861; repr. New York: Norton, 2001); Larry Neal, "The Black Arts Movement," in *Visions of a Liberated Future: Black Arts Movement Writings*, ed. Michael Schwartz (New York: Thunder's Mouth Press, 1989), 62–78; Hans Ostrom, *A Langston Hughes Encyclopedia* (Westport, CT:

Greenwood Press, 2002); Anthony Reed, *Freedom Time: The Poetics and Politics of Black Experimental Writing* (Baltimore, MD: Johns Hopkins University Press, 2014); Margaret Anne Reid, *Black Protest Poetry: Polemics from the Harlem Renaissance and the Sixties* (New York: Peter Lang, 2001); Robert E. Washington, *The Ideologies of African American Literature: From the Harlem Renaissance to the Black Nationalist Revolt. A Sociology of Literature Perspective* (Lanham, MD: Rowman & Littlefield, 2001).

R

Rap

A musical genre initially introduced in the 1960s as an experimental form of poetry featuring spoken word and poetry over jazz music. Over time, rap evolved into various rhythmic and lyrical styles that use rhetorical content and nontraditional musical instruments not only to disseminate information concerning historical and contemporary Black or oppressive experiences but also to evoke dance from an audience. Similar to the way blues and jazz were literary protests during the Harlem Renaissance and the Black Arts Movement, respectively, rap music's infancy was a literary vehicle to register the latter half of the Black Power movement. Since the 1970s, rap has remained one of the most indelible musical forms from which its crafters can foreground the Black experience in forums outside of music, including literature, theater, and art, and rap is hip-hop culture's foundation.

Although the Bronx, New York, is often named as the birthplace of rap music, literary evidence demonstrates that rap, like other musical genres created within African American culture, is planted in the soil of slave songs, work songs, field calls, protest songs, and slave spirituals. Rap music and its lyrics represent an outgrowth of the slave experience and form one of its residual branches. The rhythm of slave and work songs is a traditional call-and-response in which the leader makes a call, "We are going down to Georgia, boys," and the chorus offers a response, "Aye-Aye." Call-and-response in a rap format imitates that structure, as the lead calls, "Everybody say Hey! Ho!," and the audience replies, "Hey! Ho!" (Naughty by Nature). Additionally, rap lyrics share sociopolitical arguments and purpose with field calls, protest songs, and slave spirituals. Much of the historical discourse concerning race as seen in such songs, in some form or another, remains current. In other words, although racism today is practiced and spoken in a language differing from that of the nineteenth century, racial concerns of the past remain unreconciled, and rap music serves as a contemporary sounding board for those concerns.

Hailing the Sugar Hill Gang as rap's first artists is also an issue of contention in the historical account of the genre. However, publication of literature and lyrics produced and performed by The Last Poets and Gil Scott-Heron demonstrates that the latter are the first artists to combine poetic commentary and African rhythms and beats on an audio recording. In rap's infancy, lyrics articulated Black responses to specific social issues, such as police brutality, poverty, and institutional racism in a way that educated the mainstream public. Scott-Heron's "The Revolution Will Not Be Televised," first appeared in *New Black Poet: Small Talk at 125th and Lenox* and was released on the Flying Dutchman label in 1970. Also released in a book of poetry of the same name that year, the poem/lyric argues that there will not be a technological or drug-induced escape from the ongoing Black revolution; rather, it will be "live," and by default, all Americans will participate in the discourse and actions concerning issues of race. The Last Poets' "Niggers Are Scared of Revolution," also released in 1970, is a scathing attack against Blacks who willingly participate in stereotypical activities rather than supporting the unavoidable movement at hand.

In 1979, the Sugar Hill Gang introduced what is known as Mickey Mouse rap, songs with lyrics addressing no particular social issue. The group's first album was also the first commercially released collection of rap songs, and their live shows introduced three groundbreaking ideas to rap performance. First, the Sugar Hill Gang popularized written poetry, in that they demonstrated how poems could be converted into rap songs with a beat. Second, the group's lyrical ability introduced labyrinthine lyrics to rap music, a competitive practice as seen in the work of Mystical and Twista today. Finally, the Sugar Hill Gang's performances evoked dance, rather than political thought, and made the music a commercial enterprise marketable to the mainstream public (Light).

In the 1980s, rap music began branching off. As the audience grew internationally, rap music was being created in cultures outside of Black America. In the United States, since the 1980s, the Black aesthetic and experience have remained the corpus for rap music. Notwithstanding commercially viable performances of rap music by artists outside of African-American culture, such as the Beastie Boys, Vanilla Ice, Eminem, and Bubba Sparkxxx, the Black experience and its agenda remain the foundational topics discussed in rap music. Rap's history, however, does not negate the multicultural participation that has always been present in rap music, particularly in marketing and production.

Rap music is inherently politically and racially charged. In 1988, Public Enemy, the most anthologized rap group, began publishing lyrics that applied not only to Blacks' historical past but also to contemporary issues concerning the treatment of Blacks by White institutions and the American government. Their second album, *It Takes a Nation of Millions to Hold Us Back*, attacks a range of issues, from the introduction of crack cocaine into Black America to the military.

The years 1989–1992 were pivotal in rap music's critique of America's police departments. During this time, N.W.A., Ice-T, and Public Enemy released lyrical content directly addressing police brutality. N.W.A.'s "Fuck the Police" argued against racial profiling, Ice-T.'s "Cop Killer" stated that Blacks should defend themselves when attacked by police, and Public Enemy humorously presented the Black community's belief that contacting 911 in an emergency is "a joke." From local radio shows to members of Congress and the Reagan administration, mainstream America cited N.W.A., Ice-T, and Public Enemy as promoters of violence against police, and argued for a ban of rap music on radio and television.

Since the mid-1980s, Black activists and supporters of the First Amendment have cited documented accounts of police brutality against Blacks across America's urban centers. Their persistence and the lyrics of rap artists collectively re-lifted the veil shrouding the violence against and within the Black experience by revealing formidable racial realities to the mainstream. Rap's ability to bring local racial conflicts to an international forum and pose questions regarding the state's relationship with the Black community, have been considered dangerous, having the potential to incite violence, which is also documented. However, in 1989, the Stop the Violence

All-Stars, which consisted of KRS-One, Stetsasonic, Kool Moe Dee, MC Lyte, Just-Ice, Doug E. Fresh, Heavy D, Public Enemy, and Ms. Melodie, composed the lyric "Self Destruction," released on a twelve-inch recording. In the song, each rapper presents a resolution to violence, demonstrating that rap music's crafters have always been proactive in nonviolent discourse.

Because rap music is produced and consumed predominantly by men, one of the central arguments for discarding the First Amendment in what are deemed extreme cases is that its representations of women are inherently subjective. Therefore, it is argued that when fielding and inscribing notions of womanhood, motherhood, rape, and sexuality, any lyrical content produced in such an illusory environment cannot be policed by its male crafters. Regardless of the ebb and flow of femininity in rap's discourse, the discussion has not gone unanswered by Black women, scholars and crafters alike. In both rap lyrics and African American literature, Black women have participated in the dialogue on issues of female representations.

Rap's survivability lies not only in the messages it relays but also in its continued marketability and overwhelming profitability. Rather than banning the music outright, the option to record self-censored versions is popular among record companies housing Eminem, Ludacris, R. Kelley, and Lil' John and the East Side Boyz, who are easy prey for contemporary proponents of censorship.

By the mid-1990s, as America settled into the realization that rap music is not a fad, but a mainstay of American music, manifestations of rap were seen and heard throughout the arts. African American literature, the American mainstream, and mass media have been affected by rap music. In the late 1990s, after the murders of Tupac Shakur and the Notorious B.I.G. (Christopher Wallace), rap music, and the contemporary Black experience, generated not only new discourse but also new literary styles and language presented in Black writing. Rap music's language, an outgrowth of African-American vernacular, is demonstrated in scholarship, fiction, and poetry written and published by Blacks. Rappers and scholars alike access the language of rap music to argue the Black agenda and present the Black experience. Historically, poets, rap lyricists, and scholars bear these points out.

Poetry written by Nikki Giovanni, Sonia Sanchez, Amiri Baraka, Carolyn M. Rodgers, and Ntozake Shange are recited in rhythm, sometimes with Afrocentric beats and sounds, a further demonstration of the foundational links between Black poetry and rap music. Additionally, poets from the Black Arts Movement recognize and communicate the origins of rap music by contributing to literary discourse as essayists and cultural theorists, for instance, Giovanni's *Racism 101* and Baraka's "Somebody Blew Up America." Lyricists also publish essays, fiction, autobiography, and collections of poetry, and not only are a growing population of contributors to African American literature, but also have increased the readership of Black fiction. Sister Souljah, rapper-turned-lecturer, penned two novels in the 1990s, *No Disrespect* and *The Coldest Winter Ever.* In 1996, The Last Poets' published *On a Mission: Selected Poems and a History of the Last Poets.* After twenty years in the rap industry as producer, writer, and rapper, KRS-One published a book of essays, *Ruminations* (2003), a historical account of rap music and the relevance of the Black aesthetic to the art form's presentation, organization, and themes.

Increasingly, scholars are incorporating rap music into their work, and for some, the music is the basis of their work. Houston A. Baker Jr.'s *Black Studies, Rap, and the Academy* (1993) is one of the first scholarly works to argue that rap music represents an authentic Black experience and therefore should not be discounted in postsecondary Black Studies programs. Similarly, Tricia Rose's *Black Noise: Rap Music and Black Culture in Contemporary America* (1994) postulates rap music as intellectual property and work, suggesting that rap is a viable discourse worthy of discussion and study. In *Open Mike: Reflections on Philosophy, Race, Sex, Culture, and Religion* (2002) and *Holler If You Hear Me: Searching for Tupac Shakur* (2001), Michael Eric Dyson either peppers the vernacular with the language of rap music or uses the music as the basis for his observations and arguments. Born from students' usage of Black vernacular and its relationship to the language of rap music, language diversity is often the subject of pedagogical theory. The discourse's response to students' language rights sometimes employs rap's language as a point of entry into the debate.

Both the language and the themes of rap lyrics and video presentations have a place in the pages of contemporary Black fiction as well, further suggesting that rap music is a significant part of African American literature. Novelists such as Omar Tyree, Terry McMillan, Carol Taylor, E. Lynn Harris, and Jamis L. Dames access the intrasocial themes presented in rap. Topics including gang and police violence, paternity, monogamy, family, dating, homosexuality, and the underground economy are critiqued and framed in rap music. Rapping has bred a new wave of Black poets. Mos Def, Common, Cee-Lo, Jill Scott, and Floetry have successfully converted the art of spoken word, song, and lyricism into poetry and vice versa.

As such, rap music is the catalyst for a new generation of African American literature. From poems, songs, and lyrics to scholarship, literary criticism, and fiction, rap music informs, performs, and reports the Black aesthetic and experience to a global audience. Despite suggestions that rap is derogatory, denigrating, or demonizing, the music is responsible for maintaining an open forum discussion concerning events, social issues, and experiences pertaining to African Americans. Rap's contributions can be seen in African American literature, theater, film, television and marketing, art, politics, and of course music.

Rap music provides a stage for social and racial debates that is heavily accessed by young and/or oppressed people who enter the discourse from diverse cultural environments. As a disseminator of cultural information, the music exports the Black experience throughout the world and imports the cultural experiences of others into the American psyche. Rap music has converted street rhymers into writers, poets, businessmen, and millionaires. Through rap music, myriad youth races, cultures, and languages have been integrated, helping proponents of the genre demonstrate not only the need for multicultural educational and social environments, but also their revenue-generating potential.

Ellesia Ann Blaque

See also: Hip-Hop; Protest Literature; Vernacular.

Resources

Houston A. Baker, *Black Studies, Rap, and the Academy* (Chicago: University of Chicago Press, 1993); Adam Bradley and Andrew DuBois, *The Anthology of Rap* (New

Haven, CT: Yale University Press, 2010); Kawachi Clemmons, "I'm Hip: An Exploration of Rap Music's Creative Guise," in *Soul Thieves: The Appropriation and Misrepresentation of African American Popular Culture*, ed. Tamara Lizette Brown and Baruti N. Kopano (New York: Palgrave Macmillan, 2014), 51–60; Michael W. Clune, "Rap, Hip Hop, Spoken Word," in *The Cambridge Companion to American Poetry since 1945*, ed. Jennifer Ashton (Cambridge, UK: Cambridge University Press, 2013), 202–215; Nelson George, *Hip Hop America* (New York: Penguin, 1999); Keith Gilyard, "Holdin' It Down," in *Rhetoric and Composition as Intellectual Work*, ed. Gary A. Olson (Carbondale: Southern Illinois University Press, 2002), 118–129; Cheryl L. Keyes, *Rap Music and Street Consciousness: Music in American Life* (Urbana, IL: University of Illinois Press, 2002); Alan Light, *The Vibe History of Hip Hop* (New York: Three Rivers Press, 1999); Bryan J. McCann, *The Mark of Criminality: Rhetoric, Race, and Gangsta Rap in the War-on-Crime Era* (Tuscaloosa, AL: University of Alabama Press, 2017); Matt Miller, *Bounce: Rap Music and Local Identity in New Orleans* (Amherst, MA: University of Massachusetts Press, 2012); Naughty by Nature, "Hip Hop Hooray," by V. Brown, K. Gist, and A. Criss, on *19 Naughty III* (New York: Tommy Boy, 1993); "An Old Boat Song," in *Call and Response: The Riverside Anthology of the African American Literary Tradition*, ed. Patricia Liggins-Hill (Boston: Houghton Mifflin, 1998), 33; Alexs Pate, *In the Heart of the Beat: The Poetry of Rap* (Lanham, MD: Scarecrow, 2010); William E. Perkins, *Droppin' Science: Critical Essays on Rap Music and Hip Hop Culture* (Philadelphia: Temple University Press, 1996); Anthony B. Pinn, ed., *Noise and Spirit: The Religious and Spiritual Sensibilities of Rap Music* (New York: New York University Press, 2003); Public Enemy, "911's a Joke," by W. Drayton, K. Shocklee, and E. Sadler, on *Fear of a Black Planet* (New York: Def Jam, 1989); Robin Roberts, "Ladies First: Queen Latifah's Afrocentric Feminist Music Video," *African American Review* 28, no. 2 (1994), 245–257; Tricia Rose, *Black Noise: Black Music and Culture in Contemporary America* (Middletown, CT: Wesleyan University Press, 1994); Jeffrey Severs, "'Is It Like a Beat Without a Melody?': Rap and Revolution in *Hamilton*," *Studies in Musical Theatre* 12, no. 2 (2018), 141–152; Miles White, *From Jim Crow to Jay-Z: Race, Rap, and the Performance of Masculinity* (Urbana, IL: University of Illinois Press, 2011).

Realism

Mode of literature. Realism emerged in American literature as a reaction against romanticism (Abrams). Although critics do not agree on the exact time period in which realism flourished, they more or less agree that American realism arose between 1860 and 1914 and that Mark Twain, Williams Dean Howells, and Henry James are among its most important representative authors (McQuade).

Charles Waddell Chesnutt is considered an important African American writer in the tradition of realism. His novel *The Conjure Woman* puts the White narrator and his wife in conflict with an African American trickster/folklorist named Uncle Julius. Chesnutt's short story "The Wife of His Youth" features a very light-skinned mulatto leader of the elitist Blue Vein Society. After years of separation from her, he acknowledges his dark-skinned plantation wife, thus triumphing over his prejudices. James Weldon Johnson's novel *Autobiography of an Ex-Colored Man* (1912) is also written in the tradition of realism. Johnson uses the novel to explore the issue of race and identity of the African American.

Realism is vividly evident in the novel *Invisible Man* (1952) by Ralph Ellison, even though in other respects the novel is considered to be an excellent example of modernism. In this novel, Ellison portrays the African American as "invisible" to White society. He also represents the anger and insignificance felt by African Americans, and therefore he represents psychological realism. Thus, works of literature written well after the era of realism (1860–1914) may still draw on elements of the realist literary mode.

The short stories and novels of Zora Neale Hurston, including *Their Eyes Were Watching God* (1937), come out of a realist tradition, use the vernacular, and focus on the predicaments of working-class African American women and men.

Langston Hughes's poetry often springs from a straightforward, accessible realist mode and concerns itself with the lives and situations of ordinary people. His novel *Not Without Laughter* (1930) is clearly in the realist mode, relating the coming-of-age of a young African American man in the Midwest. His poem "Mother to Son" (1922) concerns a life lesson a mother is relating to her son. She tells him that regardless of the troubles he encounters in life, he must continue to persevere in the face of social adversity. Hughes's poem "I, Too" (1925) uses a realistic analogy, placing the issue of racial equality in the context of a family in which the narrator is "the darker brother" who must "Eat in the kitchen." In the poem "Middle Passage," Robert Hayden recreates the history of Africans being brought to America aboard slave ships. Hayden's use of language includes names of slave ships, lyrics to "Trinity Hymnal #497," and vocabulary from the vernacular. His realistic portrayal elicits a deep, disturbing connection with the Africans on the ships, effectively juxtaposing the readers' consciousness with the experiences of the Africans during their journey through the historic middle passage. Similarly, Arna Bontemps, in the poem "Southern Mansion," implicitly suggests not only that slavery and its oppression of African Americans was cruel when it occurred but also that forms of African American enslavement and oppression persist. From Charles Chesnutt and James Weldon Johnson through Zora Neale Hurston, Langston Hughes, Arna Bontemps, Robert Hayden, and African American writers of today, realism remains a useful mode of literature.

DaNean Pound

See also: Hughes, Langston; Petry, Ann Lane; Sanchez, Sonia; Wright, Richard.

Resources

M. H. Abrams, *A Glossary of Literary Terms*, 7th ed. (Fort Worth, TX: Harcourt Brace, 1999), 260–261; Russell Ames, "Social Realism in Charles W. Chesnutt," *Phylon* 14, no. 2 (Spring 1953), 199–206; Arna Bontemps, "Southern Mansion," in *American Negro Poetry: An Anthology*, ed. Bontemps (1963; repr. New York: Hill and Wang, 1995), 80; Charles W. Chesnutt, *The Conjure Woman* (Durham, NC: Duke University Press, 1993); Madhu Dubey, "Post-Postmodern Realism?" *Twentieth-Century Literature* 57, nos. 3–4 (2011), 364–371; Michael A. Elliott, *The Culture Concept: Writing and Difference in the Age of Realism* (Minneapolis, MN: University of Minnesota Press, 2002); Ralph Ellison, *Invisible Man* (1952; repr. New York: Random House, 1995); Henry Louis Gates Jr., and Nellie Y. McKay, eds., *The Norton Anthology of African American Literature* (New York: Norton, 1996); Robert Hayden, *Collected Poems*, ed. Frederick Glaysher (New York: Liveright, 1996); Langston Hughes: "Mother to Son" and "I, Too," in *The Collected Poems of Langston Hughes*, ed. Arnold Rampersad (New York: Vintage Classics, 1994); *Not Without Laughter* (New York: Knopf, 1930);

Zora Neal Hurston, *Their Eyes Were Watching God* (1937; repr. New York: HarperCollins, 1969); Gene Andrew Jarrett, *Deans and Truants: Race and Realism in African American Literature* (Philadelphia: University of Pennsylvania Press, 2007): James Weldon Johnson, *The Autobiography of an Ex-Colored Man* (1912; repr. New York: Dover, 1995); Donald McQuade et al., eds., *The Harper Single Volume American Literature*, 3rd ed. (New York: Longman, 1999), 1354–2086; Stacy I. Morgan, *Rethinking Social Realism: African American Art and Literature*, 1930–1953 (Athens, GA: University of Georgia Press, 2004); Mark Twain, *The Adventures of Huckleberry Finn* (1885; repr. New York: Pocket Books, 1973); Andreá N. Williams, "African American Literary Realism, 1865–1914," in *A Companion to African American Literature*, ed. Gene Andrew Jarrett (Malden, MA: Wiley-Blackwell, 2010), 185–199.

Reed, Ishmael (1938–)

Novelist, short-story writer, poet, essayist, dramatist, editor, and publisher. One of the most innovative, controversial, and prolific literary figures of his era, Reed describes himself in a 1968 interview as a literary "anarchist" (Sheppard, 6), one who aims to challenge Western literary conventions as well as the African American literary canon. Satiric in temperament and experimental in practice, Reed has little regard for many established literary conventions and seeks to create an alternative Black aesthetic (which he calls "neoamerican hoodooism") that relies on ancient African rituals such as conjuring, magic, and voodoo to counter dominant Western influences and to foster a multicultural consciousness in U.S. society. Although versatile and prolific, Reed is best known for his postmodernist novels, which satirize and parody the fundamental style of African American narrative, from the confessional mode of slave narratives to the modern autobiographical fiction of Richard Wright, Zora Neale Hurston, James Baldwin, and Ralph Ellison. As editor and publisher, Reed cofounded the Yardbird Publishing Company (1971), Reed, Cannon, and Johnson Communications (1973), and the Before Columbus Foundation (1976), all of which have promoted and helped define U.S. multicultural literature. Since 1980, the Before Columbus Foundation has sponsored the American Book Awards, which have drawn considerable attention to outstanding texts of U.S. multiethnic literature.

Ishmael Scott Reed was born in Chattanooga, Tennessee, to Henry Lenoir and Thelma Coleman on February 22, 1938. His surname comes from his stepfather, Bennie Stephen Reed, an autoworker. In 1942, Reed moved with his mother to Buffalo, New York, where he grew up and attended public schools. From 1956 to 1960, he was enrolled in the University of Buffalo (now the State University of New York at Buffalo), but financial difficulties forced him to drop out without a degree (Boyer). In 1962, he moved to New York City to begin his career as writer and editor. In 1967, the same year his first novel, *The Free-lance Pallbearers*, was published, he moved to Berkeley, California, and took up a teaching position in the University of California. Although the University of California at Berkeley denied him tenure in 1977, Reed has continued to teach there. In 1979, he moved to a working-class neighborhood in Oakland. He also has taught at the University of Washington, the State University of New York at Buffalo, Columbia, Yale, Dartmouth, Harvard, and the University of California at Santa Barbara. Reed's prolific literary accomplishments (nine novels, five volumes of poetry, five collections of essays, four plays, and numerous edited volumes and articles on various subjects) have been widely recognized. Notable accolades include two nominations for the National Book Award (for *Mumbo Jumbo* and *Conjure*) and one for a Pulitzer Prize (for *Conjure*), a Guggenheim Memorial Foundation Award, a Rosenthal Foundation Award, and a Pushcart Award.

In *The Free-lance Pallbearers*, Reed burlesques the traditional confessional style of African American narrative through Bukka Doopeyduk's search for selfhood in a corrupt, cannibalistic society called Harry Sam. *Yellow Back Radio Broke-Down* (1969), his second novel, explores the themes of social strife. In *Mumbo Jumbo* (1972), his most successful novel, and *The Last Days of Louisiana Red* (1974), Reed creates a mythic hoodoo (voodoo) detective called Papa LaBas, who attempts to counter Judeo-Christian influences in African American life by "neoamerican hoodooism." The neoamerican hoodooism seeks to recast ancient Egyptian myths and West Indian magic and blend them. Set in Harlem, New York, and New Orleans, Louisiana, during the 1920s, *Mumbo Jumbo* depicts the conflict between two opposing forces of American society: Jes Grew, a spontaneous outburst of Black artistic energy in the form of dance, and Wallflower Order, embodiment of the Atonist faith that underlies White rationalism. *The Last Days of Louisiana Red* is set in Berkeley, California, and narrates the investigation of the murder of Ed Yellings, by Papa LaBas, who uses voodoo to cure Louisiana Red of a mental condition that causes conflicts within the African American community. However, it is the subplot about the Moochers (his name for radical Black feminists) that has drawn fiery outrage: feminist writers and critics vehemently deny Papa LaBas's charge that Black women conspire

with the White establishment to hold Black men down.

In his later novels, Reed moves away from his "neoamerican hoodooism" and focuses on sociopolitical satire. Set in the Civil War, *Flight to Canada* (1976) satirizes both the traditional Slave Narrative and abolitionist-inspired novels (particularly Harriet Beecher Stowe's *Uncle Tom's Cabin*) with a deliberate, playful anachronism: jumbo jets and television alongside Abraham Lincoln and Robert E. Lee frame runaway slave Raven Quickskill's escape to Canada. Reed's twin novels on social and racial politics, *The Terrible Twos* (1982) and *The Terrible Threes* (1989), take aim at the Reagan era cultural conservatism and rampant commercialism. Both rework Charles Dickens's *A Christmas Carol* to showcase the glaring disparity between the extravagance of the rich and the dire condition of the poor. In *The Terrible Twos*, President Clift (a former model turned president) is representative of a social elite supported by new money and unconcerned about the well-being of the working classes. In *The Terrible Threes*, Reed's indictment of capitalism's greed and callousness turns into a condemnation of the Neo-Nazi mentality of the government that conspires to purge the country of its "unwanted" citizens with nuclear weapons. Reed's novels *Reckless Eyeballing* (1986) and *Japanese by Spring* (1993) deal with literary and academic politics. *Reckless Eyeballing* depicts a conspiracy between White male publishers and Black female writers to perpetuate racist stereotypes of Black men as rapists and muggers in literature. The novel is a variation, then, of the subplot of *The Last Days of Louisiana Red*. *Japanese by Spring* satirizes an opportunistic Black academic who, in an effort to gain tenure at his predominantly White institution, speaks out against affirmative action and multiculturalism. In his novel *Juice!* (2011), Reed takes the O. J. Simpson trial of 1994–1995 as the point of departure for a wide-ranging examination and critique of the corporate media, sensationalism, and politics and culture of America at the end of the twentieth and the beginning of the twenty-first century.

Like his fiction, Reed's poetry demonstrates his preoccupation with developing an alternative aesthetic and fighting against the social, political, and economic injustices of U.S. society. Major collections include *catechism of d neoamerican hoodoo church: poems* (1970), *Conjure: Selected Poems, 1963–1970* (1972), *Chattanooga: Poems* (1973), *A Secretary to the Spirits* (1978), and *New and Collected Poems* (1988). In *catechism*, Reed shows a strong preference for the lowercase (as reflected in the title of the collection), omission of vowels and punctuation, and the use of typographical shorthand such as the slash and the ampersand in lieu of words, a practice that befits his agenda of challenging the dominant Judeo-Christian influence through neo-American hoodooism. *Conjure*, which includes most of the poems in *catechism*, is more varied in subject matter and typographical format. However, Reed continues to promote neo-American hoodooism (for example, in "For Cardinal Spellman Who Hated Voo Doo" and "New-HooDoo Manifesto") and to satirize the misdeeds of the capitalist "monster," the military–industrial complex. *Chattanooga*, Reed's most personal collection, explores the historical significance of the city of his birth as he imbues it with personal memory and reflection. In *A Secretary to the Spirits*, Reed adds a visual dimension to his multicultural aesthetic by incorporating Betye Saar's Egyptian collage illustrations, which complement Reed's verbal message. *New and Collected Poems* demonstrates Reed's broadened scope and vision. In "Points of View," the section containing his new poems, his subject matter includes the U.S. invasion of Grenada, a California earthquake, the British royal family, the Ayatollah Khomeini, and Jesus.

Reed's major collections of essays include *Shrovetide in Old New Orleans* (1978), *God Made Alaska for the Indians* (1982), *Writin' Is Fightin': Thirty-seven Years of Boxing on Paper* (1988), *Airing Dirty Laundry* (1993), and *Another Day at the Front: Dispatches from the Race War* (2003). Selections from these books appear in *The Reed Reader* (2000). His essays are often marked by a contentious style and complement his exploration of multicultural themes in his novels and poetry. Reed's recent works of political and cultural criticism include *Going Too Far: Essays About America's Nervous Breakdown* (2012) and *Why No Confederate Statues in Mexico* (2019).

Wenxin Li

See also: Black Arts Movement; Jazz in Literature; Novel; Postmodernism; Trickster; Wright, Richard.

Resources

Primary Sources: Ishmael Reed: *Another Day at the Front: Dispatches from the Race War* (New York: Basic Books, 2003); *Barack Obama and the Jim Crow Media: The Return of the Nigger Breakers* (Montréal: Baraka Books, 2010); *Blues City: A Walk in Oakland* (New York: Crown, 2003); *Conjugating Hindi* (Victoria, TX: Dalkey Archive Press, 2018); *Flight to Canada* (1976; repr. New York: Scribner's, 1998); *The Free-lance Pallbearers* (1967; repr. Normal, IL: Dalkey Archive, 1999); *Going Too Far: Essays About America's Nervous Breakdown* (Montréal: Baraka Books, 2012); *Ishmael Reed: The Plays* (Champaign, IL: Dalkey Archive Press, 2009); *Japanese by Spring* (1993; repr. New

York: Penguin, 1996); *Juice!* (Champaign, IL: Dalkey Archive Press, 2011); *The Last Days of Louisiana Red* (1974; repr. New York: Harper, 1983); *Mumbo Jumbo* (1972; repr. New York: Scribner's, 1996); *New and Collected Poems, 1964–2007* (Boston: Da Capo Press, 2007); *Reckless Eyeballing* (1986; repr. Normal, IL: Dalkey Archive Press, 2000); *The Reed Reader* (New York: Perseus, 2000); *The Terrible Threes* (New York: Atheneum, 1989); *The Terrible Twos* (1982; repr. Normal, IL: Dalkey Archive Press, 1999); *Why No Confederate Statues in Mexico* (Montréal: Baraka Books, 2019).

Secondary Sources: Jay Boyer, *Ishmael Reed* (Boise, ID: Boise State University Press, 1993); Bruce Dick and Amritjit Singh, eds., *Conversations with Ishmael Reed* (Jackson, MS: University Press of Mississippi, 1995); Bruce Dick and Pavel Zemliansky, eds., *The Critical Response to Ishmael Reed* (Westport, CT: Greenwood Press, 1999); John Domini, "Ishmael Reed: A Conversation with John Domini," *American Poetry Review* 7, no. 1 (1978), 32–36, repr. in Dick and Singh, pp. 128–143; Nicholas Donofrio, "Multiculturalism, Inc.: Regulating and Deregulating the Culture Industries with Ishmael Reed," *American Literary History* 29, no. 1 (2017), 100–128; Anita Felicelli, "Satire and Subversion in Ishmael Reed's *Conjugating Hindi*," *Los Angeles Review of Books*, September 8, 2018, https://lareviewofbooks.org/article/satire-and-subversion-in-ishmael-reeds-conjugating-hindi/#!; Henry Louis Gates Jr., "The 'Blackness of Blackness': A Critique of the Sign and the Signifying Monkey," *Critical Inquiry* 9 (1983), 685–723; Shelley Ingram, "'To Ask Again': Folklore, *Mumbo Jumbo*, and the Question of Ethnographic Metafictions," *African American Review* 45, nos. 1–2 (2012), 183–196; "Ishmael Reed," in *African American Writers*, ed. Lea Baecher and A. Walton Litz (New York: Scribner's, 1991), 361–377; Jennifer A. Jordan, "Ideological Tension: Cultural Nationalism and Multiculturalism in the Novels of Ishmael Reed," in *Contemporary African American Fiction: New Critical Essays*, ed. Dana A. Williams (Columbus,

OH; Ohio State University Press, 2009), 37–61; Madeleine Monson-Rosen, "Messenger Bug: Ishmael Reed's Media Virus," *Cultural Critique* 88 (2014), 28–53; Elisabeth Oyler, "Creating a Neo-Hoodoo Mythology: Past, Present, and Future in Ishmael Reed's Multidirectional Memory," in *Mapping Generations of Traumatic Memory in American Narratives*, ed. Dana Mihăilescu, Roxana Oltean, and Mihaela Precup (Newcastle upon Tyne, UK; Cambridge Scholars, 2014), 103–128; Robert Scholes, "Review of *The Last Days of Louisiana Red*," *New York Times Book Review*, November 10, 1974, p. 2; Elizabeth A. Settle and Thomas A. Settle, *Ishmael Reed: A Primary and Secondary Bibliography* (Boston: G. K. Hall, 1982); Walt Sheppard, "When State Magicians Fail: An Interview with Ishmael Reed," *Nickel Review* (August 28– September 10, 1968), 72–75; Dana A. Williams, *African American Humor, Irony, and Satire: Ishmael Reed, Satirically Speaking* (Newcastle upon Tyne, UK: Cambridge Scholars, 2007); Shamoon Zamir, "An Interview with Ishmael Reed," *Callaloo* 17 (1994), 1131–1157, repr. in Dick and Singh, pp. 271–302.

Research Resources: Electronic Works

The refinement of digital technology has revolutionized access to information, making it possible for students and scholars to research an enormous and rapidly growing body of literature by and about African Americans. The *MLA* (Modern Language Association) *International Bibliography* is the premier database for literature in general, including African American literature. However, the overview of sources listed in this entry focuses specifically on databases related to African American literature. The overview is not intended to be exhaustive but instead to provide a reasonable range of databases that serve different research needs. Some of the databases are commercial products, while others are freely available on the World Wide Web.

The publisher Chadwyck-Healey offers a number of commercial products for researching African American literature. *African American Poetry, 1750–1900* is a collection of 3,000 poems by fifty-four African American poets writing in the late eighteenth and nineteenth centuries. It is based on William French's bibliography, *Afro-American Poetry and Drama, 1760–1975*. Poems by many well-known poets are included—Paul Laurence Dunbar, for example—as well as poems by lesser known authors, including James Corrothers and Albery Allson Whitman, author of *An Idyl of the South: An Epic Poem in Two Parts* (1901). The *Database of Twentieth Century African-American Poetry* provides access to the full text of thousands of poems written by the most important and influential African American poets from the early twentieth century to the present. The works of Rita Dove, Robert Hayden, Audre Lorde, and Langston Hughes are among those in the database. Biographical profiles accompany the text. *International Index to Black Periodicals Full Text* covers humanities-related disciplines drawn from more than 150 international journals, newspapers, and newsletters. The full texts of over forty periodicals are included from 1998 forward. Titles include *The Langston Hughes Review, Obsidian, Research in African Literatures*, and the *African American Review*. *African American Biographical Database* brings together the biographical profiles of thousands of African Americans. The content is primarily drawn from *Black Biographical Dictionaries, 1790–1950* and includes extended narratives of African American literary figures.

The commercial provider of database resources BiblioLine offers the *Black Studies Database*, which includes material from over 150 journals, magazines, newspapers, newsletters, and reports between 1948 and 1986.

The Schomburg Center for Research in Black Culture, a division of the Research Libraries of the New York Public Library, holds the country's largest collection of works by and about Africans and the people of African descent. In addition to books, the Center collects pamphlets, photographs, microforms, sound recordings, films, periodicals, art, and ephemera, from all countries and in all languages. The New York Public Library has made available *Black Studies on Disc*, an annually updated CD-ROM database that contains all the Schomburg catalogs. It is accompanied by the *Index to Black Periodicals*, an index to articles in Black journals and magazines since 1989. *African American Women Writers of the 19th Century* is the Schomburg Center's digital collection of biography, autobiography, fiction, poetry, and essays written by Black women prior to 1920.

An independent not-for-profit organization, JSTOR, provides electronic access to back issues of important scholarly journals in the humanities, social sciences, and sciences. Within the *Language and Literature Collection*, there are extensive archives of core African American literary journals, including *Callaloo, Phylon, African American Review*, and the *Journal of Black Studies*.

The University of Virginia Library's Electronic Text Center has a long history of providing public access to electronic texts. *African American Writers: Online E-texts* is a browsable and searchable database of African American writers ranging from Phillis Wheatley to Maya Angelou.

Black Drama provides access to English-language plays written by Black authors from North America, the Caribbean, and Africa, from 1850 to the present. The database also includes selected playbills, production photographs, and other ephemera related to the plays. There is a concentration of materials from the Harlem Renaissance, contemporary African American authors, and twentieth-century African playwrights.

Lori Ricigliano

See also: E-Zines, E-News, E-Journals, and E-Collections; Research Sources: Reference Works

Resources

African American Biographical Database (Alexandria, VA: Chadwyck-Healey, 2003), http://aabd.chadwyck.com; *African American Poetry* (Alexandria, VA: Chadwyck-Healey, 1996), http://collections.chadwyck.com/marketing/products/about_ilc.jsp?collection=daap; *African American Studies* (New York: JSTOR, 2004), https://www.jstor.org/subject/africanamericanstudies; *African American Studies: Oxford Bibliographies* (New York: Oxford University Press, 2006), www.oxfordbibliographies.com/obo/page/african-american-studies; *Black Drama* (Alexandria, VA: Alexander Street Press and the University of Chicago, 2003), https://bldr.alexanderstreet.com/; *Black Studies Center* (Alexandria, VA: Chadwyck-Healy, 2004), http://bsc.chadwyck.com/marketing/; *Black Studies on Disc* (New York: G. K. Hall, 2003), CD-ROM; *Twentieth-Century African American Poetry* (Alexandria, VA: Chadwyck-Healey, 1996), http://collections.chadwyck.com/marketing/products/about_ilc.jsp?collection=20daap; *Digital Schomburg: African American Women Writers of the 19th Century* (New York: Schomburg Center, New York Public Library, Center for Research in Black Culture, 1999), http://digital.nypl.org/schomburg/writers_aa19/; *International Index to Black Periodicals Full Text* (Alexandria, VA: Chadwyck-Healey, 2003), http://iibp.chadwyck.com; *MLA International Bibliography* (New York: Modern Language Association, 2004), https://www.mla.org/Publications/MLA-International-Bibliography.

Research Sources: Reference Works

Reference works provide access to information about African American authors, their works, and criticism of their works.

Reference works are designed to provide access to specific items of information rather than to be read consecutively, the way a novel or a story is read, for example. Reference works may be in print or electronic form. For the purposes of this entry, print reference works will be discussed; for electronic sources, see Research Sources: Electronic Works.

For literature, reference works may be divided into two major categories: bibliographies/indexes and source works. A bibliography/index reference work is "a systematically produced descriptive list of records" (Katz, 7) that provides a citation or some indication of the existence of a work and where it may be found. Source-type works are synoptic; that is, they provide summaries or digests of information. They do so directly rather than simply pointing out where information may be found. Source works include almanacs, biographical sources, dictionaries, encyclopedias, handbooks, and yearbooks (summaries of events in a given single year, such as 1954 or 1989).

Reference works relevant to literature tend to focus upon biographical information about authors, to give an indication of the existence of works, to provide a plot summary and list of characters and themes of a particular work, or to give access to criticism and reviews of works. There are several reference sources specifically for African American literature. Many of the major literary reference sources include references to at least a few writers of African descent. Literary reference sources may be retrospective, covering authors, works and criticism of the past, or current, covering contemporary authors, works, and criticism.

A selected list of reference works for African American literature, with brief annotation, follows. The list is divided into bibliography/index sources and dictionary/encyclopedia/handbook sources. A brief description follows each item. Items are listed alphabetically by the title of the work.

Bibliographic and Index Sources

African American Authors, 1745–1945: A Bio-Bibliographical Critical Sourcebook. Emmanuel S. Nelson, ed. Westport, CT: Greenwood, 2000. This sourcebook provides biographical, critical, and bibliographic information about seventy-eight African American writers, including both well-known and lesser-known authors.

African American Literature: A Guide to Reading Interests. Alma Dawson and Connie Van Fleet. Westport, CT: Libraries Unlimited, 2004. This readers' advisory guide describes and categorizes more than 700 works of African American literature in all genres.

African-American Literature: Overview and Bibliography. Paul Q. Tilden, ed. New York: Nova Science Publishers, 2003. This work provides an overview of African American literature as well as a bibliography of literature and criticism of works by African American authors.

Afro-America Fiction, 1853–1976: A Guide to Information Sources. Edward Margolies and David Bakish. Detroit: Gale, 1979.

This source provides a checklist of novels, anthologies, and short stories, and an annotated list of bibliographies on Black fiction. It has author, title, and subject indexes.

The Afro-American Novel, 1965–1975: A Descriptive Bibliography of Primary and Secondary Material. Helen Ruth Houston. Troy, NY: Whitston, 1977. This volume provides biographical notes about fifty-six African American writers as well as listings of their novels, criticism, and reviews of their works.

Afro-American Poetry and Drama, 1760–1975: A Guide to Information Sources. William P. French et al. Detroit: Gale, 1979. This work provides a listing of poetry and dramatic works and criticism.

The Afro-American Short Story: A Comprehensive, Annotated Index with Selected Commentaries. Preston M. Yancy, comp. Westport, CT: Greenwood Press, 1986. This source provides an index to 800 short stories, by over 300 authors, written between 1950 and 1982.

Best Literature by and About Blacks. Phillip M. Richards and Neil Schlager. Detroit: Gale, 2000. This source is a selective bibliography of literary works by and about African Americans.

A Bibliographical Guide to African-American Women Writers. Casper LeRoy Jordan, comp. Westport, CT: Greenwood Press, 1993. This is one of the most comprehensive bibliographies of writing by African American women, with entries on 900 writers. Listings of primary and secondary sources are provided.

Black American Women in Literature. Ronda Gliken, comp. Jefferson, NC: McFarland, 1989. This volume provides bibliographic coverage of 300 African American women writers.

Black American Writers, 1773–1949: A Bibliography and Union List. Geraldine O. Matthews, comp. Boston: G. K. Hall, 1975. A bibliography and union list of monographs by 1,600 African American authors.

Black Authors: A Selected Annotated Bibliography. James Edward Newby. New York: Garland, 1991. This source is a selected bibliography of 3,000 books, monographs, and essays published between 1783 and 1990. The annotations vary in length but tend to be brief and are arranged in nine broad categories. There is a title index and an author index.

Black Image on the American Stage: A Bibliography of Plays and Musicals, 1770–1970. James Vernon Hatch. New York: DBS, 1970. This source provides a bibliography of plays, musicals, reviews, and operas either written by an African American or containing at least one African American character or theme from 1767 to 1970. There is an author index.

Black Literature, 1827–1940. Henry Louis Gates Jr., ed. Alexandria, VA: Chadwyck-Healy, 1990. This source is a printed guide to a microfiche collection of 3,000 sources. Author, title, and genre indexes are on separate microfiches. Over 50,000 separate items are listed.

Books by African-American Authors and Illustrators for Children and Young Adults. Helen E. Williams. Chicago: American Library Association, 1991. This source is arranged by age range and provides an annotated bibliography to children's and young-adult literature and sources by African American authors and illustrators written between 1900 and 1989.

The Harlem Renaissance: An Annotated Bibliography and Commentary. Margaret Perry. New York: Garland, 1982. This work provides an annotated bibliography of articles and books about the Harlem Renaissance. Major authors are highlighted. There is an author index and a title index.

Index to Black American Writers in Collective Biographies. Dorothy Campbell. Littleton, CO: Libraries Unlimited, 1983. This volume provides an index to nearly 270 biographical sources published from 1837 to 1982. There are over 1,900 authors listed in this work.

The Pen Is Ours: A Listing of Writings by and About African-American Women Before 1910 with Secondary Bibliography to the Present. Jean Fagan Yellin and Cynthia D. Bond, comps. New York: Oxford University Press, 1991. This source provides a bibliography of writing by and about African American women with an emphasis on coverage of items appearing from 1773 to 1910. The items are arranged in five broad categories; there is also a name index.

Southern Black Creative Writers, 1829–1953: Bio-Bibliographies. Mamie Marie Booth Foster, comp. Westport, CT: Greenwood Press, 1988. This volume provides brief biographical notes for 200 African American writers and a bibliography of monographs, periodicals, and anthologies. There are author, state, and period indexes.

Dictionary, Encyclopedia, Handbook Sources

African American Dramatists: An A-to-Z Guide. Emmanuel Nelson, ed. Westport, CT: Greenwood Press, 2004. This source is a biographical dictionary of African American dramatists. A bibliography of their works and criticism is included.

African American Poets: Lives, Works, and Sources. Joyce Owens Pettis. Westport, CT: Greenwood Press, 2002. This source is a biographical dictionary with bibliographies of selected poets from the eighteenth century to contemporary times.

African American Writers. Lea Baechler and A. Walton Litz, eds. New York: Scribner's, 1991. This source provides biographical and critical essays about thirty-four African American authors.

African-American Writers. Philip Bader. New York: Facts on File, 2004. This is a biographical guidebook to selected African American writers.

Black Authors and Illustrators of Children's Books: A Biographical Dictionary. Barbara Rollock. 2nd ed. New York: Garland, 1992. This is a biographical dictionary of 150 writers and illustrators of children's books published between 1930 and 1990.

Black Literature Criticism: Classic & Emerging Authors since 1950, Second Edition. Jelena O. Kristovic, ed. Detroit: Gale Cengage Learning 2008. This source provides biographical information, information about major works and their critical reception, and suggestions for further reading for eighty writers of African descent whose works have been published since 1950. It serves as a complement to *Black Literature Criticism Excerpts from Criticism of the Most Significant Works of Black Authors over the Past 200 Years* (Detroit: Gale, 1992).

Black Literature Criticism: Excerpts from Criticism of the Most Significant Works of Black Authors over the Past 200 Years. James P. Draper, ed. Detroit: Gale, 1992. This source provides biographical and critical information on 125 writers of African descent. Each entry provides a biographical sketch of an author, a listing of his/her works, and excerpts from authoritative critical essays.

Black Plots & Black Characters: A Handbook for Afro-American Literature. Robert L. Southgate. Syracuse, NY: Gaylord, 1979. This source provides plot summaries of 100 works (speeches, novels, plays, and long poems) by African American authors appearing between 1619 and 1978. There is an author index and a chronological index.

Contemporary African-American Novelists: A Bio-Bibliographical Critical Sourcebook. Emmanuel S. Nelson, ed. Westport, CT: Greenwood Press, 1999. This source provides biographical essays and critical analyses of the works of seventy-nine contemporary authors.

The Handbook of African American Literature. Hazel Arnett Ervin. Gainesville: University Press of Florida, 2004. This source provides entries on themes (ambiguity, memory, representation, signification, etc.) relevant to African American literature.

Masterpieces of African-American Literature. Frank N. Magill, ed. New York: HarperCollins, 1992. This volume provides the plot summary, list of characters and excerpts of critical analyses of 149 titles by 96 African American writers. It includes an author index and a title index.

Modern Black Writers. Steven R. Serafin, ed. New York: Continuum, 1995. This volume contains excerpts of criticism of the works of 125 literary authors from 32 countries with an emphasis on works published in English and French during the twentieth century.

The Oxford Companion to African American Literature. William L. Andrews et al., eds. New York: Oxford University Press, 1997. This volume provides brief biographical sketches of 400 authors and plot descriptions for over 150 books and literary characters. There are also entries on issues pertinent to literature, genres, and themes. The coverage is from the colonial times to the present.

Kimberly Black-Parker

See also: E-Zines, E-News, E-Journals, and E-Collections; Gates, Henry Louis, Jr.; Major, Clarence; Research Resources: Electronic Works.

Resources

Robert Balay, *Guide to Reference Books*, 11th ed. (Chicago: American Library Association, 1996); Ron Blazek and Elizabeth Aversa, *The Humanities: A Selective Guide to Information Sources*, 5th ed. (Englewood, CO: Libraries Unlimited, 2000); James L. Harner, *Literary Research Guide: An Annotated Listing of Reference Sources in English Literary Studies*, 5th ed. (New York: Modern Language Association, 2008); William A. Katz, *Introduction to Reference Work*, 8th ed., vol. 1 (New York: McGraw-Hill, 2002).

Rodgers, Carolyn Marie (1945–2010)

Poet, prose writer, critic, publisher, and lecturer. A noted figure in the Black Arts Movement of the 1960s, Rodgers, based in Chicago, Illinois, was known for her innovation in poetic voice and form and for her sensitive exploration of a range of thematic concerns: racism, revolution, gender roles, relationships, identity, family conflict, spirituality, and survival. Her poetry documents the struggle to speak authentically as an African American woman during an era of dramatic social change, in a genre long dominated by Anglo-European tradition.

Rodgers began writing poems early in her school career, but an encounter with Gwendolyn Brooks on the Roosevelt University campus served as inspiration to take her avocation seriously. While employed as a social worker in the mid-1960s, Rodgers worked on her BA, attended workshops conducted by Brooks, and joined OBAC Writers Workshop. With fellow OBAC participants Haki R. Madhubuti (Don L. Lee) and Johari Amini (Jewel Latimore), she founded Third World Press, a vehicle for new work in the spirit of cultural revolution.

Encouraged by Brooks and by Hoyt Fuller (OBAC founder and the editor of *Negro Digest*), Rodgers had her first collection, *Paper Soul*, distributed by Third World Press in 1968. Her work earned her the first Conrad Kent Rivers Memorial Fund Award, and subsequent publications, *Two Love Raps* (1969) and *Songs of a Black Bird* (1969), brought her the Poet Laureate Award of the Society of Midland Authors and a grant from the National Endowment for the Arts. Rodgers's bold articulation of the tensions and contradictions in contemporary African American life led to a continuing series of lectureships and residencies at colleges and universities. It also triggered criticism from some of her poet peers, those discomfited by her unconventional spellings, her mix of street language and Standard English, and/or her expression of certain themes and attitudes associated with the militant Black male. Rodgers directly addressed the pressure to represent "the new Black Womanhood" as "a softer self" in "The Last M. F." (*Black Bird*), a poem that simultaneously acquiesces to the demands of her artistic community and defends (and reiterates) her linguistic choices.

How I Got Ovah: New and Selected Poems (1975), published by Doubleday's Anchor Press, marks Rodgers's abandonment of her earlier political persona and further development of more introspective themes. Nominated for the National Book Award, this collection addresses such topics as love, loneliness, religion, and family (especially maternal) ties. *The Heart as Ever Green* (1978) likewise explores an evolving, meditative self in the context of community, notably through images of the natural world. In the title poem, the speaker's resilient heart is "ever green," "like buds or shoots, / determined to grow."

After publication with Doubleday, Rodgers established Chicago's Eden Press with support from the Illinois Arts Council, and her subsequent collections have appeared under that imprint. Sustaining her commitment to higher education, she earned an MA from the University of Chicago in the early 1980s. Carolyn Rodgers's work as a writer and educator has continued to receive commendation, and among her honors are the Carnegie Award and multiple

PEN awards. Her remarkable oeuvre includes fiction, essays, reviews, and musical compositions.

Janis Butler Holm

See also: Feminism/Black Feminism; Lyric Poetry.

Resources

Primary Sources: "Black Poetry—Where It's At," in *SOS—Calling All Black People: A Black Arts Movement Reader*, ed. John H. Bracey Jr., Sonia Sanchez, and James Smethurst (Amherst, MA: University of Massachusetts Press, 2014), 188–198; *Eden and Other Poems* (Chicago: Eden, 1983); *Finite Forms: Poems* (Chicago: Eden, 1985); *For Flip Wilson* (Detroit: Broadside, 1971); *For H. W. Fuller* (Detroit: Broadside, 1970); *The Girl with Blue Hair* (Chicago: Eden, 1996); *The Heart as Ever Green: Poems* (Garden City, NY: Anchor-Doubleday, 1978); *How I Got Ovah: New and Selected Poems* (Garden City, NY: Anchor-Doubleday, 1975); *A Little Lower Than the Angels* (Chicago: Eden, 1984); *Long Rap/Commonly Known as a Poetic Essay* (Detroit: Broadside, 1971); *Morning Glory: Poems* (Chicago: Eden, 1989); *Now Ain't That Love* (Detroit: Broadside, 1970); *Paper Soul* (Chicago: Third World, 1968); *Salt* (Chicago: Eden, 1998); *Songs of a Black Bird* (Chicago: Third World, 1969); *A Train Called Judah* (Chicago: Eden, 1996); *Translation: Poems* (Chicago: Eden, 1980); *Two Love Raps* (Chicago: Third World, 1969); *We're Only Human* (Chicago: Eden, 1994).

Secondary Sources: Fahamisha Patricia Brown, "Rodgers, Carolyn M.," in *American Women Writers: A Critical Reference Guide*, ed. Taryn Benbow-Pfalzgraf, 2nd ed. (Detroit: St. James, 2000); Jean Davis, "Carolyn M. Rodgers," in *Dictionary of Literary Biography*, vol. 41, *Afro-American Poets Since 1955* (Detroit: Gale, 1985); Mari Evans, ed., *Black Women Writers (1950–1980): A Critical Evaluation* (Garden City, NY: Anchor-Doubleday, 1984); Karen Jackson Ford, *Gender and the Poetics of Excess: Moments of Brocade* (Jackson: University Press of Mississippi, 1997); Barbara J. Griffin, "Carolyn Rodgers," in *Notable Black American Women*, ed. Jessie Carney Smith, vol. 2 (Detroit: Gale, 1996); Angela Jackson, "The Blackbird Flies: Remembering Carolyn M. Rodgers," *Callaloo* 33, no. 4 (2010), 919–925; Joyce Pettis: "Carolyn Rodgers," in her *African American Poets: Lives, Works, and Sources* (Westport, CT: Greenwood Press, 2002); "Rodgers, Carolyn (Marie)," in *African-American Writers: A Dictionary*, ed. Shari Hatch and Michael Strickland (Santa Barbara, CA: ABC-CLIO, 2000); "Rodgers, Carolyn M(arie)," in *Black Writers: A Selection of Sketches from Contemporary Authors*, ed. Sharon Malinowski, 2nd ed. (Detroit: Gale, 1994); Carmen L. Phelps, *Visionary Women Writers of Chicago's Black Arts Movement* (Jackson, MS: University Press of Mississippi, 2012); Marsha C. Vick, "Rodgers, Carolyn M.," *The Oxford Companion to African American Literature* (New York: Oxford University Press, 1997); Jon Woodson, "Rodgers, Carolyn M.," in *The Oxford Companion to Women's Writing in the United States*, ed. Cathy Davidson and Linda Wagner-Martin (New York: Oxford University Press, 1995).

Romance Novel

One of the most popular literary forms the world over, the romance novel engages with the affective and sexual dynamics of human intimacy by way of recognizable narrative conventions. Romantic themes preoccupied even the earliest of African American novelists, but it was not until the late twentieth century that Black writers had the opportunity to take up or even have access to romance as a precise mode of genre writing. Contemporary African American romance novelists have moved beyond the form's historically White and heterosexist contexts and preoccupations to depict the fullness of

Black love in its multiply racialized, classed, and gendered dimensions.

Early Black novels were prone to articulate critiques of slavery and White domination in romantic plots. William Wells Brown's historical (anti)romance *Clotel* (1853) is loosely based on Thomas Jefferson's rumored liaisons with his slave Sally Hemings. The novel was originally published in London and did not appear in the United States until the 1860s. In telling the story of Clotel, daughter of Jefferson and his slave mistress, Currer, Brown makes explicit the sexual violence visited upon Black women as a means of reproducing the institution of slavery. A forerunner to such more famous twentieth-century historical novelists as Frank Yerby and Margaret Abigail Walker, Brown shows how White men's falling in "love" with their slaves was ultimately a cover for socioeconomic interest and racial domination. Frances Ellen Watkins Harper's *Iola Leroy* (1892) and Pauline Elizabeth Hopkins's *Contending Forces* (1900) are sentimental novels that explore similar themes in postbellum contexts; their female characters are able to pass in middle-class society but ultimately become credits to their race according to a logic of virtuous Black womanhood. Charles Waddell Chesnutt's widely read *The House Behind the Cedars* (1900) is a novel of passing in which the mulatto Rena Walden passes as the White Rowena Warwick to win the affection of the aristocrat George Tryon. Here Rena's desire is a function of upward mobility and heterosexual longing, with the tragic result being the impossibility of consummating her love for Tryon.

In the 1920s and 1930s, the Harlem Renaissance witnessed the publication of a number of modernist-realist romances that upend traditional notions of race and racial uplift. The bourgeois women of Jessie Redmon Fauset's "novel without a moral," *Plum Bun* (1929), and Nella Larsen's self-reflexively urbane *Passing* (1929) determine passing to be an extraordinary gift and a tiresome burden at the same time. The color of Angela Murray's skin in *Plum Bun* enables her to experience the pleasures and delights of the proverbial "New Woman" but at the cost of recognizing her own kin in the city. The famed encounter at the end of *Passing*, between Irene Redfield and Clare Kendry, which leaves Clare dead from a fall, is the culmination of Irene's anxious policing of her racial and sexual identities throughout the story. In contrast to Fauset's and Larsen's novels, Jean Toomer's *Cane* (1923), Claude McKay's *Home to Harlem* (1928), and Zora Neale Hurston's *Their Eyes Were Watching God* (1937) reveal the thwarted and at times thriving loves of the Northern urban working class and the Southern rural folk, none of whom has the ability or the desire to pass. Their lusty, quasi-romantic narratives reveal a division in class and Labor relations in the way African American novelists, even those writing today, deal with questions of affect and sexuality.

James Baldwin's *Giovanni's Room* (1956) would prove to be the most powerful yet unusual "Black" romance of its time, for all the main characters are White, the story is set in Paris, France, and the most convincing sexual bond develops between two men, the American expatriate David and the Italian bartender Giovanni. More than anything else, it may have been Baldwin's lyrical prose that signaled a new direction in the way African Americans engaged with the genre. Black romance novelists could now write about love's triumphs and tragedies without being overly sentimental in style or overly reductive in plot. Furthermore, following in the footsteps of McKay as well as Baldwin, they would not need to confine their writing to heterosexual romance. Interestingly enough, these developments came to fruition only after Black women writers responded to the misogynistic, antiromance sentiment of 1960s Black Nationalism in novels of their own: Gayl Jones's *Corregidora* (1975) and *Eva's Man* (1976); Alice Walker's *Meridian* (1976) and *The Color Purple* (1982); and Gloria Naylor's *The Women of Brewster Place* (1982) and *Mama Day* (1988). In *Sula* (1974), *Tar Baby* (1981), *Jazz* (1992), and *Love* (2003), Toni Morrison has fashioned one of the most remarkable single-authored oeuvres in world literature about the various shades and contours of Black love.

On a different level of the field of literary production, which requires a slightly different definition of the romance genre, the industry-leading romance publisher Harlequin did not bring out its first book featuring African Americans in the lead roles until 1984. Sandra Kitt's *Adam and Eva*, set in the Virgin Islands with a vacationing woman and a single father, opened the door for African American romance authorship in the genre-oriented mainstream. There was no turning back. Kitt would go on to produce several other novels, mostly starring White characters, for the Harlequin American imprint, and although her career there gradually tailed off, she became the first author to be published by Kensington Publishing's Arabesque imprint in 1994. That series was founded when the chairman overheard two Black women in a New York City bookstore complaining about the lack of romantic fare for them. Coupled with the amazing success of Terry McMillan's *Waiting to Exhale* in 1992, which ushered in a renaissance of Black popular writing in the United States more generally, the Arabesque line helped turn Black romance

publishing into a full-blown enterprise. Women writers in particular became household names: Rochelle Alers, Gwynne Forster, Donna Hill, and Margie Walker. Kensington managed to do this in a little less than five years; in 1998, the company sold Arabesque to Black Entertainment Television (BET), where it continues to flourish.

Like McMillan, Connie Briscoe, Bebe Moore Campbell, and other contemporary quasi-romantic novelists, African American men have gone beyond the genre's plot and character conventions to represent their unique perspectives on Black and interracial intimacy. Omar Tyree's *Flyy-Girl* (1993) and *A Do Right Man* (1997) paved the way for Black male romance writing, with *A Do Right Man* introducing readers to a strong yet sensitive, attractive yet self-conscious, African American man in search of true love. Eric Jerome Dickey's *Sister, Sister* (1996) and *Friends and Lovers* (1997) are renowned for their emotionally complex Black female protagonists; his *Milk in My Coffee* (1998) explores the interracial sexual and family dynamics between Jordan Greene, a Black urban professional, and Kimberly Chavers, a White artist. Carl Weber employs sharp humor to tackle serious issues of masculine anxiety in *Married Men* (2001) and *Baby Momma Drama* (2003). One might say work by these men serves as a generational counterpoint to representations of Black masculinity not only in structural state racism, particularly when it comes to racial profiling and incarceration rates, but also in the Black female-authored novels of the 1970s and 1980s, where African American men tended to exercise dominant, patriarchal authority.

E. Lynn Harris is arguably the most popular and important gay romance novelist in the United States today. *Invisible Life*

(1991), *Just as I Am* (1994), and *And This Too Shall Pass* (1996) are heartfelt, intelligent explorations of contemporary Black sexuality, which Harris refuses to categorize as being either essentially heterosexual or deviantly homosexual. His African American men struggle to bridge the gap between personal attraction and social or familial expectations. They usually find themselves torn between stereotypically "straight" identities in public—the ladies' man in college, the professional athlete, the well-respected businessman—and ostensibly "gay" sexual practices, which they keep private at the expense of being honest with their wives or girlfriends. The covert practices have come to be known as "living on the down low" or "the DL" in American social and cultural politics. Harris takes pains not to pathologize his characters, but to understand and sympathize with their complex motivations. He handles such topics as adultery, promiscuity, and AIDS with an unflinching yet deeply mature aesthetic.

Romance novelists from Kitt to Harris have established diverse and loyal audiences for their work. Their success has led to increased opportunities for African American romance authorship on at least three levels. First, popular imprints of major U.S. publishing houses have dedicated significant portions of their catalogs to Black romance fiction. Random House's Villard Books has released Tajuana Butler's *Hand-Me-Down Heartache* (2001), C. Kelly Robinson's *Between Brothers* (2001), and Tracy Price-Thompson's *Black Coffee* (2002). Simon and Schuster's Atria Books has come out with Jervey Tervalon's *All the Trouble You Need* (2002), Zane's *The Heat Seekers* (2002), and the 2004 reprint of Sister Souljah's *The Coldest Winter Ever* (1999). Since the sale of Arabesque to BET in 1998, Kensington has developed its Dafina Books imprint, which publishes the prolific novelists Roslyn Carrington, Margaret Johnson-Hodge, Timmothy B. McCann, Mary Monroe, Mary B. Morrison, and Kimberla Lawson Roby.

Second, and on a smaller but no less significant scale of production, independent presses have supported first-time, regional, and underground romance novelists whose work draws the avid, less crossover-minded reader. These books tend to embrace poor or working-class settings and protagonists more readily than their big-name counterparts. Of note here is Genesis Press of Columbus, Mississippi, the largest Black privately owned book publishing company in the United States, whose Indigo and Indigo Love Spectrum imprints compete quite well with BET's Arabesque and Kensington's Dafina series. An author of note is Wahida Clark, who, with the help of Black Print Publishing based in Brooklyn, New York, has penned hardcore "romances" of the street, *Thugs and the Women Who Love Them* (2002) and *Every Thug Needs a Lady* (2003), while incarcerated in a women's federal prison in Lexington, Kentucky.

Finally, online publishing practices as well as work, neighborhood, and circle-of-friends book clubs have democratized the literary field by forging communities of readers and writers who are in it for the books, so to speak. Black romance websites such as Zane's www.eroticanoire.com are at the forefront of the revolution in and outside of print, turning literary nonprofessionals into published authors. Moreover, African American women's reading groups have sprung up across the nation in response not only to the inaugural season of Oprah's Book Club (1996) but also to the need felt by mothers, daughters, sisters, and friends to come together to talk about their favorite stories about Black love.

Based on these observations alone, one might conclude that the romance novel has been the most influential literary form in making this a critical era for Black literary production, measured in terms of best-selling books written by African Americans. But it is also worth pointing out that the McMillan-romance boom has stirred interest in African American Erotica in short stories and anthologies. Though not technically romance novels, volumes such as *Brown Sugar* (2001), *After Hours* (2002), and *Black Silk* (2002), among a host of others, collect daring narratives of Black lust and desire that take their cue from the previously cited texts. Erotica has always occupied the margins of the literary field, denounced as pornography in public yet consumed as art in private. Black erotica sees this sort of readerly transgression as an occasion to deconstruct long-standing stereotypes about the hypersexual African American body. It accomplishes this not by policing the bounds of Black lust or desire but by expanding them through representations of both raw sensuality and passionate feeling. Zane's *The Sex Chronicles* (1999) is the most illustrative single-author book of this sort; hers is also one of the more provocative depictions of the sexual fantasies of modern Black women.

The romance novel has continued to flourish over the course of the past decade as a major genre of African American literature, assuming multiple forms and engaging even wider and more diverse audiences. Beverly Jenkins, for instance, chronicles the lives and loves of the residents of the fictional town of Henry Adams, founded by freed slaves, in her "Blessings" series (2009–2018) and takes readers to the United States' Western frontier in her "Old West" series (2016–2018). Alyssa Cole's novels, including the postapocalyptic *Radio Silence* (2015) and *An Extraordinary Union* (2018), which is set during the Civil War, look to both the historical past and an imagined future as settings for complex, vividly realized love stories, while James Earl Hardy's "B-Boy Blues" series (1994–2018), including *Love the One You're With* (2013) and *A House in Not a Home* (2013), explores same-sex romance in present-day New York City. The romance novel promises to continue engaging with perennial concerns and contemporary issues as it explores the complications and rewards of interpersonal relationships within African American communities.

Kinohi Nishikawa

See also: Novel.

Resources

Michael Awkward, *Inspiriting Influences: Tradition, Revision, and Afro-American Women's Novels* (New York: Columbia University Press, 1989); Houston A. Baker Jr., *Workings of the Spirit: The Poetics of Afro-American Women's Writing* (Chicago: University of Chicago Press, 1991); Devon W. Carbado, Dwight A. McBride, and Donald Weise, eds., *Black Like Us: A Century of Lesbian, Gay, and Bisexual African American Fiction* (San Francisco: Cleis, 2002); Hazel V. Carby, *Reconstructing Womanhood: The Emergence of the Afro-American Woman Novelist* (New York: Oxford University Press, 1987); Barbara Christian, *Black Women Novelists: The Development of a Tradition, 1892–1976* (Westport, CT: Greenwood Press, 1980); Patricia Hill Collins, *Black Sexual Politics: African Americans, Gender, and the New Racism* (New York: Routledge, 2004); Rita Dandridge, *Black Women's Activism: Reading African American Women's Historical Romances* (New York: Peter Lang, 2004); Kimberly Chabot Davis, "Generational Hauntings: The Family Romance in Contemporary Fictions of Raced History," *Modern Fiction Studies* 48, no. 3 (2002), 727–736; Robert Fleming, ed., *After Hours: A*

Collection of Erotic Writing by Black Men (New York: Plume, 2002); Calvin C. Hernton, *The Sexual Mountain and Black Women Writers: Adventures in Sex, Literature, and Real Life* (New York: Anchor, 1987); Deborah E. McDowell, *"The Changing Same": Black Women's Literature, Criticism, and Theory* (Bloomington: Indiana University Press, 1995); Retha Powers, ed., *Black Silk: A Collection of African American Erotica* (New York: Warner, 2002); Marjorie Pryse and Hortense J. Spillers, eds., *Conjuring: Black Women, Fiction, and Literary Tradition* (Bloomington: Indiana University Press, 1985); Carol Taylor, ed., *Brown Sugar: A Collection of Erotic Black Fiction* (New York: Plume, 2001).

S

Sanchez, Sonia (1934–)

Poet, activist, playwright, editor, and teacher. Sonia Sanchez was born Wilsonia Benita Driver in Birmingham, Alabama. Her mother died when she was one, and after the death of her grandmother, she spent several years with a variety of relatives before finally settling in New York City with her father, Wilson Driver, a successful jazz musician. From the age of nine, Sanchez was acquainted with the music of famous jazz musicians, including John Coltrane and Nina Simone. Shortly after she received her bachelor's degree in political science from Hunter College in 1955, she married Albert Sanchez, a Puerto Rican immigrant, whose surname she continues to use when writing. During the racial turbulence of the early 1960s, Sanchez was a supporter of integration and CORE (Congress of Racial Equality). However, Sanchez turned her attention to a more separatist view after considering the ideas of Malcolm X. After hearing Malcolm X's speeches, Sanchez became more acutely aware of the political predicament of Blacks during this era. During this same time, Sanchez began to study creative writing formally with Louise Bogan, who encouraged her to pursue a literary career. Sanchez initially published poetry in small magazines and Black periodicals, such as *The Liberator*, the *Journal of Black Poetry*, *Black Dialogue*, and *Negro Digest*. Sanchez later formed a writers' collective called the Broadside Quartet. The group consisted of young poets and was promoted by Dudley Randall, founder of Broadside Press.

Randall and Sanchez were associated with the Black Arts Movement. Sanchez is one of the most influential women members of that movement. Joyce A. Joyce asserts that "Sonia Sanchez remains one of the proudest and the most vibrant of those [Black Arts Movement] figures whose works manifest this spiritual link between art and politics" (62). Like the work of Amiri Baraka and Haki Madhubuti, Sanchez's poetry is chiefly in free verse and often uses the vernacular. Joyce observes,

If we are to appreciate Sonia Sanchez' poetry, we must wash away all Euro-American, middle class notions of what can and cannot be said in poetry and even of how a poem should look on the printed page. Abrasively strong in content and challenging in form, Sonia Sanchez' poetry addresses itself to the Black community. (64)

Sanchez began a long teaching career in 1965 at the Downtown Community School in New York and later moved to the San Francisco Bay Area, where she was a pioneer in developing Black Studies courses at San Francisco State University. In 1968, Sanchez married the activist/poet Etheridge Knight, with whom she had three children; however, the marriage was troubled and might have made her more acutely aware of the increasing tensions between Black men and Black women. This awareness might have been the impetus for many of her poems. Her first three volumes of poetry—*Home Coming* (1969), *We a BaddDDD People* (1970), and *It's a New Day* (1971)—include poems on the construction of the Black family, drug abuse, domestic violence, and interracial relationships. Sanchez was also a member of the Nation of Islam between 1972 and 1975; however, she left the Nation of Islam due mostly to what she considered its repression of women. In her book *Love Poems* (1973), her Islamic ideology is apparent, and she experiments with the haiku form. Sanchez has also written *Blues Book for Blue Black Magical Women* (1974). She joined the teaching staff of Temple University in Philadelphia, Pennsylvania, in 1977, serving as professor in the departments of English and Women's Studies. While Sanchez is best known for her poetry, she is also a playwright. Her plays include *Sister Son/ji* (1969), and *Uh Huh: But How Do It Free Us?* (1975).

Sanchez's later poetry reflects a shift toward an interest in feminism and women's rights. In 1978, she published *I've Been a Woman* and, in 1984, *Homegirls & Handgrenades* (1984), one of her most celebrated works and the winner of the 1985 American Book Award from the Before Columbus Foundation. *Under a Soprano Sky* (1987) and *Wounded in the House of a Friend* (1995) are more recent books. The latter concerns the devastation of rape and AIDS but also the need for triumph and hope. Sanchez's other poetry volumes include *Does Your House Have Lions?* (1997), which was nominated for a National Book Critics Circle Award; *Like the Singing Coming off the Drums: Love Poems* (1998); and *Shake Loose My Skin* (1999). Sanchez received the Poetry Society of American's Frost Medal in 2001 and served from 2012 until 2014 as Philadelphia's first Poet Laureate.

Recently, much like the poet Nikki Giovanni, Sanchez has celebrated the contemporary hip-hop movement. In an article in *Black Issues Book Review*, she explains, with rapper Mos Def, why modern-day rap artists should be taken seriously as poets and why the Black Arts Movement and hip-hop really exist on a continuum (Cook). Besides the American Book Award, Sanchez has received the prestigious Robert Frost Medal in poetry. Although Sanchez is arguably one of the most prolific women poets in American literary history, criticism and scholarship about her work is, at this writing, relatively scarce. Joyce writes, "The dearth of essays on Sonia Sanchez' craft as well as the simplistic and superficial reviews of her poetry testify to the lack of serious attention given to her 'vitriolic verse'" (63).

Gail L. Upchurch-Mills

See also: Black Arts Movement; Feminism/ Black Feminism; Lyric Poetry; Protest Literature.

Resources

D. A. Cook, "The Aesthetics of Rap," *Black Issues Book Review* (March/April 2000), 22–27; Richard A. Iadonesi, "Writing the (Revolutionary) Body: The Haiku of Sonia Sanchez," in *African American Haiku: Cultural Visions*, ed. John Zheng (Jackson, MS: University Press of Mississippi, 2016), 129–146; Joyce Ann Joyce, *Ijala: Sonia Sanchez and the African Poetic Tradition* (Chicago: Third World Press, 1996); Susan Kelly, "Discipline and Craft: An Interview with Sonia Sanchez," *African American Review* 50, no. 4 (2017), 1033–1041; D. H. Melhem, *Heroism in the New Black Poetry* (Lexington, KY: University Press of Kentucky, 1990); Sonia Sanchez: *Blues Book for Blue Black Magical Women* (Detroit: Broadside Press, 1974); *Does Your House Have Lions?* (Boston: Beacon Press, 1997); *Home Coming* (Detroit: Broadside Press, 1969); *Homegirls & Handgrenades* (New York: Thunder's Mouth Press,

1984); *I'm Black When I'm Singing, I'm Blue When I Ain't and Other Plays*, ed. Jacqueline Wood (Durham, NC: Duke University Press, 2010); *It's a New Day* (Detroit: Broadside Press, 1971); *I've Been a Woman* (Sausalito, CA: Black Scholar Press, 1978); *Like the Singing Coming off the Drums: Love Poems* (Boston: Beacon Press, 1998); *Love Poems* (New York: Third Press, 1973); *Morning Haiku* (Boston: Beacon Press, 2011); *Shake Loose My Skin* (Boston: Beacon Press, 1999); *Under a Soprano Sky* (Trenton, NJ: Africa World Press, 1987); *We a BaddDDD People* (Detroit: Broadside Press, 1970); *Wounded in the House of a Friend* (Boston: Beacon Press, 1995); Meta L. Schettler, "An African High Priestess of Haiku: Sonia Sanchez and the Principles of a Black Aesthetic," in *African American Haiku: Cultural Visions*, ed. John Zheng (Jackson, MS: University Press of Mississippi, 2016), 111–128.

Satire

Satire may be defined as a mode of writing that has at its heart an attitude of criticism of personal and social values and that aims to produce laughter as it highlights vice and folly. Working in many forms and genres, the satirist writes from the core values of his/her culture, attacking deviations from that core that he/she sees as sinful, foolish, aberrant, or otherwise detrimental to social order. The satirist, like the trickster, always carries a two-edged sword, as it were; his verbal instruments, including irony and exaggeration, can cut friend and foe alike if the subject seems to the satirist to have strayed from the acceptable paths of traditional culture.

African American folk traditions exhibited the satiric impulse, even when the expression of views critical of slaveholders and supporters of "the peculiar institution" might be severely punished; the slaves found a voice in folktales and orature for criticism of Mr. Charley and Miss Anne, the prototypical master and mistress of the plantation. A satiric impulse is so well disguised in many of the animal fables in which small, powerless creatures such as rabbits and spiders defeat the large and powerful elephant and lion that they were absorbed into American folklore with little understanding of their mordancy. The slaves also created stories featuring John the trickster slave who continually outwitted his master. These tales show John winning the kind of small victories that reminded the powerless slaves that the master was not a god, but a fallible human being just like themselves. When African Americans began to write fiction, stories of this type soon surfaced; Paul Laurence Dunbar's "Mr. Cornelius Johnson, Office Seeker" and Charles Waddell Chesnutt's "The Passing of Grandison"—indeed, many of Chesnutt's stories—contain satiric elements drawn directly from the folk tradition of the trickster slave. Nor did the satiric impulse die out with emancipation. A line of folk narratives concerning Shine, an imaginary African American survivor of the *Titanic* disaster, reminds listeners that the high and mighty White folks on the doomed ship were as mortal, and perhaps less resourceful, than Shine the stoker. The captain and various passengers appeal to Shine for help, offering money, status, and sexual favors, but Shine tells them they are on their own; if they hope to be saved, he says, they would be advised to "get your ass in the water and swim like me."

During the Harlem Renaissance period, writers found satire an appropriate mode for the expression of their double-edged attitudes toward their equally double-edged experience. Many writers in the period felt that the enthusiasm for the work of African

American artists expressed by White readers, critics, and supporters was based on racial fascination and paternalism, not on aesthetic judgments. Wallace Thurman, in his *Infants of the Spring* (1932), mocked the pretensions of fellow Black artists, even as he exposed the false amity of White admirers. Rudolf J. C. Fisher's *The Walls of Jericho* (1928) explores class and color conflict among African Americans in Harlem through a satiric lens. The most distinguished satirist of the period was George Schuyler, who pilloried African Americans' desire for acceptance by Whites in *Black No More* (1931), in which most of the African American population undergoes scientific treatment to turn them White. Zora Neale Hurston, in *Moses, Man of the Mountain* (1939), retells the Moses story in the idiom of the Black South, satirizing both White obsessions with the religiosity of African Americans and the presumption that the figures of Scripture and legend are best understood as Whites. Many of the short stories in Langston Hughes's collections *The Ways of White Folks* (1934) and *Laughing to Keep from Crying* (1952) exhibit a highly ironic, even satiric edge. In his newspaper sketches featuring Jesse B. Simple (the first spelling was "Semple," but Hughes changed it to "Simple" in all the later tales), Hughes gently commented on the gap between the ideals of educated Blacks and the common sense of the Black masses; in another set of newspaper sketches, later collected as *Like One of the Family*, Alice Childress dramatized the relationships between African American domestics and their bourgeois White employers.

While there are satiric elements in the fiction of Richard Wright, Ralph Ellison, and James Baldwin, the next generation of African American writers was more thoroughly engaged in satirizing American failures to achieve national values such as universal civil rights and African American deviations from core values. The prescriptions of the Black Power theorists that art should expose the enemy and further the revolution were responded to in various ways. William Melvin Kelley's *dem* (1967) exposed the enemy—White supremacy—in a wildly comic tale of a casually racist young WASP advertising executive whose wife bears one White and one Black twin. John Oliver Killens's *The Cotillion* (1971) contrasts the racial ambivalence of the Femmes Fatales with the trickster militancy of the narrator, Ben Ali Lumumba, in the struggle to win over the heroine. Fran Ross's novel *Oreo* (1974) used the myth of Theseus in a satiric send-up of such high-culture fictions as James Joyce's *Ulysses* in an extravagant tale about a Black teenage Philadelphian in search of her Jewish father in New York. Kristin Hunter Lattany's novels *The Landlord* (1966) and *The Lakestown Rebellion* (1978) both turn on the trickster element in African American culture to show how the community can defeat White power and authority. Hal Bennett's novels, exemplified by *Lord of Dark Places* (1970), take up the American fascination with the Black male body. Bennett's hero worships his own phallic self, and services both men and women to survive molestation in childhood, Civil Rights Era assaults, the Vietnam War, and urban violence. Bennett ultimately indicts both Whites and Blacks for fetishizing the Black male body. Douglas Turner Ward's one-act play *Day of Absence: A Satirical Fantasy* (1966), described as "a reverse minstrel show done in white face," and Amiri Baraka's *The Great Goodness of Life: A Coon Show* (1967) both focused on mocking the stereotypical images used by the White majority to contain and suppress African Americans. Later plays, such as Robert Alexander's *I Ain't Yo Uncle* (1996), continued to work this satiric vein.

The major figure among African American satirists in the Black Arts Movement is Ishmael Reed. In poems and novels written between the late 1960s and the turn of the twenty-first century, Reed skewered many aspects of Anglo American and African American culture, including western movies, the Nixon administration, Japan mania, even Black Power militants. His masterpiece, *Mumbo Jumbo* (1972), rewrites the history of Western civilization as a struggle between Jes' Grew, the principle of dance and spontaneity, connected to the ancient Egyptian, West African, and Haitian mysteries, and the Wallflower Order, representative of everything Nordic, over-regimented, stiff, and authoritarian. Reed's impressive revisions of history, manipulations of racial stereotypes, and interpellation of scholarship, advertisements, journalism, drawings and photographs no more detract from the book's hilarity than does its imitation of the detective novel form. Al Young's parodic fictional creation, the poet O. O. Gabugah, turned the tables on the Black Arts Movement's prescriptive theorizing in a series of mock revolutionary utterances that went undetected as frauds.

Writers of the post–Black Arts Movement period (since 1980) often write in a satiric vein. This so-called hip-hop satire retains affinities with such popular culture forms as rap music and experimental fictional forms while exploring the complexities of African American identity that result from increases in the experiences of integration, higher education, and miscegenation. These writers redefine and reuse the stereotypes created by both Blacks and Whites to define racial and cultural

authenticity, and frequently write about racially isolated individuals. Thus, Trey Ellis's novel *Platitudes* (1988) used a Chinese box structure of narrative within narrative to explore adolescent sexuality and new possibilities for fiction. Darius James's novel *Negrophobia* (1992) is a carnival of the grotesque, obscene, and scatological, designed to "subvert the perversion" of American racist culture. Paul Beatty's *The White Boy Shuffle* (1996) explores enduring questions of African American leadership and the gap between the masses and the privileged that have been raised by predecessors like Hughes, Ellison, Killens, Kelley, and Reed. Beatty's hero finds himself as leader ironically advocating that African Americans commit mass suicide. These works all confront the despair arising from "a dream deferred," the failure of the nation to meet the expectations raised by the Civil Rights Movement. Like rap music and other artistic products of African American culture at the end of the twentieth century, they are in-your-face, bold, and uncompromising. Hilarious as they often are, these hip-hop satires are dark presences, reminding readers how much remains to be done before the nation achieves its democratic ideals, if it ever can—and how hard the work of getting there will be.

Joseph T. Skerrett Jr.

See also: Hughes, Langston; Humor; Reed, Ishmael; Schuyler, George Samuel.

Resources

Darryl Dickson-Carr, *African America Satire: The Sacredly Profane Novel* (Columbia, MO: University of Missouri Press, 2001); *Spoofing the Modern: Satire in the Harlem Renaissance* (Columbia, SC: University of South Carolina Press, 2015); Alan Dundes, ed., *Mother Wit from the Laughing Barrel: Readings in the Interpretation of African American Folklore* (Englewood Cliffs, NJ: Prentice-Hall, 1973); Robert C. Elliott, *The Power of Satire: Magic, Ritual, Art* (Princeton, NJ: Princeton University Press, 1960); Jessyka Finley, "Black Women's Satire as (Black) Postmodern Performance," *Studies in American Humor* 2, no. 2 (2016), 236–265; Lisa Guerrero, "Can I Live? Contemporary Black Satire and the State of Postmodern Double Consciousness," *Studies in American Humor* 2, no. 2 (2016), 266–279; Derek C. Maus and James J. Donahue, eds., *Post-Soul Satire: Black Identity after Civil Rights* (Jackson, MS: University Press of Mississippi, 2014); Ronald Paulson, *The Fictions of Satire* (Baltimore: Johns Hopkins University Press, 1967).

Schuyler, George Samuel (1895–1977)

Journalist, novelist, and satirist. Condemned by many for his views but also respected by many for his undeniable talent, George Samuel Schuyler has been extolled as "the premier Black journalist." According to Nicholas Stix, Schuyler is "the greatest Black journalist this country has ever produced." His writings, although controversial, significantly influenced Black journalism, in particular, and journalism, in general. During his career, Schuyler traveled extensively overseas. He was one of the first Black reporters to serve as a foreign correspondent for a major metropolitan newspaper, the *New York Evening Post*. Schuyler's writing career included positions as reporter, associate editor, and columnist for the New York office of the *Pittsburgh Courier* (1924–1966). He also wrote for magazines and journals, including *The Messenger* (1923), *The Nation* (1926), *The New Republic*, *Opportunity*, *The Crisis*, *American Mercury*, *The Call*, and *American Opinion*.

Langston Hughes's landmark essay "The Negro Artist and the Racial Mountain," written during the Harlem Renaissance, was a response to an essay Schuyler had written, "The Negro-Art Hokum," in which Schuyler ridiculed some assumptions behind the notion of "Negro" writing. Both essays are included in *The Portable Harlem Renaissance Reader* (1994), edited by David Levering Lewis.

In the longer forms of literature, Schuyler had similar impact. His novel *Slaves Today: A Story of Liberia* (1931), and the satirical science fiction novel *Black No More* (1931), sometimes called the first science fiction work by an African American, featured fierce implicit social commentary. Schuyler wrote under several pseudonyms, including William Stockton, D. Johnson, Rachel Call, Edgecombe Wright, Verne Caldwell, and John Kitchen. Additionally, he wrote the serialized novels *The Black Internationale* and *Black Empire* for the *Pittsburgh Courier* (1936–1938) under the name Samuel I. Brooks. These novels helped double the *Courier*'s circulation to 250,000. In 1991, *The Black Internationale* and *Black Empire* were published together in book form as *Black Empire*. Schuyler's political shift from the left to the extreme right became the theme of his autobiography, *Black and Conservative* (1966). Schuyler vigorously demonstrated his iconoclasm and highly unpopular ultraconservatism in his books, articles, pamphlets, reviews, and essays, including "The Negro-Art Hokum" (1926), "Blessed Are the Sons of Ham" (1927), "Our White Folks" (1927), "Our Greatest Gift to America" (1929), "The Caucasian Problem" (1944), "The Reds and I" (1968), and "Malcolm X: Better to Memorialize Benedict Arnold" (1973).

Schuyler's best-known work, the satirical science fiction novel *Black No More*, was considered pulp fiction during the 1930s. It deals with the race issue in America, featuring a Black doctor, Junius Crookman, who discovers a phenomenon that will change Black people into White people. Beginning with this science fiction premise, Schuyler examines the racial attitudes of everyone from White racists to Black intellectuals. He also offers caricatures of real-life individuals, such as W.E.B. Du Bois as Dr. Shakespeare Agamemnon Beard, James Weldon Johnson as Dr. Jackson, and Madame C. J. Walker as Madame Sisseretta Blandish. The novel's protagonist is Max Dasher (a.k.a. Matthew Fisher), one of the first to embrace and undergo Dr. Crookman's discovery. Many Blacks find this discovery to be a welcome alternative to the everyday denigration they experience. The novel poses the question, "What would America be like if there were no Blacks?" Would racism cease? Dr. Crookman's newfound marvel allows Blacks to experience the daily amenities once experienced only by White America, and eventually results in an epiphany for people of all races.

George Samuel Schuyler was born on February 25, 1895, in Providence, Rhode Island, and was raised in Syracuse, New York. His father died when he was three. His mother later married a cook and porter. When he was still very young, Schuyler's mother taught him to read and write. In 1912, he dropped out of school and joined the army, serving in World War I until 1919 and obtaining the rank of first lieutenant. During his stint in the army, Schuyler went AWOL when a "Greek immigrant shoeshine man in Philadelphia called him the 'n' word, and refused to shine his shoes." Schuyler remarked, "I'm a son-of-a-bitch if I'll serve this country any longer." He eventually turned himself in and was convicted by a military court. Schuyler was sentenced to five years in prison, but because of good behavior, he was released after serving nine months of his sentence. In 1919, Schuyler was discharged from the army.

In 1928, Schuyler married Josephine E. Cogdell, an artist, journalist, and heiress of a prominent White Texas family. He was her second husband. Their daughter Philippa Duke Schuyler was born in 1931. Josephine fed young Philippa a diet that incorporated wheat germ, cod liver oil, and uncooked foods, including raw liver, in an effort to perpetuate her concept of hybridization as a source of superior vigor and intellect. Philippa was a piano prodigy who later became a journalist for the *Union Leader*. Like her father decades earlier, she experienced racial prejudice in America. This led her to travel abroad and, for a brief period, legally change her name to Felipa Monterro y Schuyler, and pass for White. Years later, she resumed the name Philippa Schuyler. On May 9, 1967, while reporting in Vietnam and performing an unauthorized humanitarian rescue mission, Philippa died in a helicopter crash. Two years later her mother, distraught over her death, committed suicide.

Schuyler's extensive career was politically radical. In his early years, he was a member of the Socialist Party. His conservative critiques and satiric depictions of the Harlem Renaissance, the Civil Rights Movement, and of a broad range of civil rights leaders, from W.E.B. Du Bois to Martin Luther King Jr. gained him attention, as did his affiliation with the far-right John Birch Society. On August 31, 1977, Schuyler died in New York City at the age of eighty-two.

Yvonne Walker

See also: Harlem Renaissance; Satire.

Resources

Jeffrey B. Ferguson, *The Sage of Sugar Hill: George S. Schuyler and the Harlem Renaissance* (New Haven, CT: Yale University Press, 2005); Henry Louis Gates Jr., "A Fragmented Man: George Schuyler and the Claims of Race," *New York Times Book Review*, September 20, 1992, pp. 42–43; Yogita Goyal, "Black Nationalist Hokum: George Schuyler's Transnational Critique," *African American Review* 74, no. 1 (2014), 21–36; Jennifer Hislop, "Phillipa Duke Schuyler: Child Prodigy," http://www.intermix.org.uk/p%20d%20schuyler00.htm; Jennifer Jordan, "The New Literary Blackface," *Black Issues Book Review* (March–April 2002), 9, www.findarticles.com/p/articles/mi_m0HST/is_2_4/ai_83553036; Mark Gauvreau Judge, "Justice to George S. Schuyler," *Policy Review Online*, August–September 2000, 26, http://www.policyreview.org/aug00/Judge_print.html; David Levering Lewis, ed.: *The Kaiser Index to Black Studies, 1984–1986*, vol. 4 (Brooklyn, NY: Carlson), 289; *The Portable Harlem Renaissance Reader* (New York: Viking, 1994); Richard A. Long, "Renaissance Personality: An Interview with George Schuyler," *Black World* 25, no. 4 (1976), 68–78; Emmanuel S. Nelson, "George Samuel Schuyler (1895–1977)," in *African American Autobiographers: A Sourcebook*, ed. Nelson (Westport, CT: Greenwood Press, 2002), 323–327; Michael W. Peplow, "George Samuel Schuyler (1895–1977)," in *The Heath Anthology of American Literature*, ed. Paul Lauter, 4th ed. (Boston: Houghton Mifflin, 2002); Ann Rayson, "George Schuyler: Paradox Among 'Assimilationist' Writers," *Black American Literature Forum* 12 (1978), 102–106; John M. Reilly, "The Black Anti-Utopia," *Black American Literature Forum* 12 (1976), 107–109; Sonnet H. Retman, "Black No More: George Schuyler and Racial Capitalism," *PMLA* 123, no. 5 (2008), 1448–1464; Paul P. Reuben, "Chapter 9: Harlem Renaissance—George Schuyler," *PAL: Perspectives in American Literature—A Research and Reference Guide* (May 2003), www.csustan.edu/english/reuben/pal/chap9/schuyler.html; George S. Schuyler: *Black and Conservative* (New Rochelle, NY: Arlington House, 1966); *Black No More* (Boston: Northeastern University Press, 1989); Carolyn See, "So Young, So Gifted, So Sad," *Washington Post Book Review*, November 24, 1975, www.washingtonpost.com/wp-srv/style/longterm/books/reviews/composit.htm; Nicholas Stix, "George S. Schuyler and Black History Month," *Enter Stage Right*, February 23, 2004, p. 26, http://www.enterstageright.com/archive/articles/0204/0204schuyler.htm; Kathryn Talalay, *Composition in Black and White: The Life of Philippa Schuyler* (New York: Oxford University Press, 1977), also www.washingtonpost.com/wp-srv/style/longterm/books/chap1/composit.htm; Ivy G. Wilson, "The New Negro Iconoclast, or, the Curious Case of George Samuel Schuyler," in *A Companion to the Harlem Renaissance*, ed. Cherene Sherrard-Johnson (Chichester, UK: Wiley-Blackwell, 2015), 155–170.

Shange, Ntozake (1948–2018)

Playwright, poet, and novelist. Ntozake Shange combined a cultural feminism with Pan-Africanism in her distinctive contribution to African American arts. Her enormously popular choreopoem, *for colored girls who have considered suicide/when the rainbow is enuf* (1975), which combines poetry, drama, and movement, made Shange one of the preeminent African American poets.

Paulette Williams (Shange's original name) enjoyed a childhood of relative security. Surrounded by the arts, she was introduced to a wide variety of literary and artistic figures, from Dizzy Gillespie and Paul Robeson to Countee Cullen and William Shakespeare. She received a bachelor's degree from Barnard College (1970) and an MA from the

University of Southern California (1973), both in American Studies. A transforming period in her life, graduate school gave Shange more positive writing experiences. Her primary and secondary encounters were characterized by racial harassment, and debasement of Black or female subjects. She taught classes in writing and socialized with dancers, authors, and musicians. She underwent a spiritual transformation when two South African friends re-baptized her in the Pacific Ocean with the Xhosa (South African, Zulu) name Ntozake Shange, a combination of "she who comes with her own things" and "she who walks with (or like) the lions." Like other important African American writers, including playwright Amiri Baraka (formerly LeRoi Jones), she considered it an act of self-identification to relinquish her Anglo-American name in favor of a signification that identifies her exclusively as a Black woman and a feminist.

In the following two years, Shange taught humanities and women's studies in the San Francisco Bay Area. She participated in poetry recitals and experimented with African, Caribbean, and African American dance traditions. She worked with the dance company of Halifu Osumare and was inspired by Osumare's feminist/African aesthetics. Her "Stead Slingin Hash/Waltzin Proper & Wanderin Demure" appeared in the collection *Time to Greez! Incantations from the Third World* (1975). In 1974, she worked with Paula Moss, a dancer formerly with Osumare's company; The Sound Clinic (a brass trio); and Jean Desarmes and his Reggae Blues Band. Their series of poems, dances, and music would become *for colored girls*. Over the next two years, the group presented "the Show" in bars, cafés, universities, and poetry centers, receiving positive responses wherever they played. In 1976, Joseph Papp produced it at New York's Booth Theatre, where it ran for 747 performances, won the Obie and Outer Critics Circle Awards for Best Play (1977), and enjoyed successful national and international tours.

According to later interviews, Shange never anticipated presenting *for colored girls* as a mainstream theatrical production, intending only to share her personal experiences as a Black woman with the female artists of her community. Paradoxically, its personal narrative and particular community appeal have given the play its universality. Reviewers for the *Chicago Tribune*, *New York* magazine, and the *New York Times* hailed its ability to transcend the anger and suffering of being a Black woman in America, celebrated its multifaceted and dramatically viable portrait of the experience of growing up, and praised it for not losing sight of its target audience. The play also had its detractors. Some critics refused to accept its unconventional dramatic structure; others claimed it demonized Black men. Subsequent critical and scholarly opinion generally rejects a sexist reading, finding that the play, while attacking the behavior of abusive men, also holds some women responsible for allowing themselves to be victimized.

Seven performers share the text of three sections of stories on similar themes: a young Black girl comes of age, an adult Black woman deals with a debasing identity imposed upon her by outsiders, and the adult Black woman re-forms her own self-definition. Each story (poem/dance/song) moves from youth to adulthood, from ignorance to self-awareness, from particular experience to collectivity. In her rejection of linearity, Shange intends to disrupt the oppressive structures of Western language. In her emphasis on music and dance, she takes a stereotype of Blacks as performers and exploits it in revised form, attempting to reveal the cultural patterns of Black dance and song as nonverbal tools, offering protective and spiritual powers (Effiong, 124).

While no later work achieved the impact of her first Broadway production, Shange continued to be a prolific stage writer for some years. She produced a *Three Pieces* series: *Spell #7*, a choreopoem that attacks stereotypes of the past for continuing to limit racial equity by limiting possibilities in thought; *A Photograph*, an unconventionally structured piece that reaffirms the defensive powers of dance and exposes the self-destructiveness of nihilistic victimization; and *Boogie Woogie Landscapes*, an expressionistic work that brings to the surface the subconscious of "the average black girl." For many critics, these productions proved that Shange was a master poet but a mediocre playwright who had yet to find her dramatic voice.

Still, Shange had some important successes, earning a Tony award for her adaptation of Bertolt Brecht's *Mother Courage*, the *Los Angeles Times* Book Review Award for *Three Pieces*, and the Columbia University Medal of Excellence (all in 1981). Her play *Three Views from Mount Fuji/A Poem with Music* opened at the Lorraine Hansberry Theatre in 1987. Since then, Shange has turned to fiction and poetry, producing several novels. *Sassafrass, Cypress & Indigo* depicts the lives of three sisters in the aftermath of the Civil Rights Movement. Her last published works, *Daddy Says* and *Float Like a Butterfly*, are children's literature, drawing naturally on the "coming-of-age" themes developed in her early dramas.

As the second Black female playwright (after Lorraine Hansberry) to receive Broadway productions, Shange introduced a much-needed, self-consciously feminist agenda to the mainstream Black theater. From 1983 to 1986, she served as associate professor of drama at the University of Houston, and for one year as Distinguished Professor of Literature at Rice University.

Ben Fisler

See also: Feminism/Black Feminism; Novel; Poetics.

Resources
Primary Sources: *Betsy Brown: Daddy Says* (New York: Simon and Schuster, 2003); *A Daughter's Geography* (New York: St. Martin's, 1991); *Ellington Was Not a Street* (New York: Simon and Schuster, 2002); *Float Like a Butterfly* (New York: Turnaround, 2003); *For colored girls who have considered suicide/when the rainbow is enuf* (New York: Macmillan, 1977); *From Okra to Greens/A Different Kinda Love Story* (New York: Samuel French, 1983); *How I Come by This Cryin' Song* (New York: St. Martin's, 1999); *If I Can Cook, You Know God Can* (Boston: Beacon, 1998); *Liliane* (London: Minerva, 1996); *The Love Space Demands: A Continuing Saga* (New York: St. Martin's, 1992); *Nappy Edges* (New York: St. Martin's, 1978); *A Novel* (New York: St. Martin's, 1985); *Ridin' the Moon in Texas: Word Paintings* (New York: St. Martin's, 1987); *Sassafrass, Cypress & Indigo: A Novel* (New York: St. Martin's, 1982); *See No Evil: Prefaces, Reviews & Essays* (San Francisco: Momo's, 1984); *Three pieces: Spell #7, A Photograph: Lovers in Motion, Boogie Woogie Landscapes* (New York: St. Martin's, 1981); *Wild Beauty: New and Selected Poems* (New York: Atria/37 INK, 2017); Ntozake Shange and Ifa Bayeza, *Some Sing, Some Cry* (New York: St. Martin's, 2010).

Secondary Sources: Elizabeth Brown-Guillory, *Their Place on the Stage: Black Women Playwrights in America* (Westport, CT: Greenwood Press, 1988); Maria José Canelo, "Solidarity in Difference: Unveiling the

Coloniality of Power in Ntozake Shange's Sociopoetics," in *Diasporic Identities and Empire: Cultural Contentions and Literary Landscapes*, ed. Anastasia Nicéphore and David Brooks (Newcastle upon Tyne, UK: Cambridge Scholars, 2013), 40–52; Sean Carney, *Artaud, Genet, Shange: The Absence of the Theatre of Cruelty* (Ottawa: National Library of Canada, 1994); Mary K. DeShazer, "Rejecting Necrophilia: Ntozake Shange and the Warrior Re-Visioned," in *Making a Spectacle: Feminist Essays on Contemporary Women's Theatre*, ed. Lynda Hart (Ann Arbor: University of Michigan Press, 1989), 86–100; Philip Uko Effiong, *In Search of a Model for African-American Drama: A Study of Selected Plays by Lorraine Hansberry, Amiri Baraka, and Ntozake Shange* (Lanham, MD: University Press of America, 2000); Deborah R. Geis, "Distraught Laughter: Monologue in Ntozake Shange's Theater Pieces," in *Feminine Focus: The New Women Playwrights*, ed. Enoch Brater (New York: Oxford University Press, 1989), 210–225; Susan J. Hubert, "Singing a Black Girl's Song in a Strange Land: *for colored girls* and the Perils of Canonicity," *Literary Griot* 14, nos. 1–2 (2002), 94–102; Neal Lester: "At the Heart of Shange's Feminism: An Interview," *African American Review* 50, no. 4 (2017), 751–764; *Ntozake Shange: A Critical Study of the Plays* (New York: Garland, 1995); Carolyn Mitchell, "'A Laying On of Hands': Transcending the City in Ntzoke Shange's *for colored girls who have considered suicide/ when the rainbow is enuf*," in *Women Writers and the City: Essays in Feminist Literary Criticism*, ed. Susan Merrill Squier (Knoxville: University of Tennessee Press, 1984), 230–248; Tejumola Olaniyan, *Scars of Conquest/Masks of Resistance: The Invention of Cultural Identities in African, African-American, and Caribbean Drama* (New York: Oxford University Press, 1995); Bernard L. Peterson, "Ntozake Shange," in his *Contemporary Black American Playwrights and Their Plays: A Biographical Directory and Dramatic Index* (Westport, CT: Greenwood Press, 1988), 417–421; Sandra L. Richards, "Ntozake Shange," in *African American Writers*, ed. Valerie Smith, 4 vols. (New York: Scribner's, 1991); Y. S. Sharadha, *Black Women's Writing: Quest for Identity in the Plays of Lorraine Hansberry and Ntozake Shange* (New Delhi: Prestige Books, 1998); Ania Spyra, "Ntozake Shange's Multilingual Poetics of Relation," *Contemporary Literature* 54, no. 4 (2013), 785–809; Khalilah Watson, *Mothering the Self: The Novels of Ntozake Shange* (Albion, MI: Albion College Press, 1997).

Short Fiction

The literary category of short fiction can be expanded to include tales, anecdotes, fables, jokes, ballads, parables, myths, legends, sketches, and folktales; however, since the early nineteenth century, short fiction has been thought of largely as fictional narratives in the range of roughly three to thirty pages—much shorter than the novella and the novel. Short fiction is also associated with a tradition in which character-driven (as opposed to plot-driven) narratives focus on ordinary people, often on their psychological and emotional lives and less on adventurous action. However, over almost two centuries, stylistic and philosophical approaches to short fiction have varied widely, from realism and naturalism to absurdism and surrealism. African American short fiction's history is rooted in Africa insofar as it springs from the union of an oral tradition and a written tradition. Writers who draw heavily on the vernacular, for example, explicitly connect their work to both traditions.

In his preface to Terry McMillan's *Breaking Ice: An Anthology of Contemporary African-American Fiction* (1990), John Edgar Wideman asks, "What's the fate of a Black story in a white world of white stories?" (viii). The history, if not the fate, of the African American short story, as a written genre, arguably began in 1820 with the publication of Lemuel Haynes's "Mystery Developed; Or, Russel Colvin (Supposed to be Murdered) in Full Life, and Stephen and Jesse Boorn, His Convicted Murderers, Rescued from Ignominious Death by Wonderful Discoveries." It is a story based on actual events that occurred in 1819, when two brothers, Stephen and Jesse Boorn, were accused and convicted of murdering their brother-in-law, Russel Colvin. Haynes, a Black minister with a predominantly White congregation in Vermont, served as the Boorn brothers' spiritual adviser. While Haynes holds the distinction as the first African American male to write short fiction, Frances Ellen Wilkins Harper's publication of "The Two Offers" (1859), which concerns the issue of whether a woman should marry or have a career, probably makes her the first African American woman writer to publish a short story.

African American short fiction continued to develop as, in the late nineteenth century, Black writers made the transition from producing individual stories to publishing collections. Paul Laurence Dunbar's *Folks from Dixie* (1898) is the first collection of short stories published by an African American man. The first Black woman writer to publish a collection of short fiction is Alice Dunbar-Nelson; her book *Violets and Other Tales* (1895) includes short stories, essays, poetry, and sketches. In Dunbar's "Anner 'Lizer's Stumblin' Block," the genuine cadence of African American speech is captured when a preacher says to his congregation:

Now come, won't you sinnahs? De Lawd is jes' on de other side; jes' one step away, waitin' to receibe you. Won't you come to

him? Won't you tek de chance o' becomin' j'int 'ars o' dat beautiful city whar de streets is gol' an' de gates is pearl? Won't you come to him sinnah? Don't you see de pityin' look he's a-givin' you, a-sayin' come, come? (8)

In "The Short Stories of Eight Black-American Masters: A Critical Assessment," Velma P. Harrison suggests:

One of the reasons for our keen enjoyment of . . . fiction, is its ironic interconnectedness with life. As such, a work of fiction often embodies the identifying traits of a group of people bound by common customs and traditions, and acts as an insightful cultural statement. More often, the relationship between art and culture is marked by individuals who relate the details in stories to their personal circumstances or discover the motive of fellow human beings through examining the actions of literary characters. (134)

Charles Waddell Chesnutt's "The Wife of His Youth" serves as an example of the phenomenon Harrison describes. This story concerns Mr. Ryder, a man who wants to better his social and economic situation within the Blue Vein Society. He proposes to the most educated, wealthiest, and lightest-skinned Black woman in the group. Mr. Ryder is faced with a dilemma when his first wife, who has spent the past twenty-five years searching for him, shows up. Although the woman at first does not recognize Mr. Ryder as her lost husband, he eventually admits that he is the missing man. This story is replete with African American history in that, after emancipation, many Blacks spent years looking for lost relatives.

Additionally, Chesnutt's very famous story "The Goophered Grapevine" reflects the reality of African American life under the conditions of perpetual servitude. It is a story within a story. John and his wife, Annie, have moved from the North to the South because of Annie's health. John is interested in purchasing a vineyard in North Carolina. While surveying the old McAdoo plantation, John and Annie meet Julius McAdoo, who tells them the history of the vineyard. According to Julius, the vineyard was "goophered" by Aunt Peggy; that is, it has had a spell placed on it. Dugald McAdoo, the former owner of the plantation, paid $10 to Aunt Peggy to keep Blacks from eating his profits. Unfortunately, a slave named Henry, who was new to the plantation and unaware of the goopher, eats the grapes and is transformed.

Henry's transformation personifies the vineyard in that he takes on its seasonal characteristics. Dugald McAdoo takes advantage of Henry's condition by selling him for $1,500 in the spring, when he is young and strong. McAdoo buys Henry back for $500 in the winter, when Henry is old and weak. Thus, every year, McAdoo makes $1,000. In addition to selling and buying Henry, McAdoo follows the advice of a Northern stranger who convinces him that he can make more money if he uses the stranger's method for cultivating grapes. The technique proves disastrous and the vineyard is ruined. Unfortunately, once the vineyard dies, so does Henry.

This classic African American short story addresses the trinity of money, greed, and selfishness prevalent throughout American history. McAdoo's eagerness to buy and sell human beings, as well as his willingness to destroy the vineyard in an effort to satisfy his insatiable appetite for profit, exemplifies the point. The story reveals the magnitude of the problem when McAdoo uses Henry's youthful appearance to garner more wealth. In addition, the fact that the stranger in the story is a Northerner is significant, in that it implicates European Americans in the North in the exploitation of African American labor. In effect, some Black American short fiction writers become personifications of tricksters by exposing America's deep-seated denial and self-deception regarding the historical, cultural, social, psychological, and economic realities of African American life within the United States.

Like Chesnutt, Frank J. Webb, in his story "Two Wolves and a Lamb" (1870), refrains from making judgments or comments about the thoughts or actions of the characters. This lack of intrusiveness on the part of the author allows the characters to tell their own stories in their own words.

After Chesnutt and Webb, the African American short story continued to flourish. Harlem Renaissance writers who produced short fiction include Zora Neale Hurston, Langston Hughes, Dorothy West, Gwendolyn Bennett, Richard Bruce Nugent, Rudolph Fisher, Jean Toomer, and Wallace Thurman. Since Hurston was rediscovered in the 1970s, her collections of short fiction have remained in print, and her story "Sweat" is often anthologized. Hughes's first collection of stories, *The Ways of White Folks* (1934), has remained in print and includes several stories that continue to be admired: "Cora Unashamed," "The Blues I'm Playing," "Father and Son," and "Berry." Hughes went on to publish two more collections during his lifetime as well as several collections of tales featuring Jesse B. Simple, a character he created in a column for the *Chicago Defender* in the 1940s (A. S. Harper). Later Hughes edited an important anthology of short fiction, *The*

Best Short Stories by Negro Writers: An Anthology from 1899 to the Present (1967). It includes stories by Chesnutt and Hurston as well as by Ted Poston, Alice Childress, Lindsay Patterson, and John A. Williams. He also included "To Hell with Dying," an early story by Alice Walker.

The range of short fiction produced by writers of the Harlem Renaissance period is considerable. It includes earthy, folk-oriented stories such as those by Hurston, who drew heavily on the vernacular. It stretches from ironic, satirical, politically alert stories by Hughes to stylized ones by Nugent and Toomer. Nugent's "Smoke, Lillies and Jade," which was published in the magazine *Fire!!*, uses a stream-of-consciousness technique, while Toomer's *Cane* is a novel-in-stories that is considered an excellent example of Modernist prose. West's "The Typewriter," Bennett's "Wedding Day," and Thurman's "Cordelia the Crude" are naturalistic, tragic stories that show an acute awareness of issues connected with race and social-class. In addition to *Fire!!*, magazines that published short fiction by African Americans during the Harlem Renaissance included *The Crisis*, *Opportunity*, and *The Messenger*.

Since the Harlem Renaissance, African American short fiction has proliferated further. Though known more for their novels, Ralph Ellison and Richard Wright produced short fiction. Ellison's story, "King of the Bingo Game," is often anthologized, as is Wright's "The Man Who Lived Underground." Similarly, James Baldwin, known chiefly as a novelist and essayist, produced the acclaimed story "Sonny's Blues." Ann Lane Petry, also a member of this generation, wrote short fiction as well as novels.

More recently, Maya Angelou, Toni Cade Bambara, J. California Cooper, Edwidge Danticat, Samuel R. Delany, Carolivia Herron, Charles R. Johnson, William Melvin Kelley, Randall Garrett Kenan, Jamaica Kincaid, Paule Marshall, James Alan McPherson, Gloria Naylor, Ntozake Shange, Renee Simms, Alice Walker, John Edgar Wideman, and Sherley Anne Williams have produced short fiction that is considered cutting-edge. The stylistic range of short fiction these and other African American writers have produced is as wide as, if not wider than, that produced in the 1920s. Short fiction by African American women, in particular, constitutes some of the most accomplished American literature produced in the era.

African American short fiction has a long history, but criticism about African American writing in this genre has yet to catch up with the richness and variety of the literature. Hans Ostrom's *Langston Hughes: A Study of the Short Fiction*, Henry B. Wonham's *Charles W. Chesnutt: A Study of the Short Fiction*, and Keith E. Byerman's *John Edgar Wideman: A Study of the Short Fiction* provide thorough analyses of the writings of three prolific African American writers of short fiction. Elizabeth Ammons has written *Short Fiction by Black Women, 1900–1920* (1991), but more criticism about individual women writers of short fiction is needed.

Studying African American short fiction necessarily involves assessing it in terms of its own cultural and literary histories and not relying solely on the European and Anglo-American traditions of the short story, traditions based largely on the work of Edgar Allan Poe, Guy de Maupassant, Anton Chekhov, Henry James, O. Henry, and Ernest Hemingway, among others (Puschman-Nalenz; Lohafer and Clarey).

Anthologies of African American short fiction help provide a more distinct sense of the achievement in this genre. The anthologies include *Breaking Ice: An Anthology of Contemporary African-American Fiction* (1990), edited by Terry McMillan; *Calling the Wind: Twentieth Century African-American Short Stories* (1993), edited by Clarence Major; and *Children of the Night: The Best Short Stories by Black Writers, 1967 to the Present*, edited by Gloria Naylor (1995). Preston M. Yancy has compiled *The Afro-American Short Story: A Comprehensive, Annotated Index with Selected Commentaries* (1986), and Charmaine N. Ijeoma has compiled "The African American Short Story, 1820–1899: An Annotated Bibliography" (2002). Wolfgang Karrer and Puschman-Nalenz have edited *The African American Short Story, 1970–1990: A Collection of Critical Essays* (1993).

Short fiction continues to provide African American authors with a flexible and expressive medium through which to share creative, reflective, and boundary-breaking narratives. Important recent work in the genre includes Nalo Hopkinson's collection *Falling in Love with Hominids* (2017), which combines folkloric, postapocalyptic, and supernatural elements; Renee Simms' *Meet Behind Mars* (2014), which includes stories that examine the sense of place, the burden of history, and the struggle to articulate and sustain individual identity; Guy Mark Foster's short-story collection *The Rest of Us* (2014), which explores African American gay male experiences and identities; and Camille Acker's *Training School for Negro Girls* (2018), which focuses on the varied and richly nuanced experiences of African American women.

Charmaine N. Ijeoma

See also: Butler, Octavia E.; Chesnutt, Charles Waddell; Fisher, Rudolph John Chauncey; Hughes, Langston; Hurston, Zora Neale; Nugent, Richard Bruce; Simms, Renee Elizabeth; Toomer, Jean; Walker, Alice.

Resources

Camille Acker, *Training School for Negro Girls* (New York: Feminist Press/CUNY, 2018); Elizabeth Ammons, comp., *Short Fiction by Black Women, 1900–1920* (New York: Oxford University Press, 1991); Robert Bone, *Down Home: A History of Afro-American Short Fiction from Its Beginnings to the End of the Harlem Renaissance* (New York: Putnam, 1975); Peter Bruck, ed., *The Black American Short Story in the 20th Century: A Collection of Critical Essays* (Amsterdam: Grüner, 1977); Keith E. Byerman, *John Edgar Wideman: A Study of the Short Fiction* (New York: Twayne, 1998); Charles W. Chesnutt: "The Goophered Grapevine," in *Selected Writings*, ed. SallyAnn H. Ferguson (Boston: Houghton Mifflin, 2001), 118–128; "The Wife of His Youth," in *Selected Writings*, ed. SallyAnn H. Ferguson (Boston: Houghton Mifflin, 2001), 199–209; Paul Laurence Dunbar, *Folks from Dixie* (New York: Dodd, Mead, 1898); Alice Dunbar-Nelson, *Violets and Other Tales*, vol. 1 of *The Works of Alice Dunbar-Nelson*, ed. Gloria T. Hull (New York: Oxford University Press, 1988); Guy Mark Foster, *The Rest of Us* (Maple Shade, NJ: Tincture/Lethe Press, 2013); Donna Akiba Sullivan Harper, *Not So Simple: The "Simple" Stories by Langston Hughes* (Columbia: University of Missouri Press, 1995); Frances E. W. Harper, "The Two Offers," in *The Anglo-African Magazine*, ed. William Loren Katz, vol. 1 (New York: Arno, 1968), 288–291, 311–313; Velma P. Harrison, "The Short Stories of Eight Black-American Masters: A Critical Assessment," PhD diss., Northern Illinois University, 1987; Lemuel Haynes, "Mystery Developed; Or, Russel Colvin, (Supposed to be Murdered) in Full Life; and Stephen and Jesse Boorn, (His Convicted Murders) Rescued from Ignominious Death by Wonderful Discoveries," in *Black Preacher to White America: The Collected Writings of*

Lemuel Haynes, 1774–1833, ed. Richard Newman (Brooklyn, NY: Carlson, 1990), 203–212; Nalo Hopkinson, *Falling in Love with Hominids* (San Francisco: Tachyon Publications, 2015); Langston Hughes, ed., *The Best Short Stories by Negro Writers: An Anthology from 1899 to the Present* (Boston: Little, Brown, 1967); Charmaine N. Ijeoma, "The African American Short Story, 1820–1899: An Annotated Bibliography," *Bulletin of Bibliography* 59, no. 3 (September 2002), 121–126; Wolfgang Karrer and Barbara Puschmann-Nalenz, eds., *The African American Short Story 1970–1990* (Trier, Germany: Wissenschaftlicher, 1993); Randall Kenan, *Let the Dead Bury Their Dead* (San Diego: Harcourt Brace Jovanovich, 1992); Susan Lohafer and Jo Ellyn Clarey, eds., *Short Story Theory at a Crossroads* (Baton Rouge: Louisiana State University Press, 1989); Clarence Major, ed., *Calling the Wind: Twentieth Century African-American Short Stories* (New York: HarperPerennial, 1993); Charles E. May, "Short Fiction: 1840–1880," in *Critical Survey of Short Fiction*, ed. Frank N. Magill, vol. 1 (Englewood Cliffs, NJ: Salem, 1981), 173–217; Terry McMillan, ed., *Breaking Ice: An Anthology of Contemporary African-American Fiction* (New York: Viking, 1990); Gloria Naylor, ed., *Children of the Night: The Best Short Stories by Black Writers, 1967 to the Present* (Boston: Little, Brown, 1995); Hans Ostrom, *Langston Hughes: A Study of the Short Fiction* (New York: Twayne, 1993); Barbara Puschman-Nalenz, "Presentation in Prefaces and the Process of Canonization," in *The African American Short Story, 1970–1990: A Collection of Critical Essays*, ed. Wolfgang Karrer and Barbara Puschman-Nalenz (Trier, Germany: Wissenschaftlicher Verlag, 1993), 12–24; Renee Simms, *Meet Behind Mars* (Detroit: Wayne State University Press, 2018); David Lionel Smith, "The African American Short Story," in *The Columbia Companion to the Twentieth-Century American Short Story*, ed. Blanche H. Gelfant and Lawrence Graver (New York: Columbia University Press, 2001), 25–33; Frank J. Webb, "Two Wolves and a Lamb," *New Era: A Colored American National Journal* 1, nos. 1–4 (January–February 1870); John Edgar Wideman, "Preface," in *Breaking Ice: An Anthology of Contemporary African-American Fiction*, ed. Terry McMillan (New York: Viking, 1990), v–x; Henry B. Wonham, *Charles W. Chesnutt: A Study of the Short Fiction* (New York: Twayne, 1998); Preston M. Yancy, comp., *The Afro-American Short Story: A Comprehensive Annotated Index with Selected Commentaries* (Westport, CT: Greenwood Press, 1986), xi–xiv.

Simms, Renee Elizabeth (1966–)

Fiction writer, essayist, poet, attorney, and professor. Simms was born and grew up in Detroit, Michigan. She earned a Bachelor of Arts degree from the University of Michigan in 1988 and a law degree from the Wayne State University School of Law in 1992. After practicing law for several years, she completed a Master of Fine Arts degree in writing at Arizona State University (2007), where she also taught courses in writing.

Simms has published short stories in a variety of periodicals, including the *North American Review*, the *Southwest Review*, *Callaloo*, the *Oxford American*, *Duende*, and the *Hawai'i Review*. These stories were collected in her first book, *Meet Behind Mars* (2018). Her fiction explores African American parenting, urban life, racism in the United States, among other subjects. She is adept at mixing different styles of narration, including realism, surrealism, and epistolary forms. Simms has earned residencies at the Ragdale and Breadloaf artists' colonies, and she was awarded a National Endowment for the Arts fellowship in 2018.

Her essays on literature, teaching, and social issues have appeared in *Salon*, *Diverse Issues in Higher Education*, and

City Arts Magazine, among other periodicals. She also contributed an essay to *44 on 44: Forty-Four African American Writers on the Election of Barack Obama, 44th President of the United States* (2011).

Simms is an Associate Professor of African American Studies and English and a writer in residence at the University of Puget Sound in Tacoma, Washington. Her teaching areas include creative writing, Black women's writing, feminist criticism, and intersections between law and literature.

Hans A. Ostrom

See also: Feminism/Black Feminism; Postmodernism; Short Fiction.

Resources

Amina Gautier, "An Interview with Renee Simms," *Necessary Fiction*, July 3, 2018: http://necessaryfiction.com/blog/AnInterview withReneeSimms (accessed 2019); Deesha Philyaw, "Visible: Women Writer of Color: Renee Simms," [interview], *The Rumpus*, April 18, 2018: https://therumpus.net/2018/04 /visible-women-writers-of-color-renee-simms/ (accessed 2019); Renee Simms: "Go! Be a Superhero," in *44 on 44: Forty-Four African American Writers on the Election of Barack Obama, 44th President of the United States,* ed. Lita Hooper, Sonia Sanchez, and Michael Simanga (Chicago: Third World Press, 2011); "Gritty, Gray, and Familiar," *City Arts Magazine,* July 27, 2018: https://www.cityartsmaga zine.com/renee-simms-tacoma-gritty -gray-and-familiar/ (accessed 2019); *Meet Behind Mars* (Detroit: Wayne State University Press, 2018); "When a Privileged Scholar Tries to Examine Privilege," *Diverse Issues in Higher Education*, September 14, 2014: https:// diverseeducation.com/article/67028/ (accessed 2019); "Who Will Protect Us? Why I'm still Conflicted about Guns as a Black Feminist," *Salon*, November 6, 2013: https://www.salon .com/2013/11/05/who_will_protect_us_why_ im_still_conflicted_about_guns_as_a_black_ feminist/ (accessed 2019).

Slave Narrative

Slave narrative is a broad category of literature that encompasses a variety of works. These include autobiographies by escaped, manumitted, or emancipated slaves; narratives of the life experiences of former slaves recorded by the Federal Writers' Project as part of the Works Progress Administration in the late 1930s; and fictionalized accounts of life in slavery, written both during the time of slavery and since then. Also often included within the category of slave narratives are works not written by former slaves but "told to" or "related to" an editor or amanuensis (one who copies or writes from the dictation of another). Slave narratives written by former slaves reached their apogee in the pre–Civil War era. They were frequently commissioned by abolitionists to garner sympathy and support for the abolitionist movement, with nearly a hundred such narratives produced before the end of the Civil War in 1865. The first narratives were composed and published as early as 1772. Newly discovered slave narratives have emerged as recently as 2002, when Henry Louis Gates Jr. purchased at auction and subsequently published *The Bondwoman's Narrative* by Hannah Crafts. The slave narrative continues to serve important functions in African American literature as a powerful source of inspiration for autobiographical works and as the source for fictionalized accounts of slavery dependent upon the genre's originators and literary conventions.

A full understanding of slave narrative as a unique and powerful genre in African American letters requires examination of the genre's place in history, a survey of some of the dominant tropes that structure slave narratives, and analysis of the genre's impact on American literature and culture.

Nonfiction slave narratives can be divided into three distinct historical time periods: those written prior to 1830, those produced between 1830 and the end of the Civil War, and those created after the end of the Civil War and through the efforts of the Works Progress Administration's Federal Writers Project from 1936 to 1938.

Fictionalized accounts of slave narratives exist throughout American literary history, with those written after World War II best classified as neo-slave narratives.

All slave narratives combine elements of autobiography, history, and cultural critique in their telling of life in slavery. One of the first known slave narratives in English was published in 1772, *A Narrative of the Most Remarkable Particulars in the Life of James Albert Ukawsaw Gronniosaw, an African Prince*, by James Albert Ukawsaw (Gates and Andrews). Of the earliest slave narratives, Olaudah Equiano's *The Interesting Narrative of the Life of Olaudah Equiano, or Gustavus Vassa, the African. Written by Himself* (1789) is perhaps best known (Gates and Andrews). In it, Equiano relates his capture in his native land (modern-day eastern Nigeria) and his subsequent travels to the West Indies, Europe, and the American colonies. Equiano's narrative is notable largely because of its being authored by Equiano himself, rather than told to an amanuensis or created with the aid of an editor or ghostwriter. Equiano's independence in this regard perhaps contributes to the story's frank treatment of the horrors of slavery and its insistence upon immediate abolition.

Many narratives from this first period were modeled upon criminal confession narratives or religious conversion narratives, the latter of which would strive to impress its White readership with the author's piety and forgiveness. Equiano made much of his own conversion to Christianity; at the end of his *Narrative* he expresses his desire to become a Christian missionary to Africa and thereby to lobby against the African slave trade. That is, he connects his Christianity with the project of abolition, implicitly arguing that individual salvation and worldly perfection are in fact not just compatible but intrinsically linked aims. This combination of individual belief and cultural critique became the hallmark of successful slave narratives in the decades that followed. Equiano's assertion of selfhood in the claim that his narrative was "written by himself" importantly evaded possible influence by White editors and ghostwriters, a concern associated with nearly all antebellum slave narratives.

If the narratives were not in fact written by former slaves who were literate enough to produce and validate their own works, then how might the participation of White abolitionists, as editors and publishers, alter the works? Although Equiano's assertion of authorship effectively counters this concern, his embrace of Christianity raises troubling concerns about narrative authenticity because his narrative, while critical, also supports forgiveness of his former captors and the superiority of Christianity to any African faith. Similar concerns continued to receive attention in the second historical period of slave narratives, 1830 to 1865. Some other notable slave narratives from this period include: Solomon Bayley's *A Narrative of Some Remarkable Incidents, in the Life of Solomon Bayley, Formerly a Slave, in the State of Delaware, North America: Written by Himself* (1825); Venture Smith's *A Narrative of the Life and Adventures of Venture, a Native of Africa: But Resident Above Sixty Years in the United States of America. Related by Himself* (1798); and George White's *A Brief*

Account of the Life, Experience, Travels, and Gospel Labours of George White, an African: Written by Himself, and Revised by a Friend (1810).

Slave narratives from the middle period, 1830 to 1865, are marked by their increased contempt for the institution of slavery. Of the many narratives produced during this era, none is better known or more highly regarded than Frederick Douglass's *Narrative of the Life of Frederick Douglass, an American Slave, Written by Himself* (1845). Douglass's narrative stands as a powerful and moving critique of American society for its tolerance of slavery amid its avowed Christian beliefs; additionally, Douglass (and others of this period) powerfully connected the power of slaves—intellectual, moral, and physical—with manhood, thus affirming the African American slave's humanity and countering widespread notions that Africans were an inferior race suited only to forced labor. While Douglass's first narrative followed many of the conventions of the slave narrative, most notably beginning with letters affirming the authenticity of the text and the trustworthiness of the author, his later narratives, including *My Bondage and My Freedom* (1855), further distanced him from his White supporters, replacing White-authored letters of authenticity with a preface and introduction of Douglass's own creation. Douglass also stressed the importance of literacy as the foundation for freedom and the effectiveness of physical resistance to counter slavery's oppression.

Other notable narratives from this period include William Wells Brown's *Narrative of William Wells Brown, a Fugitive Slave* (1847) and Henry Bibb's *Narrative of the Life and Adventures of Henry Bibb, an American Slave. Written by himself* (1849) (Gates and Andrews). Moses Roper's *Narrative of the Adventures and Escape of Moses Roper from American Slavery* appeared in 1838; it is remarkable in part for the number of times Roper attempted to escape before finally succeeding. James W. C. Pennington's *The Fugitive Blacksmith; or, Events in the History of James W. C. Pennington, Pastor of a Presbyterian Church, New York, Formerly a Slave in the State of Maryland, United States* (1849) also belongs to this era. These works made use of the many conventions familiar to readers of slave narratives while also incorporating trickster-like figures from African American Folktales.

This period also saw the publication of some of the best-known narratives by African American women, including Mary Prince's *The History of Mary Prince, a West Indian Slave. Related by Herself. With a Supplement by the Editor. To Which Is Added, the Narrative of Asa-Asa, a Captured African* (1831). Sojourner Truth's *Narrative of Sojourner Truth, a Northern Slave, Emancipated from Bodily Servitude by the State of New York, in 1828* was first published in 1850 (Gates and Andrews), and Harriet Ann Jacobs's *Incidents in the Life of a Slave Girl, Written by Herself* was first published in 1861 (Gates and Andrews). Female-authored narratives borrowed more strongly from the sentimental literary tradition, striving to make personal their accounts of oppression and elicit sympathy in the reader through shared identification. These narratives also importantly unmasked the sexual oppression of Black women at the hands of White slave owners, often in brutal detail. Since African American women could not connect their humanity to the manly attributes of strength and determination, they instead grounded their humanity in the sentiment of feeling, stressing sympathetic identification. The combination of autobiographical accounts of life in slavery, historical details, and the sentimental literary tradition's focus on eliciting sympathetic feelings had a powerful effect on readers, and Harriet Beecher Stowe adapted this form in *Uncle Tom's Cabin* (1852), the best-selling novel of the nineteenth century widely credited with bringing abolitionism to a wider audience.

The third period of slave narratives encompasses post-emancipation works such as Booker T. Washington's *Up from Slavery* (1901); Frederick Douglass's third autobiography, *Life and Times of Frederick Douglass Written by Himself. His Early Life as a Slave, His Escape from Bondage, and His Complete History to the Present Time* (1892); and Josiah Henson's *"Uncle Tom's Story of His Life." An Autobiography of the Rev. Josiah Henson (Mrs. Harriet Beecher Stowe's "Uncle Tom"). From 1789 to 1876. With a Preface by Mrs. Harriet Beecher Stowe and an Introductory Note by George Sturge, and S. Morley* (1877). Also included in this time period are the more than 2,300 narratives collected and transcribed by the Federal Writers' Project. While most of the narratives were transcribed interviews, and few were published individually, they are a rich source for poignant and personal accounts of life in slavery, and a significant contribution to the genre of slave narratives.

While the great many slave narratives published in the United States over a period of more than a century speaks to their variety and durability, there are a few common motifs, or literary tropes, shared by a great many of the works. First and foremost, because establishing the authenticity of narratives of life in slavery as actually authored by African Americans was important, many narratives begin with prefatory letters by leading figures such as editors, authors, politicians, and abolitionists that vouch for the authenticity of the text, especially for those narratives that claimed to be written "by himself" or "by herself." Most narratives also begin in slavery in the South and conclude with successful travel to the North, where freedom awaits, often signaled by the selection of a new name (to counter the loss of the patronym in slavery), the reunion of separated family members, and frequently marriage to a lost love. Often the decision to escape from slavery is precipitated by some kind of personal crisis, such as the death of a loved one, sale of a loved one to another slave owner or removal to another state, or simply overwhelming feelings of despair. Many also conclude with some sort of dedication to the abolitionist cause, emerging free in the North and dedicated to speaking against slavery's injustices.

Despite this common narrative arc, many narratives—especially those written in the antebellum era—are careful to exclude particular details of the narrator's escape from slavery, for fear of closing off a possible avenue to freedom for others still held in slavery. Many chronicles of life in slavery highlight the dehumanizing effects of slavery on the individual through physical and psychological abuse: forced beatings, difficult labor, insufficient food, the separation of family members, lack of knowledge about one's own birth and parentage, and related horrors. Another common trope in slave narratives—particularly of the middle period—is the esteem of literacy and religion as the pathways to freedom, often in direct disobedience of strict rules against learning to read or congregating as slaves. Additionally, particularly in later slave narratives, there is a concerted effort to connect the desire for individual freedom from slavery to the desire to break free from tyranny that served as the basis for the nation's independence from Great Britain, thus marking slaves and their desire for freedom as eminently patriotic and American.

The collective impact of all these various forms taken by slave narratives on American literature and culture is incalculable. First and foremost, widespread dissemination of slave-authored accounts of life in slavery countered Southern claims of slavery as a benevolent institution and credited African Americans with qualities long denied them and essential to their humanity: feelings, intelligence, and desire for freedom. Detailed accounts of the brutality of slavery coupled with condemnations of a nation that, on the one hand, esteemed freedom from tyranny as one of its cornerstones and, on the other, turned a blind eye toward the practice of slavery gave much needed momentum and ammunition to the abolitionist cause. The slave narrative also marks the emergence of the African American literary tradition, with slave narratives comprising the majority of African American-authored texts published in the nineteenth and early twentieth centuries. Slave narratives, with their autobiographical approach and narratives of individuals overcoming great odds to achieve individual freedom and salvation, also presaged the emergence of autobiography as a dominant mode in African American letters. The influence of the slave narrative can be witnessed in such works as James Weldon Johnson's *The Autobiography of an Ex-Colored Man* (1912) and Ralph Ellison's *Invisible Man* (1952). While these novels recall the slave narrative in their autobiographical approach and narratives of individual subjugation in a racist society, the slave narrative also gave rise to an entirely new category of literature, the neo-slave narrative or fictionalized account of life in slavery. Works such as Gayl Jones's *Corregidora* (1975), Ishmael Reed's *Flight to Canada* (1976), Octavia E. Butler's *Kindred* (1979), Charles Johnson's *Middle Passage* (1990), and John Sayles's film *The Brother from Another Planet* (1984) all can be read as neo-slave narratives, connected as they are to the form, structure, and content of the slave narratives that preceded them. In all these works, the individual's triumph over racist oppression is chronicled while critique is simultaneously leveled against the nation that allows such practices to persist. The slave narrative thus constitutes a rich, varied, and ever-present literary genre central to understanding both the origins and the present of African American literature.

Matthew R. Davis

See also: Craft, William and Ellen Smith Craft; Crafts, Hannah; Douglass, Frederick; Equiano, Olaudah; Jacobs, Harriet Ann; Smith, Venture; Washington, Booker T.

Resources

Nicole N. Aljoe and Ian Finseth, Ian, eds., *Journeys of the Slave Narrative in the Early Americas* (Charlottesville, VA: University of Virginia Press, 2014); William L. Andrews, *To Tell a Free Story: The First Century of Afro-American Autobiography, 1760–1865* (Urbana: University of Illinois Press, 1986); William L. Andrews, ed., *Six Women's Slave Narratives* (New York: Oxford University Press, 1988); Sterling Lecater Bland, ed., *African American Slave Narratives: An Anthology* (Westport, CT: Greenwood Press, 2001); Arna Bontemps, ed., *Great Slave Narratives Selected and Introduced by Arna Bontemps* (Boston: Beacon Press, 1969); Hannah Crafts, *The Bondwoman's Narrative*, ed. Henry Louis Gates Jr. (New York: Warner Books, 2002); Charles T. Davis and Henry Louis Gates Jr., eds., *The Slave's Narrative* (Oxford: Oxford University Press, 1985); Kimberly Drake, ed.,

The Slave Narrative (Ipswich, MA: Grey House, 2014); Frances Smith Foster, *Witnessing Slavery: The Development of Ante-Bellum Slave Narratives* (Westport, CT: Greenwood Press, 1979); Henry Louis Gates Jr. and William L. Andrews, eds., *Slave Narratives* (New York: Library of America, 2000); Charles J. Heglar, *Rethinking the Slave Narrative: Slave Marriage and the Narratives of Henry Bibb and William and Ellen Craft* (Westport, CT: Greenwood Press, 2001); William Katz, ed., *Five Slave Narratives: A Compendium* (New York: Arno, 1968); Deborah E. McDowell and Arnold Rampersad, eds., *Slavery and the Literary Imagination* (Baltimore: Johns Hopkins University Press, 1989); Sarah Meer, "Slave Narratives as Literature," in *The Cambridge Companion to Slavery in American Literature*, ed. Ezra Tawil (New York: Cambridge University Press, 2016), 70–85; Janet Neary, *Fugitive Testimony: On the Visual Logic of Slave Narratives* (New York: Fordham University Press, 2017); Moses Roper, *Narrative of My Escape from Slavery* (Mineola, NY: Dover, 2003); Valerie Smith, *Self-Discovery and Authority in Afro-American Narrative* (Cambridge, MA: Harvard University Press, 1987).

Smith, Anna Deavere (1950–)

Actor and playwright. Anna Deavere Smith was born on September 18, 1950, in Baltimore, Maryland. The daughter of an elementary school teacher and a coffee merchant, she graduated from Beaver College in 1971 and received an MFA from the American Conservatory Theater in 1976.

Smith is best known for her "On the Road: A Search for an American Character" play series. These plays include *On the Road: A Search for an American Character* (1982), *Aye, Aye, Aye, I'm Integrated* (1984), *Fires in the Mirror: Crown Heights, Brooklyn, and Other Identities* (1992), and *Twilight, Los Angeles, 1992* (1993). They feature a range of personalities—all real, living people—played across Smith's singular body. For each of her plays, the playwright began her writing process by interviewing a large number of people and asking them to comment upon a single topic. She then condensed the tape-recorded interviews and her written notes of the interviews into a performance piece in which she, as an actress, played each of her interviewees. With the aid of an accessory, such as a hat or a tie, she performed an excerpt from each interview. The plays—the sum total of these edited, collected, and performed interviews—gave the viewer the opportunity to witness a number of differing perspectives upon often charged political issue. For example, both *Fires in the Mirror* and *Twilight: Los Angeles, 1992* center on racial prejudice and violence.

Smith has received numerous awards for her unique style of playwriting. Both *Fires in the Mirror* and *Twilight, Los Angeles, 1992* won Obie awards. The former was nominated for the Pulitzer Prize. In 1996, Smith was awarded the prestigious MacArthur Foundation "genius" grant and was named the Ford Foundation's first artist-in-residence. The MacArthur Foundation, honoring the playwright, observed that she "has created a new form of theater—a blend of theatrical art, social commentary, journalism, and intimate reverie." Her play *Let Me Down Easy*, which premiered in 2008, engages with the personal and policy dimensions of health care access and efficacy, while *The Arizona Project*, which premiered in the same year, addresses women's experiences in the justice system.

In 1997, Smith founded the Institute on the Arts and Civic Dialogue, a three-year pilot program sponsored by the Ford Foundation and hosted by Harvard University and the American Repertory Theater. The Institute brought together community activists, scholars, artists, and audiences with the goal of creating new artwork that engaged with social and political issues. It was a unique place where playwrights, actors, lawyers, professors, and community organizers worked together to create socially relevant theater.

Smith is also a successful actor. She has appeared in numerous films and televisions series: the films *The Human Stain* (2003), *The American President* (1995), *Philadelphia* (1993), *Dave* (1993), *Rent* (2005), *Life Support* (2007), and *Can You Ever Forgive Me?* (2018); the television series *The West Wing* (2000–2005) and *Black-ish* (2015–present); and the television version of *Fires in the Mirror* (1993). Smith is the recipient of the National Humanities Medal (2012) and of the Dorothy and Lilian Gish Prize (2012), and she delivered the National Endowment for the Humanities' 2015 Jefferson Lecture, "On the Road: A Search for American Character." Smith is a faculty member at New York University's Tisch School of the Arts.

Harvey Young

See also: Drama; Feminism/Black Feminism; Protest Literature.

Resources

Kimberly Rae Connor, "Negotiating the Differences: Anna Deavere Smith and Liberation Theater," in *Racing and (E)Racing Language: Living with the Color of Our Words*, ed. Ellen J. Goldner and Safiya Henderson-Holmes (Syracuse, NY: Syracuse University Press, 2001), 157–182; Joan Wylie Hall, "'Everybody's Talking': Anna Deavere Smith's Documentary Theatre," in *Contemporary African American Women Playwrights*, ed. Philip C. Kolin (London: Routledge, 2007), 150–166; Richard Schechner, "Anna Deavere Smith: Acting as Incorporation," *TDR: The Drama Review* 37, no. 4 (1993), 63–64; "There's a Lot of Work to Do to Turn This Thing Around: An Interview with Anna Deavere Smith," *TDR: The Drama Review* 62, no. 3 (2018), 35–50; Anna Deavere Smith: *Fires in the Mirror* (Garden City, NY: Anchor, 1993); *House Arrest and Piano: Two Plays* (Garden City, NY: Anchor, 2004); *Letters to a Young Artist: Straight-up Advice on Making a Life in the Arts—For Actors, Performers, Writers, and Artists of Every Kind* (New York: Random House, 2006); *Talk to Me: Listening Between the Lines* (New York: Random House, 2000); *Twilight: Los Angeles, 1992* (Garden City, NY: Anchor, 1994).

Smith, Venture (1728/1729–1805)

Autobiographer. In *Narrative of the Life and Adventures of Venture, a Native of Africa, But Resident above Sixty Years in the United States of America, Related by Himself* (1798), Smith details the African and the American sides of slavery, his entrepreneurial endeavors, and the disadvantages he suffered because he was illiterate. Born in Dukandarra, Guinea, the son of a prince, Smith (also known as Broteer Venture) was pressed into slavery at the age of eight. In a prelude that contrasts his experiences in Africa with his enslavement in America, Smith recounts his life with a farmer while his parents were estranged due to his father's third marriage. Although Smith was virtually a servant, the farmer treated him as a son. After reuniting with his family, Smith became the victim of a tribal war, saw his father tortured and killed, and was taken prisoner by still another tribe that had been armed by Europeans. While a servant to the leader of the conquering army, Smith fell victim to yet another tribal war. This conquering army sold him into slavery. Robert Mumford, a ship's steward, purchased the young boy for four gallons of rum and a piece of calico, and named him for "his own private venture."

Smith, one of the few surviving slaves not sold in Barbados, was transported to Rhode Island. There he became a house servant on Fisher's Island, performing such tasks as carding wool and pounding corn. His master and his mistress frequently beat him, and their son repeatedly harassed him. At twenty-two, Smith married Margaret (Meg), another slave in the household, and fathered four children. After an abortive escape attempt in which one of the escapees (Heddy) stole from the others, Smith redeemed himself by identifying Heddy as the ringleader. Smith was then sold to Thomas Stanton and moved to Stonington Point, Connecticut. Stanton, too, abused Smith and, when Smith was thirty-one, sold him to Colonel Smith.

Frugal and enterprising, Venture Smith earned money however he could—raising and selling vegetables, fishing, shining shoes—and purchased his freedom, adopting Smith's surname as his own. He continued to exhibit an entrepreneurial spirit, primarily as a woodcutter, watermelon farmer, and owner of a shipping business. Eventually he purchased freedom for his whole family, first buying his sons, and later his wife and daughter as well as three unrelated Black men. Smith described the latter as ungrateful because they reneged on their agreement to repay his purchase money. Smith recounted additional instances of lending money to Blacks and Whites who failed to repay him, explaining that his illiteracy, particularly his inability to use figures, made him vulnerable; however, he also attributed his exploitation to racial inequality.

When he was sixty-nine, Smith dictated his *Narrative*—presumably to Elisha Niles, a schoolteacher—complaining that "though once straight and tall, measuring without shoes six feet, one inch and a half, and every way well proportioned, I am now bowed down with age and hardship." Smith's personal tales of his exploits revealed him to be a giant of a man, a "New England John Henry" (Kaplan and Kaplan, 255). His willingness to endure privation and hardship in order to accomplish his goal of freedom for himself, his family, and others underscored the power of personal effort while it also illustrated the obstacles free Blacks faced during the eighteenth century. The 1896 edition of Smith's *Narrative*—an expanded version published by a relative—included a supplement entitled *Traditions*. This addition featured accounts corroborating his larger-than-life image as a man who possessed superhuman strength and stature.

Gloria A. Shearin

See also: Slave Narrative.

Resources

Jeannine DeLombard, "Smith, Venture," in *American National Biography*, ed. John Garraty and Mark Carnes (New York: Oxford University Press, 1999); Sidney Kaplan and Emma Nogrady Kaplan, *The Black Presence in the Era of the American Revolution*, rev. ed. (Amherst: University of Massachusetts Press, 1989); Chandler B. Saint and George A. Krimsky, *Making Freedom: The Extraordinary Life of Venture Smith* (Middletown, CT: Wesleyan University Press, 2009); Venture Smith, *Narrative of the Life and Adventures of Venture, a Native of Africa, But Resident above Sixty Years in the United States of America, Related by Himself* (New London, CT: C. Holt, 1798); James Brewer Stewart, ed., *Venture Smith and the Business of Slavery and Freedom* (Amherst, MA: University of Massachusetts Press, 2010).

Spirituals

A form of sacred music that was originally created by African Americans for African Americans during slavery times. In *The*

African American Almanac, Christopher A. Brooks describes spirituals as "the most significant musical contribution of the enslaved African population in the nineteenth century" (958). Spirituals have served as the theme, focus, and inspiration for a large body of African American literature, both yesterday and today.

Spirituals are an amalgamation of West African traditions, Protestant Christianity, and the slave experience. When slaves adopted the religion of their captors, they created songs based on Christian principles, such as God, Heaven, Jesus, and biblical stories, but they expressed them in a manner indicative of their West African heritage, creating a distinct and even unique music not found anywhere else in the world. As a result, these songs included expressive and elaborate embellishments, improvisation, and call-and-response patterns. Call-and-response is a style of singing in which an individual sings a line and another individual or group echoes it. Slaves sometimes accompanied these songs with body swaying, hand-clapping, and foot-stomping. Songs were sung at work, in rare moments of leisure, and at camp meetings. Camp meetings generally took place in secret and were a place where slaves could worship freely among themselves. True to the oral tradition of their ancestors, slaves did not document these songs in hymnals or books. Nor did their creators claim individual ownership. Spirituals belonged to the community.

Spirituals served several functions within the slave community. They provided slaves a means to express their feelings and religious beliefs. Songs such as "Mary Had a Baby, Yes, Lord," established their faith in Scripture, while songs such as "O, Brother, Don't Get Weary" provided encouragement, joy, and hope. Some songs expressed their sorrow, such as "Nobody Knows the Trouble I See," and "Sometimes I Feel Like a Motherless Child," and other songs were used in praise and worship. Spirituals also provided a means of resistance and empowerment. Within these particular songs, slaves embedded coded messages that they kept secret from White slave owners. "Go Down Moses" is an example:

Go down, Moses, / Way down in Egypt land. / Tell old Pharaoh, / "Let my people go." / When Israel was in Egypt land, / "Let my people go." / Oppressed so hard they could not stand, / "Let my people go." / Go down, Moses, / Way down in Egypt land. / Tell old Pharaoh, / "Let my people go." / "Thus saith the Lord," bold Moses said, / "Let my people go; / if not I'll smite your first-born dead. / Let my people go." / Go down, Moses, / Way down in Egypt land. / Tell old Pharaoh, / "Let my people go!"

"Go Down Moses" illustrates how slaves used biblical references as coded words and how they perceived the world around them. The Hebrews represented the slaves. Egypt represented the South, and many associate the Moses figure with Harriet Tubman, who led many slaves to freedom, and Nat Turner, who led a slave revolt. Harriet Tubman, called "The Moses of her People," was known to "[wander] along back southern roads" singing seemingly harmless spirituals (Altman, 251–252). In reality, she was singing secret messages to slaves. "Follow the Drinking Gourd" is an example of a spiritual she may have sung. This song was used to instruct slaves on how to travel north to freedom. The "drinking gourd" stood for the Big Dipper and, if followed, led north. Altogether, spirituals provided slaves a means to cope, survive, and "keep on keepin' on under the physical and psychological pressures of [slavery]" (Connor, 693).

Prior to the Civil War, many Northerners had never heard spirituals. Spirituals had been a phenomenon isolated in the slave quarters, within the confining walls of slavery. Still, Whites and African Americans made efforts to preserve these distinct songs and helped expose them to wider audiences. Collection and documentation of spirituals began as early as 1801, when Richard Allen, founder of the African Methodist Episcopal Church, published *A Collection of Spiritual Songs and Hymns from Various Authors*. This collection was used in African American churches throughout the United States. Newly freed African Americans, such as Frederick Douglass and Booker T. Washington, wrote about spirituals in their slave narratives. Thomas Wentworth Higginson, a Union colonel of a regiment of free slaves, first heard the spirituals during the Civil War and was moved to publish several songs in the *Atlantic Monthly* as well as in his memoir, *Army Life in a Black Regiment* (1870).

By the 1870s, a new trend was sweeping through the United States and Europe, one that sparked a greater interest in spirituals than ever before. This trend occurred when singing groups from African American colleges, such as Fisk University, Hampton Institute, Calhoun College, and Tuskegee Institute, decided to go on tour to raise money. Spirituals were well received, particularly in the North, by former abolitionists and sympathizers with African American causes, and throughout Europe. Spirituals were so successful in Europe that Antonín Dvořák, a Czech composer, encouraged his students to compose and arrange spirituals (Brooks, 959). While composing his famous *New World Symphony* (1893), he wrote that "the so-called plantation songs are among the most striking and appealing melodies that have been found this side of the water" (Newman).

Interest continued through the end of the nineteenth century and into the twentieth. Many African Americans were arranging old spirituals and composing new ones. Some of the best-known composers include Hall Johnson, John W. Work, Florence Price, Robert Nathaniel Dett, Clarence Cameron White, and Harry T. Burleigh. In the literary world, writers were publishing works on and about spirituals. These works include *Hampton and Its Students* (1874), *The Story of the Jubilee Singers* (1877), *Plantation Melodies* (1888), and *The Book of American Negro Spirituals* (1925). The popularity of spirituals also gave rise to African American artists who could perform these songs without fear or shame. Some of the eminent artists are Marian Anderson, Paul Robeson, Robert McFerrin, Leontyne Price, and Jesse Norman.

As the status and fame of spirituals grew, so did the criticism. The bulk of this criticism can be categorized into two major camps: those who stressed a White influence and those who emphasized the West African contribution. Scholars such as Newman Ivey White, Guy B. Johnson, and George Pullen Jackson compared White and African American songs. They concluded that spirituals, though influenced by West African folk music, replicated White music, and that White songs are their "legitimate tune-and-words forbears" (Low and Clift, 593). This argument is presented in *American Negro Folk-Songs* (1928), *Folk Culture on St. Helena Island, South Carolina* (1930), and *White Spirituals in the Southern Uplands* (1933). There was, of course, a deluge of works providing an alternative perspective on the origin of the spiritual. These works include *The Souls of*

Black Folk (1903) by W.E.B. Du Bois, *Afro-American Folksongs* (1914) by Henry E. Krehbiel, and *Sinful Tunes and Spirituals* (1977) by Dena Epstein. In these works, these writers and scholars credit and acknowledge West African culture and folk tradition as a significant influence in the making of spirituals. They point to how distinct West Africanisms influenced the tunes and expression of the music and how, when combined with Protestant Christian religion and its practices, a unique and distinct music not found anywhere else in the world was created.

More recently, commentators have focused on the role of the spiritual within the slave community, rather than its origins, in such works as James Cone's *The Spirituals and the Blues* (1972), John Lovell's *Black Song: The Forge and the Flame* (1972), and Lawrence Levine's *Black Culture & Black Consciousness* (1977) (Connor, 695).

Spirituals have played a significant role in the African American literary tradition, beginning as early as the slave narratives of the 1800s and extending to contemporary works more than a century removed from slavery. Several Harlem Renaissance writers, most notably Langston Hughes and Zora Neale Hurston, were influenced by spirituals. In *Moses, Man of the Mountain* (1939), Hurston embellishes upon the biblical story and spiritual of "Go Down, Moses." Many other writers used spirituals as a way to "structure their plots [and their characters] and advance their themes" (Connor, 695). Examples include *Blake* (1859) by Martin R. Delany, *Jubilee* (1966) by Margaret Abigail Walker, *Invisible Man* (1952) by Ralph Ellison, *Song of Solomon* (1977) by Toni Morrison, and *The Amen Corner* (1968) and *Go Tell It on the Mountain* (1953) by James Baldwin (Connor,

695). Poets such as Paul Laurence Dunbar and James Weldon Johnson also modeled their works on spirituals.

Spirituals have come a long way. From the obscurity of slavery and from the mouths of nameless authors, spirituals thrive in the works of composers, performers, writers, and poets. As a result, spirituals are recognized the world over and forever entwined with African American culture and literature.

Gladys L. Knight

See also: Du Bois, W.E.B.; Johnson, James Weldon; King, Martin Luther, Jr.

Resources

Primary Sources: Richard Allen, *A Collection of Spiritual Songs and Hymns from Various Authors* (Nashville, TN: A.M.E.C. Sunday School Union, 1987); M. F. Armstrong and Helen W. Ludlow, *Hampton and Its Students* (New York: Putnam, 1874); W.E.B. Du Bois, *The Souls of Black Folk*, ed. George Stade (1903; repr. New York: Barnes & Noble Classics, 2005); Dena Epstein, *Sinful Tunes and Spirituals: Black Folk Music to the Civil War* (Urbana: University of Illinois Press, 1977); Stephen Collins Foster, *Plantation Melodies* (Boston: J. -, 1888); Thomas Wentworth Higginson, *Army Life in a Black Regiment* (Boston: Fields, Osgood, 1870); Zora Neale Hurston, *Moses, Man of the Mountain* (Philadelphia: Lippincott, 1939); George Pullen Jackson, *White Spirituals in the Southern Uplands: The Story of the Fasola Folk, Their Songs, Singings, and "Buckwheat Notes"* (Chapel Hill: University of North Carolina Press, 1933); Guy B. Johnson, *Folk Culture on St. Helena Island, South Carolina* (Chapel Hill: University of North Carolina Press, 1930); James Weldon Johnson, ed., *The Book of American Negro Spirituals* (New York: Viking Press, 1925); Henry Edward Krehbiel, *Afro-American Folksongs: A Study in Racial and National Music*, 4th ed. (Portland, ME: Longwood Press, 1976); J.B.T.

Marsh, *The Story of the Jubilee Singers, with Their Songs*, 7th ed. (London: Hodder and Stoughton, 1877); Newman Ivey White, *American Negro Folk-Songs* (Cambridge, MA: Harvard University Press, 1928).

Secondary Sources: Susan Altman, "Harriet Tubman," in her *The Encyclopedia of African-American Heritage* (New York: Facts on File, 1997); James Baldwin: *The Amen Corner* (New York: Dial Press, 1968); *Go Tell It on the Mountain* (New York: Knopf, 1953); Christopher A. Brooks, "Sacred Music Traditions," in *The African American Almanac*, 8th ed., ed. Jessie Carney Smith and Joseph M. Palmisano (Detroit: Gale, 2000), 957–964; James Cone, *The Spirituals and the Blues* (New York: Seabury Press, 1972); Kimberly Rae Connor, "Spirituals," in *The Oxford Companion to African American Literature*, ed. William L. Andrews, Frances Smith Foster, and Trudier Harris (New York: Oxford University Press, 1997); Robert Darden, *Nothing but Love in God's Water, Volume 1: Black Sacred Music from the Civil War to the Civil Rights Movement* (University Park, PA: Pennsylvania State University Press, 2014); Martin R. Delany, *Blake* (Boston: Beacon Press, 1970); Ralph Ellison, *Invisible Man* (New York: Random House, 1952); Sandra Jean Graham, *Spirituals and the Birth of a Black Entertainment Industry* (Urbana, IL: University of Illinois Press, 2018); Charles W. Joyner and Eileen Jackson Southern, "Music: Spirituals," in *Encyclopedia of Black America*, ed. W. Augustus Low and Virgil A. Clift (New York: McGraw-Hill, 1981), 591–598; Lawrence Levine, *Black Culture and Black Consciousness* (New York: Oxford University Press, 1977); John Lovell, *Black Song: The Forge and the Flame* (New York: Macmillan, 1972); Toni Morrison, *Song of Solomon* (New York: Knopf, 1977); Richard Newman, "African American Spirituals," *Africana* 19 (October 2004), http://www.africana.com/research/encarta/tt_266.asp; Erskine Peters, ed., *Lyrics of the Afro-American Spiritual* (Westport, CT: Greenwood Press, 1993); Shana L. Redmond, *Anthem: Social Movements and the Sound of Solidarity in the African Diaspora* (New York: New York University Press, 2013); Margaret Walker, *Jubilee* (Boston: Houghton Mifflin, 1966).

T

Terry [Prince], Lucy (ca. 1730–1821)

Poet and orator. Most academic studies of African American literature date its origin at 1746, when the sixteen-year-old Terry wrote the first existing poem by an American of African descent. "Bars Fight" (1746) mourns the deaths of White colonists in an August 1746 Indian raid on Deerfield, Massachusetts. The twenty-eight-line occasional poem in irregular iambic tetrameter uses colloquial expressions and spellings, such as "bar" for "meadow" and "fout" for "fought." Its strong rhyme scheme and standard meter lend themselves to musical adaptation; however, the accompanying tune has not survived. The poem circulated in Massachusetts oral history until its publication in Josiah Gilbert Holland's *History of Western Massachusetts* (1855). Though the poem is the first extant work by an African American writer, it was not the first published one. Some of the colonial African American poets whose work was published in their lifetimes include Jupiter Hammon, Phillis Wheatley, and Lemuel Haynes. Ironically, "Bars Fight" chronicles some of the earliest racial tensions in the United States and commemorates the loss of White settlers, yet it was written by a young woman trapped in racial slavery by the same White colonists.

Lucy Terry, a resident of Deerfield, was kidnapped at approximately age five from Africa and purchased for sixty pounds off a Rhode Island slave ship by Ebenezer Wells of Deerfield in 1735. Terry met Abijah (or Obijah) Prince, a freed slave, in 1746. It took him ten years to earn the money to purchase her freedom, and they married in 1756. By 1769, the couple had six children: Cesar, Festus, Drucilla, Tatnai, Durexa, and Abijah Jr. The Princes inherited land from Abijah's former master in Northfield and later purchased property in Guilford and Sunderland. On two occasions, their White neighbors attempted to appropriate their land, and both times Lucy Terry's oratorical skills successfully defended the family's rights. In 1785, she protested the Noyes family's encroachments before the Governor's Council, and, in the 1790s, she argued her case against Col. Eli Bronson in front of Supreme Court Justice Samuel Chase. Terry did not prevail in front of the board of trustees of Williams College, however, when she argued against the school's segregation policy in an attempt to enroll her oldest son in the early 1770s. Abijah Prince, several years Terry's senior, died in 1794. Local historians remember that Terry was known for her storytelling, and her home remained a gathering place for both African Americans and White Americans until her death in 1821. No other poems or works by Lucy Terry [Prince] have been discovered.

Ann Beebe

See also: Poetry; Vernacular.

Resources

Dickson D. Bruce Jr., *The Origins of African American Literature, 1680–1865* (Charlottesville: University Press of Virginia, 2001); Frances Smith Foster, *Written by Herself:*

Literary Production by African American Women, 1746–1892 (Bloomington: Indiana University Press, 1993); Blyden Jackson, *A History of Afro-American Literature*, vol. 1, *The Long Beginning, 1746–1895* (Baton Rouge: Louisiana State University Press, 1989); Mary Louise Kete, "Claiming Lucy Terry Prince: Literary History and the Problem of Early African American Women Poets," in *A History of Nineteenth-Century American Women's Poetry*, ed. Jennifer Putzi and Alexandra Socarides (New York: Cambridge University Press, 2017), 17–36; April Langley, "Lucy Terry Prince: The Cultural and Literary Legacy of Africana Womanism," *Western Journal of Black Studies* 25, no. 3 (2001), 153–162.

Tolson, Melvin B. (1898–1966)

Poet, journalist, and educator. Melvin Tolson is a problematic character within the story of African American literature. A lifelong writer, he was, nonetheless, over forty years old before he had his first literary work professionally published. Karl Shapiro said of him that he "writes and thinks in Negro" (*Harlem Gallery, I*), however, he is more typically associated with the "White" style of high modernism. His densely allusive works have never gained the popular readership of such poets as Langston Hughes or Amiri Baraka. His work seemed to require a kind of critical rehabilitation from the White poets who wrote introductions to his collections. Tolson has more recently been granted a place among first-rate poets of the twentieth century but is still largely ignored by both the popular and the scholarly communities.

Melvin Beaunorus Tolson was born on February 6, 1898, in Moberly, Missouri. His father, Alonzo Tolson, was an itinerant Methodist preacher, holding ministerial positions throughout the Midwest during Melvin's childhood. The elder Tolson was an autodidact, having taught himself a smattering of Hebrew, Latin, and Greek. Melvin's mother, Lera Hurt Tolson, seems to have been the motivation behind his educational and literary aspirations. From her, he acquired a strong sense of storytelling and an intriguing genealogy. In a personal notebook, Tolson described his mother's family as a clan of "gun-toting preachers and hallelujahing badmen" (quoted by Flasch, 21).

In school, Tolson was studious and active in extracurricular organizations. He wrote poems for school publications and directed and performed in plays with the drama club. He graduated from Lincoln High School in Kansas City, Missouri, in 1918. He enrolled at Fisk University in the fall of 1918, but financial problems led him to transfer to Lincoln University in Oxford, Pennsylvania, for the fall term of 1919. At Lincoln, Tolson was again serious and studious, but he felt somewhat inhibited by the conservative curriculum and faculty. His growing interest in such modern poets as Carl Sandburg and Edgar Lee Masters was discouraged. One positive result of his time at Lincoln, however, was his relationship with Ruth Southall, whom he met at a dance in 1921. They were married in 1922 and raised four children together.

After graduating from Lincoln University in 1923, Tolson accepted a position as professor of English at Wiley College in Marshall, Texas. Tolson became known among Wiley students as a rather stern motivator, encouraging them to read and study beyond the requirements of their courses. He also took over direction of the school debate team, which under his guidance became a powerhouse on the debate circuit, defeating the national champion University of Southern California in 1935.

During the 1931–1932 school year, Tolson took a leave of absence from Wiley to enroll in a master's degree program at Columbia University. Writers of the Harlem Renaissance had long fascinated him, but by the time Tolson arrived in New York City, the Renaissance, though still vigorous, was on its downward slope. Tolson met Langston Hughes and other writers, yet never became part of the movement. His thesis, "The Harlem Group of Negro Writers" (completed by the end of the year, but not submitted until 1940, due to Tolson's busy schedule back at Wiley College), is largely a reiteration of ideas found in Alain Locke's *The New Negro*.

After returning to Texas, Tolson set to work on *A Gallery of Harlem Portraits*, a collection of over 150 poetic character sketches not unlike Masters's *Spoon River Anthology*. It describes an assortment of people, from heroes to rogues, saints to whores. The tone is ironic and humorous, with a great affinity for the blues. The poems often reveal inner thoughts and attitudes that the characters are unable to express. "Hester Pringle," for example, describes a secretary for the Deaconess Purity League, who, after walking in on a man as he stands naked in the shower, cannot keep licentious thoughts from her mind:

Hester saw herself naked,
Pursued [. . .]
By a bronze, hard-muscled body (47)

Tolson tried in vain to find a publisher for the collection, but it went unpublished until 1979, thirteen years after his death.

His failure to publish *A Gallery* dampened Tolson's poetic aspirations, but in 1937, he was invited to become a columnist for the *Washington Tribune*, a Black newspaper with a national readership. His columns, published between 1937 and 1944

(collected as *Caviar and Cabbage* in 1982), show a wide range of interests, an erudite manner, and an irascible humor. His strongest censure was often saved for ineffective Black politicians. In one column, he said that a particular Black Congressman did not have enough knowledge to "fill the belly of a prenatal bedbug" (130).

Tolson's poem "Dark Symphony" won first prize in a contest sponsored by the American Negro Exposition at Chicago in 1939 and was published in *Atlantic Monthly* in 1941. "Dark Symphony" then formed the center of *Rendezvous with America*, a collection published in 1944. The book sold well, and Tolson experienced what would be his highest level of popular readership. The book owes a great deal to the style of Walt Whitman, down to the inclusion of a poem titled "A Song for Myself." Tolson's "for" contrasts with Whitman's "of" and signals a need for Tolson, and perhaps the African American male, to speak *for* himself. Other poems are re-imaginings of Locke's "New Negro," described by Tolson as "Hard-muscled, Fascist-hating, Democracy-ensouled" (40).

Tolson had two important life experiences in 1947: he was invited to become the Poet Laureate of Liberia; and he left Wiley College for Langston University in Langston, Oklahoma. In Langston, Tolson became a prominent community figure, writing and directing plays for the university theater and being elected to several terms as mayor of the town. The position as Poet Laureate of Liberia, though largely symbolic, led to the publication of *Libretto for the Republic of Liberia* in 1953 and a major shift in Tolson's poetic style. *Libretto* uses an allusive, high-modernist style reminiscent of T. S. Eliot, and bristles with so many learned references to antiquity, sociology, philosophy, and foreign language that Tolson felt it necessary to include 737 explanatory notes. Despite its dense allusion, the book displays a strong sense of imagery, such as when Tolson describes Liberia as a "quicksilver sparrow that slips / The eagle's claw!" To write the introduction for the collection, a modernist of no less stature than Allen Tate was recruited. Tate noted that Tolson was "in the direct succession from [Harte] Crane," but the relationship between Tate, an unregenerate Confederate, as it were, and this African American poet seemed to confuse most critics and the public as well. (*See* Modernism.)

It would be twelve years before Tolson published another collection of poetry, but he did not relent from the modernist style established in *Libretto*. Tolson conceived *Harlem Gallery: Book I, The Curator* as the first in a multivolume epic that would "convey the reality of the black man's experience in America" and "act as one way of fixing a changing ethnic experience that might disappear altogether" (Russell, 9). The book utilizes all of Tolson's skills—dense allusion, sharp humor, clever characterization, and a strong ear for folk language—and fuses them in a sophisticated way not seen before. The poem observes the lives and attitudes of five main characters, the unnamed Curator, his friend Dr. Nkomo, the artist John Laugart, the musician Mister Starks, and the poet Hideho Heights. Through their achievements and weaknesses, the poem examines the significance of African American art and the artist's place in Black history.

In his introduction, Karl Shapiro makes the (now) embarrassing comment about Tolson writing "Negro" but also places him in a lineage with Eliot and Crane and argues for the critical attention that has yet to be directed at his work (13). With *The Harlem Gallery*, Tolson attained great prominence among African American artists and established himself as a major poet. His erudite and modernist style, however, has insulated him from a wider audience. At a time when a developing sense of the Black aesthetic called for a more politicized approach to poetry, Tolson's style seemed old-fashioned and alienated him from a greater critical reception. He died of cancer in 1966, the epic sequence begun with *The Harlem Gallery* left unfinished.

Steven R. Harris

See also: Modernism.

Resources

Primary Sources: Melvin Tolson: *Caviar and Cabbage: Selected Columns by Melvin B. Tolson from the Washington Tribune, 1937–1944*, ed. Robert M. Farnsworth (Columbia: University of Missouri Press, 1982); *A Gallery of Harlem Portraits*, ed. Robert M. Farnsworth (Columbia: University of Missouri Press, 1979); *Harlem Gallery*, book I, *The Curator*, intro. Karl Shapiro (New York: Twayne, 1965); *Libretto for the Republic of Liberia* (New York: Twayne, 1953); *Rendezvous with America* (New York: Dodd, Mead, 1944).

Secondary Sources: Michael Bérubé, *Marginal Forces/Cultural Centers: Tolson, Pynchon, and the Politics of the Canon* (Ithaca, NY: Cornell University Press, 1992); Robert M. Farnsworth, *Melvin B. Tolson, 1898–1966: Plain Talk and Poetic Prophecy* (Columbia: University of Missouri Press, 1984); Joy Flasch, *Melvin B. Tolson* (New York: Twayne, 1972); David Gold, "'Nothing Educates Us Like a Shock': The Integrated Rhetoric of Melvin B. Tolson," *College Composition and Communication* 55, no. 2 (2003), 226–253; Mariann Russell, *Melvin B. Tolson's Harlem Gallery: A Literary Analysis* (Columbia: University of Missouri Press, 1980); John Taylor, "Melvin Tolson," *Antioch Review* 69, no. 4 (2011), 716–721.

Toomer, Jean (1894–1967)

Poet, playwright, and short-story writer. Toomer is best known for *Cane*, a book that mixes fiction and poetry and remains a significant Modernist text. Nathan Eugene Toomer was born in Washington, DC; his parents were Nina Pinchback, whose father, Pinkney Benton Stewart Pinchback, had been an important Louisiana politician after the Civil War, and Nathan Toomer, an older gentleman farmer from Georgia with a poor business reputation and a rumored heritage of mixed race. Pinkney Pinchback claimed to be of mixed race himself, though he could pass for White, and his wife was White. When Nathan Toomer abandoned his wife and child, Jean and his mother moved in with her parents. To his grandparents, who would play vital roles in his early life, Jean was known as Eugene Pinchback. He lived in Washington with his grandparents from 1896 to 1906. From 1906 until 1910, he lived in Brooklyn, New York, and New Rochelle, New York, with his mother, who had remarried. After the death of Toomer's mother in 1909, Jean moved back with his grandparents. He remained in Washington until 1914. The Pinchback family had fallen on hard times and abandoned their upper-middle-class home for one in a racially mixed area of Washington.

Toomer had been enrolled in Black schools at his grandfather's insistence the entire time he lived in Washington, but he was exposed to the daily lives of African Americans for the first time in his late teens. From 1914 to 1918, he briefly attended a number of colleges, including the University of Wisconsin at Madison, the Massachusetts College of Agriculture (now the University of Massachusetts at Amherst), the University of Chicago, the American College of Physical Training in Chicago, New York University, and City College in New York City. He studied agriculture, physical education, history, sociology, and law, but he never earned a degree. He moved around the country in 1918, then returned to New York City for two years. This period exposed him to radical politics and the New York literary scene. He briefly tried to spread the word of socialism to New Jersey longshoremen. In 1919, Toomer met Waldo Frank, who would be a prominent supporter of his work; at this point in his life, Toomer had decided to devote himself to writing. Around 1920, he adopted the name Jean, under which he would publish all his best-known works; in his later life, he would go by Nathan Jean Toomer or N. Jean Toomer.

In 1920, financial problems forced Toomer to move back with his grandparents. He cared for them in exchange for a small allowance and continued to work hard on his writing. In the fall of 1921, he heard about an opportunity to serve as substitute teacher at a Black school in Sparta, Georgia, and he took the job. His experiences during this period and on another trip to the South in 1922 formed a crucial part of his artistic vision. The other main component of his vision was that of a mixed "American race," with Native American, African, and European roots; this understanding of race reflected Toomer's attitudes about himself and his work, and his search for a means to realize it would guide him through artistic pursuits, politics, and spiritual philosophies throughout his life.

Toomer's first trip to the South, which lasted until November 1921, was followed by the composition of his best-known plays, *Balo* (written in the winter of 1921–1922) and *Natalie Mann* (written in early 1922). *Balo* tells the story of the mixed-race Lee family, whose eldest son has a religious awakening and gives the play its name.

During the play, which is filled with elements of Black folk culture, a White neighbor farmer, who is very similar to the patriarch Will Lee in concerns and outlook, visits; the play stresses both the similarities between those with different skin tones and the remaining historical separation that divides them. The Lee family—the father explicitly of African, European, and Native American origin, the mother described as having a yellow complexion—serve as exemplars of Toomer's vision of a hybrid American identity. *Balo* was performed at Howard University in 1923.

Natalie Mann tells the story of the title character, a middle-class Black woman who escapes the social restrictions placed on her by her cohort to live a nonconformist life in New York City; these strictures, the play indicates, derive from a desire to gain acceptance by mimicking White middle-class culture. Through the help and example of Nathan Merilh, a worldly, intellectual Black man who embraces Leo Tolstoy as well as the heritage of African American folk life (and who serves as another representation of Toomer's ideal American hybrid), Natalie rejects the strictures placed upon her. The play was never performed because producers found it unsuitable for the American stage (McKay, 81).

Cane, Toomer's best-known work and only published literary book, was begun in November 1921 and finished by the early fall of 1922. It combines poetry, short stories, and a drama, "Kabnis," which together form a portrait of African American life in the early twentieth century. A good deal of it was inspired by Toomer's time in Georgia, though portions take place in the North. The book has three parts, which display unity of theme and create a whole. The first, highly lyrical part takes place in the rural South. It includes the well-known stories of women, "Karintha," "Becky," "Carma," "Fern," and "Esther"; and the poems "Song of the Son" (first published in the NAACP's journal *The Crisis*) and "Georgia Dusk" (which was written early and sent to *The Liberator*). The second portion of the book focuses on the North, especially Washington, DC, and Chicago. It portrays a much colder, urban life, though it also draws attention to relationships between men and women. This section is characterized by encounters in streets, theaters, and parks. The short play "Kabnis" is the third part. In it, an educated Northerner living in the South struggles with his role in life.

Images of nature echo from one text to another in *Cane*, and many of its poems bear strong connections. All portions of the book touch on elements of African folk culture. *Cane* was published by Boni and Liveright in 1923 and made Toomer's reputation as an artistic innovator. Toomer's prose and poetry in the book are highly imagistic, subtle, and evocative. Though it did not sell well, *Cane* is acclaimed as a highlight of the Harlem Renaissance, and Toomer gained admirers such as Langston Hughes, W.E.B. Du Bois, Countee Cullen, Sherwood Anderson, and Kenneth Burke. Generations of writers following *Cane* were nudged toward experimentation in style and form thanks to his work. A second edition of the book appeared in 1927. The third and fourth editions appeared only in the 1960s, one with University Place Press (1967) and one with Harper & Row (1969). These editions were largely responsible for reintroducing *Cane* and the figure of Toomer at a crucial moment in the growth of the academic study of African American literature.

After the publication of *Cane*, Toomer mostly withdrew from the literary world, largely pursuing spiritual goals, influenced partly by the ideas of George Gurdjieff. He published short stories and poems in journals such as *Little Review* and *The Dial*; *Balo* appeared in *Plays of Negro Life* (1927) and his novella *York Beach* in *The New American Caravan* in 1929; and he had a handful of aesthetic and political essays published in the 1920s and 1930s. Though he continued to write throughout his life, composing stories, novels, a play, and numerous partial autobiographies (including *Reflections of an Earth Being*, 1928–1930), the last literary pieces published during his lifetime were the poems "Brown River, Smile," which appeared in *Pagany* in 1932, and "The Blue Meridian," published in *The New Caravan* in 1936. His play *A Drama of the Southwest*, written in 1935, was published in a critical edition in 2016.

By late 1923, Toomer had become deeply involved with the teachings of George Ivanovitch Gurdjieff, an Armenian mystic philosopher who worked primarily in France. Toomer spent a summer at Gurdjieff's center and spread word of his philosophy in the United States. After meeting the White Modernist writer Margery Latimer, Toomer tried his hand at leading a Gurdjieff-inspired communal experiment near Portage, Wisconsin, Latimer's hometown. Latimer and Toomer married in 1931, living in Chicago and in an artists' colony in Carmel, California; she died days after giving birth to their daughter. In 1934, Toomer married Marjorie Content, a photographer and New York socialite who moved in Toomer's circles. They moved to Doylestown, Pennsylvania, where Toomer lived until his death. He tried to develop another communal society in Doylestown, the Mill House Experiment, but it, too, failed. Though he distanced himself from Gurdjieff in the late 1930s, Toomer never completely abandoned his belief in the philosophy. He had become interested in the Society of Friends after moving to

Pennsylvania, and after a trip to India and explorations of Scientology, Toomer joined the Quakers in 1940. He wrote for the Quaker journal *Friend's Intelligencer* and published two books on them, *An Interpretation of Friends Worship* (1947) and *The Flavor of Man* (1949).

Toomer's papers, formerly at Fisk University, are part of the James Weldon Johnson Memorial Collection at the Beinecke Rare Book and Manuscript Library at Yale University. (*See* Modernism.)

Ian W. Wilson

See also: Harlem Renaissance; Modernism.

Resources

Wesley Beal, "The Form and Politics of Networks in Jean Toomer's *Cane*," *American Literary History* 24, no. 4 (2012), 658–679; Nissa Ren Cannon, "Neither/Nor: The Productive Frustration of Classification in Jean Toomer's *Cane*," in *We Speak a Different Tongue: Maverick Voices and Modernity 1890–1939*, ed. Anthony Patterson and Yoonjoung Choi (Cambridge, UK: Cambridge Scholars, 2015), 154–167; Geneviève Fabre and Michel Feith, eds., *Jean Toomer and the Harlem Renaissance* (New Brunswick, NJ: Rutgers University Press, 2001); Barbara Foley, *Jean Toomer: Race, Repression, and Revolution* (Urbana, IL: University of Illinois Press, 2014); Karen Jackson Ford, *Split-Gut Song: Jean Toomer and the Poetics of Modernity* (Tuscaloosa, AL: University of Alabama Press, 2005); Nellie Y. McKay, *Jean Toomer, Artist: A Study of His Literary Life and Work, 1894–1936* (Chapel Hill: University of North Carolina Press, 1984); Therman B. O'Daniel, ed., *Jean Toomer: A Critical Evaluation* (Washington, DC: Howard University Press, 1988); Hans Ostrom, "Jean Toomer" (poem), *Xavier Review* 23, no. 2 (Fall 2003), 46; Jean Toomer, *Cane*, ed. Rudolph P. Byrd and Henry Louis Gates Jr. (New York: Norton, 2011); *A Drama of the Southwest: The Critical Edition of a Forgotten Play*, ed. Carolyn Decker

(Albuquerque, NM: University of New Mexico Press, 2016); *The Wayward and the Seeking: A Collection of Writings by Jean Toomer*, ed. Darwin T. Turner (Washington, DC: Howard University Press, 1980); Mark Whalan, "Jean Toomer and the Avant-Garde," *The Cambridge Companion to the Harlem Renaissance*, ed. George Hutchinson (Cambridge, UK: Cambridge University Press, 2007), 71–81.

Trickster

A character in African American tales of heroism that originated in African oral narratives in which animals took on the personalities of human beings and overcame difficult circumstances by defeating larger animals through the use of trickery. Often taking the form of a rabbit, spider, tortoise, or monkey, the figure of the trickster, reborn in various parts of the Americas, became a symbol of heroic action and potential power for enslaved Africans who felt powerless in the face of slavery and, specifically, the plantation system. This figure became central to the African American trickster tale, which was shared through word of mouth among the slaves in order to inspire perseverance, to communicate instructions on how to outwit and/or overcome the slave masters, and, most important, to provide examples of how to obtain materials for survival under circumstances marked by want.

Trickster tales, according to John W. Roberts, were also based on the everyday life of Africans, who had to deal with "subsistence-level existence as well as chronic shortages of basic material necessities occasioned by various factors peculiar to life on the African continent" (24). The slave experience, also marked by such conditions, allowed for the transformation of such tales into ones that reflected the need for survival strategies in a new world. Regarded by Whites as childish inventions, trickster tales were thus allowed to abound, and their heroes reflected the ingenuity one could employ in dealing with the harsh realities of deprivation. Viewing these heroes with awe and, in many cases, venerating them, African slaves and their offspring adopted the personalities and characteristics of the trickster and applied them to their own experiences during enslavement. In the words of Robert Hemenway,

> Trickster tales, universal in all folklore, were especially popular [in the African American folkloric tradition] because they often emphasized the triumph of the weak over the strong; they seemed ready made for a slave situation in which foot speed—escape—was a persistent hope and tricks rather than physical force were the primary recourse for survival. (25)

Roberts characterizes the reverence for the heroes of these tales as almost a deification when he writes that the "African conception of the trickster as a sacred being, usually a god, undoubtedly influenced African attitudes toward the adaptability of behaviors embodied in trickster tales in certain kinds of situations" (27).

The best-known animal trickster is Brer Rabbit, notorious for stealing from others in the animal and human kingdoms. In one of the most popular versions of his tale, Brer Rabbit steals water from a well. A farmer erects a "tar baby" near the well in order to trap the rabbit. When Brer Rabbit tries to steal water again, he becomes stuck in the sticky mass of the tar. Finally catching the rabbit, the farmer throws him into the briar patch, from which he escapes once again. In a few other versions, Brer Rabbit's outcome is less positive; he is punished severely for maliciously duping his own kind and for creating disorder within the animal community. As Roberts makes clear, a trickster was viewed as heroic only if his tricks purposefully reflected the "most advantageous behaviors for securing individual interests without disrupting the order and harmony of society" (29). Appropriate trickster behavior, then, did not willfully bring harm to the rest of the community. Given this, in adopting the appropriate behaviors of trickster figures such as Brer Rabbit, slaves sought to weaken the master's authority while seeking to avert retaliation and punishment. Speaking of the importance of Brer Rabbit to hero formation within the slave community, Hemenway characterizes it in this way:

Shaped by a long line of oral artists, Brer Rabbit is black from the tip of his ears to the fuzz of his tail, and he defeats his enemies with a superior intelligence growing from a total understanding of his hostile environment. He is the briar-patch representative of a people living by their wits to make a way out of no way. (9)

Sharing trickster tales in secret and striving together for the rewards of the trickster, slaves often used these tales of heroism as a source of communal strength.

In addition to animal tricksters, Africans had a wealth of religious folklore from which to draw for the development of trickster tales in the Americas. The Yoruba in particular contributed to this tradition the characteristics of their most respected trickster deity, Eshu-Elegba (a.k.a. Legba, Elegbara, Esu), who outmaneuvered his fellow deities to gain the respect of the creator god and to be granted the power to make things happen; he thus became the guardian of the crossroads, where choice, destiny, and morality are mediated through communication (Roberts, 18–19). Enslaved Africans applied these attributes to the invention of supernatural figures (also known as conjurers) who would circumvent the slavocracy and subvert the oppressive structure of the plantation system. Embodying elements of animal and cosmic tricksters, individuals such as John the Conqueror were born and functioned as "mediational" characters between and within the spirit and material worlds. As Deidre Badejo emphasizes, such a figure became "man, animal, demi-god and Nature" all at once (5). The result was "not only a literary figure who dupes for self-aggrandizement but also one who challenges an established social order and probes the question of fate" (10). This character would later influence the "badman" folk heroic tradition, in which the trickster "responded to victimization with violence" (Roberts, 206).

A White Southerner who romanticized the slave system with the creation of the character of Uncle Remus, Joel Chandler Harris, best known for his *Uncle Remus* tales, became one of the first and best-known collectors of trickster tales. Despite their emphasis on comic elements that appeared to denigrate slaves, the tales received wide attention in the nineteenth century; and their popularization resulted in the recognition of the African origins of the tales and of the trickster figure as a hero in African (and later African American) folk expression. Charles Waddell Chesnutt's *The Conjure Woman* (1899) further added to the interest in tricksters and conjurers in Southern folklore. Modern retellings of particular tales featuring the trickster figure include

Zora Neale Hurston's *Mules and Men* (1935) and Julius Lester's *Black Folktales* (1969).

The trickster figure continues to be used by contemporary writers and intellectuals. For example, poets such as Kamau Brathwaite and Louise Bennett have included references to Anansi the spider god in their verses. The novelist Toni Morrison rewrites the tale of Brer Rabbit and the tar baby in *Tar Baby* (1981), and Erna Brodber focuses on the supernatural communicative powers of tricksters within Black folk communities in *Myal* (1988) and *Louisiana* (1994). Finally, such literary theorists as Jay Edwards and Henry Louis Gates Jr. with his theory of "signifyin(g)," have highlighted the complex structures of trickster tales and the subversive elements in the language used by trickster figures in such narratives from the African oral tradition to the modern literary one.

Deonne N. Minto

See also: Chesnutt, Charles Waddell; Folklore; Gates, Henry Louis, Jr.; Reed, Ishmael.

Resources

Barbara Babcock-Abrahams, "'A Tolerated Margin of Mess': The Trickster and His Tales Reconsidered," *Journal of the Folklore Institute* 2 (1975), 147–186; Deidre L. Badejo, "The Yoruba and Afro-American Trickster: A Contextual Comparison," *Présence Africaine* 147, no. 3 (1988), 3–17; Jay Edwards, *The Afro-American Trickster Tale: A Structural Analysis* (Bloomington: Folklore Publications Group, Indiana University, 1978), 9–13; Arthur Huff Fauset, "American Negro Folk Literature," in *The New Negro*, ed. Alain Locke (New York: Albert and Charles Boni, 1925), 238–244; Henry Louis Gates Jr., *The Signifying Monkey: A Theory of Afro-American Literary Criticism* (New York: Oxford University Press, 1988); Robert Hemenway, "Introduction: Author, Teller, and Hero," in *Uncle Remus: His Songs and Sayings*, by Joel Chandler Harris (1880; repr. New York: Penguin, 1982), 7–31; Gretchen Martin, *Dancing on the Color Line: African American Tricksters in Nineteenth-Century American Literature* (Jackson, MS: University Press of Mississippi, 2015); Babacar M'Baye, *The Trickster Comes West: Pan-African Influence in Early Black Diasporan Narratives* (Jackson, MS: University Press of Mississippi, 2009); Annie Reed, "Brer Rabbit and the Briar Patch," in *Talk That Talk: An Anthology of African-American Storytelling*, ed. Linda Goss and Marian E. Barnes (New York: Simon and Schuster, 1989), 30–31; John W. Roberts, *From Trickster to Badman: The Black Folk Hero in Slavery and Freedom* (Philadelphia: University of Pennsylvania Press, 1989); Robert Farris Thompson, *Flash of the Spirit: African and Afro-American Art and Philosophy* (New York: Vintage Books, 1984); Roger M. Valade III, "Trickster Tale," in *The Essential Black Literature Guide* (Detroit: Visible Ink Press, 1996), 361.

Troupe, Quincy Thomas, Jr. (1943–)

Poet, editor, educator, and biographer. Quincy Troupe is best known for award-winning poetry, which blends jazz and be-bop rhythms, cadences, and language in order to explore social justice issues connected with being a person of color and, in particular, an African American man. Troupe has received the National Endowment for the Arts Award in Poetry (1978) and has twice won the American Book Award from the Association of American Publishers (in 1980 for *Snake-back Solos* and in 1990 for *Miles: The Autobiography*). He won the Peabody Award in 1991 for coproducing and writing *The Miles Davis Radio Project*, and he has twice been the winner of the World Heavyweight Championship Poetry Bout at the Taos

Poetry Circus. In 1972, Troupe was awarded a $10,000 International Institute of Education travel grant, which he used to visit Senegal, Ivory Coast, Guinea, Ghana, and Nigeria. He also received a $6,000 grant from the New York State Council of the Arts in 1979. In 2002, he was named the first Poet Laureate of California; he subsequently resigned from the post and from his faculty position at the University of California at San Diego in response to controversy surrounding his falsification of his bachelor's degree on his curriculum vitae.

Quincy Troupe was born on July 23, 1943, to Dorothy Marshall and Quincy Troupe Sr., a Negro League baseball player. He grew up in St. Louis, Missouri, and later moved to Louisiana and then to Los Angeles, California. In 1964, he published his first poem, "What Is a Black Man?" in *Paris Match*. In Los Angeles, he taught creative writing for the Watts Writers' movement from 1966 until 1968, and, in 1968, he published the anthology *Watts Poets: A Book of New Poetry and Essays*. He also served as associate editor of *Shrewd* magazine that year and taught creative writing at the University of California at Los Angeles and the University of Southern California. He has also taught creative writing and literature at Ohio University, where he was the founding editor of *Confrontation: A Journal of Third World Literature*, which published works by Chinua Achebe, Toni Cade Bambara, Audre Lorde, Herberto Padilla, Amos Tutuola, and Alice Walker, among others. Troupe also edited *American Rag*. He subsequently taught creative writing and literature classes at Richmond College, Columbia University, the University of California at Berkeley, California State University at Sacramento, the University of Ghana at Legon, and the University of California at San Diego.

In 1975, Troupe and Rainer Schulte edited the acclaimed *Giant Talk: An Anthology of Third World Writings*, a volume that includes poetry, folktales, short stories, and novel excerpts from African American, African, Native American, Caribbean, and Latin American authors. Troupe and Schulte identify as Third World writers "those who identify with the historically exploited segment of mankind who confront the establishment on their behalf" (Slater).

Troupe's earliest poetic influences were Pablo Neruda, John Joseph Rabearivello, Aimé Césaire, Cesar Vallejo, Jean Toomer, and Sterling A. Brown. A *Publishers Weekly* review of Troupe's collection of poetry *Avalanche* noted that his poetry often manifests as a "cold, smacking, 'rush of objects.'" Troupe's first collection dedicated entirely to his own poetry, *Embryo, 1967–1971*, published in 1972, includes the poem "Impressions/of Chicago: For Howlin' Wolf," which demonstrates his flurry of music imagery and metaphor. In 1978, he published *Snake-back Solos: Selected Poems, 1969–1977*. Imagery of music saturates the collection and contributes to the varied tones in the poetry.

Troupe's other volumes of poetry include *Skulls Along the River* (1984); *Weather Reports: New and Selected Poems* (1991); *Avalanche: Poems* (1996); *Choruses: Poems* (1999); *Take It to the Hoop, Magic Johnson* (2000); *Transcircularities: New and Selected Poems* (2002); *Little Stevie Wonder* (2005); *The Architecture of Language* (2006); and *Errançities* (2012). In addition to the poetry collections, Troupe wrote *The Inside Story of TV's "Roots"* (with David L. Wolper), which explores the story behind the Alex Haley novel and subsequent miniseries (1978), and *Soundings* (1988), a collection of essays. He edited *James Baldwin: The Legacy* (1989), a collection of tributes from famous writers and others, compiled after James Baldwin's death, and he recorded Baldwin's poetry for the Library of Congress on two separate occasions. In 1989, Troupe and Miles Davis wrote the critically acclaimed *Miles: The Autobiography*. Troupe garnered the American Book Award for *Miles* and attracted a new throng of admirers. He went on to write *Miles and Me*, his reflections on interviewing Miles Davis for the autobiography. Douglas Henry Daniels of the *African American Review* called the book an "invaluable work." Troupe co-wrote *The Pursuit of Happyness* (2006) with Chris Gardner, and he has published numerous articles in magazines and journals.

Alicia Kester

See also: Jazz in Literature.

Resources

Jan Garden Castro, "Quincy Troupe: An Interview," *American Poetry Review* 34, no. 2 (2005), 49–57; Horace Coleman, "Quincy Thomas Troupe, Jr.," in *Dictionary of Literary Biography*, vol. 41, *Afro-American Poets Since 1955*, ed. Trudier Harris and Thadious M. Davis (Detroit: Gale, 1985), 334–338; Douglas Henry Daniels, "Review of *Miles and Me*," *African American Review* 35, no. 1 (Spring 2001), 152–153; Tom Dent, "Snake-Back Solos," *Freedomways* 20 (Second Quarter 1980), 104–107; Chris Gardner and Quincy Troupe, *The Pursuit Happyness* (New York: Amistad, 2006); Henry Louis Gates Jr. and Nellie Y. McKay, eds., *The Norton Anthology of African American Literature* (New York: Norton, 1979), 2002–2007; Michael Harper: Review of *Avalanche*, *Publishers Weekly*, March 18, 1996, p. 66; "Review of *Snake-back Solos*," *New York Times Book Review*, October 21, 1979, pp. 18–21; "Quincy (Thomas) Troupe, (Jr.)," in *Contemporary Authors*, New Revision Series, vol. 126 (Detroit: Gale, 2004), 403–408; Jack Slater, "Review of *Giant Talk*," *New York Times Book Review*, November 30, 1975, pp. 56–57; Quincy Troupe: *The Architecture of Language* (Minneapolis, MN: Coffee House Press, 2006); *Avalanche: Poems* (Minneapolis, MN: Coffee House Press, 1996); *Choruses* (Minneapolis, MN: Coffee House Press, 1999); *Embryo Poems, 1967–1971* (New York: Barlenmir, 1972); *Errançities* (Minneapolis, MN: Coffee House Press, 2012); *Little Stevie Wonder* (Boston: Houghton Mifflin, 2005); *Miles and Me* (Berkeley, CA: University of California Press, 2000); *Skulls along the River* (New York: I. Reed Books, 1984); *Snake-Back Solos: Selected Poems, 1969–1977* (New York: I. Reed Books, 1978); *Soundings* (New York: Writers & Readers, 1988); *Take It to the Hoop, Magic Johnson* (New York: Jump at the Sun, 2000); *Transcircularities: New and Selected Poems* (Minneapolis, MN: Coffee House Press, 2002); *Weather Reports: New and Selected Poems* (New York: Writers & Readers, 1991); Quincy Troupe, ed.: *James Baldwin: The Legacy* (New York: Simon & Schuster, 1989); *Watts Poets: A Book of New Poetry and Essays* (Los Angeles: House of Respect, 1968); Quincy Troupe and Miles Davis, *Miles: The Autobiography* (New York: Simon & Schuster, 1989); Quincy Troupe and Rainer Schulte, eds., *Giant Talk: An Anthology of Third World Writings* (New York: Random House, 1975); Quincy Troupe and David L. Wolper, *The Inside Story of TV's "Roots"* (New York: Warner Books, 1978); Mel Watins, "Hard Times for Black Writers," *New York Times Book Review*, February 21, 1981, pp. 3, 26.

Truth, Sojourner (1797–1883)

Itinerant preacher, abolitionist, feminist, social reformer, and singer. Sojourner Truth is best known for her speech "Ain't I a Woman?," delivered in May 1851 to the Women's Rights Convention in Akron, Ohio. Born into a slave-owning Dutch family in Ulster County, New York, probably in

1797, Truth was originally known as Isabella Baumfree. She was sold away from her parents at the age of nine. She was later married to a fellow slave named Thomas and birthed five children. In 1826, a year before slavery was outlawed in New York, she left the house of her master, Mr. Dumont, where she had experienced physical and sexual abuse and, with one of her children, found shelter with Isaac and Maria Van Wagenen. She worked as their domestic servant and successfully sued for the custody of another of her children who had been illegally sold into the South as a slave. The Van Wagenens paid her old master for the services of Truth and her child. She was known as Isabella Van Wagenen from this point until about 1843.

After her conversion to Christianity by way of a visitation from God, she dedicated her life to God's work, at first "under the influence of Millerite Second Adventism" (Painter, "Sojourner Truth," 738). She moved to New York City in 1828 with her son. During her fourteen years there, Truth joined various churches but left that "Sodom" at God's command to go east as an evangelist (Gilbert). She set forth, with fairly traditional Christian beliefs, to "set the world right side up." She met Olive Gilbert, an abolitionist, feminist, and friend of William Lloyd Garrison of the abolitionist movement. Gilbert recorded Truth's story in *The Narrative of Sojourner Truth: A Bondswoman of Olden Time*, published in Boston in 1850. Proceeds from the sale of the book helped maintain Truth's family financially. The sale of her photograph also earned income. She often said, "I sell the shadow to support the substance" (Samra).

Although the veracity of the account of her 1851 Akron speech, as transcribed by Frances D. Gage, the President of the Women's Rights Convention, has been questioned, this address established Truth's role as a cultural icon (Sánchez-Eppler; Samra). (Painter credits Gage with turning "ain't I a woman?" into a "refrain" in Truth's speeches in 1863 ["Sojourner Truth", 738]). Truth's lifelong illiteracy was, she said, the result of slavery, which robbed her of an education. In such statements as "I can tell you I can't read a book, but I can read de people" (Mabee and Newhouse), however, Truth occasionally revised the traditional notion of literacy. Because her speeches and her narrative were actually written by others, the authenticity of the accounts has sometimes been in question (Humez). Depending upon who transcribed Truth's autobiographical accounts and speeches, Truth's dialect may appear Northern or Southern, her views informed or uninformed.

In 1853, Truth and her grandson, Samuel Banks, made an uninvited visit to Harriet Beecher Stowe in Andover, Massachusetts, remaining for several days. Stowe later recorded her impressions in "Sojourner Truth, the Libyan Sibyl," an article published a decade later in *The Atlantic Monthly* (Stowe; Terry; Lebedun). Its subtitle refers to a statue inspired by Truth and sculpted by William Wetmore Story that was displayed at the World's Fair in London in 1862. Stowe records her conversations with and impressions of Truth's striking stature (she stood nearly six feet tall) and powerful personal presence. Truth informed Stowe that her name used to be Isabella but that when she left "the house of bondage," the Lord renamed her Sojourner Truth because of her mission as a traveling, truth-declaring preacher. God made her, she says, "a sign unto this nation" of the sins against her people. In 1857, drawn to a Quaker-related group of reformers living in Battle Creek, Michigan, Truth moved there from

Northampton, Massachusetts. From the 1850s to the 1870s, she continued to advocate at various meetings and rallies for the rights of African Americans and women. In 1864, a year after the Emancipation Proclamation, Truth visited Washington, DC, "to see the freedmen of [her] people." On October 29 of that year, she met with President Lincoln at the White House. The nature of their discussion and Lincoln's attitude toward Truth remain a matter of dispute. She thereafter worked with freed slaves in Washington, resettling some with her own money in Rochester, New York, and Battle Creek, Michigan. Scandalized that freed Blacks were still relying on the government in 1870, she promoted their education so that they might be better able to support themselves. She was also in favor of their settlement in the West, based on the model of the Indian reservation. She kicked off a resettlement campaign in February 1870 and toured New England and the mid-Atlantic states, collecting signatures in its support. The campaign was not successful.

Although Truth was reputed to have been involved with the Underground Railroad, no evidence for this claim exists. Tragically, Truth's grandson, Samuel Banks, died in 1875 at the age of twenty-four, depriving Truth of a beloved traveling companion. Truth also experienced severe health difficulties at this time, including the paralysis of her right side and permanent gangrenous ulcers on her legs. Frances Titus, a New England Quaker who also worked to bring freed slaves to Battle Creek, helped support Truth financially and assisted in revising her *Narrative*. The 1875 edition includes Truth's "Book of Life," a compendium of clippings and letters from her scrapbooks. Although Titus preserved these documents, which scholars have used, she also romanticized Truth, misrepresented various crucial dates,

and poorly edited older documents. She did, however, endorse Truth's argument that the nation owed Blacks a debt for having profited for generations from their unpaid labor.

In her last years, Truth lived with her daughters in Battle Creek, Michigan, where she frequently had visitors. After several months of intense suffering, she died there before dawn on November 26, 1883. Nearly a thousand people attended her funeral, and some of Battle Creek's most prominent citizens acted as pallbearers. Titus's 1884 edition of Truth's *Narrative* includes a "Memorial Chapter." In one of the tributes to her in that chapter, Frederick Douglass describes Truth as "Venerable for age, distinguished for insight into human nature, remarkable for independence and courageous self-assertion, devoted to the welfare of her race, . . . [and] for the last forty years an object of respect and admiration to social reformers everywhere" (Gilbert, "Memorial Chapter" 14).

Carol Margaret Davison

See also: Feminism/Black Feminism; Protest Literature.

Resources

Olive Gilbert, ed., *The Narrative of Sojourner Truth: A Bondswoman of Olden Time* (Battle Creek, MI: Review and Herald Office, 1884); Darcy Grimaldo Grigsby, *Enduring Truths: Sojourner's Shadows and Substance* (Chicago: University of Chicago Press, 2015); Jean M. Humez, "Reading *The Narrative of Sojourner Truth* as a Collaborative Text," *Frontiers: A Journal of Women Studies* 16, no. 1 (1996), 29–52; Jean Lebedun, "Harriet Beecher Stowe's Interest in Sojourner Truth, Black Feminist," *American Literature: A Journal of Literary History, Criticism, and Bibliography* 46, no. 3 (1974), 359–363; Carleton Mabee and Susan Mabee Newhouse, *Sojourner Truth: Slave, Prophet, Legend* (New York: New York University Press, 1993); Nell Irvin Painter: "Sojourner Truth," in *The Oxford Companion to African American Literature*, ed. William L. Andrews, Frances Smith Foster, and Trudier Harris (New York: Oxford University Press, 1997), 738; *Sojourner Truth: A Life, a Symbol* (New York: Norton, 1996); Isabelle Kinnard Richman, *Sojourner Truth: Prophet of Social Justice* (New York: Routledge, 2016); Matthew K. Samra, "Shadow and Substance: The Two Narratives of Sojourner Truth," *Midwest Quarterly: A Journal of Contemporary Thought* 38, no. 2 (1997), 158–171; Karen Sánchez-Eppler, "Ain't I a Symbol," review of Nell Irvin Painter, *Sojourner Truth*, *American Quarterly* 50, no. 1 (1998), 149–157; Harriet Beecher Stowe, "Sojourner Truth, the Libyan Sibyl," *The Atlantic Monthly* 11 (1863), 473–481; Esther Terry, "Sojourner Truth: The Person Behind the Libyan Sibyl," *Massachusetts Review: Quarterly of Literature, the Arts, and Public Affairs* 26, nos. 2–3 (1985), 425–444; Margaret Washington, *Sojourner Truth's America* (Urbana, IL: University of Illinois Press, 2009).

Tubman, Harriet Ross (ca. 1820–1913)

Escaped slave, conductor on the Underground Railroad, Union Army spy and scout, nurse, and activist. Harriet Tubman was born Araminta Ross on the Brodas plantation in Dorchester County, Maryland, to parents who were descended from the Ashanti tribe of West Africa. She later changed her name to Harriet, her mother's name. At around the age of five, she became a house servant, and later a field slave. Her master often "sold her out" to other plantations, and she was beaten regularly (Shaw). An overseer struck her on the head with a two-pound weight when she tried to defend a fleeing slave at the age of twelve. From then on, she suffered from narcoleptic seizures or blackouts (Shaw). In 1844, when she was about twenty-five years old, she married John Tubman, a free African American man. She worked as a slave by day but was allowed to stay with her husband at night.

Despite her injuries, Tubman was a strong and capable woman who could navigate by the stars and practice wood-crafting because of her former fieldwork. These skills came in handy when she escaped from slavery in 1849 and went to Philadelphia, Pennsylvania, because she heard that she was about to be sold following her master's death. Tubman did not tell her husband about her plans because she knew he would turn her in (Shaw). The only person she told was her sister. Eventually, she settled in Auburn, New York, among many supporters of the abolitionist movement. Because she wanted other slaves to be free as well, Tubman saved money and came back to the South approximately nineteen times as a conductor on the Underground Railroad. The Railroad consisted of a group of African Americans and White Americans who helped slaves escaped to the North through a series of tunnels, dirt roads, and hidden rooms in homes. Over the next ten years, Tubman personally helped free about 300 slaves, including all her family members, and she never lost an escapee. On her third trip back home to help slaves escape, she went to get her husband, only to discover he had remarried and did not want to leave with her. She nonchalantly moved on to free others.

Tubman's success rate had to do with her strategic planning, wit, and courage. All her escapes occurred on Saturday nights because she knew the slave owners could not put up Wanted posters until Monday. Tubman went undetected because she seemed to be a harmless woman who walked and sang songs, when in fact she usually carried a gun. The songs' lyrics contained clues alerting slaves that she came to help them escape.

Known as "The Moses of Her People," she was such a threat that slave owners offered a $40,000 reward for her capture. However, Tubman was never captured, because of her ingenuity. Once she escaped capture by pretending to read her own Wanted poster. One legend claims that she had a narcoleptic blackout underneath one of her Wanted posters and never realized it.

To end slavery, Tubman worked with such abolitionists as Frederick Douglass and William Still. Fortunately, Tubman was too ill to participate in the doomed raid on Harper's Ferry with John Brown in 1859. Later that year, she was physically assaulted by the police when she helped a runaway slave named Charles Nalle escape to Canada. During the Civil War, Tubman's duties as a Union spy, scout, and nurse made her a major asset. On June 2, 1863, she organized and led the Combahee River raid in South Carolina that freed more than 750 slaves. It remains the only military raid in U.S. history that was planned and led by a woman. Even though Tubman fought valiantly for the Union cause, she was denied a pension for many years.

After the Civil War ended, Tubman settled with her family back in Auburn and married Nelson Davis in 1870. They lived together until his death eighteen years later. With Tubman's cooperation and assistance, Sarah Elizabeth Bradford wrote Tubman's biography, *Scenes in the Life of Harriet Tubman*, in 1869. Tubman tried to build a home for elderly ex-slaves in Auburn with the profits from this book and her military pension. Eventually, for lack of funds, she gave the land to the African Methodist Episcopal Zion Church, which completed the home in 1908. She later moved into the home, which today is known as the Harriet Tubman Home. Besides this endeavor, Tubman tried to establish schools in North Carolina for free Blacks and fought for many social issues such as women's rights. Tubman died of pneumonia, at around the age of ninety-three, on March 10, 1913. She was buried with military honors in Auburn's Fort Hill Cemetery. Shortly after her death, a bronze plaque was placed at the Cayuga County Courthouse and a civic holiday was declared in her honor. In 1944, Eleanor Roosevelt christened a ship *Harriet Tubman*. The U.S. postal service issued stamps to honor her in 1978 and 1995. Numerous books about her and a 1978 movie, *A Woman Called Moses*, have celebrated Tubman's life.

Tubman's bravery and ingenuity, as she worked against seemingly staggering odds, make her an American hero. She freed herself and other African Americans. Many regard her feats as timeless and inspirational.

Devona Mallory

See also: Feminism/Black Feminism.

Resources

Susan Altman: "Harriet Tubman," in *Encyclopedia of African-American Heritage* (New York: Facts on File, 2001); "Harriet Tubman," *The New York History Net: The Harriet Tubman Home*, http://www.nyhistory.com/harriettubman/life.htm; "Harriet Tubman: A Legacy of Resistance" (Special Issue), *Meridians: Feminism, Race, Transnationalism* 12, no. 2 (2014); K. B. Shaw, "Harriet Tubman," *SPECTRUM Home & School Magazine*, http://www.incwell.com/Spectrum.html; Paul Wendkos, dir., *A Woman Called Moses* (New York: Xenon 2 Studios, 1978; VHS format, 1999).

V

Vernacular

For African American communities, the term "vernacular" usually refers to the language used by many African Americans in a comfortable setting. This variety of language is often called African American Vernacular English (AAVE), Black English (BE), Ebonics, or Non-standard English. Although in some contexts these terms are synonymous, the more accepted terms are AAVE and BE. The term "Ebonics," linguistically, does not necessarily mean the English spoken by African Americans—although in recent years the general population has made that association. It was coined by Robert Williams and a group of other Black linguists in 1973 at a conference on language development in Black children and refers to the similarity in the way languages of the African diaspora sound. (The African diaspora is the term used for the scattering of Black people throughout the world as a result of the slave trade.) Although not all the slaves taken from Africa speak the same language, the sound systems of their languages were similar, influencing the language used by descendants of African slaves, to which the name Ebonics refers—Ebony + phonics.

The use of "Ebonics" became popularly recognizable in 1996 when the Oakland, California, School Board attempted to pass the Ebonics Resolution, which addressed language-variation issues and their impact on the learning environment. Since then, the terms AAVE and Ebonics have become almost synonymous; however, their meanings are strikingly different linguistically. To a general audience, Ebonics carries a more negative connotation: language that is looked down upon or language of an uneducated group of people. The use of the term often connotes a negative image of Black people incapable of speaking Standard English. AAVE, on the other hand, does not always conjure up such negative feelings in the general population. Linguistically, however, neither of these terms has negative implications; they are just terms used to help describe variations in language use.

Vernacular, AAVE, or BE is neither slang nor incorrect language. Linguistically speaking, there is no such thing as incorrect language, because as long as someone is talking and is being understood by the person listening, communication occurs between speaker and listener—making language neither wrong nor right. Standardized rules that seem to govern language (e.g., do not use double negatives) are only prescriptive, meaning that someone at some time decided to add this rule to language. However, it is not a rule at all, but a way of evaluating language, for a rule of language is a feature that, if violated, renders the language unable to be understood. Avoiding double negatives is not a rule for English. For example, the use of double or even multiple negatives does not make the sentence positive, but instead makes it even more negative. Consider for a moment the sentence "There is no tea." This clearly means no tea is available, which is obvious by the one negative in the sentence. Now consider the sentence "We don't have no tea." The use of two negatives in this sentence does not make it positive. There is still no tea. However, the second sentence seems to show more of a negative sentiment. The use of a double negative does not make the sentence less understandable, but it does place the sentence in a different variety of language, one that might be called the vernacular.

Many would consider the use of double negatives as incorrect grammar or as slang. It is not incorrect grammar but a grammatical construction that is not considered *standard*. Because it is still understandable, it is not grammatically incorrect. For something to be grammatically incorrect, it cannot be understood by listeners. Slang is not the use of incorrect grammar and is not a variety of English on its own; slang words or phrases can be used within any variety that is spoken. Therefore, one could use slang with a more formal variety of language or, more commonly, in a casual setting when the vernacular is being used.

Most linguists suggest that African Americans, in a broad sense, speak differently from White Americans, even if this difference is noticeable only in the vernacular. Not all African Americans speak AAVE, however. Moreover, not all speakers of AAVE are African American. People can often tell a person's ethnicity by the way he or she speaks without even seeing the person. That recognition of ethnicity or culture without visual representation is not insulting, but it does acknowledge that there are variations in language based on race or culture. Rickford and Rickford state emphatically, "The fact is that most African Americans *do* talk differently from whites and Americans of other ethnic groups, or at least most of us [African Americans] can when we want to. And the fact is that most Americans, Black and white, know this to be true" (4). The question, therefore, becomes what distinguishes African American speech from that of White Americans. In other words, what is AAVE? The descriptions of AAVE are not always positive. H. L. Menken declared that AAVE "may be called the worst English in the world" (cited in Smitherman, 74). Other early critics of AAVE have called it "baby talk," "infantile English," and "slovenly and careless" (75). Although most current descriptions are less caustic, negative attitudes toward AAVE still exist. The effort to recognize the language of African Americans as something other than deficient and substandard has resulted in countless studies that have deconstructed AAVE into its most salient features. Still, supporters of the language have found it difficult to define exactly what AAVE is, though it is clear why people use this form of vernacular.

People of any culture use their vernacular variety for a number of reasons. First, people tend to use the vernacular because it is the language they learned at home. It is the language their family and friends use when they are at ease with each other. It is a language that people do not have to worry about "getting right" because it is their first language, so it comes naturally. A vernacular "retains the associations of warmth and closeness for the many . . . who first learn it from their mothers and fathers and other family members; it expresses camaraderie and solidarity among friends" (Rickford and Rickford, 10).

Therefore, it is not surprising that some writers of African American literature would use the vernacular in the development of characters. The use of vernacular in literature is a stylistic choice. Vernacular has been used in fiction by many, from early African American writers to contemporary ones. The use of the vernacular in writing has many purposes. It can connect a character to a social group or location without the author having to explicitly give the reader the information. Using the vernacular helps authors make their characters more real and believable, and therefore is used often. However, the use of vernacular in writing is not a formalized or standardized process. Often, writers attempt to represent the speech of the characters they create in inventive and individual ways. They use variations of English spelling because vernacular is difficult to represent with standardized English spelling, and they take liberties with how they present the vernacular. Therefore, the representation of the vernacular varies by text and by author.

The vernacular is used in many ways and for many purposes. It can help give characters personality beyond what the author describes. It can also help readers connect and identify with characters. When authors incorporate the vernacular in their texts, they do so purposefully. On the other hand, the use of the vernacular in everyday life might not always be so intentional. People use the vernacular when they are in comfortable settings and know their language is not being judged. This switch is often not noticeable; sometimes, however, it can be very intentional. People often switch their language to the vernacular to show solidarity with other speakers or to make it obvious to others where they come from, what their experiences have been, and with whom they identify. Despite the reasons for using the vernacular, one thing is clear: the vernacular of everyday people is a true and correct language and is worthy of recognition.

Iyabo F. Osiapem

See also: Baraka, Amiri; Black Arts Movement; Blues Poetry; Chesnutt, Charles Waddell; Dialect Poetry; Dunbar, Paul Laurence; Folklore; Hip-Hop; Hughes, Langston; Hurston, Zora Neale; Major, Clarence; Performance Poetry; Rap.

Resources

Katherine Clay Bassard, "The Significance of Signifying: Vernacular Theory and the Creation of Early African American Literary Study," *Early American Literature* 50, no. 3 (2015), 849–854; Arna Bontemps, "A Summer Tragedy," in *African American Literature: An Anthology of Nonfiction, Fiction, Poetry, and Drama*, ed. D. A. Worley and Jesse Perry (Lincolnwood, IL: National Textbook Company, 1993), 40–49; Ernest J. Gaines, *A Lesson Before Dying* (New York: Knopf, 1993); Zora Neale Hurston, *Mules and Men* (1935; repr. Bloomington: Indiana University Press, 1978); Hans Ostrom, *A Langston Hughes Encyclopedia* (Westport, CT: Greenwood Press, 2002); A. Philip Randolph and Chandler Owen, "The Steel Drivin' Man," in *African American Literature: An Anthology of Nonfiction, Fiction, Poetry, and Drama*, ed. D. A. Worley and Jesse Perry (Lincolnwood, IL: National Textbook Company, 1993), 72–77; J. R. Rickford and R. J. Rickford, *Spoken Soul: The Story of Black English* (New York: Wiley, 2000); Ntozake Shange, "one thing i dont need," in *African American Literature: An Anthology of Nonfiction, Fiction, Poetry, and Drama*, ed. D. A. Worley and Jesse Perry (Lincolnton, IL: National Textbook Company, 1993), 154–157; G. Smitherman, *Talkin' That Talk: Language, Culture, and Education in African America* (New York: Routledge, 2000).

W

Walker, Alice (1944–)

Novelist, essayist, poet, literary critic, and activist. Born in Eatonton, Georgia, Alice Malsenior Walker was the youngest of eight children born to sharecroppers Willie Lee and Minnie Grant Walker. As a young child, Walker was blinded in one eye when one of her brothers shot her with a BB gun. After this incident, her exuberance was replaced with a quiet retreat into literature and writing. Early on, Walker was greatly influenced by Russian novelists such as Dostoyevsky, Gogol, and Tolstoy. She read them as if "they were a delicious cake" (Gentry, 33). Walker studied at Spelman College for her first two years of undergraduate school (1961–1963). However, she knew that her need to react politically to the mistreatment of Blacks was at odds with the aims of Spelman. Consequently, she transferred to Sarah Lawrence College in Bronxville, New York, where she earned a bachelor's degree in 1965. Her first book of poems, *Once* (1968), was written during her senior year at Sarah Lawrence after she had experienced thoughts of suicide and undergone an abortion. Walker's mentor, the poet and professor Muriel Rukeyser, helped Walker publish her first volume of poetry.

Walker was active in the Civil Rights Movement of the 1960s, and, in 1967, she married civil rights attorney Mel Leventhal. Soon thereafter, the couple moved to Mississippi to volunteer with the voter-registration drives. They were the only interracial married couple in their community. That same year, Walker received a McDowell

Fellowship, which allowed her to complete her first novel, *The Third Life of Grange Copeland* (1970). From 1968 to 1972, she was a writer-in-residence and professor of women's studies at Jackson State University, Tougaloo College, and Wellesley College. Later, Walker published a collection of short stories, *In Love and Trouble* (1973). She published a children's book titled *Langston Hughes: American Poet* (1974), a biography of the Harlem Renaissance poet, whom she had met during her college years. Hughes also helped Walker publish her first short story, "To Hell with Dying."

Walker was instrumental in recovering the lost works of another crucial participant in the Harlem Renaissance, Zora Neale Hurston. At Wellesley, Walker began to notice certain Black women writers who were shrouded in obscurity. She was particularly taken with Hurston's use of the vernacular. In spite of her success as a writer, Hurston had died poor and was buried in an unmarked grave in the Garden of Heavenly Peace Cemetery in Florida. In 1973, Walker journeyed to the gravesite and placed a marker on what she believed was Hurston's grave in Fort Pierce, Florida. The marker lauded Hurston a "genius of the south." Walker published an essay in *Ms.* magazine entitled "In Search of Zora Neale Hurston" (1974), detailing her experiences resurrecting Hurston's lost works. Today, all of Hurston's major works are again in print, due largely to Walker's efforts. Walker published another novel, *Meridian* (1976), which dealt with the Civil Rights Movement. Several years later, she edited a

Zora Neal Hurston reader titled *I Love Myself When I Am Laughing ... and Then Again When I Am Looking Mean & Impressive* (1979). Walker published a book of short stories, *You Can't Keep a Good Woman Down*, in 1981.

While these works received good critical notices, it was Walker's third novel, *The Color Purple* (1982), that made her a widely acclaimed, internationally known writer. The novel was nominated for the National Book Critics Circle Award, won the American Book Award, and won the Pulitzer Prize for fiction. *The Color Purple* is told in a series of letters written by Celie, the novel's heroine, to God and to her younger sister, Nettie. In the novel, Celie is a poor Black woman who is raped by her father and beaten by her husband. However, despite these hardships, Celie prevails in the end by finding both her own independent voice and strength in other female characters in the novel, Sophia and Shug Avery. By the end of the novel, the men in the story are transformed, and healing begins for Celie. Despite the popularity of this work, Walker received some harsh criticism. The harshest came from critics who focused on the allegedly stereotypical manner in which Black men are portrayed in the work (Early; Harris). Critics chided Walker for her portrayal of men as overly aggressive and violent. Others focused on what they perceived to be Walker's failure to produce a historically accurate novel (Early).

The Color Purple was adapted into a film by Steven Spielberg and released in 1985. It received eleven Academy Award nominations, including a Best Picture nomination; a Best Supporting Actress nomination for Oprah Winfrey in her role as Sophia; and a Best Actress nomination for Whoopi Goldberg for her role as Celie. About ten years after the release of the film version, Walker wrote *The Same River Twice: Honoring the Difficult* (1996). Here she details some of her disappointment with the critics' reception of the novel and film, and she explains how her own screenplay adaptation of the novel was not accepted by Spielberg.

Walker later published *Living by the Word: Selected Writings, 1973–1977* (1988), a collection of essays, and *The Temple of My Familiar* (1989), a romantic novel. Her other novel, *Possessing the Secret of Joy* (1992), underscores Walker's activism with woman's issues, namely, the brutality of female genital mutilation practices, particularly in Africa. Walker published a second book on this subject, *Warrior Marks: Female Genital Mutilation Practices and the Sexual Blinding of Women* (1993). Walker's other works include: *By the Light of My Father's Smile* (1998); *The Way Forward Is with a Broken Heart* (2000); *Sent by Earth: A Message from the Grandmother Spirit after the Bombing of the World Trade Center and the Pentagon* (2001); the novel *Now Is the Time to Open Your Heart* (2004); the poetry collections *Hard Times Require Furious Dancing: New Poems* (2010) and *Taking the Arrow Out of the Heart* (2018); and the memoir *The Chicken Chronicles* (2012).

Among Walker's many awards, in addition to the Pulitzer Prize, include: the Lillian Smith Award from the National Endowment for the Arts; the Rosenthal Award from the National Institute of Arts and Letters; a nomination for the National Book Award; a Radcliffe Institute Fellowship; a Merrill Fellowship; a Guggenheim Fellowship; a Townsend Prize; a Lynhurst Prize; the Front Page Award for best magazine criticism from the Newswoman's Club of New York; a Global Exchange's Domestic Human Rights Award; and a LennonOno Grant for Peace.

Gail L. Upchurch-Mills

See also: Feminism/Black Feminism; Lesbian Literature; Novel.

Resources

Primary Sources: Alice Walker: *By the Light of My Father's Smile* (New York: Random House, 1998); *The Chicken Chronicles: Sitting with the Angels Who Have Returned with My Memories: Glorious, Rufus, Gertrude Stein, Splendor, Hortensia, Agnes of God, the Gladyses, & Babe: A Memoir* (New York: The New Press, 2012); *The Color Purple* (New York: Harcourt Brace Jovanovich, 1982); *Hard Times Require Furious Dancing: New Poems* (Novato, CA: New World Library, 2010); *In Love and Trouble* (New York: Harcourt Brace Jovanovich, 1973); *In Search of Our Mothers' Gardens* (San Diego, CA: Harcourt Brace Jovanovich, 1983); "In Search of Zora Neale Hurston," *Ms.* 3 (March 1975), 74–90; *Langston Hughes: Poet* (New York: Crowell, 1974); *Living by the Word: Selected Writings, 1973–1977* (San Diego, CA: Harcourt Brace Jovanovich, 1988); *Meridian* (New York: Harcourt Brace Jovanovich, 1976); *Now Is the Time to Open Your Heart* (New York: Random House, 2004); *Once* (New York: Harcourt, Brace, and World, 1968); *Possessing the Secret of Joy* (New York: Harcourt Brace Jovanovich, 1992); *The Same River Twice: Honoring the Difficult* (New York: Scribner's, 1996); *Sent by Earth: A Message from the Grandmother Spirit after the Bombing of the World Trade Center and the Pentagon* (New York: Seven Stories Press, 2001); *Taking the Arrow Out of the Heart* (New York: 37 INK, 2018); *The Temple of My Familiar* (San Diego, CA: Harcourt Brace Jovanovich, 1989); *The Third Life of Grange Copeland* (New York: Harcourt Brace Jovanovich, 1970); *Warrior Marks: Female Genital Mutilation Practices and the Sexual Blinding of Women* (New York: Harcourt Brace, 1993); *The Way Forward Is with a Broken Heart* (New York: Random House, 2000); *You Can't Keep a Good Woman Down* (New York: Harcourt Brace Jovanovich, 1981); Alice Walker, ed., *I Love Myself When I Am Laughing ... and Then Again When I Am Looking Mean and Impressive* (Old Westbury, NY: Feminist Press, 1979).

Secondary Sources: Rudolph P. Bird, *The World Has Changed: Conversations with Alice Walker* (New York: The New Press, 2010); Gerald Early, "*The Color Purple* as Everybody's Protest Art," *Antioch Review* 44, no. 3 (1986), 261–275; Tony Gentry, *Alice Walker* (New York: Chelsea House, 1993); Trudier Harris, "On *The Color Purple*, Stereotypes, and Silence," *Black American Literature Forum* 18, no. 4 (1994), 155–161; Maria Lauret, *Alice Walker* (New York: Palgrave Macmillan, 2011); Evette Porter, "Absolute Alice," *Black Issues Book Review*, March/April 2003, 34–38; Gloria Wade-Gayles, "Black, Southern, Womanist: The Genius of Alice Walker," in *Southern Women Writers: The New Generation*, ed. Tonette Bond Inge (Tuscaloosa, AL: University of Alabama Press, 1990); Margaret Walsh, "The Enchanted World of *The Color Purple*," *Southern Quarterly* 25, no. 2 (1987), 89–101.

Walrond, Eric Derwent (1898–1966)

Short-story writer and essayist. Walrond was one of the great early writers of the West Indian diaspora, and like Claude McKay, he played a central role in the Harlem Renaissance before leaving the United States for Europe. Today he is known chiefly for one collection of ten stories, *Tropic Death* (1926), which along with McKay's *Gingertown*, Jean Toomer's *Cane*, and Langston Hughes's *The Ways of White Folks*, constitute the major short fiction collections of the Harlem Renaissance. Like the Jamaican native McKay, Walrond was a promoter of racial pride who incorporated primitivist elements in his work. He was not interested in publishing for the "Talented Tenth" of the African American community, and like McKay, he did not flinch from presenting topics, such as murder and prostitution, which some Black writers wished to avoid. Walrond, a pioneer in writing in West Indian dialects, used a vivid impressionistic style that carefully incorporated symbolist elements. Although he did write stories on New York City, most notably "Miss Kenny's Marriage" and "City Love," all the stories of *Tropic Death* are set in the Caribbean: British Guiana, Barbados, the Panama Canal Zone, and on shipboard. The plots are slight, and the characters too briefly described to escape being types. What is remarkable is the style, the creation of atmosphere, and the use of language to capture regional dialects. Walrond is excellent at portraying folk customs and the problems that develop around nationality, language, and race. He presents both the positive and the negative aspects of rural Caribbean life, and he never idealizes his Black and mulatto characters. He depicts African Americans as often subject to a self-defeating color consciousness, but he shows them holding on in the face of White exploitation as well.

Walrond was born in Georgetown, British Guiana. His father moved to the Canal Zone, deserting his family. Walrond's mother was an evangelical Protestant, and although he respected some elements of this tradition, he was not associated with it in later life. His early years were spent in Barbados, but then he moved with his mother to Panama, where she attempted to find her husband. After he came to the United States in 1918, Walrond was attracted to Marcus Garvey's Universal Negro Improvement Association and was an editor of his publication *The Negro World* from 1921 to 1923. Walrond studied at City College of New York (1922–1924) and at Columbia University (1924–1926) and spent a semester as a Zone Gale fellow at the University of Wisconsin (1928), but he never received a BA degree.

Walrond developed quickly as a writer, from short articles to sketches to short stories from 1925 to 1927 and was at the height of his powers in 1926 to 1928 when he left the United States to work on a book on the Panama Canal, which he was never able to complete. He traveled to the Canal Zone and then, after stopping in Haiti and the Dominican Republic, went on to France, where he stayed for several years, at one point joining Nancy Cunard's circle, before moving to England in 1932. Walrond lived in London from 1932 to 1939, when he moved to Bradford-on-Avon. From 1936 to 1938, he contributed short pieces to Marcus Garvey's periodical *Black Man*. He died in London of a heart attack in 1966. There is no biography of Walrond. Parascandola summarizes much of what is known about his life in his Introduction to *Winds Can Wake Up the Dead* (11–42).

Peter Glenn Christensen

See also: Harlem Renaissance; Novel.

Resources

Primary Sources: Louis J. Parascandola, ed., *Winds Can Wake Up the Dead: An Eric Walrond Reader* (Detroit: Wayne State University Press, 1998); Louis J. Parascandola and Carl A. Wade, eds., *In Search of Asylum: The Later Writings of Eric Walrond* (Gainesville, FL: University Press of Florida, 2011); Eric Walrond, *Tropic Death* (1926; repr. New York: Collier, 1972); Eric Walrond and Rosey E. Pool, eds., *Black and Unknown Bards: A Collection of Negro Poetry* (Aldington, UK: Hand & Flower Press, 1958, 1971; repr. Ann Arbor, MI: University Micro-films, 1991).

Secondary Sources: Cora Agatucci, "Eric Walrond," in *African American Authors, 1745–1945: A Bio-Bibliographical Critical Sourcebook*, ed. Emmanuel S. Nelson

(Westport, CT: Greenwood Press, 2000), 429–439; Jay Berry, "Eric Walrond," in *Dictionary of Literary Biography*, vol. 51, *Afro-American Writers from the Harlem Renaissance to 1940*, ed. Trudier Harris (Detroit: Gale, 1987), 296–300; Enid E. Bogle, "Eric Walrond," in *Fifty Caribbean Writers: A Bio-Bibliographical Critical Sourcebook*, ed. Daryl Cumber Dance (Westport, CT: Greenwood Press, 1986), 474–482; James C. Davis, *Eric Walrond: A Life in the Harlem Renaissance and the Transatlantic Caribbean* (New York: Columbia University Press, 2015); Tony Martin, "The Defectors—Eric Walrond and Claude McKay," in his *Literary Garveyism* (Dover, MA: Majority Press, 1983), 124–138; Kenneth Ramchand, "The Writer Who Ran Away: Eric Walrond and *Tropic Death*," *Savacou* (Kingston, Jamaica) 2 (September 1970), 67–75; Carl A. Wade, "African-American Aesthetics and the Fiction of Eric Walrond: *Tropic Death* and the Harlem Renaissance," *CLA Journal* 42, no. 4 (June 1999), 403–429.

Washington, Booker T. (1856–1915)

Autobiographer, orator, human rights advocate, and educator. Owing to his nonconfrontational approach to race relations and his belief that vocational training would allow African Americans to succeed in business as in life, Washington became one of the most influential leaders of the late nineteenth century. However, the late twentieth-century scholarly consensus, which is revealed, for example, in his being mentioned in only two passing citations in a *Publications of the Modern Languages Association* special issue on African American literature, casts him as a post-Reconstruction puppet who attempted to counteract the radicalism of rival Black leaders, including, but certainly not limited to, W.E.B. Du Bois. But this view of

Washington, as Mark Bauerlein has pointed out, overlooks larger historical contexts, including the realities and consequences of Jim Crow laws and other conditions with which African Americans had to contend. The view may also underestimate the extent to which Washington covertly sponsored activism and protest. Much of the information about Washington's life comes from his reflections on what he was able to achieve as a result of his unflagging effort and determination. *The Story of My Life and Work* (1896) was written primarily for Black readers and was sold door-to-door, while *Up from Slavery* (1901), written with the journalist Max Bennett Thrasher, was designed to reach a wider audience. Washington's aim in writing these works was to present his own story as an exemplar for aspiring Blacks, and to encourage the next generation to face the new era of opportunity, after Reconstruction, with pride and courage.

Because Booker Taliaferro Washington was born into slavery, the property of James Burroughs of Virginia, the exact date of his birth is not known. Even though his mother was a plantation cook, his childhood was one of privation, and conditions for his family seem only to have worsened after emancipation. His family moved to Malden, West Virginia, where his stepfather had found work packing salt. Washington was expected to work at the salt facility as well, and he recalls the deep impression made on him by the sight of White children studying in a schoolroom that he was unable to attend. He managed to get night lessons, and at last his parents allowed him to attend day school, but he was still required to put in several hours at the salt furnace, beginning at sunrise. Later, as he writes in the chapter "The Struggle for Education" (in *Up from Slavery*), while working in the coal mines, he overheard men talking about a school for "colored people" in Virginia, and so, in 1872, at the age of sixteen, he walked approximately 200 miles to enroll in the Hampton Normal and Agricultural Institute. Having arrived without money for tuition or board, he paid his way working as a janitor. The school was founded and run by General Samuel Chapman Armstrong, who profoundly influenced Washington's life and philosophy of education. In addition to learning the value of hard work and good study habits, Washington readily accepted Armstrong's doctrines of self-discipline, self-reliance, morality, and cleanliness. Armstrong was dedicated to showing the world that former slaves could learn menial trades and could become teachers. His vision was one of uplift for Blacks, brought about through a serious and sustained effort to provide general education for anyone with a sincere desire to persevere.

Following graduation from the Hampton Institute, Washington took a teaching job in Tinkersville, West Virginia, near his family home. He left in 1878 to attend Wayland Seminary in Washington, DC, for six months. The following year, Armstrong invited him to return to Hampton as a teacher and, in 1881, recommended him as the principal of a new school called Tuskegee Normal and Industrial Institute in Alabama's Black Belt (named for the rich, heavy soil). When he arrived, the main buildings were a stable and a hen house that the first thirty students, male and female, converted into living space. Classes were held in the African Methodist Episcopal Zion Church. As part of what was to become a hallmark of the Tuskegee educational tradition, the first permanent building, constructed a year later, was designed and built by instructors and students. In addition to

pursuing basic academic subjects, students learned skills that were of immediate and practical value: brickmaking, woodworking, cooking, farming, animal husbandry, dressmaking, and weaving. They made mattresses, brooms, rugs, shoes, and soap, and eventually sold the surplus to people in the area to bring in extra money. Soon they had their own print shop, and new tools, instruments, and machines were acquired every year.

The first students graduated in 1885. By 1888, the school owned 540 acres of land and had over 400 students. In the next decade, Washington hired George Washington Carver to teach agriculture and help the school take advantage of the fertile soil surrounding the campus. Carver's innovative farming research is now legendary, but the early years of Tuskegee were filled with many shortages and setbacks. As his writings make clear, Washington was keenly aware that the success or failure of his enterprise would significantly affect future opportunities for African Americans in the South. Consequently, he traveled widely to solicit donations, endorsements, supplies, and publicity. He became a well-known speaker and, because of his warm personality and devotion to his educational mission, he eventually became a welcome guest in the homes of some of the wealthiest men and women in the United States.

Washington was asked to speak at the opening of the 1895 Atlanta Cotton States and International Exposition. No such honor had ever been given to a Southern Black. The impact of that fifteen-minute speech was phenomenal. It was later reprinted and widely circulated, along with letters of congratulation from eminent statesmen and prospective benefactors, and headlines from around the country. Speaking directly to Whites and indirectly to Blacks who shunned manual labor, he advocated economic and moral advancement rather than political agitation and legal wrangling as the surest pathway to citizenship.

This willingness to compromise drew criticism from some Black leaders of the day, most notably Du Bois, who, in *The Souls of Black Folk* (1903), denounced Washington's gradualism and his stated policy of accommodation; moreover, Du Bois distrusted the beneficence of such wealthy White industrialists as Andrew Carnegie, Collis P. Huntington, and John D. Rockefeller—all of whom regularly gave money to Washington for his work at the Tuskegee Institute. Washington's increasing comfort among powerful White businessmen and politicians, coupled with his wide-ranging knowledge of people and activities concerned with Black advancement, led him to be a frequent, if unofficial, adviser to presidents Cleveland, McKinley, Theodore Roosevelt, and Taft. In fact, at the invitation of Theodore Roosevelt, Washington attended a dinner at the White House in 1901, the first Black to do so. Washington maintained that he helped in a more substantial way "by assisting in the laying of the foundation of the race through a generous education of the hand, head, and heart" (*Up from Slavery*, 41).

In addition to expanding program offerings at Tuskegee, Washington instituted a variety of programs for rural extension work, and, in 1900, he helped establish the National Negro Business League. He received honorary degrees from Harvard University (1896) and Dartmouth College (1901) and wrote more than a dozen books, including *The Future of the American Negro* (1902), *Working with the Hands* (1904), and *My Larger Education* (1911). In all his writings, he frequently comments on the love of labor, not for financial gain alone but for its own sake, and the satisfaction that comes from doing something that needs to be done. His moral essays reiterate the value of good work. Washington had faith that markets and consumers cared more about the products of labor than the skin color of the laborer. This theme emerges often in his autobiographical works and in occasional writings on the benefits of clean living and hard work. Washington served on the boards of trustees of Fisk and Howard universities and directed philanthropic initiatives nationwide.

Despite his high visibility and extensive publication, Washington was a complex, discreet, and private man. We learn almost nothing from his autobiography about what he actually advised powerful politicians to do, and even less about his domestic life. While in New York in 1915, he was admitted to St. Luke's Hospital, suffering from arteriosclerosis. He insisted on returning home to Tuskegee, where, a little more than a week later, on November 14, he died. His funeral was attended by over 8,000 people. In 1940, he was the first American of African descent to appear on a U.S. postage stamp.

Bill Engel

See also: Autobiography; Slave Narrative.

Resources

Mark Bauerlein, *Negrophobia: A Race Riot in Atlanta, 1906* (San Francisco: Encounter Books, 2001); Michael Scott Bieze and Marybeth Gasman, eds., *Booker T. Washington Rediscovered* (Baltimore, MD: Johns Hopkins University Press, 2012); Kenneth M. Hamilton, *Booker T. Washington in American Memory* (Champaign, IL: University of Illinois Press, 2017); Louis R. Harlan: *Booker T. Washington: The Making of a Black Leader, 1856–1901* (New York: Oxford University Press, 1972); *Booker T. Washington: The*

Wizard of Tuskegee, 1901–1915 (New York: Oxford University Press, 1983); Robert J. Norrell, *Up from History: The Life of Booker T. Washington* (Cambridge, MA: Belknap Press, 2009); Booker T. Washington: *The Future of the American Negro* (Boston: Small, Maynard, 1902); *My Larger Education* (Garden City, NY: Doubleday, Page & Co., 1911); *Up from Slavery* (1901; New York: Dover, 1995); *Working with the Hands* (New York: Doubleday, Page & Co., 1904).

West, Cornel (1953–)

Philosopher, professor, activist, essayist, actor, and cultural critic. Scholar-activist Cornel West is one of the most widely recognized Black public intellectuals based in the U.S. academy today. His views have been articulated and disseminated through the main channels of the popular media. A philosopher by trade and liberation theologian in spirit, West has produced a body of social and cultural criticism that theorizes the ethical and political responsibilities to social justice in African Americanist scholarship.

West was born in Tulsa, Oklahoma, in 1953. His parents were educated at Fisk University in Nashville, Tennessee, and worked hard to be part of the consolidated Black middle class at midcentury. His mother was a schoolteacher; his father worked for the U.S. Air Force. The family eventually moved to Sacramento, California, where West's precocious activities as a child were nurtured into a keen and outspoken intellect by continued involvement in the Baptist Church as well as contact with the militant politics of the Black Panther Party. West excelled in his studies and won a scholarship to Harvard University in 1970.

It took West only three years to graduate from Harvard magna cum laude with a degree in Near Eastern languages and literature. He went on to study Western philosophy at Princeton University, where he worked with Richard Rorty and earned an MA in 1975 and a PhD in 1980. West's dissertation, which reflects the varied influences on his early liberationist thinking, was revised and published as *The Ethical Dimensions of Marxist Thought* in 1991. During his time at Princeton and Union Theological Seminary in New York City, where he began teaching in 1977, West developed a philosophical worldview that fused the most progressive elements of Christian theology, Marxist dialectics, and American pragmatism, with nods to Emersonian transcendentalism and insurgent Black politics. Teasing out the intricacies of this worldview led West to shun intellectual orthodoxy and dogmatism and to stress the modes by which critical theory and theology enable radical political praxis. Two early monographs prove instructive here: *Prophesy Deliverance!* (1982) and *The American Evasion of Philosophy* (1989).

The period since the 1980s has seen West continue to develop his liberationist thinking while occupying positions of enormous influence at the most prestigious institutions of higher education in the United States. Barely into his thirties, West was awarded a full professorship in religion and philosophy at Yale Divinity School, where he served from 1984 to 1987. In 1988, he returned to Princeton to direct its Program in Afro-American Studies. In 1994, West was on the move again, leaving Princeton for his other Ivy League alma mater, Harvard. In 1998, West was named the first Alphonse Fletcher Jr. University Professor.

In 2001, West was at the center of an academic dispute that made national headlines. Behind closed doors, newly appointed Harvard President and former U.S. Treasury

Secretary Lawrence Summers allegedly questioned West's involvement in national politics—the Million Man March in 1995, Russell Simmons's ongoing Hip-Hop Summit, the 2000 presidential campaigns of Bill Bradley and Ralph Nader—at the expense of his teaching duties and scholarly productivity. Also allegedly subjected to professional scrutiny was West's intriguing hip-hop/soul/spoken word record *Sketches of My Culture* (2001), produced by Derek "D.O.A." Allen and dedicated to "the preservation, persistence, and prevailing of our foremothers and forefathers." When news of the private meeting leaked, the news media were quick to pit West's defenders, who accused Summers of professional discrimination, against critics who branded West's extracurricular activities anti-intellectual. Even after an attempted reconciliation with Summers, West said that he had felt "attacked and insulted" by the president's words.

The fiasco left West disillusioned with Harvard, and, in 2002, he returned to Princeton, where he served as Class of 1943 University Professor of Religion and Professor of African American Studies. A resolute critic of George W. Bush, he took up the banner of national politics once again by advising Al Sharpton's presidential campaign in 2004. West has also appeared in the much-lauded cameo role of Zion elder Councilor West in two parts of the Hollywood blockbuster *Matrix* trilogy, *The Matrix Reloaded* (2003) and *The Matrix Revolutions* (2003).

The publication of West's most famous book to date, the best-selling *Race Matters* (1993), sparked renewed interest in a multifaceted yet accessible national dialogue on race in the midst of the political conservatism of the post–Reagan "culture wars." The pithy collection of eight essays addresses topics ranging from affirmative action and the "crisis in black political leadership" to predominant myths of Black sexuality and the worrisome state of Black-Jewish relations. *Race Matters* might be fruitfully compared with James Baldwin's *The Fire Next Time* (1963) in the way it attempts to convey the African American sermon of liberation, delivered especially but not exclusively to an African American audience, in prose.

West mediated the popularity of *Race Matters* with more academic fare such as the two-volume *Beyond Eurocentrism and Multiculturalism* (1993) and *Keeping Faith* (1993). The mid-to-late 1990s saw West author a handful of books with academic colleagues and other comrades in struggle. Two are explicitly geared toward changes and improvements in U.S. domestic policy: *The War Against Parents* (1998), with Sylvia Ann Hewlett, and *The Future of American Progressivism* (1998), with Roberto Mangabeira Unger. Two offer dialogues on the state of Black–Jewish and Black-on-Black relations in the United States: *Jews and Blacks* (1995), with Rabbi Michael Lerner, and *The Future of the Race* (1996), with Gates. West's millennial project with Gates, *The African-American Century* (2000), is the most difficult to categorize of these texts. Part critical argument about the achievements of Blacks in the twentieth century, part photographic exhibit of 100 African American celebrities and icons, it is perhaps best described as a wonderfully instructive coffee table book.

Over a decade after *Race Matters* was met with critical acclaim and widespread national interest, West published *Democracy Matters* (2004), which signals perhaps the most dramatic intellectual transformation in the career of this longtime critic of

U.S. social relations. Here the focus is on the world stage: West explains how the ideals of American democracy have been compromised by the perpetuation of domestic racism and imperial expansion into the twenty-first century. He understands Islamic fundamentalism and U.S. militarism as two sides of the same terrible coin. In order to stem the tide of ideologically driven violence, West calls for a revitalization of the Christian universalist notion of democracy, a notion put into prophetic words by Dr. Martin Luther King Jr.

West supported Barack Obama's candidacy for president in 2008 but subsequently criticized Obama's economic and military policies, including ongoing military engagement in Iraq. West and Tavis Smiley have engaged in activism and advocacy targeting economic inequality and injustice and together published *The Rich and the Rest of Us: A Poverty Manifesto* in 2012. In the same year, West left Princeton and returned to Union Theological Seminary; he has continued to teach on an occasional basis at Princeton, where he is Class of 1943 University Professor Emeritus in the Center for African American Studies. Since 2016, West has been Professor of the Practice of Public Philosophy both at Harvard Divinity School and in Harvard's Department of African and African American Studies.

Kinohi Nishikawa

See also: Essay; Protest Literature.

Resources

Primary Sources: Cornel West: *The American Evasion of Philosophy: A Genealogy of Pragmatism* (Madison, WI: University of Wisconsin Press, 1989); *Beyond Eurocentrism and Multiculturalism*, vol. 1, *Prophetic Thought in Postmodern Times* (Monroe, ME: Common Courage, 1993); *Brother West:* *Living and Loving Out Loud, A Memoir* (New York: SmileyBooks, 2009); *Democracy Matters: Winning the Fight Against Imperialism* (New York: Penguin, 2004); *The Ethical Dimensions of Marxist Thought* (New York: Monthly Review, 1991); *Freedom Is a Constant Struggle: Ferguson, Palestine, and the Foundations of a Movement* (Chicago: Haymarket Books, 2016); *Keeping Faith: Philosophy and Race in America* (New York: Routledge, 1993); *Prophesy Deliverance! An Afro-American Revolutionary Christianity* (Philadelphia: Westminster, 1982); *Race Matters* (Boston: Beacon, 1993); *Street Knowledge* (Rancho Murieta, CA: Roc Diamond Records, 2003), CD; Cornel West and Christa Buschendorf, *Black Prophetic Fire* (Boston: Beacon Press, 2014); Cornel West and Henry Louis Gates Jr., *The African-American Century: How Black Americans Have Shaped Our Country* (New York: Free Press, 2000); *The Future of the Race* (New York: Knopf, 1996); Cornel West and Sylvia Ann Hewlett, *The War Against Parents: What We Can Do for America's Beleaguered Moms and Dads* (Boston: Houghton Mifflin, 1998); Cornel West and bell hooks, *Breaking Bread: Insurgent Black Intellectual Life* (Boston: South End, 1991); Cornel West and Michael Lerner, *Jews and Blacks: Let the Healing Begin* (New York: Putnam, 1995); Cornel West and Tavis Smiley, *The Rich and the Rest of Us: A Poverty Manifesto* (Chicago: Third World Press, 2012); Cornel West and Roberto Mangabeira Unger, *The Future of American Progressivism: An Initiative for Political and Economic Reform* (Boston: Beacon, 1998).

Secondary Sources: Rosemary Cowan, *Cornel West: The Politics of Redemption* (Malden, MA: Polity, 2003); Gary Dorrien, "Imagining Social Justice: Cornel West's Prophetic Pragmatism," *CrossCurrents* 58, no. 1 (2008), 6–42; Clarence Sholé Johnson, *Cornel West and Philosophy: The Quest for Social Justice* (New York: Routledge, 2003); Anders Stephanson, "Interview with Cornel West," in *Universal Abandon? The Politics of Postmodernism*, ed. Andrew Ross (Minneapolis: University of Minnesota Press, 1988), 269–286;

Mark David Wood, *Cornel West and the Politics of Prophetic Pragmatism* (Urbana, IL: University of Illinois Press, 2000).

West, Dorothy (1907–1998)

Novelist, short-story writer, columnist, and editor. Dorothy West's death in 1998 marked the passing of the last surviving member of the Harlem Renaissance and the end of a seventy-year writing career. West was the only child of Rachel Benson and Isaac West, members of the Black middle class in Boston, Massachusetts. Both were grandchildren of slave masters, in South Carolina and Virginia respectively; her father, a generation older than her mother, was emancipated during the Civil War. Industrious, he was known as Boston's Black Banana King; her mother presided over a household that included three of her sisters and their children. West therefore grew up within a transplanted Southern household that nevertheless exuded the decorum of Boston's exclusive Brahmin caste. By the age of seven, she knew she wanted to be a writer; by her 1923 graduation from the Girls Latin School, she had established herself.

West's career began with the *Boston Post*. She recalled,

> I don't think I was anymore than fourteen or fifteen when the *Post* did a daily short story. At the end of the week, they gave $2, $5, and $10 prizes. . . . Eight times out of ten or seven times out of ten, I got the $10 prize and contributed to the family pot. When I got the $2 or the $5 prize, everybody in the family was indignant. (McDowell, 269)

Her future was secured in 1926 when she tied with Zora Neale Hurston for second place in the short-story category of the *Opportunity* Awards. West was accompanied to New York by Helene Johnson, a cousin with whom she'd been raised and who had merited an honorable mention in the poetry category.

The Harlem Renaissance welcomed the two, whom Wallace Thurman pleasantly memorialized in his otherwise biting novel *Infants of the Spring*:

> They were characterized by a freshness and naiveté which he and his cronies had lost. And, surprisingly enough for Negro prodigies, they actually gave promise of possessing literary talent. . . . He was also amused by their interest and excitement. (230–231)

Hurston became attached to the cousins, sharing her apartment and forming a genuine friendship with West. Others also took interest in the young, quiet girl whom they perceived as in need of their protection and guidance. A'Lelia Walker (African American bon vivant and patron of the arts) chastised Carl Van Vechten (art critic, novelist, patron, and friend of Langston Hughes) for his improper advances to West, who received marriage proposals from Countee Cullen, Claude McKay, and Langston Hughes—among others (Dalsgard, 33; Steinberg, 35; McDowell, 270; Roses, 49). While she admitted that she loved them all, she credited McKay with the greatest influence upon her writing: "I don't know how much I would have written, if it hadn't been for him" (Dalsgard, 33). West's short story "The Typewriter" is considered one of the most memorable pieces of short fiction to have been written during the Harlem Renaissance.

Like many writers of the era, West depended upon other sources for income. In

1929, she became an extra in the Theatre Guild's original production of *Porgy* by DuBose Heyward, traveling to London for three months (Newson, 22). Three years later, West was one of twenty-two African Americans who journeyed to Russia. The group included Langston Hughes, Henry Lee Moon, and Ted Poston. A group in Russia planned to make a film about American racism as a means of advancing Communist interests, but was thwarted by American threats to stall the building of the Dnieper Dam (McDowell, 272). Langston Hughes noted that the Russians seemed to know nothing about African Americans (*I Wonder*). West nevertheless remembered that year as her most carefree and recorded her memories of Sergei Eisenstein in "An Adventure in Moscow."

West's return to America was precipitated by the death of her father, followed by that of Thurman. West recalled, "For me, Wally's [Thurman] death in [1934] meant the end of the Harlem Renaissance" (Roses, 49). Disappointed by the Great Depression's impact upon creative writers, in 1934 West launched the magazine *Challenge*, promoting it as "an organ for the new voices ... to bring out the prose and poetry of newer Negroes ... by those who were the new Negroes now challenging them to better our achievements. For we did not altogether live up to our fine promise." While some disliked the suggestion that they had failed, West received support from Cullen, Hughes, Hurston, McKay, Van Vechten, and others (Cromwell, 354–355). The larger detractions came from those who demanded an explicitly socialist production. Accordingly, *Challenge* became *New Challenge* in 1937, with West as coeditor and Richard Wright as associate editor, and included Ralph Ellison's first published piece and Wright's "Blueprint for Negro Writing." Opposed to communism, West ultimately ceased its publication.

While unsupportive of the Left, West was sympathetic to America's poor. Two years with the Public Welfare Department during the Depression exposed her to the extremes of poverty (Cromwell, 353). Her time with the Works Progress Administration's Federal Writers' Project allowed her to chronicle the effects of the Depression had upon the residents of Harlem, New York, and the strategies they deployed to preserve their dignity in the face of economic and spiritual stress. West dated the end of her apprenticeship to this era: "My own writing was now more mature. I saw life with a larger eye. But important magazines were not in the market for stories about blacks. They surmised that neither were their readers." A chance submission to the *New York Daily News* in 1940 led to West's arrangement to provide the newspaper with two stories a month, thus keeping her "writing hand ready and her mind alert" and initiating a relationship that lasted almost twenty years (*The Richer, the Poorer*, 3–4).

Throughout the excitement of the 1920s and the hardship of the 1930s, West remained sustained by memories of her childhood and summers at Oak Bluffs, Martha's Vineyard. West retired to Oak Bluffs in 1947 to write her first novel, *The Living Is Easy*. It was originally to have been serialized by the *Ladies' Home Journal*, but editors feared subscription cancellations by Southern readers (Steinberg, 35). Nevertheless, reviews were favorable: drawn from West's family, the novel chronicles the manipulations of a young matron to gather her Southern sisters and their children around her in Boston, exploiting her husband's financial success. The novel also included a thinly veiled portrait of Monroe Trotter—West had been a pupil of his sister

Bessie and a goddaughter of his sister Maude (Roses, 48).

Following the publication of her first novel, West, who had returned to her youth in so much of her writing, permanently moved to her childhood summer home. While continuing to write, West also became a clerical worker at the *Vineyard Gazette* in 1965 (Cromwell, 350). She soon replaced the local bird columnist, and in 1968 began a regular column, "Cottagers' Corner," covering the activities of vacationing African Americans (Saunders and Shackelford, 6). By 1973, West was reporting on all Oak Bluffs residents—human and animal. From the late 1960s through the 1980s, West spent summers as a restaurant cashier, leaving her little time for work on her novel *The Wedding*, begun in the 1960s (Cromwell, 351). West acknowledged that the politics of the 1960s also negatively affected its completion. Admitting she cared "very deeply" about the goals of the Black Revolution, she disliked its contempt for the bourgeois: "I had a suspicion that the reviewers, who were white, would not know how to judge my work in that prevailing climate" (McDowell, 278; Steinberg, 35). Publishers likewise proved hesitant to risk a novel about the Black middle class (McDowell, 277–278) (*see* Black Arts Movement).

Despite these setbacks, West's writings for *Vineyard Gazette* eventually brought her to the attention of another Vineyard vacationer, an editor at Doubleday. She urged West to return to *The Wedding*, and they forged a friendship evident in the novel's dedication: "To the memory of my editor, Jacqueline Kennedy Onassis. Though there was never such a mismatched pair in appearance, we were perfect partners." Whereas the republication of *The Living Is Easy* in 1982 generated academic interest in West, this second novel secured popular

interest in the last surviving writer of the Harlem Renaissance, and several collections of various works followed as well as a miniseries of *The Wedding*. West died in 1998, content with her belated recognition: "It gratifies me now at the end of my life that I am not afraid of dying. I'm leaving you my legacy" (McDowell, 282).

Jennifer Harris

See also: Novel.

Resources

Primary Sources: Dorothy West: *The Dorothy West Martha's Vineyard: Stories, Essays and Reminiscences by Dorothy West Writing in the* Vineyard Gazette, ed. James Robert Saunders and Renae Nadine Shackelford (Jefferson, NC: McFarland, 2001); *The Living Is Easy* (1948; repr. Old Westbury, NY: Feminist Press, 1982); *The Richer, the Poorer: Stories, Sketches, and Reminiscences* (New York: Doubleday, 1995); *The Wedding* (New York: Doubleday, 1995).

Secondary Sources: Lionel C. Bascom, ed., *A Renaissance in Harlem: Lost Voices of an American Community* (New York: Avon, 1999), includes work by West; Adelaide M. Cromwell, "Afterword," in West's *The Living Is Easy*, 349–364; Katrine Dalsgard, "Alive and Well and Living on the Island of Martha's Vineyard: An Interview with Dorothy West, October 29, 1988," *Langston Hughes Review* (Fall 1993), 28–44; Langston Hughes, "Moscow Movie," "Scenario in Russian," and "The Mammy of Moscow," in *I Wonder as I Wander* (New York: Rinehart, 1956), 69–86; Deborah E. McDowell, "Conversations with Dorothy West," in *The Harlem Renaissance Re-examined*, ed. Victor A. Kramer (New York: AMS, 1987), 265–282; Lorraine Elena Roses, "Interviews with Black Women Writers: Dorothy West at Oak Bluffs, Massachusetts," *Sage* (Spring 1985), 47–49; James Robert Saunders and Renae Nadine Shackelford, "Introduction," in *The Dorothy West Martha's Vineyard*, 1–11;

Cherene Sherrard-Johnson, *Dorothy West's Paradise: A Biography of Class and Color* (New Brunswick, NJ: Rutgers University Press, 2012); Sybil Steinberg, "Dorothy West: Her Own Renaissance," *Publishers Weekly*, July 3, 1995, pp. 34–35; Wallace Thurman, *Infants of the Spring* (1932; repr. New York: AMS, 1975).

Wheatley, Phillis (ca. 1753–1784)

Poet and literary pioneer. Wheatley was the second woman and the first African American to publish in colonial America. Even though Africans had published previously in America, her work arguably started "African American literature" because of the United States' shift from a British colony to a free country during her lifetime. Although many scholars place her birth in Senegal, Wheatley claimed in her work that she was born in Gambia, West Africa. Little is known of Wheatley's childhood in Africa. She claimed to have remembered only her mother pouring water on the ground to honor the rising sun every morning. This ritual suggested that her mother adhered to sun worship, perhaps Islam. However, when she was around seven years old, Wheatley was captured and sold into slavery on July 11, 1761. She was bought by the Wheatley family, who resided in Boston, Massachusetts, and was named for the slave ship, the *Phillis*, upon which she arrived (Gates; Robinson).

The Wheatleys were a wealthy family who provided Phillis with the sort of thorough education that was usually reserved for the Caucasian elite of that time. Her adjustment to her new life was so phenomenal that she learned to read and write English and Latin in four years, and at around fourteen, she published her first poem, "On Messrs. Hussey and Coffin," on December 21, 1767, in the *Newport Mercury*. Wheatley utilized her classical training to enhance her poetry. Besides becoming a budding classical scholar and poet, she converted to Christianity on August 18, 1771 (Robinson).

In 1772, she tried to publish her first volume of poetry in America. Because of her race and gender, many learned people of the time period doubted that Wheatley actually wrote the poems, especially because of her command of the English language and her references to Greek and Roman figures and mythology. Therefore, Wheatley appeared in a room filled with men of the Boston elite (including Governor John Hancock and Rev. Mather Byles) to prove that she knew English and Latin and that she wrote the poems. Little is known about that meeting except that she impressed the men so much that they added an attestation page to her volume to inform the public that it was her work (Robinson). Even with this ringing endorsement, however, Wheatley still could not get published in America and had to turn to England. Fortunately, Selena Hastings, the Countess of Huntingdon, financed the publishing. Wheatley's first volume of poetry, *Poems on Various Subjects, Religious and Moral*, appeared in 1773. This publication made her the first African American to gain freedom from slavery through literary work.

Wheatley's poems demonstrate not only classical learning but also an awareness of the changing world around her. As a history-maker herself, she was very popular with the elite in America and in Europe, the first African American to gain this acknowledgment. Most of her poems were elegies, poems dedicated to the memory of important people she knew in colonial America. Furthermore, she dedicated poems to such historical figures as George Washington and Benjamin Franklin, and eventually she regularly corresponded with both. Besides her first volume of poetry, many of her letters and miscellaneous poems still exist.

Unfortunately for Wheatley, her freedom did not bring her happiness because she encountered many new problems. In 1778, she married John Peters, a free African American. Her first two children died as infants. Peters left Wheatley after she gave birth to their last child. Because of the Revolutionary War (and the death of many of the people who signed the attestation), Wheatley's fame diminished greatly. In vain, Wheatley tried numerous times to garnish subscribers to a new volume of poetry dedicated to Benjamin Franklin in 1779. After her husband abandoned her, she was forced to work as a domestic. In September 1784, her last advertisement for subscribers appeared. In December of that year, because of her hardships and lifelong poor health, Wheatley was found dead with her third child. She was in her thirties. After her death, it is believed that Peters sold the only copy of her second volume of poetry. Most of these poems are still undiscovered.

Wheatley's legacy has possibly been the most reviled of any African American writer. Dismissed by Caucasian scholars such as Thomas Jefferson as not a good poet because of her race, Wheatley has also been maligned by African American critics such as James Weldon Johnson and Amiri Baraka. Initially embraced by African American readers because of her history-making attributes, Wheatley was subsequently seen by some as having denounced her African heritage when she converted to Christianity. Her life and career, at any rate, became points of contention. To be fair, most of Wheatley's poetry has been rediscovered slowly over the centuries, so many scholars were not aware of her acknowledgment, in some of her poems, of her heritage. Now, since most of her

extant poems were put into a collection titled *The Collected Works of Phillis Wheatley* in 1988, scholars have a clearer view of her work. Since the 1980s, some scholars, such as John C. Shields and James A. Levernier, have reexamined her work to the extent that some perceive a strain of subversiveness in her verse. They do not view Wheatley as catering to her "betters." Indeed, even though she became a Christian, she criticized slavery and racism in her poetry. No matter what point of view one takes on her Christian conversion, the style of her poetry, or how subversive she was, Wheatley's contributions to African American literature and culture cannot be ignored or denied.

Devona Mallory

See also: Formal Verse; Lyric Poetry.

Resources

G. J. Barker-Benfield, *Phillis Wheatley Chooses Freedom: History, Poetry, and the Ideals of the American Revolution* (New York: New York University Press, 2018); Henry Louis Gates Jr., *The Trials of Phillis Wheatley* (New York: Basic Civitas Books, 2003); James Weldon Johnson, *The Book of American Poetry* (New York: Harcourt Brace, 1922); LeRoi Jones (Amiri Baraka), "The Myth of 'Negro Literature,'" in *Within the Circle: An Anthology of African American Literary Criticism from the Harlem Renaissance to the Present*, ed. Angelyn Mitchell (Durham, NC: Duke University Press, 1994), 165–171; James A. Levernier, "Style as Protest in the Poetry of Phillis Wheatley," *Style* 27, no. 2 (1993), 173–193; William H. Robinson, *Phillis Wheatley and Her Writings* (New York: Garland, 1984); John C. Shields, *The American Aeneas: Classical Origins of the American Self* (Knoxville, TN: University of Tennessee Press, 2001); *Phillis Wheatley and the Romantics* (Knoxville, TN: University of Tennessee Press, 2010); John C. Shields, ed., *The Collected Works of Phillis Wheatley*

(New York: Oxford University Press, 1988); John C. Shields and Eric D. Lamore, eds., *New Essays on Phillis Wheatley* (Knoxville, TN: University of Tennessee Press, 2011).

Wideman, John Edgar (1941–)

Novelist, short-story writer, essayist, professor, and editor. Born in Washington, DC, John Edgar Wideman spent his early childhood in the African American community of Homewood in Pittsburgh, Pennsylvania. He studied English at the University of Pennsylvania, where he captained the basketball team and won all–Ivy League status, and later was inducted into Philadelphia's Big Five Basketball Hall of Fame. (The importance of basketball emerges in Wideman's works, in which the physical and symbolic space of the basketball court represents a space of infinite potential, though it is never idealized or utopian). In 1963, Wideman won a Rhodes Scholarship; the only other African American to have done so was Alain Locke. He completed his MA at Oxford University in 1966, writing a thesis on the beginnings of the novel form. He is the only writer to have won the PEN/Faulkner Award twice, in 1983 for *Sent for You Yesterday* and in 1990 for *Philadelphia Fire*. Wideman also numbers the American Book Award, the MacArthur Award (1993), and a Lannan Foundation Fellowship (1991) among his accolades.

In 1966, Wideman began work on his first novel, *A Glance Away*, which was published in 1967. Both *A Glance Away* and *Hurry Home* (1970), Wideman's second novel, are experimental, fractured narratives in which the structures reflect the characters' feelings of communal and existential alienation and dislocation. At this time, Wideman lectured at the University of Pennsylvania; at his students' request, in 1968, he fashioned the university's first African American literature course. He spent three years as director of the university's Afro-American Studies program.

In *The Lynchers* (1973), Wideman produced a more raw, less obviously wrought novel. The bleak lyricism of the first two novels was transformed into a powerful, claustrophobic evocation of the pressures that accumulate during centuries of racial oppression. In 1975, Wideman, his wife, and his three children moved to Laramie, where he spent eleven years as a professor of English at the University of Wyoming.

Wideman describes the eight-year hiatus between the publication of *The Lynchers* and his next works, the novel *Hiding Place* and the short-story collection *Damballah* (both 1981), as a time in which he explored the breadth of African American literary production. The later works formed two parts of Wideman's Homewood Trilogy (which concluded with *Sent for You Yesterday*). Wideman's literary Homewood remains a central presence in his writing, reappearing in various guises in the memoir *Brothers and Keepers* (1984) and the novel *Reuben* (1987). The Homewood Trilogy pays tribute to the ways in which voices of larger-than-life figures in the family and community maintained the Homewood of his childhood through the circulation of foundational and everyday stories. Through this exchange of stories, Wideman explores what community can mean as well as the difficulties of maintaining a true, open exchange between individuals, which represents the ideal of community.

Wideman's writing shows an unflinching personal bravery; his fiction (in the novels *Hiding Place* and *Philadelphia Fire* as well as short stories from *Damballah*) and memoirs (*Brothers and Keepers*) address the imprisonment of his brother Robby (who was imprisoned for life in 1976 for his part in an armed robbery that turned into a murder) and of Wideman's son Jacob, sentenced to life in prison for the murder of a bunkmate while at camp. Wideman acknowledges the potential for pain on the parts of both writer and subject when working with biographical material, while underlining the potential of storytelling to allow people to face traumatic separations and to reconnect.

In 1986, Wideman moved to the University of Massachusetts at Amherst, where he taught as a professor in the creative writing program. In the title short story of his collection *Fever* (1989), Wideman began to explore in depth the concept that history repeats itself in the present.

In *Philadelphia Fire*, Wideman dwells on the bombing of the MOVE house on Osage Avenue on May 13, 1985. The bombing, ordered by Mayor Wilson Goode, resulted in the deaths of eleven of the house's thirteen inhabitants. In *The Cattle Killing* (1996), Wideman continues to draw on historical sources, using Richard Allen's *The Life, Experience, and Gospel Labours of the Rt. Rev. Richard Allen* to focus on the yellow fever epidemic in Philadelphia in 1793, and the ways in which the biological contagion mirrors the sickness of racism.

In the novel *Two Cities: A Love Story* (1998), the basketball memoir *Hoop Roots* (2001), and the travel memoir *The Island: Martinique* (2003), Wideman focuses on love and its role in community formation. Once again, these texts show Wideman's signature blurring of the boundaries between autobiography, biography, and fiction. In 2001, he edited the anthology *My Soul Has Grown Deep: Classics of Early African-American Literature*. In *Writing to Save a Life: The Louis Till File* (2016), which explores the intertwined tragedies of Emmett Till and his father Louis Till, Wideman calls into question the legitimacy of the senior Till's conviction on charges of rape and murder, for which he was executed by military authorities in 1945, and the manipulation of these events to influence public opinion and judicial proceedings following Emmett Till's murder in 1955.

Despite Wideman's examination of love, his literary vision is often criticized as bleak, perhaps even nihilistic. His vision, though certainly unflinching when regarding material forms of oppression and suffering, is nonetheless idealistic, as his characters find ways to negotiate personal connections, even love, across class divides, prison walls, years of separation, and even beyond death. At the core, Wideman's work, like that of Alice Walker, Gloria Naylor, and Toni Morrison, displays a faith in such personal connections and in the sense of belonging created by inclusive community models which are not based on racial, gendered, or class exclusion.

Scott Bunyan

See also: Novel; Postmodernism.

Resources

Primary Sources: John Edgar Wideman: *All Stories Are True* (New York: Vintage, 1993); *American Histories: Stories* (New York: Scribner, 2018); *Briefs* (Morrisville, NC: Lulu Press, 2010); *Brothers and Keepers* (New York: Holt, Rinehart and Winston, 1984); *The Cattle Killing* (Boston: Houghton Mifflin, 1996); *Damballah* (1981; repr. New York: Vintage, 1988); *Fanon* (Boston: Houghton Mifflin, 2008); *Fever: Twelve Stories* (New York: Henry Holt, 1989); *A Glance Away* (1967; repr. New York: Holt, Rinehart and Winston, 1985); *God's Gym* (Boston: Houghton Mifflin, 2005); *Hiding Place* (1981; repr. New York: Vintage, 1988); *The Homewood Trilogy* (New York: Avon, 1985); *Hoop Roots*

(Boston: Houghton Mifflin, 2001); *Hurry Home* (New York: Harcourt, Brace & World, 1970); *Identities: Three Novels* (New York: Henry Holt, 1994); *The Island: Martinque* (Washington, DC: National Geographic, 2003); *Lynchers* (New York: Harcourt Brace Jovanovich, 1973); *Philadelphia Fire: A Novel* (New York: Henry Holt, 1990); *Reuben* (New York: Henry Holt, 1987); *Sent for You Yesterday* (New York: Avon, 1983); *The Stories of John Edgar Wideman* (New York: Pantheon, 1992); *Two Cities* (Boston: Houghton Mifflin, 1998); *Writing to Save a Life: The Louis Till File* (New York: Scribner, 2016); John Edgar Wideman, ed., *My Soul Has Grown Deep: Classics of Early African-American Literature* (Philadelphia: Running Press, 2001).

Secondary Sources: James W. Coleman: *Black Male Fiction and the Legacy of Caliban* (Lexington, KY: University Press of Kentucky, 2001); *Blackness and Modernism: The Literary Career of John Edgar Wideman* (Jackson, MS: University Press of Mississippi, 1989); *Writing Blackness: John Edgar Wideman's Art and Experimentation* (Baton Rouge, LA: University Press of Louisiana, 2010); Ulrich Eschborn, *Stories of Survival: John Edgar Wideman's Representations of History* (Trier, Germany: Wissenschaftlicher Verlag Trier, 2011); Tracie Church Guzzio, *All Stories Are True: History, Myth, and Trauma in the Work of John Edgar Wideman* (Jackson, MS: University Press of Mississippi, 2011); D. Quintin Miller, *Understanding John Edgar Wideman* (Columbia, SC: University of South Carolina Press, 2018); Bonnie TuSmith, ed., *Conversations with John Edgar Wideman* (Jackson, MS: University Press of Mississippi, 1998); Bonnie TuSmith and Keith E. Byerman, eds., *Critical Essays on John Edgar Wideman* (Knoxville, TN: University of Tennessee Press, 2006).

Wilson, August (1945–2005)

Playwright and cultural critic. August Wilson was the most popular American playwright producing new works and the only African American playwright to win the Pulitzer Prize for drama twice in his career. He pursued a project to chronicle the African American experience in the twentieth century, through an ongoing series of plays capturing specific moments in each decade. His most important plays include *Ma Rainey's Black Bottom* (1985), *Fences* (1986), *Joe Turner's Come and Gone* (1988), *The Piano Lesson* (1990), *Two Trains Running* (1992), *Seven Guitars* (1996), *Jitney* (1996), and *King Hedley II* (2000).

Wilson was born Frederick August Kittel on April 27, 1945. His youth was spent on "The Hill," a racially mixed, low-income neighborhood in Pittsburgh, Pennsylvania, a location that would become the setting for nearly all his major dramas. His father was a White German baker named Frederick Kittel; his mother was Daisy Wilson, a Black domestic worker. The elder Kittel, an absent father to August, died in 1965. His relationship with his stepfather, David Bedford, was a difficult one as well. Growing up without a positive male role model, Frederick eventually abandoned his biological father's name, adopting August Wilson to represent his far deeper connection to his mother (Bogumil, 1).

While in high school, Wilson wrote a paper on Napoleon Bonaparte and was falsely accused of plagiarism. Considering this the final humiliation at the hands of an educational system with which he was already discouraged, Wilson dropped out of school and began a regimen of independent study, devouring works by Langston Hughes, James Baldwin, Ralph Ellison, and Richard Wright. The year of his father's death, he moved into a boardinghouse in his hometown to pursue writing.

Wilson became interested in theater before he ever saw or wrote a play, founding, with his writer/teacher friend Robert

Lee Penny, the Black Horizons Theater (1968). He directed a play by Penny and began to explore poetry and drama more vigorously, including works by Dylan Thomas, John Berryman, and Amiri Baraka. His marriage to a Muslim woman named Brenda Burton began and ended around this time (1969–1973), though not before the birth of his first daughter, Sakina Ansari. His first drama, *Recycle*, was a semiautobiographical piece about his first marriage. In 1976, he was inspired to write his first major work while listening to a "Ma" Rainey album.

Ma Rainey's Black Bottom simultaneously criticizes White commercialization of Black culture and the way violent behavior compromises Black unity. In Chicago, Illinois, in 1927, Ma Rainey's band is preparing to record the song "Black Bottom" but Ma takes some time to arrive, and once she does, she makes a number of difficult demands of the White producer, Sturdyvant. During the various delays, the band members share stories from family histories, such as the trumpeter Levee's tale of his father, who was lynched for killing a number of White men who had raped his wife.

Ma Rainey demonstrates what many critics recognized early about Wilson's work. While the author's talents were nursed on the radical, sometimes "agit-prop" dramas of the Black Arts Movement, his craft became one that is conscious of the burdens of slavery and segregation, without the alienating excesses of overt denunciation of Whites (Shafer, 9). In a 1990 article in *Applause* magazine, Wilson articulated values of responsibility and a new concern for culture that he felt were becoming paramount during his entry into adulthood. It is almost certainly his deep historical and cultural awareness, married to profoundly

moral themes, that challenges both Whites and Blacks to take responsibility for the effects of their actions on society, that have garnered Wilson his mainstream critical and financial success. *Ma Rainey* was originally produced by the O'Neill Workshop in Waterford, Connecticut (1982).

Fences, Wilson's first Pulitzer winner, depicts the family conflicts in the household of Troy Maxson, a Pittsburgh garbage collector. A flawed hero, Troy articulates the systematic forms of racial oppression in the 1950s, especially targeting professional baseball—he was once a hopeful in the Jackie Robinson tradition—and achieves equal opportunity in his workplace. He lectures his son about the importance of responsibility over feelings, yet fathers a child with a woman who is not his wife. Rose, his wife, is a strong and well-drawn foil to Troy, challenging his self-serving platitudes and asserting her dignity against her husband's humiliations. *Fences* was a marked success, earning Wilson a Drama Critics Circle Award and a Tony Award for Best New Play. It was nearly made into a feature film, but Wilson ultimately rejected the offer from Paramount Studios because the producers were unwilling to meet his demand for a Black director. It is currently one of the most commonly anthologized plays by an African American author.

Joe Turner's Come and Gone showcases the personal histories and personalities of a group of people at a 1911 Pittsburgh boardinghouse. The main character, Herald Loomis, is deeply wounded by years of forced labor on a chain gang and the unlawful conviction that put him there. In a series of spiritual revelations, involving a mysterious "shiny man" and the boardinghouse's resident shaman, he discovers the inner strength to persevere against the injustices of the world.

The Piano Lesson earned Wilson his second Pulitzer, his second Tony Award, and his fourth Drama Critics Circle Award. The action centers on a piano that has been in the Charles family since being stolen from its White owners. During slavery, a grandfather decorated it with images memorializing the abuses of enslavement and the family's history. In the present (1936), Berniece Charles, the current owner of the piano, and her brother, Boy Willie, disagree about its future. Boy Willie has been offered a good price for it by a White man, but Berniece cannot give up what her ancestor died for (he had been burned to death in retribution for the theft). Boy Willie tries to sell it without her permission, but in the end, the piano remains the family's treasured possession. The presence of a threatening apparition called Sutter (the name of the slave-owning family of Charles's past) adds a supernatural undercurrent to an otherwise realistic drama. *The Piano Lesson* has enjoyed a healthy production history, becoming the only Wilson play to be adapted into a feature film (1995).

Wilson's last four plays deal with the shared psychic trauma of racism and the spiritual/familial strategies African Americans use to empower themselves while retaining a commitment to preserving history and offering a complex critique of American Black and White society. *Two Trains Running* uses the imminent closing of the restaurant of Memphis Lee (part of Pittsburgh city renovation), in the 1960s, to explore the consequences of Black migration to the North. *Seven Guitars*, set in the 1940s, depicts an older man named Hedley, who believes owning a plantation will serve as recompense for his father's suffering at the hands of White people.

Jitney, a revamp of Wilson's 1980 drama, deals with an unsuccessful father/son reconciliation involving a taxi service owner, Becker, who dies before he can articulate his feelings for his ex-convict son, Booster. Despite heavy bitterness and near pathos, the play is rich in atmosphere; Wilson dexterously portrays the racial divisions and economics of urban renewal in his hometown (Sternlicht, 209). *King Hedley II* struggles with the need for forgiveness. Hedley, a recently released murderer (he killed a man who assaulted him), tries to leave behind his criminal life by starting a business. Hedley is destitute and his wife is pregnant, but his planting of a garden symbolizes undying possibility (Sternlicht, 212). In both *Two Trains* and *Seven Guitars*, characters either manage to retain or rediscover hope, to achieve security in the face of adversity, or to believe in the future against the losses of the past.

Wilson had many successes, from Pulitzer Prizes to Tony Awards, from a Guggenheim Fellowship (1986) to membership in the American Academy of Arts and Letters (1995). Nevertheless, he had considerable misgivings about the sincerity of those successes, suspecting his career is a mere token when set against the generally limited support for Black artists. In his keynote address to the Theatre Communications Group National Conference (1996), Wilson criticized funding of White theaters for Black plays, arguing that those monies should go to legitimate Black theaters. He also challenged the American stage's dependence on colorblind casting to give roles to Black actors, saying it distracted the theater from encouraging more new Black playwrights. He attacked Robert Brustein for charging him with "separatism" and for his "sophomoric assumptions" about theater outside a White tradition (Bogumil, 7). The speech, and Brustein's response, led to a heated debate that culminated in a public forum moderated by Anna Deavere Smith (1997). Despite the unusual opportunity for a playwright and critic to discuss the purpose and future of drama, the event turned into a public heckling and a hostile stand-off (Shafer, 14). Wilson continued to advocate and focus public efforts on increasing opportunities for African American playwrights, while standing as one of the world's most important active dramatists.

Ben Fisler

See also: Drama; Postmodernism; Vernacular.

Resources

Primary Sources: August Wilson: "August Wilson Responds," *American Theatre* (October 1996), 101–107; *Fences* (New York: New American Library, 1986); *The Ground on Which I Stand* (New York: Theatre Communications Group, 2001); "In His Own Words," *Applause* (January 1990), 5; "The Janitor," in *Short Pieces from the New Dramatists*, ed. Stan Chervin (New York: Broadway Play Publishing, 1985); *Jitney* (New York: Samuel French, 2002); *Joe Turner's Come and Gone* (New York: New American Library, 1988); *King Hedley II* (New York: Theatre Communications Group, 2005); "The Legacy of Malcolm X," *Life*, Dec. 1992, 84; *Ma Rainey's Black Bottom* (New York: New American Library, 1985); *The Piano Lesson* (New York: Plume, 1990); *The Piano Lesson*, dir. Lloyd Richards (Artisan Pictures, 1995); *Seven Guitars* (New York: Dutton, 1996); *Two Trains Running* (New York: Dutton, 1992).

Secondary Sources: Harold Bloom, ed., *August Wilson* (Broomall, PA: Chelsea House, 2002); Mary L. Bogumil, *Understanding August Wilson* (Columbia, SC: University of South Carolina Press, 1999); Margaret Booker, *Lillian Hellman and August Wilson: Dramatizing a New American Identity* (New York: Peter Lang, 2003); Keith Clark, *Black Manhood in James Baldwin, Ernest J. Gaines, and August Wilson* (Urbana, IL: University of Illinois Press, 2002); Harry Justin Elam, *The Past as Present in the Drama of August Wilson* (Ann Arbor: University of Michigan Press, 2004); Marilyn Elkins, ed., *August Wilson: A Casebook* (New York: Garland, 1994); Joan Herrington, *I Ain't Sorry for Nothin' I Done: August Wilson's Process of Playwriting* (New York: Limelight Editions, 1998); Alan Nadel, ed.: *August Wilson: Completing the Twentieth-Century Cycle* (Iowa City, IA: University of Iowa Press, 2010); *May All Your Fences Have Gates: Essays on the Drama of August Wilson* (Iowa City, IA: University of Iowa Press, 1994); Kim Pereira, *August Wilson and the African American Odyssey* (Urbana, IL: University of Illinois Press, 1995); Yvonne Shafer, *August Wilson: A Research and Production Sourcebook* (Westport, CT: Greenwood Press, 1998); Sandra G. Shannon: *August Wilson's Fences: A Reference Guide* (Westport, CT: Greenwood Press, 2003); *The Dramatic Vision of August Wilson* (Washington, DC: Howard University Press, 1995); Sandra G. Shannon, ed., *August Wilson's Pittsburgh Cycle: Critical Perspectives on the Plays* (Jefferson, NC: McFarland, 2015); Sandra G. Shannon and Sandra L. Richards, eds., *Approaches to Teaching the Plays of August Wilson* (New York: Modern Language Association, 2016); Sanford V. Sternlicht, *A Reader's Guide to Modern American Drama* (Syracuse, NY: Syracuse University Press, 2002); Qun Wang, *An In-depth Study of the Major Plays of African American Playwright August Wilson: Vernacularizing the Blues on Stage* (Lewiston, NY: Edwin Mellen, 1999); Peter Wolfe, *August Wilson* (New York: Twayne, 1999).

Wilson, Harriet E. (1825–1900)

Novelist. Originally published in 1859, Harriet Wilson's *Our Nig; or, Sketches from the Life of a Free Black (Our Nig)* was the first novel published by a free African American woman. (Hannah Crafts is likely the very first African American woman to write a novel.) Written as plea for financial support,

Our Nig garnered little critical attention at the time of its publication and remained in obscurity until Henry Louis Gates Jr. rediscovered the novel in 1981 and republished it in 1983. Many of the scant facts known about Wilson's life are the result of painstaking research by Gates and more recent investigative work by Barbara White. Wilson was born Harriet Adams in New Hampshire in 1825. She was a servant in the wealthy Milford, New Hampshire, household of Nehemiah and Rebecca Hayward, and she endured both physical and psychological abuse inflicted upon her by Mrs. Hayward. That abuse would later become the focus of *Our Nig*. On October 6, 1851, Wilson married Thomas Wilson, who was from Virginia. By the time her novel was published, she was living in Boston, Massachusetts. Wilson wrote her novel in an effort to raise funds for her son George's medical care. Her son died in 1860, shortly after its publication. Wilson died in Quincy, Massachusetts, in 1900.

Alice Walker's response to *Our Nig*, which appeared on the front cover of the 1983 edition, best sums up the book's significance to African American literature:

> I sat up most of the night reading and pondering the enormous significance of Harriet Wilson's novel *Our Nig*. It is as if we'd just discovered Phillis Wheatley—or Langston Hughes. . . . She represents a similar vastness of heretofore unexamined experience, a whole new layer of time and existence in American life and literature.

Indeed, *Our Nig* launched the literary tradition in fiction by African American women writers. Its distinctiveness lies in its narrative hybridity; like Hannah Crafts's *The Bondwoman's Narrative*, *Our Nig* is at once a sentimental novel, a domestic novel, a slave narrative, and an autobiography. Wilson makes use of overtly sentimental language to elicit an emotional response from her readers to sympathize with the plight of Frado, the abandoned and then orphaned "tragic mulatta." Borrowing from what Nina Baym terms the overplot, a stock device in popular domestic novels by White women, Wilson features Frado's long and difficult journey to self-realization and independence. That journey includes regular beatings by her mistress, Mrs. Bellmont. Unlike White heroines such as Gertrude Flint in *The Lamplighter*, Frado's hard work and virtue are not rewarded with a happy marriage and stability. Instead, debilitated by ill health as a result of overwork and extreme poverty, she leaves readers responsible for her fate (and by this time we know that Frado and Wilson are doubles): "Reposing on God, she has thus far journeyed securely. Still an invalid, she asks for your sympathy, gentle reader" (Wilson, 130).

Since its second edition in 1983 (and a reissue in 2002), *Our Nig* has inspired a variety of scholarship. Eric Gardner provides a comprehensive overview of its publishing history, and Carla Peterson argues that the function of the narrative is to "expose the romanticization of this figure [the tragic mulatta] and point to its economic basis" (165). Cynthia Davis argues that "it is pain, not sexuality, which explicitly determined Frado's physical experiences, which makes her body visible" (393). Lois Leveen focuses on the racial and spatial implication of the Bellmont house, contending that "Wilson's authorial strategy in depicting the house of oppression contests the very assumptions that serve as the foundation for the racial and spatial practices in that house" (570).

Rebecca R. Saulsbury

See also: Novel.

Resources

Nina Baym, *American Women Writers and the Work of History, 1790–1860* (New Brunswick, NJ: Rutgers University Press, 1995); Cynthia J. Davis, "Speaking the Body's Pain: Harriet Wilson's *Our Nig*," *African American Review* 27 (Fall 1993), 391–404; Eric Gardner, "'This Attempt of Their Sister': Harriet Wilson's *Our Nig* from Printer to Readers," *New England Quarterly* 66, no. 2 (June 1993), 226–246; Henry Louis Gates Jr., "Introduction," in *Our Nig; or, Sketches from the Life of a Free Black*, by Harriet Wilson (New York: Vintage, 1983), xi–lv; Lois Leveen, "Dwelling in the House of Oppression: The Spatial, Racial and Textual Dynamics of Harriet Wilson's *Our Nig*," *African American Review* 35, no. 4 (Winter 2001), 561–581; Emmanuel S. Nelson, "Harriet E. Wilson," in *African American Authors, 1745–1945: A Bio-Bibliographical Critical Sourcebook*, ed. Nelson (Westport, CT: Greenwood Press, 2000), 483–487; Carla L. Peterson, *"Doers of the Word": African-American Women Speakers and Writers in the North* (New Brunswick, NJ: Rutgers University Press, 1998); Alice Walker, Comment on back cover of *Our Nig; or, Sketches from the Life of a Free Black*, ed. Henry Louis Gates Jr. (New York: Vintage, 1983); Barbara A. White, "Afterword: New Information on Harriet E. Wilson and the Bellmont Family," in *Our Nig; or, Sketches from the Life of a Free Black*, 2nd ed., ed. Henry Louis Gates Jr. (New York: Vintage, 2002), iii–liv; Harriet E. Wilson, *Our Nig; or, Sketches from the Life of a Free Black*, ed. Henry Louis Gates Jr. (New York: Vintage, 1983).

Wright, Richard (1908–1960)

Novelist, essayist, short-story writer, and poet. Wright is best known for his novel *Native Son* (1940) and for being one of the most important, critically acclaimed, and popular American fiction writers active in the middle of the twentieth century. Although *Native Son* is considered his master work, he wrote a number of other important novels, essays, autobiographies, and short stories. Richard Nathaniel Wright was born on September 4, 1908, in Roxie, Mississippi, to Nathaniel Wright and Ella Wilson Wright. By 1912, his parents' marriage had dissolved, and he experienced great hunger and severe poverty. As a consequence, he and his younger brother, Leon, were shuffled among relatives. Although this situation caused his formal education to be disrupted, Wright was eventually able to immerse himself in the world of fiction. While he was staying with his grandparents, a lodger there introduced Wright to the story of Blue Beard. Wright would explain years later—in his best-selling autobiography, *Black Boy: A Record of Childhood and Youth* (1945)—that as she told him the story, "reality changed, the look of things altered, and the world became peopled with magical presences. … The sensations the story aroused in me were never to leave me" (39). Wright nurtured these passions well into his teen years, and in the spring of 1925, he published his first story in a Jackson, Mississippi, newspaper.

By November 1927, Wright had left the South to escape the brutalities of racism. Unfortunately, as he would explain in *Black Boy*, the North was hardly the utopia he envisioned: "My first glimpse of the flat black stretches of Chicago depressed and dismayed me, mocked all my fantasies" (261). Although the harsh realities of the Great Depression dimmed his hopes, Chicago, Illinois, proved to be crucial to his development as a writer and an intellectual. He read literary periodicals and studied the techniques of such writers as Gertrude Stein, e. e. cummings, T. S. Eliot, and

William Faulkner. By 1932 he had joined the John Reed Club, a literary society organized by the Communist Party. The club provided Wright with the opportunity to discuss fiction and share ideas. By 1933 he had joined the Communist Party and was excited by its promise to unite the working classes all over the world. During this period, Wright began writing poetry and first published it in the journals *New Masses* and *Left Front*. The poems that he produced were intended to inspire the proletariat to rise up against the bourgeois capitalist system.

Though Communist Party ideology had a profound effect on his development, Wright's first novel was devoid of these influences. In spite of his interest in revolutionary fiction, he did not intend *Lawd Today!* to serve as a symbolic representation of African American workers. Upon its completion in 1937 the novel was originally called *Cesspool*, a title reflecting its thematic content. *Lawd Today!/Cesspool* is replete with vain, ignorant braggarts who crave the approval of other men. Structurally, Wright relies upon tone more than the finer points of plot; it is a story full of moments of irony, sardonic humor, and poignancy.

Unfortunately for Wright, publishers were uninterested in his Chicago-based novel, which was released posthumously in 1967. Wright was undeterred, however, and he earned critical acclaim for his first published book, *Uncle Tom's Children* (1938). *Uncle Tom's Children* is a collection of five short stories focusing on African American manhood. Unlike *Lawd Today!* these stories were intended to be symbolic portraits of his race. All five stories—including the autobiographical essay "The Ethics of Living Jim Crow"—attempt to demystify the American South.

Rebellion and Black male survival are the subjects of Wright's most successful novel, *Native Son* (1940), which is loosely based on the experiences of a convicted Chicago murderer, Robert Nixon. Wright tells the story of Bigger Thomas, whose profound instincts for survival enable him to recognize his own humanity. Bigger is a poor African American youth living in a single-parent home on Chicago's South Side. While employed as a chauffeur for a rich White family, he accidentally murders the daughter. What ensues is a wild scheme to dispose of the body and demand a ransom for her safe return. Eventually, Bigger is hunted down by the police and brought to trial. Just like his real-life counterpart, Bigger Thomas is sentenced to death by an all-White jury.

One of themes of the novel concerns the American Dream. Wright constructs a narrative in which this established ideal is exposed as an empty myth maintained at the expense of African American lives. Bigger Thomas's victimization and tragic end are meant to establish this point. In this regard Bigger is intended to signify the revolutionary potential of the African American masses. At the same time, Wright constructs Bigger Thomas as a despicable figure. He is a morally ambivalent character whom readers often champion for his fierce survival instincts yet revile for his deviousness: he murders two women, betrays an acquaintance, and attempts to defraud the White family that employed him. Although his actions are depraved, the narration leads readers to find the United States culpable for creating its Bigger Thomases.

In October 1941, Wright coauthored a photo documentary about the history of African American suffering. Titled *Twelve Million Black Voices: A Folk History of the Negro*, it was, according to Hazel Rowley, a work that inspired passion in Wright: "Wright's empathy for his own people is more evident [in *12 Million Black Voices*] than in any of his fiction" (237). Even as Wright continued to work and travel, he found time to enrich his personal life. On March 12, 1941, he married fellow Communist Party member Ellen Poplowitz.

As Wright's career flourished, the political mood of the nation was shifting. The United States was growing less tolerant of political dissent and more apprehensive of communism. Wright, too, was finding his relationship with the Communist Party to be intolerable. The party did not share Wright's artistic vision and was dismayed by his unrelenting focus on African American political issues. They felt that he would better serve them as an author of non-racialized, proletarian-based fiction. By 1944 Wright regarded the Communist Party as a hindrance to Black liberation, and he publicly severed ties with them by penning the essay "I Tried to Be a Communist."

Wright's most renowned piece of nonfiction was released to the public in March 1955. *Black Boy* is an autobiography intended, arguably, to function as an allegorical biography of his race. It narrates Wright's life from his humble origins in Mississippi up to his abandonment of the South. The episodes address the symbolic and physical violence that intrude upon African American life—moments that parallel the events in *Uncle Tom's Children*. In particular, Wright focuses on the almost casual emasculations that African American men experience on a daily basis. But this work differed from his volume of short stories significantly in that he intended to juxtapose Southern racism and Northern racism. Unfortunately, Wright's publishers pressured him to lift this latter section from *Black Boy*. *American Hunger*, the second

part of his autobiography, was not published until 1977, well after Wright's death.

In midcareer, Wright was in a unique position as an African American novelist. No longer beholden to anyone, he was able to serve as a spokesperson for his race and speak out against American racial injustice. In spite of his fame, Wright was reconsidering his American citizenship—unwilling to raise his daughter in a society committed to segregation. In 1946, he and his family toured France, and by August 1947, they had become residents. Wright's expatriation produced a ripple effect in the lives of African American authors.

Transplanting himself from the United States to Europe provided Wright with renewed inspiration. The self-educated author of two best sellers had long studied sociological theory, Marxism, Freudian theory, and the literary techniques of Modernism and naturalism. European residency introduced Wright to existentialism and the Négritude literary movement. From these experiences he published two novels: *The Outsider* (1953), an existential investigation of racial identity, and *Savage Holiday* (1954), a Freudian novel about a neurotic White businessman. Both works reflect Wright's interest in deviant behavior and criminal motivation. Neither work received positive reviews in the United States. Critics began to suggest that Wright's expatriation was handicapping his talents. Moreover, with the emergence of new writers, critics were asserting that Wright was out of touch with the African American experience. Nevertheless, these novels further the signature themes that reverberate in his body of work: psychological despair, interracial conflict, and Black American manhood.

As African nations struggled for their independence, Wright became increasingly interested in the "Mother Land." He decided to visit the Gold Coast, now known as Ghana, in June 1953. In *Black Power: A Record of Reactions in a Land of Pathos* (1954) Wright observes colonialism as it affects the formally educated elite and the tradition-faithful masses. He was troubled by the clashing belief systems of these two groups. He questioned how a country could modernize while tied to tribal identity. Wright was befuddled by observance of ancient cultural rites, even among the Western-educated.

Considering the extent of Wright's international travels, his productivity during the 1950s was phenomenal. He followed *Black Power* with an analysis of the political aspirations of Third World nations in *The Color Curtain: A Report on the Bandung Conference* (1956) and social criticism of Spain, detailed in *Pagan Spain* (1957). With renewed vigor Wright recommitted himself to fiction. In 1957, he published a collection of essays on class, culture, and the construction of literary ideas: *White Man, Listen!*

Rather than revisit the theme of alienation, Wright returned in his final novel to a rural setting and the problematic relationship between American Whites and Blacks. Today *The Long Dream* (1958) is deemed by many scholars to be an exceptional effort, second only to his *Native Son*. *The Long Dream* focuses on the Tucker family and their identification with American capitalism. Once again, Wright constructs morally ambivalent figures to address a larger point about the economic system of the United States and the values that are sacrificed in order to maintain it. The Tucker father and son must reconcile their manipulation of the African American community with their victimization by the White power structure.

Wright's death from heart failure on November 28, 1960, marked the passing of one of the most important authors in American history and modern literary history. Toward the end of his life, he returned to poetry as a creative outlet. Haiku proved to be liberating for Wright, enabling him to focus on essences rather than structure and character motivation. Owing to his exposure to new peoples and ideas, many scholars are left with the impression that he was going through a transitional stage in his career. Wright's legacy, and the impact of *Native Son*, was strongest during the Chicago Renaissance, the Protest Literature era, and the Black Arts Movement. Richard Wright's body of work contributes to the fields of sociology, political science, cultural studies, Whiteness Studies, gender studies, queer theory, and many other facets of American literature and criticism.

Lawrence A. Davis

See also: Novel; Protest Literature; Realism.

Resources

Primary Sources: Richard Wright: *Black Boy (American Hunger): A Record of Childhood and Youth* (1945; repr. New York: HarperPerennial, 1998); *Black Power: A Record of Reactions in a Land of Pathos* (1954; repr. Westport, CT: Greenwood Press, 1974); *The Color Curtain: A Report on the Bandung Conference* (1956; repr. Jackson, MS: Banner Books, 1995); *Eight Men* (1961; repr. New York: HarperPerennial, 1996); *Haiku: This Other World* (New York: Arcade, 1998); "I Tried to Be a Communist," *Atlantic Monthly*, August–September 1944, repr. in *The God That Failed*, ed. Richard Crossman (Chicago: Regnery, 1983); *Lawd Today!* (1963; repr. Boston: Northeastern University Press, 1991); *The Long Dream* (1958; repr. Boston: Northeastern University Press, 1986); *Native Son* (1940; repr. New York: HarperPerennial, 1998); *The Outsider* (1953; repr. New York: HarperPerennial, 1993); *Pagan Spain* (1957; repr. Jackson, MS: Banner Books, 2002); *Savage Holiday* (1954; repr. Jackson, MS:

Banner Books, 1994); *Uncle Tom's Children* (1938; repr. New York: HarperPerennial, 1993); *White Man, Listen!* (1957; repr. New York: HarperPerennial, 1995).

Secondary Sources: James Baldwin, *Notes of a Native Son* (1963; repr. Boston: Beacon Press, 1984); Alice Craven and William Dow, eds., *Richard Wright: New Readings in the 21st Century* (New York: Palgrave Macmillan, 2011); William Dow, Alice Craven, and Yoko Nakamura, *Richard Wright in a Post-Racial Imaginary* (New York: Bloomsbury, 2014); Michel Fabre, *The Unfinished Quest of Richard Wright*, trans. Isabel Barzun, 2nd ed. (Urbana, IL: University of Illinois Press, 1993); Henry Louis Gates Jr. and K. A. Appiah, eds., *Richard Wright: Critical Perspectives Past and Present* (New York: Amistad, 1993); Addison Gayle, *Richard Wright: Ordeal of a Native Son* (Garden City, NY: Doubleday, 1980); James B. Haile III, *Philosophical Meditations on Richard Wright* (Lanham, MD: Lexington Books, 2012); Yoshinobu Hakutani, *Richard Wright and Haiku* (Columbia, MO: University of Missouri Press, 2014); *Richard Wright and Racial Discourse* (Columbia, MO: University of Missouri Press, 1996); Joyce Ann Joyce, *Richard Wright's Art of Tragedy* (Iowa City, IA: University of Iowa Press, 1986); Sachi Nakachi, "Richard Wright's Haiku; or, The Poetry of Double Voice," in *African American Haiku: Cultural Visions*, ed. John Zheng (Jackson, MS: University Press of Mississippi, 2016), 25–34; Susan Scott Parrish, "Richard Wright's Environments: Mediating Personhood through the South's Second Nature," in *Reading African American Autobiography: Twenty-First-Century Contexts and Criticism*, ed. Eric D. Lamore (Madison, WI: University of Wisconsin Press, 2017), 117–144; Hazel Rowley, *Richard Wright: The Life and Times* (New York: Henry Holt, 2001); Virginia Whatley Smith, ed., *Richard Wright: Writing America at Home and from Abroad* (Jackson, MS: University Press of Mississippi, 2016); *Richard Wright's Travel Writings* (Jackson, MS: University Press of Mississippi, 2001); Tyler Stovall, *Paris Noir: African Americans in the City of Light* (Boston: Houghton Mifflin, 1996); Ellen Wright and Michel Fabre., eds., *Richard Wright Reader* (New York: Da Capo Press, 1997).

General Bibliography and List of Organizations, Museums, and Research Centers

Reference Sources (Compiled by Lori Ricigliano)

Aberjhani, and Sandra L. West. *Encyclopedia of the Harlem Renaissance*. New York: Facts on File, 2003.

Andrews, William L., Frances Smith Foster, and Trudier Harris, eds. *The Oxford Companion to African American Literature*. New York: Oxford University Press, 1997.

Arata, Esther Spring, and Nicholas John Rotoli. *Black American Playwrights, 1800 to the Present: A Bibliography*. Metuchen, NJ: Scarecrow, 1976.

Arata, Esther Spring, et al. *More Black American Playwrights: A Bibliography*. Metuchen, NJ: Scarecrow, 1978.

Asante, Molefi K., and Mark T. Mattson. *The African-American Atlas: Black History and Culture. An Illustrated Reference*. New York: Macmillan, 1998.

Bassett, John Earl. *Harlem in Review: Critical Reactions to Black American Writers, 1917–1939*. Selinsgrove, PA: Susquehanna University Press, 1992.

Beaulieu, Elizabeth Ann. *The Toni Morrison Encyclopedia*. Westport, CT: Greenwood Press, 2003.

Bruccoli, Matthew J., and Judith S. Baughman, eds. *Modern African American Writers*. New York: Facts on File, 1994.

Campbell, Dorothy W. *Index to Black American Writers in Collective Biographies*. Littleton, CO: Libraries Unlimited, 1983.

Chapman, Dorothy Hilton. *Index to Black Poetry*. Boston: G. K. Hall, 1974.

Chapman, Dorothy Hilton, comp. *Index to Poetry by Black American Women*. Westport, CT: Greenwood Press, 1986.

Davis, Thadious M., and Trudier Harris, eds. *Afro-American Fiction Writers after 1955. Dictionary of Literary Biography*, vol. 33. Detroit: Gale, 1984. Also *Literature Resource Center*, http://www.galegroup.com.

Davis, Thadious M., and Trudier Harris, eds. *Afro-American Writers after 1955: Dramatists and Prose Writers. Dictionary of Literary Biography*, vol. 38. Detroit: Gale, 1985. Also *Literature Resource Center*, http://www.galegroup.com.

Dickson-Carr, Darryl. *The Columbia Guide to Contemporary African American Fiction*. New York: Columbia University Press, 2005.

Draper, James P., ed. *Black Literature Criticism: Excerpts from Criticism of the Most Significant Works of Black Authors over the Past 200 Years*. 3 vols. Detroit: Gale, 1992.

Edwards, Erica R., Roderick A. Ferguson, and Jeffrey O.G. Ogbar, eds. *Keywords for African American Studies*. New York: New York University Press, 2018.

Elliot, Emory, ed. *Columbia Literary History of the United States*. New York: Columbia University Press, 1988.

Fairbanks, Carol, and Eugene A. Engeldinger. *Black American Fiction: A Bibliography*. Metuchen, NJ: Scarecrow, 1978.

Frankovich, Nicholas, and David Larzelere, eds. *The Columbia Granger's Index to*

African-American Poetry. New York: Columbia University Press, 1999.

French, William P., and Geneviève Fabre. *Afro-American Poetry and Drama, 1760–1975: A Guide to Information Sources*. Detroit: Gale, 1979.

Gavin, Christy, ed. *African American Women Playwrights: A Research Guide*. New York: Garland, 1999.

Graham, Maryemma, ed. *The Cambridge Companion to the African American Novel*. New York: Cambridge University Press, 2004.

Harris, Trudier, ed. *Afro-American Writers, 1940–1955. Dictionary of Literary Biography*, vol. 76. Detroit: Gale, 1988. Also *Literature Resource Center*, http://www.galegroup.com.

Harris, Trudier, and Thadious M. Davis, eds. *Afro-American Poets Since 1955. Dictionary of Literary Biography*, vol. 41. Detroit: Gale, 1985. Also *Literature Resource Center*, http://www.galegroup.com.

Harris, Trudier, and Thadious M. Davis, eds. *Afro-American Writers before the Harlem Renaissance. Dictionary of Literary Biography*, vol. 50. Detroit: Gale, 1986. Also *Literature Resource Center*, http://www.galegroup.com.

Harris, Trudier, and Thadious M. Davis, eds. *Afro-American Writers from the Harlem Renaissance to 1940. Dictionary of Literary Biography*, vol. 51. Detroit: Gale, 1987. Also *Literature Resource Center*, http://www.galegroup.com.

Hatch, James V., and Omanii Abdullah, comps. and eds. *Black Playwrights, 1823–1977: An Annotated Bibliography of Plays*. New York: Bowker, 1977.

Hatch, Sheri Dorantes, ed. *Encyclopedia of African-American Writing: Five Centuries of Contribution: Trials & Triumphs of Writers, Poets, Publications and Organizations*. 2nd ed. Amenia, NY: Grey House Pub., 2009.

Hedgepeth, Chester M., Jr. *Twentieth-Century African-American Writers and Artists*.

Chicago: American Library Association, 1991.

Hill, Michael D., and Lena M. Hill. *Ralph Ellison's* Invisible Man*: A Reference Guide*. Westport, CT: Greenwood Press, 2008.

Hudson, J. Blaine. *The Encyclopedia of the Underground Railroad*. Jefferson, NC: McFarland Publishing, 2006.

Hunter, Jeffrey W., and Jerry Moore, eds. *Black Literature Criticism: Excerpts from Criticism of the Most Significant Works of Black Authors over the Past 200 Years. Supplement*. Detroit: Gale, 1999.

Jordan, Casper LeRoy, comp. *A Bibliographical Guide to African-American Women Writers*. Westport, CT: Greenwood Press, 1993.

Kallenbach, Jessamine S., comp. *Index to Black American Literary Anthologies*. Boston: G. K. Hall, 1979.

Kutenplon, Deborah, and Ellen Olmstead. *Young Adult Fiction by African American Writers, 1968–1993: A Critical and Annotated Guide*. New York: Garland, 1996.

Magill, Frank N., ed. *Masterpieces of African-American Literature*. New York: HarperCollins, 1992.

Magill, Frank N., ed. *Masterplots II: African American Literature Series*. 3 vols. Pasadena, CA: Salem, 1994.

Margolies, Edward, and David Bakish. *Afro-American Fiction, 1853–1976: A Guide to Information Sources*. Detroit: Gale, 1979.

Metzger, Linda, et al., eds. *Black Writers: A Selection of Sketches from Contemporary Authors*. Detroit: Gale, 1989.

Miller, R. Baxter. *Langston Hughes and Gwendolyn Brooks: A Reference Guide*. Boston: G. K. Hall, 1978.

Miller, Randall M., and John David Smith, eds. *Dictionary of Afro-American Slavery*. Westport, CT: Greenwood Press, 1988.

Moll, Kirk. "Reference Works on African American Literature: A Bibliographic

Guide." *Collection Building*, 2002, Vol. 21(3), p. 85.

Murphy, Barbara Thrash, and Deborah Murphy, eds. *Black Authors and Illustrators of Books for Children and Young Adults: A Biographical Dictionary*. 4th ed. New York: Routledge, 2007.

Nelson, Emmanuel S., ed. *African American Authors, 1745–1945: A Bio-Bibliographical Critical Sourcebook*. Westport, CT: Greenwood Press, 2000.

Nelson, Emmanuel S., ed. *African American Dramatists: An A to Z Guide*. Westport, CT: Greenwood Press, 2004.

Nelson, Emmanuel S., ed. *Contemporary African American Novelists: A Bio-Bibliographical Critical Sourcebook*. Westport, CT: Greenwood Press, 1999.

Ostrom, Hans. *A Langston Hughes Encyclopedia*. Westport, CT: Greenwood Press, 2002.

Ostrom, Hans, and J. David Macey, ed. *The Greenwood Encyclopedia of African American Literature*. 5 volumes. Westport, CT: Greenwood Press, 2005.

Page, Yolanda Williams, ed. *Encyclopedia of African American Women Writers*. 2 vols. Westport, CT: Greenwood Press, 2007.

Peavy, Charles D. *Afro-American Literature and Culture since World War II: A Guide to Information Sources*. Detroit: Gale, 1979.

Peterson, Bernard L. *Early Black American Playwrights and Dramatic Writers: A Biographical Directory and Catalog of Plays, Films, and Broadcasting Scripts*. Westport, CT: Greenwood Press, 1990.

Peterson, Bernard L., Jr. *Contemporary Black American Playwrights and Their Plays: A Biographical Directory and Dramatic Index*. Westport, CT: Greenwood Press, 1988.

Pettis, Joyce Owens. *African American Poets: Lives, Works, and Sources*. Westport, CT: Greenwood Press, 2002.

Richards, Phillip M., and Neil Schlager. *Best Literature by and about Blacks*. Detroit: Gale, 2000.

Roses, Lorraine Elena, and Ruth Elizabeth Randolph. *Harlem Renaissance and Beyond: Literary Biographies of 100 Black Women Writers, 1900–1945*. Boston: G. K. Hall, 1990.

Rush, Theressa Gunnels, Carol Fairbanks Myers, and Esther Spring Arata. *Black American Writers Past and Present: A Biographical and Bibliographical Dictionary*. 2 vols. Metuchen, NJ: Scarecrow, 1975.

Shockley, Ann Allen, ed. *Afro-American Women Writers, 1746–1933: An Anthology and Critical Guide*. Boston: G. K. Hall, 1988.

Smith, Valerie, ed. *African American Writers*. 2nd ed. New York: Scribner's, 2001.

Southgate, Robert. *Black Plots & Black Characters: A Handbook for Afro-American Literature*. Syracuse, NY: Gaylord, 1979.

Valade, Roger M. *The Essential Black Literature Guide*. Detroit: Visible Ink, 1996.

Werner, Craig. *Black American Women Novelists: An Annotated Bibliography*. Pasadena, CA: Salem, 1989.

Williams, Dana A. *Contemporary African American Female Playwrights: An Annotated Bibliography*. Westport, CT: Greenwood Press, 1998.

Witalec, Janet, ed. *The Harlem Renaissance: A Gale Critical Companion*. 3 vols. Detroit: Gale, 2003.

Yancy, Preston M., comp. *The Afro-American Short Story: A Comprehensive, Annotated Index with Selected Commentaries*. Westport, CT: Greenwood Press, 1986.

Yellin, Jean Fagan, and Cynthia D. Bond, comps. *The Pen Is Ours: A Listing of Writings by and about African-American Women before 1910 with Secondary Bibliography to the Present*. New York: Oxford University Press, 1991.

Anthologies

Abrahams, Roger D. *African American Folktales: Stories from Black Traditions in the New World*. New York: Pantheon, 1999.

Akinyemi, Nia Sadé. *For Colored Girls Growing Like a Rose From Concrete: An Anthology.* Atlanta: Sade/Literary Revolutionary Press, 2017.

Branch, William B. *Black Thunder: An Anthology of Contemporary African American Drama.* New York: Signet, 1995.

Brown, Leslie, ed. *African American Voices: A Documentary Reader from Emancipation to the Present.* Hoboken, NJ: Wiley & Blackwell, 2014.

Brown, Sterling Allen, Arthur P. Davis, and Ulysses Grant Lee, eds. *The Negro Caravan: Writings by American Negroes.* New York: Citadel, 1941.

Collier-Thomas, Bettye, comp. and ed. *A Treasury of African American Christmas Stories.* 2 vols. New York: Henry Holt, 1997–1999.

Courlander, Harold. *A Treasury of Afro-American Folklore: The Oral Literature, Traditions, Recollections, Legends, Tales, Songs, Religious Beliefs, Customs, Sayings, and Humor of Peoples of African American Descent in the Americas.* Repr. ed. New York: Marlowe, 2002.

Dance, Daryl Cumber, ed. *From My People: 400 Years of African American Folklore.* New York: Norton, 2002.

Dance, Daryl Cumber, ed. *Honey, Hush! An Anthology of African American Women's Humor.* New York: Norton, 1998.

Davis, Arthur P., and J. Saunders Redding, eds. *Cavalcade: Negro American Writing from 1760 to the Present.* Boston: Houghton Mifflin, 1971.

Donalson, Melvin Burke, ed. *Cornerstones: An Anthology of African American Literature.* New York: Bedford/St. Martin's, 1996.

Dungy, Camille T., ed. *Black Nature: Four Centuries of African American Nature Poetry.* Athens: University of Georgia Press, 2009.

Emanuel, James A., and Theodore L. Gross, eds. *Dark Symphony: Negro Literature in America.* New York: Free Press, 1968.

Gabbin, Joanne V., ed. *Furious Flower: African American Poetry from the Black Arts Movement to the Present.* Charlottesville: University Press of Virginia, 2004.

Gates, Henry Louis, Jr., ed. *The Classic Slave Narratives.* New York: Signet Classics, 2002.

Gates, Henry Louis, Jr., and Maria Tatar, eds. *The Annotated African American Folktales.* New York: Liveright/W.W. Norton, 2017.

Gates, Henry Louis, Jr., Nellie Y. McKay, et al., eds. *The Norton Anthology of African American Literature.* 3rd ed. 2 vols. New York: Norton, 2014.

Gilbert, Derrick I. M., ed. *Catch the Fire!! A Cross-Generational Anthology of Contemporary African-American Poetry.* New York: Riverhead, 1998.

Gilyard, Keith, ed. *Spirit & Flame: An Anthology of Contemporary African American Poetry.* Syracuse, NY: Syracuse University Press, 1997.

Guy-Sheftall, Beverly, ed. *Words of Fire: An Anthology of African-American Feminist Thought.* New York: The New Press, 1995.

Hamalian, Leo, and James V. Hatch, eds. *The Roots of African American Drama: An Anthology of Early Plays, 1858–1938.* Detroit: Wayne State University Press, 1991.

Hamilton, Virginia. *The People Could Fly: American Black Folktales.* New York: Knopf, 1985.

Harper, Michael, and Anthony Walton, eds. *The Vintage Book of African American Poetry.* New York: Vintage, 2000.

Harris, Juliette, and Pamela Johnson, eds. *Tenderheaded: A Comb-Bending Collection of Hair Stories.* New York: Atria, 2001.

Harrison, Paul Carter, ed. *Totem Voices: Plays from the Black World Repertory.* New York: Grove, 1989.

Hatch, James, and Ted Shine, eds. *Black Theatre USA: Plays by African Americans from 1847 to Today*. Rev. and enl. ed. New York: Free Press, 1996.

Hill, Patricia Liggins, Bernard W. Bell, Trudier Harris, William J. Harris, R. Baxter Miller, and Shondra A. O'Neale, eds. *Call and Response: The Riverside Anthology of the African American Literary Tradition*. Boston: Houghton Mifflin, 1998.

Hughes, Langston, ed. *The Best Short Stories by Negro Writers: An Anthology from 1899 to the Present*. Boston: Little, Brown, 1967.

Hughes, Langston, and Arna Bontemps, eds. *The Book of Negro Folklore*. New York: Dodd, Mead, 1958.

Jarrett, Gene Andrew, ed. *African American Literature beyond Race: an Alternative Reader*. New York: New York University Press, 2006.

Jarrett, Gene Andrew, ed. *The Wiley Blackwell Anthology of African American Literature. Volume 1, 1746–1920*. Hoboken: John Wiley & Sons, 2014.

Jarrett, Gene Andrew, ed. *The Wiley Blackwell Anthology of African American Literature. Volume 2. 1920 to the Present*. Chichester, West Sussex, UK: Wiley Blackwell, 2014.

Johnson, E. Patrick, and Mae G. Henderson, eds. *Black Queer Studies: A Critical Anthology*. Durham, NC: Duke University Press, 2005.

Johnson, James Weldon, ed. *The Book of American Negro Poetry*. New York: Harcourt, Brace, 1931.

Jones, LeRoi, and Larry Neal, eds. *Black Fire: An Anthology of Afro-American Writing*. New York: Morrow, 1968.

King, Woodie, Jr., ed. *The National Black Drama Anthology: Eleven Plays from America's Leading African-American Theaters*. New York: Applause, 1995.

King, Woodie, Jr., and Ron Milner, eds. *Black Drama Anthology*. New York: Columbia University Press, 1972.

Lee, Valerie, ed. *The Prentice Hall Anthology of African American Women's Literature*. New York: Pearson, 2005.

Lewis, David Levering, ed. *The Portable Harlem Renaissance Reader*. New York: Viking, 1994.

Logan, Shirley Wilson, ed. *With Pen and Voice: A Critical Anthology of Nineteenth-Century African-American Women*. Carbondale: Southern Illinois University Press, 1995.

Mance, Ajuan Maria, ed. *Before Harlem: An Anthology of African American Literature from the Long Nineteenth Century*. Knoxville: University of Tennessee Press, 2016.

Marable, Manning, and Leith Mullings, eds. *Let Nobody Turn Us Around: An African American Anthology*. 2nd ed. Lanham, MD: Rowan & Littlefield, 2009.

McMillan, Terry, ed. *Breaking Ice: An Anthology of Contemporary African American Fiction*. New York: Penguin, 1990.

Mitchell, Angelyn, ed. *Within the Circle: An Anthology of African American Literary Criticism from the Harlem Renaissance to the Present*. Durham, NC: Duke University Press, 1994.

Naylor, Gloria, ed. *Children of the Night: The Best Short Stories by Black Writers, 1967 to the Present*. Boston: Little, Brown, 1995.

Newman, Richard, Patrick Rael, and Philip Lapsansky. *Pamphlets of Protest: An Anthology of Early African American Protest Literature, 1790–1860*. New York: Routledge, 2001.

Nielsen, Aldon Lynn, and Lauri Ramey, eds. *Every Goodbye Ain't Gone: An Anthology of Innovative Poetry by African Americans*. Tuscaloosa: University of Alabama Press, 2006.

Norris, Keenan, ed. *Street Lit.: Representing the Urban Landscape*. Lanham, MD: Rowman & Littlefield, 2013.

Oliver, Clinton, ed. *Contemporary Black Drama*. New York: Scribner's, 1971.

Patton, Venetia K., and Maureen Honey, eds. *Double-Take: A Revisionist Harlem Renaissance Anthology*. New Brunswick, NJ: Rutgers University Press, 2001.

Powell, Kevin, ed. *Step into a World: A Global Anthology of the New Black Literature.* New York: Wiley, 2000.

Rampersad, Arnold, and Hilary Herbold, eds. *The Oxford Anthology of African-American Poetry.* Oxford and New York: Oxford University Press, 2005.

Riggs, Marcia Y., and Barbara Holmes, eds. *Can I Get a Witness?: Prophetic Religious Voices of African American Women: An Anthology.* Ossining, NY: Orbis Books, 1997.

Robbins, Hollis, and Henry Louis Gates, Jr., eds. *The Portable Nineteenth-Century African American Women Writers.* New York: Penguin Books, 2017.

Ruff, Shawn Stewart, ed. *Go the Way Your Blood Beats: An Anthology of Lesbian and Gay Fiction by African American Writers.* New York: Henry Holt, 1996.

Sherman, Joan R. *African American Poetry: An Anthology, 1773–1927.* Mineola, NY: Dover, 1997.

Smith, Jay Clay, Jr., ed. *Rebels in Law: Voices in History of Black Women Lawyers.* Ann Arbor: University of Michigan Press, 1998.

Smith, Rochelle, and Sharon L. Jones, eds. *The Prentice Hall Anthology of African American Literature.* Upper Saddle River, NJ: Prentice Hall, 2000.

Watkins, Mel, ed. *African American Humor: The Best Black Comedy from Slavery to Today.* Chicago: Lawrence Hill, 2002.

Williams-Myers, Albert James, ed. *In Their Own Words: Voices from the Middle Passage.* Trenton, NJ: Africa World Press, 2009.

Wilson, Sondra Kathryn, ed. *The* Crisis *Reader: Stories, Poetry, and Essays from the N.A.A.C.P.'s* Crisis *Magazine.* New York: Modern Library, 1999.

Wilson, Sondra Kathryn, ed. *The* Opportunity *Reader: Stories, Poetry, and Essays from the Urban League's* Opportunity *Magazine.* New York: Modern Library, 1999.

Worley, Demetrice A., and Jesse Perry, Jr., comps. *African American Literature: An Anthology,* 2nd ed. Lincolnwood, IL: NTC, 1998.

Yetman, Norman R., ed. *Voices from Slavery: 100 Authentic Slave Narratives.* Mineola, NY: Dover, 2000.

Young, Al. *African American Literature: A Brief Introduction and Anthology.* New York: HarperCollins, 1996.

Young, Harvey, ed. *The Cambridge Companion to African American Theatre.* Cambridge: Cambridge University Press, 2013.

Zoboi, Ibi, ed. *Black Enough: Stories of Being Young & Black in America.* New York: Balzer & Bray/HarperCollins, 2019.

Criticism

Andrews, William L. *To Tell a Free Story: The First Century of Afro-American Autobiography, 1760–1865.* Urbana: University of Illinois Press, 1986.

Armengol, Josep M. *Masculinities in Black and White: Manliness and Whiteness in (African) American Literature.* New York: Palgrave MacMillan, 2014.

Asante, Molefi K. *The Afrocentric Idea.* Rev. and enl. ed. Philadelphia: Temple University Press, 1998.

Baker, Houston A. *Blues, Ideology, and Afro-American Literature: A Vernacular Theory.* Chicago: University of Chicago Press, 1984.

Baker, Houston A. *Modernism and the Harlem Renaissance.* Chicago: University of Chicago Press, 1987.

Baker, Houston A., Jr. *Afro American Poetics: Revisions of Harlem and the Black Aesthetic.* Madison: University of Wisconsin Press, 1988.

Baraka, Amiri. *Daggers and Javelins: Essays, 1974–1979.* New York: Morrow, 1984.

Barr, Marleen S., ed. *Afro-Future Females: Black Writers Chart Science Fiction's Newest New-Wave Trajectory.* Columbus: Ohio State University Press, 2008.

Birnbaum, Michele. *Race, Work, and Desire in American Literature, 1860–1930.* New York: Cambridge University Press, 2003.

Bolden, Tony. *Afro-Blue: Improvisations in African American Poetry and Culture.* Urbana: University of Illinois Press, 2004.

Bone, Robert. *The Negro Novel in America.* New Haven, CT: Yale University Press, 1958.

Brooks, Joanna. *American Lazarus: Religion and the Rise of African-American and Native American Literatures.* New York: Oxford University Press, 2003.

Brown, Fahamisha Patricia. *Performing the Word: African-American Poetry as Vernacular Culture.* New Brunswick, NJ: Rutgers University Press, 1999.

Carby, Hazel V. *Reconstructing Womanhood: The Emergence of the Afro-American Woman Novelist.* New York: Oxford University Press, 1987.

Christian, Barbara. *Black Feminist Criticism: Perspectives on Black Women Writers.* New York: Pergamon, 1985.

Christian, Barbara. *Black Women Novelists: The Development of a Tradition, 1892–1976.* Westport, CT: Greenwood Press, 1980.

Claborn, John. *Civil Rights and the Environment in African-American Literature, 1895–1941.* London: Bloomsbury Academic, 2018.

Collins, Patricia. *Black Feminist Thought: Knowledge, Consciousness, and the Politics of Empowerment.* Rev. ed. New York: Routledge, 2000.

Cook, Mercer, and Stephen E. Henderson. *The Militant Black Writer in Africa and the United States.* Madison: University of Wisconsin Press, 1969.

Davis, Arthur P. *From the Dark Tower: Afro-American Writers (1900 to 1960).* Washington, DC: Howard University Press, 1974.

Demirtürk, E. Lâle. *The Twenty-First Century African American Novel and the Critique of Whiteness in Everyday Life: Blackness as Strategy for Social Change.* Lanham, MD: Rowman & Littlefield, 2017.

Edwards, Brent Hayes. *Epistrophies: Jazz and the Literary Imagination.* Cambridge: Harvard University Press, 2017.

Elam, Harry J., Jr., and David Krasner, eds. *African-American Performance and Theater History: A Critical Reader.* New York: Oxford University Press, 2001.

Fabi, M. Giulia. *Passing and the Rise of the African American Novel.* Urbana: University of Illinois Press, 2001.

Feinstein, Sascha. *Jazz Poetry: From the 1920s to the Present.* Westport, CT: Greenwood Press, 1997.

Ferguson, Roderick A. *Aberrations in Black: Toward a Queer of Color Critique.* Minneapolis: University of Minnesota Press, 2004.

Furlonge, Nicole Brittingham. *Race Sounds: The Art of Listening in African American Literature.* Iowa City: University of Iowa Press, 2018.

Gates, Henry Louis, Jr. *Loose Canons: Notes on the Culture Wars.* New York: Oxford University Press, 1992.

Gates, Henry Louis, Jr., ed. *Reading Black, Reading Feminist: A Critical Anthology.* New York: Merdian, 1990.

Gates, Henry Louis, Jr. *The Signifying Monkey: A Theory of Afro-American Literary Criticism.* New York: Oxford University Press, 1988.

Gayle, Addison, Jr. *The Black Aesthetic.* Garden City, NY: Doubleday, 1971.

Gayle, Addison, Jr. *The Way of the New World: The Black Novel in America.* Garden City, NY: Anchor, 1975.

Gibson, Donald B., ed. *Five Black Writers: Essays on Wright, Ellison, Baldwin, Hughes, and LeRoi Jones.* New York: New York University Press, 1970.

Gilroy, Paul. *The Black Atlantic: Modernity and Double Consciousness.* Cambridge, MA: Harvard University Press, 1993.

Gilyard, Keith. *Let's Flip the Script: An African American Discourse on Language, Literature, and Learning.* Detroit: Wayne State University Press, 1996.

Gordon, Lewis R., ed. *Existence in Black: An Anthology of Black Existential Philosophy.* New York: Routledge, 1997.

Hack, Daniel. *Reaping Something New: African American Transformations of Victorian Literature.* Princeton: Princeton University Press, 2017.

Harris, Trudier. *Martin Luther King Jr., Heroism, and African American Literature.* Tuscaloosa: University of Alabama Press, 2014.

Harris-Lopez, Trudier. *The Power of the Porch: The Storyteller's Craft in Zora Neale Hurston, Gloria Naylor, and Randall Kenan.* Athens: University of Georgia Press, 1996.

Harris-Lopez, Trudier. *Saints, Sinners, Saviors: Strong Black Women in African American Literature.* New York: Palgrave, 2001.

hooks, bell. *Ain't I a Woman: Black Women and Feminism.* Boston: South End Press, 1981.

hooks, bell. *Feminist Theory: From Margin to Center.* Boston: South End Press, 1984.

Hubbard, Dolan, ed. *Recovered Writers/Recovered Texts: Race, Class, and Gender in Black Women's Literature.* Knoxville: University of Tennessee Press, 1997.

Hubbard, Dolan. *The Sermon and the African American Literary Imagination.* Columbia: University of Missouri Press, 1994.

Hutchinson, George. *The Harlem Renaissance in Black and White.* Cambridge, MA: Belknap Press of Harvard University Press, 1995.

Jackson, Ronald L., II, and Elaine B. Richardson, eds. *Understanding African American Rhetoric: Classical Origins to Contemporary Innovations.* New York: Routledge, 2003.

Levy-Hussen, Aida. *How to Read African American Literature: Post–Civil Rights Fiction and the Task of Interpretation.* New York: New York University Press, 2016.

Lock, Graham, and David Murray, eds. *Thriving on a Riff: Jazz and Blues Influences in African American Literature and Film.* Oxford and New York: Oxford University Press, 2009.

McDowell, Deborah E., and Arnold Rampersad, eds. *Slavery and the Literary Imagination.* Baltimore: Johns Hopkins University Press, 1989.

McHenry, Elizabeth. *Forgotten Readers: Recovering the Lost History of African American Literary Societies.* Durham, NC: Duke University Press, 2002.

Melancon, Trimiko. *Unbought and Unbossed: Transgressive Black Women, Sexuality, and Representation.* Philadelphia: Temple University Press, 2014.

Miller, R. Baxter. *The Art and Imagination of Langston Hughes.* Lexington: University of Kentucky Press, 2006.

Miller, R. Baxter, ed. *Black American Poets between Worlds, 1940–1960.* Knoxville: University of Tennessee Press, 1986.

Miller, R. Baxter, ed. *Langston Hughes.* Ipswich, MA: Salem Press, 2013.

Mills, Charles W. *Blackness Visible: Essays on Philosophy and Race.* Ithaca, NY: Cornell University Press, 1998.

Nadel, Alan, ed. *May All Your Fences Have Gates: Essays on the Drama of August Wilson.* Iowa City: University of Iowa Press, 1994.

Nelson, Emmanuel S., ed. *Critical Essays: Gay and Lesbian Writers of Color.* New York: Haworth Press, 1993.

Omry, Keren. *Cross-Rhythms: Jazz Aesthetics in African-American Literature.* London and New York: Continuum, 2008.

Ostrom, Hans. *Langston Hughes: A Study of the Short Fiction.* New York: Twayne, 1993.

Posnock, Ross. *Color & Culture: Black Writers and the Making of the Modern Intellectual.* Cambridge, MA: Harvard University Press, 1998.

Rampersad, Arnold. *The Art and Imagination of W.E.B. Du Bois.* Cambridge, MA: Harvard University Press, 1976.

Redmond, Eugene. *Drumvoices: The Mission of Afro-American Poetry. A Critical History.* Garden City, NY: Anchor, 1976.

Roth, Benita. *Separate Roads to Feminism: Black, Chicana, and White Feminist Movements in America's Second Wave.* New York: Cambridge University Press, 2004.

Royster, Jacqueline Jones. *Traces of a Stream: Literacy and Social Change among African American Women.* Pittsburgh: University of Pittsburgh Press, 2000.

Schwarz, A. B. Christa. *Gay Voices of the Harlem Renaissance.* Bloomington: Indiana University Press, 2003.

Shandell, Jonathan. *The American Negro Theatre and the Long Civil Rights Era.* Iowa City: University of Iowa Press, 2018.

Sherman, Joan R. *Invisible Poets: Afro-Americans of the Nineteenth Century.* 2nd ed. Urbana: University of Illinois Press, 1989.

Smethurst, James Edward. *The New Red Negro: The Literary Left and African American Poetry, 1930–1946.* New York: Oxford University Press, 1999.

Stepto, Robert B. *From behind the Veil: A Study of Afro-American Narrative.* Urbana: University of Illinois Press, 1979.

Thompson, Robert Farris. *Flash of the Spirit: African and Afro-American Art and Philosophy.* New York: Random House, 1983.

Tracy, Steven C. *Langston Hughes and the Blues.* Urbana: University of Illinois Press, 1988.

Wall, Cheryl A. *On Freedom and the Will to Adorn: The Art of the African American Essay.* Chapel Hill: University of North Carolina Press, 2019.

Wallace, Maurice O. *Constructing the Black Masculine: Identity and Ideality in African American Men's Literature and Culture, 1775–1995.* Durham, NC: Duke University Press, 2002.

West, Cornel. *Race Matters.* New York: Vintage, 1994.

Wilburn, Reginald A. *Preaching the Gospel of Black Revolt: Appropriating Milton in Early African American Literature.* Pittsburgh: Duquesne University Press, 2014.

Williams, Roland Leander. *African American Autobiography and the Quest for Freedom.* Westport, CT: Greenwood Press, 2000.

Wintz, Cary D. *Black Culture and the Harlem Renaissance.* Houston, TX: Rice University Press, 1988.

Zabel, Darcy. *The Underground Railroad in African American Literature.* New York: Peter Lang, 2004.

Selected Organizations, Museums, and Research Centers

African American Museum & Library at Oakland
Oakland Public Library
659 14th St.
Oakland, CA 94612
(510) 637-0200

African American Museum in Philadelphia
701 Arch Street
Philadelphia, PA 19106
(215) 574-0380
http://www.ushistory.org/tour/tour_afro.htm

Amistad Research Center
Tilton Hall
Tulane University
6823 St. Charles Avenue
New Orleans, LA 70118
(504) 865-5535
http://www.amistadresearchcenter.org

Anacostia Museum & Center for African American History & Culture
Smithsonian Institution
1901 Fort Place SE
Washington, DC 20020
(202) 287-3306
http://www.si.edu

Association for African American Museums
P.O. Box 23698
Washington, DC 20026
info@blackmuseums.org

Association for the Study of African American Life and History
CB Powell Building, Suite C142
Howard University

525 Bryant Street
Washington, DC 20059
(202) 865-0053; fax (202) 265-7920
http://www.asalh.com

*The Carter G. Woodson Institute for African-
American and African Studies*
PO Box 400162
108 Minor Hall
Charlottesville, VA 22904
University of Virginia

Center for Black Genealogy
P.O. Box 53108
Chicago, IL 60653-0108
info@BlackGenealogy.org

*Center for the Study of African American
Language*
University of Massachusetts
Amherst, MA 01003

*Charles Wright Museum of African American
History*
315 E. Warren Ave.
Detroit, MI 48201-1443
(313) 494-5800; fax (313) 494-5855
http://www.maah-detroit.org

Delta Blues Museum
#1 Blues Alley
P.O. Box 459
Clarksdale, MS 38614
http://www.deltabluesmuseum.org

Douglass-Truth Branch
Seattle Public Library
African American Collection
2300 E. Yesler Way, Seattle, WA 98122
Seattle, WA

*Givens Collection of African American
Literature*
University of Minnesota
Elmer L. Andersen Library, Suite 213
222 21st Avenue South
Minneapolis, MN 55455

*Harris Collection of American Poetry and
Plays*

Brown University Library
Providence, RI 02912

James Weldon Johnson Collection
Beinecke Rare Book and Manuscript Library
Yale University
130 Wall Street
New Haven, CT 06520-8240
(203) 432-1810
http://www.library.yale.edu/beinecke/ycaljwj
.htm

Museum of Afro-American History
Administrative Office
14 Beacon St., Suite 719
Boston, MA 02108
(617) 725-0022
http://www.afroammuseum.org

*National Association of African American
Studies & Affiliates*
P.O. Box 325
Biddeford, ME 04005-0325
(207) 839-8004
e-mail: naaasgrp@webcom.com
http://www.naaas.org

*National Museum of African American His-
tory & Culture*
1400 Constitution Ave NW
Washington, DC 20560

Race & Pedagogy Institute
University of Puget Sound
Tacoma, WA 98416-1023
https://www.pugetsound.edu/academics
/academic-resources/race-pedagogy
-institute/

*Schomburg Center for Research in Black
Culture*
515 Malcolm X Blvd.
New York, NY 10037-1801
(212) 491-2200
http://www.nypl.org/research/sc/sc.html

United States National Slavery Museum
1320 Central Park Boulevard
Fredericksburg, VA 22401

About the Editors and Contributors

EDITORS

HANS A. OSTROM is a widely published writer and scholar, and author of two books on Langston Hughes and many articles. He cofounded the African American Studies program at the University of Puget Sound. At Puget Sound, he has won several awards for teaching. He has also taught at Uppsala University in Sweden and Johannes Gutenberg University in Germany.

J. DAVID MACEY is an award-winning professor of English, who, with Hans Ostrom, edited the *Greenwood Encyclopedia of African American Literature* (five volumes). He is a graduate of Yale University and earned his PhD at Vanderbilt University. He has served as an assistant vice president for diversity and global educational initiatives at the University of Central Oklahoma.

CONTRIBUTORS

ANTONY ADOLF received his BA from the University of Illinois at Chicago and his MA from the University of British Columbia and is currently editor in chief of the c/art-el collective language group.

SHARON L. BARNES is an associate professor of interdisciplinary and special programs at the University of Toledo, where she teaches academic writing and women's studies.

RACHAEL BARNETT earned her PhD in literature from the University of Washington in 2001. She teaches American literature and writing with a comparative multiethnic focus.

ANN BEEBE is an associate professor of English at the University of Texas at Tyler.

CHRIS BELL earned a PhD in disability studies at the University of Illinois at Chicago.

EMILY BERNARD is the Julian Lindsay Green and Gold Professor at the University of Vermont in Burlington.

KIMBERLY BLACK-PARKER received her BS from Central State University and her MS and PhD from Florida State University. She is currently academic chair of the Chicago State University library system.

ELLESIA ANN BLAQUE is an assistant professor at Kutztown University.

SCOTT BUNYAN, a faculty member in the Language Studies Department at Mohawk

College in Ontario, received his PhD from the University of Sussex.

DAVID CARRELL (PhD, Purdue University, 1994) is an assistant professor of English at Langston University, where he teaches American literature, Victorian literature, and composition.

WARREN J. CARSON is a Governor's Distinguished Professor and chair of the Department of Languages, Literature, and Composition at the University of South Carolina Upstate.

THOMAS J. CASSIDY received his PhD in English from Binghamton University in 1991.

PETER GLENN CHRISTENSEN is an assistant professor of English at Cardinal Stritch University in Milwaukee, Wisconsin. He received a PhD in comparative literature from the State University of New York at Binghamton.

JULIE CLAGGETT is a director of Impacting Leaders, an Atlanta-based leadership development and organizational growth firm.

PATRICIA E. CLARK is an associate professor of English at the State University of New York at Oswego.

JEFF CLEEK holds an MA in English and serves an advisor at Colorado Early Colleges, Colorado Springs.

BILL CLEM earned a PhD with emphases in multicultural American literatures and feminist theory, at Northern Illinois University. He teaches at Waubonsee Community College.

AMANDA DAVIS teaches in the Department of Women, Gender, and Sexuality at the University of Virginia.

LAWRENCE A. DAVIS earned his PhD in American studies at Purdue University, where he specialized in African American literature. Currently he is a postdoctoral fellow at the University of Michigan.

MATTHEW R. DAVIS is an assistant professor of English at the University of Wisconsin, River Falls.

CAROL MARGARET DAVISON is a professor of English literature at the University of Windsor, Canada.

VANESSA HOLFORD DIANA is a professor of English and coordinator of the Women's Studies program at Westfield State College in Westfield, Massachusetts, where she teaches courses in multicultural American literature and women's studies.

HEATH A. DIEHL is a lecturer in the General Studies writing program at Bowling Green State University, where he teaches courses in composition, literature, and women's studies.

BILL ENGEL (PhD, University of California, Berkeley) is an independent scholar and educational consultant.

KEITH FELDMAN is an associate professor of comparative ethnic studies at the University of California, Berkeley.

BEN FISLER is an associate professor of theater at Otero College in La Junta, Colorado.

LAKISKA FLIPPIN completed her MA at Brooklyn College of the City University of New York. She is a writer for Newcomb Integrated Marketing Solutions.

ERIC GARDNER is a professor of English at Saginaw Valley State University.

STEPHANIE GORDON, PhD, teaches English at Auburn University.

DELANO GREENIDGE-COPPRUE graduated from Columbia University with a PhD in English and comparative literature. He teaches composition and literature on the Rose Hill campus of Fordham University, New York.

ANGELENE J. HALL is a professor emerita of literature and popular culture in the Department of African and African American Studies at the University of Cincinnati.

JOHN GREER HALL received a bachelor's degree in African American studies and American literature from the University of Massachusetts in Boston and a master's degree in education from Converse College in Spartanburg, South Carolina.

JOHN J. HAN is a professor of English at Missouri Baptist University, where he teaches American, minority, and world literature.

ROXANNE HARDE, a postdoctoral fellow at Cornell University, earned her doctorate in American literature at Queen's University. She teaches at the University of Alberta.

JENNIFER HARRIS is an assistant professor of English at Mount Allison University

and managing editor of the Alphabet City book series.

STEVEN R. HARRIS is Assistant Dean of Libraries at the University of Nevada, Reno. He is a graduate of Weber State College (BA, 1982), the University of Utah (MA, 1985), and the University of Arizona.

MELISSA HAMILTON HAYES lives in Lincoln, Nebraska, and teaches at Doane College.

KEVIN M. HICKEY is an associate professor of English at Albany College of Pharmacy, New York.

SUSANNA HOENESS-KRUPSAW is an associate professor of English at the University of Southern Indiana in Evansville. She earned her doctorate at Southern Illinois University in Carbondale.

LAURA A. HOFFER is a senior lecturer at the University of Tennessee in Knoxville.

JANIS BUTLER HOLM is an associate professor of English at Ohio University, where she has served as associate editor for the film journal *Wide Angle*.

IMELDA HUNT, PhD, has taught at Bowling Green State University. She is the author of *The History of Art Tatum, 1909–1932* (2018).

CHARMAINE N. IJEOMA taught at Abington College of Penn State University and is Homeless Veterans Outreach Officer at Montgomery County Veterans Affairs.

REGINA JENNINGS teaches African American literature, culture, and resistance in the Department of Ethnic Studies at California State University, Stanislaus.

JAMES B. KELLEY holds a PhD in English from the University of Tulsa and teaches at Mississippi State University, Meridian.

MAUREEN A. KELLY is an assistant professor of Library Science at Oregon State University.

ALICIA KESTER lives in Northern California and is currently working on a collection of poetry.

GLADYS L. KNIGHT is a former manager of the African American Museum in Tacoma, Washington. She is author of *Icons of African American Protest: Trailblazing Activists of the Civil Rights Movement* (Greenwood Press).

TRUONG LE is a poet and writer who has published a memoir, a collection of short stories, a novel, and six books of poetry, including one in Vietnamese, English, and French.

LEWIS T. LENAIRE received his BA in English from the University of Central Oklahoma in 2001. He is an attorney in Oklahoma City, Oklahoma.

WENXIN LI is an assistant professor of English at the State University of New York at Old Westbury.

ELIZABETH BLAKESLEY LINDSAY earned an MLS and an MA in comparative literature at Indiana University. She is Assistant Dean of Libraries for Public Services and Outreach, Washington State University Libraries.

DEVONA MALLORY teaches in the English Department at Albany State University in New York.

BARBARA MCCASKILL is a professor and the codirector of the Civil Rights Digital Library at the University of Georgia.

GRACE MCENTEE is a professor at Appalachian State University, where she teaches nineteenth-century American literature and African American literature.

D. QUENTIN MILLER is a professor of English at Suffolk University.

R. BAXTER MILLER is a professor of English and director of African American studies at the University of Georgia.

DEONNE N. MINTO teaches English at Broward College in Florida.

KAREN MUNRO is the literature librarian at the University of Oregon. She holds an MFA in creative writing from the Iowa Writers' Workshop and a BA in English literature from McGill University, Montreal, Canada.

TAMIKO NIMURA taught at the University of Puget Sound. She is a freelance writer whose work has appeared in *New California Writing* and *Discover Nikkei*.

KINOHI NISHIKAWA earned a PhD in Literature at Duke University and is an assistant professor at Princeton University.

BRIAN J. NORMAN teaches ethnic American literatures at Loyola University in Chicago.

IYABO F. OSIAPEM is Senior Lecturer of Africana Studies and Linguistics at the College of William & Mary.

DANEAN POUND teaches English at Enterprise State Community College in Alabama.

PAMELA RALSTON received her doctorate in comparative literature and critical theory at the University of Washington. She teaches English and American ethnic and gender studies at Tacoma Community College.

LINDSEY RENUARD is managing editor of the *Skiatook Journal* in Skiatook, Oklahoma.

LORI RICIGLIANO earned her MLIS at the University of Washington Information School. She is a librarian at the University of Puget Sound.

REBECKA RYCHELLE RUTLEDGE is an associate professor of English and Comparative Literature at the University of North Carolina at Chapel Hill.

REBECCA R. SAULSBURY is an associate professor of English at Florida Southern College, where she teaches American literature, African American literature, and women's studies, and directs the minor in African American studies.

A. B. CHRISTA SCHWARZ is an independent lecturer in American literature at Freie Universität in Berlin, Germany. She is author of *Gay Voices of the Harlem Renaissance* (2002).

SHAWNTAYE M. SCOTT resides in Pittsburgh, Pennsylvania, and is webmaster for Toastmasters International.

GLORIA A. SHEARIN is professor emerita in the Department of Liberal Arts at Savannah State University in Savannah, Georgia.

REGINALD SHEPHERD was the author of four books of poetry: *Otherhood* (2003), *Wrong* (1999), *Angel, Interrupted* (1996), and *Some Are Drowning* (1994), which won the 1993 Associated Writing Programs Award in Poetry.

JOSEPH T. SKERRETT Jr. is a professor of English at the University of Massachusetts, Amherst, where he has taught American literature since 1973.

STEPHEN M. STECK earned a PhD from the Department of English Studies at the University of Montreal.

DOUGLAS STEWARD has taught American literature and critical theory at Truman State University and Franklin & Marshall College and now works for the Modern Language Association.

STEVEN C. TRACY is a professor of Afro-American literature at the University of Massachusetts, Amherst.

MARK TURSI has taught creative writing, literature, and rhetoric at the University of Denver. He is the author of *Shiftless Days*.

AIMABLE TWAGILIMANA is a professor of English at the State University of New York, Buffalo State College. He teaches African American literature, world literature, postcolonial theory, literature of Continental Europe, and comparative literature.

GAIL L. UPCHURCH-MILLS is a professor of English at Dutchess Community College in New York.

ELIZABETE VASCONCELOS is an adjunct in the Department of English at the University of Georgia in Athens.

YVONNE WALKER is an adjunct instructor of creative writing and African American literature at Empire State College of the State University of New York.

LINDA S. WATTS is a professor of interdisciplinary arts and sciences at the University of Washington, Bothell.

IAN W. WILSON is completing his doctoral dissertation in the curriculum of comparative literature at the University of North Carolina at Chapel Hill. He is an associate professor in German and humanities and chair of German Studies at Centre College in Danville, Kentucky.

HARVEY YOUNG is Dean of the College of Fine Arts at Boston University.

Index

Page numbers in **bold** indicate the location of main entries.